General Conference Addresses

JOURNAL EDITION | APRIL 2024

General Conference Addresses

JOURNAL EDITION | APRIL 2024

SALT LAKE CITY, UTAH

Book design © Deseret Book Company

Cover photo: Pobytov/Getty Images
Interior photos: pages 1, 35, 77, 106, 145: sevector/Adobe Stock

Visit us at deseretbook.com

978-1-63993-261-0

Printed in the United States of America
Sun Print Solutions, Salt Lake City, UT

10 9 8 7 6 5 4 3 2 1

CONTENTS

SATURDAY MORNING SESSION

Motions of a Hidden Fire 2
PRESIDENT JEFFREY R. HOLLAND

Put Ye On the Lord Jesus Christ 7
SISTER J. ANETTE DENNIS

Pillars and Rays 13
ELDER ALEXANDER DUSHKU

Covenant Confidence through Jesus Christ 19
ELDER ULISSES SOARES

Integrity: A Christlike Attribute 25
ELDER JACK N. GERARD

All Will Be Well Because of Temple Covenants 30
PRESIDENT HENRY B. EYRING

SATURDAY AFTERNOON SESSION

"Be Still, and Know That I Am God" 36
ELDER DAVID A. BEDNAR

Rise! He Calleth Thee 42
ELDER MASSIMO DE FEO

A Record of What I Have Both Seen and Heard 47
ELDER BRENT H. NIELSON

Jesus Christ at the Center of Our Lives 52
ELDER JOSE L. ALONSO

All Things for Our Good 57
ELDER GERRIT W. GONG

In Support of the Rising Generation 64
BROTHER MICHAEL T. NELSON

Be One with Christ. 70
ELDER QUENTIN L. COOK

SATURDAY EVENING SESSION

Miracles, Angels, and Priesthood Power 78
ELDER SHAYNE M. BOWEN

Foreordained to Serve 83
ELDER STEVEN R. BANGERTER

Faithful to the End 88
SISTER ANDREA MUÑOZ SPANNAUS

Fruit That Remains 93
ELDER MATTHEW L. CARPENTER

A Higher Joy 99
ELDER DIETER F. UCHTDORF

SUNDAY MORNING SESSION

Words Matter. 107
ELDER RONALD A. RASBAND

Pray, He Is There 113
PRESIDENT SUSAN H. PORTER

The Powerful, Virtuous Cycle of the Doctrine of Christ 117
ELDER DALE G. RENLUND

Trust in the Lord 123
ELDER PAUL B. PIEPER

God's Intent Is to Bring You Home 128
ELDER PATRICK KEARON

Swallowed Up in the Joy of Christ 133
ELDER BRIAN K. TAYLOR

Covenants and Responsibilities 139
PRESIDENT DALLIN H. OAKS

SUNDAY AFTERNOON SESSION

The Testimony of Jesus 146
ELDER D. TODD CHRISTOFFERSON

Call, Don't Fall 153
ELDER TAYLOR G. GODOY

Bridging the Two Great Commandments 158
ELDER GARY E. STEVENSON

Opposition in All Things 165
ELDER MATHIAS HELD

Temples, Houses of the Lord Dotting the Earth 170
ELDER NEIL L. ANDERSEN

It Is Wisdom in the Lord That We Should Have the Book of Mormon . . . 177
PRESIDENT MARK L. PACE

Rejoice in the Gift of Priesthood Keys 183
PRESIDENT RUSSELL M. NELSON

Saturday Morning Session

APRIL 6, 2024

MOTIONS OF A HIDDEN FIRE

PRESIDENT JEFFREY R. HOLLAND

Acting President of the Quorum of the Twelve Apostles

Brothers and sisters, I have learned a painful lesson since I last occupied this pulpit in October of 2022. That lesson is: if you don't give an acceptable talk, you can be banned for the next several conferences. You can see I am assigned early in the first session of this one. What you can't see is that I am positioned on a trapdoor with a very delicate latch. If this talk doesn't go well, I won't see you for another few conferences.

In the spirit of that beautiful hymn with this beautiful choir, I *have* learned some lessons recently that, with the Lord's help, I wish to share with you today. That will make this a very personal talk.

The most personal and painful of all these recent experiences has been the passing of my beloved wife, Pat. She *was* the greatest woman I have ever known—a perfect wife and mother, to say nothing of her purity, her gift of expression, her spirituality. She gave a talk once titled "Fulfilling the Measure of Your Creation." It seems to me that she fulfilled the measure of *her* creation more successfully than anyone could have dreamed possible. She was a complete daughter of God, an exemplary woman of Christ. I was the most fortunate of men to spend 60 years of my life with her. Should I prove worthy, our sealing means I can spend eternity with her.

Another experience began 48 hours after my wife's burial. At that time, I was rushed to the hospital in an acute medical crisis. I then spent the first four weeks of a six-week stay in and out of intensive care and in and out of consciousness.

Virtually all my experience *in* the hospital during that first period is lost to my memory. What is *not* lost is my memory of a journey *outside* the hospital, out to what seemed the edge of eternity. I cannot speak fully of that experience here, but I can say that part of what I received was an admonition to return to my ministry with more urgency, more consecration, more focus on the Savior, more faith in His word.

I couldn't help but feel I was receiving my own personal version of a revelation given to the Twelve nearly 200 years ago:

"Thou shalt bear record of my name . . . [and] send forth my word unto the ends of the earth. . . .

" . . . Morning by morning; and day after day let thy warning voice go forth; and when the night cometh let not the inhabitants of the earth slumber, because of thy speech. . . .

"Arise[,] . . . take up your cross, [and] follow me."[1]

My beloved sisters and brothers, since that experience, I have tried to take up my cross more earnestly, with more resolve to find where I can raise an apostolic voice of both warmth and warning in the morning, during the day, and into the night.

That leads me to a *third* truth that came in those months of loss, illness, and distress. It was a renewed witness of and endless gratitude for the resolute prayers of this Church—your prayers—of which I have been the beneficiary. I will be eternally grateful for the supplication of thousands of people who, like the importuning widow,[2] repeatedly sought heaven's intervention in my behalf. I received priesthood blessings, and I saw my high school class fast for me, as did several random wards across the Church. And my name must have been on the prayer roll of virtually every temple in the Church.

In my profound gratitude for all this, I join G. K. Chesterton, who said once "that thanks are the highest form of thought; and . . . gratitude is happiness doubled by wonder."[3] With my own "happiness doubled by wonder," I thank all of you and thank my Father in Heaven, who heard your prayers and blessed my life.

Brothers and sisters, I testify that God hears *every* prayer we offer and responds to each of them according to the path He has outlined for our perfection. I recognize that at roughly the same time so many were praying for the restoration of my health, an equal number—including me—were praying for the restoration of my wife's health. I testify that both of those prayers were heard *and* answered by a divinely compassionate Heavenly Father, even if the prayers for Pat were *not* answered the way I asked. It is for reasons known only to God why prayers are answered differently than we hope—but I promise you they *are* heard and they *are* answered according to His unfailing love and cosmic timetable.

If we "ask not amiss,"[4] there are no limits to when, where, or about what we should pray. According to the revelations, we are to "pray always."[5] We are to pray, Amulek said, for "those who are around you,"[6] with the belief that the "fervent prayer of a righteous [people] availeth much."[7] Our prayers ought to be vocal when we have the privacy to so offer them.[8] If that is not practical, they should be carried as silent utterances in our heart.[9] We sing that prayers are "motion[s] of a hidden fire,"[10] always to be offered, according to the Savior Himself, to God the Eternal Father in the name of His Only Begotten Son.[11]

My beloved friends, our prayers are our sweetest hour,[12] our most "sincere desire,"[13] our simplest, purest form of worship.[14] We should pray individually, in our families, and in congregations of all sizes.[15] We are to employ prayer as a shield against temptation,[16] and if there be any time we feel *not* to pray, we can be sure that hesitancy does *not* come from God, who yearns to communicate with His children at any and all times. Indeed, some efforts to keep us from praying come directly from the adversary.[17] When we don't know how or exactly for what to pray, we should begin, and continue, until the Holy Spirit guides us into the prayer we should be offering.[18] This approach may be the one we have to invoke when praying for our enemies and those who despitefully use us.[19]

Ultimately, we can look to the example of the Savior, who prayed so very, very often. But it has always been intriguing to me that Jesus felt the need to pray at all. Wasn't He perfect? About what did He need to pray? Well, I have come to realize that He too, with us, wanted to "seek [the Father's] face, believe his word, and trust his grace."[20] Time after time, He retreated from society to be alone before piercing heaven with His prayers.[21] At other times, He prayed in the company of a few companions. Then He would seek heaven on behalf of multitudes who would cover a hillside. Sometimes prayer glorified His clothing.[22] Sometimes it glorified His countenance.[23]

Sometimes He stood to pray, sometimes He knelt, and at least once He fell on His face in prayer.[24]

Luke describes Jesus's descent into His expiation as requiring Him to pray "more earnestly."[25] How does one who was perfect pray more earnestly? We assume that all of His prayers were earnest, yet in fulfilling His atoning sacrifice and through the pain that attended its universal reach, He felt to pray ever more pleadingly, with the weight of His offering finally bringing blood from every pore.

Against that backdrop of Christ's victory over death and His recent gift to me of a few more weeks or months in mortality, I bear solemn witness of the reality of eternal life and the need for us to be serious in our planning for it.

I bear witness that when Christ comes, He needs to recognize us—not as nominal members listed on a faded baptismal record but as thoroughly committed, faithfully believing, covenant-keeping disciples. This is an urgent matter for all of us, lest we ever hear with devastating regret: "I never knew you,"[26] or, as Joseph Smith translated that phrase, "[You] never knew me."[27]

Fortunately, we have help for this task—lots of help. We need to believe in angels and miracles and the promises of the holy priesthood. We need to believe in the gift of the Holy Ghost, the influence of good families and friends, and the power of the pure love of Christ. We need to believe in revelation and prophets, seers, and revelators and President Russell M. Nelson. We need to believe that with prayer and pleading and personal righteousness, we really can ascend to "Mount Zion, . . . the city of the living God, the heavenly place, the holiest of all."[28]

Brothers and sisters, as we repent of our sins and come boldly to the "throne of grace,"[29] leaving before Him there our alms and our heartfelt supplications, we will find mercy and compassion and forgiveness at the benevolent hands of our Eternal Father and His obedient, perfectly pure Son. Then, with Job and all the refined faithful, we will behold a world "too wonderful"[30] to understand. In the name of Jesus Christ, amen.

Notes

1. Doctrine and Covenants 112:4–5, 14.
2. See Luke 18:1–8.
3. G. K. Chesterton, *A Short History of England* (1917), 72.
4. 2 Nephi 4:35.
5. Luke 21:36; see also Alma 13:28; 34:27; Doctrine and Covenants 23:6.
6. Alma 34:27; see also 2 Thessalonians 1:11; Alma 34:21.
7. James 5:16.
8. See Psalm 55:17.
9. See Mosiah 24:10–12; Alma 34:27; 3 Nephi 20:1; Doctrine and Covenants 19:28.
10. "Prayer Is the Soul's Sincere Desire," *Hymns*, no. 145.
11. See 3 Nephi 18:19–21.
12. See "Sweet Hour of Prayer," *Hymns*, no. 142.
13. *Hymns*, no. 145.
14. See Alma 33:3.
15. See Matthew 14:23; 18:19–20; 3 Nephi 18:16, 21–24, 30; Helaman 3:35.
16. See Matthew 6:13; Luke 22:40; 3 Nephi 18:15; Doctrine and Covenants 10:5.
17. See 2 Nephi 32:8; Joseph Smith—History 1:15–16.
18. See Romans 8:26; 3 Nephi 19:24; Doctrine and Covenants 50:30.
19. See Matthew 5:44.
20. *Hymns*, no. 142.
21. See Matthew 14:23.
22. See Matthew 17:2; Mark 9:3; Luke 9:29; 3 Nephi 19:25.
23. See Matthew 17:2; Luke 9:29; 3 Nephi 19:25.
24. See Matthew 26:39; Mark 14:35.
25. Luke 22:44.
26. Matthew 7:23.
27. Joseph Smith Translation, Matthew 7:33 (in Matthew 7:23, footnote *a*).
28. Doctrine and Covenants 76:66.
29. Hebrews 4:16.
30. Job 42:3.

PUT YE ON THE LORD JESUS CHRIST

SISTER J. ANETTE DENNIS

First Counselor in the Relief Society General Presidency

As my two youngest children were growing, I discovered books that were entertaining and engaging but also used symbolism in their stories. As we read together in the evenings, I loved helping my children understand the symbolism the author was using to teach deeper principles, even gospel principles.

I knew this was sinking in one day when my younger son was in his early teens. He had started a new book and just wanted to enjoy the story, but his mind kept trying to find the deeper meaning in everything he was reading. He was frustrated, but I was smiling inside.

Jesus taught through stories and symbols[1]—a mustard seed to teach the power of faith,[2] a lost sheep to teach the worth of souls,[3] a prodigal son to teach the character of God.[4] His parables were symbols through which He could teach deeper lessons to those who had "ears to hear."[5] But those not seeking the deeper meaning would not understand,[6] just as many who read those same books I read to my children never knew there were deeper meanings and so much more to get out of those stories.

When God the Father offered His Only Begotten Son as a sacrifice for us, Jesus Christ Himself became the highest symbol of our Father in Heaven's undying love for each of us.[7] Jesus Christ became the Lamb of God.[8]

We have the privilege and blessing of being invited into a covenant relationship with God, in which our own lives can become a symbol of that covenant. Covenants create the kind of relationship that allows God to mold and change us over time and lift us to become more like the Savior, drawing us closer and closer to Him and our Father[9] and eventually preparing us to enter Their presence.

Each person on earth is a beloved son or daughter of God.[10] When we choose to be part of a covenant, it enhances and deepens our relationship with Him. President Russell M. Nelson has taught that when we choose to make covenants with God, our relationship with Him can become much closer than it was before our covenant, and it enables Him to bless us with an extra measure of His mercy and love, a covenantal love referred to as *hesed* in the Hebrew language.[11] The covenant path is all about our relationship with God—our *hesed* relationship with Him.[12]

Our Father wants a deeper relationship with all His sons and daughters,[13] but it is our choice. As we choose to draw nearer to Him through a *covenant* relationship, it allows Him to draw nearer to us[14] and more fully bless us.

God sets the conditions and obligations of the covenants we make.[15] When we choose to enter into that relationship, we witness to Him, through the symbolic actions of each covenant, that we are willing to abide by the conditions He has set.[16] Through honoring our covenants, we enable God to pour out the multitude of promised blessings associated with those covenants,[17] including increased power to change and become more like our Savior. Jesus Christ is at the center of all covenants we make, and covenant blessings are made possible because of His atoning sacrifice.[18]

Baptism by immersion is the symbolic gate through which we enter into a covenant relationship with God. Being immersed in the water and coming up again is symbolic of the Savior's death and Resurrection to new life.[19] As we are baptized, we symbolically die and are born again into the family of Christ and show we are willing to take His name upon us.[20] We ourselves embody that covenant symbolism. In the New Testament we read, "For as many of you as have been baptized into Christ have put on Christ."[21] With our baptism we symbolically put on Christ.

The ordinance of the sacrament also points to the Savior. The bread and water are symbolic of Christ's flesh and blood shed for us.[22] The gift of His Atonement is symbolically offered to us each week when a priesthood holder, representing the Savior Himself, offers us the bread and water. As we perform the action of eating and drinking the emblems of His flesh and blood, Christ symbolically becomes a part of us.[23] We again put on Christ as we make a new covenant each week.[24]

As we make covenants with God in the house of the Lord, we further deepen our relationship with Him.[25] Everything we do in the temple points to our Father's plan for us, at the heart of which is the Savior and His atoning sacrifice.[26] The Lord will teach us line upon line[27] through the symbolism of the ordinances and covenants as we open our hearts and prayerfully seek to understand the deeper meanings.

As part of the temple endowment, we are *authorized* to wear the garment of the holy priesthood. It is both a sacred obligation and a sacred privilege.

In many religious traditions, special outer clothing is worn as a symbol of a person's beliefs and commitment to God,[28] and ceremonial clothing is often worn by those leading worship services. Those sacred vestments carry deep meaning for those who wear them. We read in scripture that in ancient times, sacred ceremonial clothing was also worn in conjunction with temple rituals.[29]

As members of The Church of Jesus Christ of Latter-day Saints, those of us who have chosen to make covenants with God in the house of the Lord wear sacred ceremonial outer clothing during temple worship, symbolic of the clothing worn in ancient temple rituals. We also wear the garment of the holy priesthood, both during temple worship *and* in our everyday lives.[30]

The garment of the holy priesthood is deeply symbolic and *also* points to the Savior. When Adam and Eve partook of the fruit and had to leave the Garden of Eden, they were given coats of skins as a covering for them.[31] It is likely that an animal was sacrificed to make those coats of skins—symbolic of the Savior's own sacrifice for us. *Kaphar* is the basic Hebrew word for atonement, and one of its meanings is "to cover."[32] Our temple garment reminds us that the Savior and the blessings of His Atonement cover us throughout our lives. As we put on the garment of the holy priesthood each day, that beautiful symbol becomes a part of us.

In the New Testament book of Romans, we read: "The night is

far spent, the day is at hand: let us therefore cast off the works of darkness, and let us put on the armour of light. . . . Put ye on the Lord Jesus Christ."[33]

I am so grateful for the privilege of wearing the garment of the holy priesthood to remind me that the Savior and the blessings of His infinite Atonement constantly cover me throughout my mortal journey. It also reminds me that as I keep the covenants I have made with God in the house of the Lord, I have symbolically put on Christ, who Himself is an armor of light. He will protect me from evil,[34] give me power and increased capacity,[35] and be my light and guide[36] through the darkness and difficulties of this world.

There is deep and beautiful symbolic meaning in the garment of the holy priesthood and its relationship to Christ. I believe that my willingness[37] to wear the holy garment becomes *my* symbol to Him.[38] It is my own personal sign to God, not a sign to others.[39]

I am so grateful for my Savior, Jesus Christ.[40] His atoning sacrifice for us became the greatest symbol of His and our Father in Heaven's infinite love for each of us,[41] with the tangible symbols of that love and sacrifice—the marks in the Savior's hands, feet, and side—remaining even after His Resurrection.[42]

As I keep my covenants and obligations with God, including wearing the garment of the holy priesthood, my very life can become a personal symbol of my love and deep gratitude for my Savior, Jesus Christ, and my desire to have Him with me always.

If you have not yet done so, I invite you to choose a deeper relationship with God by making covenants with Him in the house of the Lord. Study the talks of our prophet (including the beautiful teachings in the footnotes of his talks, which most conference talks have). He has spoken repeatedly about covenants for years and especially since becoming President of the Church. Learn from his teachings about the beautiful blessings and increased power and capacity that can be yours through making and keeping covenants with God.[43]

The *General Handbook* states that it is not required to have a mission call or be engaged to be married to make temple covenants.[44]

A person must be at least 18 years old, no longer be attending high school or the equivalent, and be a member of the Church for at least one year. There are also standards of personal holiness required.[45] If you have the desire to deepen your relationship with your Father in Heaven and Jesus Christ by making sacred covenants in the house of the Lord, I invite you to speak with your bishop or branch president and let him know of your desires. He will help you know how to prepare to receive and honor those covenants.

Through a covenant relationship with God, our own lives can become a living symbol of our commitment to and deep love for our Father in Heaven, our *hesed* for Him,[46] and our desire to progress and eventually become like our Savior, being prepared to one day enter Their presence. I testify that the great blessings of that covenant relationship are well worth the price. In the name of Jesus Christ, amen.

Notes

1. See Mark 4:33–34.
2. See Matthew 17:20.
3. See Luke 15:3–7.
4. See Luke 15:11–32.
5. Matthew 13:9.
6. See Matthew 13:10–13.
7. See John 3:16–17.
8. See John 1:29; 1 Nephi 11:20–22; see also Russell M. Nelson, "The Atonement," *Ensign*, Nov. 1996, 34–35.
9. "By entering into a covenant with us, God not only binds us to Him, but It is as if He straps us on His back and takes us where only He can go" (Kerry Muhlestein, *God Will Prevail: Ancient Covenants, Modern Blessings, and the Gathering of Israel* [2021], 8). See Doctrine and Covenants 133:53.
10. "All human beings—male and female—are created in the image of God. Each is a beloved spirit son or daughter of heavenly parents, and, as such, each has a divine nature and destiny" ("The Family: A Proclamation to the World," Gospel Library).
11. "*Hesed* is a . . . term describing a covenant relationship in which both parties are bound to be loyal and faithful to each other. . . . Because God has *hesed* for those who have covenanted with Him, . . . He will continue to work with them and offer them opportunities to change. . . . And should they stray, He will help them find their way back to Him," just as He did time and time again with His covenant people in Old Testament times. "When we enter a covenant with God, we have made a covenant with Him who will always keep His word. He will do everything He can, without infringing on our agency, to help us keep ours" (Russell M. Nelson, "The Everlasting Covenant," *Liahona*, Oct. 2022, 6, 11; see also Muhlestein, *God Will Prevail*, 9–12; Deuteronomy 7:9).
12. God will never abandon His covenant relationships. "He will never tire in His efforts to help us, and we will never exhaust His merciful patience with us" (Russell M. Nelson, "The Everlasting Covenant," 6). We are joyfully bound together through an everlasting covenant.
13. See Jeremiah 31:33; 1 Nephi 17:40; Russell M. Nelson, "Let God Prevail," *Ensign* or *Liahona*, Nov. 2020, 92.

14. See James 4:8; Doctrine and Covenants 88:63.
15. See Russell M. Nelson, "Covenants," *Ensign* or *Liahona*, Nov. 2011, 86.
16. See Mosiah 5:5; 18:8–10.
17. See Russell M. Nelson, "Spiritual Treasures," *Ensign* or *Liahona*, Nov. 2019, 77; Russell M. Nelson, "The Temple and Your Spiritual Foundation," *Liahona*, Nov. 2021, 94; Russell M. Nelson, "Overcome the World and Find Rest," *Liahona*, Nov. 2022, 96; Camille N. Johnson, "Jesus Christ Is Relief," *Liahona*, May 2023, 82; Dale G. Renlund, "Accessing God's Power through Covenants," *Liahona*, May 2023, 35–37; Jean B. Bingham, "Covenants with God Strengthen, Protect, and Prepare Us for Eternal Glory," *Liahona*, May 2022, 66.
18. See Russell M. Nelson, "The Everlasting Covenant," 7.
19. See Romans 6:3–4; Colossians 2:12.
20. See 2 Nephi 31:13; Moroni 6:3; Doctrine and Covenants 20:77.
21. Galatians 3:27.
22. See Luke 22:19–20.
23. See John 6:56.
24. President Russell M. Nelson said: "Often, I hear the expression that we partake of the sacrament to renew covenants made at baptism. While that's true, it's much more than that. I've made a new covenant. You have made new covenants" (in Dale G. Renlund, "Unwavering Commitment to Jesus Christ," *Ensign* or *Liahona*, Nov. 2019, 25, footnote 18).
25. See Russell M. Nelson, "The Everlasting Covenant," 10.
26. See Russell M. Nelson, "The Temple and Your Spiritual Foundation," 93–94.
27. See 2 Nephi 28:30.
28. See "Sacred Temple Clothing," ChurchofJesusChrist.org.
29. See Exodus 28; 40:12–13.
30. See "Sacred Temple Clothing," ChurchofJesusChrist.org.
31. See Genesis 3:21.
32. See Russell M. Nelson, "The Atonement," 34.
33. Romans 13:12, 14.
34. See Ephesians 6:10–18.
35. See Mosiah 24:13–15; David A. Bednar, "Bear Up Their Burdens with Ease," *Ensign* or *Liahona*, May 2014, 88–89.
36. See Psalm 119:105; 1 Nephi 17:13.
37. Elder Neal A. Maxwell taught, "The submission of one's will is really the only uniquely personal thing we have to place on God's altar" ("Swallowed Up in the Will of the Father," *Ensign*, Nov. 1995, 24).
38. Not because of personal preference, inconvenience, or style, but because of certain medical conditions, for some people, wearing the garment is much more difficult. The Lord knows our hearts and understands our desires to honor our commitments with Him. See, for example, Mosiah 4:24–25.
39. We should not seek to judge others' use of the temple garment. See Alma 41:14; see also Dieter F. Uchtdorf, "The Merciful Obtain Mercy," *Ensign* or *Liahona*, May 2012, 70, 75.
40. See Jeffrey R. Holland, "None Were with Him," *Ensign* or *Liahona*, May 2009, 86–88.
41. See John 3:16–17; 15:12–13; Doctrine and Covenants 34:3.
42. See Isaiah 49:14–16.
43. See Russell M. Nelson, "The Everlasting Covenant," 4–11; Russell M. Nelson, "Spiritual Treasures," 76–79; Russell M. Nelson, "Let God Prevail," 92–95; Russell M. Nelson, "The Temple and Your Spiritual Foundation," 93–96; Russell M. Nelson, "Overcome the World and Find Rest," 95–98; Russell M. Nelson, "A Plea to My Sisters," *Ensign* or *Liahona*, Nov. 2015, 95–97.
44. See *General Handbook: Serving in The Church of Jesus Christ of Latter-day Saints*, 26.5.1, 27.2.2, Gospel Library.
45. See Russell M. Nelson, "Closing Remarks," *Ensign* or *Liahona*, Nov. 2019, 121.
46. See Russell M. Nelson, "The Everlasting Covenant," 11.

PILLARS AND RAYS

ELDER ALEXANDER DUSHKU
Of the Seventy

My message is for those who worry about their testimony because they haven't had overwhelming spiritual experiences. I pray that I can provide some peace and assurance.

The Restoration of the gospel of Jesus Christ began with an explosion of light and truth! A teenage boy in upstate New York, with the very ordinary name of Joseph Smith, enters a grove of trees to pray. He's worried about his soul and his standing before God. He seeks forgiveness for his sins. And he's confused about which church to join. He needs clarity and peace—he needs light and knowledge.[1]

As Joseph kneels to pray and "offer up the desires of [his] heart to God," a thick darkness envelops him. Something evil, oppressive, and very real tries to stop him—to bind his tongue so he cannot speak. The forces of darkness get so intense that Joseph thinks he's going to die. But he "exert[s] all [his] powers to call upon God to deliver [him] out of the power of this enemy which [has] seized upon [him]." And then, "at the very moment when [he's] ready to sink into despair and abandon [him]self to destruction," when he doesn't know if he can hang on any longer, a glorious brilliance fills the grove, scattering the darkness and the enemy of his soul.[2]

A "pillar of light" brighter than the sun gradually descends upon him. One personage appears, and then another.[3] Their "brightness and glory defy all description." The first, our Heavenly Father, speaks his name, "pointing to the other—[Joseph!] *This is My Beloved Son. Hear Him!*"[4]

And with that overwhelming burst of light and truth, the Restoration has begun. A veritable flood of divine revelation and blessings will follow: new scripture, restored priesthood keys, apostles and prophets, ordinances and covenants, and the reestablishment of the Lord's true and living Church, which will someday fill the earth with the light and witness of Jesus Christ and His restored gospel.

All that, and much more, began with a boy's desperate prayer and a pillar of light.

We too have our own desperate needs. We too need freedom from spiritual confusion and worldly darkness. We too need to know for ourselves.[5] That is one reason President Russell M. Nelson has invited us to "immerse [ourselves] in the glorious light of the Restoration."[6]

One of the great truths of the Restoration is that the heavens are open—that we too can receive light and knowledge from on high. I testify that is true.

But we must be wary of a spiritual trap. Sometimes faithful Church members become discouraged and even drift away because they haven't had overwhelming spiritual experiences—because they haven't experienced their own pillar of light. President Spencer W. Kimball warned, "Always expecting the spectacular, many will miss entirely the constant flow of revealed communication."[7]

President Joseph F. Smith likewise recalled, "The Lord withheld marvels from me [when I was young], and showed me the truth, line upon line, precept upon precept, here a little and there a little."[8]

That is the Lord's typical pattern, brothers and sisters. Rather than sending us a pillar of light, the Lord sends us a ray of light, and then another, and another.

Those rays of light are continuously being poured down upon us. The scriptures teach that Jesus Christ "is the light and . . . life of the world,"[9] that His "Spirit giveth light to every man [and woman] that cometh into the world,"[10] and that His light "fill[s] the immensity of space," giving "life to all things."[11] The Light of Christ is literally all around us.

If we have received the gift of the Holy Ghost and are striving to exercise faith, repent, and honor our covenants, then we are worthy to receive these divine rays constantly. In Elder David A. Bednar's memorable phrase, "we are 'living in revelation.'"[12]

And yet, every one of us is different. No two people experience God's light and truth in exactly the same way. Take some time to think about how you experience the light and Spirit of the Lord.

You may have experienced these bursts of light and testimony as "peace [spoken] to your mind concerning [a] matter" that has worried you.[13]

Or as an impression—a still, small voice—that settled "in your mind and in your heart"[14] and urged you to do something good, such as helping someone.

Perhaps you've been in a class at church—or at a youth camp—and felt a strong desire to follow Jesus Christ and stay faithful.[15] Maybe you even stood and shared a testimony that you hoped was true and then felt it was.

Or maybe you've been praying and felt a joyful assurance that God loves you.[16]

You may have heard someone bear testimony of Jesus Christ, and it touched your heart and filled you with hope.[17]

Perhaps you were reading in the Book of Mormon and a verse spoke to your soul, as if God had put it there just for you—and then you realized that He did.[18]

You may have felt the love of God for others as you served them.[19]

Or maybe you struggle to feel the Spirit in the moment because of depression or anxiety but have the precious gift and the faith to look back and recognize past "tender mercies of the Lord."[20]

My point is that there are many ways to receive heavenly rays of testimony. These are just a few, of course. They may not be dramatic, but all of them form part of our testimonies.

Brothers and sisters, I have not seen a pillar of light, but, like you, I have experienced many divine rays. Over the years, I've tried to treasure such experiences. I find that as I do, I recognize and remember even more of them. Here are some examples from my own life. They may not be very impressive to some, but they are precious to me.

I remember being a rowdy teenager at a baptism. As the meeting was about to begin, I felt the Spirit urge me to sit down and be reverent. I sat down and stayed quiet the rest of the meeting.

Before my mission, I was afraid my testimony wasn't strong

enough. No one in my family had ever served a mission, and I didn't know if I could do it. I remember studying and praying desperately to receive a more certain witness of Jesus Christ. Then one day, as I pled with Heavenly Father, I felt a powerful sense of light and warmth. And I knew. I just knew.

I remember being awakened one night years later by a feeling of "pure intelligence" telling me I would be called to serve in the elders quorum.[21] Two weeks later I was called.

I remember a general conference where a beloved member of the Quorum of the Twelve Apostles spoke the exact words of testimony I had told a friend I hoped to hear.

I remember kneeling with hundreds of brethren to pray for a dear friend who lay unconscious on a ventilator in a small, faraway hospital after his heart had stopped. As we united our own hearts to plead for his life, he woke up and pulled the ventilator out of his own throat. He serves today as a stake president.

And I remember waking up with strong spiritual feelings after a vivid dream of a dear friend and mentor who passed away far too early, leaving an enormous hole in my life. He was smiling and joyful. I knew he was OK.

These are some of my rays. You have had your own experiences—your own light-filled bursts of testimony. As we recognize, remember, and gather these rays "together in one,"[22] something wonderful and powerful begins to happen. "Light cleaveth unto light"—"truth embraceth truth."[23] The reality and power of one ray of testimony reinforces and combines with another, and then another, and another. Line upon line, precept upon precept, here a ray and there a ray—one small, treasured spiritual moment at a time—there grows up within us a core of light-filled, spiritual experiences. Perhaps no one ray is strong enough or bright enough to constitute a full testimony, but together they can become a light that the darkness of doubt cannot overcome.

"O then, is not this real?" Alma asks. "I say unto you, Yea, because it is light."[24]

"That which is of God is light," the Lord teaches us, "and he that receiveth light, and continueth in God, receiveth more light; and that light groweth brighter and brighter until the perfect day."[25]

That means, brothers and sisters, that in time and through "great diligence,"[26] we too can have our own pillar of light—one ray at a time. And in the midst of that pillar, we too will find a loving Heavenly Father calling us by name, pointing us to our Savior, Jesus Christ, and inviting us to "Hear Him!"

I bear witness of Jesus Christ, that He is the light and life of the whole world—and of your personal world and mine.

I testify that He is the true and living Son of the true and living God and that He stands at the head of this true and living Church, guided and directed by His true and living prophets and apostles.

May we recognize and receive His glorious light and then choose Him over the darkness of the world—always and forever. In the name of Jesus Christ, amen.

Notes

1. See Joseph Smith—History 1:10–13.
2. See Joseph Smith—History 1:14–16.
3. See Joseph Smith, Journal, Nov. 9–11, 1835, 24, josephsmithpapers.org.
4. Joseph Smith—History 1:17.
5. See Joseph Smith—History 1:20. When Joseph Smith returned home after the First Vision, his mother asked if he was OK. He replied, "I am well enough off. . . . *I have learned for myself* that Presbyterianism is not true" (emphasis added).
6. Russell M. Nelson, "Closing Remarks," *Ensign* or *Liahona*, Nov. 2019, 122.
7. Spencer W. Kimball, in Conference Report, Munich Germany Area Conference, 1973, 77; quoted in Graham W. Doxey, "The Voice Is Still Small," *Ensign*, Nov. 1991, 25.
8. *Teachings of Presidents of the Church: Joseph F. Smith* (1998), 201: "When I as a boy first started out in the ministry, I would frequently go out and ask the Lord to show me some marvelous thing, in order that I might receive a testimony. But the Lord withheld marvels from me, and showed me the truth, line upon line, precept upon precept, here a little and there a little, until he made me to know the truth from the crown of my head to the soles of my feet, and until doubt and fear had been absolutely purged from me. He did not have to send an angel from the heavens to do this, nor did he have to speak with the trump of an archangel. By the whisperings of the still small voice of the Spirit of the living God, he gave to me the testimony I possess. And by this principle and power he will give to all the children of men a knowledge of the truth that will stay with them, and it will make them to know the truth, as God knows it, and to do the will of the Father as Christ does it."
9. Mosiah 16:9.
10. Doctrine and Covenants 84:46; see also John 1:9.
11. Doctrine and Covenants 88:12–13.
12. David A. Bednar, *The Spirit of Revelation* (2021), 7.
13. Doctrine and Covenants 6:23.
14. Doctrine and Covenants 8:2; see also Helaman 5:30.
15. See Mosiah 5:2; Doctrine and Covenants 11:12.
16. See 2 Nephi 4:21; Helaman 5:44.

17. The Lord has identified the ability to believe on the testimony of others as a spiritual gift (see Doctrine and Covenants 46:13–14).
18. Modern revelation teaches that the words of scripture "are given by my Spirit unto you, . . . and save it were by my power you could not have them; wherefore, you can testify that you have heard my voice, and know my words" (Doctrine and Covenants 18:35–36).
19. See Mosiah 2:17; Moroni 7:45–48.
20. 1 Nephi 1:20. Elder Gerrit W. Gong has spoken of "look[ing] with eyes to see and rejoic[ing] in the Lord's many tender mercies in our lives" ("Ministering," *Liahona*, May 2023, 18) and of how "the Lord's hand in our lives is often clearest in hindsight" ("Always Remember Him," *Ensign* or *Liahona*, May 2016, 108). The gift of gratefully recognizing and acknowledging the hand of the Lord in our lives, even if we didn't recognize it or feel it in the moment, is powerful. The scriptures speak often of the spiritual power of remembering (see Helaman 5:9–12; Doctrine and Covenants 20:77, 79), which can be a precursor to revelation (see Moroni 10:3–4).
21. Joseph Smith taught, "A person may profit by noticing the first intimation of the spirit of revelation; for instance, when you feel pure intelligence flowing into you, it may give you sudden strokes of ideas, so that by noticing it, you may find it fulfilled the same day or soon; (i.e.) those things that were presented unto your minds by the Spirit of God, will come to pass; and thus by learning the Spirit of God and understanding it, you may grow into the principle of revelation, until you become perfect in Christ Jesus" (*Teachings of Presidents of the Church: Joseph Smith* [2007], 132).
22. Ephesians 1:10.
23. Doctrine and Covenants 88:40: "For intelligence cleaveth unto intelligence; wisdom receiveth wisdom; truth embraceth truth; virtue loveth virtue; light cleaveth unto light."
24. Alma 32:35. Alma emphasized that these light-filled experiences, although often small, are real in every sense. Their reality becomes even more powerful when they are combined together to form a powerful whole.
25. Doctrine and Covenants 50:24.
26. Alma 32:41.

COVENANT CONFIDENCE THROUGH JESUS CHRIST

ELDER ULISSES SOARES

Of the Quorum of the Twelve Apostles

My beloved brothers and sisters, I pray that we may be spiritually renewed by the inspired messages from our leaders this weekend and rejoice in what I love to call "covenant confidence through Jesus Christ." This confidence is the quiet yet certain assurance of receiving the blessings that God promises for those who keep their covenants and is so needed amid the challenging circumstances of our day.

The construction of new houses of the Lord across the world, under the inspired leadership of President Russell M. Nelson, has caused great rejoicing among Church members and serves as an important symbol of the expansion of the Lord's kingdom.

Reflecting on my awe-inspiring experience at the dedication of the Feather River California Temple last October, I wondered if sometimes we get lost in the excitement of having new temples in our cities and communities and neglect the holier purpose of the sacred covenants made in the temple.

Inscribed on the front of each temple is a solemn statement: "Holiness to the Lord."[1] These inspired words are a clear invitation that when we enter the Lord's house, we embark on a sacred journey of learning to become higher and holier disciples of Christ. As we make covenants in holiness before God and commit to follow the Savior, we receive the power to change our hearts, renew our spirits, and deepen our relationship with Him. Such an endeavor brings sanctification to our souls and forms a sacred bond with God and Jesus Christ, who promise that we can inherit the gift of eternal life.[2] The result of this sacred journey is that we obtain a holier and higher confidence for our day-to-day lives within our covenants made through Jesus Christ.

Such confidence is the pinnacle of our divine connection with God and can help us increase our devotion to and gratitude for Jesus

Christ and His atoning sacrifice. It fortifies our ability to love and serve others, and it strengthens our souls to live in an unholy world that is increasingly dark and discouraging. It empowers us to overcome the seeds of doubt and despair, fear and frustration, heartache and hopelessness that the enemy tries to drive deep into our hearts, especially when life is hard, trials are long, or circumstances are difficult. A biblical verse offers sound advice for each of us as we lean into the stiff wind of today's worldly challenges: "Cast not away therefore your confidence."[3]

Dear brothers and sisters, those who gain genuine confidence in the covenants made in the house of the Lord through Jesus Christ possess one of the most powerful forces that we can access in this life.

As we have studied the Book of Mormon in *Come, Follow Me* this year, we have witnessed how Nephi beautifully exemplified the power of this type of covenant confidence through his faithfulness when he faced setbacks and challenges, like getting the plates as commanded by the Lord. Nephi, despite being exceedingly sorrowful for the fear and lack of faith of Laman and Lemuel, remained confident that the Lord would deliver the plates to them. He said unto his brothers, "As the Lord liveth, and as we live, we will not go down unto our father in the wilderness until we have accomplished the thing which the Lord hath commanded us."[4] Because of Nephi's confidence in the Lord's promises, he was able to accomplish what he had been commanded to do.[5] Later, in his vision, Nephi beheld the influence of this type of confidence, writing, "I, Nephi, beheld the power of the Lamb of God, that it descended upon the saints of the church of the Lamb, and upon the covenant people of the Lord, . . . and they were armed with righteousness and with the power of God in great glory."[6]

I have seen firsthand the Lord's loving promises and power flowing into the lives of God's children, strengthening them to face life's circumstances. The other day my wife came home after her worship in the temple and told me how deeply touched she was by what she experienced there. As she entered the house of the Lord, she saw a man in a wheelchair moving very slowly and a woman walking with great difficulty using a cane, both courageously coming to worship the Lord in His house. As my wife walked into the initiatory area, she saw a sweet sister who was missing one arm—and had only part of another arm—beautifully and celestially performing any tasks she was given.

As my wife and I talked about that experience, we concluded that only pure and heartfelt confidence in the eternal promises God provides through the holy covenants made with Him in His house could cause those marvelous disciples of Christ to leave their homes on that very freezing day, despite their personal life circumstances.

My dear friends, if there is one thing we could possess—and one thing we could pass on to our children and grandchildren that would help each in the tests and trials ahead—it would be confidence in the covenants made through Jesus Christ. Obtaining such a divine possession will help them live as the Lord promised His faithful followers: "My disciples shall stand in holy places, and shall not be moved."[7]

How do we gain such confidence through Jesus Christ? It comes through humility, centering our lives on the Savior, living by the principles of the gospel of Jesus Christ, receiving the ordinances of salvation and exaltation, and honoring the covenants we make with God in His holy house.

In his closing remarks at the October 2019 general conference, our dear prophet reminded us about an important step in achieving covenant confidence, saying: "Individual worthiness to enter the Lord's house requires much individual spiritual preparation. . . . Individual worthiness requires a total conversion of mind and heart to be more like the Lord, to be an honest citizen, to be a better example, and to be a holier person."[8] Therefore, if we change our preparation to enter the temple, we will change our experience in the temple, which will transform our lives outside of the temple. "Then shall thy confidence wax strong in the presence of God; and the doctrine of the priesthood shall distil upon thy soul as the dews from heaven."[9]

A bishop I know refers to the oldest class in Primary not as a "Primary" class but as a "temple preparation" class. In January the bishop has the class members and their teachers come to his office, where they talk about how they will spend the entire year preparing to enter the temple. The bishop takes time to go through the applicable temple recommend interview questions, which are then included in their Primary lessons. He invites the children to be prepared so that when they come to the bishop's office in one year, they will be confident, covenant confident, ready to receive a temple recommend and enter the Lord's house. This year the bishop had four young girls who were so excited, prepared, and confident to go to the temple that they wanted the bishop to print their recommends on New Year's Day at 12:01 a.m.

Preparation isn't just for those going to the temple for the first time. We all should be perpetually preparing to go to the house of the Lord. One stake I know has adopted the motto "Home centered, Church supported, and temple bound." *Bound*[10] is an interesting word in that it means focused on a direction, but it also means fastened to or secured by, resolved and determined, sure. So being temple bound secures us to the Savior, giving us proper direction and stability while ensuring we have covenant confidence through Jesus Christ. Therefore, all of us should intentionally enhance such binding by having our next appointment scheduled with the Lord in His holy house, whether the temple is near or far away.[11]

Our dear prophet, President Russell M. Nelson, reminds us about these vital principles by saying: "The temple lies at the center of strengthening our faith and spiritual fortitude because the Savior and His doctrine are the very heart of the temple. Everything taught in the temple, through instruction and through the Spirit, increases our understanding of Jesus Christ. His essential ordinances bind us to Him through sacred priesthood covenants. Then, as we keep our covenants, He endows us with *His* healing, strengthening power. And oh, how we will need His power in the days ahead."[12]

The Savior desires that we become prepared to understand, with great clarity, exactly how to act as we make covenants with our

Heavenly Father in His name. He wants us to be prepared to experience our privileges, promises, and responsibilities; to be prepared to have the spiritual insights and awakenings that we need in this life. I know that when the Lord sees even a spark of desire or a flicker of righteous effort in our willingness to center our lives on Him and on the ordinances and covenants we make in His house, He will bless us, in His perfect way, with the miracles and tender mercies we need.

The house of the Lord is where we can be transformed in higher and holier ways. So, when we walk out of the temple, transformed by our hope in the promises of the covenants, armed with power from on high, we take the temple with us into our homes and lives. I assure you that having the spirit of the Lord's house in us changes us, completely.

We also know from the temple that if we want the Spirit of the Lord to be unrestrained in our lives, we simply cannot and must not have unkind feelings toward anyone. Giving place in our hearts or minds for unkind feelings or thoughts will produce unkind words and actions, whether on social media or in our homes, causing the Spirit of the Lord to withdraw from our hearts. Therefore, please cast not away your confidence, but rather, let your confidence wax strong.

The ongoing and accelerating building of temples will continue to excite, inspire, and bless us. Yet more important, as we change our preparation to enter the temple, we will change our experience in the temple, which will transform our lives outside of the temple. May this transformation fill us with confidence in our holy covenants made with God through Jesus Christ. God lives, Jesus is our Savior, and this is His restored Church on earth. I reverently declare these truths in the sacred name of our Savior, Jesus Christ, amen.

Notes

1. See Exodus 28:36; 39:30; Psalm 93:5. Translated equivalents are used on temples in non-English-speaking localities.
2. See Doctrine and Covenants 14:7; 132:19–20, 24.
3. Hebrews 10:35.
4. 1 Nephi 3:15.

5. See 1 Nephi 4:6–38.
6. 1 Nephi 14:14.
7. Doctrine and Covenants 45:32.
8. Russell M. Nelson, "Closing Remarks," *Ensign* or *Liahona*, Nov. 2019, 121–22.
9. Doctrine and Covenants 121:45.
10. See *Merriam-Webster.com Dictionary*, "bound."
11. See Russell M. Nelson, "Becoming Exemplary Latter-day Saints," *Ensign* or *Liahona*, Nov. 2018, 114.
12. Russell M. Nelson, "The Temple and Your Spiritual Foundation," *Liahona*, Nov. 2021, 93–94.

INTEGRITY: A CHRISTLIKE ATTRIBUTE

ELDER JACK N. GERARD

Of the Seventy

In the closing hours of the Savior's ministry, He went to the Mount of Olives into a garden called Gethsemane and invited His disciples to wait.[1] Now alone, He petitioned His Father, "If thou be willing, remove this cup from me."[2] Being in agony, His suffering caused Him, "even God, the greatest of all, to tremble because of pain, and to bleed at every pore, . . . and would that [He] might not drink the bitter cup, and shrink."[3] Yet in the moment of deep despair, the Savior did not shrink "but partook and finished [His] preparations unto the children of men."[4]

As the Only Begotten of the Father, Jesus Christ had power over death, pain, and suffering but did not shrink. He fulfilled the covenant He had made with His Father and, in doing so, manifested a Christlike attribute increasingly important in the world in which we live—the attribute of integrity. He remained true to God, to each of us, and to His divine identity.

Integrity

Jesus Christ is our Exemplar. Living a life of integrity requires us to be true to God, to each other, and to our divine identity. Integrity flows from the first great commandment to love God. Because you love God, you are true to Him at all times. You understand that there is right and wrong and there is absolute truth—God's truth. Integrity means we do not lower our standards or behavior to impress or to be accepted by others.[5] You "do what is right" and "let the consequence follow."[6] Recent revisions to the *Preach My Gospel* missionary manual notably added integrity as a Christlike attribute.[7]

A number of years ago, Elder Uchtdorf was assigned to reorganize our stake. During our interview, he asked me a question I have not forgotten: "Has there been anything in your life that, if brought to the attention of the public, would be an embarrassment to you or the Church?" Surprised, my mind quickly raced over my entire life, trying to recall those moments when I may have fallen short and asking myself, "If others knew everything I had done, what would they think of me or the Church?"

In the moment, I thought Elder Uchtdorf was only asking about worthiness, but I've come to understand it was really a question about integrity. Was I true to what I professed? Would the world see consistency between my words and my deeds? Would others see God through my conduct?

President Spencer W. Kimball taught, "Integrity" is our "willingness and ability to live by our beliefs and commitments."[8]

True to God

A life of integrity requires us to first and foremost be true to God.

From our early childhood, we learned the story of Daniel in the lions' den. Daniel was always true to God. His jealous peers "sought to find occasion against [him]"[9] and contrived a decree mandating prayers to their gods alone. Daniel knew of the decree but went home and—with "his windows being open"[10]—knelt and prayed three times a day to the God of Israel. As a result, Daniel was cast into the lions' den. On the morn, the king found Daniel's God had delivered him and issued a new decree that all should "tremble and fear before the God of Daniel: for he is the living God."[11]

The king came to know God through Daniel's integrity. Others see God through ours—words and deeds. Just like Daniel, being true to God will increasingly set us apart from the world.

The Savior reminds us, "In the world ye shall have tribulation: but be of good cheer; I have overcome the world."[12] President Russell M. Nelson counseled: "[Overcoming the world] means overcoming the temptation to care more about the things of this world than the things of God. It means trusting the doctrine of Christ more than the philosophies of men."[13] Likewise, we must resist the temptation to walk "in [our] own way, and after the image of [our] own god, whose image is in the likeness of the world."[14]

The oppositional pull of this world is an essential part of God's plan of salvation. How we respond to the pull is the essence of who we are—a measure of our integrity. The worldly pull can be as direct as to destroy fidelity in marriage or as subtle as posting anonymous comments critical of Church doctrine or culture. Exercising integrity in our choices is an outward expression of an inner commitment to follow the Savior Jesus Christ.

True to Others

Just as integrity flows from the first great commandment to love God, being true to each other flows from the second, to love our neighbors as ourselves. A life of integrity is not a life of perfection; it is a life in which we strive every day to foremost be true to God and within that context to be true to others. President Oaks reminds us, "Our zeal to keep [the] second commandment must not cause us to forget the first."[15]

The world increasingly grapples with integrity by imposing codes of conduct or ethical rules that govern the relationships between people and institutions. While good, these rules are generally not anchored in absolute truth and tend to evolve based on cultural acceptance. Similar to the question posed by Elder Uchtdorf, some organizations train employees to consider what their decisions or decision-making process would look like if published online or on the front page of a major newspaper. As the Church comes out of obscurity and darkness,[16] we, like Daniel, must rise above the worldly expectations and become the face of the true and living God at all times and in all places.[17]

Saying we have integrity is insufficient if our actions are inconsistent with our words. Likewise, Christian kindness is not a substitute for integrity. As a covenant people, and as leaders of His Church, we must be beyond reproach and aligned with the standards the Lord has set.

Acting with integrity builds faith and trust and reassures others that we seek only to do the will of the Lord. In our councils, we resist outside influences and follow the Lord's revealed process, seeking insights from each woman and man and acting consistent with the inspired counsel received.[18]

Our focus is on the Savior, and we are careful to avoid actions that may be perceived as serving our own interests, benefiting our family, or favoring someone at the expense of another. We go out of our way to avoid any perception that our actions may be influenced by the honors of men,[19] to receive personal recognition, generate more likes, be quoted or published.

True to Our Divine Identity

Finally, a life of integrity requires us to be true to our divine identity.

We know some who were not. Of particular significance is the anti-Christ Korihor, who led away the hearts of many, appealing to their "carnal mind."[20] Yet, in the final moments of his life, he confessed, "I always knew that there was a God."[21] President Henry B. Eyring has taught that lying "is contrary to the nature of our spirits,"[22] our divine identity. Korihor deceived himself, and the truth was not in him.[23]

In contrast, the Prophet Joseph Smith confidently proclaimed, "I knew it, and I knew that God knew it, and I could not deny it."[24]

Joseph's brother Hyrum was loved by the Lord "because of the integrity of his heart."[25] He and Joseph remained true to the end—true to their divine identity, the light and knowledge they received, and true to the person they knew they could become.

Conclusion

May we reconcile ourselves "to the will of God"[26] and develop the Christlike attribute of integrity. May we follow our Exemplar, the Savior of the world, and not shrink but live a life that is true to God, to each other, and to our divine identity.

As Job said, "Let me be weighed in an even balance, that God may know mine integrity."[27] In the sacred name of Jesus Christ, amen.

Notes

1. See Matthew 26:30, 36; Luke 22:39–41.
2. Luke 22:42.
3. Doctrine and Covenants 19:18.
4. Doctrine and Covenants 19:19.
5. See *Preach My Gospel: A Guide to Sharing the Gospel of Jesus Christ* (2023), 129.
6. "Do What Is Right," *Hymns*, no. 237.
7. See *Preach My Gospel*, 128–29.
8. *Teachings of Presidents of the Church: Spencer W. Kimball* (2006), 126.
9. Daniel 6:4.
10. Daniel 6:10.
11. Daniel 6:26.
12. John 16:33.
13. Russell M. Nelson, "Overcome the World and Find Rest," *Liahona*, Nov. 2022, 96.
14. Doctrine and Covenants 1:16.
15. Dallin H. Oaks, "*Two* Great Commandments," *Ensign* or *Liahona*, Nov. 2019, 73.
16. See Doctrine and Covenants 1:30.
17. See Mosiah 18:9.
18. See Doctrine and Covenants 42:2–3; see also *General Handbook: Serving in The Church of Jesus Christ of Latter-day Saints*, 4.3, Gospel Library.
19. See Doctrine and Covenants 121:35.
20. Alma 30:53.
21. Alma 30:52.
22. Henry B. Eyring, "Going Home" (Brigham Young University devotional, Nov. 18, 1986), 5, speeches.byu.edu.
23. See 1 John 1:8.
24. Joseph Smith—History 1:25.
25. Doctrine and Covenants 124:15.
26. 2 Nephi 10:24.
27. Job 31:6.

ALL WILL BE WELL BECAUSE OF TEMPLE COVENANTS

PRESIDENT HENRY B. EYRING
Second Counselor in the First Presidency

My beloved brothers and sisters, this session of general conference has been, for me, a sacred time. I am grateful for the assignment to speak to the millions of Latter-day Saints and our friends across the world. I love you, and I know the Lord loves you.

Over 50 years ago, I had the privilege to serve as the president of Ricks College in Rexburg, Idaho. On the morning of June 5, 1976, my wife, Kathy, and I drove from Rexburg to the Idaho Falls Idaho Temple to attend the sealing of a close friend. Of course, with four young boys in our home at the time, our temple trip could be only accomplished with the help of a courageous babysitter! We left our precious children in her care and made the short, 30-minute drive.

Our experience in the temple that day was wonderful, as it always was. However, after the conclusion of the temple sealing—and as we were preparing to return home—we noticed many temple workers and patrons nervously conversing in the lobby of the temple. Within moments, one of the temple workers told us that the newly constructed Teton Dam in eastern Idaho had collapsed! More than 80 billion gallons (300 million cubic meters) of water were flowing through the dam and into the 300 square miles (775 square km) of neighboring valleys. Much of the city of Rexburg was underwater, with homes and vehicles carried away by floodwaters. Two-thirds of the 9,000 residents were suddenly homeless.[1]

As you might imagine, our thoughts and concerns turned to the safety of our dear children, hundreds of college students and faculty, and a community we loved. We were less than 30 miles (50 km) from home, and yet on this day, long before cell phones and text messaging, we had no way of communicating immediately with our children, nor could we make the drive from Idaho Falls to Rexburg, as all the roads had been closed.

Our only option was to stay the night in a local motel in Idaho

Falls. Kathy and I knelt together in our motel room and humbly pleaded with Heavenly Father for the safety of our dear children and the thousands of others affected by the tragic event. I recall Kathy pacing the floors into the early hours of the morning with worry about her children. Despite my own concerns, I was able to put my mind at ease and fall asleep.

It wasn't long thereafter that my sweet eternal companion woke me and said, "Hal, how can you sleep at a time like this?"

These words then came clearly to my heart and mind. I said to my wife: "Kathy, whatever the outcome, all will be well because of the temple. We have made covenants with God and have been sealed as an eternal family."

At that moment, it was as if the Spirit of the Lord confirmed in our hearts and minds what we both already knew to be true: the sealing ordinances, found only in the house of the Lord and administered by proper priesthood authority, had bound us together as husband and wife, and our children had been sealed to us. There truly was no need to fear, and we were grateful later to learn that our boys were safe.

Perhaps this statement from President Thomas S. Monson best illustrates what Kathy and I felt on that unforgettable night. "As we attend the temple, there can come to us a dimension of spirituality and a feeling of *peace*. . . . We will grasp the true meaning of the words of the Savior when He said: 'Peace I leave with you, my peace I give unto you. . . . Let not your heart be troubled, neither let it be afraid [John 14:27].'"[2]

I have been blessed to feel that peace every time I enter the sacred temple. I recall the first day I walked into the Salt Lake Temple. I was a young man.

I looked up at a high white ceiling that made the room so light it seemed almost as if it were open to the sky. And in that moment, the thought came into my mind in clear words: "I have been in this lighted place before." But then immediately there came into my mind, not in my own voice, these words: "No, you have never been here before. You are remembering a moment before you were born. You were in a sacred place like this where the Lord could come."

Brothers and sisters, I humbly testify that as we attend the temple, we can be reminded of the eternal nature of our spirits, our relationship with the Father and His divine Son, and our ultimate desire to return to our heavenly home.

In recent conference addresses, President Russell M. Nelson taught:

"The safest place to be *spiritually* is living *inside* your temple covenants!"

"*Everything* we believe and *every* promise God has made to His covenant people come together in the temple."[3]

"Each person who makes covenants . . . in temples—and keeps them—has increased access to the power of Jesus Christ."[4]

He also taught that "once we make a covenant with God, we leave neutral ground forever. God will not abandon His relationship with those who have forged such a bond with Him. In fact, all those who have made a covenant with God have access to a special kind of love and mercy."[5]

Under President Nelson's inspired leadership, the Lord has accelerated, and will continue to accelerate, the building of temples across the world. This will allow all of God's children the opportunity to receive the ordinances of salvation and exaltation and to make and keep sacred covenants. Qualifying to make sacred covenants is not a one-time effort but a lifetime pattern. The Lord has said it will take our full heart, might, mind, and strength.[6]

Frequent participation in the ordinances of the temple can create a pattern of devotion to the Lord. When you keep your temple covenants and remember them, you invite the companionship of the Holy Ghost to both strengthen and purify you.

You may then experience a feeling of light and hope testifying that the promises are true. You will come to know that every covenant with God is an opportunity to draw closer to Him, which will then create a desire in your heart to keep temple covenants.

We have been promised, "Because of our covenant with God,

He will never tire in His efforts to help us, and we will never exhaust His merciful patience with us."[7]

It is through the sealing covenants in the temple that we can receive the assurance of loving family connections that will continue after death and last for eternity. Honoring marriage and family covenants made in temples of God will provide protection from the evil of selfishness and pride.

Consistent care of brothers and sisters for each other will come only with persistent efforts to lead your family in the Lord's way. Give children opportunities to pray for each other. Discern quickly the beginnings of discord, and positively recognize acts of unselfish service, especially to one another. When siblings pray for each other and serve each other, hearts will be softened and turned to each other and to their parents.

In part, that is what is described by Malachi as he foretold of the coming of the prophet Elijah: "He shall plant in the hearts of the children the promises made to the fathers, and the hearts of the children shall turn to their fathers. If it were not so, the whole earth would be utterly wasted at his coming."[8]

Trials, challenges, and heartaches will surely come to all of us. None of us are immune from "thorns of the flesh."[9] Yet, as we attend the temple and remember our covenants, we can prepare to receive personal direction from the Lord.

When Kathy and I were married and sealed in the Logan Utah Temple, then-Elder Spencer W. Kimball performed our sealing. In the few words he spoke, he gave this counsel: "Hal and Kathy, live so that when the call comes, you can walk away easily."

Initially, we did not understand what that counsel meant for us, but we did our best to live our lives in such a way that we would be prepared to leave to serve the Lord when the call came. After we had been married nearly 10 years, an unanticipated call did come from the Commissioner of Church Education, Neal A. Maxwell.

The loving counsel given by President Kimball in the temple to be able to "walk away easily" became a reality. Kathy and I received a call to leave what seemed an idyllic family situation in California to serve in an assignment and in a place that I knew nothing about. However, our family was ready to leave because a prophet, in a holy temple, a place of revelation, saw a future event for which we were then prepared.

My dear brothers and sisters, I bear witness that there is nothing more important than honoring the covenants you have made or may make in the temple. No matter where you are on the covenant path, I urge you to qualify and become eligible to attend the temple. Visit as frequently as circumstances will allow. Make and keep sacred covenants with God. I can assure you of the same truth I shared with Kathy in the middle of the night nearly five decades ago in an Idaho Falls motel room: "No matter the outcome, all will be well because of temple covenants."

I give you my sure witness that Jesus is the Christ. He lives and leads His Church. Temples are houses of the Lord. President Russell M. Nelson is God's living prophet on the earth. I love him, and I love each of you. In the sacred name of Jesus Christ, amen.

Notes

1. See "1976: The Teton Dam Failed, KTVB Captured the Aftermath from the Air," ktvb.com.
2. Thomas S. Monson, "Blessings of the Temple," *Ensign* or *Liahona*, May 2015, 91–92; emphasis added.
3. Russell M. Nelson, "The Temple and Your Spiritual Foundation," *Liahona*, Nov. 2021, 96, 94.
4. Russell M. Nelson, "Overcome the World and Find Rest," *Liahona*, Nov. 2022, 96.
5. Russell M. Nelson, "The Everlasting Covenant," *Liahona*, Oct. 2022, 5.
6. See Doctrine and Covenants 59:5.
7. Russell M. Nelson, "The Everlasting Covenant," 6.
8. Joseph Smith—History 1:39.
9. See 2 Corinthians 12:7–10.

Saturday Afternoon Session

APRIL 6, 2024

"BE STILL, AND KNOW THAT I AM GOD"

ELDER DAVID A. BEDNAR
Of the Quorum of the Twelve Apostles

During a recent open house and media day for a new house of the Lord, I led a group of journalists on a tour through the sacred structure. I described the purposes of temples in The Church of Jesus Christ of Latter-day Saints and responded to their many excellent questions.

Before entering the celestial room, I explained that this particular room in the house of the Lord symbolically represents the peace and beauty of the heavenly home to which we can return after this life. I indicated to our guests that we would not speak while in the celestial room, but I would be happy to answer any questions after we moved to the next stop on the tour.

After exiting the celestial room and as we gathered at the next location, I asked our guests if they had any observations they wanted to share. One of the journalists said with great emotion, "I have never experienced anything like that in my entire life. I did not know quiet like that existed in the world; I simply did not believe such stillness was possible."

I was struck by both the sincerity and the starkness of this person's statement. And the journalist's reaction highlighted one important aspect of stillness—overcoming and tuning out the commotion of our external environment.

As I later pondered the journalist's comment and reflected on the often hectic pace of our modern lives—the busyness, noise, diversions, distractions, and detours that so often seem to demand our attention—a scripture came to my mind: "Be still, and know that I am God."[1]

I pray the Holy Ghost will enlighten each of us as we consider a higher and holier dimension of stillness in our lives—an inner spiritual stillness of the soul that enables us to know and remember that God is our Heavenly Father, we are His children, and Jesus Christ is our Savior. This remarkable blessing is available to all Church members who are striving faithfully to become "covenant people of the Lord."[2]

Be Still

In 1833, the Saints in Missouri were the targets of intense persecution. Mobs had driven them from their homes in Jackson County, and some Church members had tried to establish themselves in other nearby counties. But the persecution continued, and the threats of death were many. In these challenging circumstances, the Lord revealed the following instruction to the Prophet Joseph Smith in Kirtland, Ohio:

"Therefore, let your hearts be comforted concerning Zion; for all flesh is in mine hands; *be still* and know that I am God."[3]

I believe the Lord's admonition to "be still" entails much more than simply not talking or not moving. Perhaps His intent is for us to remember and rely upon Him and His power "at all times and in all things, and in all places that [we] may be in."[4] Thus, "be still" may be a way of reminding us to focus upon the Savior unfailingly as the ultimate source of the spiritual stillness of the soul that strengthens us to do and overcome hard things.

Build upon the Rock

True faith is always focused in and on the *Lord Jesus Christ*—in Him as the Divine and Only Begotten Son of the Eternal Father and on Him and the redemptive mission He fulfilled.

"For he hath answered the ends of the law, and he claimeth all those who have faith in him; and they who have faith in him will cleave unto every good thing; wherefore he advocateth the cause of the children of men."[5]

Jesus Christ is our Redeemer,[6] our Mediator,[7] and our Advocate[8] with the Eternal Father and the rock upon which we should build the spiritual foundation of our lives.

Helaman explained, "Remember, remember that it is upon the rock of our Redeemer, who is Christ, the Son of God, that ye must build *your* foundation; that when the devil shall send forth his mighty winds, yea, his shafts in the whirlwind, yea, when all his hail and his mighty storm shall beat upon you, it shall have no power over you to drag you down to the gulf of misery and endless wo, *because of the rock upon which ye are built*, which is a sure foundation, a foundation whereon if men build they cannot fall."[9]

The symbolism of Christ as the "rock" upon whom we should build the foundation of our lives is most instructive. Please note in this verse that the Savior is not the foundation. Rather, we are admonished to build our personal spiritual foundation upon Him.[10]

The foundation is the part of a building that connects it to the ground. A strong foundation provides protection from natural disasters and many other destructive forces. A proper foundation also distributes the weight of a structure over a large area to avoid overloading the underlying soil and provides a level surface for construction.

A strong and reliable connection between the ground and a foundation is essential if a structure is to remain sturdy and stable over time. And for particular types of construction, anchor pins and steel rods can be used to attach the foundation of a building to "bedrock," the hard, solid rock beneath surface materials such as soil and gravel.

In a similar way, the foundation of our lives must be connected to the rock of Christ if we are to remain firm and steadfast. The sacred covenants and ordinances of the Savior's restored gospel can be compared to the anchor pins and steel rods used to connect a building to bedrock. Every time we faithfully receive, review, remember, and renew sacred covenants, our spiritual anchors are secured ever more firmly and steadfastly to the "rock" of Jesus Christ.

"Wherefore, whoso believeth in God might with surety hope for a better world, yea, even a place at the right hand of God, which hope cometh of faith, maketh *an anchor* to the souls of men, which would make them sure and steadfast, always abounding in good works, being led to glorify God."[11]

Incrementally and increasingly "in process of time,"[12] "virtue [garnishes our] thoughts unceasingly," our "confidence [waxes stronger and stronger] in the presence of God," and "the Holy Ghost [is our] constant companion."[13] We become more grounded, rooted, established, and settled.[14] As the foundation of our lives is built upon the Savior, we are blessed to "be still"—to have a spiritual assurance that God is our Heavenly Father, we are His children, and Jesus Christ is our Savior.

Sacred Times, Holy Places, and the Home

The Lord provides both sacred times and holy places to help us experience and learn about this inner stillness of our souls.

For example, the Sabbath is God's day, a *sacred time* set apart to remember and worship the Father in the name of His Son, to participate in priesthood ordinances, and to receive and renew sacred covenants. Each week we worship the Lord during our home study and also as "fellowcitizens with the saints"[15] during sacrament and other meetings. On His holy day, our thoughts, actions, and demeanor are signs we give to God and an indicator of our love for Him.[16] Every Sunday, if we will, we can be still and know that God is our Heavenly Father, we are His children, and Jesus Christ is our Savior.

A central feature of our Sabbath worship is to "go to the house of prayer and offer up [our] sacraments upon [the Lord's] holy day."[17] The "house[s] of prayer" in which we gather on the Sabbath are meetinghouses and other approved facilities—*holy places* of reverence, worship, and learning. Each meetinghouse and facility is dedicated by priesthood authority as a place where the Spirit of the Lord may dwell and where God's children may come "to the knowledge of their Redeemer."[18] If we will, we can "be still" in our holy places of worship and know ever more surely that God is our Heavenly Father, we are His children, and Jesus Christ is our Savior.

The temple is another *holy place* specifically set apart for worshipping and serving God and learning eternal truths. We think, act, and dress differently in the house of the Lord from any other places that we may frequent. In His holy house, if we will, we can be still and know that God is our Heavenly Father, we are His children, and Jesus Christ is our Savior.

The principal purposes of sacred time and holy places are exactly the same: to repeatedly focus our attention upon Heavenly Father and His plan, the Lord Jesus Christ and His Atonement, the edifying power of the Holy Ghost, and the promises associated with the sacred ordinances and covenants of the Savior's restored gospel.

Today I repeat a principle I previously have emphasized. Our homes should be the ultimate combination of both *sacred time* and *holy place* wherein individuals and families can "be still" and know that God is our Heavenly Father, we are His children, and Jesus Christ is our Savior. Leaving our homes to worship on the Sabbath and in the house of the Lord certainly is essential. But only as we return to our homes with the spiritual perspective and strength obtained in those holy places and activities can we then sustain our focus upon the primary purposes of mortal life and overcome the temptations so prevalent in our fallen world.

Our ongoing Sabbath, temple, and home experiences should fortify us with the power of the Holy Ghost, with an ongoing and stronger covenant connection to the Father and the Son, and with "a perfect brightness of hope"[19] in God's eternal promises.

As home and Church are gathered together in one in Christ,[20] we may be troubled on every side, but we will not be distressed in our minds and hearts. We may be perplexed by our circumstances and challenges, but we will not be in despair. We may be persecuted, but we will also recognize that we are never alone.[21] We can receive spiritual strength to become and remain firm, steadfast, and true.

Promise and Testimony

I promise that as we build the foundation of our lives on the "rock" of Jesus Christ, we can be blessed by the Holy Ghost to receive an individual and spiritual stillness of the soul that enables us to know and remember that God is our Heavenly Father, we are His children, Jesus Christ is our Savior, and we can be blessed to do and overcome hard things.

I joyfully witness that God is our Heavenly Father, we are His children, and Jesus Christ is our Redeemer and the "rock" of our salvation. I so testify in the sacred name of the Lord Jesus Christ, amen.

Notes

1. Psalm 46:10; see also Doctrine and Covenants 101:16.
2. 1 Nephi 14:14.
3. Doctrine and Covenants 101:16; emphasis added.
4. Mosiah 18:9.
5. Moroni 7:28.
6. See Mosiah 15:6–9.
7. See 2 Nephi 2:27–28.
8. See Moroni 7:28.
9. Helaman 5:12; emphasis added.
10. Ephesians 2:19–20 indicates that the "household of God" (the Church of Jesus Christ) is "built upon the foundation of the apostles and prophets, Jesus Christ himself being the chief corner stone." Thus, in the analogy used in Ephesians, Jesus Christ is the central component in the foundation upon which **His Church** is built.

    In contrast, Helaman 5:12 indicates that "it is upon the rock of our Redeemer, who is Christ, the Son of God, that ye must build *your* foundation" (emphasis added). Thus, the foundation upon which we should build our lives is the "rock of our Redeemer," "a sure foundation, a foundation whereon if men build they cannot fall." Thus, in the analogy used in Helaman, Jesus Christ is the "bedrock" upon which we should build **our individual lives**.
11. Ether 12:4; emphasis added.
12. See Moses 7:18, 21.
13. Doctrine and Covenants 121:45–46.
14. See Colossians 1:23; 2:7; 2 Peter 1:12; Neal A. Maxwell, "Overcome . . . Even As I Also Overcame," *Ensign*, May 1987, 70–72.
15. Ephesians 2:19.
16. See Russell M. Nelson, "The Sabbath Is a Delight," *Ensign* or *Liahona*, May 2015, 130.
17. Doctrine and Covenants 59:9.
18. Mosiah 18:30.
19. 2 Nephi 31:20.
20. See Ephesians 1:10.
21. See 2 Corinthians 4:8–9.

RISE! HE CALLETH THEE

ELDER MASSIMO DE FEO
Of the Seventy

Some time ago I asked my wife, "Can you tell me why, as far as I remember, we have never had any major problems in our lives?"

She looked at me and said, "Sure. I'll tell you why we have never had any major problems; it's because you have a very short memory!"

Her quick and smart answer made me realize once again that living the gospel of Jesus Christ does not remove pain and trials, which are necessary to grow.

The gospel is not a way to avoid challenges and problems but a solution to increase our faith and learn how to deal with them.

I had a sense of this truth a few months ago when I was walking one day and suddenly my sight became blurry, dark, and wavy. I was scared. Then the doctors told me, "If you don't begin treatment immediately, you may lose your sight even in a matter of weeks." I was even more scared.

And then they said, "You need intravitreal injections—injections right in the eye, wide-open eye—every four weeks for the rest of your life."

That was an uncomfortable wake-up call.

Then a reflection came in the form of a question. I asked myself, "OK! My physical sight is not good, but what about my spiritual vision? Do I need any treatment there? And what does it mean to have a clear spiritual vision?"

I pondered about the story of a blind man called Bartimaeus, described in the Gospel of Mark. The scripture says, "And when he heard that it was Jesus of Nazareth, he began to cry out, and say, Jesus, thou Son of David, have mercy on me."[1]

Technically, in the eyes of many, Jesus was just the son of Joseph, so why did Bartimaeus call Him "Son of David"? Simply because he recognized that Jesus was indeed the Messiah, who was prophesied to be born as a descendant of David.[2]

It is interesting that this blind man, who didn't have physical sight, recognized Jesus. He saw spiritually what he couldn't see physically, while many others could see Jesus physically but were totally blind spiritually.

From this story we learn more about clear spiritual vision.

We read, "And many charged him that he should hold his peace: but he cried the more a great deal, Thou Son of David, have mercy on me."[3]

All around him were telling him to be quiet, but he cried out even more because he knew who Jesus really was. He ignored those voices and screamed even louder.

He acted instead of being acted upon. Despite his limited circumstances, he used his faith to go beyond his limitations.

So, the *first principle* we learn is *we keep a clear spiritual vision when we focus on Jesus Christ and stay true to what we know to be true.*

Brothers and sisters, to keep our spiritual sight intact, we need to decide not to listen to the voices of the world around us. In this confusing and confused world, we must stay faithful to what we know, faithful to our covenants, faithful in keeping the commandments and reaffirm our beliefs even stronger, like this man did. We need to cry even louder our testimony of the Lord to the world. This man knew Jesus, stayed faithful to what he believed, and was not distracted by the voices around him.

There are many voices today trying to lower our voices as disciples of Jesus Christ. The voices of the world are trying to silence us, but that's exactly why we must declare our testimony of the Savior louder and stronger. Among all the voices of the world, the Lord is counting on me and you to declare our testimonies, to raise our voice, and to become His voice. If we don't do it, who will testify of Jesus Christ? Who will speak His name and declare His divine mission?

We have a spiritual charge that comes from our knowledge of Jesus Christ.

But what did Bartimaeus do after that?

At the Lord's command to *rise*, he acted again in faith.

The scripture says, "And he, casting away his garment, rose, and came to Jesus."[4]

This humble and faithful man understood that he could rise to a better life at Jesus's command. He knew that he was better than his circumstances, and the very first thing he did when he heard Jesus calling him was to throw away his beggar's coat.

Again he acted instead of being acted upon.

He might have thought, "I don't need this anymore, now that Jesus has come into my life. This is a new day. I'm done with this life of misery. With Jesus I can start a new life of happiness and joy in Him, with Him, and through Him. And I don't care what the world thinks of me. Jesus is calling me, and He will help me live a new life."

What a remarkable change!

As he threw away his beggar's coat, he got rid of all excuses.

And this is a *second principle: we keep a clear spiritual vision when we leave the natural man behind, repent, and begin a new life in Christ.*

The way to do it is by making and keeping covenants to rise to a better life through Jesus Christ.

As long as we make excuses to feel sorry for ourselves, sorry for our circumstances and problems, and sorry for all the bad things happening in our lives and even all the bad people who *we think* make us unhappy, we keep the beggar's coat on our shoulders. It is true that, at times, people (consciously or not) hurt us. But we need to decide to act with faith in Christ by removing the mental and emotional coat that we might still wear to hide excuses or sin and throw it away, knowing that He can and will heal us.

There is never a good excuse to say, "I am the way I am because of some unfortunate and unpleasant circumstances. And I cannot change, and I am justified."

When we think that way, we decide to be acted upon.

We keep the beggar's coat.

Acting in faith means to rely on our Savior, believing that

through His Atonement, we can *rise* above everything at His command.

The third principle is in the last four words: "[he] came to Jesus."

How could he go to Jesus since he was blind? The only way was to walk toward Jesus by hearing His voice.

And this is a *third principle: we keep a clear spiritual vision when we hear the voice of the Lord and allow Him to guide us.*

Just as this man raised his voice over the voices around him, he was able to listen to the voice of the Lord in the middle of all other voices.

This is the same faith that allowed Peter to walk on water as long as he kept his spiritual focus on the Lord and was not distracted by the winds around him.

Then the story of this blind man ends with the words "he received his sight, and followed Jesus in the way."[5]

One of the most important lessons in this story is that this man exercised true faith in Jesus Christ and received a miracle because he asked with *real intent*, the *real intent* to follow Him.

And this is the ultimate reason for the blessings we receive in our lives, which is to follow Jesus Christ. It is about recognizing *Him*, making and keeping covenants with God *because of Him*, changing our very nature *through Him*, and enduring to the end by following *Him*.

For me, keeping a clear spiritual vision is all about focusing on Jesus Christ.

So is my spiritual sight clear as I get my eye injections? Well, who am I to say? But I am grateful for what I see.

I clearly see the hand of the Lord in this sacred work and in my life.

I see the faith of many wherever I go who strengthen my own faith.

I see angels all around me.

I see the faith of many who don't see the Lord physically but recognize Him spiritually, because they know Him intimately.

I testify that this gospel is the answer for everything, because

Jesus Christ is the answer for everyone. I am grateful for what I can see as I follow my Savior.

I promise that as we hear the voice of the Lord and allow Him to guide us on the Savior's covenant path, we will be blessed with clear vision, spiritual understanding, and peace of heart and mind throughout our lives.

May we cry our testimony of Him louder than the voices around us in a world that needs to hear more of Jesus Christ and not less. May we remove the beggar's coat that we might still wear and rise above the world to a better life in and through Christ. May we get rid of all excuses not to follow Jesus Christ and find all good reasons to follow Him as we hear His voice. This is my prayer in the name of Jesus Christ, amen.

Notes

1. Mark 10:47.
2. See Isaiah 11:1; Jeremiah 23:5; Matthew 21:9.
3. Mark 10:48.
4. Mark 10:50.
5. Mark 10:52.

A RECORD OF WHAT I HAVE BOTH SEEN AND HEARD

ELDER BRENT H. NIELSON

Of the Presidency of the Seventy

After I graduated from law school, my wife, Marcia, and I chose to join a law firm that specialized in trial law. As I began my on-the-job training, I spent much of my time preparing witnesses to testify at trial. I quickly learned that facts were determined in a courtroom as witnesses, under oath, testified to the truthfulness of what they had both seen and heard. As witnesses testified, their words were both recorded and preserved. The importance of credible witnesses was always at the forefront of my preparation.

It didn't take long for me to realize that the very same terms I was using every day as a lawyer were also the terms I used in my gospel conversations. "Witness" and "testimony" are terms that we use as we share our knowledge and feelings about the truthfulness of the gospel of Jesus Christ.

When I was sustained as a new Area Seventy, I opened the scriptures to learn my duties and read Doctrine and Covenants 107:25, which states, "The Seventy are also called . . . to be especial witnesses unto the Gentiles and in all the world." As you can imagine, my eyes were drawn to the term "especial witnesses." It became clear to me that I had a responsibility to bear my witness—to testify of the name of Jesus Christ—wherever I traveled in the world.

There are many examples in the scriptures of those who were eyewitnesses and who testified to what they both saw and heard.

As the ancient prophet Mormon begins his record, he writes, "And now I, Mormon, make a record of the things which I have both seen and heard, and call it the Book of Mormon."[1]

The Savior's Apostles Peter and John healed a man in the name of Jesus Christ of Nazareth.[2] When commanded not to speak in the name of Jesus, they responded:

"Whether it be right in the sight of God to hearken unto you more than unto God, judge ye.

"For we cannot but speak the things which we have seen and heard."[3]

Another compelling testimony comes from the Book of Mormon Saints who witnessed the visit of the Savior Jesus Christ. Listen to this description of their witness: "And after this manner do they bear record: The eye hath never seen, neither hath the ear heard, before, so great and marvelous things as we saw and heard Jesus speak unto the Father."[4]

Brothers and sisters, today I declare my witness and make a record of what I have both seen and heard during my sacred ministry as a Seventy of the Lord Jesus Christ. In doing so, I testify to you of a loving Heavenly Father and His benevolent Son, Jesus Christ, who suffered, died, and rose again to offer eternal life to God's children. I testify of "a marvelous work and a wonder"[5] and that the Lord has set His hand once again to restore His gospel on the earth through His living prophets and apostles.[6] I testify that based upon what I have both seen and heard, there has never been a better time to be a member of The Church of Jesus Christ of Latter-day Saints than today. I know this of my own knowledge, independent of any other source, because of what I have both seen and heard.

During my senior year of high school, to graduate from seminary I had to identify all 15 temples of the Church. A picture of each temple was at the front of our classroom, and I had to know where each was located. Now, years later, it would be an enormous challenge—with 335 operating or announced temples—to identify each one. I have personally seen many of these houses of the Lord and testify that the Lord is offering His blessings and ordinances to more and more of His children across the world.

My friends at FamilySearch have taught me that over one million new names are added to FamilySearch each day. If you didn't find your ancestor yesterday, I invite you to look again tomorrow. When it comes to gathering Israel on the other side of the veil, there has never been a better time to be a member of The Church of Jesus Christ of Latter-day Saints than today.

As we raised our children in Twin Falls, Idaho, our perspective of the worldwide Church was limited. When I was called to be a General Authority, Marcia and I were assigned to serve in the Pacific Area, a place we had never been. We were pleased to find stakes from the top of New Zealand to the bottom, with a temple that was dedicated in 1958. It was one of those 15 I had to memorize in seminary. We found temples in every major city of Australia, with stakes across that continent. We had assignments in Samoa, where there are 25 stakes, and Tonga, where almost half the population are members of the Church. We had an assignment on the island of Kiribati, where we found two stakes. We had assignments to visit stakes in Ebeye in the Marshall Islands and Daru in Papua New Guinea.

After our service in the Pacific Islands, we were assigned to serve in the Philippines. To my surprise, the Church of Jesus Christ in the Philippines is growing beyond anything I had realized. There are now 125 stakes, 23 missions, and 13 operating or announced temples. I witnessed a church of over 850,000 members in that country. How had I missed the establishment of Christ's Church across the world?

After three years in the Philippines, I was asked to serve in the Missionary Department. My assignment took us to missions all over the world. My view of the Savior's worldwide Church expanded exponentially. Marcia and I were assigned to visit missions in Asia. We found a beautiful stake center in Singapore, with amazing, faithful members. We visited members and missionaries in a chapel in Kota Kinabalu, Malaysia. We met missionaries in Hong Kong and participated in a wonderful stake conference with faithful, devoted Saints.

This experience was repeated as we met missionaries and members across Europe, in Latin America, in the Caribbean, and in Africa. The Church of Jesus Christ is experiencing tremendous growth in Africa.

I am an eyewitness to the ongoing Restoration of the gospel of Jesus Christ and the fulfilling of the prophecy of Joseph Smith that "the truth of God will go forth boldly, nobly, and independent, till it has penetrated every continent, visited every clime, swept every country, and sounded in every ear."[7]

Our wonderful missionaries who now cover the globe are 74,000 strong. Working together with members, they baptize over 20,000 people every month. It has recently been 18-, 19-, and 20-year-old young men and young women who, with the help of the Lord, have produced this mighty miracle of gathering. We find these young women and young men in the small villages of Vanuatu and in the large cities of New York, Paris, and London. I have watched them teach about the Savior in remote congregations in Fiji and larger gatherings in places like Texas, California, and Florida in the United States.

You will find missionaries in every corner of the earth speaking 60 different languages and fulfilling the Savior's great commission in Matthew 28: "Go ye therefore, and teach all nations, baptizing them in the name of the Father, and of the Son, and of the Holy Ghost."[8] I honor the past and current missionaries of the Church and remind our rising generation of President Russell M. Nelson's invitation to come and gather Israel.[9]

I testify today that I have observed this profound Restoration of the Savior's gospel with my own eyes and heard it with my own ears. I am a witness of God's work across the world. There has never been a better time to be a member of The Church of Jesus Christ of Latter-day Saints than today.

Perhaps the most inspiring miracle of the Restoration that I have witnessed is you, the faithful members of the Church in every land. You, the Latter-day Saints, are described by Nephi in the Book of Mormon as he saw our day and testified, "And it came to pass that I, Nephi, beheld the power of the Lamb of God, that it descended upon the saints of the church of the Lamb, and upon the covenant people of the Lord, who were scattered upon all the face of the earth; and they were armed with righteousness and with the power of God in great glory."[10]

I testify that I have seen with my own eyes what Nephi saw—you, the covenant Saints in every land, armed with righteousness and the power of God. As I was at the pulpit in one of these great nations of the world, the Lord impressed upon my mind something that King Benjamin taught in Mosiah 2 in the Book of Mormon. Brent, "I would desire that ye should consider on the blessed and happy state of those that keep the commandments of God. For behold, they are blessed in all things, both temporal and spiritual."[11]

I witness to you that I have seen this with my own eyes and heard it with my own ears as I have met you, faithful Saints of God across the earth who keep the commandments. You are the covenant children of the Father. You are disciples of Jesus Christ. You also know what I know because you have received your personal witness of the truthfulness of the restored gospel of Jesus Christ. The Savior taught, "But blessed are your eyes, for they see: and your ears, for they hear."[12]

Under the direction of the Lord and the leadership of His prophets and apostles, we will continue to prepare missionaries, make and keep sacred covenants, establish Christ's Church across the world, and receive the blessings that come as we keep the commandments of God. We are united. We are God's children. We know Him and we love Him.

I join all of you, my friends, as we unitedly testify that these things are true. We make a record of what we have both seen and heard. You and I are witnesses who testify. It is with the power of this united witness that we continue to move forward with faith in the Lord Jesus Christ and His gospel. I declare my witness that Jesus Christ lives. He is our Savior and our Redeemer. In the name of Jesus Christ, amen.

Notes

1. Mormon 1:1.
2. See Acts 3:6.
3. Acts 4:19–20.
4. 3 Nephi 17:16.
5. 2 Nephi 27:26; see also Isaiah 29:14.
6. See 2 Nephi 29:1.
7. *Teachings of Presidents of the Church: Joseph Smith* (2007), 444.
8. Matthew 28:19.
9. See Russell M. Nelson, "Hope of Israel" (worldwide youth devotional, June 3, 2018), Gospel Library; Russell M. Nelson, "Preaching the Gospel of Peace," *Liahona*, May 2022, 6–7.
10. 1 Nephi 14:14.
11. Mosiah 2:41.
12. Matthew 13:16.

JESUS CHRIST AT THE CENTER OF OUR LIVES

ELDER JOSE L. ALONSO
Of the Seventy

As we journey through mortality, we are at times beset by trials: the severe pain of the loss of loved ones, the arduous fight against illness, the sting of injustice, the harrowing experiences of harassment or abuse, the shadow of unemployment, familial tribulations, the silent cry of loneliness, or the heartrending consequences of armed conflicts.[1] In such moments, our souls yearn for refuge.[2] We seek earnestly to know: Where may we find the balm of peace?[3] In whom can we place our trust to help us with the confidence and strength to surmount these challenges?[4] Who possesses the patience, the encompassing love, and the omnipotent hand to uplift and sustain us?

The profound questions of the soul, those that surface in our darkest hours and highest trials, are addressed through the unwavering love of Jesus Christ.[5] In Him, and through the promised blessings of His restored gospel,[6] we find the answers we seek. It is through His infinite Atonement that we are offered a gift beyond measure—one of hope, healing, and the assurance of His constant, enduring presence in our lives.[7] This gift is available to all who reach out with faith, embracing the peace and redemption He so freely offers.

The Lord extends His hand to each of us, a gesture that is the very essence of His divine love and kindness. His invitation to us transcends a simple call; it is a divine pledge, reinforced by the enduring power of His grace. In the scriptures, He lovingly assures us:

"Come unto me, all ye that labour and are heavy laden, and I will give you rest.

"Take my yoke upon you, and learn of me; for I am meek and lowly in heart: and ye shall find rest unto your souls.

"For my yoke is easy, and my burden is light."[8]

The clarity of His invitation "come unto me" and "take my yoke" affirms the profound nature of His promise—a promise so vast and complete that it embodies His love, offering us a solemn guarantee: "Ye shall find rest."

As we diligently seek spiritual guidance,[9] we embark on a deeply transformative odyssey that strengthens our testimonies. As we comprehend the vastness of our Heavenly Father's and Jesus Christ's perfect love,[10] our hearts are filled with gratitude, humility,[11] and a renewed desire to pursue the path of discipleship.[12]

President Russell M. Nelson taught that "when the focus of our lives is on God's plan of salvation . . . and Jesus Christ and His gospel, we can feel joy regardless of what is happening—or not happening—in our lives. Joy comes from and because of Him."[13]

Alma, speaking to his son Helaman, declared: "And now, O my son Helaman, behold, thou art in thy youth, and therefore, I beseech of thee that thou wilt hear my words and learn of me; for I do know that whosoever shall put their trust in God shall be supported in their trials, and their troubles, and their afflictions, and shall be lifted up at the last day."[14]

Helaman, speaking to his sons, taught about this eternal principle of putting the Savior at the center of our lives: "Remember, remember that it is upon the rock of our Redeemer, who is Christ, the Son of God, that ye must build your foundation."[15]

In Matthew 14 we learn that after hearing of John the Baptist's death, Jesus sought solitude. However, a large crowd followed Him. Moved by compassion and love, and not allowing His grief to distract Him from His mission, Jesus welcomed them, healing the sick among them. As evening approached, the disciples faced a daunting challenge: a multitude of people with scant food available. They proposed that Jesus send the crowd away to procure food, but Jesus, with high love and high expectations, asked the disciples to feed them instead.

While the disciples were preoccupied with the immediate challenge, Jesus demonstrated His trust in and love for His Father, coupled with an unwavering love for the people. He directed the crowd to sit on the grass, and taking only five loaves and two fish,

He chose to give thanks to His Father, acknowledging God's provision over His authority and power.

After He gave thanks, Jesus broke the bread, and the disciples distributed it to the people. Miraculously, the food not only sufficed but was abundant, with 12 baskets of leftovers. The group fed included five thousand men, along with women and children.[16]

This miracle teaches a profound lesson: when confronted with challenges, it's easy to become engrossed in our difficulties. However, Jesus Christ exemplified the power of focusing on His Father, offering gratitude, and acknowledging that solutions to our trials do not always lie within ourselves but with God.[17]

When we encounter difficulties, we naturally tend to concentrate on the obstacles we face. Our challenges are tangible and command our attention, yet the principle of surmounting them is in our focus. By placing Christ at the core of our thoughts and deeds, we align ourselves with His outlook and strength.[18] This adjustment does not discount our struggles; instead, it helps us to navigate through them under divine guidance.[19] As a result, we discover solutions and support that arise from a higher wisdom. Adopting this Christ-centric perspective empowers us with the fortitude and insight to turn our trials into victories,[20] reminding us that with the Savior, what seems like a major problem can become a pathway to greater spiritual progress.

The story of Alma the Younger in the Book of Mormon presents a compelling narrative of redemption and the profound impact of centering one's life around Christ. At first, Alma stood as an opponent of the Lord's Church, leading many astray from the path of righteousness. However, a divine intervention, marked by an angelic visitation, awakened him from his wrongdoings.

In his darkest hour, tormented by guilt and desperate to find a way out of his spiritual anguish, Alma remembered his father's teachings about Jesus Christ and the power of His Atonement. With a heart yearning for redemption, he earnestly repented and pleaded fervently for the Lord's mercy. This crucial moment of complete surrender, bringing Christ to the forefront of his thoughts as Alma earnestly sought His mercy, triggered a remarkable transformation. The heavy chains of guilt and despair vanished and were replaced by an overwhelming sense of joy and peace.[21]

Jesus Christ is our hope and the answer to life's greatest pains. Through His sacrifice, He paid for our sins and took upon Himself all of our suffering—pain, injustice, sorrow, and fear—and He forgives and heals us when we trust in Him and seek to change our lives for the better. He is our Healer,[22] comforting and repairing our hearts through His love and power, just like He healed many during His time on earth.[23] He is the living water, fulfilling the deepest needs of our souls with His constant love and kindness. This is like the promise He made to the Samaritan woman at the well, offering "a well of water springing up into everlasting life."[24]

I bear solemn witness that Jesus Christ lives, that He presides over this, His sacred Church, The Church of Jesus Christ of Latter-day Saints.[25] I testify that He is the Savior of the world, the Prince of Peace,[26] the King of kings, the Lord of lords,[27] the Redeemer of the world. I affirm with certainty that we are ever present in His mind and heart. As a testament to this, He has restored His Church in these latter days and has called President Russell M. Nelson as His prophet and the President of the Church at this time.[28] I know that Jesus Christ gave His life so that we might have eternal life.

As we strive to place Him at the center of our lives, revelations unfold to us, His profound peace envelops us, and His infinite Atonement brings about our forgiveness and healing.[29] It is in Him that we discover the strength to overcome, the courage to persevere, and the peace that surpasses all understanding. May we strive each day to draw nearer to Him, the source of all that is good,[30] the beacon of hope in our journey back to the presence of our Heavenly Father. In the sacred name of Jesus Christ, amen.

Notes

1. See Psalm 23:4; 2 Corinthians 1:3–4.
2. See Psalm 46:1.
3. See Jeremiah 8:22.
4. See Isaiah 41:10; Ether 12:27.
5. See John 3:16; Romans 8:38–39.

6. See Acts 3:20–21; 3 Nephi 20:29–31.
7. See Isaiah 53:5; Alma 34:10–14.
8. Matthew 11:28–30.
9. See Proverbs 3:5–6; James 1:5.
10. See Romans 8:39; 1 John 4:16.
11. See 1 Thessalonians 5:18; Mosiah 4:11.
12. See Matthew 16:24; 2 Nephi 31:19–20.
13. Russell M. Nelson, "Joy and Spiritual Survival," *Ensign* or *Liahona*, Nov. 2016, 82.
14. Alma 36:3.
15. Helaman 5:12.
16. See Matthew 14:13–21.
17. See Proverbs 3:5–6; Philippians 4:6–7.
18. See 2 Corinthians 12:9–10.
19. See Psalm 32:8; Ether 12:27.
20. See Romans 8:28; 1 Nephi 3:7.
21. See Alma 36:5–20.
22. See Psalm 147:3; 1 Peter 2:24.
23. See Isaiah 53:4–5.
24. John 4:14; see also Isaiah 12:3.
25. See Matthew 16:18; Ephesians 1:22–23.
26. See Isaiah 9:6.
27. See 1 Timothy 6:15.
28. See Amos 3:7; Doctrine and Covenants 1:38.
29. See John 3:16; Alma 34:14.
30. See Deuteronomy 31:6; Philippians 4:13; Moroni 10:32.

ALL THINGS FOR OUR GOOD

ELDER GERRIT W. GONG
Of the Quorum of the Twelve Apostles

Today is April 6, the anniversary of Jesus Christ restoring His latter-day Church—and part of the Easter season, when we joyfully testify of Jesus Christ's perfect life, atoning sacrifice, and glorious Resurrection.

A Chinese story begins as a man's son finds a beautiful horse.

"How fortunate," the neighbors say.

"We'll see," says the man.

Then the son falls off the horse and is permanently injured.

"How unfortunate," the neighbors say.

"We'll see," says the man.

A conscripting army comes but doesn't take the injured son.

"How fortunate," the neighbors say.

"We'll see," says the man.

This fickle world often feels tempest tossed, uncertain, sometimes fortunate, and—too often—unfortunate. Yet, in this world of tribulation,[1] "we know that all things work together for good to them that love God."[2] Indeed, as we walk uprightly and remember our covenants, "all things shall work together for your good."[3]

All things for our good.

A remarkable promise! Comforting assurance from God Himself! In a miraculous way, the purpose of Creation and the nature of God are to know beginning and end,[4] to bring about all that is for our good, and to help us become sanctified and holy through Jesus Christ's grace and Atonement.

Jesus Christ's Atonement can deliver and redeem us from sin. But Jesus Christ also intimately understands our every pain, affliction, sickness,[5] sorrow, separation. In time and eternity, His triumph over death and hell can make all things right.[6] He helps heal the broken and disparaged, reconcile the angry and divided, comfort the lonely and isolated, encourage the uncertain and imperfect, and bring forth miracles possible only with God.

We sing hallelujah and shout hosanna! With eternal power and infinite goodness, in God's plan of happiness all things can work together for our good. We can face life with confidence and not fear.

Left on our own, we may not know our own good. When "I choose me," I am also choosing my own limitations, weaknesses, inadequacies. Ultimately, to do the most good, we must be good.[7] Since none save God is good,[8] we seek perfection in Jesus Christ.[9] We become our truest, best selves only as we put off the natural man or woman and become a child before God.

With our trust and faith in God, trials and afflictions can be consecrated for our good. Joseph, sold into slavery in Egypt, later saved his family and people. The Prophet Joseph Smith's incarceration in Liberty Jail taught him "these things shall give thee experience, and shall be for thy good."[10] Lived with faith, trials and sacrifices we would never choose can bless us and others in ways never imagined.[11]

We increase faith and trust in the Lord that all things can work together for our good as we gain eternal perspective;[12] understand our trials may be "but for a small moment";[13] recognize affliction can be consecrated for our gain;[14] acknowledge accidents, untimely death, debilitating illness, and disease are part of mortality; and trust loving Heavenly Father does not give trials to punish or judge. He would not give a stone to someone asking for bread nor a serpent to one asking for a fish.[15]

When trials come, often what we most want is for someone to listen and be with us.[16] In the moment, cliché answers can be unhelpful, however comforting their intent. Sometimes we yearn for someone who will grieve, ache, and weep with us; let us express pain, frustration, sometimes even anger; and acknowledge with us there are things we do not know.

When we trust God and His love for us, even our greatest heartbreaks can, in the end, work together for our good.

I remember the day I received word of a serious car accident which involved those I love. At such times, in anguish and faith, we can only say with Job, "The Lord gave, and the Lord hath taken away; blessed be the name of the Lord."[17]

Across the worldwide Church, some 3,500 stakes and districts and some 30,000 wards and branches provide refuge and safety.[18] But within our stakes and wards, many faithful families and individuals confront difficult challenges, even while knowing that (without yet knowing how) things will work together for our good.

In Huddersfield, England, Brother Samuel Bridgstock was diagnosed with stage-four cancer shortly before the calling of a new stake president. Given his dire diagnosis, he asked his wife, Anna, why he would even go to be interviewed.

"Because," Sister Bridgstock said, "you're going to be called as stake president."

Initially given a year or two to live, President Bridgstock (who is here today) is now in his fourth year of service. He has good and hard days. His stake is rallying with increased faith, service, and kindness. It is not easy, but his wife and family live with faith, gratitude, and understandable sadness they trust will become eternal joy through Jesus Christ's restoring Atonement.[19]

When we are still, open, and reverent, we may feel the beauty, purpose, and serenity of the covenant belonging the Lord offers. In sacred moments, He may let us glimpse the larger eternal reality of which our daily lives are part, where small and simple things work together for the good of givers and receivers.

Rebekah, the daughter of my first mission president, shared how the Lord answered her prayer for comfort with an unexpected opportunity to answer someone else's prayer.

Late one evening, Rebekah, grieving her mother's recent passing, had a clear impression to go buy gas for her car. When she arrived at the station, she met an elderly woman struggling to breathe with a large oxygen tank. Later, Rebekah was able to give the woman her mother's portable oxygen machine. This sister gratefully said, "You've given me back my freedom." Things work together for good when we minister as Jesus Christ would.

A father assigned with his teacher-age son as ministering companions explained, "Ministering is when we go from being neighbors who bring cookies to trusted friends, spiritual first responders." Covenant belonging in Jesus Christ comforts, connects, consecrates.

Even in tragedy, spiritual preparation may remind us Heavenly Father knew when we felt most vulnerable and alone. For example, a family whose child was taken to the hospital later found comfort in remembering the Holy Ghost had whispered in advance what to expect.

Sometimes the larger eternal reality the Lord lets us feel includes family across the veil. A sister found joy in conversion to Jesus Christ's restored gospel. Yet two traumas had deeply impacted her life—seeing a boating accident and tragically losing her mother, who had taken her own life.

Yet this sister overcame her fear of water enough to be baptized by immersion. And on what became a very happy day, she witnessed someone, acting as proxy for her deceased mother, be baptized in the temple. "Temple baptism healed my mother, and it freed me," the sister said. "It was the first time I felt peace since my mother died."

Our sacred music echoes His assurance that all things can work together for our good.

> *Be still, my soul: Thy God doth undertake*
> *To guide the future as he has the past.*
> *Thy hope, thy confidence let nothing shake;*
> *All now mysterious shall be bright at last.*[20]
> *Come, come, ye Saints, no toil nor labor fear;*
> *But with joy wend your way.*
> *Though hard to you this journey may appear,*
> *Grace shall be as your day. . . .*
> *And should we die before our journey's through,*
> *Happy day! All is well!*[21]

The Book of Mormon is evidence we can hold in our hand that Jesus is the Christ and God fulfills His prophecies. Written by inspired prophets who saw our day, the Book of Mormon begins with raw drama—a family dealing with deep differences. Yet, as we study and ponder 1 Nephi 1 through to Moroni 10, we are drawn to Jesus

Christ with a firm testimony that what happened there and then can bless us here and now.

As the Lord, through His living prophet, brings more houses of the Lord closer in more places, temple blessings work together for our good. We come by covenant and ordinance to God our Father and Jesus Christ and gain eternal perspective on mortality. One by one, name by name, we offer beloved family members—ancestors—sacred ordinances and covenant blessings in the Lord's pattern of saviors on Mount Zion.[22]

As temples come closer to us in many places, a temple sacrifice we can offer is to seek holiness in the house of the Lord more frequently. For many years, we have saved, planned, and sacrificed to come to the temple. Now, as circumstances permit, please come even more often to the Lord in His holy house. Let regular temple worship and service bless, protect, and inspire you and your family—the family you have or the family you will have and become someday.

Also, where your circumstances permit, please consider the blessing of owning your own temple clothes.[23] A grandmother from a humble family said of anything in the world, what she most wanted were her own temple clothes. Her grandson said, "Grandma whispered, 'I will serve in my own temple clothes, and after I die, I will be buried in them.'" And when the time came, she was.

As President Russell M. Nelson teaches, "*Everything* we believe and *every* promise God has made to His covenant people come together in the temple."[24]

In time and eternity, the purpose of Creation and the nature of God Himself are to bring all things together for our good.

This is the Lord's eternal purpose. It is His eternal perspective. It is His eternal promise.

When life is cluttered and purpose isn't clear, when you want to live better but don't know how, please come to God our Father and Jesus Christ. Trust They live, love you, and want all things for your good. I testify They do, infinitely and eternally, in the sacred and holy name of Jesus Christ, amen.

Notes

1. See John 16:33.
2. Romans 8:28.
3. Doctrine and Covenants 90:24. The popular phrase "It's all good" often implies things are OK and in order, without necessarily meaning they are actually for our good.
4. See Moses 1:3.
5. See Alma 7:11.
6. See 2 Nephi 9:10–12. God respects moral agency, sometimes allowing even the unrighteous acts of others to affect us. But as we willingly seek to do all we can, Jesus Christ's grace and His enabling and atoning power can cleanse, heal, bind up, reconcile us with ourselves and each other, on both sides of the veil.
7. See Moroni 7:6, 10–12. Professor Terry Warner writes perceptively on this topic.
8. See Romans 3:10; Moroni 10:25.
9. See Moroni 10:32.
10. See Doctrine and Covenants 122:4, 7.
11. We learn by experiences we would never choose. Sometimes bearing burdens with the Lord's help can increase our capacity to bear those burdens; Mosiah 24:10–15 illustrates the Lord's promise to "visit my people in their afflictions" and to "strengthen them that they could bear up their burdens." Alma 33:23 teaches that our "burdens may be light, through the joy of his Son." Mosiah 18:8 reminds us that when we are "willing to bear one another's burdens . . . they may be light."
12. The prophet Isaiah speaks of the Messiah: "The Spirit of the Lord God is upon me; because the Lord hath anointed me to preach good tidings unto the meek; he hath sent me to bind up the brokenhearted, . . . to comfort all that mourn; to appoint unto them that mourn in Zion, to give unto them beauty for ashes, the oil of joy for mourning, the garment of praise for the spirit of heaviness" (Isaiah 61:1–3). Likewise, the psalmist offers the Lord's promised perspective: "Weeping may endure for a night, but joy cometh in the morning" (Psalm 30:5). This includes the glorious promises for the righteous on the morning of the First Resurrection.
13. Doctrine and Covenants 122:4. Believing trials may be for what is in eternity a "small moment" does not mean to downplay or make less trying or challenging the agonizing pain or suffering we may experience day after day in this life, the unbearable sleepless nights, or the excruciating uncertainties of each new day. Perhaps the promise of being able to look back and see our mortal suffering in light of God's compassion and eternal view adds some perspective to our understanding of mortality and our hope to endure with faith and trust in Him to the end. Also, when we have eyes to see, there is often good in the now; we need not necessarily wait for a future time to see good.
14. See 2 Nephi 2:2.
15. See Matthew 7:9–10. Letting God prevail in our lives is not passively to accept whatever comes. It is actively to believe that Heavenly Father and our Savior, Jesus Christ, want only and always what is best for us. When tragedy strikes, we can ask with faith, not "Why me?" but "What can I learn?" And we can mourn with broken hearts and contrite spirits, knowing, in His time and way, compensating blessings and opportunities will come.
16. We have covenanted to mourn with those who mourn and comfort those who stand in need of comfort (see Mosiah 18:9).
17. Job 1:21.
18. See Doctrine and Covenants 115:6.
19. Faith in the face of difficulty is the opposite of the existential anguish and despair the Book of Mormon describes of those who "curse God, and wish to die" but who "nevertheless . . . would struggle with the sword for their lives" (Mormon 2:14).
20. "Be Still, My Soul," *Hymns*, no. 124.
21. "Come, Come, Ye Saints," *Hymns*, no. 30. Consider also:

    How great the wisdom and the love. . . .
    Redemption's grand design,
    Where justice, love, and mercy meet
    In harmony divine!

    ("How Great the Wisdom and the Love," *Hymns*, no. 195.)

Amid life's uncertainties, we know redemption's grand design will bring justice, love, and mercy together for our good.

22. See Obadiah 1:21. The Prophet Joseph Smith taught: "How are they [the Latter-day Saints] to become saviors on Mount Zion? By building their temples, erecting their baptismal fonts, and going forth and receiving all the ordinances . . . in behalf of all their progenitors who are dead" (*Teachings of Presidents of the Church: Joseph Smith* [2007], 473).
23. Members attending the temple for the first time can purchase temple clothes at a significant discount.
24. Russell M. Nelson, "The Temple and Your Spiritual Foundation," *Liahona*, Nov. 2021, 94.

IN SUPPORT OF THE RISING GENERATION

BROTHER MICHAEL T. NELSON

Second Counselor in the Young Men General Presidency

In preparing to speak to you, I have been drawn to the story of Helaman and the stripling sons of the people of Ammon. I have felt the power of Book of Mormon prophets teaching parents, bishops, and ward members through studying this account.

Helaman was a man that the young Ammonites could trust. He helped them develop and mature in righteousness. They knew and loved him and "would that [he] should be their leader."[1]

Helaman loved these young men like sons and saw their potential.[2] Elder Dale G. Renlund taught that "to effectively serve others we must see them . . . through Heavenly Father's eyes. Only then can we begin to comprehend the true worth of a soul. Only then can we sense the love that Heavenly Father has for all . . . His children."[3] Bishops today are blessed with discernment to see the divine identity of the youth in their care.

Helaman "numbered"[4] the young men in his care. He prioritized building strong relationships with them.

At a critical time when life and death hung in the balance, Helaman and his young warriors lost track of the army pursuing them. Helaman counseled with the youth:

"Behold, we know not but they have halted for the purpose that we should come against them. . . .

"Therefore what say ye, my sons . . . ?"[5]

These faithful young men responded, "Father, behold our God is with us, and he will not suffer that we should fall; then let us go forth."[6] The day was won, as Helaman supported these young men in their resolve[7] to act.[8]

The young Ammonites had a great cause and were valiant in "the support of the people."[9] "This little force," led by Helaman, spread "great hopes and much joy"[10] into the hearts of the experienced Nephite armies. Bishops today can lead their uniquely gifted youth in blessing the ward and gathering Israel. President Russell M. Nelson has taught that this is the mission "for which [they] were sent to earth."[11]

Like these young Ammonites who were "true at all times in whatsoever thing they were entrusted,"[12] Helaman faithfully followed his leaders. No matter the challenge or setback, Helaman always remained "fixed with a determination"[13] to advance their purpose. When he was directed to "march forth with [his] little sons,"[14] he obeyed.

The youth today are blessed as bishops follow the guidance of our leaders to "counsel with the ward Young Women president[s]."[15] Stake presidents ensure that bishops and Young Women presidents are instructed in fulfilling their responsibilities for the youth.[16]

Helaman honored covenants. When Ammon taught the gospel to the parents of the stripling young men, these parents embraced it with open hearts. They were so committed to their new life of righteous discipleship that they made a covenant to "lay down the weapons of their rebellion."[17] The only thing that caused them to consider breaking this covenant, going back to their familiar past of fighting, was seeing the Nephites in danger.

The Ammonites wanted to help these people who had offered them a safe home. Helaman, along with others, persuaded them to keep their covenant never to fight. He trusted more in the strength that God would provide than in the strength these Ammonites could have provided with their swords and arrows.

When Helaman and his young warriors faced daunting challenges, Helaman was resolute. "Behold, it mattereth not—we trust God will deliver us."[18] In one instance, when they were on the verge of starving to death, their response was to "pour out [their] souls in prayer to God, that he would strengthen [them] and deliver [them]; . . . [and] the Lord . . . did visit [them] with assurances that he would deliver [them]"[19] "because of their exceeding faith in that which they had been taught to believe."[20]

We learn from Helaman that these young men were supported by their parents. These faithful parents knew they had the primary responsibility for teaching their children. They taught their children to keep the commandments and "walk uprightly"[21] before God. Their mothers taught them "that if they did not doubt, God would deliver them."[22] Their fathers set a powerful example of covenant making.[23] These former warriors knew the horrors of battle. They entrusted their inexperienced sons to Helaman's care and supported them by sending "many provisions."[24]

Helaman wasn't alone as he served his young army. He had people around him whom he turned to for support and guidance. He reached out to Captain Moroni for help, and it came.

No one serving in the Lord's kingdom serves alone. The Lord has blessed us with wards and stakes. Through His restored organization, we have the resources, wisdom, and inspiration to meet any challenge.

A bishop provides guidance for the ward through councils.[25] He promotes quarterly ministering interviews and then encourages the elders quorum and Relief Society to fulfill their responsibility of ministering to families. These presidencies take the lead in assessing needs and finding inspired solutions. Stake presidents offer support by instructing the elders quorum and Relief Society presidencies in these responsibilities.

The needed guidance for leaders and parents is found in the Gospel Library and the Gospel Living apps. In these inspired resources, we can find the scriptures, teachings of modern prophets, and the *General Handbook*. The Youth tab in the Gospel Library has many resources for quorum and class presidencies[26] and has *For the Strength of Youth: A Guide for Making Choices*. As all members of the ward study these inspired sources and seek guidance from the Spirit, everyone will be directed by the Lord in strengthening the youth.

The entire ward will be blessed and strengthened as members focus on the rising generation. Despite our imperfections and shortcomings, Heavenly Father invites each of us, through the companionship of His Spirit, to reach out to others. He knows that we grow and are sanctified as we follow the promptings of the Holy Ghost.[27] It doesn't matter that our efforts are imperfect. When we partner with the Lord, we can trust that our efforts will be in line with what He would do for the youth.

By following the direction of the Holy Ghost in reaching out to the youth, we become witnesses of Heavenly Father's love in their lives. Acting on promptings from the Lord builds relationships of love and trust. It is relationships in the lives of the youth that have the greatest influence on their choices.

The youth will learn the pattern of revelation as they participate with us in the process of seeking and acting upon promptings to serve others. As the youth turn to the Lord for this inspired guidance, their relationships with and trust in Him will deepen.

We express our confidence in the youth by offering support and direction without taking over.[28] As we step back and allow the youth to learn through counseling together, choosing an inspired course, and putting their plan into action, they will experience true joy and growth.

President Henry B. Eyring taught that "what will matter most is what they learn from [you] about who they really are and what they can really become. My guess is that they won't learn it so much from lectures. They will get it from feelings of who you are, who you think they are, and what you think they might become."[29]

Our youth amaze us with their courage, their faith, and their abilities. As they choose to be fully engaged disciples of Jesus Christ, His gospel will be etched upon their hearts. Following Him will become a part of who they are, not just what they do.

Helaman helped the young Ammonites to see how a valiant disciple of Jesus Christ lives. We can be powerful examples to the youth of how disciples of Christ live today. Faithful parents are praying for these examples in the lives of their children. No program can replace the influence of loving, covenant-keeping adults.

As the president of the priests quorum, the bishop can set an example for the youth of how to be a loyal husband and a loving father[30] through protecting, providing, and presiding[31] in righteous ways. Bishops, with a "laser-like focus on [the] youth,"[32] will have an influence that will last for generations.

The youth today are among Heavenly Father's most noble[33] spirits. They were among the stalwart defenders of truth and agency in the premortal world.[34] They were born in these days to gather Israel through their powerful witness of the Lord Jesus Christ. He knows each one of them and knows their great potential. He is patient as they grow. He will redeem and protect them. He will heal and guide them. He will inspire them. We, their parents and leaders, have been prepared to support them. We have the Savior's Church to assist us as we raise the next generation.

I bear witness that Christ's Church, restored through the Prophet Joseph Smith and led today by President Russell M. Nelson, is organized to help the youth fulfill their great purpose in these latter days. In the name of Jesus Christ, amen.

Notes

1. Alma 53:19.
2. "If you choose to, if you want to, . . . you can be a big part of something big, something grand, something majestic! . . . You are among the best the Lord has *ever* sent to this world. You have the capacity to be smarter and wiser and have more impact on the world than any previous generation!" (Russell M. Nelson, "Hope of Israel" [worldwide youth devotional, June 3, 2018], Gospel Library).
3. Dale G. Renlund, "Through God's Eyes," *Ensign* or *Liahona,* Nov. 2015, 94.
4. Alma 56:55.
5. Alma 56:43–44.
6. Alma 56:46.
7. "Our Heavenly Father's goal in parenting is not to have His children *do* what is right; it is to have His children *choose* to do what is right" (Dale G. Renlund, "Choose You This Day," *Ensign* or *Liahona,* Nov. 2018, 104).
8. "As we empower the youth by inviting and allowing them to act, the Church will move forward in miraculous ways" (from a meeting with Elder David A. Bednar; see also 2020 Temple and Family History Leadership Instruction, Feb. 27, 2020, Gospel Library).
9. Alma 53:22.
10. Alma 56:17.
11. Russell M. Nelson, "Hope of Israel," Gospel Library.
12. Alma 53:20.
13. Alma 58:12.
14. Alma 56:30.
15. *General Handbook: Serving in The Church of Jesus Christ of Latter-day Saints,* 7.1.2, Gospel Library.
16. See *General Handbook,* 6.7.2.
17. Alma 23:7.
18. Alma 58:37.
19. Alma 58:10–11.
20. Alma 57:26.
21. Alma 53:21.
22. Alma 56:47.
23. See Alma 23:7; 24:17–19.
24. Alma 56:27.

25. See *General Handbook*, 7.1.1.
26. "As we seek eternal truth, the following two questions can help us recognize whether a concept comes from God or from another source: Is the concept taught consistently in the scriptures and by living prophets? Is the concept confirmed by the witness of the Holy Ghost? God reveals doctrinal truths through prophets, and the Holy Ghost confirms those truths to us and helps us apply them" (John C. Pingree Jr., "Eternal Truth," *Liahona*, Nov. 2023, 100).
27. See Doctrine and Covenants 4:2–4.
28. "If [our] youth are too underwhelmed [by God's work], they are more likely to be overwhelmed by the world. . . . How many deacons and teachers quorum presidencies consist of merely calling on someone to offer a prayer or pass the sacrament? Brethren, these really are special spirits, and they can do things of significance if given a chance!" (Neal A. Maxwell, "Unto the Rising Generation," *Ensign*, Apr. 1985, 11).
29. Henry B. Eyring, "Teaching Is a Moral Act" (address given at the Brigham Young University annual conference, Aug. 27, 1991), 3, speeches.byu.edu.
30. See "Aaronic Priesthood Quorum Theme," Gospel Library.
31. See "The Family: A Proclamation to the World," Gospel Library.
32. "It is our hope that bishoprics will give great emphasis and focus to the priesthood responsibilities of young men and help them in their quorum duties. Capable adult Young Men advisers will be called to assist the Aaronic Priesthood quorum presidencies and the bishopric in their duties. We are confident that more young men and young women will rise to the challenge and stay on the covenant path because of this laser-like focus on our youth" (Quentin L. Cook, "Adjustments to Strengthen Youth," *Ensign* or *Liahona*, Nov. 2019, 41).
33. "Our Heavenly Father has reserved many of His most noble spirits—perhaps, I might say, His finest team—for this final phase. Those noble spirits—those finest players, those heroes—are *you*!" (Russell M. Nelson, "Hope of Israel," Gospel Library).
34. "The teenager you love may well have been one of the valiant warriors on the side of agency and truth. . . . We can help in the way we react to their determination to choose for themselves. They will sense whether we see them as if they could well have been one of the faithful warriors from the premortal existence, committed still to the defense of moral agency and aware of its great value to bring them happiness. If we can see them as faithful warriors from the premortal existence, we may also see their claims of independence as a sign of their potential, a sign that they are testing the power of agency that will bring them happiness" (Henry B. Eyring, "A Life Founded in Light and Truth" [Brigham Young University devotional, Aug. 15, 2000], 3, 4, speeches.byu.edu).

BE ONE WITH CHRIST

ELDER QUENTIN L. COOK
Of the Quorum of the Twelve Apostles

I have felt deeply about the Atonement of Jesus Christ since I was quite young, but the reality of the Savior's Atonement came home to me when I was 25. I had just graduated from Stanford Law School and was studying for the California bar exam. My mother called and said that my grandfather Crozier Kimball, who lived in Utah, was dying. She said if I wanted to see him, I had better come home. My grandfather was 86 and very ill. I had a wonderful visit. He was so pleased to see me and share his testimony with me.

When Crozier was just three years old, his father, David Patten Kimball, died at age 44.[1] Crozier hoped that his father and his grandfather Heber C. Kimball would approve of his life and feel he had been true to his heritage.

My grandfather's primary counsel to me was to avoid any sense of entitlement or privilege because of these faithful ancestors. He told me my focus should be on the Savior and the Savior's Atonement. He said we are all children of a loving Heavenly Father. Regardless of who our earthly ancestors are, each of us will report to the Savior on how well we kept His commandments.

Grandpa referred to the Savior as the "Keeper of the Gate," a reference to 2 Nephi 9:41. He told me he hoped he had been sufficiently repentant to qualify for the Savior's mercy.[2]

I was deeply touched. I knew he had been a righteous man. He was a patriarch and served several missions. He taught me that no one can return to God by good works alone without the benefit of the Savior's Atonement. I can remember to this day the great love and appreciation Grandpa had for the Savior and His Atonement.

In 2019 during an assignment in Jerusalem,[3] I visited an upper room which may have been near the site where the Savior washed His Apostles' feet prior to His Crucifixion. I was spiritually touched and thought of how He commanded His Apostles to love one another.

I recalled the Savior's pleading Intercessory Prayer in our behalf. This prayer occurred in literally the closing hours of His mortal life as recorded in the Gospel of John.

This prayer was directed to followers of Christ, including all of us.[4] In the Savior's petition to His Father, He pleaded "that they all may be one; as thou, Father, art in me, and I in thee, that they also may be one in us." The Savior then continues, "And the glory which thou gavest me I have given them; that they may be one, even as we are one."[5] *Oneness* is what Christ prayed for prior to His betrayal and Crucifixion. Oneness with Christ and our Heavenly Father can be obtained through the Savior's Atonement.

The Lord's saving mercy is not dependent on lineage, education, economic status, or race. It is based on being one with Christ and His commandments.

The Prophet Joseph Smith and Oliver Cowdery received the revelation on Church organization and government in 1830, soon after the Church was organized. What is now section 20 was read by the Prophet Joseph at the first Church conference and was the first revelation approved by common consent.[6]

The content of this revelation is truly remarkable. It teaches us the significance and role of the Savior and how to access His power and blessings through His atoning grace. The Prophet Joseph was 24 years old and had already received numerous revelations and completed the translation of the Book of Mormon by the gift and power of God. Both Joseph and Oliver are identified as ordained Apostles, thus having authority to preside over the Church.

Verses 17 through 36 contain a summary of essential Church doctrine, including the reality of God, the Creation of mankind, the Fall, and Heavenly Father's plan of salvation through the Atonement of Jesus Christ. Verse 37 contains the essential requirements for baptism into the Lord's Church. Verses 75 through 79 set forth the sacrament prayers we utilize every Sabbath.

The doctrine, principles, sacraments, and practices that the Lord established through Joseph Smith, the Prophet of the Restoration, are truly seminal.[7]

The requirements for baptism, while profound, are uniquely simple. They primarily include humility before God, a broken heart and contrite spirit,[8] repenting of all sins, taking upon us the name of Jesus Christ, enduring to the end, and showing by our works that we have received of the Spirit of Christ.[9]

It is significant that all the qualifications for baptism are spiritual. No economic or social attainment is necessary. The poor and the rich have the same spiritual requirements.

There are no race, gender, or ethnicity requirements. The Book of Mormon makes it clear that *all* are invited to partake of the Lord's goodness, "black and white, bond and free, male and female; . . . all are alike unto God."[10] "All men are privileged the one like unto the other, and none are forbidden."[11]

Given our "likeness" before God, it makes little sense to emphasize our differences. Some have wrongly encouraged us "to imagine people to be much more different from ourselves and from each other than they actually are. [Some] take real but small differences and magnify them into chasms."[12]

In addition, some have wrongly assumed that because all people are invited to receive His goodness and eternal life, there are no conduct requirements.[13]

However, the scriptures attest that all accountable persons are required to repent of sins and keep His commandments.[14] The Lord makes it clear that all have moral agency and "are free to choose liberty and eternal life, through the great Mediator of all men, . . . and hearken unto his great commandments; and be faithful unto his words, and choose eternal life."[15] To receive the blessings of the Savior's Atonement, we must affirmatively exercise our moral agency to choose Christ and obey His commandments.

During my life, the meaning of "agency" and "free will" has been dissected and debated. There have been and continue to be many intellectual arguments on these topics.

On the recent cover of a major university alumni publication, a prominent biologist-professor asserts, "There's no room for free will."[16] Not surprisingly, the professor is quoted in the article as saying, "There's no such thing as God, . . . and there's no free will, . . . and this is a vast, indifferent, empty universe."[17] I could not disagree more strongly.

A fundamental doctrine of our faith is that we do have moral agency,[18] which includes free will.[19] Agency is the ability to choose and act. It is essential to the plan of salvation. Without moral agency, we could not learn, progress, or choose to be one with Christ. Because of moral agency, we "are free to choose liberty and eternal life."[20] In the premortal Council in Heaven, the Father's plan included agency as an essential element. Lucifer rebelled and "sought to destroy the agency of man."[21] Accordingly, the privilege of having a mortal body was denied to Satan and those who followed him.

Other premortal spirits exercised their agency in following Heavenly Father's plan. Spirits blessed by birth to this mortal life continue to have agency. We are free to choose and act, but we do not control the consequences. "Choices of good and righteousness lead to happiness, peace, and eternal life, while choices of sin and evil eventually lead to heartache and misery."[22] As Alma said, "Wickedness never was happiness."[23]

In this extremely competitive world, there is a constant effort to excel. Striving to be the best we can be is a righteous and worthwhile endeavor. It is consistent with the Lord's doctrine. Efforts to diminish or deprecate others or create barriers to their success are contrary to the Lord's doctrine. We cannot blame circumstances or others for a decision to act contrary to God's commandments.

In today's world, it is easy to focus on material and occupational success. Some lose sight of eternal principles and choices that have eternal significance. We would be wise to follow President Russell M. Nelson's counsel to "think celestial."[24]

The most significant choices can be made by almost everyone regardless of talents, abilities, opportunities, or economic circumstances. An emphasis on putting family choices first is essential. This is clear throughout the scriptures. Think of the account in 1 Nephi where Lehi "departed into the wilderness. And he left his house, and the land of his inheritance, and his gold, and his silver, and his precious things, and took nothing with him, save it were his family."[25]

As we face the vicissitudes of life, many events occur over which we have little or no control. Health challenges and accidents obviously can fit into this category. The recent COVID-19 pandemic has severely impacted people who did everything right. For the most important choices, we do have control. Going back to my missionary days, Elder Marion D. Hanks, our mission president, had all of us memorize part of a poem by Ella Wheeler Wilcox:

> *There is no chance, no destiny, no fate,*
> *Can circumvent or hinder or control*
> *The firm resolve of a determined soul.*[26]

On matters of principle, conduct, religious observance, and righteous living, we are in control. Our faith in and worship of God the Father and His Son, Jesus Christ, is a choice that we make.[27]

Please understand I am not advocating less interest in education or occupation. What I am saying is that when efforts relating to education and occupation are elevated above the family or being one with Christ, the unintended consequences can be significantly adverse.

The clear and simple doctrine set forth in Doctrine and Covenants 20 is touching and compelling as it amplifies and clarifies sacred spiritual concepts. It teaches that salvation comes as Jesus Christ justifies and sanctifies repentant souls because of the Savior's grace.[28] It sets the stage for the preeminent role of His Atonement.

We should strive to include others in our circle of oneness. If we are to follow President Russell M. Nelson's admonition to gather scattered Israel on both sides of the veil, we need to include others in our circle of oneness. As President Nelson has so beautifully taught: "On every continent and across the isles of the sea, faithful people are being gathered into The Church of Jesus Christ of Latter-day Saints. Differences in culture, language, gender, race, and nationality fade into insignificance as the faithful enter the covenant path and come unto our beloved Redeemer."[29]

We are united by our love of and faith in Jesus Christ and as children of a loving Heavenly Father. The essence of truly belonging is to be one with Christ. The ordinances of baptism and the sacrament set forth in Doctrine and Covenants 20, together with our temple covenants, unite us in special ways and allow us to be one in every eternally significant way and to live in peace and harmony.

I bear my sure and certain witness that Jesus Christ lives, and because of His Atonement, we can be one with Christ. In the sacred name of Jesus Christ, amen.

Notes

1. David, at age 17, had helped carry some of the Saints across the ice-filled Sweetwater River when they were stranded on the high plains of Wyoming (see *Saints: The Story of the Church of Jesus Christ in the Latter Days*, volume 2, *No Unhallowed Hand, 1846–1893* [2020], 237).
2. See Moroni 7:27–28.
3. The Chief Rabbi of Norway, Rabbi Michael Melchior, and I were the keynote speakers at a Jewish–Latter-day Saint scholars' dialogue held on June 5, 2019, at the BYU Jerusalem Center in Israel.
4. See John 17:20.
5. John 17:21–22.
6. See "The Conference Minutes and Record Book of Christ's Church of Latter Day Saints, 1838–1839, 1844" (commonly known as the Far West Record), June 9, 1830, Church History Library, Salt Lake City; Steven C. Harper, *Making Sense of the Doctrine and Covenants* (2008), 75.
7. Doctrine and Covenants 20 was the first revelation published in the Church newspaper and was utilized by missionaries with respect to both doctrine and the administration of the ordinances of baptism and the sacrament (see Harper, *Making Sense of the Doctrine and Covenants*, 75).
8. See 2 Nephi 2:7.
9. See Doctrine and Covenants 20:37.
10. 2 Nephi 26:33.
11. 2 Nephi 26:28.
12. Peter Wood, *Diversity: The Invention of a Concept* (2003), 20.
13. Nehor took this position (see Alma 1:4).
14. See Doctrine and Covenants 29:49–50.
15. 2 Nephi 2:27–28.
16. *Stanford* (publication of the Stanford Alumni Association), Dec. 2023, cover.
17. In Sam Scott, "As If You Had a Choice," *Stanford*, Dec. 2023, 44. The article identifies the professor as Robert Sapolsky, a Stanford professor of biology, neurology, and neurosurgery and a best-selling author of science books. The article contains opposing views, including from Alfred Mele, a professor of philosophy at Florida State University who headed a large John Templeton Foundation project on free will. He stated, "Scientists most definitely have not proved that free will—even ambitious free will—is an illusion" (in Scott, "As If You Had a Choice," 46).
18. See D. Todd Christofferson, "Moral Agency" (Brigham Young University devotional, Jan. 31, 2006), speeches.byu.edu.
19. See Doctrine and Covenants 58:27.
20. 2 Nephi 2:27.
21. Moses 4:3.
22. *True to the Faith: A Gospel Reference* (2004), 12.
23. Alma 41:10.
24. See Russell M. Nelson, "Think Celestial!," *Liahona*, Nov. 2023, 117–20.
25. 1 Nephi 2:4.

26. *Poetical Works of Ella Wheeler Wilcox* (1917), 129.
27. I have always loved the quote shared by Elder Neal A. Maxwell that stated this in a most succinct fashion: "If you have not chosen the kingdom of God first, it will in the end make no difference what you have chosen instead" (attributed to William Law, an 18th-century English clergyman; quoted in Neal A. Maxwell, "Response to a Call," *Ensign*, May 1974, 112).
28. See Doctrine and Covenants 20:29–31. Calvinist theology emphasized justification and sanctification of fallen souls through the grace of Jesus Christ. It taught that once God had predestined a soul for salvation, nothing could change the outcome. Doctrine and Covenants 20 makes a clean break with Calvinism. It reads, "There is a possibility that man may fall from grace and depart from the living God" (see Doctrine and Covenants 20:32–34; Harper, *Making Sense of the Doctrine and Covenants*, 74).
29. Russell M. Nelson, "Building Bridges," *New Era*, Aug. 2018, 6; *Liahona*, Dec. 2018, 51.

Saturday Evening Session

APRIL 6, 2024

MIRACLES, ANGELS, AND PRIESTHOOD POWER

ELDER SHAYNE M. BOWEN
Of the Seventy

Many today say that miracles no longer exist, that angels are fictional, and that the heavens are closed. I testify that miracles have not ceased, angels are among us, and the heavens are truly open.

When our Savior, Jesus Christ, was on the earth, He gave priesthood keys to His chief Apostle, Peter.[1] Through these keys, Peter and the other Apostles led the Savior's Church. But when those Apostles died, the keys of the priesthood were taken from the earth.

I testify that the ancient keys of the priesthood have been restored. Peter, James, and John and other ancient prophets appeared as resurrected beings, bestowing upon the Prophet Joseph Smith what the Lord described as "the keys of my kingdom, and a dispensation of the gospel."[2]

Those same keys have been passed from prophet to prophet until today. The 15 men we sustain as prophets, seers, and revelators use them to lead the Savior's Church. As in ancient times, there is one senior Apostle who holds and is authorized to exercise all priesthood keys. He is President Russell M. Nelson, prophet and President of the restored Church of Christ in our day: The Church of Jesus Christ of Latter-day Saints.

Through the Savior's Church, we receive the blessings of the priesthood—including the power of God to help us in our lives. Under authorized priesthood keys, we make sacred promises to God and receive sacred ordinances that prepare us to live in His presence. Beginning with baptism and confirmation and then in the temple, we move forward on a path of covenants that leads us back to Him.

With hands laid on our heads, we also receive priesthood blessings, including direction, comfort, counsel, healing, and the power to follow Jesus Christ. Throughout my life I have been blessed by this great power. As it has been revealed in scripture, we refer to it as the power of the holy Melchizedek Priesthood.[3]

In my youth I gained a great respect for this power, especially as it was manifest in priesthood blessings. While serving as a young missionary in Chile, my companion and I were arrested and separated. We were never told why. It was a time of great political upheaval. Thousands of people were taken into custody by the military police and never heard from again.

After being interrogated, I sat alone in a jail cell, not knowing if I would ever see my loved ones again. I turned to my Heavenly Father, fervently pleading: "Father, I have always been taught that Thou watcheth over Thy missionaries. Please, Father, I am nothing special, but I have been obedient and I need Thy help tonight."

The seeds of this help had been planted many years earlier. After my baptism, I was confirmed a member of the Church and given the gift of the Holy Ghost. As I prayed, alone, behind bars, the Holy Ghost immediately came to me and comforted me. He brought to my mind a very special passage from my patriarchal blessing, which is another blessing of the priesthood. In it, God promised me that through my faithfulness I would be able to be sealed in the temple for time and eternity to a woman full of beauty and virtue and love, that we would become the parents of precious sons and daughters, and that I would be blessed and magnified as a father in Israel.

Those inspired words about my future filled my soul with peace. I knew that they had come from my loving Heavenly Father, who always keeps His promises.[4] In that moment, I had the assurance that I would be released and live to see those promises fulfilled.

About a year later, Heavenly Father did bless me with a wife who is full of beauty and virtue and love. Lynette and I were sealed in the temple. We were blessed with three precious sons and four precious daughters. I became a father, all according to God's promises in the patriarchal blessing I received as a 17-year-old boy.

"Wherefore, my beloved brethren [and sisters], have miracles ceased because Christ hath ascended into heaven? . . .

" . . . Nay; neither have angels ceased to minister unto the children of men."[5]

I testify that miracles and ministrations are continually occurring in our lives, often as a direct result of priesthood power. Some priesthood blessings are fulfilled immediately, in ways we can see and understand. Others are unfolding gradually and will not be fully realized in this life. But God keeps all of His promises, always, as illustrated in this account from our family history:

My paternal grandfather, Grant Reese Bowen, was a man of great faith. I vividly remember hearing him recount how he received his own patriarchal blessing. In his journal, he recorded: "The patriarch promised me the gift of healing. He said, 'The sick shall be healed. Yea, *the dead shall be raised under your hands*.'"

Years later, Grandfather was piling hay when he felt prompted to return to the house. He was met by his father coming toward him. "Grant, your mother has just passed away," his father said.

I quote again from Grandfather's journal: "I didn't stop but went hurrying into the house and out on the front porch where she lay on a cot. I looked at her and could see there was no sign of life left in her. I remembered my patriarchal blessing and the promise that if I were faithful, through my faith the sick would be healed; and the dead would be raised. I placed my hands on her head, and I told the Lord that if the promise that He had made to me by the patriarch was true, to make it manifest at this time and raise my mother back to life. I promised Him if He would do this, I should never hesitate to do all in my power for the building up of His kingdom. As I prayed, she opened her eyes and said, 'Grant, raise me up. I have been in the spirit world, but you have called me back. Let this always be a testimony to you and to the rest of my family.'"

President Russell M. Nelson has taught us to seek and expect miracles.[6] I testify that because the priesthood has been restored, the power and authority of God are upon the earth. Through callings and councils, men and women, young and old, can participate in priesthood work. It is a work of miracles, attended by angels. It is the work of heaven, and it blesses all God's children.

In 1989, our family of seven was returning from a ward outing. It was late. Lynette was expecting our sixth child. She felt a strong prompting to fasten her seat belt, which she had forgotten to do. Shortly thereafter we came around a bend in the road; a car crossed the line into our lane. Going about 70 miles (112 km) an hour, I swerved to avoid hitting the oncoming car. Our van rolled, skidded down the highway, and slid off the road, finally coming to a stop, landing with the passenger side in the dirt.

The next thing I remember hearing was Lynette's voice: "Shayne, we need to get out through your door." I was hanging in the air by my seat belt. It took a few seconds to get oriented. We started lifting each of the children out of the van through my window, which was now the ceiling of the van. They were crying, wondering what had happened.

We soon realized that our 10-year-old daughter, Emily, was missing. We yelled her name, but there was no response. Ward members, who were also traveling home, were at the scene frantically looking for her. It was so dark. I looked in the van again with a flashlight and, to my horror, saw Emily's tiny body trapped under the van. I called out desperately, "We have to lift the van off of Emily." I grabbed the roof and pulled back. There were only a few others lifting, but the van miraculously flipped onto its wheels, exposing Emily's lifeless body.

Emily was not breathing. Her face was the color of a purple plum. I said, "We need to give her a blessing." A dear friend and ward member knelt with me, and by the authority of the Melchizedek Priesthood, in the name of Jesus Christ, we commanded her to live. In that moment, Emily took a long raspy breath.

After what seemed like hours, the ambulance finally arrived. Emily was rushed to the hospital. She had a collapsed lung and a severed tendon in her knee. Brain damage was a concern because of the time she was without oxygen. Emily was in a coma for a day and a half. We continued to pray and fast for her. She was blessed with a full recovery. Today, Emily and her husband, Kevin, are the parents of six daughters.

Miraculously, everyone else was able to walk away. The baby Lynette was carrying was Tyson. He too was spared any harm and was born the next February. Eight months later, after receiving his earthly body, Tyson returned home to Heavenly Father. He is our guardian angel son. We feel his influence in our family and look forward to being with him again.[7]

Those who lifted the van off of Emily observed that the van seemed to weigh nothing. I knew that heavenly angels had joined with earthly angels to lift the vehicle off of Emily's body. I also know that Emily was brought back to life by the power of the holy priesthood.

The Lord revealed this truth to His servants: "I will go before your face. I will be on your right hand and on your left, and my Spirit shall be in your hearts, and mine angels round about you, to bear you up."[8]

I testify that "the Holy Priesthood, after the Order of the Son of God"[9]—the Melchizedek Priesthood—with its keys, authority, and power has been restored to the earth in these latter days. I know that while not all circumstances turn out like we may hope and pray for, God's miracles will always come according to His will, His timing, and His plan for us.

If you desire the blessings of the priesthood, including miracles and the ministry of angels, I invite you to walk the path of covenants God has made available to each of us. Members and leaders of the Church who love you will help you take the next step.

I testify that Jesus Christ, the Son of God, lives and leads His Church through living prophets who hold and exercise priesthood keys. The Holy Ghost is real. The Savior gave His life to heal us, reclaim us, and bring us home.

I witness that miracles have not ceased, angels are among us, and the heavens are open. And oh, how open they are! In the name of Jesus Christ, amen.

Notes

1. See Matthew 16:17–19; Doctrine and Covenants 13; 110; 128:18, 21.
2. See Doctrine and Covenants 27:12–13.
3. See Doctrine and Covenants 107:1–4.
4. See Doctrine and Covenants 82:10.
5. Moroni 7:27, 29.
6. See Russell M. Nelson, "The Power of Spiritual Momentum," *Liahona*, May 2022, 99–100.
7. See Shayne M. Bowen, "Because I Live, Ye Shall Live Also," *Ensign* or *Liahona*, Nov. 2012, 16.
8. Doctrine and Covenants 84:88.
9. Doctrine and Covenants 107:3.

FOREORDAINED TO SERVE

ELDER STEVEN R. BANGERTER
Of the Seventy

This evening, I speak to the youth of the Church, the rising generation of young men and young women who are the standard bearers for the next generation.

In October 2013, our beloved prophet, President Russell M. Nelson, declared: "Your Heavenly Father has known you for a very long time. You, as His son or daughter, were chosen by Him to come to earth at this precise time, to be a leader in His great work on earth."[1]

Two years ago, President Nelson continued:

"Today I reaffirm strongly that the Lord has asked *every* worthy, able young man to prepare for and serve a mission. For Latter-day Saint young men, missionary service is a priesthood responsibility. You young men have been reserved for this time when the promised gathering of Israel is taking place. . . .

"For you young and able sisters, a mission is also a powerful, but *optional*, opportunity. . . . Pray to know if the Lord would have you serve a mission, and the Holy Ghost will respond to your heart and mind."[2]

Our prophet's references to the Lord holding the youth of our day in reserve for this time in the gathering of Israel and his invitation to pray to know what the Lord would have you do are, in part, references to the life you lived and blessings you received from God before you were born on this earth.[3] All of us who are born on this earth first lived with our Heavenly Father as His spirit children.[4] The Lord declared to Moses, "I, the Lord God, created all things . . . spiritually, before they were naturally upon the face of the earth."[5]

When He created you spiritually, He loved you as His spirit sons and daughters and embedded within each of you a divine nature and eternal destiny.[6]

During your premortal life, you "developed [your] identity and increased [your] spiritual capabilities."[7] You were blessed with the gift of agency, the ability to make choices for yourself, and you did make important decisions, such as the decision to follow Heavenly Father's plan of happiness, which is to "obtain a physical body and gain earthly experience to progress . . . and ultimately realize [your] divine destiny as heirs of eternal life."[8] This decision affected your life then, in your premortal life, and it continues to affect your life now.[9] As a child of God living in your premortal life, you "grew in intelligence and learned to love the truth."[10]

Before you were born, God appointed each of you to fulfill specific missions during your mortal life upon the earth.[11] If you remain worthy, the blessings of that premortal decree will enable you to have all kinds of opportunities in this life, including opportunities to serve in the Church and to participate in the most important work happening on the earth today: the gathering of Israel.[12] Those premortal promises and blessings are called your foreordination. "The doctrine of foreordination applies to all members of the Church."[13] Foreordination does not guarantee that you will receive certain callings or responsibilities. These blessings and opportunities come in this life as a result of your righteous exercise of agency, just as your foreordination in your premortal life came as a result of righteousness.[14] As you prove yourself worthy and progress along the covenant path, you will receive opportunities to serve in your Young Women class or priesthood quorum. You will be blessed to serve in the temple, to become a ministering brother or sister, and to serve a mission as a disciple of Jesus Christ.

Why does it matter to seek to know and understand your foreordination? In a day when questions abound, when so many seek to know their true identity, the fact that God knows and has blessed each one of us individually before we were ever born on this earth with "essential characteristic[s] of . . . premortal, mortal, and eternal identity and purpose" brings sweet peace and assurance to our mind and heart.[15] Knowing who you are begins with understanding God's foreordained blessings bestowed upon you before you were ever born on this earth. Our Heavenly Father desires to reveal to you your personal foreordination, and He will do so as you seek to learn and follow His will.[16]

I love to read President Nelson's Instagram posts. One of my favorites was on July 20, 2022. He wrote:

"I believe that if the Lord were speaking to you directly, the first thing He would make sure you understand is your true identity. My dear friends, you are literally spirit children of God. . . .

" . . . Make no mistake about it: Your potential is divine. With your diligent seeking, God will give you glimpses of who you may become."[17]

May I share with you how my earthly father taught me to discover my identity and God's plan in my life?

One Saturday morning when I was 13 years old, I was mowing the grass as part of my weekly chores. When I finished, I heard the door close at the back of our house and looked to see my father calling me to join him. I walked to the back porch, and he invited me to sit with him on the steps. It was a beautiful morning. I still recall him sitting so close to me that our shoulders were touching. He began by telling me he loved me. He asked me what my goals were in life. I thought, "Well, that's easy." I knew two things for sure: I wanted to be taller, and I wanted to go camping more often. I was a simple soul. He smiled, paused for a moment, and said: "Steve, I'd like to share something with you that's very important to me. I've prayed that our Heavenly Father will cause what I say now to be indelibly imprinted in your mind and on your soul so that you'll never forget."

My father had my full attention in that moment. He turned and looked at me in the eyes and said, "Son, protect the private times of your life." There was a long pause as he let the meaning sink deep into my heart.

He then continued, "You know, those times when you're the only one around and no one else knows what you're doing? Those times when you think, 'Whatever I do now doesn't affect anyone else, only me'?"

Then he said, "More than any other time in your life, what you do during the private times of your life will have the greatest impact on how you confront challenges and heartache you will face; and what you do during the private times of your life will also have a greater impact on how you confront the successes and joy you will experience than any other time in your life."

My father received the wish of his heart. The sound and cadence of his voice, and the love I felt in his words, were indelibly imprinted in my mind and on my soul that day.

I have learned over the years that the greatest miracle of that day on the steps of my childhood home was that, in the private times of my life, I could go to God in prayer to receive revelation. My father was teaching me how I could learn of God's foreordained blessings. In those private moments, I learned the Book of Mormon is the word of God. I learned God had foreordained me to serve a mission. I learned that God knows me and hears and answers my prayers. I learned that Jesus is the Christ, our Savior and Redeemer.

Though I have made many mistakes since that memorable day with my father, striving to protect the private times of my life has remained an anchor amid the storms of life and has enabled me to seek safe haven and the healing, strengthening blessings of our Savior's love and atoning sacrifice.

My young brothers and sisters, as you protect the private times of your life with wholesome recreation; listening to uplifting music; reading the scriptures; having regular, meaningful prayer; and making efforts to receive and ponder your patriarchal blessing, you will receive revelation. In President Nelson's words, your eyes will become "wide open to the truth that this life really *is* the time when you get to decide what kind of life *you* want to live forever."[18]

Our Father in Heaven will answer your prayers, especially your prayers offered during the private times of your life. He will reveal to you your foreordained gifts and talents, and you will feel His love envelop you, if you will sincerely ask and genuinely desire to know. As you protect the private times of your life, your participation in the ordinances and covenants of the gospel will be more meaningful. You will more fully bind yourself to God in the covenants you make with Him, and you will be lifted to have greater hope, faith, and assurance in the promises He has made to you. Do you want to know God's plan for you? I bear witness He wants you to know, and He inspired His prophet to the world to invite each of us to pray and receive this eye-opening experience for ourselves.[19] I bear witness to the reality and power of our Savior's atoning sacrifice that makes it possible to live up to and enjoy all of God's foreordained blessings, in the name of Jesus Christ, amen.

Notes

1. Russell M. Nelson, "Decisions for Eternity," *Ensign* or *Liahona*, Nov. 2013, 107.
2. Russell M. Nelson, "Preaching the Gospel of Peace," *Liahona*, May 2022, 6.
3. See Russell M. Nelson, "Hope of Israel" (worldwide youth devotional, June 3, 2018), Gospel Library: "Our Heavenly Father has reserved many of His most noble spirits—perhaps, I might say, His finest team—for this final phase. Those noble spirits—those finest players, those heroes—are *you*!"
4. See Jeremiah 1:5.
5. Moses 3:5.
6. See "The Family: A Proclamation to the World," Gospel Library; "Young Women Theme," Gospel Library; "Aaronic Priesthood Quorum Theme," Gospel Library.
7. Topics and Questions, "Premortal Life: Overview," Gospel Library.
8. "The Family: A Proclamation to the World," Gospel Library.
9. See Alma 13:1–4.
10. Topics and Questions, "Premortal Life: Overview," Gospel Library; see also Doctrine and Covenants 138:55–56.
11. See Topics and Questions, "Foreordination," Gospel Library.
12. See Russell M. Nelson, "Hope of Israel."
13. Topics and Questions, "Foreordination," Gospel Library; see also Jeremiah 1:5; "What Is the Relationship between Foreordination and Agency?," *Liahona*, Oct. 2023, 47; Guide to the Scriptures, "Foreordination," Gospel Library.
14. See Alma 13:1–4; Doctrine and Covenants 130:20–21.
15. "The Family: A Proclamation to the World," Gospel Library.
16. See Jeremiah 1:5.
17. Russell M. Nelson, Instagram, July 20, 2022, Instagram.com/russellmnelson.
18. Russell M. Nelson, "Choices for Eternity" (worldwide devotional for young adults, May 15, 2022), Gospel Library.
19. See Russell M. Nelson, "Revelation for the Church, Revelation for Our Lives," *Ensign* or *Liahona*, May 2018, 93–96.

FAITHFUL TO THE END

SISTER ANDREA MUÑOZ SPANNAUS

Second Counselor in the Young Women General Presidency

Dear young friends, today I would like to speak directly to you—the youth of the Church.

It's been a year since our Young Women General Presidency was called. How much has happened in this past year!

We have met many of you and have studied the teachings of Christ together. We have sung songs, made new friends, and served with you in our communities. We have been strengthened by listening to your testimonies at youth conferences and world events. And we have worshipped together in the house of the Lord.

Each time, we have shared a message from our Lord Jesus Christ. Tonight will not be different; I have a message for you, the youth of the Church of Jesus Christ.

The Big Questions

Have you ever wondered how you can be faithful to God while living in a world of sin? Where do you get the strength to go forward and continue doing good? How do you experience true joy?

I think the experience of David and Goliath[1] can help.

David and Goliath

In the Old Testament, the army of the Philistines was battling the Israelites, and every morning and every evening, a giant Philistine named Goliath challenged any Israelite to fight him.

Among the Israelite people lived David, a young shepherd much smaller than Goliath but with a giant faith in Jesus Christ! David volunteered to fight. Even the king tried to dissuade him, but David chose to put his trust in Jesus Christ.

Previously, David had fought a lion and also a bear. From his own experience, he knew that God had protected him and made him victorious. To David, the *cause of God was the most important cause*. So, full of faith in a God who would not abandon him, he gathered five smooth stones, took up his sling, and went to face the giant.

The scriptures tell us that the first stone David threw hit Goliath's forehead, ending his life.[2]

Searching for the Answer

While David used only one stone to kill Goliath, he was prepared with five. With five! This makes me think about how I can prepare myself to face the world.

What if each of David's stones represented a strength we need to be triumphant in our lives? What could those five stones be? I thought of these possibilities:

1. The stone of *my love for God.*
2. The stone of *my faith in our Savior, Jesus Christ.*
3. The stone of *the knowledge of my true identity.*
4. The stone of *my daily repentance.*
5. The stone of *my access to God's power.*

Let's talk about how we are blessed by these strengths.

First, the stone of *my love for God.* Loving God is the first great commandment.[3] The *For the Strength of Youth* guide teaches us: "God loves you. He is your Father. His perfect love can inspire you to love Him. When your love for Heavenly Father is the most important influence in your life, many decisions become easier."[4]

Our love for God and our close relationship with Him give us the strength we need to transform our hearts and more easily overcome our challenges.

Second, the stone of *my faith in our Savior, Jesus Christ.* When Jesus Christ came to earth, He suffered for our sins,[5] and He took upon Himself our sorrows, our pains, our weaknesses, and our physical and mental illnesses. That's why He knows how to help us. Having faith in Jesus Christ means to fully trust His wisdom, His timing, His love, and His power to atone for our sins. The stone of faith in Jesus Christ will defeat any "giant" in our lives.[6] We can overcome this fallen world because He overcame it first.[7]

Number three, the stone of *the knowledge of my true identity*. Our beloved prophet, President Russell M. Nelson, taught us that our most important identities are as children of God, children of the covenant, and disciples of Jesus Christ.[8]

Everything changes when I know who I really am.[9] When I doubt my abilities, I often repeat to myself in my mind or out loud, "I am a daughter of God, I am a daughter of God," as many times as I need until I again feel confident to keep going.

Fourth, the stone of *my daily repentance*. In the *For the Strength of Youth* guide, we read: "Repentance isn't punishment for sin; it is the way the Savior frees us from sin. To repent means to change—to turn away from sin and toward God. It means to improve and receive forgiveness. This kind of change is not a one-time event; it's an ongoing process."[10]

Nothing is more liberating than feeling God's forgiveness and knowing that we are clean and reconciled with Him. Forgiveness is possible for everyone.

The fifth stone is the stone of *my access to God's power*. The covenants we make with God, such as those we make in the ordinance of baptism, give us access to the power of godliness.[11] God's power is a real power that helps us face challenges, make good decisions, and increase our capacity to endure difficult situations. It is a power with which we can grow in the specific abilities that we need.[12]

The *For the Strength of Youth* guide explains: "Covenants *connect* you to Heavenly Father and the Savior. They *increase God's power* in your life."[13]

Let's talk about that connection. Remember when Christ taught the difference between a house built on rock and one on sand?[14] Elder Dieter F. Uchtdorf explained: "A house doesn't survive in a storm because the house is strong. It also doesn't survive just because the rock is strong. The house survives the storm because it is firmly attached to that strong rock. It's the strength of the *connection* to the rock that matters."[15]

Our personal connection to Jesus Christ will give us the courage and confidence to move forward amid people who do not respect our beliefs or who bully us. Christ invites us to keep Him in our thoughts constantly; He tells us, "Look unto me in *every* thought."[16] Thinking about the Savior gives us clarity of mind to make decisions, to act without fear, and to say no to what is contrary to God's teachings.[17] When my day is difficult and I feel like I can't take any more, thinking about Christ brings me peace and gives me hope.

How can we draw upon this power of Jesus Christ? Obeying our covenants and increasing our faith in Jesus Christ are key.

I actually wish David had had one more stone; that would be the stone of *my testimony*. Our testimony is built by personal spiritual experiences in which we recognize the divine influence in our lives.[18] No one can take that knowledge from us. Knowing what we know from having lived our spiritual experiences is priceless. Being true to that knowledge gives us freedom. It gives us joy! If we love the truth, we will seek it, and once we find it, we will defend it.[19]

An Invitation

Just as I chose stone number six, I invite you to meet with your class, quorum, or family and think about what other strengths you need to acquire to remain faithful to God and, therefore, overcome the world.

A Promise

Dear friends, Christ is eager to accompany us on the journey of our lives. I promise you, as you hold on to the iron rod, you will walk hand in hand with Jesus Christ.[20] *He* will be guiding you, and *He* will be teaching you.[21] By *His* hand, you will be able to bring down every Goliath that appears in your life.

Testimony

I testify that there is joy in praying every day, in reading the Book of Mormon every day, in partaking of the sacrament every Sunday, and in going to seminary—even in the early morning! There is joy in doing good.

There is joy in being faithful to the God of the universe, the

Savior of the world, the King of kings. There is joy in being a disciple of Jesus Christ.

God is our Father. He knows your heart's desires and your possibilities, and He trusts you.

Dear youth, Jesus Christ will help you to be faithful to the end. Of these truths I bear my testimony in the name of Jesus Christ, amen.

Notes

1. See 1 Samuel 17.
2. See 1 Samuel 17:40, 45–49.
3. See Matthew 22:36–38.
4. *For the Strength of Youth: A Guide for Making Choices* (2022), 11.
5. See Alma 7:11–14.
6. See 1 Nephi 7:12.
7. See Russell M. Nelson, "Overcome the World and Find Rest," *Liahona*, Nov. 2022, 95–98.
8. See Russell M. Nelson, "Choices for Eternity" (worldwide devotional for young adults, May 15, 2022), Gospel Library.
9. See "Young Women Theme" and "Aaronic Priesthood Quorum Theme," Gospel Library.
10. *For the Strength of Youth*, 7.
11. See Russell M. Nelson, "The Power of Spiritual Momentum," *Liahona*, May 2022, 97–100; see also Doctrine and Covenants 84:19–21.
12. See *General Handbook: Serving in The Church of Jesus Christ of Latter-day Saints*, 3.5, Gospel Library.
13. *For the Strength of Youth*, 34; emphasis added.
14. See 3 Nephi 14:24–27.
15. Dieter F. Uchtdorf, "*For the Strength of Youth:* The Savior's Message to You," *For the Strength of Youth*, Mar. 2024, 38.
16. Doctrine and Covenants 6:36; emphasis added.
17. See Doctrine and Covenants 6:33–34.
18. See Dallin H. Oaks, "Testimony," *Ensign* or *Liahona*, May 2008, 26–29; see also Alma 5:46.
19. See *For the Strength of Youth*, 32: "Love the truth so much that you would never want to steal, lie, cheat, or deceive in any way—at school, at work, online, everywhere. Be the same faithful follower of Jesus Christ in public and in private."
20. See 1 Nephi 8:19, 30; 15:24–25; Helaman 3:29–30.
21. See 3 Nephi 22:13.

FRUIT THAT REMAINS

ELDER MATTHEW L. CARPENTER
Of the Seventy

As a young boy, I loved fresh, ripe peaches. To this day, the idea of biting into a juicy, ripe peach with its tangy flavor makes my mouth water. When fully matured peaches are picked, they last two to four days before they spoil. I have fond memories of joining with my mother and my siblings in our kitchen as we would preserve harvested peaches for the coming winter by sealing them in bottles. If we preserved the peaches correctly, this delicious fruit would last several years, not just two to four days. If properly prepared and heated, the fruit is preserved until the seal is broken.

Christ directed us to "go and bring forth fruit, . . . that your fruit should remain."[1] But He wasn't speaking about peaches. He was talking about God's blessings to His children. If we make and keep covenants with God, the blessings associated with our covenants can extend beyond this life and be sealed upon us, or preserved, forever, becoming fruit that remains for all eternity.

The Holy Ghost, in His divine role as the Holy Spirit of Promise, will seal each ordinance upon those who are faithful to their covenants so that it will be valid after mortality.[2] Having the Holy Ghost seal our ordinances is essential if we want to have the promised blessings for all eternity, becoming fruit that remains.

This is particularly important if we want to be exalted.[3] As President Russell M. Nelson has taught, we should "begin with the end in mind. . . . Surely, for each of us, the 'end' we would most like to achieve is to live forever with our families in an exalted state where we will be in the presence of God, our Heavenly Father, and His Son Jesus Christ."[4] President Nelson has also said: "Celestial marriage is a pivotal part of preparation for eternal life. It requires one to be married to the right person, in the right place, by the right authority, and to obey that sacred covenant faithfully. Then one may be assured of exaltation in the celestial kingdom of God."[5]

What are the blessings of exaltation? They include dwelling in

God's presence for eternity together as husband and wife, inheriting "thrones, kingdoms, principalities, and powers, . . . and a continuation of the seeds forever and ever,"[6] receiving all that God the Father has.[7]

The Lord revealed through Joseph Smith:

"In the celestial glory there are three heavens or degrees;

"And in order to obtain the highest, a man must enter into this order of the priesthood [meaning the new and everlasting covenant of marriage];

"And if he does not, he cannot obtain it.

"He may enter into the other, but that is the end of his kingdom; he cannot have an increase."[8]

We learn here that one can be in the celestial kingdom, or dwell in the presence of God, and be single. But to be exalted in the highest degree of the celestial kingdom, one must enter into marriage by the proper authority and then be true to the covenants made in that marriage. As we are faithful to these covenants, the Holy Spirit of Promise can seal our marriage covenant.[9] Such sealed blessings become fruit that remains.

What is required to faithfully keep the new and everlasting covenant of marriage?

President Russell M. Nelson has taught there are two types of bonds when we enter into this eternal marriage covenant: a lateral bond between husband and wife, and a vertical bond with God.[10] To have the blessings of exaltation sealed upon us and remain after this life, we must be true to both the lateral and the vertical bonds of the covenant.

To keep the lateral bond with your spouse, God has counseled us to "love [your] wife [or husband] with all [your] heart, and . . . cleave unto her [or him] and none else."[11] For those who are married, to cleave unto her or him and none else means you counsel together in love, you love and care for each other, you prioritize time with your spouse over outside interests, and you call upon God to help you overcome your weaknesses.[12] It also means there is no emotional intimacy or sexual relations of any kind outside of your marriage, including flirting or dating, and there is no pornography, which engenders lust.[13]

To keep the lateral bond in the covenant, each partner must desire to be in the marriage. President Dallin H. Oaks recently taught: "We also know that He [God] will force no one into a sealing relationship against his or her will. The blessings of a sealed relationship are assured for all who keep their covenants *but never by forcing a sealed relationship on another person who is unworthy or unwilling.*"[14]

What is the vertical bond referred to by President Nelson? The vertical bond is one we make with God.

To keep the vertical bond with God, we are true to the temple covenants we have made regarding the laws of obedience, sacrifice, the gospel, chastity, and consecration. We also covenant with God to receive our eternal companion and to be a righteous spouse and parent. As we keep the vertical bond, we qualify for the blessings of being part of the family of God through the Abrahamic covenant, including the blessings of posterity, the gospel, and the priesthood.[15] These blessings are also the fruit that remains.

While we hope that all who enter into the new and everlasting covenant remain true and have the blessings sealed upon them for all eternity, sometimes that ideal seems beyond our reach. Throughout my ministry I have encountered members who make and keep covenants while their spouse does not. There are also those who are single, never having the opportunity to marry in mortality. And there are those who are not faithful in their marriage covenants. What happens to individuals in each of these circumstances?

1. If you remain faithful to the covenants you made when you were endowed, you will receive the personal blessings promised to you in the endowment *even if your spouse has broken his or her covenants or withdrawn from the marriage.* If you were sealed and later divorced, and if your sealing is not canceled, the personal blessings of that sealing remain in effect for you if you remain faithful.[16]

Sometimes, due to feelings of betrayal and very real hurt, a faithful spouse may want to cancel their sealing with their unfaithful spouse to get as far away as possible from them, both on earth and for eternity. If you are concerned that you will somehow be tied to an unrepentant former spouse, remember, *you will not*! God will not require anyone to remain in a sealed relationship throughout eternity against his or her will. Heavenly Father will ensure that we will receive every blessing that our desires and choices allow.[17]

However, if a cancellation of sealing is desired, agency is respected. Certain procedures can be followed. *But this should not be done casually*! The First Presidency holds the keys to bind on earth and in heaven. Once a sealing cancellation has been granted by the First Presidency, the blessings related to that sealing are no longer in force; they are canceled both laterally and vertically. It is important to understand that to receive the blessings of exaltation, we must demonstrate that we are willing to enter into and faithfully keep this new and everlasting covenant, either in this life or the next.

2. For those who are single members of the Church, please remember that "in the Lord's own way and time, no blessings will be withheld from His faithful Saints. The Lord will judge and reward each individual according to heartfelt [desires] as well as deed."[18]
3. If you have not remained faithful to temple covenants, is there hope? Yes! The gospel of Jesus Christ is a gospel of hope. That hope comes through Jesus Christ with sincere repentance and obediently following Christ's teachings. I have seen individuals make grave mistakes, breaking sacred covenants. On a regular basis, I see those who sincerely repent, are forgiven, and return to the covenant path. If you have broken your temple covenants, I urge you to turn to Jesus Christ, counsel with your bishop, repent, and open your soul to the *mighty* healing power available because of the Atonement of Jesus Christ.

Brothers and sisters, our loving Heavenly Father has given us covenants so that we may have access to all that He has in store for us. These sacred blessings from God are more delicious than any earthly fruit. They can be preserved for us forever, becoming fruit that remains, as we are faithful to our covenants.

I testify that God has restored the authority to bind on earth and in heaven. That authority is found in The Church of Jesus Christ of Latter-day Saints. It is held by the First Presidency and Quorum of the Twelve and is exercised under the direction of President Russell M. Nelson. Those who enter into the new and everlasting covenant of marriage and keep that covenant can become perfected and eventually receive the fulness of the glory of the Father, regardless of circumstances beyond their control.[19]

These promised blessings appertaining to our covenants can be sealed upon us by the Holy Spirit of Promise and become fruit that remains forever and ever. I so testify in the name of Jesus Christ, amen.

Notes

1. John 15:16.
2. See Dale G. Renlund, "Accessing God's Power through Covenants," *Liahona*, May 2023, 35–38; Doctrine and Covenants 132:7.
3. An ordinance is sealed when it is made valid both in heaven and on earth because it is performed by one having authority and is ratified by the Holy Ghost.

   "We tend to think of the sealing authority as applying only to certain temple ordinances, but that authority is necessary to make any ordinance valid and binding beyond death. The sealing power confers a seal of legitimacy upon your baptism, for example, so that it is recognized here and in heaven. Ultimately, all priesthood ordinances are performed under the keys of the President of the Church, and as President Joseph Fielding Smith explained, 'He [the President of the Church] has given us authority, he has put the sealing power in our priesthood, because he holds those keys' [quoted by Harold B. Lee, in Conference Report, Oct. 1944, 75]" (D. Todd Christofferson, "The Sealing Power," *Liahona*, Nov. 2023, 20).

   "An act which is sealed by the Holy Spirit of Promise is one which is ratified by the Holy Ghost; it is one which is approved by the Lord. . . . No one can lie to the Holy Ghost and get by undetected. . . . These principles also apply to every other ordinance and performance in the Church. Thus if both parties [in a marriage] are 'just and true' [Doctrine and Covenants 76:53], if they are worthy, a ratifying seal is placed on their temple marriage; if they are unworthy, they are not justified by the Spirit and the ratification of the Holy Ghost is withheld. Subsequent worthiness will put the seal in force, and unrighteousness will break any seal" (Bruce R. McConkie, "Holy Spirit of Promise," in *Preparing for an Eternal Marriage Student Manual* [2003], 136).

   "*The Holy Spirit of Promise is the Holy Ghost* who places the stamp of approval upon every ordinance: baptism, confirmation, ordination, marriage. *The promise is that the blessings will be received through faithfulness.* If a person violates a covenant, whether it be of baptism, ordination, marriage or anything else, the Spirit withdraws the stamp of approval, and the blessings will not be received. Every ordinance is sealed with a promise of a reward based upon faithfulness. The Holy Spirit withdraws the stamp of approval where covenants are broken" (Joseph Fielding Smith, *Doctrines of Salvation*, comp. Bruce R. McConkie [1954], 1:45).
4. Russell M. Nelson, *Heart of the Matter: What 100 Years of Living Have Taught Me* (2023), 15.

All covenants must be sealed by the Holy Spirit of Promise if they are to have force after the resurrection of the dead (see Doctrine and Covenants 132:7).

5. Russell M. Nelson, "Celestial Marriage," *Ensign* or *Liahona*, Nov. 2008, 94.
6. Doctrine and Covenants 132:19.
7. See Doctrine and Covenants 84:38.
8. Doctrine and Covenants 131:1–4.
9. See Doctrine and Covenants 132:19–20. "That highest destination—exaltation in the celestial kingdom—is the focus of The Church of Jesus Christ of Latter-day Saints" (Dallin H. Oaks, "Kingdoms of Glory," *Liahona*, Nov. 2023, 26).
10. "Just as marriages and families share a unique *lateral* bond [which] creates a special love, so does the new relationship formed when we bind ourselves by covenant *vertically* to . . . God" when we enter into the new and everlasting covenant of marriage (Russell M. Nelson, *Heart of the Matter*, 41–42).
11. Doctrine and Covenants 42:22; see also *General Handbook: Serving in The Church of Jesus Christ of Latter-day Saints*, 38.6.16. In discussing marriage here, I am referring to marriage according to God's law, which defines marriage as the legal and lawful union between a man and a woman (see "The Family: A Proclamation to the World," Gospel Library).
12. See "The Family: A Proclamation to the World," Gospel Library.
13. See Doctrine and Covenants 42:22–24.
14. Dallin H. Oaks, "Kingdoms of Glory," 29; emphasis added.
15. See Doctrine and Covenants 86:8–11; 113:8; Abraham 2:9–11.
16. See *General Handbook*, 38.4.1.

    While I was serving a full-time mission in Switzerland, my companion and I shared the gospel with a wonderful 60-year-old Swiss couple. As we taught this couple about the restored Church of Jesus Christ, the woman showed great interest in what we were teaching. Over the next few weeks, she gained a testimony of the reality that the Church of Jesus Christ was restored with correct authority from God and that Jesus Christ directs His Church through living prophets and apostles. We looked forward to teaching this couple about one of the most sublime doctrines of the Restoration, the opportunity for eternal marriage. Surprisingly, however, as we taught this couple about the doctrine of eternal marriage, the Swiss woman remarked that she had no interest in being with her husband for all eternity. To her, heaven did not include being with her husband, to whom she had been married for 36 years. This sister was baptized, but her husband was not. They were never sealed in the temple.

    To many, however, heaven would not be heaven without being with the person to whom they are married. To be together with the spouse you love forever truly sounds like heaven. As Elder Jeffrey R. Holland shared about his dear, beloved wife, Pat, heaven would not be heaven without her (see "Scott Taylor: For Elder Holland, Heaven without His Wife and Children 'Wouldn't Be Heaven for Me,'" *Church News*, July 22, 2023, thechurchnews.com).
17. See Dallin H. Oaks, "Kingdoms of Glory," 26.
18. Russell M. Nelson, "Celestial Marriage," 94.
19. See John 15:16.

A HIGHER JOY

ELDER DIETER F. UCHTDORF
Of the Quorum of the Twelve Apostles

I have had the great blessing of speaking at general conference for three decades now. During that time, I have been asked questions relating to these messages by many around the world. Lately, one particular question keeps coming up. It usually goes something like this: "Elder Uchtdorf, I listened carefully to your last talk, but . . . I didn't hear anything about aviation."

Well, after today, I might not hear that question for a while.

On "the Tumbling Mirth of Sun-Split Clouds"[1]

It's hard to believe it was only 120 years ago when Wilbur and Orville Wright first lifted off and flew over the sands of Kitty Hawk, North Carolina. Four short flights on that December day changed the world and opened the door to one of the greatest inventions in the world's history.

Flying was risky in those early days. The brothers knew this. And so did their father, Milton. In fact, he was so terrified of losing both of his sons in a flying accident that they promised him they would never fly together.

And they never did—with one exception. Seven years after that historic day at Kitty Hawk, Milton Wright finally gave his consent and watched as Wilbur and Orville flew together for the first time. After landing, Orville convinced his father to take his first and only flight and to see for himself what it was like.

As the plane lifted from the ground, the 82-year-old Milton got so caught up in the exhilaration of flight that all fear left him. Orville rejoiced as his father shouted with delight, "Higher, Orville, higher!"[2]

This was a man after my own heart!

Perhaps the reason I speak about aviation occasionally is that I know something of what the Wrights felt. I too have "slipped the surly bonds of Earth and danced the skies on laughter-silvered wings."[3]

The Wright brothers' first flight, which happened a mere 37 years before my birth, opened doors of adventure, wonder, and pure joy into my life.

And yet, as amazing as that joy is, there is an even higher kind of joy. Today, in the spirit of Milton Wright's delighted cry, "Higher, Orville, higher," I would like to speak about this higher joy—where it comes from, how it enters our hearts, and how we can experience it in greater measure.

The Whole Aim of Human Existence

It probably goes without saying that everyone wants to be happy.[4] Nevertheless, it also goes without saying that not everyone is happy. Sadly, it seems that for many people, happiness is hard to find.[5]

Why is that? If happiness is the one thing we humans desire most, why are we so unsuccessful at finding it? To paraphrase a country song, maybe we've been looking for joy in all the wrong places.[6]

Where Can We Find Happiness?

Before we discuss how to find joy, allow me to acknowledge that depression and other difficult mental and emotional challenges are real, and the answer is not simply "Try to be happier." My purpose today is not to diminish or trivialize mental health issues. If you face such challenges, I mourn with you, and I stand beside you. For some people, finding joy may include seeking help from trained mental health professionals who devote their lives to practicing their very important art. We should be thankful for such help.

Life is not an endless sequence of emotional highs. "For it must needs be, that there is an opposition in all things."[7] And if God Himself weeps, as the scriptures affirm He does,[8] then of course you and I will weep as well. Feeling sad is not a sign of failure. In this life, at least, joy and sorrow are inseparable companions.[9] Like all of you, I have felt my share of disappointment, sorrow, sadness, and remorse.

However, I have also experienced for myself the glorious dawn that fills the soul with joy so profound that it can scarcely be kept in. I have discovered for myself that this peaceful confidence comes from following the Savior and walking in His Way.

The peace He gives us is not like what the world gives.[10] It's better. It's higher and holier. Jesus said, "I am come that they might have life, and that they might have it more abundantly."[11]

The gospel of Jesus Christ is truly the "good news of great joy"![12] It is a message of matchless hope! A message of yoke-bearing and burden-lifting.[13] Of light-gathering. Of heavenly favor, higher understanding, holier covenants, eternal security, and everlasting glory!

Joy is the very purpose of God's plan for His children. It's what you were created for—"that [you] might have joy"![14] You were built for this!

Our Father in Heaven has not hidden the path to happiness. It is not a secret. It is available to all![15]

It is promised to those who walk the path of discipleship, follow the teachings and example of the Savior, keep His commandments, and honor covenants they make with God. What a remarkable promise!

God Has Something More to Offer

We all know people who say that they don't need God to be happy, that they are happy enough without religion.

I acknowledge and respect these feelings. Our beloved Father in Heaven wants all His children to have as much happiness as possible, so He has filled this world with beautiful, wholesome pleasures and delights, "both to please the eye and . . . gladden the heart."[16] For me, flying brought great happiness. Others find it in music, in art, in hobbies, or in nature.

By inviting everyone and sharing the Savior's good news of great joy, we do not discount any of these sources of joy. We're simply saying that God has something more to give. A higher and more profound joy—a joy that transcends anything this world offers. It is a joy that endures heartbreak, penetrates sorrow, and diminishes loneliness.

Worldly happiness, by contrast, does not last. It cannot. It is the nature of all earthly things to grow old, decay, wear out, or become stale. But godly joy is eternal, because God is eternal. Jesus Christ came to lift us out of the temporal and replace corruption with incorruption. Only He has that power, and only His joy is perpetual.

If you feel there could be more of this kind of joy in your life, I invite you to embark on the journey of following Jesus Christ and His Way. It is a journey of a lifetime—and beyond. Please let me suggest a few beginning steps on this worthy journey of discovering pure joy.

Draw Near unto God[17]

Do you remember the woman in the New Testament who endured a bleeding illness for 12 years?[18] She had spent all she had on physicians, but things only grew worse. She had heard of Jesus; His power to heal was well known. But could He heal her? And how could she even get near Him? Her sickness made her "unclean" according to the law of Moses, and therefore she was required to stay away from others.[19]

Approaching Him openly and asking for healing seemed out of the question.

Still, she thought, "If I may touch but his clothes, I shall be whole."[20]

At last, her faith overcame her fear. She braved the censure of others and pressed toward the Savior.

Finally, she was within reach. She extended her hand.

And she was healed.

Aren't we all somewhat like this woman?

There may be many reasons why we hesitate to draw near to the Savior. We may face ridicule or condemnation by others. In our pride, we may dismiss the possibility of something so simple being of so much value. We may think that our condition somehow disqualifies us from His healing—that the distance is too great or our sins too many.

Like this woman, I have learned that if we draw near to God and reach out to touch Him, we can indeed find healing, peace, and joy.

Look for It

Jesus taught, "Seek, and ye shall find."[21]

I believe this simple phrase is not only a spiritual promise; it is a statement of fact.

If we seek reasons to be angry, to doubt, to be bitter or alone, we will find them too.

However, if we seek joy—if we look for reasons to rejoice and to happily follow the Savior, we will find them.

We rarely find something we are not looking for.

Are you looking for joy?

Seek, and ye shall find.

Bear One Another's Burdens[22]

Jesus taught, "It is more blessed to give than to receive."[23]

Can it be that in our search for joy, the best way to find it is to bring joy to others?

Brothers and sisters, you know and I know this is true! Joy is like a barrel of flour or a jar of oil that will never run out.[24] True joy multiplies when it is shared.

It doesn't require something grand or complicated.

We can do simple things.

Like praying for someone with all our heart.

Giving a sincere compliment.

Helping someone feel welcome, respected, valued, and loved.

Sharing a favorite scripture and what it means to us.

Or even just by listening.

"When ye are in the service of your fellow beings ye are only in the service of your God,"[25] and God will repay your kindness generously.[26] The joy you give to others will return to you in "good measure, pressed down, and shaken together, and running over."[27]

"What Shall We Do Then?"[28]

During the coming days, weeks, and months, may I invite you to:

- Spend time in a sincere, full-hearted effort to draw near to God.
- Seek diligently for everyday moments of hope, peace, and joy.
- Bring joy to others around you.

My dear brothers and sisters, dear friends, as you search the word of God for a deeper understanding of God's eternal plan, accept these invitations, and strive to walk in His Way, you will experience "the peace of God, which passeth all understanding,"[29] even in the midst of sorrows. You will feel a greater measure of God's unsurpassable love swelling within your heart. The dawn of celestial light will penetrate the shadows of your trials, and you will begin to taste the unspeakable glories and wonders of the unseen, perfect, heavenly sphere. You will feel your spirit lifting away from the gravity of this world.

And like good Milton Wright, perhaps you will raise your voice in rejoicing and shout, "Higher, Father, higher!"

May we all seek and find the higher joy that comes from devoting our lives to our Heavenly Father and His Beloved Son. This is my earnest prayer and blessing in the sacred name of Jesus Christ, amen.

Notes

1. John Gillespie Magee Jr., "High Flight," poetryfoundation.org.
2. See Christopher Klein, "10 Things You May Not Know about the Wright Brothers," *History*, Mar. 28, 2023, history.com.
3. Magee, "High Flight."
4. Twenty-four hundred years ago, Aristotle observed that happiness is the one thing all humans desire most. In his treatise *Nicomachean Ethics*, he taught that the greatest good in life is the thing we pursue as an end itself (as opposed to those things we pursue that are a means to some other end). Happiness, above all else, is just such a thing. "We always desire happiness for its own sake," he said, "and never as a means to something else" (*The Nicomachean Ethics of Aristotle*, trans. J. E. C. Weldon [1902], 13–14).
5. See Harry Enten, "American Happiness Hits Record Lows," CNN, Feb. 2, 2022, cnn.com;

Tamara Lush, "Poll: Americans Are the Unhappiest They've Been in 50 Years," Associated Press, June 16, 2020, apnews.com; "The Great Gloom: In 2023, Employees Are Unhappier Than Ever. Why?" BambooHR, bamboohr.com.

6. See Wanda Mallette, Patti Ryan, and Bob Morrison, "Lookin' for Love (in All the Wrong Places)" (1980).
7. 2 Nephi 2:11.
8. See John 11:35; Moses 7:28–37.
9. See 2 Nephi 2:11.
10. See John 14:27.
11. John 10:10.
12. Luke 2:10, New Revised Standard Version.
13. See Matthew 11:28–30.
14. 2 Nephi 2:25.
15. If you have any concerns about whether or not your Father in Heaven will accept you and allow you to receive His joy, I invite you to prayerfully read Christ's parable of the prodigal son (see Luke 15:11–32). In that parable, we learn how our Heavenly Father feels about His children and how He awaits and celebrates our return after we have strayed from Him! From the moment we "come to ourselves" (see verse 17) and begin the journey home, He will see us, for He stands watching and waiting. And what is He waiting for? For us! As we draw near to Him, He will celebrate our return and call us His child.
16. Doctrine and Covenants 59:18. This revelation also explains, "It pleaseth God that he hath given all these things unto man; for unto this end were they made" (verse 20).
17. To those who draw near to God, He gives this grand promise: "I will draw near unto you" (Doctrine and Covenants 88:63; see also James 4:8).
18. See Mark 5:24–34.
19. See Bible Dictionary, "Clean and unclean."
20. Mark 5:28.
21. Matthew 7:7.
22. By bearing each other's burdens, we "fulfil the law of Christ" (Galatians 6:2; see also Mosiah 18:8).
23. Acts 20:35.
24. See 1 Kings 17:8–16.
25. Mosiah 2:17.
26. In his Epistle to the Romans, Paul states that God "will render to every man according to his deeds: to them who by patient continuance in well doing seek for glory and honour and immortality, eternal life: . . . glory, honour, and peace, to every man that worketh good" (Romans 2:6–7, 10).
27. Luke 6:38. Our very salvation and eternal happiness may depend on our compassion and kindness to others (see Matthew 25:31–46).
28. Luke 3:10.
29. Philippians 4:7.

Sunday Morning Session

APRIL 7, 2024

WORDS MATTER

ELDER RONALD A. RASBAND

Of the Quorum of the Twelve Apostles

Brothers, sisters, and friends across the world, I am honored to address this vast audience, many of whom are members of our Church and many of whom are friends and new listeners to this conference broadcast. Welcome!

The messages shared from this pulpit are communicated in words. They are given in English and translated into nearly 100 different languages. Always the base is the same. Words. And words matter a lot. Let me say that again. Words matter!

They are the bedrock of how we connect; they represent our beliefs, morals, and perspectives. Sometimes we speak words; other times we listen. Words set a tone. They voice our thoughts, feelings, and experiences, for good or bad.

Unfortunately, words can be thoughtless, hasty, and hurtful. Once said, we cannot take them back. They can wound, punish, cut down, and even lead to destructive actions. They can weigh heavily on us.

On the other hand, words can celebrate victory, be hopeful and encouraging. They can prompt us to rethink, reboot, and redirect our course. Words can open our minds to truth.

That is why, first and foremost, the Lord's words matter.

In the Book of Mormon, the prophet Alma and his people in ancient America encountered endless warfare with those who had disregarded the word of God, hardened their hearts, and corrupted their culture. The faithful could have fought, but Alma counseled: "And now, as the preaching of the word had a great tendency to lead the people to do that which was just—yea, it had had more powerful effect upon the minds of the people than the sword, or anything else, which had happened unto them—therefore Alma thought it was expedient that they should try the virtue of the word of God."[1]

The "word of God" surpasses all other expressions. It has been so since the Creation of the earth when the Lord spoke: "Let there be light: and there was light."[2]

From the Savior came these assurances in the New Testament: "Heaven and earth shall pass away, but my words shall not pass away."[3]

And this: "If a man love me, he will keep my words: and my Father will love him, and we will come unto him, and make our abode with him."[4]

And from Mary, the mother of Jesus, came this humble testimony: "Behold the handmaid of the Lord; be it unto me according to thy word."[5]

Believing and heeding the word of God will draw us closer to Him. President Russell M. Nelson has promised, "If you will study His words, your ability to be more like Him will increase."[6]

Don't we all want to be, as the hymn says, "more blessed and holy—more, Savior, like thee"?[7]

I picture young Joseph Smith on his knees hearing the words of his Father in Heaven: "[Joseph,] This is My Beloved Son. Hear Him!"[8]

We "hear Him" in the words of scripture, but do we let them just sit on the page, or do we recognize He is speaking to us? Do we change?

We "hear Him" in personal revelation and promptings from the Holy Ghost, in answers to prayer, and in those moments when only Jesus Christ, through the power of His Atonement, can lift our burdens, grant us forgiveness and peace, and embrace us "in the arms of his love."[9]

Second, the words of prophets matter.

Prophets testify of the divinity of Jesus Christ. They teach His gospel and show His love for all.[10] I bear my witness that our living prophet, President Russell M. Nelson, hears and speaks the word of the Lord.

President Nelson has a way with words. He has said, "Keep on the covenant path,"[11] "Gather Israel,"[12] "Let God prevail,"[13] "Build bridges of understanding,"[14] "Give thanks,"[15] "Increase your faith in

Jesus Christ,"[16] "Take charge of your testimony,"[17] and "Become a peacemaker."[18]

Most recently, he has asked us to "think celestial." "When you are confronted with a dilemma," he said, "think celestial! When tested by temptation, think celestial! When life or loved ones let you down, think celestial! When someone dies prematurely, think celestial. . . . When the pressures of life crowd in upon you, think celestial! . . . As you think celestial, your heart will gradually change, . . . you will view trials and opposition in a new light, . . . [and] your faith will increase."[19]

When we think celestial, we see "things as they really are, and . . . really will be."[20] In this world burdened with confusion and contention, we all need that perspective.

Elder George Albert Smith, long before becoming President of the Church, spoke of sustaining the prophet and heeding his words. He said: "The obligation that we make when we raise our hands . . . is a most sacred one. . . . It means . . . that we will stand behind him; we will pray for him; . . . and we will strive to carry out his instructions as the Lord shall direct."[21] In other words, we will diligently act upon our prophet's words.

As one of 15 prophets, seers, and revelators sustained yesterday by our worldwide Church, I want to share with you one of my experiences sustaining the prophet and embracing his words. It was for me much like the prophet Jacob, who recounted, "I had heard the voice of the Lord speaking unto me in very word."[22]

Last October my wife, Melanie, and I were in Bangkok, Thailand, as I was preparing to dedicate what would be the Church's 185th temple.[23] For me, the assignment was both surreal and humbling. This was the first temple on the Southeast Asia peninsula.[24] It was masterfully designed—a six-story, nine-spired structure, "fitly framed"[25] to be a house of the Lord. For months I had contemplated the dedication. What had settled in my soul and mind was that the country and the temple had been cradled in the arms of prophets and apostles. President Thomas S. Monson had announced the temple[26] and President Nelson the dedication.[27]

I had prepared the dedicatory prayer months earlier. Those sacred words had been translated into 12 languages. We were ready. Or so I thought.

The night before the dedication, I was awakened from my sleep with an unsettled, urgent feeling about the dedicatory prayer. I tried to set aside the prompting, thinking the prayer was in place. But the Spirit would not leave me alone. I sensed certain words were missing, and by divine design they came to me in revelation, and I inserted these words in the prayer near the end: "May we think celestial, letting Thy Spirit prevail in our lives, and strive to be peacemakers always."[28] The Lord was reminding me to heed the words of our living prophet: "Think celestial," "let the Spirit prevail," "strive to be peacemakers." Words of the prophet matter to the Lord and to us.

Third, and so very important, are our own words. Believe me, in our emoji-filled[29] world, our words matter.

Our words can be supportive or angry, joyful or mean, compassionate or tossed aside. In the heat of the moment, words can sting and sink painfully deep into the soul—and stay there. Our words on the internet, texting, social media, or tweets take on a life of their own. So be careful what you say and how you say it. In our families, especially with husbands, wives, and children, our words can bring us together or drive a wedge between us.

Let me suggest three simple phrases that we can use to take the sting out of difficulties and differences, lift, and reassure each other:

"Thank you."

"I am sorry."

And "I love you."

Do not save these humble phrases for a special event or catastrophe. Use them often and sincerely, for they show regard for others. Talk is growing cheap; do not follow that pattern.

We can say "thank you" on the elevator, in the parking lot, at the market, in the office, in a queue, or with our neighbors or friends. We can say "I am sorry" when we make a mistake, miss a meeting, forget a birthday, or see someone in pain. We can say "I love you," and those words carry the message "I am thinking about you," "I care about you," "I am here for you," or "You are everything to me."

Let me share a personal example. Husbands, take heed. Sisters, this is going to help you too. Before my full-time assignment in the Church, I traveled widely for my company. I was gone a fair amount of time to far reaches of the world. At the end of my day, no matter where I was, I always called home. When my wife, Melanie, picked up the phone and I reported in, our conversation always led us to expressing "I love you." Every day, those words served as an anchor to my soul and my conduct; they were a protection to me from evil designs. "Melanie, I love you" spoke of the precious trust between us.

President Thomas S. Monson used to say, "There are feet to steady, hands to grasp, minds to encourage, hearts to inspire, and souls to save."[30] Saying "thank you," "I am sorry," "I love you" will do just that.

Brothers and sisters, words do matter.

I promise that if we "feast upon the words of Christ"[31] that lead to salvation, our prophet's words that guide and encourage us, and our own words that speak of who we are and what we hold dear, the powers of heaven will pour down upon us. "The words of Christ will tell you all things what ye should do."[32] We are Heavenly Father's children and He is our God, and He expects us to speak with "the tongue of angels"[33] by the power of the Holy Ghost.[34]

I love the Lord Jesus Christ. He is, in the words of the Old Testament prophet Isaiah, "Wonderful, Counsellor, The mighty God, The everlasting Father, The Prince of Peace."[35] And as the Apostle John made clear, Jesus Christ Himself is "the Word."[36]

Of this I testify as an Apostle called to the Lord's divine service—to declare His word—and called to stand as a special witness of Him. In the name of the Lord Jesus Christ, amen.

Notes

1. Alma 31:5.
2. Genesis 1:3.
3. Matthew 24:35.
4. John 14:23.
5. Luke 1:38.

6. Russell M. Nelson, "I Studied More Than 2,200 Scriptures about the Savior in Six Weeks: Here Is a Little of What I Learned," *Inspiration* (blog), Feb. 28, 2017, ChurchofJesusChrist.org.
7. "More Holiness Give Me," *Hymns*, no. 131.
8. Joseph Smith—History 1:17.
9. The prophet Lehi describes "the arms of his love" in his declaration to his sons: "But behold, the Lord hath redeemed my soul from hell; I have beheld his glory, and I am encircled about eternally in the arms of his love" (2 Nephi 1:15).
10. President Russell M. Nelson said, "Prophets testify of Jesus Christ—of His divinity and of His earthly mission and ministry" ("Sustaining the Prophets," *Ensign* or *Liahona*, Nov. 2014, 74).
11. Russell M. Nelson, "As We Go Forward Together," *Ensign* or *Liahona*, Apr. 2018, 7.
12. Russell M. Nelson, "Hope of Israel" (worldwide youth devotional, June 3, 2018), Gospel Library.
13. Russell M. Nelson, "Let God Prevail," *Liahona*, Nov. 2020, 92.
14. Russell M. Nelson, "President Nelson Shares Social Post about Racism and Calls for Respect for Human Dignity," June 1, 2020, newsroom.ChurchofJesusChrist.org.
15. Russell M. Nelson, in Sarah Jane Weaver, "President Nelson Invites Us to #GiveThanks," *Church News*, Nov. 20, 2020, thechurchnews.com.
16. Russell M. Nelson, "Overcome the World and Find Rest," *Liahona*, Nov. 2022, 98.
17. Russell M. Nelson, "Choices for Eternity" (worldwide devotional for young adults, May 15, 2022), Gospel Library.
18. Russell M. Nelson, "Peacemakers Needed," *Liahona*, May 2023, 99; see also facebook.com/reel/277880588051925.
19. Russell M. Nelson, "Think Celestial!," *Liahona*, Nov. 2023, 118–19.
20. Jacob 4:13.
21. *Teachings of Presidents of the Church: George Albert Smith* (2011), 64.
22. Jacob 7:5.
23. The Bangkok Thailand Temple was dedicated on October 22, 2023.
24. The temple district reaches beyond Thailand's borders, spanning Cambodia to Pakistan, Nepal to Indonesia.
25. Ephesians 2:21.
26. See Thomas S. Monson, "Blessings of the Temple," *Ensign* or *Liahona*, May 2015, 91.
27. See "News for Temples in Five Nations," Mar. 27, 2023, newsroom.ChurchofJesusChrist.org.
28. See dedicatory prayer for the Bangkok Thailand Temple, temples.ChurchofJesusChrist.org.
29. An emoji, often a little yellow face, is a pictogram embedded in an electronic message to convey a feeling, expression, or idea.
30. Thomas S. Monson, "To the Rescue," *Ensign*, May 2001, 48; *Liahona*, July 2001, 57.
31. 2 Nephi 32:3.
32. 2 Nephi 32:3.
33. 2 Nephi 32:2.
34. Nephi wrote, "For when a man speaketh by the power of the Holy Ghost the power of the Holy Ghost carrieth it unto the hearts of the children of men" (2 Nephi 33:1).
35. Isaiah 9:6.
36. John 1:1.

PRAY, HE IS THERE

PRESIDENT SUSAN H. PORTER
Primary General President

Brothers and sisters, I feel joy as I respond to an impression to speak to children!

Girls and boys, wherever you are in the world, I want to share something with you.

Our Heavenly Father loves you! You are His child. He knows you. He wants to bless you. I pray with all my heart that you will feel His love.

Do you like to receive gifts? I want to talk to you about a very special gift that Heavenly Father has given to you to help you. It is the gift of prayer. What a blessing prayer is! We can talk to Heavenly Father anytime, anywhere.

When Jesus was on the earth, He taught us to pray. He said, "Ask, and ye shall receive."[1]

What gifts can you pray for? There are many, but today I want to share three:

1. Pray to know.
2. Pray to grow.
3. Pray to show.

Let's talk about each one.

First, Pray to Know

What do you need to *know*?

There is a song about prayer that Primary children sing all over the world. It starts with a question. Do you know what song it is? If I were really brave, I would sing it to you!

"Heavenly Father, are you really there? And do you hear and answer ev'ry child's prayer?"[2]

How can you know that Heavenly Father is really there, even when you can't see Him?

President Russell M. Nelson has invited you to "pour out your heart to your Heavenly Father. . . . And then listen!"[3] Listen to what you feel in your heart and to thoughts that come to your mind.[4]

Heavenly Father has a glorified body of flesh and bones and is the Father of your spirit. Because Heavenly Father has all power and knows all things, He can see all His children[5] and can hear and answer every prayer. You can come to *know* for yourself that He is there and that He loves you.

When you know that Heavenly Father is real and that He loves you, you can live with courage and hope! "Pray, he is there; speak, he is list'ning."[6]

Have you ever felt alone? One day when our granddaughter Ashley was six years old, she was the only one without a friend to play with on the school playground. As she stood there, feeling unimportant and unseen, a specific thought came into her mind: "Wait! I'm not alone! I have Christ!" Ashley knelt down right in the middle of the playground, folded her arms, and prayed to Heavenly Father. The moment she opened her eyes, a girl her age was standing there asking her if she wanted to play. Ashley came to know, "We are important to the Lord, and we are never truly alone."

Sometimes you may want to *know* why something hard is happening in your life or why you didn't receive a blessing you prayed for. Often the best question to ask Heavenly Father is not *why* but *what*.

Do you remember when Nephi and his family were hungry while they were traveling in the wilderness? When Nephi and his brothers went to hunt for food, Nephi broke his bow. But he didn't ask why.

Nephi made a new bow and asked his father, Lehi, where he could go to get food. Lehi prayed, and the Lord showed them where Nephi could go.[7] Heavenly Father will guide you when you ask Him *what* you can do and *what* you can learn.

Second, Pray to Grow

Heavenly Father wants to help you *grow*! He loves us so much that He sent His Son, Jesus Christ, to show us the way to live.[8] Jesus suffered, died, and was resurrected so we can be forgiven of our sins and *grow* to become more like Him.

Do you want to *grow* in patience or in honesty? Do you want to *grow* in a skill? Maybe you are shy and want to *grow* in courage. "Pray, he is there"![9] Through His Spirit, your heart can change, and you can receive strength.

My new friend Jonah wrote: "I often feel nervous on my way to school in the morning. I worry about things like being late, forgetting something, and taking tests. When I was 10, I started saying prayers on my drive to school with my mom. I ask for the help I need, and I pray for my family too. I also think of the things I'm grateful for. [Praying to Heavenly Father has] helped me. Sometimes I don't feel the relief right as I get out of the car, but by the time I'm at my classroom, I feel peaceful."[10]

Jonah's faith is *growing* as he prays every day and then moves forward.

Third, Pray to Show

You can pray for help to *show* Heavenly Father's love to others.[11] Through His Spirit, Heavenly Father will help you notice someone who is sad so you can comfort them. He can help you *show* His love by forgiving someone. He can give you courage to serve someone and share with them that they are a child of God. You can help others come to know and love Jesus and Heavenly Father as you do.[12]

For my whole life I prayed that my father would become a member of The Church of Jesus Christ of Latter-day Saints. Even as a young girl, I knew how many blessings *he* could receive. Our *family* could receive the blessings of being sealed for eternity. My family, friends, and I prayed often for him, but he didn't join the Church. Heavenly Father does not force anyone to make a choice.[13] He can send us answers to our prayers in other ways.

When I was old enough, I received my patriarchal blessing. In the blessing, the patriarch told me the best thing I could do to help my family be together in heaven was to be an example of the gospel of Jesus Christ. That's what I could do!

My father lived to be 86. Five days after he died, I received a sacred feeling of joy. Heavenly Father let me know through His Spirit that my father wanted to receive the blessings of the gospel of Jesus Christ! I will never forget the day I knelt around the altar in the temple with my sister and brothers to be sealed to my parents. I had started praying for this blessing when I was in Primary, and I received it when I was a grandmother.

Perhaps you are praying for blessings for your family and others you love. Don't give up! Heavenly Father will *show* you what you can do.

Share with Heavenly Father what is in your heart.[14] As you sincerely ask for His help, you will receive His Spirit to guide you.[15] Praying every day will fill you with love for Heavenly Father and Jesus Christ. This will help you want to follow Them your whole life!

Imagine what would happen if all the children in Africa, South America, Asia, Europe, North America, and Australia prayed every day. The whole world would be blessed with more of God's love!

I invite you to *pray to know* Heavenly Father is there, *pray to grow* to become like Him, and *pray to show* His love to others. I know He lives and loves *you.* "Pray, he is there." In the sacred name of Jesus Christ, amen.

Notes

1. John 16:24; see also 3 Nephi 27:29.
2. "A Child's Prayer," *Children's Songbook*, 12.
3. Russell M. Nelson, "Revelation for the Church, Revelation for Our Lives," *Ensign* or *Liahona*, May 2018, 95.
4. See Doctrine and Covenants 11:13.
5. See Moses 1:6–8, 27–29, 35.
6. "A Child's Prayer," 12.
7. See 1 Nephi 16:18, 23–24.
8. See John 3:16–17.
9. "A Child's Prayer," 12.
10. Personal correspondence.
11. See John 13:34–35.
12. See Alma 20:26–27; 22.
13. See 2 Nephi 2:27; Helaman 14:30.
14. See Mosiah 24:12; Alma 37:37.
15. See Doctrine and Covenants 19:38.

THE POWERFUL, VIRTUOUS CYCLE OF THE DOCTRINE OF CHRIST

ELDER DALE G. RENLUND
Of the Quorum of the Twelve Apostles

Years ago, my wife, Ruth; our daughter, Ashley; and I joined other tourists on a kayaking excursion in the state of Hawaii in the United States. A kayak is a low-to-the-water, canoe-like boat in which the rower sits facing forward and uses a double-bladed paddle to pull front to back on one side and then on the other. The plan was to row to two small islands off the coast of Oahu and back again. I was confident because, as a young man, I had paddled kayaks across mountain lakes. Hubris never bodes well, does it?

Our guide gave us instructions and showed us the ocean kayaks we would use. They differed from the ones I had previously paddled. I was supposed to sit on top of the kayak, instead of down inside it. When I got onto the kayak, my center of gravity was higher than I was accustomed to, and I was less stable in the water.

As we started out, I rowed faster than Ruth and Ashley. After a while, I was far ahead of them. Though proud of my heroic pace, I stopped paddling and waited for them to catch up. A large wave—about 13 centimeters[1]—hit the side of my kayak and flipped me over into the water. By the time I had turned the kayak upright and struggled to get back on top, Ruth and Ashley had passed me by, but I was too winded to resume paddling. Before I could catch my breath, another wave, this one truly enormous—at least 20 centimeters[2]—hit my kayak and flipped me over again. By the time I managed to right the kayak, I was so out of breath I feared I would not be able to climb on top.

Seeing my situation, the guide rowed over and steadied my kayak, making it easier for me to climb on top. When he saw that I was still too breathless to row on my own, he hitched a towrope to my kayak and began paddling, pulling me along with him. Soon I caught my breath and began paddling adequately on my own. He let go of the rope, and I reached the first island without further assistance. Upon arrival, I flopped down on the sand, exhausted.

After the group had rested, the guide quietly said to me, "Mr. Renlund, if you just keep paddling, maintaining your momentum, I think you're going to be fine." I followed his advice as we paddled to the second island and then back to our starting point. Twice the guide rowed by and told me I was doing great. Even larger waves hit my kayak from the side, but I was not flipped over.

By consistently paddling the kayak, I maintained momentum and forward progress, mitigating the effect of waves hitting me from the side. The same principle applies in our spiritual lives. We become vulnerable when we slow down and especially when we stop.[3] If we maintain spiritual momentum by continually "rowing" toward the Savior, we are safer and more secure because our eternal life depends on our faith in Him.[4]

Spiritual momentum is created "over a lifetime as we repeatedly embrace the doctrine of Christ."[5] Doing so, President Russell M. Nelson taught, produces a "powerful virtuous cycle."[6] Indeed, the elements of the doctrine of Christ—such as faith in the Lord Jesus Christ, repentance, entering a covenant relationship with the Lord through baptism, receiving the gift of the Holy Ghost, and enduring to the end[7]—are not intended to be experienced as one-time, check-the-box events. In particular, "enduring to the end" is not really a separate step in the doctrine of Christ—as though we complete the first four elements and then hunker down, grit our teeth, and wait to die. No, enduring to the end is repeatedly and iteratively applying the other elements of the doctrine of Christ, creating the "powerful virtuous cycle" that President Nelson described.[8]

Repeatedly means that we experience the elements of the doctrine of Christ over and over throughout our lives. *Iteratively* means that we build on and improve with each repetition. Even though we repeat the elements, we are not just spinning in circles without a forward trajectory. Instead, we draw closer to Jesus Christ each time through the cycle.

Momentum involves both speed and direction.[9] If I had paddled the kayak vigorously in the wrong direction, I could have created significant momentum, but I would not have reached the intended destination. Similarly, in life, we need to "row" toward the Savior to come unto Him.[10]

Our faith in Jesus Christ needs to be nourished daily.[11] It is nourished as we pray daily, study the scriptures daily, reflect on the goodness of God daily, repent daily, and follow the promptings of the Holy Ghost daily. Just as it is not healthy to defer eating all our food until Sunday and then binge our weekly allotment of nutrition, it is not spiritually healthy to restrict our testimony-nourishing behavior to one day in the week.[12]

When we assume responsibility for our own testimonies,[13] we gain spiritual momentum and gradually develop bedrock faith in Jesus Christ, and the doctrine of Christ becomes central to the purpose of life.[14] Momentum likewise builds as we strive to obey the laws of God and repent. Repentance is joyful and allows us to learn from our mistakes, which is how we progress eternally. We will undoubtedly have times when we flip over in our kayaks and find ourselves in deep water. Through repentance, we can get back on top and continue, no matter how many times we have fallen off.[15] The important part is that we do not give up.

The next element of the doctrine of Christ is baptism, which includes the baptism of water and, through confirmation, the baptism of the Holy Ghost.[16] While baptism is a singular event, we renew our baptismal covenant repeatedly when we partake of the sacrament. The sacrament does not replace baptism, but it links the initial elements in the doctrine of Christ—faith and repentance—with reception of the Holy Ghost.[17] As we conscientiously partake of the sacrament,[18] we invite the Holy Ghost into our lives, just like when we were baptized and confirmed.[19] As we keep the covenant described in the sacrament prayers, the Holy Ghost becomes our companion.

As the Holy Ghost exerts a greater influence in our lives, we progressively and iteratively develop Christlike attributes. Our hearts change. Our disposition to do evil diminishes. Our inclination to do good increases until we only want "to do good continually."[20] And we thereby access the heavenly power needed to endure to the end.[21] Our faith has increased, and we are ready to repeat the powerful, virtuous cycle again.

Forward spiritual momentum also propels us to make additional covenants with God in the house of the Lord. Multiple covenants draw us closer to Christ and connect us more strongly to Him. Through these covenants, we have greater access to His power. To be clear, baptismal and temple covenants are not, in and of themselves, the source of power. The source of power is the Lord Jesus Christ and our Heavenly Father. Making and keeping covenants create a conduit for Their power in our lives. As we live according to these covenants, we eventually become inheritors to all that Heavenly Father has.[22] The momentum produced by living the doctrine of Christ not only powers the transformation of our divine nature into our eternal destiny but also motivates us to help others in appropriate ways.

Consider how the expedition guide helped me after I flipped over in the kayak. He did not shout from afar an unhelpful question such as, "Mr. Renlund, what are you doing in the water?" He did not paddle up and chide me, saying, "Mr. Renlund, you would not be in this situation if you were more physically fit." He did not start towing my kayak while I was just trying to get on top of it. And he did not correct me in front of the group. Instead, he gave me the help I needed at the time I needed it. He gave me advice when I was receptive. And he went out of his way to encourage me.

As we minister to others, we do not need to ask unhelpful questions or state the obvious. Most people who are struggling know that they are struggling. We should not be judgmental; our judgment is neither helpful nor welcome, and it is most often ill-informed.

Comparing ourselves to others can lead us to make pernicious errors, especially if we conclude that we are more righteous than those who are struggling. Such a comparison is like drowning hopelessly in three meters[23] of water, seeing someone else drowning in four meters[24] of water, judging him a greater sinner, and feeling good about yourself. After all, we are all struggling in our own way. None of us earns salvation.[25] We never can. Jacob, in the Book of Mormon, taught, "Remember, after [we] are reconciled unto God, that it is only in and through the grace of God that [we] are saved."[26] We all need the Savior's infinite Atonement, not just part of it.

We do need all our compassion, empathy, and love as we interact with those around us.[27] Those who are struggling "need to experience the pure love of Jesus Christ reflected in [our] words and actions."[28] As we minister, we encourage others frequently and offer help. Even if someone is not receptive, we continue to minister as they allow. The Savior taught that "unto such shall ye continue to minister; for ye know not but what they will return and repent, and come unto me with full purpose of heart, and I shall heal them; and ye shall be the means of bringing salvation unto them."[29] The Savior's job is to heal. Our job is to love—to love and minister in such a way that others are drawn to Jesus Christ. This is one of the fruits of the powerful, virtuous cycle of the doctrine of Christ.

I invite you to live the doctrine of Christ repeatedly, iteratively, and intentionally and help others on their way. I testify that the doctrine of Christ is central to Heavenly Father's plan; it is, after all, His doctrine. As we exercise faith in Jesus Christ and His Atonement, we are propelled along the covenant path and motivated to help others become faithful disciples of Jesus Christ. We can become heirs in Heavenly Father's kingdom, which is the culmination of faithfully living the doctrine of Christ. In the name of Jesus Christ, amen.

Notes

1. Only about five inches.
2. Only about eight inches.
3. In physics, momentum = mass × velocity. When we stop, the velocity is zero. Therefore, the product of mass and velocity becomes zero, regardless of our prior momentum or the mass.
4. See Russell M. Nelson, "The Power of Spiritual Momentum," *Liahona*, May 2022, 98. President Nelson counseled, "We have never needed *positive* spiritual momentum more than we do now." That's the best way to move "forward amid . . . fear and uncertainty." See also 2 Nephi 2:6–7; 9:23–24.
5. Russell M. Nelson, "Overcome the World and Find Rest," *Liahona*, Nov. 2022, 97.
6. Russell M. Nelson, "Overcome the World," 97.
7. The phrase "the doctrine of Christ" means the same as the phrase "the gospel of Jesus Christ." See 2 Nephi 31:2–21; 3 Nephi 9:14–22; 11:7–41; 27:1–21.
8. Disengaging from any of the elements in the doctrine of Christ slows or stops our spiritual momentum. See 2 Nephi 28:30; Alma 12:10–11; Doctrine and Covenants 20:31–34; 50:24.

9. In physics, momentum = mass × velocity. Velocity is the speed in combination with the direction of motion of an object. Velocity is a vector and is inherently directional.
10. See 2 Nephi 2:6–7; 9:23–24.
11. See Russell M. Nelson, "The Power of Spiritual Momentum," 99.
12. See Colossians 2:6–7.
13. See Russell M. Nelson, "Overcome the World," 97. Underlining the importance of our testimonies in maintaining spiritual momentum, the statement by President Nelson to take charge of our testimonies was also quoted by President M. Russell Ballard (see "Follow Jesus Christ with Footsteps of Faith," *Liahona*, Nov. 2022, 35) and Elder Quentin L. Cook (see "Be True to God and His Work," *Liahona*, Nov. 2022, 120).
14. See "The Restoration of the Fulness of the Gospel of Jesus Christ: A Bicentennial Proclamation to the World," Gospel Library; Russell M. Nelson, "A Plea to My Sisters," *Ensign* or *Liahona*, Nov. 2015, 97.
15. See Mosiah 26:30; Alma 34:31; Moroni 6:8; Doctrine and Covenants 58:42.
16. See 2 Nephi 31:13.
17. Elder James E. Talmage wrote, "In the course of our study of the principles and ordinances of the Gospel, as specified in the fourth of the Articles of Faith, the subject of the Sacrament of the Lord's Supper very properly claims attention, the observance of this ordinance being required of all who have become members of the Church of Christ through compliance with the requirements of faith, repentance, and baptism by water and of the Holy Ghost" (*The Articles of Faith*, 12th ed. [1924], 171).
18. See Doctrine and Covenants 59:9.
19. See Dallin H. Oaks, "Special Witnesses of Christ," *Ensign*, Apr. 2001, 13; *Liahona*, Apr. 2001, 14.
20. Mosiah 5:2.
21. See, for instance, 2 Nephi 31:2–21; 3 Nephi 11:23–31; 27:13–21; Moroni 4:3; 5:2; 6:6; Doctrine and Covenants 20:77, 79; 59:8–9.
22. See Doctrine and Covenants 14:7; 84:33–38.
23. About 10 feet.
24. About 13 feet.
25. See Ephesians 2:8–9.
26. 2 Nephi 10:24.
27. President Jeffrey R. Holland taught: "When a battered, weary swimmer tries valiantly to get back to shore, after having fought strong winds and rough waves which he should never have challenged in the first place, those of us who might have had better judgment, or perhaps just better luck, ought not to row out to his side, beat him with our oars, and shove his head back underwater. That's not what boats were made for. But some of us do that to each other" ("A Robe, a Ring, and a Fatted Calf" [Brigham Young University devotional, Jan. 31, 1984], 5, speeches.byu.edu).
28. Russell M. Nelson, "Peacemakers Needed," *Liahona*, May 2023, 100.
29. 3 Nephi 18:32.

TRUST IN THE LORD

ELDER PAUL B. PIEPER
Of the Seventy

In our family, we sometimes play a game we call "The Crazy Trust Exercise." You may have played it too. Two people stand a few feet apart, one with their back toward the other. On a signal from the person behind, the person in front falls backward into the waiting arms of their friend.

Trust is the foundation of all relationships. A threshold question to any relationship is "Can I trust the other person?" A relationship forms only when people are willing to place trust in each other. It is not a relationship if one person trusts completely but the other does not.

Each of us is a beloved spirit son or daughter of a loving Heavenly Father.[1] But while that spiritual genealogy provides a foundation, it does not of itself create a meaningful relationship with God. A relationship can be built only when we choose to trust in Him.

Heavenly Father desires to build a close, personal relationship with each of His spirit children.[2] Jesus expressed that desire when He prayed, "That they all may be one; as thou, Father, art in me, and I in thee, that they also may be one in us."[3] The relationship God seeks with each spirit child is one so close and personal that He will be able to share all He has and all He is.[4] That kind of deep, enduring relationship can develop only when built upon perfect, total trust.

For His part, Heavenly Father has worked from the beginning to communicate His absolute trust in the divine potential of each of His children. Trust underlies the plan He presented for our growth and progression prior to our coming to earth. He would teach us eternal laws, create an earth, provide us with mortal bodies, give us the gift to choose for ourselves, and permit us to learn and grow by making our own choices. He wants us to choose to follow His laws and return to enjoy eternal life with Him and His Son.

Knowing that we would not always make good choices, He

also prepared a way for us to escape from the consequences of bad choices. He provided us a Savior—His Son, Jesus Christ—to atone for our sins and make us clean again on condition of repentance.[5] He invites us to use the precious gift of repentance regularly.[6]

Every parent knows how difficult it is to trust a child enough to let them make their own decisions, especially when the parent knows the child is likely to make mistakes and suffer as a result. Yet Heavenly Father allows us to make the choices that will help us reach our divine potential! As Elder Dale G. Renlund taught, "[His] goal in parenting is not to have His children *do* what is right; it is to have His children *choose* to do what is right and ultimately become like Him."[7]

Notwithstanding God's trust in us, our relationship with Him will grow only to the degree we are willing to place our trust in Him. The challenge is that we live in a fallen world and have all experienced a betrayal of trust as the result of dishonesty, manipulation, coercion, or other circumstances. Once betrayed, we may struggle to trust again. These negative trust experiences with imperfect mortals may even impact our willingness to trust in a perfect Heavenly Father.

Several years ago, two friends of mine, Leonid and Valentina, expressed interest in becoming members of the Church. As Leonid began to learn the gospel, he found it difficult to pray. Earlier in his life, Leonid had suffered from manipulation and control by superiors and had developed a distrust of authority. These experiences affected his ability to open his heart and express personal feelings to Heavenly Father. With time and study, Leonid gained a better understanding of God's character and experienced feeling God's love. Eventually, prayer became a natural way for him to express thanks and the love he was feeling for God. His increasing trust in God eventually led him and Valentina to enter into sacred covenants to strengthen their relationship with God and each other.

If prior loss of trust is keeping you from trusting God, please follow Leonid's example. Patiently continue to learn more about Heavenly Father, His character, His attributes, and His purposes.

Look for and record experiences feeling His love and power in your life. Our living prophet, President Russell M. Nelson, has taught that the more we learn about God, the easier it will be for us to trust Him.[8]

Sometimes the best way to learn to trust God is simply by trusting Him. Like "The Crazy Trust Exercise," sometimes we just need to be willing to fall backward and let Him catch us. Our mortal life is a test. Challenges that stretch us beyond our own capacity come frequently. When our own knowledge and understanding are inadequate, we naturally look for resources to help us. In an information-saturated world, there is no shortage of sources promoting their solutions to our challenges. However, the simple, time-tested counsel in Proverbs provides the best advice: "Trust in the Lord with all thine heart."[9] We show our trust in God by turning to Him first when confronted with life's challenges.

After I finished law school in Utah, our family faced the important decision of where to work and make our home. After counseling with each other and the Lord, we felt directed to move our family to the eastern United States, far from parents and siblings. Initially, things went well, and we felt confirmed in our decision. But then things changed. There was downsizing at the law firm, and I faced the prospect of no job or insurance at the very time our daughter Dora was born with serious medical challenges and long-term special needs. While confronting these challenges, I was extended a call to serve that would require significant time and commitment.

I had never faced such a challenge and was overwhelmed. I began to question the decision we had made and its accompanying confirmation. We had trusted in the Lord, and things were supposed to work out. I had fallen backward, and it now appeared that no one was going to catch me.

One day the words "Don't ask why; ask what I want you to learn" came distinctly into my mind and heart. Now I was even more confused. In the very moment I was struggling with my earlier decision, God was inviting me to trust Him even more. Looking back, this was a critical point in my life—it was the moment when

I realized that the best way to learn to trust in God was simply by trusting Him. In the subsequent weeks, I watched with amazement as the Lord miraculously unfolded His plan to bless our family.

Good teachers and coaches know that intellectual growth and physical strength can happen only when minds and muscles are stretched. Likewise, God invites us to grow by trusting His spiritual tutoring through soul-stretching experiences. Therefore, we can be sure that whatever trust we may have demonstrated in God in the past, another trust-stretching experience lies yet ahead. God is focused on our growth and progress. He is the Master Teacher, the complete coach who is always stretching us to help us realize more of our divine potential. That will always include a future invitation to trust Him just a little bit more.

The Book of Mormon teaches the pattern God uses to stretch us in order to build strong relationships with us. In *Come, Follow Me*, we recently studied about how Nephi's trust in God was tested when he and his brothers were commanded to return to Jerusalem to obtain the brass plates. After their initial attempts failed, his brothers gave up and were ready to return without the plates. But Nephi chose to place his complete trust in the Lord and was successful in obtaining the plates.[10] That experience likely strengthened Nephi's confidence in God when his bow broke and the family was facing starvation in the wilderness. Again, Nephi chose to trust in God, and the family was saved.[11] These successive experiences gave Nephi even stronger confidence in God for the enormous, trust-stretching task he would soon face of building a ship.[12]

Through these experiences, Nephi strengthened his relationship with God by consistently and continuously trusting Him. God uses the same pattern with us. He extends us personal invitations to strengthen and deepen our trust in Him.[13] Each time we accept and act on an invitation, our trust in God grows. If we ignore or decline an invitation, our progress stops until we're ready to act on a new invitation.

The good news is that regardless of the trust we may or may not have chosen to place in God in the past, we can choose to trust

God today and every day going forward. I promise that each time we do, God will be there to catch us, and our relationship of trust will grow stronger and stronger until the day that we become one with Him and His Son. Then we can declare like Nephi, "O Lord, I have trusted in thee, and I will trust in thee forever."[14] In the name of Jesus Christ, amen.

Notes

1. See "The Family: A Proclamation to the World," Gospel Library.
2. See Doctrine and Covenants 88:63.
3. John 17:21.
4. See Doctrine and Covenants 84:38.
5. See Alma 34:15–17.
6. "Nothing is more liberating, more ennobling, or more crucial to our individual progression than is a regular, daily focus on repentance. Repentance is not an event; it is a process" (Russell M. Nelson, "We Can Do Better and Be Better," *Ensign* or *Liahona*, May 2019, 67).
7. Dale G. Renlund, "Choose You This Day," *Ensign* or *Liahona*, Nov. 2018, 104.
8. See Russell M. Nelson, "Christ Is Risen; Faith in Him Will Move Mountains," *Liahona*, May 2021, 103.
9. Proverbs 3:5.
10. See 1 Nephi 3–4.
11. See 1 Nephi 16:18–31.
12. See 1 Nephi 17:8.
13. God's personal invitations to each of us come through reading the scriptures, from living prophets, and by the whisperings of the Holy Ghost.
14. 2 Nephi 4:34.

GOD'S INTENT IS TO BRING YOU HOME

ELDER PATRICK KEARON

Of the Quorum of the Twelve Apostles

I would like to express gratitude for your prayers as I have started the process of adjusting to the call, through President Nelson, to serve as an Apostle of the Lord Jesus Christ. You can probably well imagine how humbling this has felt, and it has been a time of extraordinary upheaval and sobering self-examination. It is, however, indeed a great honour to serve the Saviour, in any capacity, and to be engaged with you in sharing the good news of His gospel of hope.

Beyond that, it has been said that behind every new Apostle stands an astonished mother-in-law. I don't know if that has actually been said, but in this case, it certainly could be. And I suspect that the fact that my mother-in-law is no longer with us does nothing to reduce her astonishment.

Several months ago, when my wife and I were visiting another country for various Church assignments, I woke up early one morning and looked blearily outside our hotel window. Down below on the busy street, I saw that a roadblock had been set up with a policeman stationed nearby to turn cars around as they reached the barrier. At first, only a few cars traveled along the road and were turned back. But as time went by and traffic increased, queues of cars began to build up.

From the window above, I watched as the policeman seemed to take satisfaction in his power to block the flow of traffic and turn people away. In fact, he seemed to develop a spring in his step, as if he might start doing a little jig, as each car approached the barrier. If a driver got frustrated about the roadblock, the policeman did not appear helpful or sympathetic. He just shook his head repeatedly and pointed in the opposite direction.

My friends, my fellow disciples on the road of mortal life, our Father's beautiful plan, even His "fabulous" plan,[1] is designed to bring you home, *not* to keep you out.[2] No one has built a roadblock and stationed someone there to turn you around and send you away.

In fact, it is the exact opposite. God is in relentless pursuit of you. He "wants all of His children to choose to return to Him,"[3] and He employs every possible measure to bring you back.

Our loving Father oversaw the Creation of this very earth for the express purpose of providing an opportunity for you and for me to have the stretching and refining experiences of mortality, the chance to use our God-given moral agency to choose Him,[4] to learn and grow, to make mistakes, to repent, to love God and our neighbour, and to one day return home to Him.

He sent His precious Beloved Son to this fallen world to live the full range of the human experience, to provide an example for the rest of His children to follow, and to atone and redeem. Christ's great atoning gift removes every roadblock of physical and spiritual death that would separate us from our eternal home.

Everything about the Father's plan for His beloved children is designed to bring everyone home.

What do God's messengers, His prophets, call this plan in Restoration scripture? They call it the plan of redemption,[5] the plan of mercy,[6] the great plan of happiness,[7] and the plan of salvation, which is unto all, "through the blood of mine Only Begotten."[8]

The intent of the Father's great plan of happiness is your *happiness*, right here, right now, and in the eternities. It is not to prevent your happiness and cause you instead worry and fear.

The intent of the Father's plan of redemption is in fact your *redemption*, your being rescued through the sufferings and death of Jesus Christ,[9] freed from the captivity of sin and death. It is not to leave you as you are.

The intent of the Father's plan of mercy is to *extend mercy* as you turn back to Him and honour your covenant of fidelity to Him. It is not to deny mercy and inflict pain and sorrow.

The intent of the Father's plan of salvation is in fact your *salvation* in the celestial kingdom of glory as you receive "the testimony of Jesus"[10] and offer your whole soul to Him.[11] It is not to keep you out.

Does this mean anything goes with regard to how we live our

lives? That the way we choose to use our agency doesn't matter? That we can take or leave God's commandments? No, of course not. Surely one of Jesus's most consistent invitations and pleas during His mortal ministry was that we change and repent and come unto Him.[12] Fundamentally implicit in all of His teachings to live on a higher plane of moral conduct[13] is a call to personal progression, to transformative faith in Christ, to a mighty change of heart.[14]

God wants for us a radical reorientation of our selfish and prideful impulses, the eviction of the natural man,[15] for us to "go, and sin no more."[16]

If we believe the intent of the Father's all-reaching plan is to save us, redeem us, extend mercy to us, and thereby bring us happiness, what is the intent of the Son through whom this great plan is brought about?

The Son tells us Himself: "For I came down from heaven, not to do mine own will, but the will of him that sent me."[17]

Jesus's will is the benevolent Father's will! He wants to make it possible for every last one of His Father's children to receive the end goal of the plan—eternal life with Them. None is excluded from this divine potential.

If you are prone to worry that you will never measure up, or that the loving reach of Christ's infinite Atonement mercifully covers everyone else but not you, then you misunderstand. *Infinite* means infinite. *Infinite* covers you and those you love.[18]

Nephi explains this beautiful truth: "He doeth not anything save it be for the benefit of the world; for he loveth the world, even that he layeth down his own life that he may draw all men unto him. Wherefore, he commandeth none that they shall not partake of his salvation."[19]

The Saviour, the Good Shepherd, goes in search of His lost sheep until He finds them.[20] He is "not willing that any should perish."[21]

"Mine arm of mercy is extended towards you, and whosoever will come, him will I receive."[22]

"Have ye any that are sick among you? Bring them hither. Have ye any that are lame, or blind, or halt, or maimed, or leprous, or that are withered, or that are deaf, or that are afflicted in any manner? Bring them hither and I will heal them, for I have compassion upon you."[23]

He did not cast away the woman with the issue of blood; He did not recoil from the leper; He did not reject the woman taken in adultery; He did not refuse the penitent—no matter their sin. And He will not refuse you or those you love when you bring to Him your broken hearts and contrite spirits. That is *not* His intent or His design, nor His plan, purpose, wish, or hope.

No, He does not put up roadblocks and barriers; He removes them. He does not keep you out; He welcomes you in.[24] His entire ministry was a living declaration of this intent.

Then of course there is His atoning sacrifice itself, which is harder for us to understand, beyond our mortal capacity to comprehend. But, and this is an important "but," we do understand, can comprehend, the holy, saving intent of His atoning sacrifice.

The veil of the temple was rent in twain when Jesus died upon the cross, symbolising that access back to the presence of the Father had been ripped wide open—to all who will turn to Him, trust Him, cast their burdens on Him, and take His yoke upon them in a covenant bond.[25]

In other words, the Father's plan is not about roadblocks. It never was; it never will be. Are there things we need to do, commandments to keep, aspects of our natures to change? Yes. But with His grace, those are within our reach, not beyond our grasp.

This is the good news! I am unspeakably grateful for these simple truths. The Father's design, His plan, His purpose, His intent, His wish, and His hope are all to heal you, all to give you peace, all to bring you, and those you love, home. Of this I am a witness in the name of Jesus Christ, His Son, amen.

Notes

1. Russell M. Nelson, "Think Celestial!," *Liahona*, Nov. 2023, 117, 118.
2. See 2 Nephi 26:25, 27.
3. *General Handbook: Serving in The Church of Jesus Christ of Latter-day Saints*, 1.1, Gospel Library.
4. See Moses 7:33.

5. See Jacob 6:8; Alma 12:30.
6. See Alma 42:15.
7. See Alma 42:8, 16.
8. Moses 6:62.
9. See Doctrine and Covenants 45:4.
10. Doctrine and Covenants 76:50–70.
11. See Omni 1:26.
12. See Matthew 4:17.
13. See Matthew 5–7. For example, in Matthew 5:43–44, the Savior taught His disciples that it was not enough to "love thy neighbour, and hate thine enemy." To follow Him, they also needed to "love [their] enemies."
14. See Mosiah 5:2. In order for the mercy of Jesus Christ to be able to come into play in our lives, we must turn back to Him. Alma the Younger teaches that this glorious "plan of redemption could not be brought about, only on conditions of repentance . . . ; for except it were for these conditions, mercy could not take effect" (Alma 42:13).
15. See Mosiah 3:19.
16. John 8:11.
17. John 6:38.
18. See Russell M. Nelson, "The Atonement," *Ensign*, Nov. 1996, 35: "His Atonement is infinite—without an end. It was also infinite in that all humankind would be saved from never-ending death. It was infinite in terms of His immense suffering. It was infinite in time, putting an end to the preceding prototype of animal sacrifice. It was infinite in scope—it was to be done once for all. And the mercy of the Atonement extends not only to an infinite number of people, but also to an infinite number of worlds created by Him. It was infinite beyond any human scale of measurement or mortal comprehension."
19. 2 Nephi 26:24.
20. See Luke 15:4.
21. 2 Peter 3:9; see also Doctrine and Covenants 18:11–12.
22. 3 Nephi 9:14.
23. 3 Nephi 17:7; see also verse 6.
24. In Jesus Christ's teachings indicating that some individuals will not inherit the kingdom of heaven, He makes it clear that this outcome is not His desire for them but is a result of their own choices (see Matthew 7:13–14, 21–25).
25. See Matthew 27:50–51; Hebrews 9:6–12.

SWALLOWED UP IN THE JOY OF CHRIST

ELDER BRIAN K. TAYLOR
Of the Seventy

We love you, Elder Kearon. May I borrow that accent for 10 minutes?

Yearned-for Miracles

In the New Testament we learn of blind Bartimaeus, who cried out to Jesus desiring a miracle. "Jesus said unto him, Go thy way; thy faith hath made thee whole. And *immediately* he received his sight."[1]

On another occasion a man in Bethsaida longed for healing. In contrast, this miracle *did not come instantly*. Rather, Jesus blessed him *twice* before he "was restored."[2]

In a third example, the Apostle Paul "*besought the Lord thrice*" in his affliction,[3] and yet, to our knowledge, *his earnest supplication was not granted.*

Three different people. Three unique experiences.

Thus, a question: Why do some receive their yearned-for miracles quickly, while others patiently endure, waiting upon the Lord?[4] We may not know the *why*, yet gratefully, we know He *who* "loveth [us]"[5] and "[doeth] all things for [our] welfare and happiness."[6]

Divine Purposes

God, who sees the end from the beginning,[7] reassures, "Thine adversity and thine afflictions shall be but a small moment,"[8] and they shall be consecrated "for thy gain."[9]

Helping us find further meaning in our trials, Elder Orson F. Whitney taught: "No pain that we suffer, no trial that we experience is wasted. It ministers to our education. . . . All . . . that we [patiently] endure . . . builds up our characters, purifies our hearts, expands our souls, and makes us more tender and charitable. . . . It is through sorrow and suffering, toil and tribulation, that we gain the education that we come here to acquire and which will make us more like our [heavenly parents]."[10]

Understanding that "the power of Christ [would] rest upon [him]" in his afflictions, the Apostle Paul said humbly, "For when I am weak, then am I strong."[11]

Life's trials prove us.[12] Even the Savior "learned . . . obedience by" and was made "perfect through sufferings."[13]

And one day He will compassionately declare, "Behold, I have refined *thee*, I have chosen *thee* in the furnace of affliction."[14]

Coming to trust in God's divine purposes breathes hope into weary souls and kindles determination in seasons of anguish and heartache.[15]

Divine Perspectives

Years ago, President Russell M. Nelson shared this valuable insight: "As we look at all things with eternal perspective, it will significantly lighten our load."[16]

My wife, Jill, and I recently witnessed this truth in the faithful lives of Holly and Rick Porter, whose 12-year-old son, Trey, passed away in a tragic fire. With hands and feet severely burned in a heroic attempt to save her dear son, Holly later testified in ward sacrament meeting of the great peace and joy the Lord had poured out upon her family in their anguish, using words such as *miraculous*, *incredible*, and *amazing*.

This precious mother's unbearable grief was replaced by surpassing peace with this thought: "My hands are not the hands that save. Those hands belong to the Savior! Instead of looking at my scars as a reminder of what I was not able to do, I remember the scars my Savior bears."

Holly's witness fulfills our prophet's promise: "As you think celestial, you will view trials and opposition in a new light."[17]

Elder D. Todd Christofferson stated: "I believe that the challenge of overcoming and growing from adversity appealed to us when God presented His plan of redemption in the premortal world. We should approach that challenge now knowing that our Heavenly Father will sustain us. *But it is crucial that we turn to Him.*

Without God, the dark experiences of suffering and adversity tend to despondency, despair, and even bitterness."[18]

Divine Principles

To avoid the darkness of discontent and instead find greater peace, hope, and even joy during life's difficult challenges, I share three divine principles as invitations.

One—stronger faith comes by putting Jesus Christ first.[19] "Look unto me in every thought," He declares; "doubt not, fear not."[20] President Nelson taught:

"[Our] eternal life is dependent upon [our] faith in [Christ] and in His Atonement."[21]

"As I have wrestled with the intense pain caused by my recent injury, I have felt even deeper appreciation for Jesus Christ and the incomprehensible gift of His Atonement. Think of it! The Savior suffered 'pains and afflictions and temptations of every kind' so that He can comfort us, heal us, [and] rescue us in times of need."[22]

He continued: "My injury has caused me to reflect again and again on 'the greatness of the Holy One of Israel.' During my healing, the Lord has manifested His divine power in peaceful and unmistakable ways."[23]

"In the world ye shall have tribulation: but be of good cheer," our Savior encourages; "I have overcome the world."[24]

Two—brighter hope comes by envisioning our eternal destiny.[25] In speaking of the power inherent in keeping "a vision of our Father's incredible promised blessings . . . before our eyes every day," Sister Linda Reeves testified: "I do not know why we have the many trials that we have, but it is my personal feeling that the reward is so great, . . . so joyful and beyond our understanding that in that day of reward, we may feel to say to our merciful, loving Father, 'Was that all that was required?' . . . What will it matter . . . what we suffered here if, in the end, those trials . . . qualify us for eternal life . . . in the kingdom of God?"[26]

President Nelson shared this insight: "Consider the Lord's response to Joseph Smith when he pleaded for relief in Liberty Jail.

The Lord taught the Prophet that his inhumane treatment would give him experience and be for his good. 'If thou endure it well,' the Lord promised, 'God shall exalt thee on high.' The Lord was teaching Joseph to think celestial and to envision an eternal reward rather than focus on the excruciating difficulties of the day."[27]

Joseph's change in perspective brought deepening sanctification, as reflected in this letter to a friend: "After having been inclosed in the walls of a prison for five months it seems to me that my heart will always be more tender after this than ever it was before. . . . I think I never could have felt as I do now if I had not suffered the wrongs that I have suffered."[28]

Three—greater power comes by focusing on joy.[29] During eternity's most crucial, agonizing hours, our Savior did not shrink but partook of the bitter cup.[30] How did He do it? We learn, "For the joy that was set before him [Christ] endured the cross,"[31] His will "being swallowed up in the will of the Father."[32]

This phrase "swallowed up" deeply moves me. My interest was heightened when I learned that in Spanish, "swallowed up" is translated as "consumed"; in German, as "devoured"; and in Chinese, as "engulfed." Thus, when life's challenges are most painful and overwhelming, I remember the Lord's promise—that we "should suffer no manner of afflictions, save it [be] swallowed up [consumed, devoured, and engulfed] in the joy of Christ."[33]

I see in so many of you this joy, which "[defies] . . . mortal comprehension,"[34] even though your bitter cups have not yet been removed. Thank you for keeping your covenants and standing as witnesses for God.[35] Thank you for reaching out to bless us all, while "in [your] quiet heart is hidden sorrow that the eye can't see."[36] For when you bring the Savior's relief to others, you will find it for yourselves, taught President Camille N. Johnson.[37]

Divine Promises

Now, return with me to the sacrament meeting where we witnessed the miracle of Holly Porter's family being succored by the Lord.[38] On the stand while pondering what I might say to offer comfort to this remarkable family and their friends, this thought came: "Use the Savior's words."[39] So I close today as I did on that Sabbath, with His words, "which healeth the wounded soul."[40]

"Come unto me, all ye that labour and are heavy laden, and I will give you rest."[41]

"I will also ease the burdens which are put upon your shoulders, that even you cannot feel them upon your backs, even while you are in bondage; . . . that ye may know of a surety that I, the Lord God, do visit my people in their afflictions."[42]

"I will not leave you comfortless: I will come to you."[43]

My Witness

With joyful reverence, I witness our Savior lives and "His promises are sure."[44] Especially for you who are troubled or who are "afflicted in any manner,"[45] I testify that our Heavenly Father hears your tearful pleadings[46] and will always respond in perfect wisdom.[47] "May God grant unto you," as He has done for our family in times of great need, "that your burdens may be light,"[48] even "swallowed up in the joy of Christ."[49] In the holy name of Jesus Christ, amen.

Notes

1. Mark 10:52; emphasis added.
2. Mark 8:25.
3. 2 Corinthians 12:8; emphasis added.
4. See Psalm 130:5.
5. 1 Nephi 11:17.
6. Helaman 12:2; see also 2 Nephi 26:24.
7. See Abraham 2:8.
8. Doctrine and Covenants 121:7.
9. 2 Nephi 2:2.
10. Orson F. Whitney, in *Teachings of Presidents of the Church: Spencer W. Kimball* (2006), 16.
11. 2 Corinthians 12:9–10.
12. See Abraham 3:25–26.
13. Hebrews 5:8; 2:10.
14. 1 Nephi 20:10; emphasis added.
15. See 2 Nephi 4:19–35.
16. Personal conversation with Elder Russell M. Nelson, Apr. 2011.
17. Russell M. Nelson, "Think Celestial!," *Liahona*, Nov. 2023, 118.
18. D. Todd Christofferson, "The Refining Fire of Affliction," *Liahona*, Mar. 2022, 7; emphasis added.
19. See Russell M. Nelson, "Let God Prevail," *Ensign* or *Liahona*, Nov. 2020, 94.
20. Doctrine and Covenants 6:36.
21. Russell M. Nelson, "Think Celestial!," 118.
22. Russell M. Nelson, "Think Celestial!," 117. President Jeffrey R. Holland taught: "When you struggle, when you are rejected, when you are spit upon and cast out and made a hiss and a

byword, you are standing with the best life this world has ever known, the only pure and perfect life ever lived. You have reason to stand tall and be grateful that the Living Son of the Living God knows all about your sorrows and afflictions" ("Missionary Work and the Atonement," *Ensign*, Mar. 2001, 15).
23. Russell M. Nelson, "Think Celestial!," 117; see also Alma 7:11–12.
24. John 16:33.
25. See 2 Nephi 31:20; Ether 12:4; Moroni 7:48.
26. Linda S. Reeves, "Worthy of Our Promised Blessings," *Ensign* or *Liahona*, Nov. 2015, 11.
27. Russell M. Nelson, "Think Celestial!," 118.
28. Joseph Smith, letter to Presendia Huntington Buell, Mar. 15, 1839, josephsmithpapers.org.
29. See Russell M. Nelson, "Joy and Spiritual Survival," *Ensign* or *Liahona*, Nov. 2016, 81–84.
30. See Mark 14:35–41.
31. Hebrews 12:2.
32. Mosiah 15:7.
33. Alma 31:38; see also Psalm 30:5; John 15:10–11; 1 Thessalonians 1:6; Joseph Smith Translation, James 1:2 (in James 1:2, footnote *a*); 2 Nephi 2:25; 9:18; Alma 26:6–7, 11, 27, 37; 28:8; 33:23; 36:20–21; Doctrine and Covenants 109:76; Moses 5:10–11.
34. "Just as the Savior offers peace that 'passeth all understanding' [Philippians 4:7], He also offers an intensity, depth, and breadth of joy that defy human logic or mortal comprehension. For example, it doesn't seem possible to feel joy when your child suffers with an incurable illness or when you lose your job or when your spouse betrays you. Yet that is precisely the joy the Savior offers. His joy is constant, assuring us that our 'afflictions shall be but a small moment' [Doctrine and Covenants 121:7] and be consecrated to our gain" (Russell M. Nelson, "Joy and Spiritual Survival," *Ensign* or *Liahona*, Nov. 2016, 82).
35. See Mosiah 24:14; Alma 33:23. Last year, Jill and I met Paula, a beautiful young Guatemalan woman who was struggling mightily with cancer. Her response to my question of how she was feeling left an unforgettable memory in our minds and hearts: "I am grateful," this humble teenager quietly responded almost in a whisper, "that the Lord gave it to me and not to my sister." Then, although she was not feeling well, she; her sister, Sariah; and their father went on two ministering visits to two elderly widows with great personal needs and challenges of their own.
36. "Lord, I Would Follow Thee," *Hymns*, no. 220.
37. See Camille N. Johnson, "Jesus Christ Is Relief," *Liahona*, May 2023, 81; see also Luke 23:34, 43; John 19:26–27. Elder Neal A. Maxwell shared this beautiful insight, urging that "when, for the moment, we ourselves are not being stretched on a particular cross, we ought to be at the foot of someone else's—full of empathy and proffering spiritual refreshment" ("Endure It Well," *Ensign*, May 1990, 34).
38. See Alma 7:12.
39. See Dallin H. Oaks, "The Teachings of Jesus Christ," *Liahona*, May 2023, 102–5.
40. Jacob 2:8; see also Neil L. Andersen, "Wounded," *Ensign* or *Liahona*, Nov. 2018, 83–86.
41. Matthew 11:28; see also Matthew 28:20: "And, lo, I am with you alway, even unto the end of the world."
42. Mosiah 24:14.
43. John 14:18.
44. "I Am a Child of God," *Children's Songbook*, 3; see also Doctrine and Covenants 98:3.
45. 3 Nephi 17:7; see also Alma 36:3, 27.
46. See Exodus 2:24; 3:7; Mosiah 24:12.
47. See 2 Nephi 2:24; Mosiah 4:9; Isaiah 55:9. "Some blessings come soon, some come late, and some don't come until heaven; but for those who embrace the gospel of Jesus Christ, *they come*" (Jeffrey R. Holland, "An High Priest of Good Things to Come," *Ensign*, Nov. 1999, 38).
48. Alma 33:23.
49. Alma 31:38; see also Psalm 30:5; John 15:10–11; 1 Thessalonians 1:6; Joseph Smith Translation, James 1:2 (in James 1:2, footnote *a*); 2 Nephi 2:25; 9:18; Alma 26:6–7, 11, 27, 37; 28:8; 33:23; 36:20–21; Doctrine and Covenants 109:76; Moses 5:10–11.

COVENANTS AND RESPONSIBILITIES

PRESIDENT DALLIN H. OAKS

First Counselor in the First Presidency

"How does your Church differ from others?" My answer to this important question has varied as I have matured and as the Church has grown. When I was born in Utah in 1932, our Church membership was only about 700,000, clustered mostly in Utah and nearby states. At that time, we had only 7 temples. Today the membership of The Church of Jesus Christ of Latter-day Saints numbers more than 17 million in about 170 nations. As of this April 1, we have 189 dedicated temples in many nations and 146 more in planning and construction. I have felt to speak about the purpose of these temples and the history and role of covenants in our worship. This will supplement the inspired teachings of earlier speakers.

I.

A covenant is a commitment to fulfill certain responsibilities. Personal commitments are essential to the regulation of our individual lives and to the functioning of society. This idea is currently being challenged. A vocal minority oppose institutional authority and insist that persons should be free from any restrictions that limit their individual freedom. Yet we know from millennia of experience that persons give up some individual freedoms to gain the advantages of living in organized communities. Such relinquishments of individual freedoms are principally based on commitments or covenants, expressed or implied.

Here are some examples of covenant responsibilities in our society: (1) judges, (2) military, (3) medical personnel, and (4) firefighters. All of those involved in these familiar occupations make a commitment—often formalized by oath or covenant—to perform their assigned duties. The same is true of our full-time missionaries. Distinctive clothing or name tags are intended to signify that the wearer is under covenant and therefore has a duty to teach and serve and should be supported in that service. A related purpose is to remind the wearers of their covenant responsibilities. There is no magic in their distinctive clothing or symbols, only a needed reminder of the special responsibilities the wearers have assumed. This is also true of the symbols of the engagement and wedding rings and their role in giving notice to observers or reminding wearers of covenant responsibilities.

II.

What I have said about covenants being a foundation for the regulation of individual lives applies particularly to religious covenants. The foundation and history of many religious affiliations and requirements are based on covenants. For example, the Abrahamic covenant is fundamental to several great religious traditions. It introduces the holy idea of God's covenant promises with His children. The Old Testament frequently refers to God's covenant with Abraham and his seed.[1]

The first part of the Book of Mormon, which was written during the Old Testament period, clearly demonstrates the role of covenants in the Israelite history and worship. Nephi was told that the Israelite writings of that period were "a record of the Jews, which contains the covenants of the Lord, which he hath made unto the house of Israel."[2] The books of Nephi make frequent reference to the Abrahamic covenant[3] and to Israel as "the covenant people of the Lord."[4] The practice of covenanting with God or religious leaders is also recorded in the Book of Mormon writings about Nephi, Joseph in Egypt, King Benjamin, Alma, and Captain Moroni.[5]

III.

When the time came for the Restoration of the fulness of the gospel of Jesus Christ, God called a prophet, Joseph Smith. We do not know the full content of the angel Moroni's early instructions to this maturing young prophet. We do know he told Joseph that "God had a work for [him] to do" and that "the fulness of the everlasting Gospel" must be brought forth, including "the promises made to the fathers."[6] We also know that the scriptures young Joseph read most intensively—even before he was directed to organize a church—were the many teachings about covenants he was translating in the Book of Mormon. That book is the Restoration's major source for the fulness of the gospel, including God's plan for His children, and the Book of Mormon is filled with references to covenants.

Being well read in the Bible, Joseph must have known of the book of Hebrews' reference to the Savior's intent to "make a new covenant with the house of Israel and with the house of Judah."[7] Hebrews also refers to Jesus as "the mediator of the new covenant."[8] Significantly, the biblical account of the Savior's mortal ministry is titled "The New Testament," a virtual synonym for "The New Covenant."

Covenants were foundational in the Restoration of the gospel. This is evident in the earliest steps the Lord directed the Prophet to take in organizing His Church. As soon as the Book of Mormon was published, the Lord directed the organization of His restored Church, soon to be named The Church of Jesus Christ of Latter-day Saints.[9] Revelation recorded in April 1830 directs that persons "shall be received by baptism into his church" after they "witness" (which means solemnly testify) "that they have truly repented of all their sins, and are willing to take upon them the name of Jesus Christ, having a determination to serve him to the end."[10]

This same revelation directs that the Church "meet together often to partake of bread and wine [water] in the remembrance of the Lord Jesus." The importance of this ordinance is evident in the words of covenants specified for the elder or priest who officiates. He blesses the emblems of the bread for "the souls of all those who partake of it . . . , that they . . . witness unto thee, O God, the Eternal Father, that they are willing to take upon them the name of thy Son, and always remember him and keep his commandments which he has given them."[11]

The central role of covenants in the newly restored Church was reaffirmed in the preface the Lord gave for the first publication of His revelations. There the Lord declares that He has called Joseph Smith because the inhabitants of the earth "have strayed from mine ordinances, and have broken mine everlasting covenant."[12] This revelation further explains that His commandments are being given "that mine everlasting covenant might be established."[13]

Today we understand the role of covenants in the restored Church and the worship of its members. President Gordon B. Hinckley gave this summary of the effect of our baptism and our weekly partaking of the sacrament: "Every member of this church who has entered the waters of baptism has become a party to a sacred covenant. Each time we partake of the sacrament of the Lord's supper, we renew that covenant."[14]

We have been reminded by many speakers at this conference that President Russell M. Nelson often refers to the plan of salvation as the "covenant path" that "leads us back to [God]" and "is all about our relationship with God."[15] He teaches about the significance of covenants in our temple ceremonies and urges us to see the end from the beginning and to "think celestial."[16]

IV.

Now I speak more of temple covenants. In fulfillment of his responsibility to restore the fulness of the gospel of Jesus Christ, the Prophet Joseph Smith spent much of his final years directing the construction of a temple in Nauvoo, Illinois. Through him the Lord revealed sacred teachings, doctrine, and covenants for his successors to administer in temples. There persons who were endowed were to be taught God's plan of salvation and invited to make sacred covenants. Those who lived faithful to those covenants were promised eternal life, wherein "all things are theirs" and they "shall dwell in the presence of God and his Christ forever and ever."[17]

The endowment ceremonies in the Nauvoo Temple were administered just before our early pioneers were expelled to begin their historic trek to the mountains in the West. We have the testimonies of many pioneers that the power they received from being bound to Christ in their endowments in the Nauvoo Temple gave them the strength to make their epic journey and establish themselves in the West.[18]

Persons who have been endowed in a temple are responsible to wear a temple garment, an article of clothing not visible because it is worn beneath outer clothing. It reminds endowed members of the sacred covenants they have made and the blessings they have been promised in the holy temple. To achieve those holy purposes, we are instructed to wear temple garments continuously, with the only exceptions being those obviously necessary. Because covenants do not "take a day off," to remove one's garments can be understood as a disclaimer of the covenant responsibilities and blessings to which they relate. In contrast, persons who wear their garments faithfully and keep their temple covenants continually affirm their role as disciples of the Lord Jesus Christ.

The Church of Jesus Christ of Latter-day Saints is constructing temples all over the world. Their purpose is to bless the covenant children of God with temple worship and with the sacred responsibilities and powers and unique blessings of being bound to Christ they receive by covenant.

The Church of Jesus Christ is known as a church that emphasizes making covenants with God. Covenants are inherent in each of the ordinances of salvation and exaltation this restored Church administers. The ordinance of baptism and its associated covenants are requirements for entrance into the celestial kingdom. The ordinances and associated covenants of the temple are requirements for exaltation in the celestial kingdom, which is eternal life, "the greatest of all the gifts of God."[19] That is the focus of The Church of Jesus Christ of Latter-day Saints.

I testify of Jesus Christ, who is the head of that Church, and invoke His blessings on all who seek to keep their sacred covenants. In the name of Jesus Christ, amen.

Notes

1. See, for example, Genesis 17:2–9; Exodus 6:2–4; 19:5–6; Leviticus 26:42; see also 2 Nephi 9:1.
2. 1 Nephi 13:23.
3. See 1 Nephi 15:18; 17:40; 22:9; 2 Nephi 29:14.
4. See, for example, 1 Nephi 14:14; 2 Nephi 6:13; 9:1.
5. See 2 Nephi 1:5; 3:4; 31:7, 13, 14; Mosiah 5:5–8; 6:1; Alma 7:15; 46:21–22.
6. Joseph Smith—History 1:33–34, 39.
7. Hebrews 8:8.

8. Hebrews 12:24. This same description appears in Doctrine and Covenants 76:69.
9. See Doctrine and Covenants 115:4.
10. Doctrine and Covenants 20:37; see also Mosiah 18:10–13.
11. Doctrine and Covenants 20:75, 77.
12. Doctrine and Covenants 1:15.
13. Doctrine and Covenants 1:22.
14. Gordon B. Hinckley, "God Is at the Helm," *Ensign*, May 1994, 53.
15. Russell M. Nelson, "As We Go Forward Together," *Ensign* or *Liahona*, Apr. 2018, 7; Russell M. Nelson, "The Everlasting Covenant," *Liahona*, Oct. 2022, 5, 11. Also see Nephi's use of the metaphor of walking in the "path": 2 Nephi 4:32; 33:9.
16. See Russell M. Nelson, "Think Celestial!," *Liahona*, Nov. 2023, 117–20.
17. Doctrine and Covenants 76:59, 62.
18. See Church History Topics, "Nauvoo Temple," Gospel Library.
19. Doctrine and Covenants 14:7.

Sunday Afternoon Session

APRIL 7, 2024

THE TESTIMONY OF JESUS

ELDER D. TODD CHRISTOFFERSON
Of the Quorum of the Twelve Apostles

In 1832, Joseph Smith and Sidney Rigdon received a remarkable vision concerning the eternal destiny of God's children. This revelation spoke of three heavenly kingdoms. President Dallin H. Oaks spoke about these "kingdoms of glory" last October,[1] noting that "through the triumph and the glory of the Lamb,"[2] all but a relatively few individuals are eventually redeemed into one of these kingdoms, "according to the desires manifested through their choices."[3] God's plan of redemption constitutes a universal opportunity for all His children, whenever and wherever they may have lived on the earth.

While the glory of even the least of the three kingdoms, the telestial, "surpasses all understanding,"[4] our Father's hope is that we will choose—and, through the grace of His Son, qualify for—the highest and most glorious of these kingdoms, the celestial, where we may enjoy eternal life as "joint-heirs with Christ."[5] President Russell M. Nelson has urged us to "think celestial," making the celestial kingdom our eternal goal and then "carefully considering where each of [our] decisions while here on earth will place [us] in the next world."[6]

Those in the celestial kingdom are "*they who received the testimony of Jesus*, . . . who are just men made perfect through Jesus the mediator of the new covenant."[7] The inhabitants of the second, or terrestrial, kingdom are described as essentially good, including the "honorable men of the earth, who were blinded by the craftiness of men." Their principal limiting trait is that they "*are not valiant in the testimony of Jesus*."[8] By contrast, those in the lower, telestial kingdom are those who "received not the gospel, *neither the testimony of Jesus*."[9]

Note that the distinguishing characteristic for the inhabitants of each kingdom is how they relate to "the testimony of Jesus," ranging from (1) wholehearted devotion to (2) not being valiant to (3) outright rejection. On each person's reaction hangs his or her eternal future.

I.

What is the testimony of Jesus?

It is the witness of the Holy Spirit that He is the divine Son of God, the Messiah and Redeemer. It is John's testimony that Jesus was in the beginning with God, that He is the Creator of heaven and earth, and that "in him was the gospel, and the gospel was the life, and the life was the light of men."[10] It is "the testimony of the Apostles and Prophets, . . . that He died, was buried, and rose again the third day, and ascended into heaven."[11] It is the knowledge that "there is no other name given whereby salvation cometh."[12] It is the "testimony, last of all," given by the Prophet Joseph Smith, "that he lives! . . . That he is the Only Begotten of the Father—that by him, and through him, and of him, the worlds are and were created, and the inhabitants thereof are begotten sons and daughters unto God."[13]

II.

Beyond this testimony is the question, What do we do about it?

The inheritors of the celestial kingdom "receive" the testimony of Jesus in the fullest sense by being baptized, receiving the Holy Ghost, and overcoming by faith.[14] The principles and truths of the gospel of Jesus Christ govern their priorities and choices. The testimony of Jesus is manifest in what they are and what they are becoming. Their motive is charity, "the pure love of Christ."[15] Their focus is on pursuing "the measure of the stature of the fulness of Christ."[16]

At least some of those who will be found in the terrestrial kingdom also accept the testimony of Jesus, but they are distinguished by what they *don't* do about it. Not being valiant in the witness of the Savior suggests a degree of apathy or casualness—being "lukewarm"[17]— as opposed to the people of Ammon in the Book of Mormon, for example, who were "distinguished for their zeal towards God."[18]

The inhabitants of the telestial kingdom are those who reject the testimony of Jesus along with His gospel, His covenants, and His prophets. They are described by Abinadi as "having gone according to their own carnal wills and desires; having never called upon the Lord while the arms of mercy were extended towards them; for the arms of mercy were extended towards them, and they would not."[19]

III.

What does it mean to be valiant in the testimony of Jesus?

There are several possibilities that could be considered in answering this question. I will mention a few. Being valiant in the testimony of Jesus surely includes nurturing and strengthening that testimony. True disciples do not ignore the seemingly small things that sustain and strengthen their testimony of Jesus, such as prayer, study of the scriptures, Sabbath observance, partaking of the sacrament, repentance, ministering, and worship in the house of the Lord. President Nelson reminds us that "with frightening speed, a testimony that is not nourished daily 'by the good word of God' [Moroni 6:4] can crumble. Thus, . . . we need daily experiences worshipping the Lord and studying His gospel." Then he added: "I plead with you to let God prevail in your life. Give Him a fair share of your time. As you do, notice what happens to your positive spiritual momentum."[20]

Being valiant also suggests being open and public about one's witness. In baptism, we confirm our willingness "to stand as witnesses of God at all times and in all things, and in all places that [we] may be in, even until death."[21] In this Easter season especially, we joyfully, publicly, and unreservedly proclaim our witness of the resurrected, living Christ.

One aspect of being valiant in the testimony of Jesus is to heed His messengers. God does not force us into the better path, the covenant path, but He instructs His prophets to make us fully aware of the consequences of our choices. And it is not just the members of His Church. Through His prophets and apostles, He lovingly pleads with all the world to heed the truth that will make them free,[22] spare them needless suffering, and bring them enduring joy.

Being valiant in the testimony of Jesus means encouraging others, by word and example, to likewise be valiant, especially those of our own families. Elder Neal A. Maxwell once addressed "the essentially 'honorable' members [of the Church] who are skimming over the surface instead of deepening their discipleship and who are casually engaged rather than 'anxiously engaged' [Doctrine and Covenants 76:75; 58:27]."[23] Noting that all are free to choose, Elder Maxwell lamented: "Unfortunately, however, when some choose slackness, they are choosing not only for themselves, but for the next generation and the next. Small equivocations in parents can produce large deviations in their children! Earlier generations in a family may have reflected dedication, while some in the current generation evidence equivocation. Sadly, in the next, some may choose dissension, as erosion takes its toll."[24]

Years ago, Elder John H. Groberg related the story of a young family living in a small branch in Hawaii in the early 1900s. They had been members of the Church for about two years when one of their daughters fell ill with an undiagnosed disease and was hospitalized. At church the next Sunday, the father and his son prepared the sacrament as they did most weeks, but as the young father knelt to bless the bread, the branch president, suddenly realizing who was at the sacrament table, jumped up and cried, "Stop. You can't touch the sacrament. Your daughter has an unknown disease. Leave immediately while someone else fixes new sacrament bread. We can't have you here. Go." The stunned father searchingly looked at the branch president and then the congregation and, sensing the depth of anxiety and embarrassment from all, motioned to his family, and they quietly filed out of the chapel.

Not a word was said as, dejectedly, the family walked along the trail to their small home. There they sat in a circle, and the father said, "Please be silent until I am ready to speak." The young son wondered what they would do to get revenge for the shame they had suffered: would they kill the branch president's pigs, or burn his house, or join another church? Five, ten, fifteen, twenty-five minutes passed in silence.

The father's clenched fists began to relax, and tears formed. The mother began to cry, and soon each of the children was quietly weeping. The father turned to his wife and said, "I love you," and then repeated those words to each of their children. "I love all of you and I want us to be together, forever, as a family. And the only way that can be is for all of us to be good members of The Church of Jesus Christ of Latter-day Saints and be sealed by the holy priesthood in the temple. This is not the branch president's church. It is the Church of Jesus Christ. We will not allow any man or any hurt or embarrassment or pride to keep us from being together forever. Next Sunday we will go back to church. We will stay by ourselves until our daughter's sickness is known, but we will go back."

They did go back, their daughter recovered, and the family was sealed in the Laie Hawaii Temple when it was completed. Today, well over 100 souls call their father, grandfather, and great-grandfather blessed because he kept his eyes on eternity.[25]

One last aspect of being valiant in the testimony of Jesus that I will mention is our individual pursuit of personal holiness. Jesus is our essential Redeemer,[26] and He pleads, "Repent, all ye ends of the earth, and come unto me and be baptized in my name, that ye may be sanctified by the reception of the Holy Ghost, that ye may stand spotless before me at the last day."[27]

The prophet Mormon describes one group of Saints who persevered in this manner despite having "to wade through much affliction":[28]

"Nevertheless they did fast and pray oft, and did wax stronger and stronger in their humility, and firmer and firmer in the faith of Christ, unto the filling their souls with joy and consolation, yea, even to the purifying and the sanctification of their hearts, which sanctification cometh because of their yielding their hearts unto God."[29] It is this mighty change of heart—yielding our hearts to God and being spiritually reborn through the grace of the Savior—that we seek.[30]

My invitation is to act now to secure your place as one who is valiant in the testimony of Jesus. As repentance may be needed, "do not procrastinate the day of your repentance,"[31] lest "in an hour when ye think not the summer shall be past, and the harvest ended, and your souls not saved."[32] Be zealous in keeping your covenants with God. Do not be "offended [by] the strictness of the word."[33] "Remember to retain the name [of Christ] written always in your hearts, . . . that ye [may] hear and know *the voice* by which ye shall be called, and also, *the name* by which he shall call you."[34] And finally, "settle this in your hearts, that ye will do the things which [Jesus] shall teach, and command you."[35]

Our Father wants all His children who will to enjoy eternal life with Him in His celestial kingdom. Jesus suffered, died, and was resurrected to make that possible. He "hath ascended into heaven, and hath sat down on the right hand of God, to claim of the Father his rights of mercy which he hath upon the children of men."[36] I pray that we may all be blessed with a burning testimony of the Lord Jesus Christ, rejoice and be valiant in that testimony, and enjoy the fruits of His grace in our lives continually. In the name of Jesus Christ, amen.

Notes

1. See Dallin H. Oaks, "Kingdoms of Glory," *Liahona*, Nov. 2023, 26–29.
2. Doctrine and Covenants 76:39.
3. Dallin H. Oaks, "Kingdoms of Glory," 26.
4. Doctrine and Covenants 76:89.
5. Romans 8:17.
6. Russell M. Nelson, "Think Celestial!," *Liahona*, Nov. 2023, 118.
7. Doctrine and Covenants 76:51, 69; emphasis added.
8. Doctrine and Covenants 76:75, 79; emphasis added.
9. Doctrine and Covenants 76:101; emphasis added.
10. Joseph Smith Translation, John 1:4 (in the Bible appendix); see also John 1:1–3.
11. *Teachings of Presidents of the Church: Joseph Smith* (2011), 49.
12. Mosiah 5:8.
13. Doctrine and Covenants 76:22–24. The testimony of Jesus comes by the Holy Ghost, the spirit of prophecy and revelation (see Revelation 19:10; *Teachings: Joseph Smith*, 384–85).
14. See Doctrine and Covenants 76:51–53.
15. Moroni 7:47.
16. Ephesians 4:13.
17. See Revelation 3:15–16.
18. Alma 27:27.
19. Mosiah 16:12.
20. Russell M. Nelson, "The Power of Spiritual Momentum," *Liahona*, May 2022, 99.
21. Mosiah 18:9.

22. See John 8:31–32.
23. Neal A. Maxwell, "Settle This in Your Hearts," *Ensign*, Nov. 1992, 65. In addition to these remarks by Elder Maxwell, other general conference speakers in recent years have addressed this subject, including Quentin L. Cook ("Valiant in the Testimony of Jesus," *Ensign* or *Liahona*, Nov. 2016, 40–44) and Rebecca L. Craven ("Careful versus Casual," *Ensign* or *Liahona*, May 2019, 9–11).
24. Neal A. Maxwell, "Settle This in Your Hearts," 65–66.
25. See John H. Groberg, "Writing Your Personal and Family History," *Ensign*, May 1980, 48–49.
26. "He hath power given unto him from the Father to redeem [us] from [our] sins because of repentance; therefore he hath sent his angels to declare the [glad] tidings of the conditions of repentance, which bringeth unto the power of the Redeemer, unto the salvation of [our] souls" (Helaman 5:11). See also Helaman 5:10: Jesus redeems us *from* our sins, not *in* our sins.
27. 3 Nephi 27:20; see also verses 16–21; 3 Nephi 11:31–36.
28. Helaman 3:34.
29. Helaman 3:35.
30. See Mosiah 5:7; 27:24–31; Alma 5:11–15, 26; Moses 6:59–60.
31. Alma 34:33.
32. Doctrine and Covenants 45:2; see also Helaman 13:38.
33. Alma 35:15.
34. Mosiah 5:12; emphasis added.
35. Joseph Smith Translation, Luke 14:28 (in Luke 14:27, footnote *b*).
36. Moroni 7:27.

CALL, DON'T FALL

ELDER TAYLOR G. GODOY
Of the Seventy

Today I would like to begin by testifying of the complete certainty within my heart that God hears our prayers and answers them in a personalized way.

In a world going through times of uncertainty, pain, disappointment, and heartbreak, we might feel inclined to rely more on personal abilities and preferences, as well as the knowledge and security that come from the world. This could cause us to put in the background the real source of succor and support that can counter the challenges of this mortal life.

I remember an occasion when I was hospitalized for an illness, and it was difficult for me to sleep. When I turned off the lights and the room became dark, I saw a reflective sign on the ceiling in front of me that said, "Call, don't fall." To my surprise, the next day I observed the same message repeated in several parts of the room.

Why was that message so important? When I asked the nurse about it, she said, "It is to prevent a blow that might increase the pain you already have."

This life, by its nature, brings painful experiences, some inherent to our physical bodies, some due to our weaknesses or afflictions, some due to the way others use their agency, and some due to our use of agency.

Is there a promise more powerful than the one the Savior Himself made when He declared, "Ask, and it shall be given you; seek, and ye shall find; knock," or call, "and it shall be opened unto you"?[1]

Prayer is the means of communication with our Heavenly Father that allows us to "call and don't fall." However, there are circumstances in which we might think that the call has not been heard because we do not receive an immediate response or one according to our expectations.

This sometimes leads to anxiety, sadness, or disappointment. But remember Nephi's expression of faith in the Lord when he said,

"How is it that he cannot instruct me, that I should build a ship?"[2] Now, I ask you, how is it that the Lord cannot instruct you, that you do not fall?

Confidence in God's answers implies accepting that His ways are not our ways[3] and that "all things must come to pass in their time."[4]

The certainty of knowing that we are children of a loving and merciful Heavenly Father should be the motivation to "call" in devout prayer with an attitude of "pray[ing] always, and not faint[ing]; . . . that [our] performance may be for the welfare of [our] soul[s]."[5] Imagine the feelings of Heavenly Father when in each prayer we make a supplication in the name of His Son, Jesus Christ. What power and tenderness, I believe, are displayed when we do so!

The scriptures are full of examples of those who called out to God so they would not fall. Helaman and his army, while facing their afflictions, called upon God, pouring out their souls in prayer. They received assurance, peace, faith, and hope, gaining courage and determination until they achieved their goal.[6]

Imagine how Moses would have called and cried out to God when finding himself between the Red Sea and the Egyptians approaching to attack, or Abraham when obeying the mandate to sacrifice his son Isaac.

I am certain that each of you have had and will have experiences where calling will be the answer to not fall.

Thirty years ago, while my wife and I were preparing for our civil marriage and our temple marriage, we received a call informing us that civil marriages were canceled due to a strike. We received the call three days before the scheduled ceremony. After several attempts at other offices and not finding available appointments, we began to feel distressed and doubtful that we really could get married as planned.

My fiancée and I "called," pouring out our souls to God in prayer. Finally, someone told us about an office in a small town on the outskirts of the city where an acquaintance was the mayor. Without hesitation, we went to visit him and asked him if it would be possible to marry us. To our joy, he agreed. His secretary emphasized to us that we had to obtain a certificate in that city and deliver all the documents before noon the next day.

The next day, we moved to the small town and went to the police station to request the required document. To our surprise, the officer said that he would not give it to us because many young couples had been running away from their families to get married secretly in that town, which of course was not our case. Again, fear and sadness overtook us.

I remember how I silently called out to my Heavenly Father so as not to fall. I received a clear impression in my mind, repeatedly saying, "Temple recommend, temple recommend." I immediately took out my temple recommend and handed it to the officer, to my fiancée's bewilderment.

What a surprise we had when we heard the officer say, "Why didn't you tell me that you are from The Church of Jesus Christ of Latter-day Saints? I know your church well." He immediately began to prepare the document. We were even more surprised when the officer left the station without saying anything.

Fifty minutes passed, and he did not return. It was already 11:55 in the morning, and we had only until noon to deliver the papers. Suddenly he appeared with a beautiful puppy and told us it was a wedding gift and gave it to us along with the document.

We ran toward the mayor's office with our document and our new dog. Then we saw an official vehicle coming toward us. I stopped in front of it. The vehicle stopped, and we saw the secretary inside. Seeing us, she said, "I'm sorry; I told you noon. I must go on another errand."

I humbled myself in silence, calling with all my heart to my Heavenly Father, asking for help once again to "not fall." Suddenly, the miracle happened. The secretary said to us, "What a beautiful dog you have. Where could I find one like that for my son?"

"It is for you," we immediately replied.

The secretary looked at us with surprise and said, "OK, let's go to the office and make the arrangements."

Two days later, Carol and I were married civilly, as planned, and then we were sealed in the Lima Peru Temple.

Of course, we need to remember that calling is a matter of faith and action—faith to recognize that we have a Heavenly Father who answers our prayers according to His infinite wisdom, and then action consistent with what we asked for. Praying—calling—can be a sign of our hope. But taking action after praying is a sign that our faith is real—faith that is tested in moments of pain, fear, or disappointment.

I suggest you consider the following:

1. Always think of the Lord as your first option for help.
2. Call, don't fall. Turn to God in sincere prayer.
3. After praying, do all you can to obtain the blessings you prayed for.
4. Humble yourselves to accept the answer in His time and His way.
5. Don't stop! Keep moving forward on the covenant path while you wait for an answer.

Perhaps there is someone right now who, due to circumstances, feels like they are about to fall and would like to call like Joseph Smith did when he cried out: "O God, where art thou? . . . How long shall thy hand be stayed?"[7]

Even in circumstances such as these, pray with "spiritual momentum," as President Russell M. Nelson taught,[8] because your prayers are always heard!

Remember this hymn:

Ere you left your room this morning,
Did you think to pray?
In the name of Christ, our Savior,
Did you sue for loving favor
As a shield today?
Oh, how praying rests the weary!
Prayer will change the night to day.
So, when life gets dark and dreary,
Don't forget to pray.[9]

As we pray we can feel the embrace of our Heavenly Father, who sent His Only Begotten Son to relieve our burdens, because if we call out to God, I testify we will not fall. In the name of Jesus Christ, amen.

Notes

1. Matthew 7:7.
2. 1 Nephi 17:51.
3. See Isaiah 55:8.
4. Doctrine and Covenants 64:32.
5. 2 Nephi 32:9.
6. See Alma 58:10–11.
7. Doctrine and Covenants 121:1–2.
8. See Russell M. Nelson, "The Power of Spiritual Momentum," *Liahona*, May 2022, 97–100.
9. "Did You Think to Pray?," *Hymns*, no. 140.

BRIDGING THE TWO GREAT COMMANDMENTS

ELDER GARY E. STEVENSON
Of the Quorum of the Twelve Apostles

Introduction

As my wife, Lesa, and I travel on assignment throughout the world, we relish the privilege of meeting with you in congregations large and small. Your devotion to the work of the Lord buoys us up and stands as a testimony to the gospel of Jesus Christ. We return home from each trip wondering if we possibly gave as much as we received.

When traveling, we have little time for sightseeing. However, when possible, I spend a few moments in a particular passion. I have an interest in architecture and design and a special fascination with bridges. Suspension bridges amaze me. Whether it's the Rainbow Bridge in Tokyo, the Tsing Ma Bridge in Hong Kong, the Tower Bridge in London, or others I have seen, I marvel at the engineering genius built within these complicated structures. Bridges take us places we otherwise would not be able to go. (Before I continue, I note that since this message was prepared, a tragic bridge accident occurred in Baltimore. We mourn the loss of life and offer condolences to affected families.)

A Magnificent Suspension Bridge

Recently, a conference assignment took me to California, where I once again crossed the iconic Golden Gate Bridge, regarded as an engineering wonder of the world. This monumental structure intertwines beautiful form, functional purpose, and masterful engineering. It is a classic suspension bridge with bookend towers, supported by massive piers. The colossal, majestic weight-bearing twin towers soaring above the ocean were the first elements to be constructed. Together they shoulder the load of the sweeping main suspension cables and the vertical suspender cables, which cradle the roadway below. The extraordinary stabilizing capacity—the power of the tower—is the magic behind the engineering of the bridge.

Golden Gate Bridge District

Early construction images of the bridge bear testimony of this engineering principle. Each bridge element finds weight-bearing support from the symmetrical towers, both interdependently connected one to another.

When the bridge is complete, with its two powerful towers firmly in place and piers anchored in a foundation of bedrock, it is an image of strength and beauty.

Today I invite you to [consider] this stately bridge—with its ascending twin towers built on a strong foundation—through a gospel lens.

In the twilight of Jesus Christ's ministry, during what we now call Holy Week, a Pharisee who was a lawyer[1] asked the Savior a question he knew was nearly impossible to answer:[2] "Master, which is the great commandment in the law?" The lawyer, "tempting him" and seeking a legalistic answer, with seemingly deceitful intent, received a genuine, sacred, divine response.

"Jesus said unto him, Thou shalt love the Lord thy God with all thy heart, and with all thy soul, and with all thy mind.

"This is the first and great commandment." Hearkening to our bridge analogy, the first tower!

"And the second is like unto it, Thou shalt love thy neighbour as thyself." This is the second tower!

"On these two commandments hang all the law and the prophets."[3] The remaining elements of the bridge!

Let's examine each of the two great commandments, revealed and recited in Jesus Christ's response. As we do so, let the image of the magnificent suspension bridge resonate in your mind's eye.

Love the Lord

The first, to love the Lord with all your heart, soul, and mind.

In this answer, Jesus Christ condenses the essence of the law embodied in the sacred teachings of the Old Testament. To love the Lord centers first on your heart—your very nature. The Lord asks that you love with all your soul[4]—your entire consecrated being—and finally, to love with all your mind—your intelligence and intellect. Love for God is not limited or finite. It is infinite and eternal.

For me, the application of the first great commandment can sometimes feel abstract, even daunting. Gratefully, as I consider further words of Jesus, this commandment becomes much more graspable: "If ye love me, keep my commandments."[5] This I can do. I can love Heavenly Father and Jesus Christ, which then leads to prayer, scripture study, and temple worship. We love the Father and the Son through the payment of tithes, keeping the Sabbath day holy, living a virtuous and chaste life, and being obedient.

Loving the Lord is often measured in small daily deeds, footsteps on the covenant path: for young people, using social media to build up rather than tear down; leaving the party, movie, or activity where standards might be challenged; showing reverence for things sacred.

Consider this tender example. It was fast Sunday as Vance[6] and I knocked on the door of a small, humble home. We and other deacons in the quorum had come to expect the words "Please come in," yelled warmly in a thick German accent loud enough to hear through the door. Sister Muellar was one of several immigrant widows in the ward. She couldn't answer the door very easily, as she was legally blind. As we stepped inside the dimly lit home, she greeted us with kind questions: What are your names? How are you doing? Do you love the Lord? We answered and shared that we came to receive her fast offering. Even at our young age, her meager circumstances were readily apparent, and her faith-filled response was profoundly touching: "I placed a dime on the counter earlier this morning. I am so grateful to offer my fast offering. Would you be kind enough to place it in the envelope and fill out my fast-offering receipt?" Her love of the Lord lifted our faith each time we left her home.

King Benjamin promised remarkable power for those who follow the first great commandment. "I would desire that ye should consider on the blessed and happy state of those that keep the commandments. . . . They are blessed in all things, . . . and if they hold out faithful to the end they are received into heaven . . . in a state of never-ending happiness."[7]

Loving the Lord leads to eternal happiness!

Love Your Neighbor

Jesus then said, "And the second is like unto it, Thou shalt love thy neighbour as thyself."[8] This is the second tower of the bridge.

Here Jesus bridges our heavenly upward gaze, to love the Lord, with our earthly outward gaze, to love our fellow men and women. One is interdependent on the other. Love of the Lord is not complete if we neglect our neighbors. This outward love includes all of God's children without regard to gender, social class, race, sexuality, income, age, or ethnicity. We seek out those who are hurt and broken, the marginalized, for "all are alike unto God."[9] We "succor the weak, lift up the hands which hang down, and strengthen the feeble knees."[10]

Consider this example: Brother Evans[11] was surprised when he was prompted to stop his car and knock on an unknown door of an unknown family. When a widowed mother of over 10 answered the door, their difficult circumstances and great needs became readily apparent to him. The first was simple, paint for their home, which was followed by many years of temporal and spiritual ministering to this family.

This thankful mother later wrote of her heaven-sent friend: "You have spent your life reaching out to the least of us. How I would love to hear the things the Lord has to say to you as He expresses His appreciation for the good you have done financially and spiritually for the people that only you and He will ever know about. Thank you for blessing us in so many ways, . . . for the missionaries you provided for. . . . I often wonder if the Lord picked on you exclusively or if you were just the one who listened."

To love your neighbor includes Christlike deeds of kindness and service. Can you let go of grudges, forgive enemies, welcome and minister to your neighbors, and assist the elderly? You will each be inspired as you build your tower of love for neighbor.

President Russell M. Nelson taught: "Giving help to others—making a conscientious effort to care about others as much as or *more* than we care about ourselves—is our joy. Especially . . . when it is not convenient and when it takes us out of our comfort zone. *Living* that second great commandment is the *key* to becoming a true disciple of Jesus Christ."[12]

An Interdependency

Jesus further taught, "On these two commandments hang all the law and the prophets."[13] This is very instructive. There is an important interdependency between loving the Lord and loving one another. For the Golden Gate Bridge to perform its designed function, both towers are equally strong and with equal power to bear the weight of the suspension cables, the roadway, and the traffic crossing the bridge. Without this engineering symmetry, the bridge could be compromised, even leading to collapse. For any suspension bridge to do what it was built to do, its towers must function together in complete harmony. Likewise, our ability to follow Jesus Christ depends upon our strength and power to live the first and second commandments with balance and equal devotion to both.

The increasing contention in the world suggests, however, that we at times fail to see or remember this. Some are so focused on keeping the commandments that they show little tolerance of those they see as less righteous. Some find it difficult to love those who are choosing to live their lives outside of the covenant or even away from any religious participation.

Alternatively, there are those who emphasize the importance of loving others without acknowledgment that we are all accountable to God. Some refuse entirely the notion that there is such a thing as absolute truth or right and wrong and believe that the only thing required of us is complete tolerance and acceptance of the choices of others. Either of these imbalances could cause your spiritual bridge to tip or even fall.

President Dallin H. Oaks described this when he said: "We are commanded to love everyone, since Jesus's parable of the good Samaritan teaches that everyone is our neighbor. But our zeal to keep this second commandment must not cause us to forget the first, to love God with all our heart, soul, and mind."[14]

Conclusion

So the question for each of us is, How do we build our own bridge of faith and devotion—erecting tall bridge towers of both loving God and loving our neighbors? Well, we just start. Our initial efforts might look like a plan on the back of a napkin or an early-stage blueprint of the bridge we hope to construct. It might consist of a few realistic goals to understand the Lord's gospel more or to vow to judge others less. No one is too young or too old to begin.

Over time, with prayerful and thoughtful planning, rough ideas are refined. New actions become habits. Early drafts become polished blueprints. We build our personal spiritual bridge with hearts and minds devoted to Heavenly Father and His Only Begotten Son as well as to our brothers and sisters with whom we work, play, and live.

In the days ahead, when you pass over a majestic suspension bridge or even when you see a picture, with its soaring towers, I invite you to remember the two great commandments, described by Jesus Christ in the New Testament. May the Lord's instructions inspire us. May our hearts and minds be lifted upward to love the Lord and turned outward to love our neighbor.

May this strengthen our faith in Jesus Christ and His Atonement, of which I testify in the name of Jesus Christ, amen.

Notes

1. "In the New Testament, [the term *lawyer* was] equivalent to *scribe*, one who was by profession a student and teacher of the law, including the written law of the Pentateuch, and also 'the traditions of the elders' (Matt. 22:35; Mark 12:28; Luke 10:25)" (Bible Dictionary, "Lawyer").
2. Anciently, Jewish scholars had enumerated 613 commandments in the Torah and actively debated the relative importance of one versus the other. Perhaps the lawyer intended to use Jesus's answer against Him. If He said one commandment was the most important, it might allow an opening to accuse Jesus of ignoring another aspect of the law. But the Savior's response silenced those who had come to entrap Him with a foundational statement that today is the bedrock for all we do in the Church.

3. Matthew 22:36–40.
4. See Doctrine and Covenants 88:15.
5. John 14:15.
6. Both names changed in this story to protect privacy.
7. Mosiah 2:41.
8. Matthew 22:39.
9. 2 Nephi 26:33.
10. Doctrine and Covenants 81:5.
11. Name changed to protect privacy.
12. Russell M. Nelson, "The Second Great Commandment," *Ensign* or *Liahona*, Nov. 2019, 100.
13. Matthew 22:40.
14. Dallin H. Oaks, "*Two* Great Commandments," *Ensign* or *Liahona*, Nov. 2019, 73–74.

OPPOSITION IN ALL THINGS

ELDER MATHIAS HELD
Of the Seventy

Recently, while driving in a city unknown to us, I inadvertently took a wrong turn, which led my wife and me onto an express highway for endless miles without being able to turn around again. We had received a kind invitation to a friend's home and worried that we would now arrive much later than we were expected to.

While on this highway and desperately looking for a way out again, I blamed myself for not paying better attention to the navigation system. This experience caused me to think about how in our lives we sometimes make wrong decisions and how we must live with the consequences humbly and patiently until we are able to change our course again.

Life is all about making choices. Our Father in Heaven gave us the divine gift of agency precisely so that we could learn from our choices—from the right ones and also from the wrong ones. We correct our wrong choices when we repent. This is where growth happens. Heavenly Father's plan for all of us is about learning, developing, and progressing toward eternal life.

Ever since my wife and I were taught by the missionaries and joined the Church many years ago, I have always been impressed by the profound teachings that Lehi gave to his son Jacob in the Book of Mormon. He taught him that "the Lord God gave unto man that he should act for himself"[1] and that "it must needs be, that there is an opposition in all things."[2] To be able to exercise our agency, we need to have opposing options to consider. In doing so, the Book of Mormon also reminds us that we have been "instructed sufficiently"[3] and that "the Spirit of Christ"[4] has been given to every one of us to "know good from evil."[5]

In life, we constantly confront many important choices. For example:

- Choosing whether or not we will follow God's commandments.

- Choosing to have faith and recognize when miracles happen or to skeptically wait for something to happen before choosing to believe only then.
- Choosing to develop trust in God or to fearfully anticipate another challenge the next day.

As when I took a wrong turn on that highway, suffering from the consequences of *our own* poor decisions can often be especially painful because we only have ourselves to blame. Nevertheless, we can always choose to receive comfort through the divine process of repentance, make wrong things right again, and in doing so learn some life-changing lessons.

Sometimes we can also experience opposition and trials from things outside of our control, such as:

- Moments of health and periods of sickness.
- Times of peace and times of war.
- Hours of day and of night and seasons of summer and of winter.
- Times of labor followed by times of rest.

Even though we usually cannot choose between these kinds of situations because they just happen, we are still free to choose *how* to react to them. We can do so with a positive or with a pessimistic attitude. We can seek to learn from the experience and ask for our Lord's help and support, or we can think that we are on our own in this trial and that we must suffer it alone. We can "adjust our sails" to the new reality, or we can decide not to change anything. In the darkness of night, we can turn on our lights. In the cold of winter, we should choose to wear warm clothes. In seasons of sickness, we can seek medical and spiritual help. We choose how to react to these circumstances.

Adjust, learn, seek, choose are all action verbs. Remember that we are agents and not objects. Let us never forget that Jesus promised to "take upon him the pains and sicknesses of his people . . . that he may . . . succor," or help, us as we turn to Him.[6] We can choose to build our foundation on the rock that is Jesus Christ so that when the whirlwind comes, "it shall have no power over [us]."[7] He has promised that "whosoever will come [to Him], him will [He] receive; and blessed are those who come unto [Him]."[8]

Now, there is one additional principle that is especially important. Lehi said that there "must needs be . . . an opposition *in all things*."[9] This means that opposites don't exist apart from each other. They can even complement each other. We would not be able to identify joy unless we had also experienced sorrow at some point. Feeling hungry at times helps us to be especially grateful when we do have enough to eat again. We would not be able to identify truth unless we had also seen lies here and there.

These opposites are all like the two sides of one same coin. Both sides are always present. Charles Dickens provided an example of this idea when he wrote that "it was the best of times, it was the worst of times."[10]

Let me give an example from our own life. Getting married, forming a family, and having children brought to us the greatest moments of joy we have ever experienced in our lives but also the most profound moments of pain, anguish, and grief when something happened to any one of us. Infinite joy and bliss with our children were sometimes also followed by recurring periods of sicknesses, hospitalizations, and sleepless nights filled with distress, as well as finding relief in prayers and priesthood blessings. These contrasting experiences taught us that we are never alone in moments of suffering, and they also showed us how much we can carry with the Lord's succor and help. These experiences helped to shape us in wonderful ways, and it has all been totally worthwhile. Is this not what we came here for?

In the scriptures we also find some interesting examples:

- Lehi taught his son Jacob that the afflictions he suffered in the wilderness helped him know the greatness of God and that "[God] shall consecrate [his] afflictions for [his] gain."[11]
- During Joseph Smith's cruel incarceration in Liberty Jail, the

Lord told him that "all these things shall give [him] experience, and shall be for [his] good."[12]

- Finally, Jesus Christ's infinite sacrifice was certainly the greatest example of pain and suffering ever seen, but it also brought about the wonderful blessings of His Atonement to all of God's children.

Where there is sunshine, shadows must be there too. Floods can bring destruction, but they usually bring life as well. Tears of grief often turn into tears of relief and happiness. Feelings of sadness when loved ones depart are later compensated with the joy of meeting again. In periods of war and destruction, many little acts of kindness and love are also happening for those with "eyes to see, and ears to hear."[13]

Our world today is often characterized by fear and anxiety—fear of what the future might bring for us. But Jesus has taught us to trust and "look unto [Him] in every thought; doubt not, fear not."[14]

Let us constantly make a very conscious effort to see both sides of *every* coin allotted to us in our lives. Even though both sides might sometimes not be immediately visible to us, we can know and trust that they are always there.

We can rest assured that our difficulties, sorrows, afflictions, and pains do not define us; rather, it is *how* we go about them that will help us grow and draw closer to God. It is our attitudes and choices that define us much better than our challenges.

When in health, cherish and be grateful for it every moment. When in sickness, seek to patiently learn from it and know that this can change again according to God's will. When in sorrow, trust that happiness is around the corner; we often just cannot see it yet. Consciously shift your focus and elevate your thoughts to the positive aspects of challenges, because they are undoubtedly always there too! Never forget to be grateful. Choose to believe. Choose to have faith in Jesus Christ. Choose to always trust God. Choose to "think celestial," as President Russell M. Nelson recently taught us![15]

Let us always be mindful of our Heavenly Father's wonderful

plan for us. He loves us and sent His Beloved Son to help in our trials and to open for us the door to return to Him. Jesus Christ lives and stands there at every moment, waiting for us to choose to call upon Him to provide succor, strength, and salvation. Of these things I testify in the name of Jesus Christ, amen.

Notes

1. 2 Nephi 2:16.
2. 2 Nephi 2:11.
3. 2 Nephi 2:5.
4. Moroni 7:16.
5. 2 Nephi 2:5.
6. Alma 7:11, 12.
7. Helaman 5:12.
8. 3 Nephi 9:14.
9. 2 Nephi 2:11; emphasis added.
10. Charles Dickens, *A Tale of Two Cities* (1859), 1.
11. 2 Nephi 2:2.
12. Doctrine and Covenants 122:7.
13. Deuteronomy 29:4.
14. Doctrine and Covenants 6:36.
15. See Russell M. Nelson, "Think Celestial!," *Liahona*, Nov. 2023, 117–20.

TEMPLES, HOUSES OF THE LORD DOTTING THE EARTH

ELDER NEIL L. ANDERSEN
Of the Quorum of the Twelve Apostles

Don't you love the beautiful words we just sang? "I'll strengthen thee, help thee, and cause thee to stand, . . . upheld by my righteous, omnipotent hand."[1] The Lord is strengthening His Saints of all ages as they come to His holy house. From Kinshasa to Zollikofen to Fukuoka to Oakland, the youth, of their own initiative, are overflowing temple baptistries. In the past, most beloved ordinance workers had graying hair—but not anymore. Called missionaries, service missionaries, and returned missionaries are around every corner. Across the world, there is a growing feeling drawing us to the house of the Lord.

Just over a year ago, a dear family friend, age 95, living on the east coast of the United States, who had been taught by missionaries for 70 years, said to her daughter, "I want to go to the temple with you."

Her daughter replied, "Well, Mother, you first need to be baptized."

"OK," she replied, "then I want to be baptized." She was baptized. A few days later, she reverently entered the temple baptistry. And just over a month ago, she received her own endowment and sealing. "The knowledge and power of God are expanding; the veil o'er the earth is beginning to burst."[2]

Have you wondered why the Lord would direct His prophet to now dot the earth with His holy temples?[3] Why would He, at this specific time, give the needed prosperity to His covenant people that through their sacred tithes, hundreds of houses of the Lord could be built?

This morning, President Dallin H. Oaks showed a beautiful visual of the temples being constructed across the world. Kathy and I were recently in the Philippines. Think of this miracle: The Manila Temple was dedicated in 1984. It would be 26 years before the second temple, in Cebu City, was completed in 2010. Now, 14 years later, 11 temples are being constructed, designed, or prepared for dedication. From the north to the south: Laoag, Tuguegarao, Santiago, Urdaneta, Alabang, Naga, Tacloban City, Iloilo, Bacolod, Cagayan de Oro, and Davao. It is breathtaking to see the wondrous works of God!

Across the globe, houses of the Lord are coming closer to us. Why in our day?

The Last Days

The Lord warned that in the last days, there would be distress among nations,[4] people would "be lovers of their own selves,"[5] "all things [would] be in commotion,"[6] confusion would abound,[7] and "men's hearts [would] fail them."[8] We have certainly seen men's and women's hearts fail them: the enticements of the world, the distraction of alluring voices, the neglect of spiritual nourishment, the fatigue from the demands of discipleship.[9] Perhaps you have been saddened as you have seen someone you love, who at one time spoke sincerely of his or her faith in Jesus Christ, bore witness of the Book of Mormon, and eagerly helped build the kingdom of God, suddenly move away, at least for now, from his or her beliefs and toward the sidelines of the Church. My counsel to you is don't despair! All is well. For with God, nothing is impossible.[10]

With this prophesied commotion and disbelief in the world, the Lord promised that there would be a covenant people, a people eagerly awaiting His return, a people who stand in holy settings and are not moved out of their place.[11] He spoke of a righteous people resisting the deceptions of the adversary, disciplining their faith, thinking celestial, and trusting completely in the Savior Jesus Christ.

Why is the Lord now bringing hundreds of His temples closer to us? One reason is that amid the turmoil and temptations of the world, He has promised to strengthen and bless His covenant Saints, and His promises are being fulfilled!

Promises from the Kirtland Temple

How do these holy houses strengthen, comfort, and protect us? We find an answer in the pleadings of the Prophet Joseph Smith in the dedication of the Kirtland Temple. It was in this temple where the Saints sang, "We'll sing and we'll shout with the armies of heaven."[12] The Savior Himself appeared, and prophets of old returned, bestowing additional priesthood keys to the restored gospel.[13]

On that sacred occasion in the Kirtland Temple, the Prophet prayed that in the Lord's holy house, the Saints would be armed with the power of God, that the name of Jesus Christ would be upon them, that His angels would have charge over them, and that they would grow up in the Lord and "receive a fulness of the Holy Ghost."[14] These powerful supplications are fulfilled in our lives as we faithfully worship in the house of the Lord.

Armed with Power

In His house, we are literally endowed with heavenly power.[15] Our faith in Jesus Christ and our love for Him are confirmed and fortified. We are spiritually assured of our true identity and the purposes of life.[16] As we are faithful, we are blessed with protection from temptations and distractions. We feel our Savior's love as He lifts us from our difficulties and sorrows. We are armed with the power of God.

His Name upon Us

In His holy house, we take His name more completely upon us. When we are baptized, we profess our belief in Him and our willingness to keep His commandments. In the temple, we sacredly promise, through our covenants, to follow Him forever.

The youth of this Church are incredible. In a difficult world, they take upon themselves the name of Christ. In Heber City, Utah, a public meeting was held to discuss the details of a temple planned for construction. Three hundred youth filled the adjoining park to show their support for the proposed temple. One young man, speaking to government leaders in an open forum, courageously explained, "I am hoping to be married in this temple. [The temple will help] me to keep myself clean and pure." Another described the temple as a symbol of light and hope. Young men and women of the Church throughout the world are embracing the name of Jesus Christ.[17]

Angels with Us

In the Kirtland Temple, the Prophet Joseph prayed that "angels [would] have charge over [His Saints]."[18] Regularly performing ordinances for our ancestors in the temple brings a sweet and sure confirmation that life continues beyond the veil.

Although many of our experiences in the house of the Lord are too sacred to share publicly, some we can share. Forty years ago, while living in Florida, Kathy and I traveled to the temple in Atlanta, Georgia. On Wednesday night, May 9, 1984, as we completed a session in the temple, an ordinance worker approached me and asked if I had time to do just one preparatory initiatory ordinance. The name of the person I represented was unusual. His name was Eleazer Cercy.

The next day, the temple was full of Saints. As I prepared to perform my second endowment of the day, I was given the name of the person I would represent. Surprisingly, the name was the same individual from the night before, Eleazer Cercy. I felt the Spirit of the Lord as the endowment was completed. Later in the afternoon, still in the temple, Kathy saw an elderly family friend, Sister Dolly Fernandez, who now lived in Atlanta. With no male members of her family with her, she asked if I could possibly assist in the sealing of her father to her father's parents. I was of course honored.

As I knelt at the end of the altar for this sacred ordinance, I heard once again the name that was now inscribed in my mind, her father, Eleazer Cercy. I fully believe that following this life, I will meet and embrace a man known in his mortal life as Eleazer Cercy.

Most of our experiences in the house of the Lord bring joyful peace and quiet revelation more than dramatic intervention. But be assured: angels do have charge over us!

A Fulness of the Holy Ghost

The gift of the Holy Ghost is given to us as we are confirmed a member of the Church. Each week as we worthily partake of the bread and water in remembrance of our Savior, we are promised His Spirit will always be with us.[19] As we come with willing hearts to the house of the Lord, the most holy place on earth, we grow up in the Lord and can "receive a fulness of the Holy Ghost."[20] Through the power of the Holy Ghost, we are filled with peace and joy and unspeakable hope.[21] We receive the strength to remain His disciples even when we find ourselves outside of holy places.

President Russell M. Nelson has declared: "Our Savior and Redeemer, Jesus Christ, will perform some of His mightiest works between now and when He comes again. We will see miraculous indications that God the Father and . . . Jesus Christ . . . preside over this Church in majesty and glory."[22] Dotting the earth with houses of the Lord is a mighty work and miraculous indication.[23]

My beloved friends, if we are able and have not already increased our attendance at the temple, let us regularly find more time to worship in the house of the Lord. Let us pray for the temples that have been announced, that properties can be purchased, that governments will approve plans, that talented workers will see their gifts magnified, and that the sacred dedications will bring the approval of heaven and the visit of angels.

Promises

The temple is literally the house of the Lord. I promise you as you come worthily and prayerfully to His holy house, you will be armed with His power, His name will be upon you, His angels will have charge over you, and you will grow up in the blessing of the Holy Ghost.

The Lord promised, "Every soul who forsaketh his sins and cometh unto me, and calleth on my name, and obeyeth my voice, and keepeth my commandments, shall see my face and know that I am."[24] There are many different ways to see the face of Christ, and there is no better place than in His holy house.[25]

In this day of confusion and commotion, I testify that the temple is His holy house and will help preserve us, protect us, and prepare us for the glorious day when, with all His holy angels, our Savior returns in majesty, power, and great glory. In the name of Jesus Christ, amen.

Notes

1. "How Firm a Foundation," *Hymns*, no. 85.
2. "The Spirit of God," *Hymns*, no. 2.
3. There are currently 182 operating temples. Six are under renovation. Seven are awaiting dedication, with one more awaiting rededication. There are 45 under construction and 94 more which have been announced or are in planning and design.
4. See Luke 21:10.
5. 2 Timothy 3:2.
6. Doctrine and Covenants 88:91.
7. Elder David A. Bednar said: "Gospel principles are for me and you what a helm is to a ship. Correct principles enable us to find our way and to stand firm, steadfast, and immovable so we do not lose our balance and fall in the raging latter-day storms of darkness and confusion" ("The Principles of My Gospel," *Liahona*, May 2021, 126).
8. Doctrine and Covenants 45:26.
9. "If any man will come after me, let him deny himself, and take up his cross, and follow me" (Matthew 16:24).
10. See Luke 1:37.
11. See Doctrine and Covenants 87:8.
12. *Hymns*, no. 2.
13. See Doctrine and Covenants 110. Prior to this time, the Prophet Joseph Smith had received the Aaronic Priesthood and its keys from John the Baptist, and he had received the Melchizedek Priesthood and its keys from the Apostles Peter, James, and John (see Doctrine and Covenants 13:1; 27:12–13).
14. Doctrine and Covenants 109:15; see also verse 22.
15. President Russell M. Nelson said: "The temple can help us in our quest. There we are endowed with God's power, giving us the ability to overcome Satan, the instigator of *all* contention" ("Peacemakers Needed," *Liahona*, May 2023, 101).
16. See Russell M. Nelson, "Choices for Eternity" (worldwide devotional for young adults, May 15, 2022), Gospel Library.
17. Elder Colin Stauffer, personal correspondence, Jan. 30, 2024.
18. Doctrine and Covenants 109:22.
19. See Doctrine and Covenants 20:77, 79.
20. Doctrine and Covenants 109:15.
21. See Romans 15:13.
22. Russell M. Nelson, "Revelation for the Church, Revelation for Our Lives," *Ensign* or *Liahona*, May 2018, 96.
23. President Brigham Young said, "We will have hundreds of temples and thousands of men and women officiating therein for those who have fallen asleep, without having had the privilege of hearing and obeying the Gospel" (*Teachings of Presidents of the Church: Brigham Young* [1997], 312). And President Ezra Taft Benson said: "Our predecessors have prophesied that temples will dot the landscape of North and South America, the isles of the Pacific, Europe, and elsewhere. If

this redemptive work is to be done on the scale it must be, hundreds of temples will be needed" (*The Teachings of Ezra Taft Benson* [1988], 247).

24. Doctrine and Covenants 93:1.
25. Elder David B. Haight said:

    "It is true that some have actually seen the Savior, but when one consults the dictionary, he learns that there are many other meanings of the word *see*, such as coming to know Him, discerning Him, recognizing Him and His work, perceiving His importance, or coming to understand Him.

    "Such heavenly enlightenment and blessings are available to each of us" ("Temples and Work Therein," *Ensign*, Nov. 1990, 61).

IT IS WISDOM IN THE LORD THAT WE SHOULD HAVE THE BOOK OF MORMON

PRESIDENT MARK L. PACE

Sunday School General President

Dear brothers and sisters, we are so grateful for your efforts in reading the scriptures with *Come, Follow Me*. Thank you for all you are doing. Your daily connection with God and His word has profound consequences. "Ye are laying the foundation of a great work. And out of small things proceedeth that which is great."[1]

Reading the Savior's teachings in the scriptures helps us transform our homes into sanctuaries of faith and centers of gospel learning.[2] It invites the Spirit into our homes. The Holy Ghost fills our souls with joy[3] and converts us into lifelong disciples of Jesus Christ.

Over these last several years, while reading the books of holy scripture, we have observed the panorama of God's teachings to His children in all the major gospel dispensations.[4]

In every dispensation, we have seen a familiar pattern. God restores or reveals the gospel of Jesus Christ through His prophets. The people follow the prophets and are greatly blessed. However, over time, some people stop heeding the words of the prophets and distance themselves from the Lord and His gospel. This is what we call apostasy. The gospel was first revealed to Adam, but some of the children of Adam and Eve turned away from the Lord in apostasy.[5] We see a pattern of restoration and apostasy repeated in the dispensations of Enoch, Noah, Abraham, Moses, and others.

Now, today, we live in the dispensation of the fulness of times.[6] This is the only dispensation that will not end in an apostasy.[7] It is this dispensation that will usher in the Second Coming of the Savior Jesus Christ and His millennial reign.

So, what's different about this dispensation? What has the Lord provided us today, especially for our time, that will help us draw near to the Savior and never leave Him?

One answer that comes to my mind is the scriptures—and particularly the Book of Mormon: Another Testament of Jesus Christ.

While God has promised there will never be another *general* apostasy, we need to be mindful and careful to avoid a *personal* apostasy—remembering, as President Russell M. Nelson has taught, "We are each responsible for our individual spiritual growth."[8] Studying the Book of Mormon, as we are doing this year, always brings us closer to the Savior—and helps us stay close to Him.

We call it "study," and that's good because it implies effort. But we don't always need to learn some new fact. Sometimes reading the Book of Mormon is just about feeling connected to God today—nourishing the soul, being strengthened spiritually before heading out to face the world, or finding healing *after* a rough day out in the world.

We study the scriptures so the Holy Ghost, the great teacher, can deepen our conversion to Heavenly Father and Jesus Christ and help us become more like Them.[9]

With these thoughts in mind, we could consider, "What has the Holy Ghost taught us this week during our study of the Book of Mormon?" and "How does this bring us closer to the Savior?"

These are good questions for our scripture study at home. They are also excellent questions to start a Sunday class at church. We improve our teaching at church on Sunday by improving our learning at home during the week. Thus, in our Sunday classes, "he that preacheth and he that receiveth, understand one another, and both are edified and rejoice together."[10]

Here are a few verses the Spirit has impressed upon my mind from this week's Book of Mormon study:

- Nephi instructed Jacob to "preserve these plates and hand them down . . . from generation to generation. And if there were preaching which was sacred, or revelation . . . , or prophesying," Jacob should "engraven . . . them upon these plates . . . for the sake of [their] people."[11]
- Jacob later testified, "We search the [scriptures], . . . and having all these witnesses we obtain a hope, and our faith becometh unshaken."[12]

Now, these verses caused me to remember what Nephi had said previously about the brass plates:

"We had obtained the records . . . and searched them and found that they were . . . of great worth unto us, insomuch that we could preserve the commandments of the Lord unto our children.

"Wherefore, it was wisdom in the Lord that we should carry them with us, as we journeyed in the wilderness towards the land of promise."[13]

Now, if it was wisdom for Lehi and his family to have the scriptures, it is just as wise for us today. The great worth and spiritual power of the scriptures continue undimmed in our lives today.

There has never been a people in history with the access to the Book of Mormon and other scriptures that we enjoy today.[14] Yes, Lehi and his family were blessed to carry the brass plates with them, but they didn't have a copy for every tent! The most important copy of the Book of Mormon is our personal copy. It is the copy that we read.

In Lehi's vision of the tree of life, Lehi taught us the importance of personal experience with the love of God. After he partook of the fruit, Lehi saw his wife, Sariah, and his sons Nephi and Sam a little way off.

"They stood as if they knew not whither they should go.

" . . . I beckoned unto them," Lehi said, "and I also did say unto them with a *loud voice* that they should come unto me, and partake of the fruit, which was desirable above all other fruit.

"And . . . they did come unto me and partake of the fruit."[15]

I love Lehi's example of intentional parenting. Sariah, Nephi, and Sam were living good, righteous lives. But the Lord had something better, something sweeter for them. They didn't know where to find it, but Lehi did. So he called to them "with a loud voice" to come to the tree of life and partake of the fruit for themselves. His direction was clear. There could be no misunderstanding.

I am the product of a similar kind of intentional parenting.[16] When I was a young boy, maybe 11 or 12 years old, my mother asked me, "Mark, do you know for yourself, by the Holy Ghost, that the gospel is true?"

Her question surprised me. I had always tried to be a "good boy," and I thought that was enough. But my mother, like Lehi, knew that something more was needed. I needed to act and know for myself.

I replied that I had not yet had that experience. And she didn't seem surprised at all by my answer.

She then said something I have never forgotten. I remember her words to this day: "Heavenly Father wants you to know for yourself. But you must put in the effort. You need to read the Book of Mormon and pray to know by the Holy Ghost. Heavenly Father will answer your prayers."

Well, I had never read the Book of Mormon before. I didn't think I was old enough to do that. But my mother knew better.

Her question ignited in me a desire to know for myself.

So, each night, in the bedroom I shared with two of my brothers, I turned on the light above my bed and read a chapter in the Book of Mormon. Then, turning off the light, I slipped out of my bed onto my knees and prayed. I prayed more sincerely and with greater desire than I ever had before. I asked Heavenly Father to please let me know of the truthfulness of the Book of Mormon.

From the time I started reading the Book of Mormon, I felt that Heavenly Father was aware of my efforts. And I felt that I mattered to Him. As I read and prayed, comfortable, peaceful feelings rested upon me. Chapter by chapter, the light of faith was growing brighter inside my soul. In time, I realized that these feelings were confirmations of truth from the Holy Ghost.[17] I came to know for myself that the Book of Mormon is true and that Jesus Christ is the Savior of the world. How grateful I am for my mother's inspired invitation.

This experience reading the Book of Mormon as a boy started a pattern of scripture study that continues to bless me to this day. I still read the Book of Mormon and kneel in prayer. And the Holy Ghost confirms its truths over and over again.

Nephi said it right. It was wisdom in the Lord that we should carry the scriptures with us throughout our lives. The Book of Mormon is the "keystone" that makes this dispensation different from all previous dispensations. As we study the Book of Mormon and follow the living prophet, there will be no personal apostasy in our lives.[18]

The invitation to come to the tree of life by holding fast to the word of God is not just an invitation from Lehi to his family, and it is not just an invitation from my mother for me to read and pray about the Book of Mormon. It is also an invitation from our prophet, President Russell M. Nelson, to each one of us.

"I promise," he said, "that as you prayerfully study the Book of Mormon *every day*, you will make better decisions—*every day*. I promise that as you ponder what you study, the windows of heaven will open, and you will receive answers to your own questions and direction for your own life."[19]

It is my prayer that reading the Book of Mormon this year will be a joy and a blessing for each of us and will draw us ever nearer to the Savior.

Heavenly Father lives. Jesus Christ is our Savior and Redeemer. The Book of Mormon contains His words and conveys His love. President Russell M. Nelson is the Lord's living prophet on the earth today. I know these things to be true because of the confirming witness of the Holy Ghost, which witness I first received while reading the Book of Mormon as a boy. In the name of Jesus Christ, amen.

Notes

1. Doctrine and Covenants 64:33.
2. "The new home-centered, Church-supported integrated curriculum has the potential to unleash the power of families, as each family follows through conscientiously and carefully to transform their home into a sanctuary of faith. I promise that as you diligently work to remodel your home into a center of gospel learning, over time *your* Sabbath days will truly be a delight. *Your* children will be excited to learn and to live the Savior's teachings, and the influence of the adversary in *your* life and in *your* home will decrease. Changes in your family will be dramatic and sustaining" (Russell M. Nelson, "Becoming Exemplary Latter-day Saints," *Ensign* or *Liahona*, Nov. 2018, 113).
3. "Verily, verily, I say unto you, I will impart unto you of my Spirit, which shall enlighten your mind, which shall fill your soul with joy" (Doctrine and Covenants 11:13).
4. "Dispensations are time periods in which the Lord has at least one authorized servant on the earth who bears the holy priesthood and the keys, and who has a divine commission to dispense

the gospel to the inhabitants of the earth" (Topics and Questions, "Dispensations," Gospel Library).

5. See Moses 5:12–16.
6. The prophet Daniel saw our day, our dispensation, when he interpreted Nebuchadnezzar's dream. The Church of Jesus Christ of Latter-day Saints is the stone in that dream, cut out of the mountain without hands, rolling forward to fill the whole earth (see Daniel 2:34–35, 44–45; Doctrine and Covenants 65:2).
7. "God the Father and Jesus Christ called upon the Prophet Joseph Smith to be the prophet of this dispensation. All divine powers of previous dispensations were to be restored through him. This dispensation of the fulness of times would not be limited in time or in location. It would not end in apostasy, and it would fill the world" (Russell M. Nelson, "The Gathering of Scattered Israel," *Ensign* or *Liahona*, Nov. 2006, 79–80).
8. Russell M. Nelson, "Opening Remarks," *Ensign* or *Liahona*, Nov. 2018, 8.
9. See "Conversion Is Our Goal," *Come Follow Me—For Home and Church: Book of Mormon 2024*, v.
10. Doctrine and Covenants 50:22; see also verses 17–21.
11. Jacob 1:3–4.
12. Jacob 4:6.
13. 1 Nephi 5:21–22.
14. It was recently announced that 200 million copies of the Book of Mormon have been distributed in this dispensation. That is truly remarkable. The Book of Mormon has now been translated into 113 languages, with 17 new translations in process. What a blessing to have the Book of Mormon in print, digital, audio, video, and other formats. (See Ryan Jensen, "Church Distributes 200 Millionth Copy of the Book of Mormon," *Church News*, Dec. 29, 2023, thechurchnews.com.)
15. 1 Nephi 8:14–16; emphasis added.
16. "The most powerful spiritual influence in the life of a child is the righteous example of loving parents and grandparents who faithfully keep their own sacred covenants. Intentional parents teach their children faith in the Lord Jesus Christ so that they too 'may know to what source they may look for a remission of their sins' [2 Nephi 25:26]. Casual and inconsistent covenant keeping leads to spiritual casualty. The spiritual damage is often greatest on our children and grandchildren" (Kevin W. Pearson, "Are You Still Willing?," *Liahona*, Nov. 2022, 69).
17. See Doctrine and Covenants 6:22–24.
18. The Prophet Joseph Smith said, "I told the brethren that the Book of Mormon was the most correct of any book on earth, and the keystone of our religion, and a man would get nearer to God by abiding by its precepts, than by any other book" (in the introduction to the Book of Mormon).
19. Russell M. Nelson, "The Book of Mormon: What Would Your Life Be Like without It?," *Ensign* or *Liahona*, Nov. 2017, 62–63.

REJOICE IN THE GIFT OF PRIESTHOOD KEYS

PRESIDENT RUSSELL M. NELSON

President of The Church of Jesus Christ of Latter-day Saints

My dear brothers and sisters, today is an historic day for President Dallin H. Oaks and me. It was 40 years ago, on April 7, 1984, when we were sustained to the Quorum of the Twelve Apostles.[1] We have rejoiced in each and every general conference since then, including this one. We have once again been blessed with a sacred outpouring of the Spirit. I hope you will repeatedly study the messages of this conference throughout the coming months.

When I was born,[2] there were six functioning temples in the Church—one each in St. George, Logan, Manti, and Salt Lake City, Utah; as well as in Cardston, Alberta, Canada; and Laie, Hawaii. Two earlier temples had functioned briefly in Kirtland, Ohio, and Nauvoo, Illinois. As the body of the Church moved west, the Saints were forced to leave those two temples behind.

The Nauvoo Temple was destroyed by an arsonist's fire. It was rebuilt and then dedicated by President Gordon B. Hinckley.[3] The Kirtland Temple was desecrated by enemies of the Church. Later the Kirtland Temple was acquired by Community of Christ, which has owned it for many years.

Last month we announced that The Church of Jesus Christ of Latter-day Saints has purchased the Kirtland Temple, along with several significant historic sites in Nauvoo. We greatly appreciate the cordial and mutually beneficial discussions we had with leaders from Community of Christ that led to this agreement.

The Kirtland Temple has unusual significance in the Restoration of the gospel of Jesus Christ. Several events that took place there had been prophesied for millennia and were essential for the Lord's restored Church to fulfill its latter-day mission.

The most important of these events occurred on Easter Sunday, April 3, 1836.[4] On that day, Joseph Smith and Oliver Cowdery experienced a *series* of remarkable visitations. First, the Lord Jesus

Christ appeared. The Prophet recorded that the Savior's "eyes were as a flame of fire; the hair of his head was white like the pure snow; his countenance shone above the brightness of the sun; and his voice was as the sound of the rushing of great waters."[5]

During this visitation, the Lord affirmed His identity. He said, "I am the first and the last; I am he who liveth, I am he who was slain; I am your advocate with the Father."[6]

Jesus Christ then declared that He had accepted the temple as *His* house and made this stunning promise: "I will manifest myself to my people in mercy in this house."[7]

This significant promise applies to *every* dedicated temple today. I invite you to ponder what the Lord's promise means for you personally.

Following the Savior's visitation, Moses appeared. Moses conferred upon Joseph Smith the keys for the gathering of Israel and the return of the ten tribes.[8]

When this vision closed, "Elias appeared, and committed the dispensation of the gospel of Abraham" to Joseph.[9]

Then Elijah the prophet appeared. His appearance fulfilled Malachi's promise that before the Second Coming, the Lord would send Elijah to "turn the heart of the fathers to the children, and the heart of the children to their fathers."[10] Elijah conferred the keys of the sealing power upon Joseph Smith.[11]

The significance of these keys being returned to the earth by three heavenly messengers under the direction of the Lord cannot be overstated. Priesthood keys constitute the authority and power of presidency. Priesthood keys govern how the priesthood of God may be used to bring about the Lord's purposes and bless all who accept the restored gospel of Jesus Christ.

It is important to note that prior to the organization of the Church, heavenly messengers had conferred the Aaronic and Melchizedek Priesthoods upon the Prophet Joseph and had given him keys of both priesthoods.[12] These keys gave Joseph Smith authority to organize the Church in 1830.[13]

Then in the Kirtland Temple in 1836, the conferral of these

three additional priesthood keys—namely, keys of the gathering of Israel, keys of the gospel of Abraham, and keys of the sealing power—was essential. These keys authorized Joseph Smith—and all succeeding Presidents of the Lord's Church—to gather Israel on both sides of the veil, to bless all covenant children with the blessings of Abraham, to place a ratifying seal on priesthood ordinances and covenants, and to seal families eternally. The power of these priesthood keys is infinite and breathtaking.

Consider how *your* life would be different if priesthood keys had not been restored to the earth.[14] Without priesthood keys, you could not be endowed with the power of God.[15] Without priesthood keys, the Church could serve only as a significant teaching and humanitarian organization but not much more. Without priesthood keys, none of us would have access to essential ordinances and covenants that bind us to our loved ones eternally and allow us eventually to live with God.

Priesthood keys distinguish The Church of Jesus Christ of Latter-day Saints from any other organization on earth. Many other organizations *can* and *do* make your life better here in mortality. But no other organization *can* and *will* influence your life after death.[16]

Priesthood keys give us the authority to extend all of the blessings promised to Abraham to every covenant-keeping man and woman. Temple work makes these exquisite blessings available to *all* of God's children, regardless of *where* or *when* they lived or now live. Let us rejoice that priesthood keys are once again on the earth!

I invite you to consider carefully the following three statements:

1. The gathering of Israel is evidence that God loves *all* of His children everywhere.
2. The gospel of Abraham is *further* evidence that God loves *all* of His children everywhere. He invites *all* to come unto Him—"black and white, bond and free, male and female; . . . *all* are alike unto God."[17]
3. The sealing power is *supernal* evidence of how much God loves *all* of His children everywhere and wants *each* of them to choose to return home to Him.

Priesthood keys restored through the Prophet Joseph Smith make it possible for *every* covenant-keeping man and woman to enjoy incredible *personal* spiritual privileges. Here again, there is much we can learn from the sacred history of the Kirtland Temple.

Joseph Smith's dedicatory prayer of the Kirtland Temple is a tutorial about how the temple spiritually empowers you and me to meet the challenges of life in these last days. I encourage you to study that prayer, recorded in Doctrine and Covenants section 109. That dedicatory prayer, which was *received by revelation*, teaches that the temple is "a house of prayer, a house of fasting, a house of faith, a house of learning, a house of glory, a house of order, a house of God."[18]

This list of attributes is much more than a description of a temple. It is a promise about what will happen to those who serve and worship in the house of the Lord. They can *expect* to receive answers to prayer, personal revelation, greater faith, strength, comfort, increased knowledge, and increased power.

Time in the temple will help you to *think celestial* and to catch a vision of who you really are, who you can become, and the kind of life you can have forever. Regular temple worship will enhance the way you see yourself and how you fit into God's magnificent plan. I promise you that.

We are also promised that in the temple we may "receive a fulness of the Holy Ghost."[19] Imagine what *that* promise means in terms of having the heavens open for each earnest seeker of eternal truth.

We are instructed that all who worship in the temple will have the power of God and angels having "charge over them."[20] How much does it increase your confidence to know that, as an endowed woman or man armed with the power of God, you do not have to face life alone? What courage does it give you to know that angels really will help you?

Finally, we are promised that "no combination of wickedness" will prevail over those who worship in the house of the Lord.[21]

Understanding the spiritual privileges made possible in the temple is vital to each of us today.

My dear brothers and sisters, here is my promise. Nothing will help you *more* to hold fast to the iron rod[22] than worshipping in the temple as regularly as your circumstances permit. Nothing will protect you *more* as you encounter the world's mists of darkness. Nothing will bolster your testimony of the Lord Jesus Christ and His Atonement or help you understand God's magnificent plan *more*. Nothing will soothe your spirit *more* during times of pain. Nothing will open the heavens *more*. Nothing!

The temple *is* the gateway to the greatest blessings God has in store for each of us, for the temple is the only place on earth where we may receive *all* of the blessings promised to Abraham.[23] That is why we are doing all within our power, under the direction of the Lord, to make the temple blessings more accessible to members of the Church. Thus, we are pleased to announce that we plan to build a new temple in each of the following 15 locations:

- Uturoa, French Polynesia
- Chihuahua, Mexico
- Florianópolis, Brazil
- Rosario, Argentina
- Edinburgh, Scotland
- Brisbane, Australia south area
- Victoria, British Columbia
- Yuma, Arizona
- Houston, Texas south area
- Des Moines, Iowa
- Cincinnati, Ohio
- Honolulu, Hawaii
- West Jordan, Utah
- Lehi, Utah
- Maracaibo, Venezuela

My dear brothers and sisters, I testify that this *is* The Church of Jesus Christ of Latter-day Saints. He stands at its head. We are His disciples.

Let us *rejoice* in the restoration of priesthood keys, which make it possible for you and me to enjoy *every* spiritual blessing we are *willing* and worthy to receive. I so testify in the sacred name of Jesus Christ, amen.

Notes

1. I filled the vacancy in the Quorum of the Twelve left by the January 11, 1983, death of Elder LeGrand Richards. Elder Oaks filled that which was left by the January 11, 1984, death of Mark E. Petersen.
2. September 9, 1924.
3. The dedication of the rebuilt Nauvoo Illinois Temple by President Gordon B. Hinckley occurred on June 27, 2002, the 158th anniversary of the martyrdom of Joseph and Hyrum Smith.
4. Just one week after the Prophet Joseph Smith dedicated the Kirtland Temple.
5. Doctrine and Covenants 110:3.
6. Doctrine and Covenants 110:4.
7. Doctrine and Covenants 110:7.
8. See Doctrine and Covenants 110:11.
9. Doctrine and Covenants 110:12. This was a perpetuation of the promise the Lord had made to Abraham thousands of years earlier (see Genesis 18:18; 1 Nephi 15:18).
10. See Malachi 4:5–6.
11. See Doctrine and Covenants 110:13–16.
12. See Doctrine and Covenants 13; 27:7–8, 12.
13. See Doctrine and Covenants 20:1–4.
14. When the Lord told Joseph Smith that this dispensation is the time when "nothing shall be withheld" (Doctrine and Covenants 121:28), it was because these priesthood keys had been returned to the earth.
15. See Doctrine and Covenants 95:8; 109:22.
16. See Doctrine and Covenants 132:45–46.
17. 2 Nephi 26:33; emphasis added.
18. Doctrine and Covenants 109:8.
19. Doctrine and Covenants 109:15.
20. Doctrine and Covenants 109:22.
21. See Doctrine and Covenants 109:24–26.
22. Meaning the word of God.
23. See Doctrine and Covenants 110:12; 132:29–30.

A Christ Centered Christmas

Sharon Velluto Suzanne Meredith

Illustrated by Sal Velluto

ISBN 0-9667633-0-0

Printed in the United States of America

Published by
SVI Inc.
West Jordan, Utah

Dedicated to our children:
Alex, Daniela, Kurt, Sara, Nate, and McKell.

HOW TO USE THIS BOOK

This book has been designed to satisfy the needs of all families; from those with small children to those whose children are grown, as well as singles and seniors. The book was written with the intent to help families escape the commercialism so prevalent during the season, and to focus on the true spirit and meaning of Christmas.

This volume is a compilation of 24 short devotionals, one for each day of December up to Christmas Eve.

Each devotional contains:

A short Christ-centered lesson, based on a familiar Christmas symbol.

A simple ornament, depicting a traditional Christmas symbol, designed to accompany the lesson. These ornaments are fun and easy to color, cut out and assemble.

Suggestions for fun activities to reinforce concepts.

A comprehensive list of suggested hymns and songs from the Children's Song Book to lift and inspire.

Additional scriptural references from the four Standard Works and suggested stories from the children's scripture readers. (*Old Testament Stories, New Testament Stories, Book of Mormon Stories, and Doctrine and Covenants Stories.*)

Optional materials including thoughts, inspirational articles, stories, poetry, games, recipes, finger puppets, and more.

The chapters are designed so that each family may select the materials suitable to their own needs, and time constraints. On days which are hectic, a family may choose to just sing a song, read a poem, or simply tell about the main idea of the lesson. The lessons can be as simple or complex as desired. A brief summary of the lesson, "*In A Nutshell,*" is provided with each lesson, and can be used by itself as a brief thought, if desired. The family may elect to utilize only a few devotionals from this volume, if they do not wish to use them on a daily basis.

Many of the ideas in this manual could be used to supplement Family Home Evenings, Primary lessons and other activities throughout the year.

Each lesson is presented on two facing pages in an easy to follow, visually organized format. The Optional Materials, found in Section 2 of the book, can be used to enrich or vary the devotional from year to year.

The ornaments can be assembled all together as a family activity, or one per day. They may be hung on the family tree, a small separate tree, or even a garland, as a visual reminder of gospel principles. The ornaments can be labeled with date and name of the family member who colored them and saved as keepsakes.

For your convenience, the materials in "Cards and Activities" and "Ornaments" sections may be photocopied. (For personal use only)

PREFACE

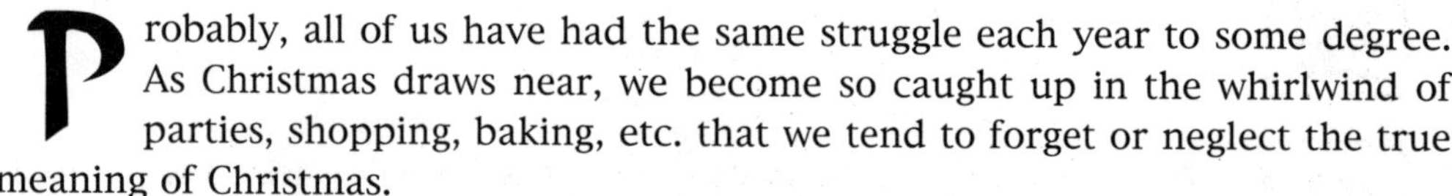

Probably, all of us have had the same struggle each year to some degree. As Christmas draws near, we become so caught up in the whirlwind of parties, shopping, baking, etc. that we tend to forget or neglect the true meaning of Christmas.

Suzanne and I had discussed our frustrations about the chaos and commercialism of this season, and we talked about some ways to bring the true Spirit of Christmas into our homes. At the time, we were working together in our ward Primary presidency, and decided to use our ideas for an Activity Day, to which we invited the children and their families. The positive feedback we received, as well as the numerous requests for additional copies of the materials used for that activity, encouraged us to consider the publication of our ideas in book format.

We tried these ideas within our ward Primary organization as well as our own families, and found them to be very successful. The devotionals provided a time when we could shut out the hurry of the world, sing songs together, and enjoy the sweet peaceful feelings of Christmas, which are often lost in the bustle of the season.

The activities were not only fun, but, through them our children learned more about the Savior and His teachings.

Because our children colored and assembled the ornaments themselves, they were very excited to learn and participate. Each day they asked, "What are we learning today?"

In publishing this book, our hope is to help people to focus on the life and mission of our Savior, that we may draw nearer to Him. May Christ truly be the center of our Christmas celebration and our light throughout the year!

Sharon Velluto

ELPFUL HINTS

The pages labeled “Cards and Activities,” and “Ornaments” may be removed from the book or may be photocopied in accordance with the copyright notice.

For tips on photocopying or information about ordering extra packets of ornaments see page 162 or 214.

When removing cardstock pages from the book, support the binding with one hand while carefully pulling the page with the other hand. This will help to preserve the spine of the book.

When assembling the cardstock ornaments, it is important to pay particular attention to folding the various elements properly. Folding is much easier, and folds are crisper if fold lines are scored first. To score, place a straight edge, such as a ruler along the fold. Run something pointed (such as a toothpick, pencil, or pen) along the fold line. Do not use anything sharp enough to tear the paper. A pen without ink is the best.

Folds can be made crisper by running the blade of a pair of dull scissors or butter knife over the fold to crease it. Do not apply too much pressure as this will considerably weaken the paper. To punch holes it is best to NOT use a standard paper punch. They are too large and the holes rip easily. Small paper punches are available in many craft stores. A riveter or a small nail also work well.

Slots are easier to cut out if the piece is folded first. If the piece does not fold, a single edged razor blade is the best to cut the slot. The slots can also be removed by scoring with a pen or needle several times and then carefully inserting a knife or scissor blade.

To glue large areas that stick flat, back to back, it is best to use a “stick flat” glue, such as spray glue or "YES"™ paste. White glue makes the paper buckle. Glue sticks have less moisture and will make the paper buckle less than white glue.

Super glue works very quickly to glue the more complicated pieces. (This should be done only with adult supervision.)

STORAGE AND PRESERVATION

After scoring coloring and cutting out the ornament, and before folding, cover with contact paper. This will help to preserve the ornaments. You may want to write your child's name and/or date on it first.

Plastic ornament boxes can be purchased or made from strips of cardboard by cutting slots which overlap to form a grid in which the ornaments can be placed. This will keep them from being smashed. Store flat ornaments on the bottom of the box.

COMMENTS AND SUGGESTIONS

Our objective in preparing this book was to make it “user friendly.” Christmas can be a hectic season, and we wanted to provide simple, ready-to-use materials, which can be put together with a minimal amount of time and effort.

We selected a binding which makes the volume easy to handle, and, allows the pages to lay flat. Each devotional is presented on two facing pages in an easy to follow, visually organized format.

We hope that we have accomplished our goal and that you enjoy the fruit of our efforts. Your comments and suggestions are welcome.

Write to us at P.O. Box 1663, West Jordan, UT, 84088, or E-Mail us at ccc@velluto.com

CONTENTS

How to use this book...v
Preface...vi
Helpful Hints; Storage and Preservation; Comments and Suggestions............................xii
Clarification of Copyright; Tips on Photocopying: Ordering Additional Copies.....162, 214

SECTION ONE: 1 Devotionals

1. Signs of Christ.............................. Pg. 2 Ornament: Samuel Star..... Pg. 229
MAIN IDEA: The star, one of our most beloved Christmas symbols, was a sign given by God to announce the birth of His Son.

2. The Gift of Prayer.......................... Pg. 4 Ornament: Praying Hands Pg. 231
MAIN IDEA: Because of the great love Heavenly Father has for His children, He gave them the gift of prayer.

3. Inviting Christ In........................... Pg. 6 Ornament: Holly / Holy....... Pg. 233
MAIN IDEA: Christmas is a time to reflect on the precious gift God gave because He "*so loved the world.*" (John 3:16)

4. The Worth of Souls......................... Pg. 8 Ornament: Gold Snowflake Pg. 235
MAIN IDEA: We are all children of God. Each of us is important and valuable to Him.

5. Brotherhood.................................. Pg. 10 Ornament: Bow................. Pg. 237
MAIN IDEA: By understanding and appreciating the differences in others, we become tied in unity.

6. Look to God and Live...................... Pg. 12 Ornament: Christmas Tree Pg. 239
MAIN IDEA: The evergreen tree serves as a reminder of our need to always reach heavenward toward eternal sources of spiritual light.

7. Glad Tidings.................................. Pg. 14 Ornament: Angel.............. Pg. 241
MAIN IDEA: God sends messengers to enlighten and bring joy to His children.

8. Seek and Ye Shall Find................... Pg. 16 Ornament: Shepherd/Cane Pg. 243
MAIN IDEA: After hearing the angel's joyous message, the shepherds went to Bethlehem to seek the baby Jesus.

9. Joy to the World............................ Pg. 18 Ornament: Book of Carols Pp. 231,245
MAIN IDEA: Good music can uplift and inspire us, and singing is a way to praise God.

10. The Lost Sheep and the Good Shepherd Pg. 20 Ornament: Bell................ Pg. 247
MAIN IDEA: Our Savior's love for us is unconditional.

11. **The Lamb of God................Pg. 22 Ornament: Sheep.............Pg. 249**
MAIN IDEA: The lamb which the Jews sacrificed during Passover was a special symbol of the sacrifice the "Lamb of God" would one day make for mankind.

12. **In Wisdom's Path...............Pg. 24 Ornament: Wise Men........Pg. 251**
MAIN IDEA: Because the Wise Men studied ancient prophecy, they learned of and followed the star which led them to Jesus.

13. **Gifts for a Newborn King.....Pg. 26 Ornament: Treasure Chest Pg. 253**
MAIN IDEA: Like the Wise Men, each of us can worship and honor the Savior by offering gifts of love, obedience and service to others.

14. **Gifts from God...................Pg. 28 Ornament: Gift Box..........Pp. 255**
MAIN IDEA: Christmas gifts remind us of the many gifts Heavenly Father and Jesus have given us.

15. **Families Can Be Forever......Pg. 30 Ornament: Wreath..........Pg. 257**
MAIN IDEA: Families need to develop charity, which is everlasting love.

16. **Light of the World.............Pg. 32 Ornament: Candle.......... Pp. 259, 261**
MAIN IDEA: Jesus Christ is the light of the world. His teachings can guide us safely through the darkness back to our heavenly home.

17. **The Least of These.............Pg. 34 Ornament: Manger..........Pp. 247, 263, 265**
MAIN IDEA: Heavenly Father and Jesus know each of us, our true selves, and love us for who we are. They have asked that we love and serve "the least" of our fellow men.

18. **Peace...............................Pg. 36 Ornament: Dove.............Pg. 265**
MAIN IDEA: Living the principles of the gospel will bring the blessing of peace.

19. **Victory Over Death............Pg. 38 Ornament: Poinsettia......Pp. 245,261, 267**
MAIN IDEA: Jesus gave us victory over physical and spiritual death.

20. **The Bread of Life...............Pg. 40 Ornament: Bread............Pg. 243**
MAIN IDEA: Bread is a symbol of the saving truths Jesus taught and of the atoning sacrifice made so that all may obtain eternal life.

21. **Living Water.....................Pg. 42 Ornament: Well.............Pp. 271, 273**
MAIN IDEA: Jesus said that He offered "living water" to all who were thirsty. This is spiritual water which refreshes and cleanses the soul.

22. **Christ the King................. Pg. 44 Ornament: Crown...........Pg. 241**
MAIN IDEA: Jesus was the Christ of whom the prophets testified. He will one day reign upon earth as King of Kings.

23. **Follow the Prophets...........Pg. 46 Ornament: Christmas Light Pg. 261**
MAIN IDEA: Prophets teach us what Jesus wants us to know, and can guide us back to Him.

24. **Jesus Christ Is Born!..........Pg. 48 Ornament: Nativity........Pg. 275**
MAIN IDEA: Christmas is a time to ponder God's great gift to man, and to feel a loving reverence for Jesus Christ, the Son of God.

SECTION TWO: Optional Materials

Lesson 1
- Additional References.............................. 52
- He Is Born (Article)...................................53
- Though Quietly the Witness Borne (Poem) 54
- A Light to Remember Him (Activity Sheet)...163
- Put Up a Star (Poem and Activity Sheet).....165
- Street Signs (Activity).............................167
- Samuel the Lamanite (Cut outs)..........213,215

Lesson 2
- Additional References...............................55
- In Tune (Poem)...55
- Open Invitation (Poem)............................. 56
- Prayer (Poem)... 56
- With Thoughtless Hands (Poems)...............56
- The Lord's Prayer (Poem)..........................56
- An Informal Prayer (Poem).........................56
- "Hello...?" (Story).................................... 57
- Ye Have Not Because (Poem).......................58
- Apology (Poem)...58
- The Larger Prayer (Poem).......................... 58
- Thoughts on Prayer.....................................58

Lesson 3
- Additional References............................... 59
- Ralph Waldo Emerson (Quote).................... 59
- My Gift (Poem)..59
- Wrapped Up (Poem)................................... 60
- Christmas Story (Poem)............................. 60
- Did You Have a Good Christmas? (Poem)....... 60
- Prepared for Christmas (Poem).................. 61
- The Proportions of Christmas (Story)...........61
- Monkey Traps (Article)...............................62
- Cards: "Treasures in Heaven" (Game)...169-173

Lesson 4
- Additional References.............................. 63
- I Have Wept in the Night (Poem)................63
- Thoughts on Self-Worth............................ 63
- A Commonplace Life (Poem).......................64
- Cocoon (Poem)... 64
- What a Soul is Worth (Poem).......................64
- Weighing the Baby (Poem)......................... 64
- Like Him (Poem).. 64
- The Royal Highway.....................................65
- Bushel (Activity).......................................175

Lesson 5
- Additional References.............................. 66
- I Know Something Good About You (Poem).....66
- Insight (Poem)...63
- The Master's Touch (Poem).........................67
- A Morning Prayer (Poem)............................67
- One Smile (Poem)....................................... 67
- Outwitted (Poem)....................................... 67
- The Empty Box (Poem)...............................68
- Good Samaritan (Flannel board. figures).......217
- Empty Box (Pattern With Poem)................219

Lesson 6
- Additional References................................69
- Mom's Butter Cookies (Recipe)...................69
- Oh Christmas Tree (Song Lyrics)................70
- What's Better for Me (Poem).......................70
- Passive Faith (Poem)...................................70
- Being Content (Poem)................................. 70
- Change (Poem)... 70
- Surrender (Poem),,,,,,...................................70
- I Surrender (Article).................................71
- Wait On (Poem).. 73

Lesson 7
- Additional References.................................74
- Quotes about Angels...................................74
- They That Be with Us...(Article).................75
- Are You an Angel Too? (Poem)...................77
- One Day (Poem)..77
- Cards for "Who's That Angel? (Game).......179

Lesson 8
- Additional References.................................78
- Hide and Seek (Poem).................................78
- Taffy (Recipe)..79
- The Search (Poem)...................................... 79
- Seek and Ye Shall Find (Poem)...................79
- Il Presepe (Article)......................................80
- My Brother's Keeper (Game).......................181

Lesson 9
- Additional References.................................84
- I Have a Song (Story)..................................84
- Elizabeth Goudrian Weenig (Story).............85
- Quote by Elder David B. Haight................. 86
- Quote by Elder Dallin H. Oaks....................86
- President Spencer W. Kimball (Quote)..........87
- Voice (Poem).. 87
- I May Have Sung There Too! (Poem)..............87
- There's a Song in the Air (Poem).................87
- Cards for music activity (Game).............. 183

Lesson 10
- Additional References.................................88
- Shepherds of Israel (Article)........................88
- Consider the Fisherman (Article)................89
- The Good Shepherd (Poem).........................92

Lesson 11
- Additional References.................................93
- Lamb Hunt (Activity)..................................93
- Wandering in the Wilderness (Activity)......94
- Behold the Lamb (Poem).............................95
- The Coming Child (Poem)...........................95
- Passover (Recipes)...................................... 95
- The Passover (Article).................................96
- Lambs for "Lamb Hunt" (Activity)....185-187

Lesson 12
- Additional References....101
- Wisdom (Poem)....101
- He Who Knows (Poem)....101
- Excerpt from "Children" (Poem)....102
- The Wisdom of Innocents (Article)....102
- Two Prayers (Poem)....104
- Tell it to Children (Poem)....104
- Scripture Treasure Hunt (Cards)....189
- Action Words Guessing Game (Cards)....191

Lesson 13
- Additional References....105
- For We Have Seen His Star (Article)....105
- Wise Men (Poem)....108
- What Shall I Bring? (Poem)....108
- Pattern and tags for shoe (Activity)....221

Lesson 14
- Additional References....109
- A Reason for Rejoicing (Article)....109
- Conversation with a 3 Year Old (Story)....112
- Hands (Poem)....112
- Heaven's Gift (Poem)....113
- Perspective (Poem)....113
- All That I Have (Poem)....113
- Gratitude (Poem)....113

Lesson 15
- Additional References....114
- Christmas Eve (Story)....114
- Fight for Freedom and Family (Article)....115
- Quote by Elder Neal A. Maxwell....116
- Marriage, Home and Family (Poem)....117
- Two and a Half (Poem)....117
- Children Don't Keep (Poem)....117
- Tally Sheet (Poem)....117
- Circles (Poem)....117
- Cookies (Recipes)....118

Lesson 16
- Additional References....119
- My Little Light (Poem)....119
- Benjamin Franklin (Quote)....119
- When Life Just Seems (Poem)....119
- Adjudication (Poem)....120
- Two Overtures (Poem)....120
- Sight (Poem)....120
- The Hold Up (Story)....121
- Open Your Eyes (Article)....122
- My Little Light (Activity sheet)....191

Lesson 17
- Additional References....124
- Trusting in His Hand (A Tribute)....124
- His Plan (Poem)....125
- The Great Potato Discourse (Article)....125
- A Bag of Tools (Poem)....126
- Labels (Poem)....127
- Only He Could See (Poem)....127
- My "Mite" (Poem)....127
- Quote by Edwin H. Chapin....127

Lesson 18
- Additional References....128
- In Search of Peace (Poem)....128
- Prayer for Peace by St. Francis (Poem)....129
- The Prince of Peace (Poem)....129
- Conquests (Poem)....129
- Psalms 23....129
- Peacemaker Cake (story and recipe)....130
- The Puzzle (Article)....131
- Pie (Illustration for activity)....195

Lesson 19
- Additional References....134
- It Pleased Him (Article)....134
- The Kind Friend (Parable)....136
- Stone (Poem)....137
- Empty (Poem)....137
- Two Keys (Poem)....137
- He Is Not Here (Poem)....137
- (See also The Sacramental Covenant)....157

Lesson 20
- Additional References....138
- So Close and Yet... (Article)....138
- Living Bread (Poem)....140
- Do I Hunger After Righteousness? (Poem) 141
- Scripture Cookies and Muffins (Recipes)....141

Lesson 21
- Additional References....142
- Can You Imagine (Article)....142
- Come to the Well (Poem)....145
- House Upon the Rock (Activity sheet)....223

Lesson 22
- Additional References....146
- Nathanael and the Preacher (Story)....146
- So it was Done (Poem)....152
- Moses, Builder, Savior, King (Poem)....153
- Crown (Poem)....153
- Paradox (Poem)....153
- Yet I Know (Poem)....153

Lesson 23
- Additional References....154
- We Thank Thee, ... (article)....154
- A Prophet's Word (Poem)....156
- Realization (Poem)....156
- Beacons (Poem)....156
- Why is It? (Poem)....156
- Brightly Beams Our Father's Mercy (Poem)..156
- Biographic Outlines... (Activity)....197
- Pictures of the Prophets....225-227

Lesson 24
- Additional References....157
- Excerpts from "The Sacramental Covenant" by Melvin J. Ballard....157
- Christmas Greetings (Poem)....159
- The Language of Christmas (Poem)....160
- Ponder These Things (Poem)....160
- Keeping Christmas (Poem)....160

SECTION THREE: *Cards and Activity Pages*

A Light to Remember Him (Activity sheet) .... Lesson 1.................... 163
Put Up a Star (Poem and Activity sheet).............. Lesson 1.................... 165
Street Signs (Activity).. Lesson 1.................... 167
Cards: Treasures in Heaven (Game)...................... Lesson 3.................... 169-173
Bushel (Activity).. Lesson 4.................... 175
Cards for "Who's That Angel?"(Game).................. Lesson 7.................... 179
My Brother's Keeper (Game)................................. Lesson 8.................... 181
Cards for music activity (Game)........................... Lesson 9.................... 183
Lambs for "Lamb Hunt" (Activity)........................ Lesson 11.................. 185-187
Scripture Treasure Hunt (Cards).......................... Lesson 12.................. 189
Action Words Guessing Game (Cards).................. Lesson 12.................. 191
My Little Light (Activity sheet).......................... Lesson 16.................. 193
Pie (Illustration)... Lesson 18.................. 195
Biographic Outlines of the Prophets..................... Lesson 22.................. 197-211
Samuel the Lamanite (Cut outs).......................... Lesson 1, 24.............. 213-215
The Good Samaritan (Flannel Board Figures)........ Lesson 5.................... 217
Empty Box (Pattern With Poem)........................... Lesson 5.................... 219
Pattern and tags for shoe (Activity).................. Lesson 13.................. 221
House Upon the Rock (Activity sheet)................. Lesson 21.................. 223
Pictures of the Prophets...................................... Lesson 23.................. 225-227

SECTION FOUR: *Ornaments*

1. Samuel Star............................... 2 pieces.. 229
2. Praying Hands........................... 2 pieces.. 231
3. Holly /Holy............................... 2 pieces.. 233
4. Gold Snowflake......................... 3 pieces.. 235
5. Bow.. 2 pieces.. 237
6. Christmas Tree......................... 2 pieces.. 239
7. Angel... 1 piece.. 241
8. Shepherd/Candy Cane............... 2 pieces.. 243
9. Book of Carols.......................... 2 pieces.. 231, 245
10. Bell.. 2 pieces.. 247
11. Sheep....................................... 7 pieces.. 249
12. Wise Men.................................. 2 pieces.. 251
13. Treasure Chest.......................... 1 piece.. 253
14. Gift Box.................................... 1 piece (3 copies).......................... 255
15. Wreath...................................... 2 pieces.. 257
16. Candle...................................... 3 pieces.. 259, 261
17. Manger..................................... 3 pieces.. 247, 263, 265
18. Dove... 2 pieces.. 265
19. Poinsettia................................. 4 pieces.. 245, 261, 267
19. Poinsettia petals....................... white copy..................................... 269
20. Bread.. 2 pieces.. 243
21. Well.. 2 pieces.. 271, 273
22. Crown....................................... 2 pieces.. 241
23. Christmas Light........................ 1 piece.. 261
24. Nativity.................................... 2 pieces.. 275

Devotionals

Signs of Christ

IN A NUTSHELL

Signs are an important part of daily life. They help to keep us safe by telling us what to expect. Because our Heavenly Father loves us and wants us to be safe, He often uses signs to tell His children of important events. Long before Jesus was born, prophets told their people what to watch for and what to expect. One of these prophets was Samuel the Lamanite who prophesied of the night when Jesus Christ would be born. He foretold the appearance of a new star and a night in which there would be no darkness.

LESSON

Signs are an important part of our everyday life. In our society, we use signs for many different reasons. (Use Street Signs, Optional Materials, page 167)

1. Signs keep us safe.
2. Signs tell us the speed we should go, or when to stop, go, yield or slow down. (Merge, Stop, Yield, Stop light)
3. Signs tell us where we are, which direction to travel, and how far we need to go to reach our destination. (Directional signs, speed limit, welcome to, etc.)
4. Signs tell us which way we should not go, and things we should not do. (No Turn, One Way, Do Not Enter, Don't Walk, No Parking, etc.)
5. Signs tell us where we can go to find help. (Hospital, Police, etc.)
6. Signs warn us to be careful, by telling us of things to watch for and expect. (Railroad, Sharp Curve, Pedestrian, Slippery When Wet, Steep Hill, etc.)

Signs are often seen in nature also. One old adage tells us:

Red sky in the morning,
Sailors take warning.
Red sky at night,
Sailors delight.

Red leaves tell us that winter is approaching, while, new blossoms announce the coming of springtime. The American Indians have many proverbs predicting the weather. According to folklore, some of nature's signs for rain are : birds flying low or making lots of noise, fish breaking water and biting easily, flies gathering in houses, dogs or horses rolling on their backs, and silver maple and cottonwood leaves turning over.

During Jesus' day, the Pharisees asked him for a sign from heaven. Jesus reproved them for knowing the signs of nature and not knowing the "signs of the times," which were signs of vital importance. (See Matthew 16:1-3)

Heavenly Father uses signs for many of the same reasons already mentioned. To Noah, He gave the sign of a rainbow as a promise that the earth would never again be flooded. (See Genesis 9:13)

Because Heavenly Father loves us, He wants us to be safe. He wants to warn us of dangers which might harm us. He wants us to know what is coming and what to expect.

The birth of His Son, Jesus Christ was one of the most important events to occur in the earth's history. He wanted the people of the earth to recognize Him, and to know of His birth, so He told people of the signs they should watch for, long before Jesus was born. Isaiah lived about 700 years before Jesus' birth, and wrote some of the most important prophesies that exist about the Savior. "*For unto us a child is born, unto us a son is given; and the government shall be upon his shoulder; and his name shall be called Wonderful, Counselor, The mighty God, The everlasting Father, The Prince of Peace.* (Isaiah 9:6) *He hath no form nor comeliness; and when we shall see him, there is no beauty that we should desire him. He is despised and rejected of men; a man of sorrows, and acquainted with grief; ...Surely he hath borne our griefs and carried our sorrows*; (See Isaiah 53 for full prophesy)

In the Americas, God had other children. He wanted them to know of the coming of His Son also. So, as God always does, He told a prophet to tell the people of His coming and warned them that they should repent and get ready. The prophet's name was Samuel. He was a righteous Lamanite. Most of the Nephites were wicked and God sent Samuel to warn them. The Nephites threw him out of their city, and he was about to return to his home.

But, God had a message for Samuel to deliver and sent him back. Samuel told the Nephites to repent and believe in Christ. He told them that Christ would be born in five years. God would give the people a sign so they might know that what Samuel had said was the truth. They would see a new star in the heavens, and the night of Jesus' birth there would be no darkness. They would watch the sun set and rise again, but it would not get dark. (See Helaman 14:2-6)

Just as God had promised, the sign came, so all of the people would know of this very important event, the birth of Jesus Christ.

ACTIVITY IDEAS

- Leave a light on throughout the Christmas Season, or use the enclosed picture A LIGHT TO REMEMBER HIM (page 163) color it and hang it in your home, as a reminder of the true meaning of Christmas.
- Using the figures in the Optional Materials, pages 213-215, have children act out or tell the story of Samuel the Lamanite and the birth of Jesus.
  (These figures can be mounted on wooden sticks, backed with flannel or used as finger puppets by attaching a small loop to the back of the figure, or mount a long triangular stand to the backs of the pictures and stand the figures on a flat surface. These figures can also be used with Lesson 24. To do a scripture reading of the story of Samuel the Lamanite, use Helaman 13:1-7; 14: 1-12; 15:1-3. For younger children, see Book of Mormon Stories, *Samuel the Lamanite Tells about Jesus Christ*, and the *Signs of Christ's Birth*.
- Use the picture and poem in the Optional Materials, PUT UP A STAR, page 165. For each act of kindness shown, children can glue a star (metallic foil) into the sky.
- Study the references in the Optional Materials, Additional References section, *Signs of the Second Coming*, page 52. Discuss which of these signs have been fulfilled, which are in the process of being fulfilled, and which are yet to be fulfilled.
- Using the STREET SIGNS found in Optional Materials, page 167, place them individually in various parts of the room as if it were a roadway. Have each child pretend to be driving along the roadway. The children must obey each sign as it is passed. Discuss what each sign means, and what the driver must do. Discuss what would happen if the signs were ignored. What would happen if signs such as Hospital, Railroad, Stop etc. were all taken down? Compare this to how we should respect and watch for the signs that Heavenly Father sends to us.

SUGGESTED SONGS *Christmas songs in Italics*

CHILDREN'S SONGBOOK

Samuel Tells of the Baby Jesus............36
Stars Were Gleaming..............................37
The Nativity Song.................................52
He Sent His Son....................................34
Had I Been a Child.............................80
When He Comes Again......................82

HYMNS

Joy to the World......................................201
Silent Night..204
Away in a Manger............................206
O Little Town of Bethlehem....................208
With Wondering Awe.............................210
The First Noel (verse 2)........................213
I Believe in Christ....................................134
Jesus, Once of Humble Birth.....................196

ORNAMENT

Samuel Star

- This ornament consists of two pieces, found on page 229.

The Gift of Prayer

IN A NUTSHELL

Following Samuel's prophecy, things became very difficult for those who believed in Jesus Christ. The unbelievers established a day in which all believers would be killed, unless the sign was given. Nephi, the leader of the Church, prayed fervently in behalf of his people. His prayers were answered. That night Samuel's prophecies were fulfilled. Like Nephi, we can receive help and guidance from our Heavenly Father through the wonderful gift of prayer.

LESSON

After Samuel, the Lamanite prophet, foretold the coming of Christ, many people believed what he had taught. They repented of their sins and were baptized, and became strong and loyal members of the Church. Steadfastly, they watched for the signs spoken of by Samuel, "*that they might know that their faith had not been in vain.*" (3 Nephi 1:6)

But there were many wicked Nephites who hated the members of the Church. They began to say that the time was past for Samuel's words to be fulfilled, and they began to persecute and ridicule those who still trusted in Samuel's prophecies. These wicked people who did not believe what the prophets had foretold, set aside a day to kill all those who did believe unless the sign of Christ's birth came.

Nephi was the leader of the Church in the land of Zarahemla. He was worried and sorrowful for those faithful few who believed in Christ. He did not want them to be hurt or killed. So, he went out and bowed himself down upon the earth, and cried mightily to his God in behalf of his people, for "*those who were about to be destroyed because of their faith.*" (3 Nephi 1:11) Nephi prayed fervently all day long.

God let Nephi know that he didn't need to worry any more. The voice of the Lord came to him saying: *"Lift up your head and be of good cheer; for behold the time is at hand, and on this night shall the sign be given, and on the morrow come I into the world."* (3 Nephi 1:13)

That night, just as Samuel had prophesied, the sun set in the western sky. But it didn't get dark. The people saw for themselves that the testimonies of the prophets were true.

God keeps all of his promises. When He says that He will do something, we can trust that He will do as He has said. When we need help, when we are worried, when we have questions or when we simply want to express thanks, we can pray as Nephi did and receive guidance, and help.

Anciently, many kings would not allow their subjects to approach them without being first given permission to do so. Addressing the king without his consent was often punishable by death. It is for this reason that the story of Queen Esther is so touching. Even though Esther was the wife of the king, she was under the same restrictions, and was forbidden to talk with her own husband unless asked to do so. Esther risked her own life when she approached the king in an effort to save her people from destruction.

Our Father in Heaven, the greatest King of all, has given to His children the gift of prayer, the privilege of approaching and communicating with Him. Too often this priceless gift is taken for granted and treated in a most casual manner. And far too often, prayer is used only when a serious need arises. " *In the day of their peace they esteemed lightly my counsel; but in the day of their trouble, of necessity they feel after me.*" (D&C 101:8) We have been counseled repeatedly to "pray without ceasing." (See 1 Thessalonians 5:17, Alma 26:22) By keeping a prayer in our hearts, we will be ready to listen and able to understand when God wants to communicate His will to us. Prayer is a blessing which helps us to keep our lives more finely tuned to the will of God. Brigham Young said,

"*Prayer keeps a man from sin and sin keeps a man from prayer.*" (*Richard Evans Quote Book,* Salt Lake City: Bookcraft, 1971, p. 137)

During His ministry, Jesus labored diligently to teach the Jews of their relationship with God. He taught that God was actually their Father, who loved them, was aware of them, cared about them, and stood ready and waiting to help them. Elder Richard L. Evans taught,

"*He who has ceased to pray, has lost a great friendship.*" (Ibid, p. 132)

Before we ever reach out our hand to God, before our prayers ever wing heavenward, He is already waiting with outstretched hand. Putting one's hand in God's is surer than a light in darkness, and is safer than a known and well traveled path.

Even midst a raging storm, ultimately, Peter was far safer walking on the water with his eyes fixed on the Master, than he ever could have been in a small Judean fishing boat. God is infinitely greater than our greatest need, wiser than our greatest dilemma and more merciful than our greatest sin.

ACTIVITY IDEAS

- Share personal experiences you have had with prayer.
- Disassemble a flashlight, making three piles.
  One: the batteries (the power source or God)
  Two: the empty flashlight case (the connections or prayer)
  Three: the light bulb (us)
  Explain that even though the batteries (The Power Source) might not be inside of the flashlight, they still contain stored energy and once they are inserted properly, can give power to the flashlight. The bulb can do nothing by itself, and will not light up by merely touching it to the batteries.
- Heavenly Father has established a connection between Himself and us. That connection is prayer. Without God, we are nothing, but with His help, guidance and power, all things are possible. (See Luke 1:37) Prayer is a wonderful gift from our Heavenly Father which provides light for our lives, and power which comes from a divine and never ending source. Unlike the batteries, God's love and long-suffering care for his children is eternal.
- Using a radio with a tuning knob, show your children how they can tune into a radio station, even those far away. Talk about how a radio can pick up a signal from a great distance away and bring it into our homes. Prayer works in the same way for us. When our lives are out of tune through sin, the radio signal is still there, we just can't receive it as easily, because there is interference. The poem "*In Tune*" in the Optional Materials, page 55, goes well with this activity.
- Draw a circle and then draw a line through the middle of it, cutting the circle into two equal parts. Label one half "*I talk, God listens.*" Label the other half "*God talks, I listen.*" Explain that in order for prayer to be complete, we need both parts. Sometimes we don't enjoy the benefits of prayer because we don't allow for the other half to be fulfilled. Often we need to overcome some obstacles to enjoy the full benefits of prayer. Some of these obstacles are: not allowing enough time, too many distractions, not understanding the answer given, not accepting the will of Heavenly Father, not having enough faith in God.

SUGGESTED SONGS

Christmas songs in Italics

CHILDREN'S SONGBOOK

Samuel Tells of the Baby Jesus................36
Stars Were Gleaming.................................37
There Was Starlight on the Hillside..........40
A Child's Prayer......................................12
A Prayer..22
I Love to Pray..25
I Feel My Savior's Love.............................74
Seek the Lord Early................................108
Search, Ponder, and Pray.........................109

HYMNS

Away in a Manger................................206
Hark! the Herald Angels Sing..............209
With Wondering Awe............................210
I Need Thee Every Hour.........................98
Did You Think to Pray..........................140
Sweet Hour of Prayer...........................142
Secret Prayer..144
Prayer Is the Soul's Sincere Desire.....145
Abide with Me; 'Tis Eventide...............165
Abide with Me..166

ORNAMENT

Praying Hands

- This ornament consists of two pieces found on page 231.

Inviting Christ In

IN A NUTSHELL

Our Heavenly Father and Jesus are willing and anxious to come into the lives of any who will "open the door." One day Jesus taught his dear friend, Martha, a very valuable lesson. He explained the importance of "seeking the needful thing." Sometimes, with the hustle and hurry of the season, it is easy to forget the true reason for the celebration. Christmas is a time for rejoicing as we remember the precious gift God gave because He "so loved the world." (John 3:16)

LESSON

Behold, I stand at the door, and knock; if any man hear my voice, and open the door, I will come in to him, and will sup with him and he with me. (Revelation 3:20) Many artists have portrayed the message of this scripture on canvas. The Master stands at a door which has no handle; a door which must be opened from the inside. (See L.D.S. picture packet 237) Jesus Christ is waiting outside the door of our heart, ready and anxious to come into our lives, to show us the way to live, if we will but open the door and let him in.

Christmas should be a time to reflect on the birth and life of our Savior, but often, the shiny, showy things of the world drown out the simple beauty of what Christmas truly is.

Jesus often retired to Bethany to be with His friends, Mary, Martha and Lazarus. On one of these occasions recorded in Luke 10, Mary sat at the feet of Jesus to be fed spiritually, while her sister Martha was "cumbered about much serving", preparing for what she perceived to be the physical needs of her guest. Martha petitioned Jesus, for some needed help from her sister. She asked, "*Lord, dost thou not care that my sister hath left me to serve alone? Bid her therefore that she help me.*" Tenderly Jesus addressed her, "*Martha, Martha, thou art careful and troubled about many things: But one thing is needful; and Mary hath chosen that good part, which shall not be taken away from her.*" (See Luke 10:40-42)

Mary came that day to the Savior, with open heart, hungering and thirsting for the spiritual food which He had to offer. Martha, a kind and generous woman, had momentarily become caught up in the immediate temporal needs of her guest, and had forgotten the "needful things." * (See footnote)

Though each of us as mortal men need temporal food to sustain life, we also need that food which is spiritual to nourish our soul.

Paul taught," *For now we see through a glass, darkly; but then face to face: now I know in part; but then shall know even as I am known.*" (1 Corinthians 13:12) In this life, our vision is limited, and our perspective a little distorted. It is easy at times to lose our eternal focus.

Especially at Christmas time, it is easy to be swept away by the deluge of demands; to be caught up in the frenzy of gift giving, decorations, baking etc, that we neglect the most essential part of Christmas, the "reason for the season".

It should never be forgotten that Christmas began almost two thousand years ago, in a humble stable. There were no sparkling lights, no tinseled tree, no golden ribbons, no holly wreaths. Instead, there were two weary travelers, a humble stable, a holy infant, a promised star.

Holly is the festive and fun part of the holiday, but should never overshadow or detract from the *holy*, which is "the needful thing." Let us "open our door" this Christmas, as we remember the birth of Him who stands knocking.

Holly or Holy

Mom said to bring out the H-O-L-L-Y,
But I seem to have misplaced an "L."
So instead, I will bring out the H-O-L-Y
And I'm sure that we'll like that as well

Sharon Velluto

*Often, Martha is judged a bit unfairly, because of this particular incident in her life. Martha, this day "was cumbered about much serving" To her had fallen the duty of being hostess to One she recognized as divine. She felt a great need to attend to the physical needs of her guest. It is possible that she had petitioned Mary for help up to this time and had not received it. Perhaps she was a bit envious of her younger sister. It is likely that she, too, wished to sit at the Master's feet and hear the blessed words which fell from His lips. It cannot be supposed that Martha's spirituality or personal righteousness was in any way inferior to that of Mary. The fervent witness born by Martha of the Savior's divinity and divine Sonship on the occasion when her brother Lazarus was raised from death is one of the most powerful recorded in scripture. (See John 11: 1-46 especially verses 21-28. See also Bruce R. McConkie, *The Mortal Messiah,* Book 3, Salt Lake City:Deseret Book, 1980, P.183.)

ACTIVITY IDEAS

- In the toe of a Christmas stocking place a tiny pearl. Then, push a long piece of tinsel on top of it. Pull the tinsel out, leaving the pearl hidden in the toe of the stocking, unnoticed. Then pull the pearl out. Explain that the pearl is small and simple and harder to find. In fact, unless it is searched for carefully, it may be missed altogether. The tinsel is bright and shiny and easily grabs attention. When the two are placed side by side, the tinsel is the first thing noticed, but the pearl is of far greater value. Read Matthew 13:45-46
- TREASURES IN HEAVEN GAME: Cut out the cards in the Optional Materials: Treasures in Heaven. pp. 169-173 (Mounting the cards on card stock or covering them with contact paper, will help to preserve them.) Place the cards in a bowl or brown paper bag. On the floor, establish a starting line and a finish line. Beginning with the youngest family member, each player draws a card out, reads it, and then moves the number of steps indicated on the card. (Make certain that each child reaches the finish line or "Heaven." Be careful that this game is fun and not used to criticize and point fingers. Everyone is a winner no matter how soon or late they reach the finish line. The family may want to give a cheer each time a player reaches the finish line. Add extra cards as needed to meet your own family's needs.

  OPTIONAL IDEA: On two pieces of paper, bowls, sacks etc., draw clouds for heaven and a circle for the earth. Have the children decide if the card is a "heavenly decision" or an "earthly decision". Place card in appropriate bowl.
- Wrap a box and label it "*A Gift for Jesus*" Tape onto the package this scripture: "*Inasmuch as ye have done it unto one of the least of these my brethren, ye have done it unto me.*" (Matthew 25:40) Explain that the most beautiful gift we can give at Christmas, is the gift of ourselves to someone else, for it is truly a gift to the Savior. Leave the box in a prevalent place as a reminder to serve one another. Read the poem *My Gift* in Optional Materials page 59, or *One Smile* on page 67.

SUGGESTED SONGS

Christmas songs in Italics

CHILDREN'S SONGBOOK

Song	Page
Once within a Lowly Stable	41
Mary's Lullaby	44
Christmas Bells	54
I Need My Heavenly Father	18
Jesus Wants Me for a Sunbeam	60
To Think about Jesus	71
I'm Trying to Be like Jesus	78
Every Star Is Different	142
I Am like a Star	163
I Will Follow God's Plan	164

HYMNS

Hymn	Page
Oh, Come, All Ye Faithful	202
Silent Night	204
O Little Town of Bethlehem	208
I Heard the Bells on Christmas Day	214
I Need Thee Every Hour	98
More Holiness Give Me	131
Know This, That Every Soul Is Free	240
Who's on the Lord's Side?	260
Teach Me to Walk in the Light	304

ORNAMENT

Holly /Holy

- This ornament consists of two pieces, found on page 233.

The Worth of Souls

IN A NUTSHELL

Gold is a precious metal of great worth. It was one of the gifts brought by the Wise Men to the baby Jesus. Gold is an important color of Christmas because it shimmers and shines as it reflects light. Each of Heavenly Father's children is precious and valuable to Him , even more valuable than gold. The knowledge that we are all children of our Heavenly Father should inspire us to treat others with kindness and respect. Jesus taught that we should treat others the way we would like to be treated. This is called the Golden Rule. By loving and respecting each of God's children, as Jesus taught us to do, we reflect the light of God making the world a better place.

LESSON

The Bible lists three gifts brought by the Wise Men to the Christ Child. The first one mentioned is gold. (Matthew 2:11)

The color gold is a special part of Christmas, because the it reflects light. It even seems to take on a light of its own. When a gold ornament is hung near a light on a Christmas tree, it sparkles and shines almost as brightly as the light itself. It is like doubling the light. The tree becomes twice as bright without using any extra energy.

We are very precious and valuable to God; much more valuable than gold. "*I will make a man more precious than fine gold...*" (Isaiah 13:12)

We are His children. *"The Spirit itself beareth witness with our spirit, that we are the children of God. And if children then heirs; heirs of God, and joint-heirs with Christ;* (Romans 8:16-17)

He loves us just as our earthly parents love us, except His love is perfect and complete. When we are surrounded by the light of His love, we desire to reflect that light, and we take on a light of our own, making the world a brighter place.

Knowing that we are children of God, helps us realize that we, also, can become like Him. " *I have said, Ye are gods; and all of you are children of the most High.*" (Psalms 82:6)

Babies are born and grow until at last they become adults like their parents. Very often, they even look and act like their parents. When we realize that God is our Father, we recognize that we are of royal birth. Heavenly Father helps us to become the best we can be.

We can give the gift of ourselves to God, by our obedience to His commandments, and by showing others that we know, they also are children of our Heavenly Father. We can treat them like a brother or sister. We all are of great worth! "*Remember the worth of souls is great in the sight of God.*" (D&C 18:10)

Because Jesus knew that we are all children of our Heavenly Father, He gave us an important guideline for living. He taught, "*All things whatsoever ye would that men should do to you, do ye even so to them:*" (Matthew 7:12) This is called the Golden Rule.

THE GOLDEN RULE

"Do unto others
as you would have them do to you."
It's the Golden Rule
and I find it true.
When I treat others kindly
They're kinder to me
I can make a difference
for all to see.
When I light my lamp
To make it glow
The light shines 'round
and seems to grow.
So if I care for others
I'll try
To lift my light
Way up high.

- Suzanne Meredith-

"*Ye are the light of the world. A city that is set on an hill cannot be hid. Neither do men light a candle and put it under a bushel, but on a candlestick; and it giveth light unto all that are in the house. Let your light shine before men, that they may see your good works, and glorify your Father which is in heaven.* " (Matthew 5:14-16)

ACTIVITY IDEAS

- Using a light and a gold ornament, show how the light is reflected.
- Assemble the BUSHEL found in the Optional Materials p. 175 and tape or glue it to a glass bottle. Light a candle and let the flame burn for a few minutes. Put the bottle over the candle, and let children watch through the top glass as the candle flickers and goes out. Read Matthew 5:14-16 and/or Luke 11:33-36 Discuss what happened to the flame when it was hidden under the bushel, and how it is useless to ourselves and to others. Liken this to our testimonies.
- Gather some pictures of baby animals and talk about how they grow up to be like their parents. A baby kitten will never grow up to be an elephant. As children of God, we will grow up to be like Him. (See D&C 132:20. See also the quotes by Lorenzo Snow in Lesson 23, page 202: "*A Son of God...*" and "*As man now is...*" See also the poem "*Like Him*" in Optional Materials, page 64)
- Spray paint small stones or hardened salt dough nuggets with gold spray paint. Attach a note for each family member— maybe something like: "*You're worth your weight in gold,*" "*Your golden smile warms my heart.*" etc.

  SALT DOUGH RECIPE

  Mix well 1 Cup Salt, 1/2 Cup water, 2 Tablespoons oil. Add 2 cups flour. Shape and bake at 250 degrees for several hours until hard.
- Have a gold rush. Tie legs of two family members together, like a three legged race and hunt for gold nuggets. (Either the salt dough nuggets or some of the many gold candies available. Discuss Moses 1:39. The work of God is not to gather gold, but to gather souls, which to Him are far more precious, and bring them eternal life.
- Cut the bottoms from plastic strawberry crates. Cover with glue and sprinkle with gold glitter to make snowflakes. Or, make paper snowflakes and sprinkle with glitter. Emphasize that each snowflake is unique, just as people are, but each one is beautiful, even though they are different.

SUGGESTED SONGS *Christmas songs in Italics*

CHILDREN'S SONGBOOK

Once within a Lowly Stable.....41
Sleep, Little Jesus.....47
I Am a Child of God.....2
I'm Trying to Be like Jesus.....78
Love One Another.....136
Every Star Is Different.....142
Shine On.....144
Kindness Begins with Me.....145
I Want to Live the Gospel.....148
We Are Different.....263

HYMNS

Far, Far Away on Judea's Plains (vs.3).....212
The First Noel.....213
The Lord Is My Light.....89
I Believe in Christ.....134
Because I Have Been Given Much.....219
Lord, I Would Follow Thee.....220
Each Life that Touches Ours for Good.....293
Teach Me to Walk in the Light.....304
Brightly Beams Our Father's Mercy.....335

ORNAMENT

Gold Snowflake

- This ornament consists of three pieces found on page 235.

Brotherhood

IN A NUTSHELL

Part of God's eternal plan of happiness for man was that each of his children would be born different and unique. These differences help us to learn and grow as we lift others, and then in turn we are helped by them. In the parable of "The Good Samaritan", and by His own example, Jesus taught that the only true path to peace is through "good will toward men."

LESSON

When a ribbon is woven around with great care, a beautiful bow is the result. Just as the ribbon is tied together to make a bow, all mankind can and should be tied together in unity and caring.

Each person is strong in some areas and weak in others. We each have our own personality and talents. We can either judge one another harshly because of differences and weaknesses, or we can use our strengths to support and help those around us. These differences are part of God's plan of happiness for us. We can learn from one another because of these differences. We can lend our talents to lift others and to help in times of need. Then, when we are feeling weak and in need of support, there will be someone there to help us. Wrapped in the bow of brotherhood, we can all be stronger and more beautiful.

"*Peace on earth, good will toward men*," has been God's message to all since the very first Christmas. (Luke 2:14)

The Savior gave us a wonderful example of the way we should treat one another with brotherly love, when he taught this parable:

A certain man went down from Jerusalem to Jericho, and fell among thieves, which stripped him of his raiment, and wounded him, and departed, leaving him half dead.

And by chance there came down a certain priest that way: and when he saw him, he passed by on the other side.

And likewise a Levite, when he was at the place, came and looked on him, and passed by on the other side.

But a certain Samaritan, as he journeyed, came where he was: and when he saw him, he had compassion on him,

And went to him, and bound up his wounds, pouring in oil and wine, and set him on his own beast, and brought him to an inn, and took care of him.

And on the morrow when he departed, he took out two pence, and gave them to the host, and said unto him, Take care of him; and whatsoever thou spendest more, when I come again, I will repay thee.

Which now of these three thinkest thou, was neighbor unto him that fell among thieves? And he said, He that shewed mercy on him. Then said Jesus unto him, Go, and do thou likewise." (Luke 10:30-37)

TIED IN BROTHERHOOD

Sometimes life can feel so frustrating
'Cause you don't see the way I see.
It seems I know what I'd have done
If things had been up to me.

Then when we talk and you tell me
Why you did it just that way.
It helps me to understand you,
We can begin a brand new day.

A day there's tolerance of weakness,
And differences are good,
A day in which we clearly see
We are tied in brotherhood.

Suzanne Meredith

"*And the Lord make you to increase and abound in love one toward another, and toward all men....*" (1 Thessalonians 3:12)

ACTIVITY IDEAS

- Fill a 11"x 13" cake pan about 3/4 - 1 inch with whole milk. (Use whole milk because of the fat content. Effects are most easily seen when using a clear glass pan) Drop a few drops of different colors of food coloring into the milk. in different parts of the pan, at least 2-3 inches apart. Talk about the differences and beauty of each color. Squirt a little dish soap into bowl. Colors will swirl together, making beautiful color patterns. Though we may differ in color, talents, size etc., we all are important to our Heavenly Father. He loves us for who we are and what we can become. Each has something he can offer. Without yellow there could never be green or orange. As we mix and lend our strength to each other, we make life more beautiful. Having charity towards others, and accepting them for who they are, makes our lives richer and happier.
- Use the figures of "*The Good Samaritan*," found in Optional Materials p. 217 (These figures may be backed with flannel or a piece of hook and loop to be used as flannel board figures. It is helpful to cover with contact paper before attaching hook and loop. The back of most couches will work as a flannel board. The figures can also be glued to wooden craft sticks or a loop may be attached to make finger puppets. Children learn a great deal by acting out or retelling the story themselves.) Children should understand that the Samaritans were enemies of the Jews and were despised by them. The man who fell among thieves was a Jew. Priests and Levites were also Jews and were considered to be the most upright among the people.
- Demonstrate tying a bow as you teach about brotherhood. You may want to have enough ribbon for each family member to tie a bow on the tree. Other variations: tie a bow onto the tree for each act of brotherly kindness. Give each family member a long piece of ribbon. Sit in a circle. Each person uses the end of his own piece of ribbon and ties it to the end of the person's ribbon sitting to his right.
- Learn to see another person's point of view. Have everyone write answers to questions such as: What is your favorite color, movie, food, memory? etc. What scares you most, makes you happiest, etc. Gather the papers. Read one at a time. Guess who made the list. Discuss similarities and differences. When differences of opinion exist, we have a tendency to think the other person is wrong. Often there is not a right way and a wrong way, just two different ways.
- Give each family member a toothpick and have them break it in half. Talk about the effort it takes to break it. Now give everyone a bundle of toothpicks and have them try to break it. Discuss how being united and lending our strength and support to one another can make us stronger. The pioneers are a good example. (The activity also works with string.)
- Make an EMPTY BOX for someone you want to share your love with. The pattern is found in the Optional Materials on page 219, See also the poem "*The Empty Box*" on page 68.

SUGGESTED SONGS *Christmas songs in Italics*

CHILDREN'S SONGBOOK

He Sent His Son..........34
Have a Very Merry Christmas!..........51
Jesus Said Love Everyone..........61
Love One Another..........136
I'll Walk with You..........140
"Give," Said the Little Stream..........236
Friends Are Fun..........262
We Are Different..........263

HYMNS

Silent Night..........204
Far, Far Away on Judea's Plains..........212
Because I Have Been Given Much..........219
Lord, I Would Follow Thee..........220
Have I Done Any Good?..........223
Let Us Oft Speak Kind Words..........232
Each Life that Touches Ours for Good..........293
Love One Another..........308

ORNAMENT
Bow

- This ornament consists of two pieces, found on page 237.

Look to God and Live

IN A NUTSHELL

As we look to God and become dependent on Him, we find added strength and power. Jesus taught this principle when He said, *"I am the vine and ye are the branches."* (See John 15) While in the wilderness, God sent poisonous serpents to punish the faithless Israelites, and then provided a way for them to be saved. If they would but look to the serpent held up on the staff of Moses, they would be healed. Jesus taught, *"I am the way the truth and the life; no man cometh unto the Father but by me."* (John 14:6) The evergreen tree serves as a reminder of our need to always look heavenward toward eternal sources of spiritual light.

LESSON

Select and show some baby pictures of your children. Explain that there is very little that a tiny baby can do by itself. He needs help to eat and drink. Someone must change him and dress him. A baby cannot talk, so he can't even say what he needs. If he is cold, or hot, or wet, or hungry, or if he just wants to be held, he cries to get what he wants.

As a baby grows, he begins to be able to do things on his own. He can walk, or eat, or move to places he wants to go. As he grows older, he begins to talk and ask for things he wants. As we grow older it is fun to do things by ourselves.

When we were tiny we were "dependent". That means that we rely on someone else for help. We need someone to help us. We "depend" on them.

As we grow older, we become "independent". That means that we can do things on our own, without any help. We don't have to "depend" on others.

A plant is "dependent". It depends on the soil for its food. It also needs water, air and sunlight in order to stay alive. Notice how the leaves of a house plant turn toward the window. This is because plants need lots of sunlight. They are dependent.

Even though it may seem that we are old enough to be totally "independent", we are still dependent on sunlight, air, and food to maintain physical life.

Jesus taught that spiritually we should be dependent on a higher source than ourselves. He said," *I am the vine and ye are the branches.*" (See John 15:1-8) When a branch is severed from the main vine, it withers and dies. Spiritually, if we cut ourselves off from our heavenly source of "light and truth" we likewise will perish.

When Moses was leading the Israelites in the wilderness they lost faith in God and began to complain. God sent poisonous serpents which bit the Israelites.

The Lord, then directed Moses to make a serpent of brass, put it on his on his staff and hold it up for all of the Israelites to see. If they would look upon it, they would be healed. Many did not believe Moses and refused to perform such a seemingly juvenile and meaningless act. Because of their refusal to look to the staff, they perished. (Numbers 21: 5-9, Alma 33:19-21, 1 Nephi 17:41)

Pine trees are majestic and beautiful, and a perfect symbol of Christmas. These trees are also called "evergreen," because they stay green all year round, reminding us of the gift of eternal life, given to man. With needles pointing heavenward, they stand as a reminder of our need to "look up," a symbol of trust in God.

CHRISTMAS TREE

Upon a winter hillside
There stands a solemn sign,
Dark against the silent white--
A tall and stately pine.

While all the earth lies wilted
Anticipating spring,
The pine tree on the mountainside
Remains forever green.

With needles pointed upward,
A constant heav'nward reach,
And, dauntless under heavy snow
Their silent lessons teach.

On one cold, distant hillside--
A place called Calvary,
A tree loomed, silhouetted;
Innocence, between two thieves.

The King of Men reached heav'nward,
His crowning gift to give
Of everlasting life to all
Who'll look to God and live!

Sharon Velluto

Just as a plant must reach its leaves toward the light, just as the Israelites had to look up to the staff to be saved, we also need to look to the Savior. Only through His atonement can we be saved. "*I am the way, the truth, and the life; no man cometh unto the Father, but by me.*" (John 14:6)

Look unto me, and be ye saved, all the ends of the earth: for I am God, and there is none else (Isaiah 45: 22)

ACTIVITY IDEAS

- Soak a pine cone in water overnight. Remove from the water and sprinkle the pine cone with grass seed. Place it in a sunny spot, in a shallow bowl, containing a small amount of water. In a few weeks a little tree will grow. It will need to be shaped a little with scissors. Observe with your children, how the needles point upward toward the light. (You'll need to start now in order to have your tree by Christmas.)
- Make sugar cookie trees. (See the recipe, "*Mom's Butter Cookies*" in Optional Materials, page 69)
- An old Reader's Digest, or similar magazines, can be folded to make paper trees. Fold each individual page as shown in the illustration to the right. Making folds crisp, makes the tree look better. Spray paint gold, silver, white or green, or use spray snow.

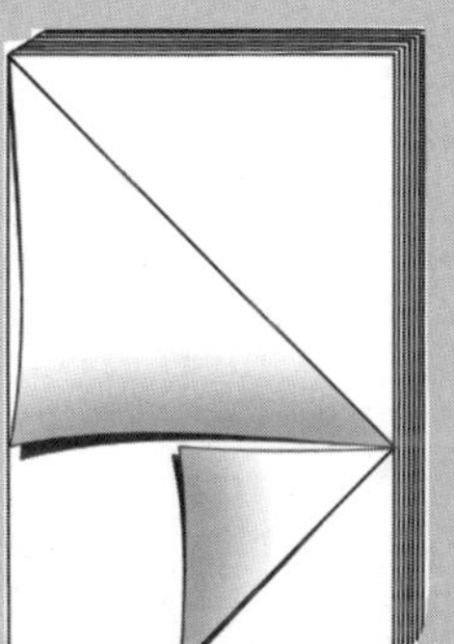

- Learn the song *Oh Christmas Tree* or *O Tannenbaum.* Words are found in Optional Materials, page 70.
- Fill a bucket with rocks, wood, or toys. Place it on the floor and mark another spot on the floor about 3 feet away. Work as a team to move the bucket from its place on the floor to the other space marked, without using hands. Discuss what it means to be dependent on someone else. What is the difference between depending on the "arm of flesh" and depending on God? See Jeremiah 17:5, and Topical Guide, "*Trust Not in the Arm of Flesh.*"

SUGGESTED SONGS

Christmas songs in Italics

CHILDREN'S SONGBOOK

Song	Page
He Sent His Son	34
Who Is the Child	46
Sleep, Little Jesus	47
Oh, Hush Thee, My Baby	48
He Died That We Might Live Again	65
To Think about Jesus	71
Help Us, O God, to Understand	73
On a Golden Springtime	88
Seek the Lord Early	108
I Want to Live the Gospel	148
I Will Follow God's Plan	164

HYMNS

Song	Page
Once in Royal David's City	205
Away in a Manger	206
How Firm a Foundation (all verses)	85
How Great Thou Art	86
I Need Thee Every Hour	98
Nearer, Dear Savior, to Thee	99
Precious Savior, Dear Redeemer	103
Come, Follow Me	116
When Faith Endures	128
Jesus, the Very Thought of Thee (vs.3)	141
Lord, I Would Follow Thee	220

ORNAMENT

Christmas Tree

- This ornament consists of two pieces, found on page 239.

Glad Tidings

IN A NUTSHELL

Angels are divine messengers, sent to minister for the Lord. Throughout history, our Heavenly Father has sent angels to teach, enlighten and bring joy to His children. The angel Gabriel was sent to Mary, bringing her the joyous message of the birth of Christ. Gabriel also brought news to Zacharias about the birth of his son, John. And it was angels who brought glad tidings of Christ's birth to the shepherds that first Christmas night.

LESSON

There are angels on top of many Christmas trees. There are angels that move and angels that hang. Just about anywhere there are Christmas decorations, you are likely to see an angel or two. What exactly are angels and why are they a part of the Christmas celebration?

Angels are divine messengers sent to minister for the Lord. It was the angel Gabriel who brought the remarkable message to Mary that she would be the mother of God's Son.

The angel Gabriel, also told Zacharias about a miracle son that would be born to him and Elisabeth. His name would be John. Later known as "The Baptist," John would prepare the way for Jesus Christ. (See Luke 1:11-25, 57-64)

"...The angel Gabriel was sent from God unto a city of Galilee, named Nazareth,

To a virgin espoused to a man whose name was Joseph, of the house of David; and the virgin's name was Mary.

And the angel came in unto her, and said, Hail, thou that art highly favored, the Lord is with thee: blessed art thou among women.

And when she saw him, she was troubled at his saying, and cast in her mind what manner of salutation this should be.

And the angel said unto her, fear not, Mary: for thou hast found favour with God.

And, behold, thou shalt conceive in thy womb, and bring forth a son, and shalt call his name JESUS.

He shall be great, and shall be called the Son of the Highest: and the Lord God shall give unto him the throne of his father David:

And he shall reign over the house of Jacob for ever; and of his kingdom there shall be no end.

Then said Mary unto the angel, How shall this be, seeing I know not a man?

And the angel answered and said unto her, The Holy Ghost shall come upon thee, and the power of the Highest shall overshadow thee: therefore also that holy thing which shall be born of thee shall be called the Son of God.

And, behold, thy cousin Elisabeth, she hath also conceived a son in her old age: and this is the sixth month with her, who was called barren.

For with God nothing shall be impossible.

And Mary said, Behold the handmaid of the Lord; be it unto me according to thy word. And the angel departed from her.

And Mary said, My soul doth magnify the Lord, And my spirit hath rejoiced in God my Savior." (Luke 1: 26-38, 46-47)

Joseph, Mary's husband, had also seen an angel in a dream, who gave him instruction about the course he was to follow. (See Matthew 1:18-25, 2:13) And it was angels who brought the glad tidings of Christ's birth to the shepherds that very first Christmas.

"And there were in the same country shepherds abiding in the field, keeping watch over their flock by night.

And, lo, the angel of the Lord came upon them, and the glory of the Lord shone round about them: and they were sore afraid.

And the angel said unto them, Fear not: for, behold, I bring you good tidings of great joy, which shall be to all people.

For unto you is born this day in the city of David a Savior, which is Christ the Lord.

And this shall be a sign unto you; Ye shall find the babe wrapped in swaddling clothes, lying in a manger.

And suddenly there was with the angel a multitude of heavenly host praising God, and saying, Glory to God in the highest, and on earth peace, good will toward men." (Luke 2:8-14)

Angels a sacred watch were keeping
Even while the newborn Christ was sleeping.
They joyously praised Him
with all of their might
Telling news of Christ's birth
on that special night.

If God were to send a message to me
Would I listen? And what would it be?
I think it would be as it was then,
"Peace on earth, good will toward men."

Suzanne Meredith

Artists often render angels with halos and wings. Halos are a representation of the light which angels radiate. Wings symbolize their ability to come from and return to God's presence. (See D&C 77:4, 2 Samuel 22:11, Psalm 18:10)

Joseph Smith received many special messages from angels. He taught us that angels do not have wings. (See *Teachings of the Prophet Joseph Smith,*, Salt Lake City: Deseret book, 1976, p. 163)

Imagine, receiving a message sent from God, and brought especially to you by an angel!

ACTIVITY IDEAS

- Send all family members to different rooms or areas of the house. Parents decide on a "Glad Tiding" to be delivered by an "Angelic" family member. (Such as: "Meet in the kitchen for a special treat" or "Go get in the car, we are going Christmas shopping." etc.)
- Play a game of WHO'S THAT ANGEL? Use the cards in the Optional Materials page 179 or make up some of your own. Try to guess the angel. Another variation would be to play charades of "famous angels."
- Learn about other angels. Here are some suggestions:

  Genesis 21:17; Genesis 24:7; Genesis 31:11; Exodus 33:2; Judges 6:22; Judges 13; 1 Kings 13:18; 2 Kings 1:15; Psalms 91:11; Psalms 104:4; Daniel 3:28; Daniel 6:22; Daniel 9:21; Matthew 4:6; Matthew 4:11; Matthew 17:3; Matthew 28:2; Luke 1:11-20; Luke 1:26-38; Luke 2:9-14; Luke 15:10; Luke 22:43; John 20:12; Acts 5:19; Acts 10:30; Acts 12:7-11; Acts 27: 23-24; Hebrews 1:7,14; Hebrews 13:2; Revelation 5:11-12; Revelation 14: 6; Revelation 22:16; 1 Nephi 3:29-31; 1 Nephi 11; 2 Nephi 32:3; Mosiah 3:2; Mosiah 27:18; Alma 8:14; Helaman 5:48; Helaman 16:14; D&C 13:1; D&C 27:12; D&C 103:19; D&C 110; D&C 128:20-21; Moses 5; Moses 7:27.

  OTHER REFERENCES: Topical Guide: Priesthood, Keys of; *Doctrines of Salvation*: volume. 1, p.196, volume. 2, p.110; *History of the Church*: Volume. 1 p. 69, Volume. 2, p. 428, 433; *Teachings of the Prophet Joseph Smith*, p. 158, p. 265; Mormon Doctrine, pp. 341-342

SUGGESTED SONGS

Christmas songs in Italics

CHILDREN'S SONGBOOK

Stars Were Gleaming...............................37
There Was Starlight on the Hillside.......40
Once within a Lowly Stable.........................41
Who Is the Child?...............................46
Sleep, Little Jesus..................................47
Oh, Hush Thee, My Baby..........................48
Picture a Christmas...............................50
The Nativity Song...................................52
An Angel Came to Joseph Smith..............86
The Golden Plates......................................86
On a Golden Springtime............................88
Book of Mormon Stories (Verse 3)...........118

HYMNS

Angels We Have Heard on High............203
Silent Night...204
It Came upon the Midnight Clear............207
Hark! the Herald Angels Sing...............209
While Shepherds Watched Their Flocks....211
Far, Far, Away on Judea"s Plains..............212
The First Noel.......................................213
The Spirit of God.......................................2
Israel, Israel, God Is Calling (vs. 3).........7
Come, Rejoice (vs.2)................................9
What Was Witnessed in the Heavens?..........11
An Angel from on High..........................13
I Saw a Mighty Angel Fly..........................15
What Glorious Scenes Mine Eyes...(vs 2)......16

ORNAMENT

Angel

- This ornament consists of one piece, found on page 241.

Seek and Ye Shall Find

IN A NUTSHELL

The Christmas candy cane is shaped like a shepherd's crook, to serve as a reminder of the role of the shepherds that first Christmas. After hearing the angel's joyous message, the shepherds went to Bethlehem to seek *"the babe wrapped in swaddling clothes, lying in a manger."* (Luke 2:12) When at last they found Him, they rejoiced. Like the shepherds, each honest soul has been challenged to seek and to find Him.

LESSON

Because of ancient prophesies, the Israelites were anxiously awaiting a mighty King, a Messiah, who would come to save them.

Israel knew that the Messiah would be a descendent of King David, (Isaiah 11:1) and would be born in Bethlehem, David's city of birth. (Micah 5:2) They knew that He would to be born of a virgin. (Isaiah 7:14)

In fulfillment of these prophesies, *"There went out a decree from Caesar Augustus, that all the world should be taxed."* (Luke 2:1) Each person, according to Jewish tradition, went to the city of their ancestry. Joseph and Mary, both of David's line, went to Bethlehem to be counted on the census and taxed. The journey from Nazareth to Bethlehem was 80 long, difficult miles, and Mary was *"great with child." "And so it was, that, while they were there, the days were accomplished that she should be delivered. And she brought forth her first born son, and wrapped him in swaddling clothes, and laid him in a manger; because there was no room for them in the inn."* (Luke 2:6-7)

On the hillsides of Bethlehem, shepherds were keeping watch over their sheep by night. *"And, lo, the angel of the Lord came upon them, and the glory of the Lord shone round about them: and they were sore afraid. And the angel said unto them, Fear not: for, behold, I bring you good tidings of great joy, which shall be to all people. For unto you is born this day in the city of David a Saviour, which is Christ the Lord."* (Luke 2:9-11)

Bethlehem, was crowded to overflowing with caravans of people who had come from many different cities and countries to be taxed, just as Joseph and Mary had. With the multitudes of tax payers in the city that night, there would surely be many infants. How could the shepherds know which baby was the infant King? *"And this shall be a sign unto you;"* explained the angel, *"Ye shall find the babe wrapped in swaddling clothes, lying in a manger."* (Luke 2:12)

Swaddling clothes are pieces of fabric which are wound tightly around a baby to keep him warm and make him feel safe. These swaddling clothes were very common at the time. It would not be an uncommon thing to find many newborns wrapped in them. It would be unusual, however, to find a newborn baby laying in a manger, which is a dirty, germ-filled trough used for feeding animals.

After giving his God-given message to the shepherds, *"there was with the angel a multitude of heavenly host praising God, and saying, Glory to God in the highest, and on earth peace, good will toward men. And it came to pass, as the angels were gone away from them into heaven, the shepherds said one to another, Let us now go even unto Bethlehem, and see this thing which is come to pass, which the Lord hath made known unto us."* (Luke 2:13-15) The shepherds hurried from inn to inn, from stable to stable. These inns, or *kahn,* as they were often called were usually large stone buildings with a large inner court in the center, where the animals were tethered. This central court was surrounded by little recesses which had no front door. Everything was open, and everything which took place was in full view to all. There was no furniture inside, and the kahn were often dirty. In Bethlehem many of these"inns" were located in large caves which are very common to that area.

After searching diligently for the baby, the shepherds finally, *" found Mary, and Joseph, and the babe lying in a manger. And when they had seen it, they made known abroad the saying which was told them concerning this child. And all that heard it wondered at those things which were told them by the shepherds. And the shepherds returned, glorifying and praising God for all the things which they had heard and seen, as it was told unto them."* (Luke 2:16-18, 20)

Imagine, being told by an angel of God, after 4000 years of waiting, that very night, in their own, small town of Bethlehem, the Son of God had been born! Imagine what those humble shepherds must have felt as they searched for the Baby!

Although we may not have been a shepherd that eventful night in Bethlehem, each honest, searching, human soul has been given the same commission -- to seek Him and to find Him.

ACTIVITY IDEAS

- SEARCH FOR THE CHRIST CHILD. Dress a few dolls and put them in different rooms of the house. Dress one in swaddling clothes and lay it in a box with shredded newspaper. (manger) The other dolls may be dressed normally, or in swaddling clothes. Place them on pillows or in beds. Have the "shepherds" go from door to door to search for the Christ Child. As each baby is found, discuss why it is not the baby Jesus.
- Shepherds use a long wooden crook to gently lead straying sheep back to the safety of the flock. Our Christmas candy cane is shaped like a shepherd's crook reminding us of the role of the shepherds in the Christmas story. Use the recipe for taffy in Optional Materials, page 79. Divide the taffy in half and work red food coloring into one half, leaving the other half white. After the taffy has been cooled and pulled, give each child a small piece of white and a small piece of red to twist together and make a candy cane.
- Simple candy canes can also be made by twisting red and white chenille wires, or by threading red and white beads alternately onto a chenille stem. Colored cookie dough, rolled into snakes is also a fun way to make candy canes. Use the cookie recipe on page 69, or one of the recipes on page 118. (Go "find" a neighbor or someone else who needs a visit, and give the candy canes to them. By finding a way to serve others, we are really "finding" Jesus)
- Play MY BROTHER'S KEEPER game in Optional Materials, page 181.
- Try a new variation of "*Hide and Seek*" called "*Sardines.*" One person is chosen to seek while the other members of the family go to hide. However, everyone must squeeze into the same hiding place.
- Read the three parables Jesus told: *The Lost Coin, The Lost Sheep,* and *The Prodigal Son.* Why would Jesus tell three stories about things that are lost? Study and discuss the ways they became lost. The coin was lost by accident or negligence, the lamb wandered off away from the flock, the Prodigal Son made a poor choice. These are the same ways people become lost as well.

SUGGESTED SONGS

Christmas songs in Italics

CHILDREN'S SONGBOOK

Stars Were Gleaming 37
The Shepherd's Carol..............................40
Once within a Lowly Stable.....................41
Away in a Manger..................................42
Who Is the Child...................................46
Sleep, Little Jesus..................................47
The Nativity Song...................................52
I Pray in Faith..14
Seek the Lord Early...............................108
Search, Ponder, And Pray.......................109

HYMNS

Oh, Come, All Ye Faithful.........................202
While Shepherds Watched Their Flocks....211
Far, Far Away on Judea's Plains.............212
The First Noel.......................................213
The Lord Is My Shepherd........................108
The Lord My Pasture Will Prepare.........109
Come, Ye Disconsolate...........................115
Come, Follow Me....................................116
Ye Simple Souls Who Stray.......................118
Dear to the Heart of the Shepherd............221

ORNAMENT

Shepherd/Candy Cane

- This ornament consists of 2 pieces, found on page 243.

Joy to the World

IN A NUTSHELL

Music has a powerful influence on both the spirit and the mind of men. It has power for both good and evil. While bad music can "pollute and poison" the mind, good music can uplift and inspire, and help one to replace negative or degrading thoughts. Singing hymns of praise is an effective way to worship our Heavenly Father, who loves to hear our songs. "*For the song of the righteous is a prayer unto me...*" (D&C 25:12)

LESSON

Have you ever noticed how music can intensify feelings? Christmas music often creates a festive feeling and brings a spirit of love. Listening to or singing Christmas carols adds fun to our holidays. Singing songs about the Savior, brings feelings of joy and peace.

Songs are a way to pray to God and praise Him. Often prayers are answered through the words of an inspired song. "*Music is an effective way to worship our Heavenly Father and his Son Jesus Christ.*" (Elder Franklin D. Richards, *Ensign*, November 1982, pages 22-25)

Heavenly Father has said that He loves to hear our songs. "*For my soul delighteth in the song of the heart; yea, the song of the righteous is a prayer unto me, and shall be answered with a blessing upon their heads.* (D&C 25:12)

Each year, millions of dollars are spent on musical scores for movies. Directors are very careful to place appropriate music in just the right places to create the mood they want their viewers to feel. By doing this, even something simple, like a candlelight dinner can be made to seem either frightening, romantic or sad just by the type of music which is played in the background.

William Gladstone, said, "*Music is one of the most forceful instruments for governing the mind and spirit of man.*"

Music has great power for both good and evil. In a Priesthood bulletin, the First Presidency stated, "*Through music man's ability to express himself extends beyond the limits of the spoken language in both subtlety and power.* " (First Presidency, "*Priesthood Bulletin,*" August 1973)

Listening to sad music can bring the spirit down without even realizing it. Some music may even dull the senses or bring evil thoughts. Uplifting music can inspire and bring peace. In fact, music is sometimes used in hospitals as a form of therapy. Many people listen to music to relax, lighten their mood, or to replace degrading thoughts.

Our leaders have taught us that the right kind of music can prepare our minds to receive inspiration, and put us in tune with the Spirit of the Lord. Elder Boyd K. Packer taught that hymns can be an effective tool to chase evil thoughts from the stage of our mind. (See Boyd K. Packer, *Ensign*, January 1979, pages 25-28 and Dallin Oaks, *Ensign*, November 1994, page 10)

"*Music has a very powerful and wonderful influence in establishing feelings and moods that can lift and elevate your thoughts and your actions. But because it is so powerful, it is cleverly used by the adversary to stimulate your thoughts, feelings and moods; to pollute and poison your mind and cause you to do things you would not otherwise consider doing.*" (Ardeth G. Kapp, *Ensign*, November 1990, page 94)

Although Christmas is a time when it seems easier to choose uplifting music, all through the year we should be careful of the type of music we allow into our minds and hearts. " *Of course we can choose; the free agency is ours, but we cannot escape the consequences of our choices. And if there is a chink in our integrity, that is where the devil concentrates his attack.*" (Spencer W. Kimball, *Ensign*, March 1980, page 2)

Elder Neal A Maxwell said, "*When we rejoice in beautiful scenery, great art and great music,it is but the flexing of instincts acquired in another place and another time.*" (Neal A. Maxwell, *Ensign*, April 1984, page 21)

"*Music is truly the universal language, and when it is excellently expressed, how deeply it moves our souls!*" (President David O. McKay, *Improvement Era*, 1945, 48:309)

Come, we that love the Lord,
And let our joys be known.
Join in a song with sweet accord,
And worship at his throne.

(Hymns # 119 Isaac Watts, 1694-1748)

ACTIVITY IDEAS

- Go Christmas caroling.
- As a family, tour some different stores, restaurants etc. and notice what type of music is played. Notice that in many stores, music is often slower because the merchant wants the buyer to take his time.
- Choose a simple melody and make up your own "Family Carol" by putting words to it, or make up a new verse to one of your favorite Christmas songs.
- Select some various types of music, ie. sad, happy, marching, scary, etc. Listen to the songs and discuss feelings felt with each piece. For younger children, give them some crayons and paper to draw what they feel. Notice colors and lines.
  OPTIONAL IDEA: Select a section of a video, turn the volume down, and listen to each type of music as the background music for the same segment.
- Check out an old silent movie to watch as a family. Pay particular attention to how the music helps tell the story.
- Choose a "song leader" to direct the family. Sing fast or slow according to the pace the leader directs. Stop, even in the middle of a word, and do not begin singing again until the leader indicates. Younger children really enjoy leading and following them can really keep you on your toes also!
- Cut out the cards in the Optional Materials, page 183 and use them to add some extra fun to your favorite songs. (ie. boys only, girls only, high, low, loud, soft, hum etc.) To better preserve the cards mount on card stock or cover with contact paper.
- Make musical instruments to accompany your favorite songs. Tape two spoons together. (Use a small ball of tape between the handles) Make a drum from an oatmeal box, (or pots and pans if you can stand the noise!) Cover one end of an empty paper roll with wax paper, secure with a rubber band, and use it as a kazoo. Make a shaker by covering both ends of a paper tube. Fill it with rice, popcorn or small beans, or put beans inside two paper plates and staple the edges together. Fill bottles or glasses with different levels of water and tap with a spoon, or blow across the tops of the bottles. Stretch rubber bands across an old tissue box or shoe box and pluck. Tape drinking straws together and blow into them like a harmonica
- Read the words to a favorite Christmas carol, leaving out any word which refers to Christ, even words like Him, His, He etc. Discuss what was missing. This can help everyone to realize that Christ is what Christmas is all about.

SUGGESTED SONGS

Christmas songs in Italics

CHILDREN'S SONGBOOK

Song	Page
All Christmas Songs on pages	34-54
Hosanna	66
Hum Your Favorite Hymn	152
Sing Your Way Home	193
"Give." Said the Little Stream	236
Lift Up Your Voice and Sing	252
Fun to Do	253

HYMNS

Hymn	Number
All Christmas Hymns Numbers	201-204
Come, Sing to the Lord	10
Come, Ye Children of the Lord	58
All Creatures of Our God and King	62
Come, We That Love the Lord	119
I Believe in Christ	134

ORNAMENT

Book of Carols

- This ornament consists of 2 pieces, found on pages 231 and 245.

The Lost Sheep and the Good Shepherd

IN A NUTSHELL

At night, in Palestine, sheep were brought to a sheep fold where one shepherd stood watch over them. In the morning, each shepherd returned to the sheep fold to gather his sheep. The sheep recognized and trusted their master's voice and came when called. To illustrate His great love for all of His Father's children, Jesus shared the parable of "The Lost Sheep." He further taught, "*I am the good shepherd; the good shepherd giveth his life for the sheep.*" (John 10:11) Our Savior's love for us is unconditional.

LESSON

In Jesus' day, at night in Palestine, sheep were brought to a safe place called a sheep fold. It had high walls with thorns on top to keep anything or anyone from getting in. Several flocks were brought into one fold and one of the shepherds (called a *porter*) would stand guard so that the other shepherds could go home to rest. In the morning, each shepherd came come to call his own flock and lead them to the pasture. The sheep knew and trusted their shepherd. They would not follow a stranger. The shepherd usually had a name for each of his sheep. They knew their master's voice and each came when he was called.

Often a shepherd hung a bell around the neck of his sheep. The sound of the bell helped the shepherd to keep track of the sheep while they grazed in the pasture. It also helped him to find any sheep that may have strayed away from the flock. The soft tinkling of the bells helped the sheep to feel safe. The sound of the shepherd's voice meant even more than safety— it meant love.

If a thief or a wild animal came to steal or kill any of the sheep, a hired man might run away because it would be too dangerous to fight for the sheep. A good shepherd, however, would risk putting himself in danger to protect the sheep because he loved them.

Just as the shepherd loves each of the sheep in his flock , our Savior loves His sheep. His love for them is unconditional. "*I am the good shepherd; the good shepherd giveth his life for the sheep.*" (John 10:11)

To illustrate His love for each of us, the Savior told the following parable:

"What man of you, having an hundred sheep, if he lose one of them, doth not leave the ninety and nine in the wilderness, and go after that which is lost, until he find it?

And when he hath found it, he layeth it on his shoulders, rejoicing.

And when he cometh home, he calleth together his friends and his neighbours, saying unto them, Rejoice with me; for I have found my sheep which was lost.

I say unto you, that likewise joy shall be in heaven over one sinner that repenteth, more than over ninety and nine just persons, which need no repentance." (Luke 15:4-7)

"*My sheep hear my voice, and I know them, and they follow me:*" (John 10:27)

Jesus promised that one day there would be one fold and one shepherd. (See Matthew 18:16 and 3 Nephi 16:3)

MARY'S LAMB
(original version)

Mary had a little lamb,
Its fleece was white as snow,
And everywhere that Mary went
The lamb was sure to go;

He followed her to school one day —
That was against the rule,
It made the children laugh and play,
To see the lamb at school

And so the Teacher turned him out,
But still he lingered near,
And waited patiently about,
Till Mary did appear;

And then he ran to her, and laid
His head upon her arm.
As if he said — 'I'm not afraid —
You'll keep me from all harm.'

'What makes the lamb love Mary so?'
The eager children cry---
'O, Mary loves the lamb, you know,'
The Teacher did reply;

'And you each gentle animal
In confidence may bind,
And make them follow at your call,
If you are always kind.'

Sarah Josepha Hale
(1788-1879)

ACTIVITY IDEAS

- Play HIDE AND SEEK with the "Shepherd" looking for the rest of the family who are his "Lost Sheep." If you have bells, each sheep can softly tinkle the bell to lead the shepherd in his search.
- Blindfold a family member and have him try to recognize another family member's voice. Liken this to the sheep who knows his master's voice.

  OPTIONAL IDEA: Have the "shepherd call out directions of how to reach an appointed place to the blindfolded "sheep" while other family members call out distractions. The sheep must listen very carefully in order to distinguish the "shepherd's " voice from the others.
- Bake an almond (or other small edible thing) into a batch of cupcakes or cookies. Be certain to warn your children that it is there before eating. Tell the parable of the lost coin in Luke 15:8-10 or New Testament Stories, *Jesus Tells Three Stories.*

  OPTIONAL IDEA: Select one family member to hide a coin and another to find it. (You can give clues "hot" and "cold" if needed.) Take turns until each person has had a chance to hide and to seek.
- Take one piece out of a favorite board puzzle. Talk about how the puzzle looks and how it feels to have lost that piece. Stress how important it is to you that each family member stays safe and strong both physically and spiritually. Read the story of "*The Prodigal Son*" in Luke 15: 11-32 or New Testament Stories, *Jesus Tells Three Stories.*

  OPTIONAL IDEA: Have you ever lost a small piece to something? To others it may have seemed insignificant but actually was really important. We are all important to our Heavenly Father. Read and discuss Matthew 11:29-32.
- Make a simple obstacle course which "the shepherd" must follow to reach the "sheep." (A rolled up sock or something similar will work as a sheep.) Discuss how a good shepherd would often even sacrifice his own safety for the safety of his sheep.
- Hide cotton balls (sheep) and have the children find their flock. (an assigned number)

  OPTIONAL IDEA: The cotton balls can be colored and a different color assigned to each shepherd, who then finds only the sheep of his flock. (Use colored chalk, tempera paint or dampened watercolors)

SUGGESTED SONGS

Christmas songs in Italics

CHILDREN'S SONGBOOK

Christmas Bells....54
Tell Me the Stories of Jesus....57
Little Lambs So White and Fair....58
Jesus Is Our Loving Friend....58
Jesus Loved the Little Children....59
Help Us, O God, to Understand....73
I Feel My Savior's Love....74
God Is Watching Over All....229

HYMNS

Oh, Come, All Ye Faithful....202
Away in a Manger....206
O Little Town of Bethlehem....208
Redeemer of Israel (vs. 2)....6
The Lord Is My Shepherd....108
The Lord My Pasture Will Prepare....109
Come, Follow Me....116
Dear to the Heart of the Shepherd....221
Come, All Ye Son's of God (vs. 2)....322

ORNAMENT

Bell

- This ornament consists of two pieces, found on page 247.

The Lamb of God

IN A NUTSHELL

The lamb which the Jews sacrificed during Passover was a special symbol of the sacrifice the "Lamb of God" would one day make. According to God's command, this special sacrificial lamb had to be a firstborn male, without blemish, in the first year. Jesus Christ, the firstborn and only begotten Son of the Father, was the lamb chosen by God, even before the foundation of the world, to be an infinite and eternal sacrifice, that all of God's children might be redeemed from the bondage of sin and death. Understanding this, John the Baptist testified, *"Behold the Lamb of God, which taketh away the sins of the world."* (John 1:29.30)

LESSON

Each year in early spring, all of the house of Israel gathered together to celebrate the Passover. The observance of this yearly celebration was a commandment of God. The feast was to serve as a reminder of their deliverance from Egyptian slavery.

When Moses was commanded to lead the children of Israel out of Egyptian bondage, the pharaoh refused to let them go. God sent ten different plagues to the Egyptians. The pharaoh didn't like the plagues of flies, and lice, and frogs and boils, and dead cattle. He told Moses to ask God to remove the plagues and then he would let the Israelites go. But, each time the plague was removed Pharaoh changed his mind, and refused to free the Israelites. God revealed to Moses that all the firstborn children in Egypt would be killed. The Israelites were told to paint the blood of a lamb on the top and sides of their doors. This would protect their families from the plague. The lamb couldn't be just any lamb, it had to be:

1. Male
2. Firstborn
3. In the first year
4. Without blemish (See Exodus 12:5)

The Israelites painted the blood of the lamb on the door and stayed in their houses all night. During the night the first born son of every home died. But, the angel of destruction passed by the homes where the blood of the lamb had been painted. Those first born children were not killed. The Passover feast was a time to remember the night that the angel of destruction "passed over" all of the houses which had the blood of the lamb painted above their doors. They remembered how the blood of the lamb had saved them.

During the Passover, every male twelve years and older was presented at the temple. Each family brought or purchased a firstborn, male lamb without spot, to be sacrificed and eaten by the family during this feast.

The lamb was to be killed and cooked in the way specified by God. The neck had to be cut, and the blood spilled out. The lamb was roasted whole without breaking any bones. The entire lamb was to be eaten that night. If the family was small, a lamb could be shared between two families, but any leftovers were to be burned. (Exodus 12:4.10) It was necessary to prepare the lamb in this special way because it was a symbol of Jesus Christ. When Jesus was crucified, no bones were broken, but the spear pierced His side and His blood was spilt. His atoning blood can save us from destruction.

To ancient Israel, God commanded that the Passover feast was to be eaten in haste, standing up, with shoes on their feet. (Exodus 12:11) This was to remind the Israelites of the night they fled from Egypt. In Jesus' day the meal was eaten while reclining on pillows. (Not at all like any of the pictures we see of the Last Supper) Laying down and relaxing was a reminder of their new life of rest, repose and freedom. (This makes it easier to understand how John could be laying on the Master's breast during the Last Supper, which was the Passover supper. See John 13:25, 21:20)

The Jews, in Jesus' day had been observing the Passover for almost 1500 years and understood well that the sacrificial lamb represented the means by which God had delivered them from Egyptian bondage. John the Baptist, whose mission it was to witness of the Christ, declared, *"Behold the Lamb of God, which taketh away the sins of the world."* (John 1:29,30) Though we may have heard this statement repeated many times and often give it little thought, John had not used this statement casually. John the Baptist selected 13 carefully calculated words to bear witness of the Christ, and he understood fully their deep meaning. John the revelator added his witness to that of John the Baptist's when he said that Jesus was the *"lamb slain from the foundation the world."* (Revelation 13:8)

Jesus Christ, the firstborn and only begotten Son of the Father , was the Lamb which God had chosen, even before the foundation of the world, as an infinite and eternal sacrifice, that all of God's children might be redeemed from the bondage of sin and death.

At the Last Supper, Jesus introduced a new "feast", a new symbol to remember Him. It was the sacrament. He said that the Passover would not be observed any longer.

ACTIVITY IDEAS

- Number some small cards from one to forty, and place .them around the house in order. Each number represents one year in the wilderness. Gather the cards from around the house. Help your family escape from Egypt, cross the Red Sea, (Blankets can be used for the parting of the water) and wander in the wilderness. (exaggerate the moaning and complaining) For additional help and ideas see "*Wandering in the Wilderness*" Optional Materials, page 94.
- THE LAMB HUNT: Hide the lambs provided in the Optional Materials pages 185 and 187 throughout the house. (You may want to dress as a shepherd and explain that you have lost your sheep) See Lamb Hunt instructions in Optional Materials, page 93 for further explanation.
- LEAVENING: Show a loaf of regular bread and a loaf of pita bread. Explain that one has leaven and one does not. Ask: "What does leaven do? It makes a gas to make bread and cakes rise. We use two kinds of leaven today. One is yeast. One is baking powder. With a funnel, put 1-2 Tablespoons of baking powder in a balloon. (yeast and sugar water works the same but takes longer) Fill a narrow mouth bottle with about a cup of vinegar. (A pop bottle works well) Stretch the balloon over the mouth of the bottle, letting all of the baking powder fall into the vinegar. The combination of these two substances creates a gas which will blow up the balloon.
- Go on a LEAVEN HUNT. Before Passover, Jews clean their entire house of leaven. What would need to be thrown out? Bread. cake, cookies, crackers, cereal, etc Explain that for Jews, cleaning their homes of leaven is a solemn thing. For eight days Jews do not eat anything made with leaven. They eat only unleavened bread called matzoh. Sometimes in the scriptures, the Passover is called the "*Feast of Unleavened Bread* ," because there is a feast of seven days following the Passover called the "*Feast of Unleavened Bread.*" Leaven is a symbol for sin. Just as Jews clean their houses of leaven, we need to clean our lives of all sin through baptism and repentance.
- Prepare a small Passover feast using the following.

  Bitter herbs (use romaine lettuce or horseradish)
  Green Herbs (lettuce, watercress, celery or parsley) dipped in water
  Haroseth *
  Matzoh or Pita bread*

  * (See the recipes in Optional Materials, page 95)

  You may also want to tell about Elijah and why the Jews open the door for him at the Passover. (See #12 in the Passover article under the "Sequence of the Seder," page 99)

SUGGESTED SONGS

Christmas songs in Italics

CHILDREN'S SONGBOOK

Song	Page
He Sent His Son	34
Little Jesus	39
Who Is the Child?	46
Little Lambs So White and Fair	58
He Died That We Might Live Again	65
To Think about Jesus	71
The Sacrament	72
Before I Take the Sacrament	73
Help Us, Oh God, to Understand	73

HYMNS

Song	Page
Joy to the World	201
Oh, Come, All Ye Faithful	202
In Humility, Our Savior	172
While of These Emblems We Partake	174
O God, the Eternal Father	175
We'll Sing All Hail to Jesus Name	182
In Remembrance of Thy Suffering	183
God Loved Us, So He Sent His Son	187
In Memory of the Crucified	190

ORNAMENT

Sheep

- This ornament consists of 7 pieces. found on page 249.

In Wisdom's Path

IN A NUTSHELL

Wisdom is a gift of the spirit given to the righteous. It is a blessing given to those who learn and apply basic eternal principles of truth. The scriptures teach of "Wise men" who came from the East to worship the Christ Child. These men had studied not only science and astronomy, but understood ancient scripture and prophecy as well. Applying what they had learned, they came to Bethlehem, in search of the Messiah. When they found Him, they bowed and worshiped Him. Those who are diligent and obedient to God's commandments, who have learned and applied gospel truths are blessed with that deep understanding of spiritual truth called wisdom.

LESSON

Sometime following the birth of Jesus there came men from the East to worship Him. These men are referred to in scripture as "Wise men." Wisdom is the ability to understand truth, and apply it to make good choices. Wisdom is a gift of the spirit given to the righteous. In order to obtain the blessing of the gift of wisdom, one must follow the basic eternal pattern set forth by God.

First: Learn the truth: The Prophet Joseph Smith said, *"A man is saved no faster than he gets knowledge, for if he does not get knowledge, he will be brought into captivity by some evil power in the other world, as evil spirits will have more knowledge and consequently more power, than many men who are on the earth. "* (*History of The Church of Jesus Christ of Latter-Day Saints*, Volume. 4, Salt Lake City: Deseret Book, 1978, page 588)

The Wise Men were very learned men. They had studied and learned much of science, astronomy, and other important subjects, but they also knew the words of God. They had studied the scriptures and knew that a new star would appear in the heavens as a sign for the Messiah's birth. Many people must have seen the star, and even marveled at it. It was prophesied that the star would be, *"such an one as ye never beheld."* (Helaman 14:5)

However, not everyone who witnessed the star understood its significance, and most must have dismissed it as some remarkable phenomenon of nature.

Second: Apply the truth: President Joseph F. Smith said, *"Pure intelligence comprises not only knowledge, but also the power to properly apply that knowledge."* (*Gospel Doctrine*, 5th ed. Salt Lake City :Deseret Book Co. 1939, page 58) The Wise Men saw the star and knew what it meant. So they gathered together some of their most valuable possessions to offer as gifts of worship, and set out to find the Infant King.

The scriptures say, *"And this is life eternal, that they might know thee the only true God, and Jesus Christ whom thou hast sent."* (See John 17:1-6,8,11) But, how is it possible to know at what point one really "knows Him?" John explained that there is a way for man to know. He said, *"And hereby we do know that we know him, if we keep his commandments. He that saith, I know him, and keepeth not his commandments, is a liar, and the truth is not in him."* (1 John 2:3-4) To "know Jesus" we must try to live as He did.

Korihor, a powerful antichrist, taught, *"Behold, ye cannot know of things which ye do not see."* (Alma 30:15) But he was wrong. There is a way to know without seeing. Jesus said, *"If any man will do his will, he shall know of the doctrine, whether it be of God, or whether I speak of myself."* (John 7:17) It has been said that the gospel is not for spectators. It must be lived. James wrote, *"Be ye doers of the word, and not hearers only, deceiving your own selves. "* (James 1:22)

President Ezra Taft Benson said, *"Brothers and sisters and friends, learn this principle. The Lord will increase our knowledge, wisdom and capacity to obey when we obey His fundamental laws.... I do not believe that a member of the Church can have an active, vibrant testimony of the gospel without keeping the commandments. A testimony is to have current inspiration to know the work is true, not something we receive only once. The Holy Ghost abides with those who honor, respect, and obey God's laws. And it is that Spirit which gives inspiration to the individual. Humbly I testify to the reality of this promise. ...Keep the commandments of God and you will have the wisdom to know and discern that which is evil. "* (*Ensign*, May 1983, pages 54-55) Wisdom involves not only hearing the voice of the Shepherd, but following it. (See John 10:27)

Third: Understand the truth: Wisdom is a gift of God, granted to those who have learned and applied the truth. Wisdom is never paraded, but is a gift to be cherished. It is best expressed by living a worthy life. There is a vast difference between wisdom and knowledge. Knowledge is understanding involving the intellect only, while wisdom is an understanding involving both mind and heart. The scriptures tell us that Jesus *"grew and waxed strong in spirit, filled with wisdom."*

(Luke 2:40) *To wax* means to become. At the age of twelve, Jesus taught the learned doctors in the temple. They were "*astonished at his understanding and answers*." (Luke 2:47) Often, after hearing the Savior teach, many were astonished and said, "*Whence hath this man this wisdom?*" (Matthew 13:54)

Yet, even the devils knew and testified that Jesus was the Christ. However, they lacked wisdom and understanding, because the basic, eternal principles of truth had never been applied. Intellectually they knew who Jesus was, and even testified. But, they lacked the spiritual understanding needed to fully recognize and "know" Him. (See Matthew 8:29, Mark 1:34, Luke 4:41) Only those who have paid the price, through obedience, are blessed with that deep understanding of spiritual truth which is called wisdom.

President Kimball made the following promise: "*May I remind all of us that if we live the gospel and follow the counsel of the leaders of the Church, we will be blessed to avoid many of the problems that plague the world. The Lord knows the challenges we face. If we keep his commandments, we will be entitled to the wisdom and blessings of heaven in solving them.*" (*Ensign*, May 1980, page 92)

ACTIVITY IDEAS

- Go on a SCRIPTURE TREASURE HUNT. Cut apart and hide the clues provided in the Optional Materials, page 189. You may want to plan a special birthday cake to remember Jesus' birthday, or some other appropriate treasure. (If covered with contact paper, these clues can be preserved and used again)
- ACTION WORDS GUESSING GAME. Cut apart the cards in Optional Materials, page 191. On each card are printed some action words, and a phrase from a song. Read the action words first and see if the other players can guess the Primary or Christmas song in which those words appear. If they cannot guess, read the phrase as a second clue.

  VARIATION: Act out or draw the title of the song. (To preserve cards, mount on card stock or cover with contact paper.)
- FIND THE STAR: Cut a star out of yellow paper. Have one child leave the room while the rest of the family hides the star. When the child reenters the room, sing the song Twinkle Twinkle little star, How I wonder *where* you are." Sing softly as the child gets further away, and sing louder as he gets nearer to the hidden star.

SUGGESTED SONGS

Christmas songs in Italics

CHILDREN'S SONGBOOK

Stars Were Gleaming....37
Sleep, Little Jesus....47
The Nativity Song....52
I Know My Father Lives....5
Search, Ponder, And Pray....109
Every Star Is Different....142
Keep the Commandments....146
I Will Be Valiant....162
I Am like a Star....163
I Will Follow God's Plan....164
The Wise Man and the Foolish Man....281

HYMNS

Oh, Come, All Ye Faithful....202
Silent Night....204
Once in Royal David's City....205
With Wondering Awe....210
Lead Me into Life Eternal....45
Lord, I Would Follow Thee....220
Choose the Right....239
I'll Go Where You Want Me to Go....270
As I Search the Holy Scriptures....277
Thy Holy Word....279
Teach Me to Walk in the Light....304

ORNAMENT

Wise Men

- This ornament consists of 2 pieces, found on page 251.

Gifts for a Newborn King

IN A NUTSHELL

Anciently, the offering of gifts was customary as an expression of respect or tribute. The Wise Men brought gifts of gold, frankincense, and myrrh to pay homage to the baby Jesus. Jesus has freely offered the gift of repentance to all. In return, He has asked only, "Come Follow Me." Often, following the Savior involves sacrifice. It may mean giving up worldly wealth or position. It may mean accepting an unwanted call to service. Like the Wise Men, we can worship and honor the Savior by offering gifts of love, obedience and service to others.

LESSON

Long ago there lived some very wise men. They had studied the scriptures and the prophesies about a Savior who would come to earth. One night they saw the sign, a new star in the eastern sky. These men gathered up their finest treasures to offer as gifts, left their homes and families and began a very long and sacred journey. These wise men probably had to sacrifice a great deal to bring these simple but valuable gifts to the baby Jesus. They brought gold, frankincense and myrrh as gifts to honor the infant King.

Gold is a precious metal. For ages, it has been a symbol of great value. No substance has ever been sought for more than gold.

Frankincense is a chunky, white resin which comes from trees found in southern Arabia and East Africa. When it is burned, frankincense emits a pleasant odor. It was used for incense burned in the temple. For centuries frankincense was a principal item of trade in the East.

Myrrh is a pale, yellow gum secreted by small trees and shrubs found principally in Arabia, and Ethiopia. When exposed to air, it turns dark and solidifies. In the ancient world, myrrh was a major ingredient in perfumes, incenses, and embalming, and was considered to be of great value.

These three gifts were brought by the Wise Men as an expression of honor for the infant King. Though their gifts were nice, the greater gift was their honor, reverence and respect for Jesus. They knew who this special Baby was, and they came to worship him.

Some humble shepherds were also invited to worship the newborn King. They had no gold, frankincense or myrrh to bring. They brought to the Savior only their humble gift of reverence. Though their gift held no earthly value, it was just as acceptable and prized as that of the Wise Men.

If you had been privileged to visit the baby Jesus, what gift would you have selected to bring?

During Christ's earthly ministry, one of the most important truths He tried to teach people was how insignificant and trivial man's quest for wealth is. Jesus repeatedly cautioned mankind to beware to not let the the cares of the world overtake their hearts. (See Luke 21:34)

"*Take heed, and beware of covetousness: for a man's life consisteth not in the abundance of the things which he possesseth. Seek ye the kingdom of God and all these things shall be added unto you,*" (See Luke 12:15-21, 31)

Jesus taught that the riches of eternity which He offered were free. They could be obtained without money and without price. (See Isaiah 52:3, 55:1, 3 Nephi 20:38)

Richard Fielder said, "*Any pleasure which keeps the heart from God, will be fatal to the soul.*"

"*In this world, it is not what we take up, but what we give up that makes us rich.*" (Henry Ward Beecher)

Jesus extended to all men the invitation, "*Come and follow me.*" (See John 12:26) There are many people in the world who ask that we follow them, but Jesus Christ was the only one worthy to ask such a thing. Sometimes following the Savior is very difficult. He asked us to take up our cross and follow Him. (See Matthew 8:38, 16:24, Mark 8:34, Luke 9:23, D&C 56:2)

Because the Savior and our Heavenly Father understand our individual strengths and weaknesses, "taking up the cross" may demand something different for each person. The rich young ruler, was asked to give up his worldly possessions. (Matthew 19:16-26) Jonah's cross was an unwanted call to service. (Book of Jonah, see also John 12:26) For Saul, it was to give up an old life in exchange for a new one. (Acts 9, see also 2 Nephi 31:10-13) Taking up the cross for both Alma and his son, meant giving up an important position in order to do the work of the Lord. (Mosiah 17:2-3, Alma 4:19) Abraham was asked to sacrifice his son whom he loved. (Genesis 22) And the cross for Joseph Smith and his brother Hyrum, was to seal their testimony with their blood.

Whatever the sacrifice asked of us, Jesus has promised that "*Take my yoke upon you,....and ye shall find rest unto your souls. For my yoke is easy and my burden is light.*" (Matthew 11:29- 30)

The best gift we can offer to the Savior is a gift of self to others. The gift of self brings far more joy and satisfaction than anything which could ever be bought, both to the giver and to the receiver.

ACTIVITY IDEAS

- ♦ Make a list of gifts which do not cost money. For example: A homemade card, a song, a coupon book of services, a poem etc. Clement C. Moore wanted to give a special Christmas gift to his children and wrote the poem, *"The Night Before Christmas."* . Give one of these Christmas gifts to a friend, neighbor, or stranger.
- ♦ Assemble the SHOE in Optional Materials, page 221. Fill with goodies and give it to someone you choose.
- ♦ Spray paint rocks, or use small balls of gold foil. Decorate a small box as a treasure chest. Put a small golden "nugget" in the treasure chest for each act of service given to someone else.
- ♦ Read and discuss the story of *The Widow's Mites* from the *New Testament Stories* or Mark 12:38-44. Jesus recognized in the widow one who may have been poor as to the things of the world, but was *"rich toward God;"* Paul described it as, " *having nothing but possessing all things.* " (2 Corinthians 6:10, see also Matthew 6:19-21)
- ♦ A fun and inexpensive ornament can be made by making a dough consisting of one third cup of cinnamon and two tablespoons of applesauce. (This may need to be adjusted slightly, depending on the consistency of the applesauce.) Roll out like cookie dough and cut out with cookie cutters. Allow these to dry in a warm place for 2-3 days. (Either make a hole in them before drying or glue a ribbon from which to hang them.) The cinnamon apple smell will last for years. Bulk cinnamon can be purchased quite inexpensively.
- ♦ MORE IDEAS FOR SERVICE: Send a letter to a missionary or serviceman, or even a nearby prison. Record a cassette tape to send to someone far from home. Add someone new to your Christmas gift list who may otherwise be forgotten. Participate in *Sub for Santa.* Do the *Twelve Days of Christmas* for someone. Shovel snow, do someone's shopping, fix meals, provide transportation, secretly do someone's chores. Remember that "presence" is often more valued than "presents!" Make a visit to someone who may be lonely. Visit a nursing home or hospital. Parents, give coupons to your children for a date with mom or dad to do a favorite activity. Time with children is much more valuable than any gift which might be purchased with money.

SUGGESTED SONGS

Christmas songs in Italics

CHILDREN'S SONGBOOK

Song	Page
He Sent His Son	34
Jesus Is Our Loving Friend	58
Jesus Wants Me for a Sunbeam	60
Love One Another	136
I'll Walk with You	140
Called to Serve	174
A Happy Helper	197
When We're Helping	198
"Give," Said the Little Stream	236
We Are Different	263

HYMNS

Song	Page
O Little Town Of Bethlehem	208
With Wondering Awe	210
I Heard the Bells on Christmas Day	214
A Poor Wayfaring Man of Grief	29
Come, Follow Me	116
More Holiness Give Me	131
Because I Have Been Given Much	219
Have I Done Any Good?	223
Let Us All Press On	243
Put Your Shoulder to the Wheel	252

ORNAMENT

Treasure Chest

- ♦ This ornament consists of 1 piece, found on page 253.

Gifts from God

IN A NUTSHELL

Christmas is a fun time for giving and receiving gifts. There are two types of gifts. One is the gift which is purchased with money. Another type of gift is one which cannot be bought. Our Heavenly Father has given many of these types of gifts to His children. The sun, the air, water, and health are all examples of gifts which money cannot buy. Christmas is a time to remember the greatest gifts ever given. "*For God so loved the world that he gave his only begotten Son. (John 3:16) Greater love hath no man than this, that a man lay down his life for his friends. Ye are my friends.*" (John 15:13-14)

LESSON

Christmas is a time of gift giving. Festively wrapped packages and exciting secrets are all around. It is great fun to choose a special gift, wrap it and give it to someone. It is also fun to receive gifts which someone has chosen for us.

There are two kinds of gifts. One kind is the kind which is bought with money. Long ago Wise Men brought gifts to Jesus, to honor Him. They brought gold, frankincense and myrrh. These were very precious and valuable gifts. These are the type of gifts which are bought with money. They are nice gifts, but they are gifts which are valuable only on this earth. They must be left behind when we die. We can't take them with us.

There is another type of gift. These are gifts which money cannot buy. Heavenly Father has given us many of these types of gifts. The sun, the air we breathe, water, and health are all examples of gifts which cannot be bought with money. Even though we buy our food from the store, it is still a gift of our Heavenly Father who created the seed and provided light and soil so that the plants could grow. Sometimes these gifts are taken for granted.

When Jesus died, the people in the Americas were in darkness for three days. There were terrible earthquakes and storms. The people could not see anything. Those people must have realized then, what a wonderful blessing the sun is. (See 3 Nephi 8:19-23)

Many years ago, some wicked people were building a tall tower so they could get to heaven. Heavenly Father wasn't happy and He mixed their language all up. When they tried to talk with each other they couldn't understand, and couldn't finish their tower. One righteous man prayed that their language would not be confused because he wanted to be able to talk with his family and friends. (See Ether 1:33-37, Genesis 11:1-9). Our language is a wonderful blessing from Heavenly Father. How awful it would be to not be able to read, write, or speak to each other!

Once a man saw Jesus' Apostles giving the gift of the Holy Ghost and working miracles. He wanted this same power and offered the Apostles some money if they would give it to him. But, priesthood is a gift from Heavenly Father and cannot be bought with money. (See Acts 8:9-24)

Children and families are a very special gift of our Father in Heaven.

King Benjamin taught that we will always be indebted to God for the blessings He gives us. He said that even if we "*should render all the thanks and praise which your whole soul has power to possess*" and "*if ye should serve him with all your whole souls yet ye would be unprofitable servants.*" When we do as God has commanded, "*he doth immediately bless you; and therefore he hath paid you. And ye are still indebted to him, and are and will be forever.*" (See Mosiah 2:20-24)

Heavenly Father wants us to have a grateful heart. The Psalmist wrote, "*It is a good thing to give thanks unto the Lord, and to sing praises unto thy name, O most High.*" (Psalms 92:1) And Alma counseled, "*let thy heart be full of thanks unto God.*" (Alma 37:37)

One day Jesus met ten lepers who asked him to heal them. He told them to go show themselves to the priests. On the way they realized that they had been healed. One man came back to give thanks to Jesus. Jesus asked, "*Were there not ten cleansed? but where are the nine? There are not found that returned to give glory to God, save this stranger.*" (Luke 17: 17-18)

Christmas is a time to remember the greatest gift that God has given to the world, the gift of His Son. "*For God so loved the world that he gave his only begotten Son.*" (John 3:16) God could have saved Jesus, but he allowed him to suffer and die for us.

Jesus also gave us a priceless gift when He atoned for our sins and gave His life for us, that we might have Eternal life. "*Greater love hath no man than this, that a man lay down his life for his friends. Ye are my friends.*" (John 15:13-14)

When you look at others with their lands and gold,
Think that Christ has promised you his wealth untold
Count your many blessings money cannot buy
Your reward in heaven nor your home on high.
Count your blessings. Name them one by one.
Count your many blessings see what God hath done.

(Hymns, #241, Thomas Ken, 1637-1711)

ACTIVITY IDEAS

- Tell your children about some of your special material gifts. for example: a wedding ring, other valuable or sentimental gifts, heirlooms etc. Go on a treasure hunt to find some of the valuable gifts you have which are bought with money. (For example: bed, car, refrigerator, T.V., clock, sink, oven, furnace, etc.) Explain why each thing is valuable to you. End the treasure hunt by finding a picture of the family and explain to them that family is one of the most valuable gifts which Heavenly Father has given us.
- Give each child a small number of beans. Sit in a circle and take turns naming gifts which money cannot by. Each time a person names a gift which money cannot buy, he drops one of his beans into the bottle. If a child cannot think of one give a hint. Here are some suggestions: Sun, water, earth, scriptures, knowledge, language, ability to reason, work, read, talents, gospel, priesthood, a testimony, etc.) Discuss what life might be like without some of these gifts. Express gratitude for these things.
- One of the most priceless gifts God has given us is the gift of our children. *"Lo children are an heritage of the Lord...Happy is the man that hath his quiver full of them."* (Psalms 127:3-5) Express gratitude for each child. Tell how you felt when they were born, how you feel about and appreciate them now.

  NOTE: This is something everyone needs to hear. Children especially need to be told frequently of their worth, and of their parent's love for them. It does NOT spoil a child or make him "conceited" to hear these expressions of love. Rather, it has an opposite effect. It gives self-assurance, and the child then gives that love back to others.
- Make a list of people who have given you "gifts without price." For example: neighbors, teachers, grandparents, postman, etc. Write a note of thanks to one, or several of them.
- Say a prayer of thanksgiving. Do not ask for anything, only give thanks.
- Select some objects from around the house. Explain how everything we possess actually comes from Heavenly Father. For example: an apple was purchased from the store, but in order to grow it needed air, sunshine and soil. Our family has been blessed with a way to earn money so that we can buy the apple.
- Read Number 21: 1-9. Discuss verse 7. After all that God had done for the Israelites, they still complained. Finally, they recognized that their lack of gratitude, was a sin. See also the story The Ten Lepers in New Testament Stories or Luke 17:12-18.

SUGGESTED SONGS

Christmas songs in Italics

CHILDREN'S SONGBOOK

Song	Page
He Sent His Son	34
Little Jesus	39
Who Is the Child	46
I Am a Child of God	2
I'm Thankful to Be Me	11
Children All Over the World	16
Every Star Is Different	142
How Dear to God Are Little Children	180
How Will they Know?	182
Home	192
Because God Loves Me	234

HYMNS

Song	Page
Joy to the World	201
Oh, Come, All Ye Faithful	202
O Little Town Of Bethlehem	208
All Creatures of Our God and King	62
God Loved Us, So He Sent His Son	187
I Stand All Amazed	193
How Great the Wisdom and the Love	195
Jesus, Once of Humble Birth	196
We Give Thee But Thine Own	218
Because I Have Been Given Much	219
Love at Home	294

ORNAMENT

Gift Box

- This ornament consists of 1 piece, (3 copies) found on pages 255.

Families Can Be Forever

IN A NUTSHELL

A circle is a shape which goes on endlessly. The Christmas wreath is a symbol of eternal life and eternal love. One of the supreme blessings promised by our Heavenly Father is that our families can be eternal. When charity, or pure love, is practiced within our families, bonds of eternal love and friendship are nourished and strengthened.

LESSON

A circle goes on forever. It never stops, but continues around endlessly. When a man and woman are married, they often exchange wedding rings. The rings are circles which symbolize eternal love.

At Christmas time we often see evergreen branches wrapped carefully into a circle. It is called a wreath. Evergreen branches are used in wreaths because they are always green, even through the winter when other plants lose their leaves and die. Evergreen leaves are a symbol of something which is forever growing. The wreath represents eternal life and eternal love.

Heavenly Father has promised us that our families can be forever. The love within a family is eternal and ever growing. What a great blessing from a loving Heavenly Father!

But, what happens when a family seems to be falling apart -- when rings come off or family members leave? Is it the end of the family circle? No! The bonds of love a family shares, really do go on forever.

Sometimes, families have problems because people have problems. When the people we love have problems, the best thing to do is to keep loving them, maybe more than ever. We must remember that people are not perfect, but love can be.

Perfect love is called "charity." Often people think that giving money or "*things*" is charity. This idea is wrong. Charity is not the gift, it is the reason for giving.

> *"And charity suffereth long, and is kind, and envieth not, and is not puffed up, seeketh not her own, is not easily provoked, thinketh no evil, and rejoiceth not in iniquity but rejoiceth in the truth, beareth all things, believeth all things, hopeth all things, endureth all things.*
>
> *Wherefore, my beloved brethren, if ye have not charity, ye are nothing, for charity never faileth. Wherefore, cleave unto charity, which is the greatest of all, for all things must fall- But charity is the pure love of Christ, and it endureth forever; and whoso is found possessed of it at the last day, it shall be well with him....*
>
> *Pray unto the Father with all energy of heart, that ye may be filled with this love which he has bestowed upon all who are true followers of his Son, Jesus Christ; that ye may become the sons of God; that when he shall appear we shall be like him, for we shall see him as he is; that we may have this hope; that we may be purified even as he is pure." (Moroni 7:47-48)*

Charity is a special kind of love. It is a forgiving love. It is the kind of love Jesus had for each of us when he chose to suffer for our sins. Charity is pure love.

If our homes were filled with charity; a love which suffers long and is still kind, a love which shows more interest and concern for the welfare of others than it does for itself, truly our homes could be like heaven!

President Spencer W. Kimball said, "*We can make our houses homes and our homes heavens.*"

"*A happy family is but an earlier heaven.*" Sir John Bowring.

Let charity begin at home!

OUR FAMILY'S LOVE

The circle of our family's love
Began long ago, and up above.
In another time and place;
A Heavenly Family, a loving face.

Now here on earth — even through tears,
Our family's love extends for years.
The circle of our love goes on
'Round forever, it will never be gone.

Suzanne Meredith

ACTIVITY IDEAS

- Sit in a circle. Discuss how a circle goes around endlessly. (A ring could be shown as well.) Go around the circle and have each family member tell something they like about the other members of the family.
- Play "*Doctor, Doctor, We Need Help*!" One family member leaves the room. The rest of the family joins hands to form a circle. Weave yourselves into a "mess" by twisting, turning and stepping over and under one another's arms without breaking the circle. (or your arms) Then call for the family member who is out of the room, "(Johnny, Johnny) we need help!" The person returns and helps the family to untangle themselves, by giving instructions such as, "Step over that arm." "Go through here." etc.

  Some other fun circle games are "*Button, Button*;" "*Duck, Duck, Goose*:" "*Telephone Wire*;" "*Spin the Bottle*;" "*Fruit Basket*," or "*Ring Around the Rosies.*"
- Use cookie dough or bread dough to make wreaths. (Frozen bread dough which has been thawed works well and saves time) See cookie recipes in the Optional Materials, page 118.
- Make a "*Handsome Wreath*". Trace each family member's hand onto colored paper. You may choose to make them all green, or the person's favorite color. Cut the hands out and glue them onto a large cardboard wreath. Curl all of the fingers down. Decorate with a bow. You may want to write some good quality that member has on the hand, before gluing it to the wreath.
- Make or purchase a wreath. Attach an item representing each family member on the wreath. Items such as pictures, or things representing hobbies and interests. Display it during the season as a symbol of your family.
- Use an old Jigsaw puzzle with small pieces. Spray paint the pieces green. Glue the pieces onto small cardboard circles, making a frame which looks like a wreath. Decorate with a bow or small red candies. Attach a family or individual picture behind the frame

SUGGESTED SONGS *Christmas songs in Italics*

CHILDREN'S SONGBOOK

Song	Page
Mary's Lullaby	44
Who Is the Child?	46
Have a Very Merry Christmas (vs. 3)	51
I Am a Child of God	2
The Hearts of the Children	92
I Love to See the Temple	95
Where Love Is	138
Family Prayer	189
Love Is Spoken Here	190
Home	192
A Happy Family	198

HYMNS

Song	Page
Silent Night	204
O Little Town of Bethlehem	208
Let Us Oft Speak Kind Words	232
God Is Love	87
Our Savior's Love	113
Turn Your Hearts	291
O My Father	292
Love At Home	294
Home Can Be a Heaven on Earth	298
Families Can Be Together Forever	300
Love One Another	308

ORNAMENT
Wreath

♦ This ornament consists of 2 pieces found on page 257.

Light of the World

IN A NUTSHELL

Each person born into this world, was given a special light to lead and guide them in the way of righteousness. It is called "The Light of Christ." Without light it is difficult to tell where we are and where we are going. Even the tiniest light can dispel the deepest darkness. Jesus taught, *"I am the light of the world..."* (John 8:12) The teachings of Jesus can guide us safely through the darkness, back to our Heavenly home.

LESSON

Have you ever lost something in the dark and tried to find it? Or, have you ever tried to find your way without a light to see where you were going? Light is a great blessing!

At birth, every person on earth was given a special light to lead and guide them. Some people call this light "conscience." It is also called "The Light of Christ." This light helps us to discern between right and wrong. When we choose the right, this light inside makes us feel warm and good. When we make a wrong choice, we feel dark and cold inside. Abraham Lincoln understood this principle when he said, *"When I do good I feel good. When I don't do good I don't feel good."* (See also Moroni 7:12-19)

In Jesus' day, Jews traveled to Jerusalem to celebrate several different feasts. One of these was called the Feast of Tabernacles. During this feast, the temple was illuminated with four large candelabra. The feast was to commemorate the sojourn in the wilderness of the children of Israel, who were finally led to the Promised land by a pillar of light which guided their way. During this celebration and afterwards, Jesus often went to the temple to teach. On one of these visits, Jesus taught *"I am the light of the world; he that followeth me shall not walk in darkness, but shall have the light of life."* (John 8:12, see also John 9:5, 12:46)

The Lord's word is a light to those who are faithful. *"Thy word is a lamp unto my feet and a light unto my path."* (Psalms 119:105) *"Then Jesus saith unto them, Yet a little while is the light with you. Walk while ye have the light, lest darkness come upon you: for he that walketh in darkness knoweth not whither he goeth. While ye have the light, believe in the light, that ye may be the children of light."* (John 12:35)

John taught, *"This then is the message which we have heard of him, and declare unto you, that God is light, and in him is no darkness at all."* (1 John 1:5)

Both physical and spiritual light help us to know where we are, and, to see where we are going. Spiritual light leads to salvation. It edifies and uplifts. (See D&C 50:23-24) It is a protection against evil, for, *" Light and truth forsake the evil one."* (See D&C 93:37) Paul counseled the saints to "cast off the works of darkness and... put on the armor of light." (Romans 13:12) For this reason the Lord commanded parents in Zion to *"bring up your children in light and truth."* (D&C 93:40-42) Heavenly Father knew that the "light of truth" would keep His children safe, and make them happy. The stronger the light, the easier it is to see through the darkness. (See Isaiah 54:13)

The gospel of Jesus Christ is a light to the world, showing all how to live happier and more peaceful lives. (See D&C 45:9) It was prophesied that the light of the gospel would *"break forth among those who sat in darkness."* (D&C 45:28-29, 36) Everyone who has experienced this wonderful light, has been asked to share it with others, lighting a safe path for them. *"Ye are the light of the world. A city that is set on an hill cannot be hid.... Let your light so shine before men that they may see your good works, and glorify your Father which is in heaven."* (Matthew 5:14-16, see also 3 Nephi 12:14-16, 15:12, 18:24)

The night Jesus was born, people in America were waiting for a sign of light to signal His birth -- a day and a night and a day in which there would be no darkness. When Jesus died, there was another sign — a sign of darkness. For three days, in the Americas, there were earthquakes and great storms. The destruction was so great that the face of the entire land was completely changed. Many cities had been completely destroyed, and the roads the people were familiar with had been broken up. Many of their loved ones had been killed. The darkness was so thick that not even a candle could be lit. The people had no light to see what had happened. Somehow, a large group had gathered at the temple and were discussing this great sign of darkness. Through the darkness the people heard the voice of Christ. The thick darkness was dispelled and Jesus descended from heaven and stood in their midst.

Sometimes it feels as though the darkness and evil which surround us are too powerful to combat. Yet, even the tiniest light can dispel the deepest darkness. In the Doctrine and Covenants Jesus said, *"Behold, I am Jesus Christ, the Son of the living God, who created the heavens and the earth, a light which cannot be hid in darkness."* (D&C 14:9) If we live by the light of His gospel we will have light to see clearly even during dark and troubled times.

ACTIVITY IDEAS

- Turn off the lights and sit in darkness for a few minutes. Talk about how important light is to be able to see. Turn a small flashlight on. (Or a flashlight with a weak battery) Discuss that no matter how big or powerful the darkness or shadow is, light is always more powerful and can chase the darkness away.
- Read the words to *Our Savior's Love*, Hymns # 113 with your family. Turn off all the lights and light one candle. Notice the size of the flame. Light a second candle with the candle which is already lit. Two things happen.
  1. There is now more light in the room.
  2. The candle which shared its light now burns brighter.

  When we share the gospel and our testimonies with others, the world is brighter and our own light also grows.

  Note: Please handle lighted candles carefully since they constitute a serious fire hazard. This activity should be done only with adult supervision and the candles should never be left unattended.
- Several accounts in the scriptures describe how Jesus opened the eyes of the blind. One man blind from birth, had never had light sufficient to see. Imagine how he must have felt to step from darkness into the light! (See John 9, Matthew 9:27-31, 20:30-34, Mark 10:46-52, Luke 18:35-43) Blindfold a child and instruct him/her to do a few things. (ie: Walk to the closet and open the door. Go get a drink of water etc.) When the blindfold is removed, ask the child to try to imagine how it would feel to have his sight restored after years of being in darkness, and the first thing they see is the face of Jesus.
- To the tune of "*This Little Gospel Light*," sing : This little light inside of me I'm going to let it shine! Repeat 2 more times...Let it shine, let it shine, let it shine!

  Vs. 2 I'm gonna choose the right, Oh Yes! I'm gonna let it shine.
  Vs. 3 If my little light goes out, I can make it shine.
  Vs. 4 I'll stop, repent, and choose the right. I'm gonna let it shine.
- Share experiences of when the light of Christ has helped you to make a right choice or when it has helped you to know that something you were doing was wrong.
- Color and cut out the flames in the Optional Materials page, 191. Mount them onto wooden sticks, (a happy and sad, or happy and mad face back to back) Have children hold up the flame which best represents the examples given. (ie: Yell at your sister, share your toys, take turns, help Mom by setting the table, fight with your sister.

SUGGESTED SONGS

Christmas songs in Italics

CHILDREN'S SONGBOOK

Song	Page
Samuel Tells of the Baby Jesus	36
Stars Were Gleaming	37
There Was Starlight on the Hillside	40
Mary's Lullaby	44
Jesus Wants Me for a Sunbeam	60
The Church of Jesus Christ	77
Every Star Is Different	142
Shine On	144
I Want to Live the Gospel	148
I Am like a Star	163
The Things I Do	170
Called to Serve	174

HYMNS

Hymn	Number
Oh, Come, All Ye Faithful	202
O Little Town of Bethlehem	208
With Wondering Awe	210
The First Noel	213
The Lord Is My Light	89
Lead Kindly Light	97
I Need Thee Every Hour	98
Jesus, Savior, Pilot Me	104
Our Savior's Love	113
Thy Spirit, Lord, Hath Stirred Our Souls	157
Teach Me to Walk in the Light	304
The Light Divine	305

ORNAMENT

Candle

- This ornament consists of 3 pieces, found on pages 259 and 261.

The Least of These

IN A NUTSHELL

There is a special message in the birth and life of our Savior. Jesus was born under the most lowly and humble of circumstances. He was taunted and persecuted by those who felt they were better, and, was even betrayed by some of His closest friends. But, Jesus understood who He really was. He understood that money, friends, possessions and position cannot make anyone a better person. Each of us is important because we are children of God. Heavenly Father and Jesus know each of us. They know our strengths and weaknesses and they love us for who we are. By precept and example, Jesus taught that we should serve "the least" of our brethren.

LESSON

Living in this materialistic world, it is easy to become confused about what is really important. Too often feelings of self-worth are based on the wrong things. A young child may base his feelings of self-worth on friends, clothes or appearance. To a teenager, a boyfriend or girlfriend, the number of dates, good grades, a popular circle of friends, being a member of an important group, or talents, can bring feelings of importance or inferiority. To adults, a nice house, a prestigious job, a good income, or possessions often become status symbols. Often, feelings of importance are based on the accomplishments of children or relationship with a spouse. Sometimes feelings of inferiority can come from how others may have treated us in the past, particularly during childhood. An elderly person may base feelings of worth on health, and the ability to be independent. Too often, feelings of self-worth are based on all of the wrong things. These things may serve as "security blankets" but they cannot change who a person really is deep down inside.

Philip James Bailey said, "*It matters not what men assume to be, or good, or bad, they are what they are.*" (*Richard Evans Quote Book*, Salt Lake City: Publishers Press, 1971, p. 209)

There is a special message in the birth and life of our Savior. The King of Kings was born in the lowliest of circumstances. He was wrapped in swaddling clothes and had a manger for His bed. Jesus later told some of His followers, "*The foxes have holes, and the birds of the air have nests; but the Son of man hath not where to lay his head.*" (Matthew 8:20) He was raised in meager circumstances, as a humble carpenter's son. Isaiah wrote of Jesus: "*He hath no form nor comeliness; and when we shall see him, there is no beauty that we should desire him.*" (Isaiah 53:2) Jesus was betrayed by some of His closest friends, and was taunted and persecuted by those who felt they were better.

Thomas à Kempis wrote, "*Thou art none the holier if thou art praised, nor the viler if thou art reproached. Thou art what thou art.*" (*Richard Evans Quote Book*, Salt Lake City: Publishers Press, 1971, p. 210)

Jesus understood who He really was. He knew that He was the Son of God and that knowledge brought self respect.

Heavenly Father knows each of us. We are His children. He knows who we really are, beneath all of the things we hide under. He knows our strengths and He knows our weaknesses. In fact, He said that He gave man weakness, to make him humble, and that through His grace weakness could be turned to strength. (See Ether 12:27)

Jesus taught that temporal things are not important. (See Matthew 16:26, Matthew 6:19-21, 33) What really matters is who we are deep down inside; who we are when we are stripped of possessions, talents, health, position etc. (See the story of Job) Elder Richard G. Scott gave some comforting counsel when he said, "*We must learn to judge ourselves not by what we are, but by what under the influence of the Lord we may become.*" (*Ensign*, November 1979, p. 70)

Jesus ministered to the humble, the lowly, the sinner. He blessed those who had been rejected, and even prayed for his enemies. He asked us to do as He had done. "*Love your enemies, bless them that curse you, do good to them that hate you, and pray for them which despitefully use you and persecute you.*" (Matthew 5:44) It is easy to serve those whom we love, but, Jesus asked that we serve the "least," not the "best." By example, Jesus taught how to overcome pride and serve those around us. (See John 13: 4-10) Service to others is one of the best ways to show our love to Heavenly Father and Jesus. Bruce R. McConkie related a story from his father's journal about his grandmother, a widow who was serving as Relief Society President:

> *Mother was president of the Moab Relief Society. A non-member who opposed the Church had married a Mormon girl. They had several children, now they had a new baby. They were very poor and Mother was going day by day to care for the child and take them baskets of food etc...Mother herself was ill, and more than once was hardly able to get*

home after doing the work at this home.

One day she returned home especially tired and weary. She slept in her chair. She dreamed she was bathing a baby, which she discovered was the Christ Child. She thought, who else has actually held the Christ Child? Unspeakable joy filled her whole being. She was aflame with the glory of the Lord. It seemed the marrow of her bones would melt. Her joy was so great, it awakened her. As she awoke, these words were spoken to her, "Inasmuch as ye have done it unto one of the least of these my brethren, ye have done it unto me." (*Relief Society Magazine*, March 1970, p. 169)

ACTIVITY IDEAS

- Gather some cans or wooden blocks, and write on them some of the things that help us feel secure. Talents, house, car, intelligence, friends, clothes, etc. Stack the blocks into a pyramid shape. (Four on the bottom row, three on the next etc.) What would happen if we lost ___? (Pull out one of the bottom blocks.) The others will fall down. (These things are all temporary and can be easily lost. For example: a head injury caused an honor student great difficulties to continue her studies, a neck injury paralyzed a talented gymnast etc) It is important to never base our feelings of self worth on the wrong things. We are of worth because we are children of our Father in Heaven. He loves us and knows what we can become.
- Go on a service scavenger hunt. Divide up in teams and give each a list. (The list may include things like: vacuum a room, dust 3 pieces of furniture, change a baby, wash dishes, fold laundry, wash a floor, wash walls, make a bed) Go through the neighborhood and perform each act of service for others.
- Select someone who may need a visit. Go and spend the evening with them.
- Make a manger from a small a box. Cut up pieces of yellow or gold paper or yarn to use as straw, and place them in a box next to the manger. For every secret act of service done for anyone, the family member places a piece of straw in the manger. Try to make the manger soft and comfortable by Christmas, by serving others.
- Show some apple seeds. Discuss what they look like and what they are capable of becoming. Discuss the saying, "*You can count the seeds inside an apple, but you can't count the apples in a seed.* "

  Wrap one package in beautiful paper, another in wrinkled or ripped paper. (Or use cans and switch the labels around.) Does what is on the outside change what is inside?

SUGGESTED SONGS

Christmas songs in *Italics*

CHILDREN'S SONGBOOK

He Sent His Son..................................34
Once within A Lowly Stable................41
Who Is the Child?..............................46
I Am a Child of God............................2
Jesus Wants Me for a Sunbeam.........60
I'm Trying to Be like Jesus...............78
Love One Another.........................136
Where Love Is..................................138
I'll Walk with You...........................140
Love Is Spoken Here.........................190
We Are Different...................................263

HYMNS

Silent Night..204
Once in Royal David's City.......................205
Away in a Manger................................206
Be Thou Humble.................................130
More Holiness Give Me.......................133
We Give Thee But Thine Own............218
Because I Have Been Given Much..........219
Lord, I Would Follow Thee..................220
You Can Make the Pathway Bright...........228
Scatter Sunshine.................................230
Each Life That Touches Ours For Good......293

ORNAMENT

Manger

- This ornament consists of 3 pieces, found on pages 247, 263, 265.

Peace

IN A NUTSHELL

Isaiah wrote," *"And the work of righteousness shall be peace; and the effect of righteousness quietness and assurance for ever."* (Isaiah 32:17) Peace is a feeling of safety and quiet that comes from the Lord. Everything Jesus did, or said, was to establish and teach the ways of righteousness which bring peace. Isaiah called Him the "*Prince of Peace.*" (Isaiah 9:6) The gospel of Jesus Christ can bring sweet feelings of peace even during times of trouble. Jesus taught, "*These things I have spoken unto you, that in me ye might have peace.*" "*Peace I leave with you, my peace I give unto you; not as the world giveth, give I unto you.Let not your heart be troubled, neither let it be afraid.*" (John 14:26-27)

LESSON

Throughout the world, the dove is used as a sign of peace. Doves are often released to signify the wish for peace among nations. Peace is not merely the absence of war. Peace is a feeling of safety, a quiet assurance which comes from the Lord. Peace is a reward given to those who live righteously and obey God's commandments. Isaiah taught, "*And the work of righteousness shall be peace; and the effect of righteousness quietness and assurance for ever.*" (Isaiah 32:17) Paul taught that one of the fruits of the Spirit is peace. (See Galatians 5:22-23) Isaiah prophesied that Jesus would be known as The Prince of Peace. (Isaiah 9:6) The night Jesus was born, angels heralded his birth by singing, "*Glory to God in the highest and on earth peace good will toward men.*" (Luke 2:14)

Before the world was created, the sign of the dove was chosen as a witness for the Holy Ghost. It is an emblem or token of truth and innocence. The devil cannot come in the sign of the dove. (See *Bible Dictionary*: Dove, Sign of, *Joseph Smith History of the Church* 5:261, Abraham Facsimile 2, Fig 7) John the Baptist knew before Jesus was baptized that the sign of the dove would come as a witness of the Messiah. When John the Baptist saw the appointed sign he testified, "*And I saw, and bare record that this is the Son of God.*" (See *Joseph Smith Translation*, John 1:31-3, page 808)

Before His crucifixion Jesus promised His disciples that He would send another comforter. Then, He said, "*Peace I leave with you, my peace I give unto you; not as the world giveth, give I unto you. Let not your heart be troubled, neither let it be afraid.*" (John 14:26-27) This comforter, the Holy Ghost, speaks with a voice of perfect stillness and peace. and was sent to comfort and guide us. (See 1 Kings 19:11-12, and 3 Nephi 11:3)

The Gospel of Jesus Christ is called "The Gospel of Peace." (See Ephesians 2:14, Romans 10:15) The Gospel brings peace because it teaches who we are and of Heavenly Father's plan for His children. It brings peace to those who are obedient for they can receive the assurance that the path they are pursuing is correct. The gospel brings peace because it teaches the ways of truth and righteousness, and "*the work of righteousness shall be peace.*" The Gospel can bring peace even when there may be trouble all around. An understanding that Heavenly Father and Jesus have all things in their hands, and our best interest in mind brings great peace. "*... for all flesh is in mine hands; be still and know that I am God.*" (D&C 101:16) "*Thou wilt keep him in perfect peace, whose mind is stayed on thee: because he trusteth in thee.*" (Isaiah 26:3) Just as Jesus stilled the storm He can quiet life's storms and give peace. Jesus taught, "*These things I have spoken unto you, that in me ye might have peace. In the world ye shall have tribulation; but be of good cheer; I have overcome the world.*" (John 16:33)

"*There was a time in ancient America when such blessings came to this land and lasted for 200 years. Peace and prosperity were everywhere. There were no wars, no crimes, no jails, no poverty, no moral corruption and none of the diseases which sins produce, not for 200 years. This is no storybook tale. It was a great reality. It was a vital chapter in world history that came but has never been repeated. Yet it can be repeated now in our day on the same terms.*" (Elder Mark E. Peterson, *Ensign*, November, 1979, page 14)

When Jesus comes again, there will be a period of one thousand years when all of God's children will live in peace. Satan will have no power over the hearts of men. He will be "bound" by their righteousness. (See 1 Nephi 22:26) Isaiah prophesied that there would come a time when "*all thy children shall be taught of the Lord; and great shall be the peace of thy children.*" (Isaiah 54:13)

There is a peace which comes from obeying the commandments of God. It is a peace which "passeth understanding" (Philippians 4:7) "*... he who doeth the works of righteousness shall receive his reward, even peace in this world and eternal life in the world to come.*" (D&C 59:23) "*But the wicked are like the troubled sea, when it cannot rest, whose waters cast up mire and dirt. There is no peace, saith my God, to the wicked.*" (Isaiah 57:20-21) "*Behold I say unto you, wickedness never was happiness.*" (Alma 41:10)

ACTIVITY IDEAS

- Cut some strips of paper or 3/4 inch ribbon to make a paper chain. Talk about acts done in your family by "peacemakers." For each one mentioned, add a link to the chain. Discuss how peacemakers can help to bind the family together in love.
- The Jewish people use the greeting "*Shalom*," which means "Peace be unto you." Read the beginning of some of Paul's letters. See how many began with this greeting.
- Use the figures of the pies in Optional Materials, page 195. Explain that peace comes when we obey the commandments of God. This does not mean that our lives will be free from trial, but it does mean that we can feel at peace, we can feel "whole" even though we may be having difficulties. When we do something wrong we feel empty-like something is missing. (Show the pictures of the pies.) Sometimes we may feel that a huge piece is missing in our life and that there is no way to feel "whole" again. (Turn the picture upside down.) No matter how big the missing piece may be, if we have faith and trust in the Lord, He can restore what is missing.
- Act out the story of Jesus stilling the storm. See Mark 4:35-41, or New Testament Stories, Jesus Commands the Wind and the Waves
- Read the words to verse 3 of *It Came Upon A Midnight Clear* Hymn #207. Discuss what it means to "*send back the song which now the angels sing*" and how we can do this.
- Make a Peacemaker Cake. See Optional Materials, page 130.
- Guess the songs which contain these phrases: ① "Sleep in heavenly peace." ② "Peace on the earth, good will to men From heav'n's all-gracious King." ③ "And praises sing to God the King, And peace to men on earth;" ④ "Peace on earth and mercy mild, God and sinners reconciled!" ⑤ "And shall not cease till holy peace In all the earth is growing." ⑥ "All glory be to God on high And on the earth be peace." ⑦ "Peace on earth, good-will to men; Peace on earth, good-will to men!" ⑧ "And wild and sweet the words repeat Of peace on earth, good will to men."

  ANSWERS: ① *Silent Night* ② *It Came upon the Midnight Clear* ③ *O Little Town of Bethlehem* ④ *Hark! the Herald Angels Sing* ⑤ *With Wondering Awe* ⑥ *While Shepherds Watched Their Flocks* ⑦ *Far, Far Away on Judea's Plains* ⑧ *I Heard the Bells on Christmas Day*

SUGGESTED SONGS *Christmas songs in Italics*

CHILDREN'S SONGBOOK

The Shepherd's Carol............................40
Sleep, Little Jesus................................47
Picture a Christmas............................50
I Know My Father Lives.........................5
I Feel My Savior's Love........................74
When I Am Baptized..........................103
The Holy Ghost................................105
Listen, Listen...................................107
Where Love Is..................................138
Keep the Commandments.........................146
Mother, Tell Me the Story.(esp. vs.2)........204

HYMNS

See the list of Hymns in Activity..............# 6
Sweet Is the Peace the Gospel Brings...........14
How Firm a Foundation (vs. 3-7).............85
Master, the Tempest Is Raging.................105
Come unto Jesus...................................117
Lean on My Ample Arm..........................120
Though Deepening Trials........................122
Oh, May My Soul Commune with Thee.......123
Be Still, My Soul...................................124
How Gentle God's Commands....................125
When Faith Endures...............................128
Where Can I Turn for Peace......................129

ORNAMENT

Dove

- This ornament consists of 2 pieces, found on page 265.

Victory Over Death

IN A NUTSHELL

When Adam and Eve partook of the forbidden fruit in the garden of Eden, they brought two kinds of death upon themselves and all mankind: physical death and spiritual death. Red and green, the Christmas colors, remind us of two priceless gifts our Savior has given us. Green reminds us of His gift of the resurrection, the victory over physical death, which is given to all men. Red reminds us of Jesus' terrible suffering in the Garden of Gethsemane and on the cross where he gained victory over spiritual death. Those who believe on Him, repent of their sins, and obey His commandments, will obtain the gift of eternal life.

LESSON

Any time a beautiful bright red and vivid green are placed side by side, we are reminded of Christmas. Red and green have been designated as the Christmas colors. Red is brilliant, rich and distinct. It is the most vibrant color and the most easily seen.

When Adam partook of the forbidden fruit, he brought two kinds of death upon himself and all of mankind -- physical death and spiritual death. In the scriptures, physical death is sometimes called "the grave. " It is the separation of the spirit from the body.

Spiritual death is often referred to as "hell." It is the separation of man from God.

When our Savior suffered in the Garden of Gethsemane, His agony was so intense that great drops of red blood fell to the ground. Jesus Christ suffered to atone for our sins so that we would not have to suffer if we would repent. He paid the price for us. His victory made it possible for us to repent and gain victory over spiritual death.

> *"For behold, I, God, have suffered these things for all, that they might not suffer if they would repent;*
>
> *But if they would not repent they must suffer even as I;*
>
> *Which suffering caused myself, even God, the greatest of all, to tremble because of pain, and to bleed at every pore, and to suffer both body and spirit — and would that I might not drink the bitter cup, and shrink —*
>
> *Nevertheless, glory be to the Father, and I partook and finished my preparations unto the children of men."* (D&C 19:16-19)

The color red is a reminder that Jesus Christ suffered and died for us .

Green is the color of tiny new leaves which push their way up out of the ground in springtime. Even plants which appear to be dead through the long winter months will burst forth with new life when the time is right. Some other trees remain green year round. They are called evergreen.

The color green represents everlasting life. The resurrection of Jesus Christ made it possible for each of our spirits to be reunited with our physical bodies. This was another victory for us through Christ — the victory over physical death.

VICTORY

When all around is well adorned
with Christmas red and green,
My heart soars with gladness
as I think on what it means.

Traditions of celebrating
last from year to year.
Will memories of the past be gone
'cause loved ones are not near?

No! When I think of the great love
offered through God's Own Begotten,
Only joy can fill my heart
and all my earthly woes forgotten.

Through Christ's redeeming blood
I know that I can be forgiven,
To live with Him and loved ones too,
and enter into heaven.

Resurrection's miracle
gives my life a whole new meaning,
Thoughts of pain and sorrow
are replaced with great rejoicing.

The red and green of Christmas colors,
and the carols that I sing,
Remind of joy and reverence
as I worship the new born King

Suzanne Meredith

"*Jesus said..., I am the resurrection, and the life: he that believeth in me, though he were dead, yet shall he live: And whosoever liveth and believeth in me shall never die...*" (John 11:25-26)

Red and green, the colors of Christmas, serve to remind us of these two priceless gifts our Savior has given to us.

ACTIVITY IDEAS

- Make puppets out of paper bags, socks, or fabric, Discuss how our hand makes the puppet move. When the hand is removed, the puppet no longer moves. Compare this to the spirit. When the spirit is separated from the body, it is called death. The spirit still lives and moves, but the body has no power to do so. Resurrection is the reuniting of the spirit with the body.
- Set up a family "store" where children can purchase small items or treats. Give each child some "money" (ie. beans, paper coins, etc. Do not give enough to buy any of the items. Explain how someone could "pay the price" for them. Discuss the atonement and how Christ paid the price for us. All he asks in return is that we repent and obey the commandments.
- Have each family member draw a picture of himself/herself and put it into a bowl. Explain that the first person to *wish* his figure out of the bowl, without touching it in any way, wins the game Of course, this can't be done. The only way for the figure to get out of the bowl is to have someone else pull it out. This is similar to our situation on earth. No amount of hard work or wishing can pull us out of our fallen situation. We need the help offered to us through the atonement of Jesus Christ.
- Choose a special gift for each child and hide it somewhere in the house. (A homemade gift would be most appropriate. ie. a poem, picture, treat, etc.) Write a short poem describing where it is hidden. Such as: "Search high, search deep, Then go and search the place you sleep." When each child has found his gift, talk about how it was selected especially for them, and the sacrifice made to provide the gift. Then discuss the gifts offered to us by our Savior through His atonement. The gift of having our bodies forever, and the gift of living with Heavenly Father again.

SUGGESTED SONGS

Christmas songs in Italics

CHILDREN'S SONGBOOK

He Sent His Son..34
Mary's Lullaby..44
I Lived in Heaven..4
Did Jesus Really Live Again?..................64
He Died That We Might Live Again..........65
To Think about Jesus............................71
Help Us, O God, to Understand................73
On a Golden Springtime.........................88

HYMNS

Oh, Come, All Ye Faithful.....................202
Silent Night...204
Once in Royal David's City...................205
Hark! the Herald Angels Sing..............209
My Redeemer Lives..............................135
I Know That My Redeemer Lives...........136
Behold the Great Redeemer Die............191
I Stand All Amazed.............................193
That Easter Morn................................198
He Is Risen!.......................................199

ORNAMENT

Poinsettia *(The colors of Christmas)*

- This ornament consists of 4 pieces, found on pages 245, 261, 267.

The Bread of Life

IN A NUTSHELL

While the Israelites dwelt in the wilderness, God rained down "*bread from heaven,*" called *Manna,* to save them from starvation. Manna was Heavenly Father's way of showing the Israelites that He was watching over them. Jesus taught, "*I am the bread of life: he that cometh to me shall never hunger...*" (John 6:35) Like manna, Jesus was sent down from heaven to offer spiritual food to those who hunger, Anyone who accepts Jesus as their Savior, and lives by His teachings is promised "living bread."

LESSON

When the Israelites escaped from Egypt, they witnessed many miracles performed by the Lord to assist and sustain them. They passed through the Red Sea on dry land. They were led by a pillar of cloud by day and a pillar of fire by night.

During their journey in the wilderness, there was a period when they had no food. Even though they had witnessed countless miracles they lost faith and began to complain against Moses. With hungry stomachs, their thoughts turned again to Egypt and the abundance of food they remembered having there. Fearing they would starve in the wilderness, they forgot all that God had done for them. They desired only to have their stomachs filled.

God showed the faithless Israelites that He was still watching over them. He rained down manna from heaven. When the Israelites saw this strange substance covering the ground, they exclaimed "Man-hu?" meaning "What is it?" That is how the manna got its name. Manna was often referred to as "heavenly bread." Manna actually didn't look like bread at all. It looked like coriander seed and tasted like wafers made with honey. (See Exodus 16:31)

For 40 years the Lord fed the Israelites with manna. When they reached the promised land they no longer received it. (See Exodus 16:2-31, 35) While in the wilderness, the Israelites gathered manna daily. They were allowed only to gather enough for one day, with the exception of the day before the sabbath, when they were to gather enough for two days. None could remain until the next day. If they disobeyed, the manna rotted, became wormy and stank.

The miracle of manna was to show the Israelites that it was really the Lord who was leading and caring for them. It was also sent to test their faith and obedience. (See Deuteronomy 8:2-3)

One of the miracles which Jesus performed was feeding a great multitude of five thousand men, and the women and children with them. One young boy had only five small loaves of bread and two fish which he gave to Jesus. Jesus gave thanks and blessed it. Everyone ate and was filled. When Jesus sent His disciples to gather up what was left, there were twelve baskets of food remaining. (See John 6:12-13)

The next day many of those people sought Jesus again. They wanted to see even greater miracles. They wanted Jesus to prove that He was the Messiah. They claimed that Moses had fed their fathers with manna for forty years. If Jesus were truly the Son of God, He should be able to prove it by doing a greater miracle than that of Moses.

Jesus corrected the people and taught that it was not Moses who provided that bread, but God. He told them their fathers had eaten manna and were dead, because like all food, manna could only sustain their bodies. Then He taught, "*I am the bread of life: he that cometh to me shall never hunger; and he that believeth on me shall never thirst...Verily, verily, I say unto you, He that believeth on me hath everlasting life.*" (John 6:35, 47)

Jesus wanted the people to understand that like manna, He had been sent from heaven to nourish them spiritually. But, like the Israelites who asked "Man-hu?" there were many who did not understand that Jesus was God's gift to us from heaven.

Jesus taught that anyone who will accept Him as their Savior, and live by His teachings has access to spiritual food, the "living bread" which will spiritually sustain him until he at last reaches the "Promised Land."

Bread is a reminder of the sacrifice Jesus made of freely offering His life so that all men might have eternal life. We partake of the "bread of life" when we live as Jesus taught us to do.

HIS WORD

With hungry heart I long to fill my soul
With sustenance which heals, restores,
makes whole.

Then feasting on His word the famine stilled;
And with the bread He offers I am filled.

No other source of strength be seen or heard,
Can heal a broken soul as does His word.

Sharon Velluto

ACTIVITY IDEAS

- Gather and cut out logos from magazines, newspapers, or the yellow pages. Make sure to remove the name. These can be logos from cars, restaurants, clothing, signs etc. Have family members guess the names of the places or products represented. Even though there are no names, just the symbol makes us think of a place or thing. (ie. most children recognize an octagon as a stop sign.) Jesus established a symbol so that we might remember Him. It is the sacrament. Discuss the important symbolism of the sacrament. For example, why the bread is broken and not cut? Why is it eaten and not just looked at? What three promises or covenants do we make when we partake of the sacrament?
- It is said that "*Bread is the staff of life.*" That means it is a support and mainstay of life. Jesus taught,"I am the bread of life." Jesus should be the "staff" of our spiritual lives. In the Lord's prayer, Jesus prayed, "*Give us this day our daily bread.*" Where can we go to find the spiritual bread we need? Where are the words of Jesus recorded? Share favorite scriptures, and tell why it is a favorite, or choose a favorite scripture to memorize, individually or as a family.
- Make *Scripture Cookies*, or *Muffins*. See recipe in Optional Materials, page 141. Copy scriptures on slips of paper and have family members look up the scripture to find what ingredient is called for.
- The following is a fun recipe for clay using bread. Remove the crusts from 15 pieces of white bread, and cut into pieces. Add one (generous) tablespoon liquid detergent, and 3/8 cup of white glue. (Depending on the consistency of the bread, if the clay is too dry, add a few more drops of glue, if it is too moist work in a few small pieces of bread) Knead until smooth. This clay is smooth and glossy when dried. Make the loaves and fishes in the New Testament story or make flat pieces shaped like bread. Write your favorite scripture on them, and use as Christmas tree ornaments.
- The October 1987 issue of *The Friend*, pages 10-11 has a fun song called *Scripture Power.* Learn it, and sing it together.

SUGGESTED SONGS

Christmas songs in Italics

CHILDREN'S SONGBOOK

He Sent His Son	34
Little Jesus	39
Once within a Lowly Stable	41
Who Is the Child?	46
I Lived in Heaven	4
Tell Me the Stories of Jesus	57
He Died That We Might Live Again	65
To Think about Jesus	71
The Sacrament	72
Help Us, O God, to Understand	73
I Feel My Savior's Love	74
When He Comes Again	82
Love One Another	136

HYMNS

O Little Town of Bethlehem	208
Hark! the Herald Angels Sing	209
A Poor Wayfaring Man of Grief (vs. 2)	29
Press Forward Saints (vs. 2)	81
In Humility, Our Savior	172
While of These Emblems We Partake	173-174
O God, the Eternal Father	175
'Tis Sweet to Sing the Matchless Love	176-177
Jesus of Nazareth, Savior and King	181
We'll Sing All Hail to Jesus Name	182
In Remembrance of Thy Suffering	183
Reverently and Meekly Now	185
In Memory of the Crucified	190

ORNAMENT

Bread

- This ornament consists of 2 pieces, found on page 243.

Living Water

IN A NUTSHELL

Water is essential for life. Without water, nothing could live or grow. There are several types of water. Salt water cannot quench thirst. Stagnant water can be very dangerous to drink. Living water is water which is clean and pure. One day, Jesus taught a woman of Samaria that He offered living water. He said, "*Whosoever drinketh of the water that I shall give him shall never thirst; but the water that I shall give him shall be in him a well of water springing up into everlasting life.*" (John 4:13-14) The water Jesus offers is spiritual. Spiritual water is essential to eternal life.

LESSON

In nature several types of water can be found.

Salt water is found in the oceans and many seas. People cannot drink salt water. It dries the mouth and the body. Men have died of thirst in the middle of the ocean, surrounded by water which they could not drink.

Another type of water is *stagnant water.* Stagnant means not flowing or moving. If water cannot run, if it is stopped or damned in any way, it becomes impure, and sometimes the bacteria in it can cause disease. The Dead Sea is a body of stagnant water. It is fed mainly by the Jordan River, but has no other outlet except evaporation. The Dead Sea is nearly six times as salty as the ocean, and because it accumulates all the minerals brought in, its water is very bitter. Except for a few microbes, it contains no other life. Sea fish which are introduced into the Dead Sea soon die. Stagnant water is very dangerous to drink. Water which cannot flow, has no ability to clean itself and harmful bacteria gets trapped inside.

Living water is water which can flow freely. High in the mountains when it is close to its source, it is clean and pure.

Well water comes from deep under the ground where there are many streams of clean, fresh, living water. By digging holes deep into the ground, man can reach and use the water from these underground streams.

Jacob's well was a very popular and productive, old well in Samaria. It was 75 feet deep. One day Jesus met a woman at this well. He was thirsty and asked for her to give Him a drink. The woman was surprised that Jesus would ask such a thing of her. Jesus was a Jew, and the Jews and Samaritans were enemies. Jesus told the woman that if she really knew who He was, she would not only have given Him water to drink, but would have asked and He would have given her "living water." The woman was unbelieving.

The well was deep and Jesus had nothing to draw water with. She asked, "*Art thou greater than our father Jacob, which gave us the well?*" (John 4:12) Jesus told the woman that whoever drank of the water from that well would thirst again, "*But whosoever drinketh of the water that I shall give him shall never thirst; but the water that I shall give him shall be in him a well of water springing up into everlasting life.*" (John 4:13-14)

The woman was interested in this type of water. She came every day to the well to draw water. It would be a great relief to never perform this chore again and she said to Jesus, "*Sir, give me this water, that I thirst not, neither come hither to draw.*" (John 4:15) Jesus wasn't talking about real water, but about spiritual water-- the kind which keeps us moving forward and helps our spirits to grow.

Water is essential for life. Nothing could live or grow without water. Water is also a great source of power. Electricity, steam engines, and water wheels are all powered by its force. Water purifies and cleanses.

Spiritual water is essential for eternal life. Through the atonement of Jesus Christ, we are given the chance to repent, be baptized and to be born again. This is a necessary step to gain eternal life. (See John 3:5, Moses 6:59) The living water which Jesus offers is a source of power. The eternal truths He taught can save us. His gospel can be a "*well springing up into everlasting life.*" (D&C 63:23, Revelation 21:6, Isaiah 12:3, 2 Nephi 22:3)

When the Israelites were in the wilderness, they spent three days in an area with no water. They began to complain to Moses. God instructed Moses to hit a rock with his staff and water would come out. The Israelites all drank freely of the water. (See Exodus 17:1-6, Psalms 78:19-35, Isaiah 48:21. 1 Nephi 17:29)

Jesus is the spiritual rock from where living waters come. He said, "*Therefore whosoever heareth these sayings of mine, and doeth them, I will liken him unto a man, which built his house upon a rock: And the rain descended, and the floods came, and the winds blew, and beat upon the house; and it fell not: for it was founded upon a rock.*" (Matthew 7:24-25)

His invitation is to all. "*Come unto me.*" (Matthew 11:28) If we live by His eternal principles and teachings He has promised that we will not fall, nor will we thirst. "*If any man thirst, let him come unto me, and drink...*(and) *out of his belly shall flow rivers of living water.*" (John 7:37-38)

ACTIVITY IDEAS

- Put several drops of blue food coloring into a glass of water. Put several drops of red food coloring into another glass of water. Put one stalk of celery into each. Within a day the stalks begin to change color. Daily we make choices about the "spiritual water" we drink. Good water and bad water both have a great influence on our spirit. Do we drink from the teachings of Jesus such as honesty, kindness, respect etc. or do we drink from wells of dishonesty, cruelty or selfishness?
- Turn off the water in the house for a half hour before the lesson and observe what happens. Talk about how important water is to our lives, and how important spiritual water is to our spirit.
- Make a "House Upon A Rock," found in Optional Materials page 223. Building our house upon a rock, means to live by the principles Jesus taught us. Each window has one of the principles Jesus taught us to live by.

  OPTIONAL IDEAS: Houses can be made with graham crackers, glued together with frosting. For younger children the story of *The Three Little Pigs* could be told and straw compared to lies, cheating etc. and sticks compared to selfishness, unkindness etc. The house of bricks is safe and secure. The way Jesus taught us to live is safe and secure. Some cereals make good straw covering for houses. Pretzels make good stick houses. Small, rectangular, dispenser- type candies can be used for bricks.
- Make card houses and sing "The foolish man built his house upon the sand..." Have children take turns being the wind, and blowing the house down.
- *The Friend,* October 1987 pages 10 and 11 has a really fun song called "Scripture Power." Find a copy and learn the song as a family. It will probably become a family favorite.
- Sing, or do a musical reading of "A Poor Wayfaring Man of Grief," Hymns # 29, particularly verses 2 and 3. Discuss the meaning of the words.
- Elder Paul H. Dunn once said, "*When we're through changing -- we're through.*" Just as stagnant water can be dangerous, remaining spiritually stagnant can also be dangerous. Discuss what happens to a muscle or a car if it doesn't move. Discuss ways we can keep keep a constant flow of "living water." in our lives. You may wish to use the poem "Perspective" on page 113. (See also Hymn #217 "*Come, Let Us Anew.*")

SUGGESTED SONGS

Christmas songs in Italics

CHILDREN'S SONGBOOK

Song	Page
Little Jesus	39
Away in a Manger	43
Have a Very Merry Christmas	51
Jesus Once Was a Little Child	55
Jesus Wants Me for a Sunbeam	60
Beautiful Savior	62
I'm Trying to Be like Jesus	78
When I Am Baptized	103
Seek The Lord Early	108
I Want to Live the Gospel	148
"Give," Said the Little Stream	236
The Wise Man and the Foolish Man	281

HYMNS

Song	Page
Once in Royal David's City	205
O Little Town of Bethlehem	208
A Poor Wayfaring Man of Grief	29
Battle Hymn of the Republic	60
How Great Thou Art	86
Come, Follow Me	116
Lean on My Ample Arm	120
I Believe In Christ	134
My Redeemer Lives	135
I Know That My Redeemer Lives	136
True to the Faith	254
I'll Go Where You Want Me to Go	270

ORNAMENT

Well

- This ornament consists of 2 pieces, found on pages 271, 273.

Christ the King

IN A NUTSHELL.

God has raised up many prophets who have testified of the coming of the Messiah. These special witnesses foretold details of His birth, His life, His mission, and His death. While many people refused to accept Jesus as the Messiah, others were convinced of His divinity, and hailed Him as their spiritual King. Jesus was the Christ of whom the prophets testified. Jesus, has fulfilled and will fulfill all of the prophecies spoken of Him. Though in life He was derided and crowned with thorns, He will one day reign upon the earth as King of kings and Lord of lords.

LESSON

In the Old Testament there are a great number of prophecies about the Messiah, the Christ, who would come and reign as King of the Jews. All Israel looked forward to his coming with great anticipation. Prophets said he would be a descendant of King David, son of Jesse. (See Numbers 24:17, Isaiah 11:1, Jeremiah 23:5-6) and that he would be born in Bethlehem, (See Micah 5:2) and that his mother would be a virgin. (See Isaiah 7:14, 2 Nephi 17:14)

The Wise Men saw His star, the sign of His birth, and came seeking Him. They inquired of King Herod, "*Where is he that is born King of the Jews? for we have seen his star in the east and are come to worship him.*" (Matthew 2:2) When the Wise Men finally found the Christ child, they recognized Him and fell down and worshiped Him.

Herod was troubled at what he had heard from the Wise Men. No doubt he had heard rumors of this great King who was to come. He asked the Wise Men to come back and report to him. But, being warned in a dream, they went home another way. Joseph was also warned by an angel, and fled into Egypt with his young family. The prophet Hosea had written, "*When Israel was a child, then I loved him, and called my son out of Egypt.*" (Hosea 11:1) This was a type of Christ. When Herod saw that he had been mocked, he was enraged and ordered all of the children in Bethlehem two years old and under to be slain, fulfilling Jeremiah's prophesy. "*Thus saith the Lord; A voice was heard in Ramah, lamentation, and bitter weeping; Rachel weeping for her children refused to be comforted for her children, because they were not.*" (Jeremiah 31:15)

When Jesus was eight days old, his parents presented him in the temple, according to Mosaic law. There in Jerusalem, was a devout man named Simeon, who was also waiting for the Messiah. The Holy Ghost had revealed to him that he would see the King of kings before he died. That day the Spirit directed him to come to the temple. Recognizing the infant King, Simeon took Jesus in his arms and blessed God saying, "*Now lettest thou thy servant depart in peace ...for mine eyes have seen thy salvation.*" (Luke 2:29-30, see also Isaiah 25:9) Also in the temple that day was a prophetess named Anna, who was a very elderly woman. She came to the temple each day to serve God with fasting and prayer. She also recognized Jesus as the promised King of Israel. After she had seen Jesus, she testified to many people that the Messiah had been born. Mary and Joseph already knew who Jesus was, and yet, they marveled at the things which were said about Him. (See Luke 2:33)

After Herod's death Joseph and Mary returned from Egypt and chose Nazareth of Galilee as their new home. Jesus came to be called Jesus of Nazareth by friend and foe alike. (See Matthew 21:11, Mark 1:24, Luke 18:37, 24:19, Acts 3:6) This fulfilled another prophecy that he would be called a Nazarene. (See Matthew 2:23) It was in a synagogue in Nazareth that Jesus testified that He was the Messiah, the Son of God, the One who fulfilled the prophesy of Isaiah. (See Isaiah 61:1-2, Luke 4:16-30, Mark 6:1-3, Matthew 13:54) The Jews laughed at Him and rejected what He had said, asking, "*Isn't this the carpenter's son? Isn't this Jesus of Nazareth?*" (See Matthew 13:55-57; Mark 6:3-4,; Luke 4:24; John 4:44) They knew that the Messiah was to be born in Bethlehem, and they believed Jesus had been born in Nazareth. Jesus replied that a prophet is not without honor, save in his own country. Even though the Jews had seen Jesus work many miracles and fulfill many Old Testament prophesies (ie. opening the eyes of the blind etc. Isaiah 42:7), still they rejected Him.

But, many of His disciples did recognize something special in Jesus. On one occasion, many of His followers sought to make Him king by force. (See John 6:15) On another occasion, Jesus was hailed as the King of Israel by his followers as He made His triumphal entry into Jerusalem on the back of a donkey. (See Zechariah 9:9, Matthew 21:1-11, Luke 19:28-40) These acts enraged the jealous Jewish leaders who had rejected Jesus as a fraud and a blasphemer. So Jesus became the stone that the builders refused, (See Psalms 118:22) a rock of offense to the Jews, (See Isaiah 8:14; Romans 9:33, 1 Peter 2:8, 2 Nephi 18:14) He was sold for 30 pieces of silver. (See Zechariah 11:13) They pierced his hands and feet, (See Psalms 22:16) and gave him "*vinegar to drink*". (See

Psalms 69:21) He gave his back to the smiters, when they flogged Him. (See Isaiah 50:6) He was wounded for our transgression, He was bruised for our iniquity. (See Isaiah 53:5) In derision, the Jews placed a crown of thorns upon his head, and draped a purple robe about his shoulders. The made fun of Him and even spit on Him.

Pilate wrote on His cross, "Jesus of Nazareth the King of the Jews." It was written in three languages. This angered the Jews. They said, "*Write not, The King of the Jews; but that he said, I am King of the Jews.*" But Pilate said, "*What I have written, I have written,*" and he refused to change it. Perhaps even he recognized in part who Jesus really was. (See John 19: 19-22)

Neal A. Maxwell said, "*I testify that He is utterly incomparable in what He is, what He knows, what He has accomplished and what He has experienced. Yet, movingly, He calls us His friends.*" (See John 15:15 and Ensign, November 1981, p. 8)

Jesus, once of humble birth, will one day in glory come to earth, as King of kings and Lord of lords. Every knee will bow and every tongue confess that Jesus is King. (See D&C 88:104, Philippians 2:10-11, D&C 76:110, see also Hymns #196)

ACTIVITY IDEAS

- Bear testimony about the life and mission of the Savior.
- Discuss some things a king does, such as: make decisions, judge, make laws, etc. Tell about some wicked kings who have lived. (*Herod*: Luke 2, Bible Dictionary; *King Laban*: 1 Nephi 3 & 4; *King Noah*: Mosiah 11& 12; *David*: 2 Samuel 11 & 12) Discuss what it would be like to live under the rule of a wicked king who made evil laws, and what it might be like when Jesus reigns as king.
- Read the words of some of the hymns listed, and discuss what the words mean. Try to memorize one of them together. Or, read only a phrase from a song referring to Jesus as the King. Guess which song the phrase comes from. There are many others than those listed. See also Hymns #39-86, 134, 136, 147, 181, 197, 215, 225.
- Let your children take turns being king and making decisions. (ie. What to eat for dinner, who says family prayer, etc.)
- Do a musical reading. Hum or play the music from "*I Stand All Amazed*" while reading the words to Nephi's vision, 1 Nephi 11, especially the following verses: 14-15, 18-21 up to Lamb of God, 24, 27-33.

SUGGESTED SONGS

Christmas songs in Italics

CHILDREN'S SONGBOOK

Song	Page
He Sent His Son	34
Samuel Tells of the Baby Jesus	36
The Shepherd's Carol	40
Mary's Lullaby (especially vs. 2)	44
I Lived in Heaven	4
Beautiful Savior	62
He Died That We Might Live Again	65
Hosanna	66
This Is My Beloved Son	76
When He Comes Again	82
When Jesus Christ Was Baptized	102

HYMNS

Song	Page
Joy to the World	201
Oh, Come, All Ye Faithful	202
Angels We Have Heard on High	203
It Came upon the Midnight Clear	207
Hark! the Herald Angels Sing	209
Come, O Thou King of Kings	59
Battle Hymn of the Republic	60
Rejoice, the Lord Is King!	66
How Great Thou Art	86
Jesus, Once of Humble Birth	196
O Savior, Thou Who Wearest a Crown	197

ORNAMENT

Crown

- This ornament consists of two pieces, found on page 241.

Follow the Prophets

IN A NUTSHELL

Imagine flying in an airplane in the blackness of night, with no working lights either outside the plane or on the instrument panel. Imagine the feeling of comfort to finally see through the darkness, the runway lights leading to safety. Like the lights on a runway, prophets provide a safe path to follow by teaching us of the divinity of Jesus Christ and His divine plan for happiness. The Lord has promised that He will do nothing without first revealing it to His prophets. (See Amos 3:7) Joseph Smith was one of Heavenly Father's prophets, chosen to help restore His gospel to earth.

LESSON

An audible sigh of relief escaped from Nelson as at last the small, long-overdue cargo plane came into view. He had been alone for hours at the remote runway waiting for the plane to bring its supplies and pick him up. It was getting dark as the pilot unloaded the cargo and replaced it with Nelson's luggage. A thick blanket of clouds covered the stars as they took off into the late evening sky. As the velvety blackness of night closed in around them, Nelson became aware that there was no light in the cabin, not even from the plane's instrument panel, which should have been softly glowing. There were no lights in the cockpit and no working radio. Alarmed, he asked the pilot how they would be able to manage through such intense darkness. Calmly, the pilot explained that he would simply keep flying until he saw the gleam from the light tower and then fly toward it.

Nelson strained to see the light which could guide them through the blackness. At last they saw the light tower. Relief swept over him and he felt the weight of worry lift. Now they had their guiding light. As they neared the tower, however, Nelson was again gripped by fear when he realized that it was too dark to see the runway. They still would not be able to land. They had come this far, but with no working radio, and no lights to land by, the danger was far from being over. Fuel was low. They felt completely helpless as they circled in the darkness.

Suddenly, two rows of lights appeared as someone heard the plane's engine and switched on the runway lights. Fear was replace by joy and gratitude as the lights guided them to safety.

Like the light tower in this story, our Savior is always there to lead us in the way we should go. He knew, however, that there would be times when dark clouds of trouble would make us lose our way. He knew we would need some extra guidance.

Like the lights on the runway, prophets provide a safe path for us to follow so that we can safely return to a loving Heavenly Father.

All prophets, from Adam to this day have testified of Jesus. Some foretold his birth and gave hope that a Savior would come. Others walked with Him on earth, learned from Him and wrote of His life, teachings and miracles. Still others testify that He lived long ago on the earth, and still lives today. Prophets witness of the Savior's divinity. They teach us what Jesus would like us to do; how following His example can help us to live happier lives now, and how we can once again return to live with Him. Heavenly Father has promised that he will never do anything without first revealing it to one of His prophets. (See Amos 3:7) He has promised that His prophets will never lead us away from the path we should be on. (See "*Excerpts from Three Addresses by President Wilford Wodruff Regarding the Manifesto,*" in the D&C; See also Marion G. Romney, *Conference Report,* Oct. 1960, page 78, *Discourses of Wilford Woodruff* pages 212-13, Joseph F. Smith, *Journal of Discourses,* 24:192)

Regardless of the time a prophet lived, their divine calling is to bear witness that Jesus is the Christ, our Savior and Redeemer, that He loves us, that only through Him, the Only Begotten of the Father, can we gain eternal life. Elder Bruce R. McConkie taught, "*A prophet is one who has the testimony of Jesus, who knows by the revelations of the Holy Ghost to his soul that Jesus Christ is the Son of God. In addition to this divine knowledge, many of them lived in special situations or did particular things that singled them out as types and patterns and shadows of that which was to be in the life of him who is our Lord.*" (*The Promised Messiah,* Salt Lake City : Deseret Book, 1981, p. 448)

Joseph Smith was the first prophet of this dispensation. The Lord used Joseph as His "tool" to restore all truth and gospel keys again to the earth in these last days. Today, December 23rd is Joseph Smith's birthday. This great prophet left us one of the most powerful testimonies ever recorded of the Savior. "*And now, after the many testimonies which have been given of him, this is the testimony, last of all, which we give of him: That he lives! For we saw him, even on the right hand of God; and we heard the voice bearing record that he is the Only Begotten of the Father -- That by him, and through him, and of him, the worlds are and were created, and the inhabitants thereof are begotten sons and daughters unto God.* (D&C 76:22-24)

Christmas lights are an important part of Christmas. Without them, a Christmas tree would be dark and somewhat dismal. Christmas just would not be the same. Without the prophets, our guiding lights, we too, would be in darkness. Our lives would not be the same. What a blessing it is to have a living prophet for a living Church. If we follow the counsel of the prophets we have the assurance of safety, and in turn we can then guide others in their quest for truth.

ACTIVITY IDEAS

- Turn off all lights except the Christmas lights. Bear your testimony in a family testimony meeting around the Christmas tree.
- Play "*The Prophet Says.*" Play it the same way as "*Simon Says.*" For example: The leader might say, "The prophet says, 'Plant a garden.'" Everyone would then act out planting a garden. "The prophet says, 'Read the scriptures.'" Everyone pretends to read the scriptures."Clean your yard." If anyone acts it out, they are out until the next round, since the leader didn't say, "The Prophet says."
- Have small lights stationed in a path leading to a "prize." These could be Christmas lights, night lights etc.) Turn off room lights so that the lights of the path show well. (Pictures of the prophets could be used next to or instead of lights.) Discuss the importance of prophets, how they lead us and show us the way to go, and how to prepare for things which we may not even expect. Prophets give us direction and lead us safely through the dark.

  OPTIONAL IDEA: Make a pretend runway, with tape or rope on the floor. Put several objects on the runway. Blindfold one player and have another direct him along the runway safely, so he misses the objects. Compare this to guidance from a prophet.
- Using the quotes in the Optional Materials pages 197-212, play "*Who Said That?*" or use the trivia questions pages 211-212 to play "*Prophet Trivia.*"
- Use the *Pictures of Prophets* on pages 225-227, to play "*Name That Prophet,*" or match pictures of prophets with their names in a game of concentration.
- Gather several tools. Show them one at a time and ask who might use it. (ie. hammer and nails=carpenter, wrench=plumber, brush=painter etc.) Explain that prophets are "tools" for Heavenly Father, who help Him in His work. We can also be His tools by being good examples, serving Him and others.

SUGGESTED SONGS

Christmas songs in Italics

CHILDREN'S SONGBOOK

Song	Page
Samuel Tells of The Baby Jesus	36
Stars Were Gleaming	37
There Was Starlight on the Hillside	40
This Is My Beloved Son	76
The Sacred Grove	87
On a Golden Springtime	88
Seek the Lord Early	108
Follow the Prophet	110
Book of Mormon Stories (vs. 3-4)	118
Nephi's Courage	120
Keep the Commandments	146

HYMNS

Song	Page
Silent Night	204
O Little Town of Bethlehem	208
With Wondering Awe	210
The First Noel	213
We Thank Thee, O God, for a Prophet	19
Come, Listen to a Prophet's Voice	21
We Listen to a Prophet's Voice	22
Joseph Smith's First Prayer	26
Praise to the Man	27
Our Savior's Love	113
Brightly Beams Our Father's Mercy	335

ORNAMENT

Christmas Light

- This ornament consists of 1 piece, found on page 261.

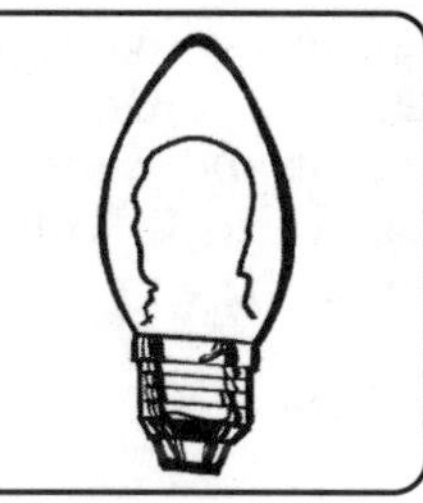

Jesus Christ Is Born!

IN A NUTSHELL

Christmas brings many different feelings: excitement, joy, wonder, happiness, closeness to family. As we take time to ponder the priceless gifts which God gives us, our hearts are filled with reverence for God's greatest gift — the gift of His Son. *"For God so loved the world, that he gave his only begotten Son, that whosoever believeth in him should not perish but have everlasting life."* (John 3:16) Jesus Christ also gave us a priceless gift — the gift of Himself, His love, His life, His atonement, His ALL. *"Thanks be unto God for his unspeakable gift."* (2 Corinthians 9:15)

LESSON

Tonight is the night! This is the reason for the celebration, the parties, the decorations, the fun secrets and gifts — Jesus Christ was born!

Christmas brings so many feelings - excitement, wonder, happiness, joy, and a special closeness to family. For some, Christmas may bring feelings of intense loneliness as they miss loved ones who are far away.

There is another feeling we feel tonight as we think about the birth of our Savior. Though it is a quiet feeling, it is deep and intense. We feel it from our head to our toes, with every fiber of our being.

> *"And thou shalt love the Lord thy God with all thine heart, and with all thy soul, and with all thy might.*
>
> *And these words, which I command thee this day, shall be in thine heart.*
>
> *And thou shalt teach them diligently unto thy children, and shalt talk of them when thou sittest in thine house, and when thou walkest by the way, and when thou liest down, and when thou risest up."* (Deuteronomy 6:5,7)

At times, this love is so intense it makes us feel as if we will burst. We feel it with our whole soul. It is a feeling which includes courtesy, honor and respect. This love is called reverence.

Reverence is more than just being quiet. It is a feeling of deep respect, love, and awe.

There were no parties and gifts on the first Christmas. It was a quiet night filled with reverence, peace and the loving tenderness of a newly formed family. There was no happy laughter or shouts of joy, just warmth, stillness and the rejoicing which comes from deep joy.

Let us take time tonight to fill our hearts with reverence. Let us take time to remember the kindest and most loving man ever to be born into this world -- Our Savior and Redeemer, Jesus Christ. Let us remember not only His birth, but His life -- a generous gift from a kind and loving Father.

"For God so loved the world, that he gave his only begotten Son, that whosoever believeth in him should not perish but have everlasting life." (John 3:16)

Let us also remember the gift given us from Jesus Christ Himself -- the gift of His love, His life, His atonement, His ALL.

REVERENCE

So small, so weak and frail He was,
A new born babe in straw because
There was no room there at the inn,
Yet in the stable starlight streamed in.
A Heavenly glow was all around
As in the field shepherds were found.

There was no one else awake at all
And angels had glad tidings to call.
They sang praises to God's name and then
Said - "Christ is born in Bethlehem!"
Oh what rejoicing then took place
Good will toward men on every face.

They found him wrapped in swaddling bands
While others saw in foreign lands
The star that shone to lead the way
To the place the Holy Baby lay.
And all who saw Him that special night
Knew He was full of Truth and Right.

This was the One all prophets said
Would come that now we could be led
To greater heights of peace and love
And to Heavenly Father up above.
So there silent, with love intense
Each knelt and worshiped in reverence.

Suzanne Meredith

"*Thanks be unto God for his unspeakable gift. (2 Corinthians 9:15) "Peace I leave with you, my peace I give unto you; not as the world giveth, give I unto you. Let not your heart be troubled, neither let it be afraid."* (John 14:27)

What will your gift be to Him? *"If ye love me, keep my commandments."* (John 14:15) *"A new commandment I give unto you, That ye love one another; as I have loved you, that ye also love one another. By this shall all men know that ye are my disciples, if ye have love one to another."* (John 13:34-35)

"*And thou shalt love the Lord thy God with all thy heart, and with all thy soul, and with all thy mind, and with all thy strength; this is the first commandment. And the second is like, namely this, Thou shalt love thy neighbor as thyself. There is none other commandment greater than these."* (Mark 12:30-31)

The greatest gift we can give is the gift of love.The night Jesus was born the angels sang, "*Glory to God in the highest, and on earth peace, good will toward men.*" (Luke 2:14)

"*What a consummation to be wished — Peace on earth! But how can that come except through the maintenance of good will toward men? And through what means could glory to God in the highest be more effectively rendered?*" (James E. Talmage, *Jesus the Christ*, Salt Lake City: Church of Jesus Christ of Latter-Day Saints, 1973, page 94)

ACTIVITY IDEAS

- Have children act out the Christmas Story. For the text use either Luke 2 or New Testament Stories, *Jesus Christ Is Born.*
  OPTIONAL IDEA: Use a nativity set, or the "*Samuel the Lamanite*" figures from Lesson 2 to tell the story of the birth of Christ. (See Optional Materials pages 213-215)
- Ask someone who might be spending Christmas alone to join you for this evening.
- Play some nice Christmas Music in the background while reading the Christmas Story from Luke 2, and Matthew 2.
- Do a Family Christmas Program, for your own family or someone else. There are two nice readings in the *Family Home Evening Resource Book* which could be used for this. "Come Let us Adore Him" pages 159-160 deals mainly with Jesus' birth, while "Easter Program" pages 153-154 deals with His life, atonement and resurrection.

SUGGESTED SONGS

Christmas songs in Italics

CHILDREN'S SONGBOOK

He Sent His Son	34
Stars Were Gleaming	37
When Joseph Went to Bethlehem	38
Little Jesus	39
Once within a *Lowly Stable*	41
Away in a Manger	42
Mary's Lullaby	44
I Think When I Read That Sweet Story	56
Jesus Is Our Loving Friend	58
Jesus Said Love Everyone	61
I Feel My Savior's Love	74
Mother, Tell Me the Story.(esp. vs.2)	204

HYMNS

Oh, Come, All Ye Faithful	202
Silent Night	204
O Little Town of Bethlehem	208
With Wondering Awe	210
The First Noel	213
How Great Thou Art	86
Come, Follow Me	116
God Loved Us, So He Sent His Son	187
How Great the Wisdom and the Love	195
Love One Another	308

ORNAMENT

Nativity

- This ornament consists of 2 pieces, found on page 275.

Optional Materials

ADDITIONAL REFERENCES

Prophecies of Jesus Christ

Numbers 24:17............ .Star out of Jacob
Psalms 22:16-18.......... They pierced His hands and feet, stared upon Him, and cast lots (Matthew 27:35; Mark 15:24; Luke 23:34; John 19:24)
Psalms 69:21............... .In my thirst they gave me vinegar (Matthew 27: 34,48; Mark 15:36; Luke 23:36; John 19:28-29)
Isaiah 7:14................. A virgin shall conceive (Matthew 1:20-23; 2 Nephi 17:14)
Isaiah 42: 7................. To open eyes of the blind (Matthew 9:27-30, 11:5, 20:30-34; Luke 7:21-22; John 9:1-7)
Isaiah 50:6.................. I gave my back to smiters (Lamentations 3:30; Matthew 26:67; Matthew 27: 26,30)
Ezekiel 37:12.............. I will open your graves (Matthew 27:52)
Hosea 11:1.................. I called my Son out of Egypt (Matthew 2:15)
Micah 5:2.................... Messiah to come from Bethlehem (Matthew 2:6; Luke 2:4,15; John 7:42)
Zechariah 9:9............... Thy King cometh unto thee riding upon an ass (Matthew 21:2-9, Luke 19: 28-40; John 12:14-15)
Zechariah 11:12-13...... I was prised at 30 pieces of silver (Matthew 26:15; 27:3-10)

Signs of the Second Coming

Isaiah 2:2.................... Lord's house established (Micah 4:1)
Ezekiel 37:16-20.......... Book of Mormon to come forth (3 Nephi 21:1-2)
Hosea 1:11................... Israel gathered (D&C 39:11)
Malachi 3:1.................. Lord's messenger to come (3 Nephi 24:1)
Malachi 4:5.................. Elijah to come
Matthew 24: 3-5........... False christs and prophets (See also verses 11, 24-26)
Matthew 24:6-7........... Wars and plagues
Matthew 24:12,37......... Iniquity will abound (2 Timothy 3:1-5, 7)
Acts 2:19..................... Signs in heavens (Matthew 24:29; Joel 3:15)
Acts 3: 19-21............... Restoration of all things
2 Thessalonians 2:3..... Apostasy
Revelation 14: 6-7........ Angel to bring back gospel
3 Nephi 21:23-25......... Zion to be established (D&C 84:3-5)
D&C 49:24................... Lamanites and Jacob to flourish
D&C 65:2..................... Gospel preached to all world (Numbers 14:21; 1 Nephi 14:12; Moses 60:62; D &C 133:37)

See Also *Mormon Doctrine*, Signs of the times

Signs

1 Corinthians 14:22...... Tongues given as a sign
Matthew 24: 32-33........ Parable of fig tree
Matthew 24: 42-51........ Watch and be diligent
D&C 63:9...................... Faith cometh not by signs
D&C 68:10.................... Believers blessed with signs

Old Testament Stories

Noah

Book of Mormon Stories

Samuel the Lamanite Tells about Jesus Christ
Alma's Mission to Ammonihah
Korihor
Nephi and Lehi In Prison
The Murder of the Chief Judge

He Is Born!

For there is nothing hid, which shall not be manifested; neither was anything kept secret, but that it should come abroad. (Mark 4:22)

English novelist, George Eliot, speaking of expectations said, "*Nothing is so good as it seems beforehand.*" But he was wrong .Our son was everything we had expected and more.

Owen Fellltham, perhaps, expressed it better when he said, "*All earthly delights are sweeter in expectation than enjoyment, but all spiritual pleasures more in fruition than expectation.*"

Certainly, our son was a very special and long awaited spiritual gift.

Three years before his birth, I had met and married my husband. He was 30, I was 31. We wanted to start our family immediately. (As we were a bit pressed for time)

But, it didn't happen that way. Instead it would be a lengthy and distressful road. But three long years, and numerous medical tests later, there he was; ten fingers, ten toes, a head full of dark hair, a pudgy nose and a somewhat pointed head. He was beautiful!

My mother-in-law and niece had traveled all the way from Italy to be with us for his birth. The Italians have a beautiful tradition of celebrating an important event by giving a gift; a small memento called a "*bomboniera*", to friends and family. The "bomboniera" serves as a remembrance of special events such as births, weddings and special anniversaries.

Sitting there in the hospital next to our son's little crib, we discussed and planned our birth announcements, and some kind of a bomboniera which we could afford on our limited budget.

Finally, I had a great idea. For the birth announcement, we would make a postcard resembling the WANTED posters of the old West.. It read: "*WANTED ALIVE! Yes we have wanted this little one for a long time!*" Then we entered all of the statistics of his birth, and put his picture inside the frame. Everyone who was aware of our difficulties, understood what we had wanted to express with this announcement.

For a bomboniera, we decided to give a little, homemade Christmas tree ornament. We made an extra one for ourselves also, as a reminder of the blessing of his birth. Each year, at Christmas, we put that little ornament on our own tree. It reminds us of the happiness we felt on that occasion, and the joy we felt then all comes flooding back.

Several months before our baby was due, we began the painstaking endeavor of selecting a name. (Which, I think, may possibly have been more difficult than labor!)

Because my husband is Italian, we wanted to choose a name which sounded good in both the Italian and English language, and one which his family would be able to pronounce without much difficulty.

I presented my husband with a long list of names which I liked. He couldn't agree on any of them. So, I read the entire baby name book to him. Still nothing. It seemed that every name brought back funny memories from his childhood of someone he knew who had been owner of that particular name, and so he wouldn't even consider it. His only suggestion was "Elvis", which didn't appeal to me a great deal.

One day he finally announced, "What about Alexander. I don't mind that name." We looked it up in our book of baby names to find out what it meant. "Helper of men." That convinced us that Alexander was the name that we wanted to give him. So Alexander it would be.

We made up our list of friends and relatives to whom we wanted to send our "glad tidings." We wanted to tell everyone, but with our limited finances, we had to reduce our list.

Two thousand years ago, our Heavenly Father's first born Son came to earth. God also announced the birth of His Son. This was not an ordinary birth but an extraordinary one, and, likewise, the announcement would be befitting the event. God was not limited to a tight budget. This was an occasion of utmost importance. There would be no restrictions made to His list of "friends and relatives." These glad tidings were to go to all people.

To the city of Bethlehem, God sent an angel choir who sang praises of honor and worship for this newborn Babe. Unborn generations filled the heavens with songs of praise and shouts of joy. But God's announcement was not limited to this select group of shepherds on a hillside in Bethlehem. Instead this glorious message was heralded around the earth, from sea to sea, to every nation and every people. A new star appeared in the heavens, as well as many magnificent signs and wonders.

Everyone who had been faithfully watching and waiting for the sign of this blessed event knew that it had come to pass.

One of our relatives accused us of not sending her a birth announcement. I assured her that, indeed, we had sent one, and I described our little homemade postcard to her. Yes, she vaguely remembered receiving something similar, but had thrown it away thinking it to be a piece of "junk mail."

So it was with our Heavenly Father. Everyone who was watching their "spiritual mailbox" for the announcement, received it with joy. There were those who disregarded the announcement and discarded it as a piece of insignificant "junk mail," some freak of nature or astronomical phenomenon. But everyone did receive the announcement. All "friends and family" were informed.

Long before His birth, God had chosen the name for his Son. An angel was sent to Mary, telling her what the baby's name would be. It was a name common in those days. In Greek, the name is Jesus. In Hebrew it is Jeshua or Joshua. It means, God is help, or God is Salvation. In that day people didn't have last names, or surnames. Instead, to differentiate one Jeshua from another, people often attached a short description as a surname. Generally, these names described where someone was from or who their father was. Two surnames often assigned to Jesus were: Jesus of Nazareth or Jesus the carpenter's son.

Often these descriptions stuck to a person and became their permanent last names. In my genealogy, I find names such as: Scott, meaning of Scotland; Vest, meaning from the West; and Jacobson, meaning the son of Jacob.

However, none of those names which were assigned to Jesus were to be the one by which he would be known throughout history. The title of "*Christ*" would be the name affixed permanently to his name, to set Him apart from all others. Christ means "The Anointed One" or" The Messiah." Jesus has come to be known by believers everywhere as Jesus the Christ.

He was the one anointed even before the foundation of the world, to bring salvation to all who would believe on His name and follow Him. He was the sinless One, who, through His atonement and the shedding of His own innocent blood would bring salvation to mankind. He was the promised baby of whom countless prophets had prophesied; the Babe of Bethlehem, born of a virgin, the Son of the Highest, The Savior and Redeemer of the World, Immanuel.

So, that holy night, in Bethlehem and around the world, God announced the birth of His Son. This was the night of all nights. The heavens resounded with exultant praises sung by a glorious and holy angel choir. Humble shepherds on a hillside in Bethlehem, hurried to find the Holy Babe. After witnessing for themselves, they "*made known abroad*" all which they had heard and seen. A gleaming star of promise, appeared in the heavens, announcing to all men everywhere, "He is born!." The glorious birth announcement was sent worldwide, to every nation and tongue.

Though the majority of the human race discounted this heavenly announcement, sent some two thousand years ago, it has, nevertheless, been carefully recorded and preserved in holy writ. That sacred account of the events which occurred that holy night is a precious gift from God, a memento for the generations yet unborn, a "bomboniera" so to speak, which affords each of us an opportunity to know of the events which took place on that hallowed night, when God announced the birth of His Son to the world.

Now as we reflect and reverence the marvels which occurred that night, our hearts are filled with joy and gladness for the birth of God's Holy Son. And we rejoice anew with the angels:

"***Glory to God in the highest, and on earth peace -- Good will toward men.***" (Luke 2:14)

THOUGH QUIETLY THE WITNESS BORNE

So modestly God's gift was giv'n
No pomp, parade or pageantry,
No garish crown of jeweled gold,
No fanfare blared, no revelry.

So privately the song was sung
To common folk, of humble stock.
A simple message, "Peace on earth!"
On Bethleh'ms hill where grazed the flock.

And softer still the shining star
In eastern sky --- appointed sign
By mindless masses, unobserved
Shone, herald of God's gift divine.

Though quietly the witness borne,
In humble hearts, it lingers on.
Still shines within their hearts His star.
Still echoes in their lives His song.

Sharon Velluto

ADDITIONAL REFERENCES

Psalms 55:17.............. I will pray evening, morning and noon
Proverbs 15:29........... He heareth the prayer of the righteous
Jeremiah 29:13........... Shall find me when ye search with all thy heart
Daniel 6:10................. Daniel kneeled three times a day,
Matthew 6:6-13........... Jesus teaches about prayer (Lord's Prayer)
Matthew 7:7-11.......... Jesus gives more instructions on prayer (See also Mark 11:24)
Mark 14:38................. Watch and pray that ye enter not into temptation (See also Matthew 26:41, Alma 13:28)
Luke 11:1.................... Lord teach us to pray
Luke 18:1-13.............. Men ought always to pray (See also D&C 88:76)
Ephesians 6:18........... Pray always
Philippians 4:6........... By prayer let your requests be made known
James 1:5-6................ If any man lacks wisdom, let him ask of God
James 4:3................... Ask and receive not, because ye ask amiss
James 5:16.................. The prayer of a righteous man availeth much
1 Peter 3:12................ His ears are open unto their prayers
2 Nephi 32:8-9........... Evil spirit teacheth a man not to pray
Enos........................... Enos prays
Alma 26:22................. Pray without ceasing to know the mysteries
Alma 31:22................. Every man offered self same prayer
Alma 34:17-27........... A prophet's instructions on prayer
Alma 37:37................. Counsel with the Lord in all thy doings
Alma 38:13................. They pray to be heard of men
3 Nephi 18:19-21....... Jesus instructs Nephite families to pray to Father in His name
Ether 2:14.................. Brother of Jared chastened for forgetting to pray
D&C 8:10.................... Do not ask for that which ye ought not
D&C 9:8...................... How to recognize answer to prayer
D&C 19:28.................. Pray vocally as well as in thy heart

Old Testament Stories
Daniel and the Lions' Den
Esther

New Testament Stories
Jesus Teaches about Prayer

Book of Mormon Stories
Lehi's Dream
Building the Ship
Enos
King Benjamin
Alma the Younger Repents
Nephi and Lehi in Prison
Jesus Christ Blesses the Children
Jesus Christ Teaches about the Sacrament and Prayer
The Jaredites leave Babel
The Jaredites Travel to the Promised Land

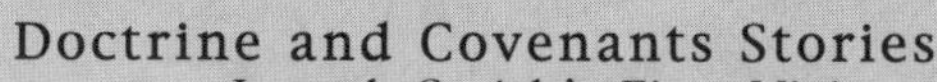

Doctrine and Covenants Stories
Joseph Smith's First Vision

IN TUNE

A radio can take a song from far across the sea--
Some soft melodious serenade--and bring that song to me.
I turn a switch, adjust a knob, to put the set in tune.
Sweet lilting notes then resonate to fill my empty room.
When I gaze into gentle skies, and know there's music there
Uncertainties all melt away-- I know God hears my prayer!

Sharon Velluto

OPEN INVITATION

We wait in lines for autographs,
Or strain our eyes to see
An athlete, or a president,
One of nobility.

To think of spending time with them
Is more than one could dream.
To be acknowledged, shake their hand
Brings praise and high esteem.

Yet when our Heavenly Father bids
Us kneel before His throne,
Receive His counsel, hear His word,
We often fail to come.

Imagine! God of heav'n and earth
The One without compare!
Oh, that we could comprehend
That wondrous gift called prayer!

Sharon Velluto

With thoughtless and impatient hands,
We tangle up the plans
The Lord has wrought
And when we cry in pain
...He saith,
"Be quiet, man, while I untie the knot."

Author Unknown

THE LORD'S PRAYER

You cannot pray the Lord's Prayer
And even once say "I".
You cannot pray the Lord's Prayer
And even once say "My".
Nor can you pray the Lord's Prayer
And not pray for another;
For when you ask for daily bread,
You must include your brother.
For others are included
In each and every plea;
From beginning to the end of it
It does not once say "Me".

Author Unknown

PRAYER

I know not by what method rare,
But this I know, God answers prayer.
I know that he has given His word,
That tells me prayer is always heard,
And will be answered, soon or late,
And so I pray and calmly wait.
I know not if the blessings sought,
Will come in just the way I thought,
But leave my prayers to Him above,
Whose ways are wiser than my own,
Assured that He will grant my quest
Or send some answer far more blessed.

Eliza M. Hickok

AN INFORMAL PRAYER

"The proper way for a man to pray,"
said Deacon Lemuel Keys,
"And the only proper attitude,
is down upon his knees."

"No, I should say the way to pray,"
said Reverend Dr. Wise,
"Is standing straight with outstretched arms
and rapt and upturned eyes."

"Oh, no, no, no," said Elder Snow,
"Such posture is too proud.
A man should pray with eyes fast closed,
and head contritely bowed."

"It seems to me his hand should be
austerely clasped in front,
With both thumbs pointed toward the ground,"
said Reverend Dr. Hunt.

"Last year I fell in Hodgekin"s well,
head first," said Cyrus Brown.
"With both my heels a-striking up,
my head a-pointin' down."

"And I made a prayer right then and there;
best prayer I ever said...
The prayin'est prayer I ever prayed,
a standin' on my head."

Author Unknown

"HELLO...?

Be thou humble; and the Lord thy God shall lead thee by the hand, and give thee answer to thy prayers. (D&C 112:10)

"It's for you, Mama," my little toddler, Alex, called to me. He padded into the kitchen, dragging his plastic, toy phone behind him. The bells clanked as the phone skipped and bounced across the floor.

He sat down at my feet on the kitchen floor, and repeated, "It's for you." holding the phone up to me. "It's Batman."

I took my hands from the soapy dishwater and put the phone to my ear. Cradling the receiver between my shoulder and my ear, I continued to wash the pile of dishes in the sink, while I talked to an imagined super hero.

I asked about his partner, his butler and a long list of villains he had been fighting recently. Then, when I felt my son was satisfied with my conversation, I politely concluded the call, handed the phone back to him and continued with the task at hand.

Alex dialed another number. "It's for you again. It's Santa Claus," he informed me.

Again I held the phone to my ear, while the dishes clinked in the sink. "How is Mrs. Santa?" I asked. "How are the elves? Are they keeping out of trouble? Are the toys almost finished? "I paused for an imaginary response after each question, adding lots of "uh-huhs" and "un-uhs" and "Ohs" into the conversation. When I had finished talking to the jolly gentleman, I gave the phone back.

The little bells rang again as Alex dialed another number. Barney, a furry purple dinosaur wanted to talk. So, I spoke with him about his friends, how much Alex liked his show, and about all the things he had been up to lately. I handed the phone back to my son, being a little wearied by the interruptions and wanting to finish the dishes.

But, Alex was enjoying this little game. He dialed another number and handed me the phone. "It's Jesus," he told me.

My stomach jumped into my throat. I was taken somewhat aback. There I stood with his little toy phone clasped in my soapy hand, and I was speechless. Jesus was on the other end and wanted to talk and I didn't know what to say.

I have since wondered why such a thing should have affected me like that. It isn't as if I never pray. I do pray. Regularly even. And I know that the Savior is the mediator in those prayers. So why should having Him on the other line bother me?

Was it that I didn't have any "small talk", which I felt worthy of His time and attention? Surely, He wasn't interested in my dirty dishes and unmade beds. Yet the scriptures tell us to pray over our fields and flocks. (See Alma 34:24-25) Was it that I considered "my fields and my flocks " to be too inconsequential and menial for His consideration?

To me a dandelion is a weed, and a nuisance which adds color to my yard. But when those little yellow blossoms are clasped in the tight, pudgy fist of my toddler, whose shining face beams up at me, "Mama, I brought you some flowers,." those weeds become a thing of charm and beauty. Wouldn't my "little weeds" be the same to a loving Father?

Could the reason for my discomfort be that my prayers are often trite and repetitious, that instead of truly praying I have been pretending? Or is it that I pray without the realization that there really is someone on the other end of the line who is actually listening to my prayers and stands ready to answer them?

I remember kneeling in prayer once, during a time of great discouragement. My heart was weighed down with a problem, and my prayers did not lift the burden but seemed to hover and settle around me like a heavy fog, refusing to rise upward. In frustration and despair, I opened my eyes and stared at the blank, white wall in front of me. "Why won't thou listen?" I asked. "Why dost thou not care?" I thought, I may as well have been praying to a wall, for all the good this was doing me.

As tears of desperation welled up in my eyes, a scripture was whispered to my heart. "*And there ye shall serve gods, the work of men's hands, wood and stone, which neither see, nor hear nor eat, nor smell.*" (Deuteronomy 4:28) I was familiar with the scripture. It was one I had used often in the mission field to teach of the evil practice of idol worship. At first I was puzzled as to why this particular scripture had been given to me, and what it had to do with my situation.

Then, in my heart I was given to understand, that there I knelt facing the wall, a work of men's hands, a wall of wood and stone, that could neither see nor hear, nor eat, nor smell. I was petitioning a God who I felt was unaware of my suffering, and was unwilling to stretch forth His hand in answer to my pleas. I understood that in my faithless prayers, I had been committing a great evil. Though I may not have been praying to an "idol" I was praying to a Being whom I perceived to be an "idle god." I had allowed my despair to so engulf me, that my prayers were being voiced with little faith that they would be heard and answered. I had forgotten that "*With God, nothing is impossible.*" (See Luke 1:37) The promise of the Lord is sure:

"*Call unto me, and I will answer thee, and shew thee great and mighty things, which thou knowest not.*" (Jeremiah 33:3)

YE HAVE NOT BECAUSE

If you had been living when Christ was on earth,
And had met the Savior kind,
What would you have asked Him to do for you,
Supposing you were blind?

The child considered and then replied,
I expect that without a doubt,
I'd have asked for a dog and a collar and chain
To lead me safely about.

And how oft' thus in our faithless prayers
We acknowledge with shame and surprise,
We have only asked for a dog and chain,
When we might have had "opened eyes".

Author Unknown

APOLOGY

Dear God, its been a long time
Since I've knelt before thy throne.
Please understand that I was doing
So well on my own.

Life's sea was calm, untroubled then,
I hope not to offend;
That now, I bow with begging hand,
I didn't need help then.

Sharon Velluto

THE LARGER PRAYER

At first I prayed for Light;
Could I but see the way,
How gladly, swiftly would I walk
To everlasting day.

And next I prayed for Strength;
That I might tread the road
With firm, unfaltering feet and win
The heaven's serene abode.

And then I asked for Faith;
Could I but trust my God,
I'd live enfolded in His peace,
Though foes were all abroad.

But now I pray for Love;
Deep love to God and man,
A living love that will not fail
However dark his plan.

And Light and Strength and Faith
Are opening everywhere;
God only waited for me, till
I prayed the larger prayer.

Edna Dow Cheney
1824-1904

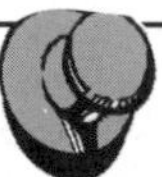

No person has a stronger weapon against the power of evil than he who with unbroken regularity goes night and morning on bended knee before our Heavenly Father in sincere and humble secret prayer.

Marion G. Romney
Ensign, January 1985, p. 5

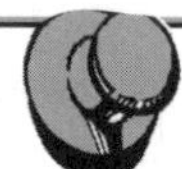

When the burdens of life become heavy, when trials test one's faith, when pain sorrow and despair cause the light of hope to flicker and burn low, communication with our Heavenly Father provides peace.

Thomas S. Monson

If you find yourself further away from God than you were yesterday, you can be sure who has moved.

Author Unknown

ADDITIONAL REFERENCES

Psalms 37:16	Little that righteous hath is better than riches of the wicked
Psalms 62:10	If riches increase, do not set heart upon them
Psalms 73:12	Ungodly who prosper
Proverbs 11:4,28	He that trusteth in riches shall fall
Proverbs 13:7	There is that maketh himself rich and hath nothing
Matthew 6:19-21	Lay up for yourselves treasures in heaven
Matthew 6:24	Cannot serve God and mammon (Luke 16:11-13)
Matthew 13:1-9,18-23	Parable of the sower (Mark 4:1-9)
Matthew 16:26	What is a man profited if he gain the world and lose his soul
Mark 4:19	Riches choke the word
Mark 12:38-44	Widow's mite
Luke 8:7,14	Choked by cares of the world
Luke 12:15-21	Beware of covetousness
Luke 12:31	Seek ye the kingdom of God
Luke 21:34	Take heed lest your hearts be overcharged with the cares of life
John 15:19; 17:16	If ye were of the world, the world would love its own
Colossians 2:8	Beware lest men spoil you after the rudiments of world
Colossians 3:2	Set your affections on the things above..not on earth
1Timothy 6:7-12	The love of money is the root of all evil
Titus 2:12	Denying ungodliness and worldly lusts
James 4:4	Friendship of world is enmity with God
2 Nephi 9:39	Carnally minded is death, spiritually minded is life eternal
2 Nephi 9:42	God will not open to those who are wise and puffed up
Jacob 2:18	Before seeking riches, seek kingdom of God
Mosiah 3:19	Natural man is an enemy to God
Alma 5:57	Come out from the wicked
Alma 31:27	Puffed up with vain things of the world.
D&C 1:16	Those who seek not the Lord shall perish
D&C 6:7	Seek not for riches but for wisdom
D&C 53:2	Commandment to forsake world
D&C 121:35-36	Hearts set on vain things of world

Book of Mormon Stories
- Lehi's Dream
- The People of Ammon
- The Zoramites and the Rameumptom

Old Testament Stories
- The Prophet Elisha

New Testament Stories
- The Rich Young Man
- The Widow's Mites
- The Ten Young Women

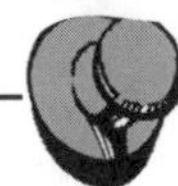

"See how the masses of man worry themselves into nameless graves, while here and there a great, unselfish soul forgets himself into immortality."

Ralph Waldo Emerson
1803-1882

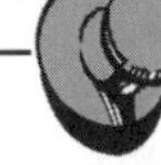

MY GIFT

Nor crown, nor robe, nor spice I bring
As offering unto Christ, my King
Yet have I brought a gift the Child
May not despise, however small;
For here I lay my heart today,
And it is full of love to all.
Take Thou the poor but loyal thing,
My only tribute, Christ, my King!

Eugene Field
1850-1895

WRAPPED UP

As I wrap these presents which are
Heaped up, high around
My heart feels rather barren,
For this season I've been found

To be so wrapped up in Christmas;
Wrapped in shining silvery things
That I think I've lost perspective
'Neath this paper, tape and string.

I fear, much like the keeper
Closed the door at Bethlh'ms Inn;
I've forgotten that this season
Is for celebrating Him.

May I see past box and bundle
Wrapped in papers red and gold,
And wrap myself in peace, good-will.
The glad news angels told.

Though somewhat insignificant,
I give my offering,
Wrapped up, my gift of self, to Him,
Who gives us everything.

Sharon Velluto

CHRISTMAS STORY

Christmas isn't the lights or the holly,
It isn't the ribbons of gold,
Not the carols, the tree, or the presents,
It's a story not oft enough told.

Of Wise Men who watched and who waited
For the sign of His birth from afar,
And hoping to witness the Promise
They followed a glistening star.

All huddled and cold on a hillside,
The shepherds who heard the glad song
Of angels who sang Hallelujah,
Peace on earth for the Savior is born!

It's the story of two weary travelers;
Foreigners, seeking for some place to stay,
And, finding no room but a stable,
And naught for a bed but some hay.

It's the tale of a wonderful baby
Wrapped tight in swaddling clothes,
And laid upon hay in a manger;
God's gift to bring hope to the world.

Sharon Velluto

DID YOU HAVE A GOOD CHRISTMAS?

"Did you have a good Christmas?" they ask me.
Now, what measuring stick does one use?
Tell me, which scale exists to determine
How successful my Christmas, I muse?

Do I number and weigh all the presents
So festively wrapped 'neath the tree?
Or do I consider the counsel---
"'Tis more blessed to give than receive?"

Does my scale slightly tip toward envy?
Or, with covetous eyes did I yen?
Or, did I employ the entreaty--
"Peace on earth, and good will toward men?"

Sharon Velluto

PREPARED FOR CHRISTMAS

My house, it looks like Christmas.
A wreath welcomes at my door,
The tree is lit and tinseled,
Gifts are piled up on the floor.

My house, it sounds like Christmas.
Secrets buzzing through the halls,
Pots clanking in the kitchen,
Children bouncing off the walls.

My house, it smells like Christmas.
Wassail, gingerbread and pine,
Caramel popcorn, Christmas cookies
Hand dipped chocolates in a line.

My house, it tastes like Christmas.
Ample candy, spice and sweets,
Christmas gifts from caring neighbors,
Cache of yummy Christmas treats.

And me, I feel like Christmas,
My budget's more than spent,
My "up and go" I started with,
"Well, it got up and went!

"Yes, I'm prepared for Christmas.
To hear, to smell, to see.
But in my heart I question,
Is this what it should be?

Is the reason for my emptiness,
A carol left unsung?
Some needy one left wanting?
Or a kindness left undone?

Am I prepared for Christmas?
Just what does that imply?
It's Christ's ideals etched in my heart,
Not glitz that greets the eye.

Sharon Velluto

THE PROPORTIONS OF CHRISTMAS

This year I will pay proper honor to the true King of Christmas.
By Ruth C. Ikerman

Ever since I was a little girl I had wanted to possess a set of nativity figures to use on the top of the bookcase at Christmas time. In a colorful market of a town in Central America my husband and I were privileged to make such a purchase for our home. In the doing, we had an adventure which taught us anew to keep the accompaniments of Christmas down to size and to exalt the Christ of Christmas.

We had been advised to seek the flower section as we walked through the market, where women sat on the ground with their colorful woven shawls and reed baskets bulging with red and green fruits. At the far corner of the square we were attracted to a little shop by the sound of squawking chickens in a basket. We turned in and passed a smiling dark-skinned lad of about six and his little sister of four who sat outdoors eating a piece of brown tortilla. They bounced to their feet and followed us, while their mother concluded her bargaining with a customer. On the shelves of the shop were rows of little figurines. On the top shelf was a set of five pieces-- the familiar figure of the beloved Child in the manger, an adoring mother, the kneeling father, patient burro, and gentle cow.

Apparently the shopkeeper loved this set and when it had not sold the year before, she had not packed it away, but kept it on display where she could enjoy it. There was not a speck of dust on any of the figures, despite the dirt and confusion of the market. As her hands caressed the pieces, turning them over to me, I could sense how much she hated to part with them.

When I asked her how much they would be, the price she named happened to be the figure I had been saving for this particular purchase. I took out a bill and handed it to her. She wiped her hand across a strand of dark hair on her perspiring forehead and looked at me intently, as though she knew I understood how much she would miss the figure of Mary with the blue cape over her white robe.

The children were now running through the big wicker baskets on the floor. Presently the boy came up from the bottom with a tiny white angel, which had a golden scroll in its hand. Little sister popped up with a wooly lamb and a shepherd boy attached to the same green ceramic base. My husband reached for coins in his pocket to pay for the angels and the shepherd.

What else did the scene need? I wondered. Suddenly I wished I could remember the Spanish words for "three kings." Then I saw in her side case three tall kings, tucked away behind faded crepe-paper flowers. I pointed to them.

A frown crossed her face and she shook her head. I put another bill on the counter and motioned toward the three tall figures of the kings on camels, their golden turbans and rich blue and red robes glittering against the bejeweled boxes on the animals they were riding. Again the woman shook her head. When my husband started to reach for them, thinking perhaps they were out of her arm's reach, she spoke a torrent of Spanish--her disapproval, at least, clearly intelligible.

Suddenly she was silent. Taking one of the kings, she placed the figure beside the beautiful manger scene in front of me. Then she picked up the king and held it behind her, hiding it from my sight. She brought the king back again to the scene and again immediately removed it, putting it behind her again, and this time barricading herself against the adobe wall of her little shop.

What queer actions, I thought. Doesn't she want to make a sale?

Then in a moment of clarity I understood what she was trying to tell me. Plainly, this woman who stood before me with eager face and work-worn hands was saying, "Don't buy these three kings to go with this lovely manger set. Can't you see that the kings are bigger than the other figures? Don't you know that if you do this, you will have your eyes always on the kings and their presents, and you will never see the Child?"

Her face framed a radiant smile when I humbly managed to say, Gracias, señora," and she knew I understood. She put her hand on my arm and held me there while she motioned to her young son and spoke to him in rapid Spanish. He placed a chair on a box and began to climb until I feared for his safety on the makeshift ladder. Down he came with a package wrapped in newspaper. Inside was an assortment of kings, each carrying a gift. And as she had known they would be, each king was in proper size in relation to my other figures.

Happily she sighed, as she pocketed the small change which these figures commanded, apparently oblivious to the larger bills she might have had for the garish kings. Hat in hand my husband stood by my side looking at the figures which we would be taking to our home. As I picked up the package, I spoke the two words of our own language which are understandable in almost any country - "Merry Christmas."

There immediately came from the lips of the shopkeeper and her children the reply, "Feliz Navidad." I hear its echo now as I arrange the manger scene on top of the bookcase in our California home. I am putting it in place early, so that as I do my shopping this year, I may be reminded to keep the true proportions of this most important of days.

This year I will pay proper honor to the true King of Christmas.

By Ruth C. Ikerman, *Devotional Programs for Every Month,* Nashville:Abingdon Press, 1957, p. 115-119 Used with permission

---

MONKEY TRAPS

"The trouble with some of us is we get caught in monkey traps. In Africa, the natives have a unique, effective way to capture monkeys. They lop the top off a coconut, remove the meat, and leave a hole in the top of the coconut large enough for the monkey to put his paw in. Then they anchor the coconut to the ground with some peanuts in it. When the natives leave, the monkeys, smelling those delicious peanuts, approach the coconuts, see the peanuts in them, put their paws in to grasp the nuts, and attempt to remove the nuts--but find that the hole is too small for their doubled up fists. The natives return with gunny sacks and pick up the monkeys--clawing, biting, screaming--but they won't drop the peanuts to save their lives.

Do you know anyone who is caught in a monkey trap, where the things that matter the most are at the mercy of those things that matter the least?

I'd like you to ponder that;...then make certain you are not caught in like fashion by the siren songs of our society...or these insidious evils Satan will place in your path in attractive packages which turn out to be empty and hollow.

Ensign , November 1980, Robert L. Backman, p. 42 Used with permission

ADDITIONAL REFERENCES

Psalms 4:6............................. Lord, lift up the light of thy countenance upon us
Psalms 82:6............................ Ye are Gods (See also D&C 76:58, John 10:34)
Jeremiah 31:3........................ I have loved thee with an everlasting love
Hosea 1:10............................. Ye are sons of the living God
Jonah 4.................................. .God explains to Jonah the worth of souls (vs. 11)
Matthew 25:32-46.................. When ye have done it unto others, ye have done it unto me
Luke 22:32............................. Strengthen thy brethren
John 3:16............................... God so loved the world
John 13:34-35........................ Ye are my disciples if ye love one another
John 15:9............................... As the Father hath loved me, I loved you
Acts 17:29............................. We are offspring of God
Romans 8:16-17..................... Spirit witnesses we are children of God
Ephesians 4:6......................... There is one God, and Father of all
1Nephi 17:36......................... Nephi explains the purpose of the creation
2 Nephi 1:15.......................... Encircled in the arms of His love
Mosiah 2:17........................... When serving others we are serving God
Alma 5:19-26......................... Reflect God's image
Alma 24:14............................ He loveth our souls
D&C 10:58............................. I am the light which shineth in darkness
D&C 18:10-16........................ Worth of souls is great in sight of God
D&C 76:24............................. Earth's inhabitants are begotten sons and daughters of God
Moses 1:39............................. This is my work and my glory

New Testament Stories
Before the New Testament
The Sermon on the Mount
The Pharisee and the Publican
Jesus Blesses the Children
The Talents

Old Testament Stories
Before the Old Testament

Book of Mormon Stories
King Benjamin
Jesus Christ Blesses the Children

I have wept in the night
For the shortness of sight
That to somebody's need made me blind;
But I never have yet
Felt a tinge of regret
For being a little too kind.

Author Unknown

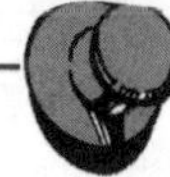

God bless you to realize where you came from and the great privileges that are yours. If the veil were rolled back and you could just see one glimpse of God's great eternal plan concerning you and who you are, it would not be hard for you to love Him, keep His commandments, and live worthy of every blessing that He has had for you since before the foundations of the world were laid.

LeGrand Richards

You give but little when you give of your possessions. It is when you give of yourself that you truly give.

Kahil Gibran
1883-1931

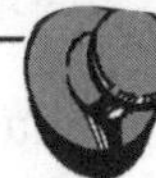

Be loyal to the royal in you.

Hugh B. Brown

A COMMONPLACE LIFE

"A commonplace life," we say as we sigh.
But why should we sigh as we say?
The commonplace sun in the commonplace sky
Makes up the commonplace day.
The moon and the stars are commonplace things
And the flower that blooms, and the bird that sings
But dark were the world and sad our lot
If flowers failed and the sun shone not.
And God who studies each separate soul,
Out of commonplace lives makes His beautiful Whole.

Author Unknown

WHAT A SOUL IS WORTH

Satan wouldn't work so hard
To thwart God's holy plan
If he didn't recognize
The worth of souls of men.

Knowing fully who they are
And what each soul could be;
Disquieting the very thought--
He works on jealously.

It's not their souls mean much to one
Whose character's so flawed;
It's more, he simply understands
Just what they're worth to God.

He, cunningly seduces them
To disregard their birth,
For Satan, too, knows very well
Just what a soul is worth!

Sharon Velluto

LIKE HIM

The mighty oak so big and tall,
Was once a little acorn small.
A puppy grows into a dog.
A tadpole will become a frog.
And what's inside an egg someday,
Will spread its wings and fly away
It makes me feel so very glad,
When someone says I look like Dad.
Each of us is a son or daughter,
Of our loving Heavenly Father.
And the still small voice within,
Whispers I can be like Him.

Sharon Velluto

COCOON

Soft cocoon of silken white,
Promise wrapped inside;
Blueprint yet, of things to be,
Monarch of the sky.

Tiny seedling, leather skinned
Entombed beneath the sod.
Diagram of fruited tree,
Monument to God.

And thou, O man, who art thou?
What plan declares thy worth?
Can'st thou proclaim thy destiny,
Or purpose of thy birth?

Thou embryo of Godhood,
Consigned from Heavenly home;
Thy soul's eternal worth declared,
By what thou may'st become!

Sharon Velluto
(See Psalms 8)

WEIGHING THE BABY

How many pounds does the baby weigh--
Baby who came but a month ago?
How many pounds from the crowning curl
To the rosy point of the restless toe?

Grandfather ties the 'kerchief knot,
Tenderly guides the swinging weight,
And carefully over his glasses peers
To read the record: "Only eight."

Softly the echo goes around;
The father laughs at the tiny girl;
The fair young mother sings the words,
While Grandmother smooths the golden curl.

And stooping above the precious thing,
Nestles a kiss, within a prayer.
Murmuring softly, "Little one,
Grandfather didn't weigh you fair."

Nobody weighed the baby's smile,
Or the love that came with the helpless one;
Nobody weighed the threads of care,
From which a woman's life is spun.

Nobody weighed the baby's soul
For here on earth, no weights there be
That would avail. God only knows
Its value in eternity.

Ethyl Lynn Beers
1827-1879

The Royal Highway

Bear ye one another's burdens, and so fulfill the law of Christ. (Galatians 6:2)

The story is told of a kind and generous king who ordered a great highway to be built for all of the subjects of his kingdom. As the highway neared completion, the king planned to have a great contest for all who desired to participate. A grand prize was to be awarded the winner. People from far and wide gathered to hear the rules of the contest. The rich and poor, the young and the old, all waited anxiously for the king's explanation. "The purpose of this contest," declared the king, "is to determine who can travel my highway the best."

The people were perplexed and looked at each other in bewilderment. The king, however, gave no further explanation, but left the citizens to wonder and question among themselves exactly what he had meant.

Some determined that certainly the one who traveled the road the best was the one who traveled it the fastest. These people began preparing their finest horses for the great race.

Some concluded that the one who traveled the road the best, must certainly be he whose vehicle was the finest. These people began cleaning and repairing their fine carriages. Wheels were greased and adjusted. The carriages were embellished with gold fringes and fine tapestries, in preparation for the great parade.

Another group concluded that to travel the road best surely referred to those who ate the finest food during the journey. Dishes were polished, and great platters of the finest breads, cheeses and pastries were prepared for the great banquet.

Others decided that he who traveled the road the best must be the one who walked, and took the time to enjoy the scenic vistas along the highway. They prepared special clothing and comfortable walking shoes for the nature hike.

Still others were certain that their fine clothing, jewelry and hats would determine the winner of the contest. Needles whirred throughout the night sewing exotic silks and linens into beautiful clothing for the royal fashion show.

The day of the great contest finally arrived . Excitedly the people gathered together at the highway and waited for the race to begin. No finer carriages, clothing or food had ever been seen in the kingdom before. Horses were sleek and their coats glistened in the sun. People had been practicing and preparing for months in anticipation of this great event.

It was a lovely day, the sun was shining and a gentle breeze was blowing in from the sea. At the trumpet's sound all began. The horses raced off leaving others behind in their cloud of dust. The carriage driver's were disgusted at the display and got out to clean their carriages the best they could. During the journey citizens dined on the finest foods, and enjoyed spectacular scenery. Others walked carefully along so as not to spoil their elegant clothing. All day the people travelled the highway, sure that their way was best. As they arrived at the highway's end, each one complained to the king that there was a great pile of rocks and debris left on the highway. They lamented that it was unsightly, had ruined their clothing and carriages, and slowed their journey. The king however offered no reply or explanation.

As the sun sank low and red in the western sky, one lone and weary traveler crossed the finish line and hesitantly approached the king. His fine clothes were now dirty and tattered, and he carried a large, heavy bag. With great respect he bowed low before the king, and said, "Great, and honorable king, today I was honored to travel your great highway. It is most grand indeed. But, along the way I found a great pile of rocks and debris, which had been left in the middle of the road. It slowed other's progress, and damaged their clothing and carriages. So, I stopped to clear the pile away. This bag of gold was at the bottom of the pile and I wish you to return it to its rightful owner.

The king smiled at the old man, and said, "You are the rightful owner of the gold."

The man looked at the king in astonishment. He had never known such wealth. He thought surely the king must be mistaken. He knew that the gold was not his.

The king assured him, "Yes, indeed you are the rightful owner of this gold. You have earned it, for it is you who won my contest. He who travels the road best is he who makes the road smoother for those who will follow."

Adapted from "*The King's Highway*" Author Unknown, *Especially for Mormons,* Kellirae Arts, 1973, Volume 2, Page 289.

ADDITIONAL REFERENCES

Ruth 1:16	Thy people shall be my people
Matthew 5:21-26,38-44	Jesus teaches higher law of brotherly love
Romans 10:12	No difference between Jew and Greek
Romans 12:10	Be kindly affectioned one to another with brotherly love
Romans 12:3-9	Be one body with differing gifts
Romans 14:10-19	Paul talks about judging and brotherhood
1 Corinthians 13	Paul teaches about charity
Galatians 3:26-29	Gospel makes us one
1 Thessalonians 4:9	Ye are taught of God to love one another
Philemon 3-5, 16	The Gospel changes a servant into a brother
1 John 2:3-11	John teaches about brotherly love
1 John 3:10-11, 16-18	John teaches about love and brotherhood
1 John 4:7-21	God loved us, we ought to love one another
Mosiah 5:7	Because of the covenant we are brothers
Mosiah 18:8-11	Alma teaches about the covenant of baptism
Moroni 7:45-48	Moroni teaches about charity (Moroni 8:17,26)
D&C 12:8	No one can assist in this work without humility and love
D&C 38:24-25	Let each man esteem his brother as himself
D&C 46:11-12	Every man is given a gift that all may profit
D&C 42:88	If thy brother offend thee (Matthew 18:15-17)

Old Testament Stories
Enoch

New Testament Stories
The Good Samaritan
The Talents

Book of Mormon Stories
King Benjamin
Peace in America

I KNOW SOMETHING GOOD ABOUT YOU

Wouldn't this old world be better
If the folks we met would say—
"I know something good about you!"
And treat us just that way?

Wouldn't it be fine and dandy
If each handclasp, fond and true,
Carried with it this assurance—
"I know something good about you!"

Wouldn't life be lots more happy
If the good that's in us all
Were the only thing about us
That folks bothered to recall?

Wouldn't life be lots more happy
If we praised the good we see?
For there's such a lot of goodness
In the worst of you and me!

Wouldn't it be nice to practice
That fine way of thinking too?
You know something good about me,
I know something good about you.

Louis C. Shimon

INSIGHT

With eyes fast closed
The soul can see,
Backwards through
-- Eternity.

Past rich and poor,
Past bond and free,
To Heaven's
Boundless family

No great or small,
No color, race,
An enemy --
With brother's face.

Though wretched
And through sin, defiled,
Each human soul
Is Heaven's child.

Oh, that humanity
Were wise
Enough to see
With heart, not eyes.

Sharon Velluto

THE MASTER'S TOUCH

He stretched forth His firm, pow'rful hand
Commanding that the waves be still.
The wind , the waves, all nature bowed,
Subservient to the Master's will.

Decaying, dying, leprous ones,
Were purified by healing touch.
Possessed, tormented, anguished souls
Released from demon's vengeful clutch.

His hands, renewed, revived, restored
Eased pain, buoyed up, gave strength, and light,
Fed hungry, yearning souls life's bread.
Restored men's hearing, speech, and sight.

And then He bade us all go forth
To still the storm, to comfort strife,
To offer blinded, broken souls
The light of hope, the path of life.

"Do unto others," Jesus said,
Benevolence to multiply.
For some sick, struggling soul may feel
His healing touch, through you or I.

Sharon Velluto

A MORNING PRAYER

Let me today do something that shall take
A little sadness from the world's vast store,
And may I be so favored as to make
Of joy's too scanty sum a little more.

Let me not hurt by any selfish deed
Or thoughtless word, the heart of foe or friend
Nor would I pass, unseeing, worthy need,
Or sin by silence when I should defend.

However meager be my worldly wealth,
Let me give something that shall aid my kind --
A word of courage, or a thought of health
Dropped as I pass for troubled hearts to find.

Let me tonight look back across the span
'Twixt dawn and dark, and to my conscience say
Because of some good act to beast or man--
The world is better that I lived today.

Ella Wheeler Wilcox
1855-1919

ONE SMILE

One smile can glorify the day
One word new hope impart;
The least disciple need not say
There are no alms to give away
If love be no the heart.

Author Unknown

OUTWITTED

He drew a circle that shut me out --
Heretic, rebel, a thing to flout.
But love and I had the wit to win;
We drew a circle that took him in.

Edwin Markham
1853-1940

THE EMPTY BOX

The final bell— and children scattered
Out into the snow.
I closed the door, and heaved a sigh,
Alone at last! But No...

He waited there beside my desk,
His clothes thread-bare and torn,
A dirty face and unkempt hair,
And shoes a little worn.

He may have lacked in wit and grace,
As well as coat and gloves,
But never void of willing hands
Nor smile of radiant love.

"Teacher, I've a gift for you,"
He offered timidly,
He drew it from behind his back,
And held it out to me.

A tiny box, wrapped carefully,
In tattered wrap, and string.
"Open it," he grinned at me;
His voice did fairly sing.

So, carefully I pulled the string,
And laid the wrap aside,
Then gently lifted up the lid,
To see what lay inside.

I hesitated, then began, bewildered, yet polite,
"There's nothing here...."
He shook his head,
"There's something there all right!"

I looked again inside the box,'
'Twas empty as can be,
"It's something you can't touch!" he said.
"It's something you can't see!"

"This box is filled with love for you,
And once you know it's there..."
He paused--- "Now can you see it?"
"Oh yes," I smiled, "It's there!"

And still it sits upon my desk,
That memento which he brought,
I'll not forget the loving child,
Nor the meaning of his box.

Sharon Velluto
(Adapted from the story *The Empty Box* , Author Unknown)

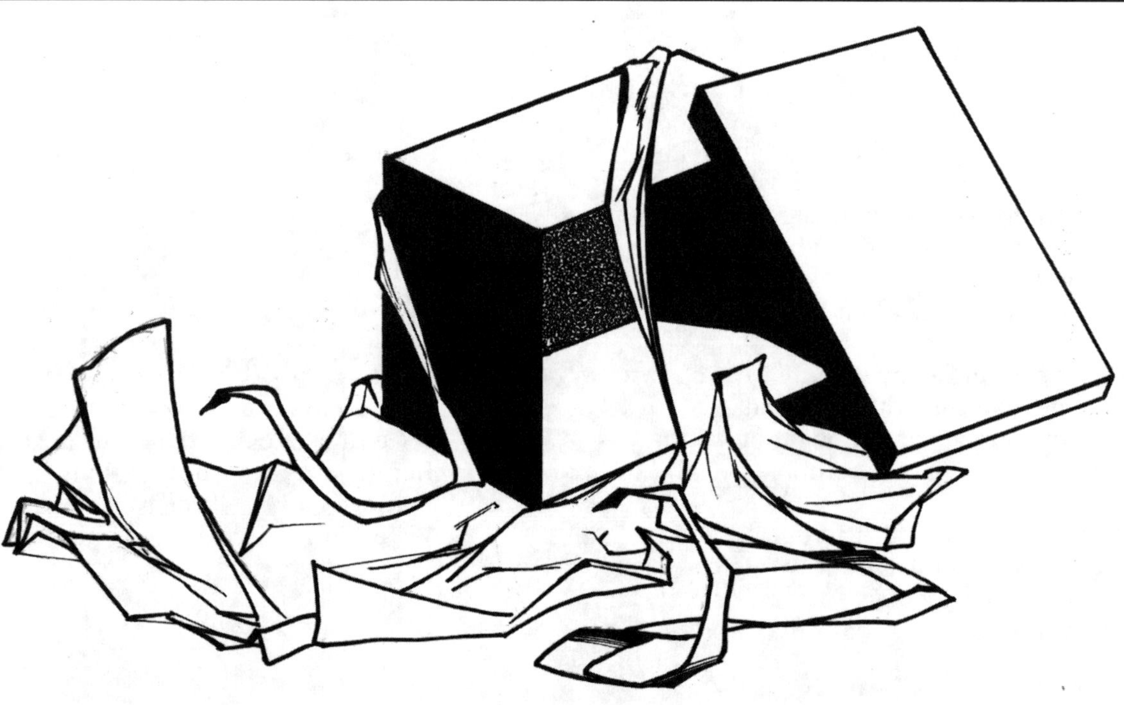

ADDITIONAL REFERENCES

Deuteronomy 4:29	Thou shalt seek the Lord
Deuteronomy 8:14-18	Israel commanded to remember the Lord
Psalms 1:1-6	Blessed is the man who walks not with the ungodly
Psalms 14:1-2	Lord looked to see if there were any to seek God
Proverbs 3:5-7	Trust in Lord with all thy heart
Proverbs 3:13-18	Understanding better than silver
Jeremiah 17:5-10	Cursed is the man who maketh flesh his arm
Ezekiel 34:12-16, 31	As shepherd I will seek out my sheep
Daniel 3:12-30	Three young men trust in God
Daniel 6	Daniel trusts in the Lord
Amos 5:4	Seek me and ye shall live
Matthew 6:33	Seek first the kingdom of God(Luke 12:31-32)
John 14:6-11	I am the way the truth and life
Hebrews 3:8-12	Take heed lest there be in you an evil heart of disbelief
Hebrews 12:1-2	Look to Jesus the finisher of our faith
2 Nephi 26:8	Righteous who watch for Christ shall not perish
2 Nephi 31:20	Press forward with steadfastness
3 Nephi 15:9	I am the light, look unto me
D&C 6:36-37	Look unto me in every thought
D&C 76:22-23	A testimony of Christ
D&C 88:63, 83	Seek me diligently and ye will find me
D&C 101:38	Seek the face of the Lord always

Old Testament Stories

Abraham and the Sacrifice of Isaac
The Prophet Moses
David and Goliath
Jonah
Job
Daniel and the Lions' Den

New Testament Stories

A Woman Touches Jesus' Clothes
Jesus Brings Lazarus Back to Life

Book Of Mormon Stories

Lehi Leaves Jerusalem
The Brass Plates
Traveling in the Wilderness
Lehi's Dream
Alma Teaches about Faith and the Word of God
Helaman and the 2,000 Young Warriors
Nephi and Lehi in Prison
The Jaredites Travel to the Promised Land

This recipe goes with Activity # 2, page 13

Mom's Butter Cookies

1 cup butter
3/4 cup sugar
1 egg
2 tablespoon cream or 1 egg yolk
3 cups flour
1 tsp baking powder
1/2 teaspoon salt
1 & 1/2 teaspoon vanilla
Food Coloring if desired

Cream butter and sugar. Add egg, cream and vanilla. Mix well. Add dry ingredients and mix. Chill 2-3 hours. Roll out on a lightly floured surface to about 1/4 inch thick and cut with cookie cutters. Bake at 350 degrees for 8-12 minutes or until golden brown.

O CHRISTMAS TREE
(O TANNENBAUM)

O Christmas tree, O Christmas tree,
Thy color never changeth. (repeat)
Thy boughs stay green through summers glow,
Through winter's frost and fallen snow.
Oh Christmas tree, O Christmas tree,
Thy color never changeth.

**O Christmas tree, O Christmas tree,
Thy branches point to heaven. (repeat)
Their upward strain exemplifies
That man must reach t'ward Heavens skies.
Oh Christmas tree, O Christmas tree,
Thy branches point to heaven.

O Tannenbaum, O Tannenbaum,
Wie treusind deine Blatter (repeat)
Du grunst nich nur zur Sommer's zeit,
Nien, auch im Winter, wennes schneit.
O Tannenbaum, O Tannenbaum,
Wie treusind deine Blatter.

Traditional German Song
** Verse added SV

PASSIVE FAITH

Passive Faith but praises in the light,
When sun doth shine.
Active Faith will praise in darkest night ---
Which faith is thine?

Author Unknown

CHANGE

I plead to God for changes.
Relief from want or pain,
A change of stage or scenery,
Some noble trait to gain.

Then heaven softly whispers that
I need to change my plea.
More than altering surroundings
The need is to change me.

Instead of asking Him, "Who am I?"
Then explaining what I need;
I should ask "Whose am I?"
And, "What would He make of me?"

Sharon Velluto

Inspired by the writing of Truman J. Madsen,
Christ and the Inner Life , page 19

WHAT'S BETTER FOR ME

So oft' in the darkness I stumble
Because I am too wise to see.
I stubbornly cling to my wishes
When God knows what's better for me.

When I'm lost in life's ominous forest
And can't see beyond the tall trees
I must trust His eternal perspective
For, His vision transcends what I see.

Oh Father, of infinite wisdom
Please, help me more clearly to see
Thy goodness, thy love, and thy mercy
Ask only what's better for me.

Sharon Velluto

BEING CONTENT

As God leads, I am content,
He will take care,
All things by His will are sent,
That I must bear,
To him I take my fear,
My wishes, while I'm here,
The way will all seem clear,
When I am "There."

Author Unknown

SURRENDER

The Master said, "Ye are the branch,
and I thy constant vine."
That cannot be until I learn
to bend my will to Thine.

God knows a man stands taller
when he yields on bended knee.
He knows that he is stronger
when he learns humility.

Deliberate dependence,
and reliance on the vine,
Will not repress, debilitate
but elevate, refine.

It is only by submitting
that a man is truly free.
One only truly finds his life
by losing it to Thee.

Sharon Velluto

I SURRENDER

Therefore let your hearts be comforted... for all flesh is in mine hands; be still and know that I am God. (D&C 101:16)

"Do you give up?" she whispered. Never, I thought. At least not yet, anyway. I was not about to admit defeat, even though she was older, bigger and sat straddling my chest, pinning my arms to the bed. Calling a truce would not be nearly as humiliating, but I was in no position to do that; she was clearly in control.

"Do you give up?" she repeated, being careful to keep her voice low so that Mom and Dad, who were in the bedroom next to us would not hear.

This scenario was repeated almost every night. My older sister would tickle me until I could not stand it anymore, and she would not relinquish her quest until I had admitted defeat. I was usually the one who got in trouble for these escapades, because as Dad always said, "You must have learned to whisper in a logging camp."

Well, tonight, I was determined that I would win. I would overthrow my captor, to nevermore be dominated by her size and age. Mustering all of my strength, I bucked her off with a giant heave of my legs. Quickly she moved to "attack" again. But before she reached me with those unmerciful, tickling fingers, I placed both feet squarely in her stomach and pushed.

She toppled off the bed, landing on the lamp cord. The moss green, metal lamp sitting on the chest of drawers fell, hitting her squarely on the head.

"What is going on in there?", Dad's voice boomed from the other room.

"Nothing," my sister groaned, rubbing her head. Quietly she climbed back into bed. We were both silent. Clearly, this had been a resounding victory for me. "One big battle won, by little sister."

In the battle of life, most of us seek to be in control; or at least we seek to control ourselves, and our own situation. Many struggle to obtain dominance and authority over others in order to gain some sense of power or prestige. Our last desire in life, is to surrender our position to become subject to another's rule.

Surrender is a difficult thing for many of us. Almost from infancy, we struggle against surrender. Many times, I have found myself walking the floor with an infant, who was completely exhausted. The more tired he got, the more he seemed to refuse to "give in", close his eyes and partake of that blessed and rare commodity that new mothers call sleep.

But that is exactly what our Maker has asked of us. Submit. Surrender.

Submission to God is seldom an easy thing. The Lord has asked that his children follow a straight and narrow way, which is generally steep and difficult.

Submit yourselves therefore to God. Resist the devil, and he will flee from you. (James 4:7)

"For the natural man is an enemy to God, and has been from the fall of Adam, and will be, forever and ever, unless he yields to the enticings of the Holy Spirit, and putteth off the natural man and becometh a saint through the atonement of Christ the Lord, and becometh as a child, submissive, meek, humble, patient, full of love, and willing to submit to all things which the Lord seeth fit to inflict upon him, even as a child doth submit to his father. (Mosiah 3:19 See also Alma 13:28)

Jonah, was asked by the Lord to go to Nineveh, to preach repentance to a people who were very wicked. The scriptures are unclear as to what his reason was for not wanting to go.

Whatever the reason, he fled to Joppa to buy passage on a ship to Tarshish. But the Lord sent out a great wind on the sea. The men in the ship were frightened and asked Jonah if he knew the reason for the storm. The fear of God came upon Jonah because of the poor choice he had made. He explained to the crew that the storm was his fault; punishment for his disobedience. He told the crew to throw him into the sea. They were reluctant to do so, but fearing for their own lives, the men threw Jonah into the raging sea.

The Lord had prepared a fish to swallow Jonah, and he spent three days in the cold, dark belly of the fish.

One can sense the deep anguish Jonah felt as he later recounted, *"I cried by reason of mine affliction unto the Lord,... out of the belly of hell,"* he said. (Jonah 2:2)

After three dark and dreary days in its belly, the fish spat Jonah out on dry land and he went immediately to Nineveh, to do as the Lord had asked in the first place.

Most of us, at least once in our lives, must answer our call to "Nineveh." Such a call came one night after praying fervently for some direction in my life. The answer had been clear and unmistakable -- I was to serve a mission.

How could the Lord ask such a thing of me? Didn't He know I was 25? Most of my friends were already married and had children. I would be 27, when I returned. How could He expect me to do such a thing? I felt that if I followed His will, it would most probably cost me the life with a companion and children, that I desired above all else. After all, hadn't my instructor in the "Celestial Marriage" class said that one becomes less "marriageable" after age 25? And according to my reasoning, marriage was a desirable and good thing!

So I did what any sensible, rebellious person would do under such circumstances. I boarded a ship for B.Y.U., the dating capital of the world. There, I did find several worthy prospects, who promptly "dumped me overboard."

I soon learned that rebellion against God, requires a "time out" period in the cold, dark belly of a fish. The light withdrew, and I found myself in a miserable state of spiritual darkness. It took me much longer than Jonah, to finally surrender. But, finally, the darkness was more than I could endure. "And I cried by reason of mine affliction unto the Lord...out of the belly of hell." If only the light would return, I would do anything He wanted. I surrendered.

Still, it was with hesitant and reluctant steps that I turned in my mission papers. I hoped that in some way the Lord would "rescue " me from this fate.

It was during this period of great fear and darkness, that I was blessed to listen to Elder LeGrand Richards speak. I no longer remember where I was, or when it was. I remember only a statement which sank deep into my soul and pierced my heart. He said, "The Lord can do more with your life in ten minutes, than you can do in ten years." It was the spark of hope that I needed to now pursue my course to Nineveh, with faith.

It is with a grateful heart that I can look back and see clearly, *"For this is the love of God, that we keep his commandments; and his commandments are not grievous."* (1 John 5:3, See also: 1 Corinthians 1:25, Proverbs 14:12, Isaiah 55:22)

My mission did more for every facet of my life than any other single event could have. What a tragedy it would have been in my life to have missed that experience. I now count that experience to be one of my deepest and richest blessings, sent by a loving Father to bless the life of His daughter. It was a blessing sent by One who knew better than I, what I really needed.

With finite vision, it is impossible to understand the infinite wisdom of God. The Lord said. *"For my thoughts are not your thoughts, neither are your ways my ways, saith the Lord. For as the heavens are higher than the earth, so are my ways higher than your ways, and my thoughts than your thoughts."* (Isaiah 55:6,8,9)

Because we cannot see the wisdom of the Lord's purposes we often stubbornly seek to follow our own agenda.

"For they being ignorant of God's righteousness, and going about to establish their own righteousness, have not submitted themselves unto the righteousness of God." (Romans 10:3)

"Trust in the Lord with all thine heart; and lean not unto thine own understanding. In all thy ways acknowledge him, and he shall direct thy paths. Be not wise in thine own eyes fear the Lord, and depart from evil." (Proverbs 3:5-7)

Experience is often short lived, however, and one is often doomed to repeat the same mistakes. When one suffers from spiritual amblyopia, that "lazy eye" doesn't see aright, and spiritual vision becomes blurred or distorted.

Shortly after returning from my mission, my life seemed to be stagnant. It didn't seem to be going anywhere, and particularly, life wasn't going in the direction I wanted it to go. I was 27 years old, fresh off a mission, unmarried, unemployed and unsatisfied with my situation. I spent much time on my knees, counseling the Lord about what would be best for me, telling Him what I expected Him to do for me. One day, while reading in the Old Testament, I stumbled onto the story of Balaam, which has become one of my favorites.

Because of his great fear of the Israelites, the King of Moab tried to bribe the prophet Balaam to curse this great nation. Since Balaam had seen the great wickedness of the Israelites, it seemed a reasonable request, so he went to the Lord to inquire about it. God told Balaam that he was not to curse the Israelites for they were blessed. The King persisted, sending bigger bribes by more notable envoys.

Not wanting to take "No," for an answer, Balaam repeatedly petitioned the Lord to allow him to go with these princes. Finally, the Lord relented, but Balaam was commanded that he should speak only what the Lord told him to say. As Balaam approached the gate of the city, an angel, with sword in hand, stood in the way. Being the sensible little animal that he was, Balaam's donkey turned out of the way, so as not to run over the angel. Balaam, however, could not see the angel and beat his donkey. He tried to turn her to the right path. This time the donkey thrust herself against the stone wall, which stood on each side of the path, smashing Balaam's foot in the process. So Balaam beat his donkey again. The angel then moved some distance forward where the path was very narrow and the pair could not turn to one side or the other. Balaam and his donkey moved forward upon the path until the poor little donkey saw the angel again. This time the animal fell down under Balaam, who by now was so angered that he beat her with a staff. Then, the Lord opened the donkey's mouth. She spoke to Balaam saying: *"What have I done unto thee, that thou hast smitten me these three times?"* (Numbers 22:28)

Balaam answered that the donkey had mocked him, and if he had a sword he would kill the disobedient beast. The donkey answered that she had been a faithful servant upon which Balaam had ridden up to that day. She explained that never before had she ever done this sort of thing. Balaam agreed, that up until now she had indeed been obedient to his orders.

Then the Lord opened the eyes of Balaam, and he saw the angel of the Lord, who reproved the disobedient prophet for his wicked choice, telling him that had it not been for his faithful beast of burden turning away these three times, Balaam would have been slain. (See Numbers 22)

After reading the story, I laughed, and I learned. How often I am like Balaam, trusting more in my own judgement than in the wisdom of the Lord. I persist in pursuing my own course until eventually I smash my foot against the wall, which causes pain or makes me angry.

How often, do we flounder in life's waters, drowning, and in our desperation, to keep our heads above the surface, stubbornly refuse to submit to Him who reaches out His arm in love to save us? But in order to allow Him to save us, we must quit thrashing about in the water and let God pull us to safety.

Jesus taught that the first and most important commandment was to love God. How better can we demonstrate our love for God than by trusting Him enough to submit to His will and obey His commandments? How better can we become "one" with them than by our total, willing submission.

By worldly standards, submission to God is a sign of weakness. Humility and strength, are seeming contradictions; faith and firmness seem to be opposites. But, by heavenly measure these are signs of great strength. Describing the humble members of the church, even amidst persecution, Mormon wrote, *"Nevertheless, they...did wax stronger and stronger in their humility, and firmer and firmer in the faith. of Christ unto the filling their souls with joy and consolation, yea even to the purifying and the sanctification of their hearts, which sanctification cometh because of their yielding their hearts unto God."* (Helaman 3:35)

Surrender to God's will takes great self-will. Submission is a process through which we obtain strength and nourishment from the vine. Jesus taught, *"I am the vine and ye are the branches; he that abideth in me, and I in him, the same bringeth forth much fruit; for without me ye can do nothing."* (John 15:5)

Never in the history of mankind has there existed one who exemplified this principle more than Jesus Christ. His submission to the Father was complete. From His early youth he was, *"about his Father's business."* (Luke 2:49) What the Father told Him to say, He said. What the Father told Him to do, He did. His submission was so complete that he said, *"I can of mine own self do nothing."* (John 5:19-20, John 12:49, John 5:3) Jesus' submission to the will of His Father was total, when He took upon himself the sins of mankind. *"Oh my Father,"* He prayed, *"if it be possible, let this cup pass from me: nevertheless, not as I will but as thou wilt."* (Matthew 26:39)

With His great atoning sacrifice, Jesus Christ submitted totally, His will to the will of His Father. He trusted fully that His Father not only knew, but would also do what was in His best interest, and the best interest of all mankind, even if it were to cause unfathomable suffering.

Herein, lies the great difference in submitting oneself to God, and submitting oneself to man. When we surrender our lives to the will of God, we can trust that what He does will be in our best interest, while submission to man offers no such guarantee. Unlike man, God does not ask for submission to fulfill selfish desires, but to fulfill eternal purposes. *"For this is my work and my glory, to bring to pass the immortality and eternal life of man."* (Moses 1:39) Knowing this, we can trust that He loves us and understands our needs.

"Men and women who turn their lives over to God, will find out that He can make a lot more out of their lives than they can. He will deepen their joys, expand their vision, quicken their minds, strengthen their muscles, lift their spirits, multiply their blessings, increase their opportunities, comfort their souls, raise up friends, and pour out peace. Whoever will lose his life to God will find he has Eternal life." (Ezra Taft Benson, "Jesus Christ, Gifts and Expectations," *The New Era,* May 1975, p. 20.)

"Look unto me in every thought; doubt not, fear not."

(D&C 6:36)

WAIT ON

To talk with God,
No breath is lost ---
Talk on!

To walk with God,
No strength is lost --
Walk on!

To wait on God,
No time is lost --
Wait on!

Dnyanodaya (Indian Poet)

Cited in Masterpieces of Religious Verse, ed. James D. Morrison, Harper & Row, New York, 1948, p. 67

ADDITIONAL REFERENCES

Genesis 24:7	Angel guides Abraham's servant to Rebekah
Numbers 22:1-35	Story of Balaam (esp. vs. 22-35)
Judges 6:22	An angel appears to deliver Israel
Daniel 9:21	Gabriel teaches Daniel about the Messiah
Matthew 28:2	Angel rolls back stone, announces resurrection
Luke 15:10	Joy of angels when sinners repent
Luke 22:43	An angel strengthens Jesus
John 20:12	Mary sees two angels at the tomb
Acts 5:19	Peter and John delivered from prison by angel
Acts 10:30	Cornelius is instructed by an angel
Acts 27: 23-24	An angel comforts Paul
Hebrews 1:7,14	Angels are God's ministers (Psalms 104:4)
Hebrews 13:2	Some have entertained angels unawares
Revelation 14: 6	John sees angel who restores the gospel.
1 Nephi 11	Angel instructs Nephi about Lehi's vision
Omni 1:25	King Benjamin tells about ministering of angels
Mosiah 3:2	Angel teaches King Benjamin before discourse
Alma 8:14	An angel comforts and strengthens Alma
Alma 12:28-29	When expedient, God sent angels
Alma 13:22-25	Voice of Lord by mouth of angels
Helaman 5:22-49	Nephi and Lehi converse with angels
3 Nephi 17:23-25	Nephite children encircled by angels
Moroni 7:35-39	Ministering of angels has not ceased
D&C 76:40-42	Glad tidings are the gospel
D&C 103:19	Missionaries are promised protection of angels
Joseph Smith History 1:29-47	Angels brought message to Joseph Smith
Joseph Smith History 1:68-72	John the Baptist restores priesthood keys
Bible Dictionary	Two classes of angels (D&C 129:1-3)
History of Church Vol. 2, p. 428, 433	Angels at dedication of Kirtland Temple

Old Testament Stories

Abraham and the Sacrifice of Isaac
Joshua
Elijah Talks with Jesus
Shadrach, Meshach, and Abednego
Daniel and the Lion's Den

New Testament Stories

Elizabeth and Zacharias
Mary and the Angel
Joseph and the Angel
Jesus is Tempted

Book of Mormon Stories

How We Got the Book of Mormon
Lehi Warns the People
The Brass Plates
Alma the Younger Repents
Alma's Mission to Ammonihah
Nephi and Lehi in Prison

Doctrine and Covenants Stories

The Angel Moroni and the Gold Plates
Joseph and Oliver Are Given the Priesthood

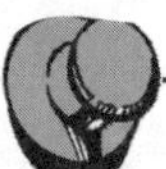

"It is contrary to the law of God for the heavens to be opened and messengers to come to do anything for man that man can do for himself."

Joseph Fielding Smith

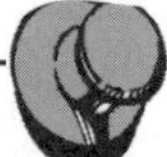

Lord with the angels we too would rejoice;
Help us to sing with the heart and voice;
Glory to God in the highest;
Peace on earth, good will to men !

John Menzies Macfarlane
1833-1892 (Hymns #212)

THEY THAT BE WITH US

I will be on your right hand and on your left, and my Spirit shall be in your hearts, and mine angels round about you, to bear you up. (D&C 84:88)

During the ministry of the prophets Elijah and Elisha (circa 914-897 B.C.) there was almost constant turmoil between the neighboring kingdoms of Judah, Israel, Syria, Moab and Edom. The house of Israel had divided into two kingdoms; the northern kingdom called Israel, and the southern kingdom of Judah. These two kingdoms were bitterly jealous and suspicious of one another. During this tumultuous period, many wars were waged in an effort to gain dominion and seize property from other kingdoms.

Syria had attacked Israel several times but was always defeated. The king of Syria was frustrated by his repeated failures and called his servants together in a secret meeting. A place was appointed where his army was to attack Israel, and capture the king.

Elisha, the prophet and seer of Israel, sent for Jehoram, king of Israel, and warned him of Syria's plan. Doubting somewhat the prophet's words, Jehoram sent spies to investigate the prophet's claim, and found Elisha's words to be true. Because of Elisha's prophesies, the king had been spared from bondage or death "*not once nor twice.*" (2 Kings 6:10)

Ben-hadad, king of Syria, was extremely troubled by his repeated failures to conquer Israel. The previous meeting had been one of utmost secrecy, and the king therefore deduced that one of his subjects must be a traitor. He called his men together to discover who had betrayed Syria. One of the soldiers assured the king that none of his men had been disloyal, but, the prophet in Israel had warned the king of the ambush. Most people would have dismissed this claim as foolish nonsense, or weak excuse, but Elisha had already gained quite a reputation.

Elisha was a disciple of the great prophet Elijah, whose mighty ministry had been marked by great miracles which had left an indelible impression on believers and unbelievers alike. At Elijah's request, the heavens had been sealed, he had been fed by ravens, had extended the meal and oil of a widow, and had raised her son from the dead. In an effort to demonstrate to the wavering Israelites the power of their God Jehovah, Elijah had called down fire from heaven, which consumed not only the sacrifice, but the wood, the stone altar, the dust and twelve barrels of water which had been poured over it. Elijah challenged the Israelites, "*How long halt ye between two opinions? If the Lord be God then follow him: but if Baal, then follow him.*" (1 Kings 18:21)

While hiding from the wicked queen Jezebel, , he was fed, strengthened and received instruction from an angel of God. There he was instructed to find Elisha and anoint him as his successor. Knowing that his earthly ministry would soon end, Elijah asked Elisha what he desired before he was taken. Elisha asked to be given a double portion of Elijah's spirit. Knowing that this was not his to grant, but the Lord's, Elijah said," "*Thou hast asked a hard thing: nevertheless, if thou see me when I am taken from thee; it shall be so unto thee; but if not it shall not be so.*" (2 Kings 2:10)

"*That request for a double portion of the spirit of Elijah provokes me to deep thought, for the spirit of Elijah, as we still may learn, is something so moving, so powerful, and something tied so closely to the most sacred authority of the priesthood, that obviously it would be glorious to be under the constant influence of even a part of that spirit, let alone a double portion.*" (Boyd K. Packer *The Holy Temple,* Salt Lake City: Bookcraft, 1980, p. 108)

Elisha was blessed to witness the chariot and horses of fire that descended, and the whirlwind that swept Elijah up into heaven. Now, Elisha was following in his master's footsteps. Already, he had healed the waters of Jericho, prophesied Israel's victory over the Moabites, removed a deadly plague from pottage, and multiplied bread during a great draught. Elisha had promised a son to a woman who had always shown him kindness, and had later raised her son from the dead. He had multiplied the oil of a faithful widow, allowing her to pay her debts, and save her son from a life of slavery.

Elisha's fame was not limited to Israel. Knowledge of his power had spread to Syria when Naaman, the mighty captain of the king's host, had been healed of his leprosy. Syria's king was no stranger to the power of Israel's prophet.

The king knew that the only way to conquer Israel would be to capture Elisha, so he sent spies who found the prophet in the city of Dothan. King Ben-hadad sent a great host of soldiers with horses and chariots, who encompassed the city by night.

Early in the morning, when Elisha's servant arose, he found the city surrounded by the powerful Syrian army. In great alarm, the servant ran to Elisha crying out, "*Alas, my master! how shall we do?*" Elisha tried to calm the young man, saying, "*Fear not; for they that be with us are more than they that be with them.*" (2 Kings 6:15-16)

The servant was not a fool. He could count! He could see clearly that they were outnumbered. The scene he beheld was that of one old man and a young boy against the mighty Syrian army! Surely, he must have wondered how acute his master's vision actually was!

Elisha, must have sensed the young man's great fear and prayed that the eyes of his servant might be opened. When the young man looked again, the veil had been removed, and he beheld that the mountain was filled with horses and chariots of fire which came down and encircled Elisha. The prophet had spoken the truth! *"They that be with us are more than they that be with them."*

That morning, Elisha's servant learned in a dramatic way one of heaven's great lessons. *"One on God's side is a majority."* (Wendell Phillips)

At Elisha's request the Lord smote the Syrian army with blindness, and then the prophet peacefully led the army into Samaria, a principal city in Israel. When, at last, the eyes of the Syrians were opened, they beheld that their entire army had been taken captive almost single-handedly. Jehoram, king of Israel, asked Elisha if he should kill the Syrians. But Elisha commanded, instead, that a feast be prepared for them. After the entire army had been fed and cared for, they were released and immediately returned to tell their king what had taken place.

Ben-hadad determined that he would no longer go in secret against Israel but would use a different strategy. He surrounded the city of Samaria, cutting off their food supply. The ensuing famine was so severe, that some citizen's had even resorted to cannibalism. As Jehoram, king of Israel, was walking along the wall one day, a woman called to him begging for his help. The king told her that he had nothing to give to her. The woman then disclosed a bargain she had made with a neighbor woman to eat their sons. Her son had been boiled and eaten first but the other woman had hidden her son. Now the desperate woman begged for the king's intervention. Jehoram was so repulsed by her story, that he rent his clothes and vowed to kill the prophet Elisha. Jehoram had never wanted to admit that this great calamity which had befallen Israel was in any way due to his own wickedness, but instead he blamed Elisha for their plight.

When Jehoram finally found the prophet, Elisha was already aware of his wicked intentions. He prophesied that the following day, a measure of fine flour would be sold for a shekel and two measures of barley for a shekel. The King's servant was incredulous. How could this be? In his mind, even if the windows of heaven were opened and food poured out, such a thing could not be possible. But with God, nothing is impossible! (See Genesis 18:14, Luke 1:37) When the king's servant voiced his disbelief in Elisha's words, the prophet told him that he would see the miracle, but not partake of it.

Early the following morning, a few starving lepers decided that they had suffered enough. By law they were to remain outside the city. If they entered to beg for food they could be killed. If they sat where they were, they would surely starve to death. If they entered the Syrian camp they would most likely be killed also, but there was the remote chance that the Syrians might spare them and give them food. They reasoned that they would probably die anyway, but their chances for survival were better if they sought food from the Syrians.

When they entered the camp, they found it deserted, except for the donkeys and horses the Syrians had left tethered there. They entered a tent, ate and drank, and carried off silver and clothing and hid them. They returned a second time, and did the same. Feeling a bit guilty for their selfishness, they decided to share their good fortune with the people of the city. When Jehoram received the news, he was suspicious, thinking it to be some kind of a trap. But, when his servants investigated, they not only found the camp to be empty, but the route the Syrian army had taken, was strewn with garments and vessels which had been discarded in their flight.

So, Israel spoiled the tents of the Syrians, and as prophesied, a measure of fine flour and two measures of barley each sold for a shekel. The king's doubtful servant had been appointed to keep the gate of the city. As he stood there, a witness to the literal fulfillment of Elisha's words, he was trampled by the people and died, never having the opportunity to partake of the bounty. (See 2 Kings 6,7)

But how were the prophet's words so miraculously fulfilled? Why had the powerful Syrian army so mysteriously and suddenly abandoned their camp? During the night, the Syrian army had been startled by the sound of a mighty army approaching. The Lord had made them hear a noise of chariots and horses. Fearing that the Israelite king had hired another nation to assist them, they had fled in terror. They left everything behind and dropped other valuables by the wayside which were too cumbersome and slowed their flight. Once again, Israel had been delivered by the Lord's host. (2 Kings Chapter 7)

A nearly identical story was repeated some one hundred years later when Syria attacked Judah. Syria had already defeated the northern kingdom of Israel, and, that once mighty kingdom no longer existed. In fact, the Syrians had captured every stronghold in the entire country with the exception of Jerusalem.

The Syrian soldiers made mighty threats against the city, and demanded that they surrender. They jeered when Judah claimed that their God would deliver them. They boasted that the god's of every other country had failed to save them, so why should Judah's god be any different. The people of Judah had every reason to fear, except for the fact that Hezekiah was a righteous king, and had been given the assurance by the prophet Isaiah that Judah would receive the Lord's protection. Hezekiah gathered his people together and told them, *"Be strong and courageous, be not afraid nor dismayed for the king of Assyria, nor for all the multitude that is with him: for there be more with us than with him. With him is an arm of flesh; but with us is the Lord our God to help us, and to fight our battles. And the people rested themselves upon the words of Hezekiah king of Judah."* (2 Chronicles 32:7-8)

That night A great plague wiped out nearly the entire Syrian camp. All who did not die, fled for their lives, and the once boastful Syrian army returned in shame. (See 2 Chronicles 32)

The Psalmist wrote, "*The angel encampeth round about them that fear him, and delivereth them.*" (Psalm 34:7)

There are times of great distress or discouragement in almost every life; times when one feels abandoned and alone. There may even come times of darkness when one feels "*surrounded by demons,...encircled about by the angels of him who hath sought to destroy our souls.*" (See Helaman 13:37)

The Savior understood that, although we may feel abandoned we are never alone. Jesus was betrayed by one of his closest friends, and a great number of people with whom he had associated daily, came to the Garden of Gethsemane to arrest Him. In an attempt to defend his Master, Peter drew his sword and cut off Malchus's ear. Jesus rebuked Peter for the act of violence, and asked, "*Thinkest thou that I cannot now pray to my Father, and he shall presently give me more than twelve legions of angels?*" (Matthew 26:51-53, John 18:10) That would be the equivalent of more than 72,000 angels!

Parley P. Pratt wrote "*Angels are ministers both to men upon the earth and to the world of spirits. They pass from one world to another with more ease and in less time than we pass from one city to another. ... O what an unspeakable blessing is the ministry of angels to mortal man! What a pleasing thought, that many who minister to us and watch over us, are our near kindred, our fathers who have died and risen again in former ages, and who watch over their descendants with all the paternal care and solicitude which characterize affectionate fathers and mothers on the earth.* " (Parley P. Pratt, *Key to Theology*, 5th ed.,Salt Lake City: George Q. Cannon & Sons Co., 1891, pages 116-118)

Heber C. Kimball, counselor to Brigham Young wrote, "*...we did not fear, nor hesitate to proceed on our journey, for God was with us, and angels went before us, and we had no fear of either men or devils. This we knew because they were seen.*"

"*I am now in my fifty fourth year; I am a Latter-day Saint, full in the faith, and not only in the faith, but I have a knowledge of the truth of this work. I know God lives and dwells in the heavens; ...He is not so very far off as many imagine. He is near by, His angels are our associates, they are with us and around about us, and watch over us and take care of us, and lead us, and guide us, and administer to our wants in their ministry and in their holy calling unto which they are appointed.*" (Orson F. Whitney, *Life of Heber C. Kimball,* 3d.ed., Salt Lake City: Bookcraft, pages 43-44, 460-61)

Wilford Woodruff added his testimony to that of President Heber C. Kimball when he said, "*I believe the eyes of the heavenly hosts are over this people;... I believe they watch over us all with great interest.* " (Wilford Woodruff, *Journal of Discourses,* volume 11, London: Latter Day Saint Book Depot, 1854-86, page 316)

God has promised to those obedient to His law, that He will be "*our refuge and our strength, a very present help in trouble,*" (Psalms 46:1) When one has gained that certainty, he can join with Paul in declaring: "*If God be for us, who can be against us?*" (Romans 8:31)

"*In the gospel of Jesus Christ, we have help from on high. 'Be of good cheer,' the Lord says, 'for I will lead you along.' (D&C 78:18)...In facing life's problems and meeting life's tasks, may we all claim that gift from God our Father, and find spiritual joy.*" (President Howard W. Hunter, *Ensign,* November 1988, page 61)

Summarized from:

Old Testament Student Manual, Volume 11, pages 261-263, 311-316, 319-339.

Josephus Complete Works, Translated by William Whiston, A.M., Michigan: Kregel Publications, 1981, pages 191-201

ARE YOU AN ANGEL TOO?

An angels brings glad tidings.
An angel bears good news.
An angel sings the songs of peace.
Are you an angel too?

An angel helps and comforts.
An angel tells what's true.
An angels blesses, lifts and cheers.
Are you an angel too?

An angel offers praises;
God's goodness brings to view
By teaching man of His great love.
Are you an angel too?

If you, too, bring glad tidings
Through what you say and do;
If your life sings of "Peace on earth,"
Then you're an angel too!

Sharon Velluto

ONE DAY

One day the world will comprehend
the wonder of that night,
When God sent His beloved Son
and blessed the world with light.

One day the world will understand
the message of the song,
And moved by Heav'ns transcendent act
will pass God's love along.

One day the world will come to know
of Him who then will reign,
And with Him usher in the peace
of which the angels sang.

Sharon Velluto

ADDITIONAL REFERENCES

Deuteronomy 4:29............... If ye seek the Lord with all thy heart, ye shall find Him
1 Chronicles 16:10-11........ Seek the Lord and his strength
1 Chronicles 28:9............... Solomon told to seek the Lord
Ezra 7:10............................ Ezra had prepared his heart to seek
Psalms 69:32-33................. The heart shall live that seeks God
Psalms 105:3-4................... Seek the Lord and his strength
Psalms 119:2....................... Blessed are they who seek
Proverbs 8:17...................... Those who seek shall find
Isaiah 55:6.......................... Seek Lord while he may be found
Jeremiah 29:13.................... Ye shall find if ye seek with whole heart
Lamentations 3:25............... The Lord is good to those who wait and seek
Ezekiel 34:12...................... As a shepherd...so will I seek my sheep
Daniel 9:3........................... Daniel seeks Lord with fasting and prayer
Amos 5:4............................ Seek me and ye shall live
Matthew 6:33...................... Seek ye first kingdom of God (See also: Luke 12:31, 3 Nephi 13:33, D&C 11:23)
Matthew 7:7-8..................... Ask, seek, knock (See also: Luke 11:9)
Matthew 18:12-13............... Parable of lost sheep (See also Luke 15:4-6)
John 10 (entire chapter)...... Christ is the Good Shepherd
Hebrews 11:6...................... God is a rewarder of them that seek him
1 Nephi 22:25..................... One fold and one shepherd (3 Nephi 16:3)
D&C 46:8-9......................... Seek the best gifts
D&C 88:63,83...................... Draw near unto me
D&C 93:1............................ Righteous who seek Lord to see his face
D&C 101:38........................ Seek the face of Lord always

New Testament Stories
Jesus Christ is Born
Jesus Tells Three Stories

Book of Mormon Stories
How We Got the Book of Mormon
Traveling in the Wilderness
Lehi's Dream
The Signs of Christ's Birth
The Signs of Christ's Crucifixion

Doctrine and Covenants Stories
Joseph Smith's First Vision

HIDE AND SEEK

Hide and Seek
is the way of a child;

His objective --
to hide so carefully--
so well
that he will not be discovered.

***

Seek and Find
is the way of God;

His desire --
to be known.

His goal--
not in the hiding
but the finding.

His promise --
ask and be answered
knock, it will be opened
seek and ye shall find.

To anyone
who makes the effort
to search
God shall be discovered.

God remains hidden
only to those
who demonstrate no initiative
to seek--
who have no desire
to find.

Sharon Velluto

TAFFY

1& 1/2 cup sugar	3/8 cup water
2 tsp butter	Pinch of salt
1/4 cup mild vinegar	1 Tablespoon Peppermint flavoring
Pinch of soda	(or any other flavor)

Combine sugar, vinegar, water, and cook to light crack about 268 degrees. Add butter, soda, salt. Pour onto marble slab or platter and let it cool until it can be dented with the finger. Work in flavoring. (Mom should pull it until it is cool enough for children to handle) Have fun. Take some to a neighbor.

This recipe goes with Activity # 2, page 17

SEEK AND YE SHALL FIND

To shepherds on a hillside,
An angel gave a sign,
Teaching what to look for,
Telling Whom they'd find.

'Knock it shall be opened,'
Jesus promised all mankind.
Ask it will be given.
Seek and ye shall find.

Heaven never asks us
To seek the Promised Land
Without a fiery pillar;
Without His outstretched hand.

His path well marked, established,
Mortals needn't stumble blind,
For, with the call to seek Him
Comes assurance we will find.

'I will not leave thee comfortless,
My Spirit's peace be thine.'
He promised all disciples —
'But first seek, if thou wouldst find.'

An eternal invitation
Which is all encompassing;
All shepherds on all hillsides
May seek and find the King!

Sharon Velluto

THE SEARCH

Confused,
I sought to find myself
Among the quiet trees.
But all insight was swept away
Elusive as a breeze.

Alone,
I sought to find my God
In vast and starry skies.
But their stark and vacant stare
Has left me no more wise.

In love,
I helped one bear the load
Along the path he trod.
It's when I lost myself that I
Found both myself and God.

Sharon Velluto

"IL PRESEPE"

I am the good shepherd and know my sheep, and am known of mine. My sheep know my voice, ...and they follow me. (John 10:14,27)

One of my favorite Italian Christmas traditions is that of the "presepe," or creche. These marvelous dioramas depict the nativity scene set in a stable, and often display the entire city of Bethlehem and its inhabitants. Some presepi are very elaborate, with intricate passage ways, stairs, trees, fountains, stone walks and walls. Most are lighted and some even have moving parts.

Presepi are found in private homes as well as public buildings. They are seen in railway stations, airports, banks, stores and churches. Many are very large, and in some homes can even fill an entire room.

The figures for these scenes are made of various materials, from terra cotta to plastic. They vary in size from an inch to life size.

On our first trip to Italy, my husband and I began collecting pieces for our own presepe. We chose some small, hand painted figures made of durable plastic. Each character depicts a different occupation or trade common to that era. There are figures of the Holy Family, shepherds, angels, three kings, and a variety of villagers.

One figure, a tired, little, shepherd boy, lays fast asleep on a hillside, while all around him a glorious angel choir is singing. I wondered how it could have been possible for someone to sleep through all of that!

I then began to notice that many of these little characters seemed oblivious to the miracle which was unfolding right before them. One shepherd boy sits cross-legged on a tree stump, huddled in a blanket. Surely he has heard the angel's announcement, but just doesn't want to leave the warmth and security of his blanket to venture out into the cold. A woman carries water from the village well. A long pole lays across her shoulders, upon which are tied two large buckets of water. Her burden seems too heavy for her to go in search of a rumored baby. Other villagers are too absorbed with their daily tasks of sharpening knives, spinning yarn, washing laundry and feeding chickens to go in search of the child. Even though a brilliant star shines overhead, none of them seem to notice.

How was it that so many didn't hear or misunderstood the Master and his message? What is it that keeps so many from seeking and finding the Savior?

In the parable of the sower Jesus describes three groups of people who failed to grasp His message. Lehi describes the same three groups of people in the vision of the tree of life.

WAKE UP!

The first group are the sleepers. As the sower cast his seeds, some fell by the wayside where the ground was hard and impenetrable. Before the seed could take root, they were gobbled up by birds. (See Matthew 13:4)

Though Lehi desperately called for Laman and Lemuel to come and partake of the fruit, either they didn't hear or didn't care enough to even commence in the path.

Although the hand of God is constantly stretched out to all of his children, many fail to recognize it. The story is told of a man who while shingling his roof, lost his footing and began to fall. In desperation he prayed for help. At that moment his pants caught on a nail which stopped his fall. "Never mind," he told God, "this nail saved me." Because God usually answers our prayers through natural means, it is easy for one person to describe an event as an act of God, while another dismisses it as luck or fate.

One day Jesus called his disciples together privately and said, "*Blessed are the eyes which see the things that ye see.*" (Luke 10:23) Many people witnessed the miracles of Jesus, and still remained unaffected by them. For some His miracles did little more than entertain or satisfy curiosity. Others dismissed them as the work of Beelzebub, prince of devils. Jesus knew that those who saw with spiritual eyes would be the ones blessed, for they received a testimony that Jesus was truly the Messiah.

Spiritual darkness is described as eyes which cannot see the workings of God, ears which are not attuned to hear the whisperings of the Spirit, hearts which are hard and impenetrable. (See Proverbs 20:12-13, Matthew 25, Mark 13)

"Awake!" has been a common cry of the prophets. Nephi urged his wayward brothers to "*awake from a deep sleep, yea even the sleep of hell.*" (2 Nephi 1:13)

In our home we have a pair of finches as pets. One day they were chirping loudly, and though I heard them, it didn't really register until my husband walked to the cage to change their food and water. "They call," he said. Since my husband is the one who takes responsibility for the birds, he heard their chirping and responded to it, while to me their chirping had virtually gone unnoticed.

Man responds to the voices he trains himself to hear. It is hard to imagine how people like Laman and Lemuel, Korihor, or the pharaoh in Moses' day could have seen all they did and still discount it. After hearing Paul's stirring testimony of his conversion, King Agrippa declared, "*Almost, thou persuadest me to be a Christian.*" (Acts 26:28) There actually are those who can sleep through angel choirs!

Wake up little shepherd!
O watchman of the sheep,
Wake up and hear the angel choir,
Awaken from your sleep!

Wake up little Shepherd!
Wake up and hear the song!
The glorious news, this holy night
The Son of God is born!

GET UP!

The second group are the sitters. These are the people who are either too fearful or too discouraged to commit themselves fully to the gospel. They are described as seeds which fell on stony ground and quickly sprang up, but the scorching sun caused them to wither and die, because they had no root in themselves. (See Matthew 13:5-6, 21) These are the people in Lehi's dream who began to press forward along the path which led to the tree, but a great mist of darkness arose and they wandered off and were lost. The fruit of the tree was inviting enough to entice them into the path, but they failed to grasp the rod of iron which would lead them securely to the tree of life.

President Spencer W. Kimball said, "*It seems to me that basically there are two major causes for the holding back which we see in the Church. First, sin which results in disinterest or immobilization and guilt; and second, the reluctance of good members of the Church to stretch just a little bit more in the service.*" (*Ensign*, May 1979, page 82)

We have been promised that we will find Him, but, only if we make the effort to seek. Yet, like the little shepherd, many prefer to remain on their stump, wrapped in a warm blanket rather than venture out into the night in search of Him. The cost of true discipleship requires sincere faith, and all of the heart, might, mind and strength. (See D&C 4:2, James 1:22) In this search, there is no looking back, no holding back.

President Gordon B. Hinckley encouraged, "*In this work there must be commitment. There must be devotion. We are engaged in a great eternal struggle that concerns the very souls of the sons and daughters of God. We are not losing, We are winning. We will continue to win if we will be faithful and true. We can do it. We must do it. We will do it. .... May we be faithful. May we be valiant. May we have the courage to be true to the trust God has placed in each of us. May we be unafraid. 'For ... God hath not given us the spirit of fear, but of power, and of love, and of sound mind. Be not therefore ashamed of the testimony of our Lord.'*" (2 Timothy 1:7-8) President Gordon B. Hinckley, *Ensign*, November 1986, pages 44-45)

Get up little shepherd!
Glad tidings you have heard.
Get up and go to Bethlehem;
Go and seek "The Word!"

Get up little shepherd!
Take courage! Brave the cold!
For soon you'll find the shelter
And the warmth within His fold.

CHEER UP!

I was very surprised once to hear a good sister say she didn't even hope to make it to the Celestial Kingdom. Like the figure of the villager, bowed beneath the great weight of her load, some find the burden of discipleship to be overwhelming. Jesus said, "*Come unto me, all ye that labor and are heavy laden, and I will give you rest. ...for my yoke is easy, and my burden is light.*" (Matthew 11:28-30) But, His yoke requires perfection, and at times, that yoke seems anything but light! (See Matthew 5:48, 3 Nephi 12:48)

In the scriptures, the Lord is often referred to as the Bridegroom, and salvation is symbolized as a marriage supper. (See Isaiah 54:5) Being married to one who is perfect would be extremely uncomfortable. Marriage to one who demands perfection of his spouse would be almost unbearable. Many would prefer divorce, rather than to pay the price which such a union might cost. There are times when the tremendous weight of the yoke of perfection seems almost unbearable.

I recall attending church one Sunday morning feeling overwhelmed by the weight of that burden. I was so discouraged with myself; my faults and imperfections. I sat alone at the back of the chapel in total despair. The music leader cheerfully led the congregation in singing, "There Is Sunshine in My Soul Today". I couldn't sing. There was no sunshine in my heart. The words of that hymn just stuck in my throat as I fought back tears of discouragement. Then, there came the soothing strains of the second verse: "And Jesus listening can hear, the songs I cannot sing!" (Hymns # 227) My burden lifted as the Savior helped me to shoulder that yoke, "His yoke."

How gentle God's commands!
How kind his precepts are!
Come, cast your burdens on the Lord
And trust his constant care.

Why should this anxious load
Press down your weary mind?
Haste to your Heav'nly Father's throne
And sweet refreshment find.

His goodness stands approved,
Unchanged from day to day;
I'll drop my burden at his feet
And bear a song away.

(Hymns, #125, Text by Philip Doddridge 1702-1751)

As our marriage partner, the Lord has promised, "*I will be with thee: I will not fail thee, nor forsake thee.*" (Joshua 1:5) He will assume our debt, help bear the burdens of life, and through Him we can become whole.

Cheer up little shepherd!
Though heavy be your load,
There's One who vowed to lift you up
And help you walk the road.

LOOK UP!

The third group are the distracted ones. In Lehi's dream, these people grasped the rod of iron, followed the path through the mists of darkness to partake of the fruit of the tree. After partaking of the tree of life, they saw a great and spacious building filled with people laughing at them. They were ashamed, and fell away and were lost.

The parable of the sower describes them as seed which were choked when they fell among thorns. Jesus explained that he that received seed among the thorns "*is he that heareth the word; and the care of this world, and the deceitfulness of riches, choke the word, and he becometh unfruitful.*" (Matthew 13:22)

Often during my youth, I heard or read the promise of Moroni, about how one can know the truth for himself. I supposed that testimony came as an automatic result of following those certain steps; somewhat like following a recipe and getting cookies as the result. I have come to realize since, that testimony is not a prize which is earned by performing certain behaviors. It is a a precious gift of the Spirit, given by God to faithful and obedient seekers of truth. I also believed that once I had received a testimony it automatically became mine to keep. I learned, however, that just as the unfaithful steward buried his talent in the earth, and it was taken from him, through disobedience or negligence, the light of spiritual knowledge may also be taken away. (See Matthew 25:14-29) That person then becomes as if he had never known the things of the Spirit. "*And that wicked one cometh and taketh away light and truth,through disobedience, from the children of men...*" (D&C 93:39. See also 2 Nephi 28:30, Hebrews 3:13, Alma 12: 9-11, D&C 78:10, Moses 5:13)

As a teenager, I had a group of friends I really enjoyed being with. All of us had a great love for sports. Several of these girls had jobs during the week, and their only day free to play was Sunday, during my Sacrament Meeting. So, I often skipped my Sacrament Meeting to play softball with them. I knew I was making a wrong choice, and my conscience bothered me. But, unfortunately, at that time, fitting in was more important to me.

One does not rebel against the Lord without suffering spiritual consequences. A deep spiritual blackness crept into my heart and settled over me. I began to wonder if the things I had been taught all my life were true. Was there really a God? It was a frightening thought, and if there were answers being sent, I couldn't hear them, because of the darkness in my heart. I was afraid.

In that state of blackness and uncertainty, there came one saving thought, a spiritual alarm, so to speak, which woke me up. There was one thing I knew for certain. There was a devil, and I felt his presence. The price of sin was darkness, and it was unbearable. I knew I needed to change. As I recommitted myself to living the principles of the gospel which I knew to be true, the light returned, and once again I was able to feel the warmth and assurance of God's presence.

Often it is not the sins of commission which cause a loss of the spirit, but the sins of omission. Like the villagers, it is easy to become so distracted by the tasks at hand, that one fails to notice the star above. Perhaps one of God's most challenging requests is to live in the world, but to not be a part of it.

Life with its many challenges and demands has a tendency at times to distract us from our spiritual goals. Sister Jeanne Inouye said, "*As I have attempted to establish priorities, I have learned that we may almost always have too much to do. As I think about our time constraints, I conclude that God has not intended that we should be able to do everything we would like to do. If there were not more to do than we are individually capable of doing, we wouldn't have to make choices and we would never realize what we value most.*" (Ensign, November 1993, page 97)

"*You will care for more things than you will be able to do things about. Wise selection of causes is one of the highest forms of the use of free agency that there is, and really, one of the ways God tests our basic wisdom and our capacity to love.*" (Neal A. Maxwell, speech delivered at Catalina Young Adult Conference, 23 Oct. 1972. See *Old Testament Student Manual*, Vol.. 2, p. 332)

David O. McKay admonished, "*With all my soul, I plead with members of the Church, and with people everywhere, to think more about the gospel, more about the development of the Spirit within; to devote more time to the real things of life and less time to those things which will perish.*" (*Conference Report*, April 1968, page 144. See also 2 Nephi 9:51)

Look up all ye shepherds!
Look to the star above!
Heralding His blessed birth;
The Gift of God's great love.

LIFT UP!

Jesus taught, "*He that receiveth seed into the good ground is he that heareth the word, and understandeth it; which also beareth fruit, and bringeth forth, some an hundred fold, some sixty, some thirty.*" (Matthew 13:23)

After partaking of the tree of life, Lehi's greatest desire was to share it with others "*for I knew it was desirable above all other fruit.*" (1 Nephi 8:11-12)

Within the presepe, there are shepherds and villagers surrounding the manger who have diligently sought Him and found Him. One is an elderly man who holds up his lantern so all in the stable can see the miracle.

Elder Marion D. Hanks stated, "*The Lord said, speaking of His servants, 'Their arm shall be my arm.' Have you ever thought about this? To me this is one of the most sacred and significant and personal commissions I can read about in the holy records or elsewhere. The Lord says that this arm of mine is His arm. This mind, this tongue, these hands, these feet, this purse — these are the only tools He has to work with.*" (Service, Brigham Young University Speeches of the Year [Provo, 15 Oct. 1958], page 3. See also *Relief Society Personal Study Guide 3,* 1991, page 187)

President Howard W. Hunter said, "*Developing spirituality and attuning ourselves to the highest influences of godliness is not an easy matter. It takes time and frequently involves a struggle. It will not happen by chance, but is accomplished only through deliberate effort and by calling upon God and keeping His commandments.*" (*Ensign*, May 1989, page 24)

President Spencer W. Kimball exemplified one whose life was spent in seeking and finding the Savior, and then in assisting others in their search. After being sustained as prophet in a Solemn Assembly of the Church, President Kimball gave one of his powerful one sentence sermons. He said, "*With our hands to the plow, looking forward; with our eyes to the light looking upward; we enter into our 'Father's business' with fear and trembling and love.*" (Ensign, May 1974, page 47) He later testified, "*I know that Jesus Christ is the Son of the living God and that He was crucified for the sins of the world. He is my friend, my Savior, my Lord, my God.*" (*Ensign*, November 1982, page 6)

Lift up, oh ye shepherds,
Your lantern burning bright!
Hold it high that all may see
The miracle this night!

(The illustrations accompanying this article were inspired by the actual figurines from our family's presepe, produced by *Presepi Fontanini s.p.a.*)

ADDITIONAL REFERENCES

Ezra 3:11.................... They sang praises of thanksgiving
Job 38:7........................ When the morning stars sang together
1 Samuel 16:16-23...... David plays music to calm King Saul
1Chronicles 16:8-10... Sing unto Him
Psalms.......................... These are actually songs (See especially those listed below)
  Psalms 92:1........... It is a good thing to give thanks and sing praises
  Psalms 96:1-2........ Sing unto the Lord all the earth
  Psalms 98:1............ Sing unto the Lord for he hath done marvelous things
  Psalms 100:2......... Come before His presence with singing
  Psalms 105:1-3...... Sing praises unto the Lord and talk of His wondrous works
  Psalms 115-118.... Probably the song Jesus sang before going to Mount of Olives
Song of Solomon........... Many scriptures are songs
Isaiah 12:2,5............... Jehovah is my song, sing to the Lord
Matthew 26:30............ Jesus sings hymn before going to Mount of Olives (Mark 14:26)
Luke 2:13- 14............. Angels sing songs at Savior's birth
Ephesians 5:19........... Saints counseled to teach with hymns
Revelation 5:9-14........ John hears every creature praising God and the Lamb
Alma 5:26..................... Have ye felt to sing the song of redemption?
D&C 25:11-12............. Hymns are pleasing to the Lord
D&C 136:28................. Praise the Lord with singing

Preface to the Hymn Book

Bible Dictionary

Under the headings of Psalms and Music

Doctrine and Covenants Stories

Joseph and Emma

I HAVE A SONG -- AND I KNOW HOW TO USE IT!

Music has power to speak to the soul,
To chase away shadows, to heal, and make whole .

Sharon Velluto

What a rough day! And it was only 10:00 a.m. All morning my four year old son had teased and tormented his nine month old sister. I had asked -- pleaded with him to stop, but to no avail. Finally I sent him to his room for a much needed "Time Out!"

I let him sit there a while before going up. He was laying on the floor in his bedroom. "I'm a bad boy," he said over and over. I assured him that he was not a bad boy, but that he had made some bad choices. We talked for some time about how wickedness did not bring happiness, but misery. Still, there was a dark cloud over him that needed to be lifted. Otherwise, I knew that I was in for more of the same behavior.

We had been learning about music in Primary. He had a weapon and I wanted him to know how to use it. I asked him if he really wanted to feel happy. He assured me that he did. I told him that Heavenly Father had given us many gifts to help us stay close to Him. One of these is music.

We first said a prayer together and then we began to sing those bad feelings away.

"*I am a child of God, and He has sent me here.*" "*I know my Father lives and loves me too.*" "*I'm trying to be like Jesus, I'm following in his ways.*" Before long the smile returned, the darkened face turned bright. "I feel better he announced."

The very next day I was feeling overwhelmed and discouraged by the critical circumstances of a dear friend.

"You don't feel very good today, do you Mama?" he asked.

"No," I told him, "I don't"

In his very finest voice he began singing his very favorite Primary song. "*Genesis, Exodus, Leviticus, Numbers...*"

I laughed.

"Do you feel better Mama?" he asked.

"Yes," I told him and gave him a hug. He had a song and he knew how to use it.

When my husband joined the Church, none of his family would attend His baptism. They were bitterly opposed to this new church, especially his mother.

Years later, he left his native country of Italy, and traveled to America for six months to visit friends. The house was empty and his mother felt alone. She began to attend church, just for the company. She found the members warm and accepting. But, each week as she joined with the members in singing the sacred hymns of the Church, her heart was touched. The music spoke to her soul.

After returning home, my husband received one of the most blessed gifts he could have ever imagined. On Christmas Day, he took the hand of his mother and led her into the waters of baptism.

After we were married, his mother visited us in America. In church, she desperately wanted to sing the hymns. We hurried to find the song in her Italian hymnbook which corresponded to the one being sung. Often, she missed the entire song while we were looking. So she began to sing any song she wanted. It didn't matter to her if the words matched the melody or not. When she sang the hymns she no longer felt like she was a stranger in a strange land, but that she spoke the universal language of the Spirit through singing the hymns. She was one in heart. She was one in voice.

The last few months of her life were spent in bed, battling cancer. My husband had flown to Italy to be with her. When we talked on the phone, he told me of her struggles. I felt so helpless. We were an ocean apart. My husband told me that often the only time during the day that she was calm was when he read my letters to her.

Knowing of her great love for music, I held a special Family Home Evening on the subject of music with my two children and we recorded it. We sang all of our favorite songs. I also purchased some of the Church hymns on cassettes and sent them to her. When she was having a particularly difficult time, the family members turned on the music. The effect was immediate. The music calmed and soothed her, and eased her suffering. Good music has power to heal and lift souls.

I had a song and I knew how to use it!

ELIZABETH GOUDRIAN WEENIG

In a very special way, the gift of music made it possible for my family to enjoy the blessings of the gospel that we rejoice in today.

Elizabeth Goudrian was born on December 17, 1979, at Krimpen a/d Ijssel, South Holland in the Netherlands. Her father, Arij Cornelis Goudriaan, was the skipper of a merchant ship that sailed from port to port delivering goods to the people. Elizabeth's mother, Henderika, became an invalid soon after she was married. She had broken her ankle in a fall while getting off a carnival merry-go-round. Medical knowledge was not like it is today and the bones were not set properly. Her leg eventually developed an infection which they called tuberculosis of the bone and she was never well from that time on.

Elizabeth was the oldest of six children; four boys and two girls. One brother and one sister passed away from diphtheria and whooping cough when they were just tiny, leaving just the four children.

Elizabeth had the opportunity to go away to school to get her education when she was six and a half. She was a very good student and graduated from the eighth grade when she was only twelve years old. The school master was so pleased with her dedication as a student that he wanted her to go on to the higher school. Since Elizabeth was only twelve, she would need her parents' permission to continue her education. It was for the purpose of obtaining this permission that Elizabeth traveled with her school master to her home in December of 1891. Upon arriving at the door of her home, Elizabeth was met by the priest of the Dutch Reformed Church to which her family belonged. He told this twelve year old girl that it was so sad that she had not come sooner; for her mother only a short time before had passed away.

The priest informed young Elizabeth that now she would never be able to see her mother again. Members of the Dutch Reformed Church believed that the dead were dead, never to rise again. How lonely and heart wrenching this news must have been for this young girl. In her later life, Elizabeth remembered walking down the dike road to the cemetery where her mother had been buried. With stick in hand, she would tap against the wooden fence along the road and say to herself over and over again, "Mother, will I ever see you again?" Unsatisfied with the answer that her family's church had given her, she studied the Bible over and over again. She felt inside that there had to be a life after death, otherwise what would have been the purpose of Jesus coming to the earth?

Elizabeth was never able to return to school after the death of her mother. Because her father had to be gone from home for days at a time with his shipping business, he feared for the safety of his four small children. It was decided that the children should be separated and sent to live for a time with relatives. Elizabeth was sent to stay with her father's sister, Taunte Bett. Taunte Bett was a widow at the time and, in order to support her family, she had taken over her husband's shipping business of three ships.

Elizabeth loved her Taunte Bett. She went with her on board her ship as she traveled through the various ports of the Netherlands as well as into Belgium, parts of France and just over the border into Germany. While on the ship, Taunte Bett told Elizabeth about a new church that she had come in contact with. Some of the members of this church had been teaching her about the religion's beliefs.

One evening, after docking in the port of Rotterdam, Elizabeth and her aunt went into town. As they approached, they noticed a group of people gathered about two young men. The young men began the meeting with prayer and then began singing a pretty song. The words of the song told of a life after death. The song seemed like an answer to her prayers. She was very interested in the words to the song, because, for the first time she realized that there were people who actually believed in a life hereafter. This was something that she hungered to know more about, for, deep in her heart, she wanted so much to see her mother again.

As the young men finished the song, Elizabeth turned to her aunt and asked if she knew the name of this beautiful song that they had just heard. Taunte Bett replied that the song was called "Oh, My Father," and that it was one of the choice songs of this new found "Mormon" religion that she had been telling Elizabeth about. Elizabeth thrilled at the hope of an eternal life, for, in her heart she already knew it to be true. She promised herself that in some way she would find this church and hear for herself of its teachings.

Finally, at Christmas time in 1898, Elizabeth was able to visit a branch of the "Mormon" Church in Rotterdam. She returned home and asked her father if she could attend this church each week to learn more of its teachings. Reluctantly, he gave his permission. For three years Elizabeth investigated the Church of Jesus Christ of Latter-day Saints in Rotterdam. Each Sunday she walked the eight kilometer distance between her home and Rotterdam alone, by herself. Occasionally she would stay the night with members of the Church and return home in the morning. However, most of the time she would walk back the entire distance by herself at night.

For three years Elizabeth attended church every Sunday, missing only one week in the winter time when the river was too dangerous to cross on account of piled up ice, and the men wouldn't let her go across.

After much prayer and pleading to know of God's will, Elizabeth said, "The more I prayed, the more I felt myself being drawn toward the Mormon Church and the teachings I received there. In the meantime, the salvation for the dead was explained to me and that was what convinced me of its truth. I sincerely thanked my Heavenly Father for the light He had given to me through the Gospel."

Elizabeth was baptized a member of the Church of Jesus Christ of Latter-day Saints on March 3, 1900 by Paul Roelofs, a missionary serving in the Netherlands. A few years later, on the 15th of March 1904, she emigrated to Utah and began the wonderful life that we, her descendants, enjoy today.

How grateful we are for her faith and her valiant spirit. We also acknowledge and are grateful for the far reaching effects that music has upon all of our lives. How blessed we are that a young girl of sixteen heard a beautiful song on a street corner in Holland a little over one hundred years ago. That song, "*Oh, My Father*," touched her heart and prepared her to receive the testimony of the Holy Ghost. In a very special way, the gift of music made it possible for my family to enjoy the blessings of the gospel that we rejoice in today.

Excerpted from the journal of Elizabeth Goudriaan Weenig and personal recounts written by her daughter Lucille W. Christopherson. Compiled by Lynda Christopherson. Used with permission.

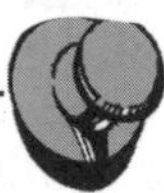

There come to ones soul heavenly thoughts as he joins in heavenly expressions coupled with heavenly melody.

Elder David B. Haight,
Ensign, May 1983, pp. 11-12

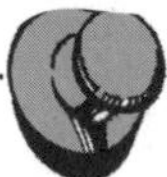

What are we saying, what are we thinking, when we fail to join in singing in our worship services?...We need to make better use of our hymns, to put us in tune with the Spirit of the Lord, to unify us and to help us teach and learn our doctrine.

Elder Dallin H.Oaks,
Ensign, November 1994, p. 11-12

PRESIDENT SPENCER W. KIMBALL

Ever frustrated and feeling inept, President Spencer W. Kimball said, "I have tried by double expenditure of energy to measure up."

Plagued for years with heart problems which slowed his pace, his feelings of inadequacy and uselessness grew.

After watching the face of his sister be eaten by cancer and a niece waste away with the dreaded disease, President Kimball received the news he most feared -- cancer of the throat.

Doctors removed one full vocal chord and half of another. Until his throat healed he was to remain silent. He typed his interviews and wrote other communication.

Miraculously, a piece of tissue grew where the vocal chord had once been, forming a false vocal chord.

His first attempts at speaking were difficult and disheartening, as he tried to find and use his "new voice. "President Kimball prayed constantly for help, and his prayers were answered. "I realize I cannot quit for anything," he wrote home to his wife, "though temptation is terrific when I stumble and stammer, and halt." (p. 312)

As he spoke, the Saints leaned forward and listened attentively, The grating, raspy voice President Kimball so worried about became a familiar and beloved voice to members worldwide. (See Spencer W. Kimball, Salt Lake City: Bookcraft Inc., 1979, pp. 249-323)

"It is sad to me to see in the congregations many people standing silent when they could be singing 'their hearts out.' I wonder constantly if they would sing happily today if for twelve years they could only move their lips through thousands of songs and could make no sound? I wonder if the silent ones can even imagine what it is like to be unable to join their fellow singers in praise to their Lord in music?" ("How To Use Music More Effectively" Reprinted in *The Teachings of Spencer W. Kimball*, ed Edward L. Kimball, Salt Lake City: Bookcraft, p. 518-519)

VOICE

A Tribute to President Spencer W. Kimball

The diagnosis cancer!
Most dreaded awful news!
And, underneath the surgeon's knife,
His vocal chords removed.

Once clear, melodic baritone;
The melody now stilled.
To ever speak or sing again,
Would be as Heaven willed.

Overwhelmed and feeling useless;
E'er longing to give voice
To burning witness in his heart;
To praise, to sing, rejoice.

He struggled to give utterance,
Then, raspy, raw, he spoke.
"I've fallen among cutthroats, thieves,
Who stole my voice," he joked.

Oh, how it saddened him to see
The Saints who would not raise
Their voice in song, while still they could,
In hymns of laud and praise.

Said he, "For years, I've only mouthed
The words I could not sing;
With aching heart e'er longing to
Sing praises to my King."

His raspy speech is silenced now,
Our prophet's voice, most dear
Is stilled. And how the Saints will miss
That voice we loved to hear.

But, on Resurrection Morning,
With joy he'll join the throng
Of Saints and angels praising God.
He'll sing on and on and on!

Sharon Velluto

I MAY HAVE SUNG THERE TOO!

One quiet night in Bethlehem,
The city lay asleep.
While on a distant hillside,
Some shepherds watched their sheep.

The silent stillness broken
By an angel song.
The night illuminated
By the heavenly throng.

Glory be to God the Highest!
This long awaited morn.
"Hallelujah! Peace on earth." they sang,
"For Jesus Christ is born!"

I wonder, was I an angel
Who joined that sacred choir,
Who sang praises at the Savior's birth,
Who filled the sky with fire?

Their message so familiar,
Piercing my heart through,.
Peace on earth! Good will to men!
I may have sung there too!

Sharon Velluto

THERE'S A SONG IN THE AIR

There's a song in the air!
There's a star in the sky!
There's a mother's deep prayer
And a baby's low cry!
And the star rains its fire while the beautiful sing,
For the manger of Bethlehem cradles a King!

Josiah Gilbert Holland
1819 - 1881

ADDITIONAL REFERENCES

Psalms 23.................................. The Lord is my shepherd
Psalms 95:7................................ Ye are the people of pasture, the sheep of his hand
Isaiah 40:11............................... He shall feed his flock and gather the lambs
Ezekiel 34:12,16......................... I will seek out my sheep
Matthew 10:6.............................. Go to the lost sheep
Luke 15:8-10.............................. The parable of the lost coin
Luke 15:11-32............................ The parable of the prodigal son
John 10:10-15............................ The hireling fleeth, the good shepherd giveth his life
John 10:16.................................. Other sheep I have (See also 3 Nephi 15:15-24)
John 21:15-17............................ Feed my sheep
1 Peter 5:1-4.............................. Feed the flock
1 Nephi 13:41............................ There shall be one God and one Shepherd
1 Nephi 22:25............................ He gathereth his children and numbereth his sheep
Mosiah 14:6................................ We like sheep have gone astray (Isaiah 5:3-6)
Mosiah 26:21.............................. He that hears my voice will be my sheep
Alma 5:38-41, 57-62................. Follow the voice of the good shepherd
Helaman 15:13........................... They shall know the shepherd, and be with his sheep
3 Nephi 18:31............................ I know my sheep and they are numbered
D&C 10:59-60............................ I will show I had other sheep

New Testament Stories

The Good Shepherd
Jesus Tells Three Stories -- The Lost Sheep, The Lost Coin, The Lost Son

Book of Mormon Stories

Jesus Christ Appears to the Nephites (His other sheep)

SHEPHERDS OF ISRAEL

by John R. Lasater

"But he that entereth in by the door is the shepherd of the sheep...and the sheep hear his voice: and he calleth his own sheep by name, and leadeth them out and the sheep follow him: for they know his voice. (John 10:2-5)

Some years ago, it was my privilege to visit the country of Morocco as part of an official United States government delegation. As part of that visit, we were invited to travel some distance into the desert to visit some ruins. Five large black limousines moved across the beautiful Moroccan countryside at considerable speed. I was riding in the third limousine, which lagged some distance behind the second. As we topped the brow of a hill, we noticed that the limousine in front of us had pulled off to the side of the road. As we drew nearer, I sensed that an accident had occurred and suggested to my driver that we stop. The scene before us has remained with me for these many years.

An old shepherd, in the long flowing robes of the Savior's day, was standing near the limousine in conversation with the driver. Nearby I noticed a small flock of sheep numbering not more than fifteen or twenty. An accident had occurred. The king's vehicle had struck and injured one of the sheep belonging to the old shepherd. The driver of the vehicle was explaining to him the law of the land. Because the king's vehicle had injured one of the sheep belonging to the old shepherd, he was now entitled to one hundred times its value at maturity. However, under the same law, the injured sheep must be slain and the meat divided among the people. My interpreter hastily added, "But the old shepherd will not accept the money. They never do."

Startled, I asked him why. And he added, "Because of the love he has for each of his sheep."

It was then that I noticed the old shepherd reach down, lift the injured lamb in his arms, and place it in a large pouch on the front of his robe. He kept stroking its head, repeating the same word over and over again. When I asked the meaning of the word, I was informed, "Oh, he is calling it by name. All of his sheep have a name, for he is their shepherd, and the good shepherds know each one of their sheep by name."

It was as my driver predicted. The money was refused, and the old shepherd with his small flock of sheep, with the injured one tucked safely in the pouch on his robe, disappeared into the beautiful deserts of Morocco.

As we continued our journey toward the ruins, my interpreter shared with me more of the traditions and practices of the shepherds of that land. Each evening at sundown, for example, the shepherds bring their small flocks of sheep to a common enclosure where they are secured against the wolves that roam the deserts of Morocco. A single shepherd then is employed to guard the gate until morning. Then the shepherds come to the enclosure one by one, enter therein, and call forth their sheep - by name. The sheep will not hearken unto the voice of a stranger but will leave the enclosure only in the care of their true shepherd, confident and secure because the shepherd knows their names and they know his voice.

The words of the Master Shepherd rang loudly in my ears: "*But he that entereth in by the door is the shepherd of the sheep. To him the porter openeth; and the sheep hear his voice: and he calleth his own sheep by name, and leadeth them out. And when he putteth forth his own sheep, he goeth before them, and the sheep follow him: for they know his voice. And a stranger will they not follow, but will flee from him: for they know not the voice of strangers.*" (John 10:2-5)

Excerpt from article entitled "*Shepherds of Israel,*" by Elder John R. Lasater, *Ensign* , May 1988, pages 74-75 . Used with permission.

CONSIDER THE FISHERMAN

"Simon, son of Jonas, lovest thou me? ... Feed my sheep." (John 20:17)

He has been described as valiant, bold, stalwart, courageous, zealous, noble, mighty. Yet, he has also been depicted as wavering, boastful, impetuous, cowardly, presumptuous. Simon, son of Jonas, later to be called Cephas, "the rock" was a man of great strength, courage and faith, yet, he was also a man who was "thoroughly human."

It seems that Peter's human weakness has been more vividly chronicled than any other apostle.

Yet, Peter was one who humbly recognized and openly admitted his weakness.

It was Andrew, Peter's brother, who first introduced him to the Lord. Andrew had been a disciple of John the Baptist. After hearing the Baptist's testimony and being taught by the Lord himself, Andrew enthusiastically told his brother, "*We have found the Messias.*" (See John 1: 32-42)

Peter followed Jesus for nearly a year and had witnessed many of His mighty works before he was called into the full time service of the Lord. He had seen the Savior turn water to wine, cleanse the temple, and heal the nobleman's son. He had heard Jesus' solemn testimony in the synagogue at Nazareth, and a similar proclamation to a woman in Samaria. By now he had spent hundreds of hours being taught by the Master, and had witnessed countless miracles.

Peter and his brother, Andrew, were fishermen by trade. In partnership with James, John, and their father Zebedee, the five had developed a successful business. They owned their own boats, and employed other men. Peter was married, and owned a home; first in Bethsaida, (See John 1:44) and later in Capernaum. (See Matthew 8:14)

The day Peter was called to the ministry, Jesus was walking beside the sea of Galilee, also called the sea of Gennesaret. Multitudes of people flocked to hear His words. Jesus boarded Simon's boat and asked him to push it out a short distance from the shore. Peter, Andrew, James and John had just returned from a discouraging night of fishing. While they washed their nets, Jesus taught the multitude from Peter's boat.

Peter and his partners needed to provide for their families' needs. Perhaps that day Peter had been weighing in his mind the cost of discipleship. How could he meet the demands of business and family, and yet at the same time follow the Savior? I picture Peter sitting with his cleaned net; half listening, half absorbed in thought, while he waited patiently for Jesus to finish teaching.

When at last Jesus finished, He asked Peter to launch his boat into the deep water and let down his nets. At first Peter argued, telling his Master that they had toiled all night and caught nothing. He was tired, and anxious to get home. But, finally, Peter relented saying, "*nevertheless at thy word I will let down the net.*" (Luke 5:5)

They launched the boat into the sea, and cast out their nets, enclosing a great number of fish. As they toiled to pull them in, their nets broke, and they called to their partners for help. Both boats were so filled with fish that they began to sink.

Seeing the miracle, Peter was overcome and sank to his knees crying out, "*Depart from me; for I am a sinful man, O Lord.*" Gently, the Savior encouraged Peter, "*Fear not; from henceforth thou shalt catch men.*" (Luke 5:7, 10) No longer was Peter to capture and kill fish, but, instead would bring the message of life and salvation to men.

"*And when they brought their ships to land, they forsook all, and followed him.*" (Luke 5:1-11 See also Matthew 4:18-22, Mark 1:16-20) Without hesitation, Peter left a thriving business in full faith that his family would be provided for.

In the Bible, there are recorded many instances when the Master openly rebuked Peter for his impulsiveness, his lack of faith, or lack of understanding.

When Peter had stepped out of his boat and walked upon a wind whipped sea, and then overcome by fear sank into the boiling waves, the Savior reproved him. "*O thou of little faith, wherefore didst thou doubt?*" (Matthew 14:31)

When Jesus foretold his own suffering and death in Jerusalem, Peter began to rebuke him, saying "*This shall not be unto thee*!"Jesus turned to Peter and reproached him saying, "*Get thee behind me, Satan: thou art an offense unto me: for thou savorest not the things that be of God, but those that be of men.*" (Matthew 16:23) Though well intending, Peter had tried to persuade Jesus to take an easier way, just as Satan had done previously. (See Matthew 4:1-11) Once lovingly described as "the rock," Peter now was chastened for being a "stumbling stone." (See Matthew 16:21-23, Mark 8:31-33)

At the last supper, when contention about precedence arose among the twelve, Peter was sternly admonished, "*He that is greatest among you, let him be as the younger; and he that is chief, as he that doth serve.*" (See Luke 22:24-27)

During supper, Jesus arose, filled a basin with water, and girded himself with a towel in the manner of a hired servant. Washing a person's dirty feet was considered one of the lowest of tasks, and Peter objected, "*Lord, dost thou wash my feet?*" Jesus explained to Peter that he didn't understand the full significance of this act now, but would later. Again Peter objected, "*Thou shalt never wash my feet.*" Jesus replied, "*If I wash thee not, thou hast no part with me." Fervently, Peter implored, "Lord, not my feet only, but also my hands and my head.*" (John 13:5-9)

That evening in the Garden of Gethsemane, Peter was chastened yet another time, "*Simon, sleepest thou? Couldest not thou watch one hour? Watch ye and pray, lest ye enter into temptation. The spirit truly is ready, but the flesh is weak.*" (Mark 14:37 See also Matthew 26:40-41)

Later, while attempting to defend and protect Jesus from an angry mob, Peter drew his sword and cut off the ear of Malchus, servant of the high priest. Jesus' severely reproached Peter, commanding him to put away his sword, saying, "*...for all they that take the sword, shall perish with the sword.*" (Matthew 26:52, John 18:10) Repeatedly Peter and the rest of the twelve were reproved by the Savior for their lack of faith and understanding. (See Matthew 14:31, 16:8, 17:17-21, Mark 4:40, Luke 8:25, 17:5)

However, "*Whom the Lord loveth he chasteneth.*" (Hebrews 12:6, See also Revelation 3:19, Mosiah 23:21, Helaman 15:3, D&C 95:1, 136:31) Those who truly love the Lord, and desire to follow Him, submit and learn from His chastening. Such a man was Simon Peter. Peter seemed to sense the divinity of the Master almost by "instinct," and possessed a humble, submissive desire to learn from and follow Him.

After Jesus gave his discourse on the bread of life, a great number of his followers could not grasp His meaning and turned away from following Him. Jesus asked the twelve, "*Will ye also go away?*" Peter's impassioned reply was, "*Lord, to whom shall we go? thou hast the words of eternal life. And we believe and are sure that thou art that Christ the Son of the living God.*" (John 6:66-69)

There were differing opinions among the Jews about who Jesus was. Some supposed Him to be a prophet or a great teacher, even Elias. Superstition and guilt even led some to believe that He was John the Baptist who had risen from the dead. Jesus wanted to know the convictions of the twelve whom he had chosen as disciples, and asked, "*But whom say ye that I am?*" With ardent devotion Peter proclaimed, "*Thou art the Christ. the Son of the living God.*" (Matthew 16:15-16)

This was not a conclusion at which Peter had arrived through some mental process of weighing facts and evidence. Nor was it a mere expression of belief. This was a conviction which burned in his soul; revealed to him by God.

Yet, notwithstanding his firm conviction Jesus later admonished him, "*Simon, Simon, behold, Satan hath desired to have you, that he may sift you as wheat: But I have prayed for thee, that thy faith fail not: and when thou art converted, strengthen thy brethren.*" (Luke 22:31-32)

Was the Lord in question of his devotion? Peter fervently declared, "*Lord, I am ready to go with thee, both into prison, and to death.*" (Luke 22:34) "*I will lay down my life for thy sake.*" (John 13:37) "*Though all men shall be offended because of thee, yet will I never be offended.*" (Matthew 26:33)

But Jesus prophesied, "*In this night, before*

the cock crow twice, thou shalt deny me thrice." (Mark 14:30)

Peter had been one of the three privileged to attend Christ on the Mount of transfiguration. (See Matthew 17:1-4) He was one of the three permitted to witness the raising of the daughter of Jairus. (See Mark 5:37) His own calloused hands had pulled a coin from the fish's mouth to pay the temple tax. (See Matthew 17:27) Jesus had taught in his home and had healed his mother-in-law. (See Mark 1:30-31) Peter had witnessed Christ's power to calm the storm, (See Mark 4:37-41) multiply bread, and fish to feed a multitude, (See Matthew 14:14-21) and heal all manner of disease and infirmity.

He had seen the worshipful reverence of the crowd, as Jesus made his triumphal entry into Jerusalem, and the miraculous manner in which the animal had been procured. (See Matthew 21:2) It was unthinkable that he could possibly deny the deep convictions which he held! Peter vehemently affirmed, "*If I should die with thee, I will not deny thee in any wise. Likewise said they all.*" (Mark 14:31)

Peter followed Jesus to Caiaphas' palace. He sat with the servants and warmed himself by the fire. Three times he was asked if he knew Jesus and three times denied, swearing, "*I know not the man.*" (Mark 14:66-72)

Hearing the cock crow for the second time, Peter remembered the words of Jesus and went out and "*wept bitterly.*" (See Matthew 26:75, Mark 14:72, Luke 22:62)

Surely, afterwards, Peter watched the agonizing scenes of suffering and torture on the cross, and felt the earth tremble at His death, as thick darkness covered the land and engulfed his heart. Oh, the ache and confusion he must have felt, to have not only lost his dearest companion, but to also realize that he had forsaken his friend during a time of great need.

On Sunday morning, Mary Magdalene and three other women ran to tell the apostles their good news. They had seen the risen Lord. In disbelief, Peter and John ran to the tomb to see for themselves, thinking the story to be merely "*idle tales*" of the women. (See Luke 24:11) John, the younger of the two apostles, outran Peter and stopped outside the door of the sepulcher to look inside. Breathlessly, Peter rushed past him, into the tomb and saw the linen burial clothes. In awe and wonder they returned to their own homes.

Peter's hopes were confirmed when Jesus later appeared to him and showed him the prints of the nails. All of the apostles were "*upbraided for their disbelief.*" (Mark 16:14)

Eight days later Jesus appeared again in the upper room, allowing a doubtful Thomas to feel the prints in his hands and feet, and to see for himself.

Jesus made an appointment to meet His apostles one week later on the mount in Galilee. During the days of waiting, Peter told his brethren, "*I go a fishing.*" (John 21:3) He launched his boat into the waters of the Sea of Tiberius. (Also called the Sea of Galilee) Six other apostles joined him: Thomas, Nathaniel, James, John and two other disciples. All night long they toiled and caught nothing. Tired and discouraged, they headed for shore. From the boat they could see a man walking on the bank by the sea, but couldn't tell who it was. The man called to them, "*Children, have ye any meat?.*"

"No," they replied.

The man called back, telling them, "*Cast the net on the right side, and ye shall find.*"

The men did as they had been instructed and let their nets back into the water, perhaps remembering a similar incident just three years earlier.

When they began to pull their nets back up, they were not able to draw it for the multitude of fish. John, ever spiritually perceptive, recognized immediately, "*It is the Lord.*" (See John 21)

Peter immediately girt on his fishers robe, hurled himself into the water, and swam for shore. The others brought the boat to shore dragging their catch. Peter waded into the shallow water to help them to pull in the fish. One hundred fifty three great fish! They marveled that the nets had not broken with such a catch.

Jesus had already kindled a fire, and invited them to come and dine.

When they had finished eating, the Master turned to Peter and asked, "*Simon, son of Jonas, lovest thou me more than these?*" Did Peter love Jesus more that these fish or the things of the world? This was Peter's livelihood, his profession.

However gently the question was put, it must have pierced the heart of Peter. Surely, his denial, his humanness and his faults must have rushed to mind.

Without hesitation Peter answered, "*Yea. Lord, thou knowest that I love thee.*" To which Jesus answered, "*Feed my sheep.*"

The question was repeated, "*Simon, son of Jonas lovest thou me?*" Again Peter affirmed, "*Yea Lord thou knowest that I love thee.*" Again came the command, "*Feed my sheep.*"

Yet a third time, Jesus posed the question to Peter, "*Simon, son of Jonas, lovest thou me?*" Peter was grieved by the Lord's repeated inquiry. His heart must have ached with each repetition of this searching question, and his response came from the depths of a pierced and contrite heart. "*Lord, thou knowest all things, thou knowest that I love thee,*" to which Jesus again replied, "*Feed my sheep.*"

Three times Peter had denied, "*I know not*

this man." and now, three times had affirmed with whole heart his love for the Savior. The man who once declared that he would die for the Savior, now committed to live for Him.

This commission, "*Feed my sheep,*" gives me great comfort. First it is comforting to know that the Lord calls men with human weakness into His service: not that Peter's weakness in any way can compensate for our own, but to know that, "*my grace is sufficient for all men that humble themselves before me; for if they humble themselves before me; and have faith in me, then will I make weak things become strong unto them.*" (Ether 12:27) Such was the case with Peter who became one of the most stalwart and faithful men to ever walk the earth. Mighty in word and deed, he eventually suffered death as a martyr for His Master, to whom he had passionately declared his love.

It is also comforting to know that Jesus would have such love for all of his sheep--the white ones and the black ones--that he would call faithful shepherds to tenderly care for them.

I remember teaching a wonderful sister about the Plan of Salvation, during my mission. It soon became clear to us that she didn't accept the fact that we had lived in a pre-existent state with God. This was unusual, for there were few people who ever argued this point. It seemed to strike a familiar chord in most people, and they readily accepted these truths. But this sister couldn't accept it. We shared with her many passages from the Bible which teach about the pre-existence, but still she could not accept it. I went home and pondered
and prayed for guidance. I felt impressed to teach her from modern scripture.

We returned, and using the Book of Mormon, Doctrine and Covenants and Pearl of Great Price, we taught her again of the grand council and war in Heaven. With every scripture we read, she protested. She wanted to see it in the Bible. Each time, we told her to wait. When finally we had finished, we turned to the Bible and read each of the passages which we had read with her previously; those she had been unable to accept. The light came on, and she understood. It was such a magnificent thing to see the understanding in her eyes. Then she shared with us the reason for her doubt, which really touched me. "The reason I couldn't accept it," she said, "was that it was too wonderful a thing to even imagine, that I was actually a child of God." What a wonderful thing it is to know that we are His children, that he loves us and cares for us. "*Behold, what manner of love the Father hath bestowed upon us, that we should be called the sons of God.*" (1 John 3:1)

Oh, the comfort which comes from the commission of the Lord to Peter, "*Simon, son of Jonas, lovest thou me? ...Feed my sheep.*" (John 20:17)

References:

Bruce R. McConkie, *The Mortal Messiah*, Salt Lake City: Deseret Book, 1980

James E. Talmage, *Jesus The Christ*, Salt Lake City: The Church of Jesus Christ of Latter-day Saints, 1973

THE GOOD SHEPHERD

The sheep are safely sheltered for the night within the fold.
The shepherd will return with dawn's first rays.
He'll call his sheep to follow Him; the lambs all know His voice.
He'll lead them to lush pastures where they'll graze.

And gently, ever gently, his staff prods the ones who stray.
He leadeth them to waters clear and deep.
The feeble ones are carried and the wand'ring ones sought out.
He numbereth and loveth all his sheep.

The hills know many shepherds with their many different flocks.
They call with voices loud, or deep or low.
Some whistle, others shout above the bleating of the sheep.
Each lamb responds unto the voice they know.

Each lamb knows his own shepherd; and each feeds with his own flock.
And hearing his familiar voice, they came.
Trusting in the love of him who'd gladly give his life.
For his sheep — The one who knew and called their name.

Sharon Velluto

ADDITIONAL REFERENCES

Exodus 12	Instructions for the Passover
Leviticus 9:3, 16:22	Scapegoat and the Day of Atonement
Isaiah 53:7	He is brought as a lamb to the slaughter
Matthew 26:2,17	Preparation for feast of Passover (See also Mark 14:12)
John 1:29	Behold the Lamb of God
John 6	Bread of life discourse
Acts 8:32	Like a sheep to the slaughter
1 Corinthians 5:7	Christ our Passover is sacrificed
Hebrews 11:28	Through faith he kept the Passover
Hebrews 9:12-14, 10:1-6	Blood of Christ to sanctify
1 Peter 1:19	Blood of Christ as lamb without blemish
Revelation 5:6	Stood as lamb as it had been slain
Revelation 7:14	Robes made white in blood of Lamb (See also 1 Nephi 12:11, Alma 13:11, Mormon 9:6)
Revelation 13:8	Lamb slain from the foundation of the world
2 Nephi 11:4	This end hath the law of Moses...the typifying of Him
Alma 7:14	Lamb of God which taketh away sins
D&C 88:106	Lamb of God hath overcome
Moses 5:6-7	Adam is taught about sacrifice

See Passover in Bible Dictionary

Old Testament Stories
The Prophet Moses
The Passover

New Testament Stories
The First Sacrament
Jesus Suffers in Gethsemane
Jesus is Crucified

Book of Mormon Stories
Jesus Christ teaches about the Sacrament and Prayer

THE LAMB HUNT ACTIVITY

Prepare the lambs in Optional Materials pages 185 and 187, according to directions. Then hide the lambs around the house.

After the children have had time to search for the lambs, have them and bring them back to the "sheepfold." Explain that there is a special holiday called the Passover. Anciently, the Israelites chose a special lamb to sacrifice and eat for the Passover feast. This is what God had commanded them to do. This lamb had to be a special lamb. Give the following directions.

1. It had to be a **male** lamb, a boy... if you have a pink lamb those are girls, put them down in front of you.

2. This special lamb had to be a **firstborn** lamb... If your lamb has a two or a three on it, that means it was born second or third. Put those in front of you because we cannot use those lambs.

3. This lamb had to be a **young** lamb. It had to be less than one year old. If you have a gray lamb, those are old lambs and they cannot be used, so put them down in front of you.

4. This special lamb had to be a lamb **without spots.** If your lamb has spots, it can't be used. Put it down in front of you.

The special lamb that the Israelites used had to be pure and white, it had to be young, it had to be the firstborn and it had to be a boy. Every family was required to choose a lamb which fit these requirements to eat for their Passover dinner. This was because the lamb was to point to Jesus.

- Jesus was a boy.
- Jesus was Heavenly Father's first son, the firstborn.
- Jesus was killed when He was very young.
- Jesus was without spot. He had no sin.

When the Israelites killed the lamb for their dinner it was called a sacrifice. It was to remind them that the blood they had painted on their doors had saved them from death. When Jesus died, that was called a sacrifice also. The blood He shed in the Garden of Gethsemane and on the cross can save us.

WANDERING IN THE WILDERNESS

To be used with activity idea #1, page 23.

1. **Crossing the Red Sea:** (Two blankets can be parted) Ask: When in our life do we go completely under water? (Baptism) When the Israelites passed through the Red Sea,they became free and they started a new life. They started on a journey to a promised land, flowing with milk and honey.

When we are baptized we become free from sin. We begin a new life. We begin a journey toward the promised land, the celestial kingdom with the riches of eternity. " *I would not that ye should be ignorant, how that all our fathers were under the cloud and all passed through the sea. And all were baptized unto Moses in the cloud and on the sea.*" (1 Corinthians 10:1-2)

2. **Being led by a pillar of fire**: (A flashlight) What do we have that is like a fire to guide us to the promised land? (Holy Ghost) Sometimes receiving of the gift of the Holy Ghost is called baptism by fire. If we watch and listen to the Holy Ghost, He will lead us safely back to Heavenly Father.

"*Moreover, thou leddest them in the day by a cloudy pillar and in the night by a pillar of fire to give them light in the way wherein they should go... Is not my word like as a fire? saith the Lord... For as many as are led by the Spirit of God, they are the sons of God... For behold again I say unto you, that if ye will enter in by the way and receive the Holy Ghost, it will show you all things that you should do.*" (Nehemiah 9:12, Jeremiah 23:24, Romans 8:14, 2 Nephi 32:5)

3. **Manna:** When the children of Israel were hungry, God provided manna for them. (Lead them to a room where some torn up bread has been placed. Have them eat a piece. You may want to show them some coriander seed. Manna is described as being small and round, like coriander seed. (See Exodus 16:14, 31) Manna kept the Israelites from starving. Jesus explained that He is the bread of life.

"Feasting on the word", by reading the scriptures and following the counsel of His prophets, helps keep the spirit healthy and alive. *"Verily, verily, I say unto you, Moses gave you not that bread from heaven, but my Father giveth you the true bread from heaven... I am the bread of life. He that cometh to me shall never hunger... I am the living bread which came down from heaven.; if any man eat of this bread he shall live forever and the bread I will give is my flesh which I will give for the life of the world.* " (John 6:32,35,51)

4. **Water from the Rock:** (Place a rock or picture of a rock near the faucet) The Israelites were very thirsty. They had nothing to drink. God commanded Moses to hit a rock with his rod and water would come out of the rock. So he did. (Hit the faucet and turn it on. Give everyone a drink.)

Jesus told a woman of Samaria that He was the living water. If we drink the living water He offers we will never be thirsty. We drink this water by learning of Jesus and living as He taught.

"*Whosoever drinketh of this water shall thirst again, but whosoever drinketh of the water that I shall give him shall never thirst. But the water that I shall give him shall be in him a well of water springing up into everlasting life... If any man thirst, let him come unto me and drink...out of his belly shall flow rivers of living water.*" (John 4:13-14, 7:37-38)

5. **Poisonous Serpents:** (A length of thick rope, a stuffed sock or any plastic toy can be used as a serpent.) While they were wandering in the wilderness, the Israelites forgot God's commandments and started to do some wicked things. God sent fiery (poisonous) serpents. They bit the Israelites. Many died. God told Moses to make a serpent of brass, and to put the serpent on his staff. God told Moses to hold his rod high in the air. If those who had been bitten would just look upon the rod they would be saved. But some were stubborn and didn't believe Moses. They wouldn't look at his rod and died. The Book of Mormon states, " *Yea and behold a type was raised in the wilderness that whosoever would look upon it might live. And many did look and live.... And as he (Moses) lifted up the brazen serpent in the wilderness, even so shall he be lifted up, who should come. And as many as should look upon that serpent should live, even so as many as should look upon the Son of God with faith, having a contrite spirit , might live, even unto that life which is eternal. And as Moses lifted up the serpent in the wilderness, even so must the Son of Man be lifted up, that whosoever believeth in him should not perish but have everlasting life.*" (Alma 33:19, Helaman 8:14-15, John 3:14-15)

Each Sunday when we partake of the sacrament, we eat bread and drink water in remembrance of what Jesus did to save us. If we will always partake of the sacrament and do so worthily we can be saved. We will go to live with Jesus and Heavenly Father again.

6. **Go to the promised land:** Sing verse 5 of *Follow the Prophet* (Children's Song Book, page 110.) It is helpful to understand that the distance between Egypt and the promised land is only about 200 miles. It took three months to travel from Egypt to Mount Sinai, where the Israelites camped for nearly a year. It took only 11 days to reach Kadesh which nearly borders the promised land. Because of their rebellion and lack of faith in God, the Israelites were made to wander up and down in the wilderness for 38 more years. All of that time they were within just a few miles of the land of Canaan. Compared to the distance the Mormon pioneers travelled, the distance the Israelites traveled was relatively small. The first company of pioneers made the trek across the plains in a little over 4 months, a distance of about 1,000 miles. That is 10 times the distance the Israelites traveled.

"BEHOLD THE LAMB"

God said, "Choose ye a lamb,
a young male, without spot.
His blood upon the door insures
that ye shall suffer not."

John recognized the Lamb;
God's Son who bore no stain.
Lamb chosen to be sacrificed.
Lamb chosen to be slain.

A Lamb whose very blood
redeemed the soul of man;
And as God's chosen witness John
declared, "Behold the Lamb."

Sharon Velluto

THE COMING CHILD

Welcome all wonders in one sight!
Eternity shut in a span!
Summer in winter, day in night!
Heaven in earth, and God in man!
Great little One! whose all-embracing birth
Lifts earth to heaven, stoops heaven to earth...

To Thee, meek Majesty! soft King
Of simple graces and sweet loves;
Each of us his lamb will bring,
Each his pair of silver doves;
Till burnt at last in fire of Thy fair eyes,
Ourselves become our own best sacrifice.

Richard Crashaw
1613? - 1649

Haroseth or Charoseth

3 tart unpeeled apples grated
1/2 cup nuts (walnuts or almonds)
1/3 cup raisins
1/4 cup grape juice or apple juice (wine is generally used, but honey or sugar could be substituted as well)
3/4 teaspoon cinnamon (or less if preferred)

Mix until ingredients are blended. Place in bowls for dipping. *(See steps 8 and 9 on page 99``)*

These recipes go with Activity # 5, page 23.

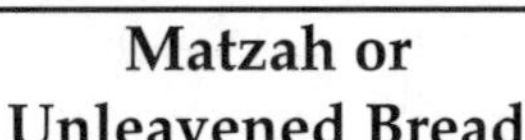

Matzah or Unleavened Bread

3 cups flour or Matzah meal
1/4 tsp salt
Water enough to make a stiff dough

Knead all ingredients until smooth. Divide into 4 parts. Roll out to about a 1/8 inch thickness. Lightly puncture the dough with a fork. Place on a lightly greased cookie sheet. Bake at 400 degrees for about 8-10 minutes or until light brown. Turn over and bake until brown.

(Commercially purchased Matzah is generally square in shape. These are covered and served whole. The leader of the seder breaks the Matzah)

THE PASSOVER

The Passover was a sacred symbol pointing forward to the great and last sacrifice which would be made by the Savior, just as the sacrament is a symbol which looks back in remembrance of that same sacrifice.

The story of the Israel's sojourn in Egypt began when Joseph was sold to Egyptians by his jealous brothers. He obtained a position of importance by interpreting the Pharaoh's dream, and warning him of an impending famine. The Egyptians stored enough food to live rather comfortably through a seven year draught. In Canaan, Israel, Joseph's father, and his sons were starving, so he sent his sons to Egypt for food. Eventually, Israel, his eleven sons and their families joined Joseph in Egypt. They numbered about 70 people. Joseph and his family were called Israelites.

Because of Joseph's position, the Israelites were well accepted. But after the pharaoh died, the new king became very suspicious of the Israelites. The descendants of Israel grew and prospered, and were blessed abundantly of God. The pharaoh became afraid of their strength.

So Pharaoh, attempting to control this race, began a series of retaliations to subdue them. When heavy taxes didn't seem to effect them, he made them slaves and placed extremely heavy burdens upon them, hoping to weaken and destroy the race. But the Israelites prospered. The heavier the burdens placed on them, the more they seemed to prosper. Pharaoh ordered that every son born to Israelites be thrown into the river.

It was during this time, that Moses was born and hidden in a reed basket by his mother. After finding him in the river, Pharaoh's daughter raised him as her own son. Though Moses was raised in Pharaoh's court, he knew that he was an Israelite. One day, Moses killed an Egyptian while defending an Israelite slave. Fearing for his life, Moses fled from Egypt and dwelt in the land of Midian for several years. From a burning bush, God commanded Moses to lead the children of Israel out of bondage so that they might worship God as they had been commanded.

So Moses went to the pharaoh and asked him to let his people go into the wilderness that they might hold a feast to God. But Pharaoh said, *"Who is the Lord that I should obey his voice to let Israel go?"* (Exodus 5:2)

Not only did the pharaoh refuse to let Israel go, he made their work harder for them. They now had to gather the straw needed to make bricks, which before had been provided for them. The people grew angry with Moses and complained that he had made their situation worse. So, Moses again prayed for guidance. The Lord assured Moses that Pharaoh would be punished and that he would see the power of God. He promised that He would deliver the children of Israel.

Egypt was cursed with ten plagues. With each plague, Pharaoh promised to let the Israelites go, and asked Moses to pray to God to lift the plague. Each time the curse was lifted, the Pharaoh went back on his word and refused to let the Israelites go. The plagues were:

1. The water in Egypt turned to <u>blood.</u> The fish died and the river began to stink. Pharaoh's magicians were able to do the same.
2. Rivers, lands and even houses were filled with <u>frogs</u>. Pharaoh's magicians imitated the curse.
3. <u>Lice</u> covered the land and people. Magicians could not copy the plague.
4. <u>Swarms of Flies</u> infested everything in Egypt but not in Goshen where the Israelites were.
5. The <u>cattle, oxen, horses, donkeys, camels and sheep</u> of the Egyptians were smitten with a disease and died. Israel's animals were unaffected.
6. The Egyptians and their animals were stricken with <u>boils.</u>
7. Fiery <u>hail</u> fell from the skies. destroying crops, breaking down trees and killing any person or animal who remained in the fields. There was no hail in Goshen.
8. Swarms of <u>locusts</u> covered the land, infested houses, and devoured all crops which had not been destroyed by the hail.
9. A thick <u>darkness</u> covered the land for three days. No one was able to see anything or move from their houses.
10. The <u>first born</u> child in every house would die.

God commanded the Israelites to choose a lamb and kill it. They were to take the blood of the lamb and paint it on their doorposts and the lintel above the door. The lamb could not just be any lamb of their choosing. God specified that it had to be a firstborn male, without blemish, of the first year. The lamb was to be roasted and eaten with unleavened bread and bitter herbs.

They were to eat it "*with your loins girded, your shoes on your feet, and your staff in your hand, and ye shall eat it in haste, it is the Lord's Passover.*" (Exodus 12:11)

That night, the angel of death would pass

through all of the land and smite the firstborn of every house. But, the houses on which the blood of the lamb appeared, the angel would "pass over" and not destroy them.

They were commanded "*This day shall be unto you for a memorial, and ye shall keep it a feast unto the Lord throughout your generations; ye shall keep it a feast by an ordinance forever.*" (Exodus 12:14)

The Israelites were to remain in their houses and not leave until the following morning. "*And it came to pass, that at midnight the Lord smote all the firstborn in the land of Egypt, from the firstborn of Pharaoh that sat on his throne unto the firstborn of the captive that was in the dungeon, and the firstborn of cattle...and there was a great cry in Egypt; for there was not a house where there was no one dead.*" (Exodus 12:29-30) This was the "final straw" for the Pharaoh and he commanded that the Israelites leave. The Israelites fled Egypt, taking with them their bread before it was leavened.

Led by Moses they went to the borders of the Red Sea. By this time the Pharaoh had changed his mind again, and sent his army to capture the Israelites. They were trapped. The Red Sea was on one side and Pharaoh's army on the other. Seeing the mighty army of Pharaoh, the Israelites lost faith and began to murmur against Moses, saying that they were better off being slaves, than to be killed there. But God was faithful to his promise and delivered them. The sea parted and they walked through on dry land.

Every year, the Israelites held a feast in remembrance of the night that the angel of death "passed over" their homes.

Most Biblical scholars believe that the ritual of sacrifice began at the time of Moses, but modern revelation indicates that it actually began with Adam and that it was "*in similitude of the Only Begotten of the Father*" (Moses 5:7) who would later come and himself be offered up as a sacrifice for sin.

The "Paschal" or "Passover" lamb was to point Israel's mind to the Savior in the following ways:

1. The lamb had to be male and without spot. Jesus was also male and the only person to ever live, who was without the blemish of sin. He was sinless and without spot. (See Exodus 12:5)

2. The sacrifice had to be a firstborn as well as being a young lamb in the first year. Jesus was the firstborn Son of the Father, and was sacrificed as a young man in the prime of his life.

3. The lamb could not be strangled or killed in any like manner. Its blood had to be spilt. Jesus' blood was shed for mankind both on the cross and in Gethsemane to atone for the sin of man and to save him, just as the blood on the doorposts saved Israel from the destroyer.

4. Israel was commanded to not break any bone of the animal. This is one reason for roasting the lamb, since boiling would require it to be cut up. Special care was taken to not break any bone.

Jesus was crucified on the first day of the Passover, which was on a Friday. The following day was to be a doubly holy day. It was the Jewish sabbath, and the second day of the feast. Jesus' body could not be left on the cross "*lest the land be defiled.*" (Deuteronomy 21:22-23) It was a common practice of the day, to break the legs of the offender with a club. This was followed by a spear being thrust into his side to finish the execution, so the body would not remain on the cross during the Sabbath. The practice of breaking the legs was to inflict additional pain. It was to compensate for the suffering that would otherwise have come, had the offender's death occurred naturally, which at times took up to five days. Since Jesus, had already died, the guards passed by His body, and did not break His legs. But, to insure that Jesus was indeed dead, a spear was thrust into His side. All of this was in fulfillment of scripture, for which the Paschal lamb was a type. For nearly 1500 years this sacrificial feast had pointed to this great and last sacrifice offered for man's salvation by the Savior.

(For further information on the procedures for crucifixion refer to *The Mortal Messiah*, by Bruce R. McConkie, Volume 4, chapter 107, See also: Psalms 22:16, 34:20; Isaiah 50:6, 53:5)

Before eating the Passover meal, the house was cleaned of all leaven, as God had commanded. (See Exodus 13:7) It was forbidden to eat leaven for the entire eight day feast. Those who ate leaven during that time, were cut off from the rest of Israel. (See Exodus 12:15,19; 13:7)

The Jews are very strict in their observance of cleanliness and purification for this event. Separate dishes are reserved specifically for the Passover meal, and different pots are used for cooking. Not only is all leaven removed from the house, but, all surfaces in the entire kitchen, including the stove and refrigerator, are cleaned and purified by glowing, purging or soaking, before food may be placed on them.

Leaven is symbolic of sin since it caused food to ferment and to mold. (See Bible Dictionary, *Leaven*) The command to clean houses of leaven and to not eat of leaven for the seven days following Passover. (Called the Feast of Unleavened Bread) is similar to the commands given us to cleanse our lives of sin.

It was a solemn occasion to clean the house of leaven, and often now is done by candlelight. Leaven was put in a separate place and was later destroyed.

Current Jewish tradition dictates that not one crumb of leaven may be left in the home. However, it seems that the original command pertained more to the consumption of leaven than the purging of it from homes. Jesus often taught about the extreme views the Jews had of cleanliness. "*There is nothing from without a man, that entering into him can defile him; but the things which come out of him, those are they that defile the man*." (Mark 7:15; See also: Matthew 15:2-14, Mark 7:3-16, Luke 11:37-54)

Fifteen hundred years after the original command to observe the Passover was given, Christ's ministry came to a close at Passover time. The Last Supper was the Passover feast. The room had been prepared, cleaned of leaven, and made ready for Christ and His apostles. Jesus observed this command and sent two of his apostles to the temple to make the sacrifice of the lamb, and to procure a place to eat. All had been prepared and made ready.

In Jesus' day, anyone who ate the Passover was required to be "ceremonially clean". They were also required to fast from the time of sacrifice the previous evening.

This Passover was called the Last Supper for two reasons. First, it was the last supper Christ would eat during his mortal life. Second, it was the last time the Passover feast was to be officially observed, and accepted of God.

During the Passover, one person is appointed to be the head of the Passover dinner, to lead the proceedings. Jesus was head of the proceedings during this last Passover.

The Passover feast is called a "*Seder,*" meaning order. This is because a specified order has been established for the feast.

The procedures for Passover have varied some throughout the thousands of years it has been practiced. The basic order for the feast as it exists today is as follows, and was similar in the day of Jesus:

1. *The* Kiddush or Kadesh: Which is the singing of the blessing over the first cup of four cups of wine. This cup is called "The cup of the blessings."

2. Urechatz: The washing of the hands prior to partaking of the green herb. It is probably at this point that Jesus varied from the established tradition and instead washed the feet of His disciples.

Afterwards, a low table was brought in. Sometimes these tables hung from the ceiling so as not touch the floor and defile it. Each person had a separate couch or pillow to recline on. They lay on their left side and leaned on the left hand for support, with their feet extending back toward the ground. They positioned themselves on three sides of the table, leaving one end open for the serving of food. (This isn't at all like the paintings we see of the Last Supper and better explains why John was lying on the Savior's bosom. (See John 13:25. 21:20)

3. Karpas: Eating and dipping of the green vegetable twice in salt water. The vegetable is generally lettuce, parsley, celery or watercress. It is dipped twice in salt water before eating it. The first time dipped represents the salty tears of their ancestors. The second time is to remember their deliverance. The greens are symbolic of spring, hope and new life.

4. Yakhatz: Breaking the Matzah, or unleavened bread. (Also called *Matzoh*) In modern Jewish tradition, Matzah represents survival, and is often called the "bread of deliverance." The Matzah is broken into three pieces to be used throughout the meal. Today, the larger piece of this is hidden for the children to find later. That piece is called the Afikomen.

It is assumed that this part of the Seder was added to the Passover to keep the children awake during the entire ceremony. This Afikomen is eaten at the very end of the meal. In modern Passover meals, Matzah replaces the lamb, which is no longer sacrificed. It is the last thing eaten, so the taste remains in the mouth.

When the Israelites fled Egypt, they took their bread before it had been leavened. Unleavened bread has since been used as a reminder of their deliverance and was part of the feast instituted by Jehovah. (See Exodus 12:8,17)

5. Maggid: Telling of the Passover story. This includes the asking of the four questions.

Questions: Why is this night different from all other nights?

1. On other nights we can eat bread or matzah, why on this night do we eat only matzah?
2. On other nights we eat any kind of vegetable, why on this night do we eat bitter herbs?
3. On other nights, we do not have to dip a vegetable even once. Why tonight do we dip it twice?
4. On other nights we sit any way we want, Why on this night do we recline on pillows?

(Note: from book to book the questions vary. There is not one set *Haggadah,* which is the book each participant uses to follow the story, but there are thousands of variations.) The four types of children (wise, scornful, simple, and naive) are spoken about at this point and their questions answered. A second cup of wine is drunk at this time called "The cup of memory."

6. Rachatz or Rakhtzah: washing the hands before the meal.

7. Motzi (Motzee) Matzoh: Saying the blessings

for the matzah. Two blessings are pronounced. One is a blessing which is said all year and one is said especially for Matzah.

8. Maror: Tasting the bitter herbs and dipping them in Haroseth. Haroseth sometimes called Charoseth or Haroset is a sweet apple nut mixture which represents the mortar used by the Israelites to make bricks for Pharaoh. (In Christ's day it was made of dates, raisins and vinegar, and was sour.) It is sweet to remind the Jews of the hope of freedom. This is probably the "sop" mentioned into which Judas dipped his hand, revealing himself as the traitor. The bitter herb used is usually horseradish. It is bitter to symbolize the afflictions suffered while in slavery.

9. Korek or Korech: Eating of a Hillel sandwich which is made of Matzah and bitter herbs together. Anciently it was also eaten with lamb. (In Jesus' day this was dipped in the Haroseth.)

10. Shulkhan Orech: Serving the traditional Passover meal. Today, this is a large and festive meal. The fare is now varied from what it was anciently, and numerous Passover cookbooks are available to ensure that food remains *"kosher."* (Clean or fit to eat, according to Judaic law). Everything up to this point has been preliminary to the meal.

11. Tzafon or Tzafun: Finding and eating the Afikomen. (See explanation in #4 above)

When the children find the Afikomen, the leader of the Seder must pay a price to "redeem" it from the children, who enjoy bartering to get the highest price possible. It is most likely that this part of modern day Passover was not practiced in Jesus' day.

12. Barekh or Berach: Saying the blessing after the meal. Some of these blessings are sung. They are called the *Hallel.* Then the third cup of wine, or "The cup of Redemption" is drunk.

It was probably during this point that Jesus instituted the sacrament. Judas had already been sent away, and only those worthy to partake were present.

After drinking the third cup of wine, the door is opened for Elijah the Prophet, and passages of scripture are read which foretell the destruction of all heathen nations. (It is interesting to note that each year during the Passover, Jews open their doors inviting Elijah to come, to fulfill the promise made in Malachi. (See Malachi 4:3) In 1836, during this Passover feast, Elijah did come. He appeared to Joseph Smith in the Kirtland temple, along with many other ancient prophets, to restore sacred priesthood keys. (See Joseph Fielding Smith, *Doctrines of Salvation,* Volume 2, pp. 100-101, and D&C 110)

13. Hallel: Singing songs of praise and drinking the fourth cup of wine. "The cup of hope and freedom." Psalms 113-118, are the Psalms known as the Hallel. Psalm 132 is known as the Great Hallel. (See Bible Dictionary, p. 698) Matthew 26:30 and Mark 14:26 both mention the singing of a hymn before Jesus went into the Garden of Gethsemane. This was probably the point where that occurred.

14. Nirtzah: Completing the Seder with traditional songs. Often at this point the Jewish holocaust is also discussed.

In celebrating the Passover with the last supper, Jesus was fulfilling Jewish law. It is safe to assume that He followed the same ordered ritual that others followed, insofar as he did not violate principles of truth. Then, building upon this ancient foundation, He instituted the ordinance of the sacrament. (See *The Mortal Messiah,* Bruce R. McConkie Volume 4, page 56)

At the last supper Jesus told his disciples that in Him, the law had been fulfilled and the practice of sacrifice had come to an end. People no longer needed to look forward to a Savior, for He had already come. Jesus was to be the *"great and last sacrifice,"* the *"sacrifice that was infinite and eternal"* (See Alma 34:10-14; 2 Nephi 2:7; 3 Nephi 9:19-20; and Hebrews 7,8,9,10) He was the *"lamb slain from the foundation of the world,"* (Revelation 13:8) *"The Lamb of God, which taketh away the sins of the world."* (John 1:29)

Sacrifice was to formally end that evening, and a new feast was instituted to replace it; not a feast which looked forward a sacrifice yet to be made, but one which was to look back in remembrance of the sacrifice already made in behalf of all mankind. The sacrament, with broken bread is a reminder of His broken flesh, and the cup of wine is taken in remembrance of the blood which He shed.

The Jews, who rejected Christ, continued to go to the temple each year to offer sacrifices. This practice continued for but a few short years until the temple at Jerusalem was destroyed. There no longer existed a holy place designated for sacrifice and thereafter, the Passover was generally observed in individual households. Gradually, the practice of the Pascal sacrifice by the Jews died out.

The full meaning of these sacrifices has become lost to the Jewish people. One writer stated that the shank bone, which is used now in place of the Paschal lamb, serves as a reminder of the lamb their ancestors sacrificed. Another wrote it was to remind them of the time that their ancestors were shepherds, while still another wrote that the sacrifice was offered by their ancestors in hopes of a good harvest.

The Passover has remained fairly consistent through many centuries, but there have been a few changes made from its original procedure. One of these changes is the roasted egg which is said to have originated in the times of the temple and symbolizes new life, a perfect symbol of Easter. Another change is the shank bone which is used today instead of the Passover lamb.

Israel was commanded to not let any stranger eat the Passover with them. (See Exodus 12:43) The Passover was a renewal of a covenant that they had made with God. The circumcision of males was a symbol of that covenant. Since a stranger had not made that covenant, they could not renew a covenant which had never been made. (This is similar to the command to not partake of the sacrament unworthily or without the baptismal covenant. Children are an exception because the sacrament serves as a reminder of the covenant they are going to make) Currently, the Jews open their doors as a symbol that all are invited to enter in and to feast with them. (See *Bible Dictionary,* under the heading *Feasts* for other changes made to the Passover ritual)

(One of the most interesting of Jewish holidays is Yom Kippur. During this festival, in ancient times, as commanded in the Bible, a young goat was forced into the wilderness. This young goat was believed to carry away all of their sins. It is believed that this is where the word scapegoat was derived from.

Yom Kippur, literally translated means the Day of Atonement. One author wrote that Jews no longer believe a goat can take away their sins. Instead they ask God for forgiveness. This goat was another type of Christ.)

An understanding of the Passover enables us to better comprehend some of the significant events in the life of the Savior. When Christ was 12 years old, under Jewish law he had become a man, and was taken to be presented at the temple with all the other Jewish males, as commanded by God. Since His parents observed Jewish law, it is probable that Jesus had been to Jerusalem with them before, but this was the first time He had been presented to God in the temple as was the custom. Since all males had to be presented, and the Passover sacrifice was to be slain in the temple, which was God's appointed place, there was a large congregation. It is estimated that close to 3 million people had come. It is easy then to see how Jesus may have become lost (at least to his parents) during this time of confusion.

Jesus' ministry began at Passover time with the first cleansing of the temple. Sacrifices were made available to the people at the temple. But in order to purchase one of these, a special temple money was used. Roman coins had an effigy of Caesar, and were considered to be his money, and hence they were not fit for use in the temple for purchasing the sacred sacrificial animals. Money changers changed coins from different countries for the temple money which was used to purchase the animals to be offered as a sacrifice.

If we were to attend Passover today, our currency would be exchanged for temple money. The Italian Lire, the English Pound, the German Marc, the French Franc, the Japanese Yen, the Mexican Peso etc. would be exchanged for temple money. But, the money changers were not honest and were robbing the people as they exchanged the money. This is what enraged Christ, not the fact that a sacrifice which was sacred and acceptable was being sold.

The Passover was a sacred symbol pointing forward to the great and last sacrifice which would be made by the Savior, just as the sacrament is a symbol which looks back in remembrance of that same sacrifice.

References:

1. Bruce R. McConkie, *Doctrinal New Testament Commentary,* Vol..1, Salt Lake City: Bookcraft, 1973 (Elder McConkie gives a full and enlightening description of the events and procedures followed during the Last Supper of our Lord, in his book *The Mortal Messiah,* Volume 4, pp. 19-67. See also Volume 1 p. 166 for a discussion of many of the symbolic inferences of the Passover.)

2. Bruce R. McConkie, *Mormon Doctrine*, Salt Lake City: Bookcraft, 1966

3. Bruce R. McConkie, *The Promised Messiah, The Mortal Messiah,* Volumes 1-4, Salt Lake City: Deseret Book, 1980

4. *Old Testament Student Manual,* Salt Lake City: The Church of Jesus Christ of Latter-Day Saints, 1982

5. *The Life And Teachings of Jesus Christ,* Salt Lake City: The Church of Jesus Christ of Latter-Day Saints, 1979

6. *Passover Program*, prepared by Victor L. Ludlow, Provo, Utah,1988

7. Frances R. AvRutick, *The Complete Passover Cookbook,* New York: Jonathan David Publishers, 1981

8. Betty Morrow and Louis Hartman, *A Holiday Book :Jewish Holidays*, Champaign, Illinois: Garrard Publishing, 1967

9. Howard Greenfield, *Passover*, Canada: Holt, Rinehart, Winston of Canada Ltd., 1978

10. Barbara Diamond Goldin, *The Passover Journey: A Seder Companion,* New York: Viking, 1994

11. Oris Sherman and Lynn Sharon Schwartz, *The Four Questions,* New York: Dial Books for Young Readers, 1989

ADDITIONAL REFERENCES

1 Kings 3:5-12; 4:29... Wisdom of Solomon
Job 32:7-9.................. Job explains wisdom
Proverbs 2:2-6............ How to obtain wisdom
Proverbs 4................. Discourse on wisdom
Matthew 7:21............ Blessings for those who obey (See also D&C 63:23; 93:26-28; 136:32-33)
Matthew 10:16-20....... Jesus teaches apostles to be wise
Matthew 22:29........... Ye err not knowing scriptures (See also Mark 12:24; D&C 1:37)
Matthew 25:1-13........ Wise and foolish virgins
John 7:31-39.............. The Holy Ghost gives wisdom (See JST verses 34,36)
John 8:12,32.............. Jesus explains knowledge and its rewards
John 14:23,25-27........ Comforter will teach all things (See also Moroni 10:3-5)
James 1:5.................... If any of you lack wisdom (See JSH:11)
1 John 2:3-7.............. We understand principles by living them. (See also John 7:17, Alma 32:26-34)
Mosiah 2:17................ King Benjamin teaches words of wisdom
Alma 5:45-46.............. Alma explains how he gained knowledge
Alma 37:34-37............ Counsel with the Lord in all thy doings
D&C 8:1-3................... Oliver taught how to know truth (See also D&C 6:7,22-24)
D&C 50:40.................. Wisdom is a process (also D&C 98:12)
D&C 88:77-86, 118..... How to learn (See also D&C 90:15, 109:7,14; 90:15)
D&C 89:18-21............ Promise of the Word of Wisdom
D&C 131:6................... Impossible to be saved in ignorance
D&C 138...................... Prophet Joseph F. Smith ponders
Moses 1:1-26.............. Moses discerns between God and Satan

Ensign
April 1982 p. 40 — H.J.Grant gets wisdom through paying tithing, Hinckley
October 1985, p. 46 — The wisdom of Daniel, Perry
May 1984 pp.62-64 — By Their Fruits Ye Shall Know Them, Derrick

Old Testament Stories
King Solomon

New Testament Stories
The Wise Men
The Boy Jesus

Book of Mormon Stories
How we Got the Book of Mormon

WISDOM

Wisdom to search and to learn of His word,
Wisdom enough to be led,
To walk in sure footsteps of those gone before,
To follow paths prophets have tread.

Wisdom to recognize Covenant Star,
Conviction to trust in its light,
Enough to forsake the enticements of earth,
To follow -- though dark be the night.

Drawn by a feeling no tongue can express;
By God's sacred promise fulfilled.
Inspired and o'ercome by God's transcendent gift
Impelled by devotion to kneel.

Wisdom to turn in a different way,
To follow a God-given dream.
To witness His birth and His glorious Name,
That others may worship the King.

Sharon Velluto

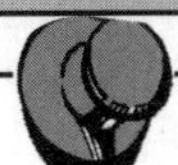

He who knows not
and knows not that he knows not
Is a fool—-shun him.

He who knows not
and knows that he knows not
Is simple—-teach him.

He who knows
and knows not that he knows
Is asleep—-waken him.

He who knows
and knows that he knows
Is wise—-follow him

Author Unknown

THE WISDOM OF INNOCENTS

They are idols of hearts and of households. They are angels of God in disguise:
The sunlight still sleeps in their tresses, His glory still gleams in their eyes.
These truants from home and from heaven, They have made me more manly and mild:
And I know now how Jesus could liken The Kingdom of God to a child.

Charles Dickens

There are several shows on television which, because of content, are not allowed in our home. However, because of the popularity of one of these particular shows, my son (then about three years old) had seen several of the previews. One day, after one of these previews had aired, he asked me, "Mom, you don't like _____ _____, do you?

I told him no, explaining that I disapproved of the way he treated his parents, family and others, and I disliked the way the characters belittled religious values. (I, too, had seen the commercials.) "No," I said, "I don't like him very much."

Thoughtfully, he looked at me and said, "But, Heavenly Father does! He loves everyone!" And off he went to play. He hadn't wanted to argue, nor to beg for permission to see the show. He had wanted only to set matters straight in his own mind, and had taught his mother a profound lesson. Though God disapproves of the sin, he still loves the sinner. Isaiah taught that in the last days, "*a little child shall lead them.*" (Isaiah 11:6)

During His ministry, Jesus seemed to be drawn to children. "*And they brought unto him also infants, that he would touch them: but when his disciples saw it, they rebuked them. But Jesus called them unto him, and said, Suffer the little children to come unto me, and forbid them not:*" And then Jesus taught a great truth, "*for of such is the kingdom of heaven.*" (Luke 16:15-16) The kingdom of God is made up of souls who have become as little children; pure and innocent before God. In order to make his meaning perfectly clear, the Savior added, "*Verily I say unto you, whosoever shall not receive the kingdom of God as a little child shall in no wise enter therein.*" (vs. 17)

It has been said that we are not mortal beings having a spiritual experience, but we are spiritual beings having a mortal experience. The great movement in recent decades of people trying to "find themselves," actually may have come about because of "homesickness;" a longing for the home we once knew. So much of what we experience here on earth is so foreign to our prior existence, that our souls naturally longs for that higher and holier sphere, which we once knew.

Christ as a God, came to earth and dwelt among mortal men in a wicked and sinful world. The acceptance and love of those trusting children was probably a refreshing change for Him, and perhaps when He was with them He briefly caught a glimmer of Heaven.

When the disciples asked Jesus which of them would be greatest in the Kingdom of Heaven, Jesus called a little child and sat him in the midst of them and said, "*Except ye be converted, and become as little children, ye shall not enter into the kingdom of heaven. Whosoever therefore shall humble himself as this little child, the same is greatest in the kingdom of heaven.*" (Matthew 18:1-4)

When the qualities of children are carefully examined, it is easy to see how the Savior could liken the Kingdom of Heaven to a child.

While studying art in college, I chose ceramics as my dominant field. I seldom had the money to buy the commercial clays, but purchased instead a cheaper recycled clay we called "Studio Mix." This was made from discarded clay which had been sent through a pug mill and repackaged. Often while pulling up the walls of a beautiful piece of pottery, I would run into a pebble or a piece of sponge, which had to be removed. Usually, this "surgery" destroyed the pot and I was forced to begin again. Occasionally, I even discovered pieces of dissecting needles, which we used to trim the pottery, which cut my hands.

It was a rare and wonderful occasion to be able to work on the potter's wheel with one of the commercial clays, which were pure and free from foreign matter.

Such has been my experience with children. During my mission, there was no concept which we taught that was so readily accepted as the fact that children were innocent before God and not in need of baptism. Rarely did anyone believe that children needed to be cleansed. Rather, most admitted that they questioned their church's practice of baptizing infants. The innocence and innate goodness of little children is easily recognized. Because of their purity of heart, children keenly sense when things are not right. I have been impressed by the sensitivity of my son who has often told me, "My heart didn't feel so good." and he had quit whatever activity it was, that he was engaged in.

One day my three year old daughter was watching a video of a famous fairy tale. I noticed that several times she ran and hid behind the couch, listening to, but not watching the parts which frightened her. She had a keen sense of what was right and what was not, and she fled and hid from the things which felt wrong.

Nephi, a man of great faith, prayed for this childlike quality, "*Wilt thou make me that I may shake at the appearance of sin?*" (2 Nephi 4:31)

I recall a disagreement my husband and I had

a few years ago. During the somewhat heated discussion, my young son shouted, "Don't fight!" However, both of us wanted the final word. Seeing that his efforts at peacemaking were going unheeded, he ran to me and clasped his hand over my mouth.

"Don't talk!" he said, "Don't fight!" He was right. We were wrong. Contention, a tool of Satan, had ruined the spirit of our home and our son not only sensed it, but had the wisdom to stop it.

When children have been taught the difference between right and wrong, they have a deep sense of loyalty to God's commandments. Recently this was brought forcefully to my attention, and I learned a great lesson from my child. We had taken our children to an action/adventure movie. As we took our seats, my son said, "I hope there are no bad words in this movie." My husband and I looked at each other and said, "That's doubtful." Then my son asked, "Isn't it kind of going against Heavenly Father when you purposely go where they don't obey the commandments?" After all the "good" rationalizations passed through my mind, I had to admit that he was right.

Children are motivated by a pure unconditional love. Expressions of their love are freely given, without measure nor expectation.

"I have a question," my little daughter tells me constantly.

"What is your question?" I ask.

"I love my mama." she says.

"Oh, what a nice question!" I tell her. That pure love creates in them an ability to quickly forgive error, both in themselves and others, and to quickly seek forgiveness for their own mistakes.

Love seems to inspire in children a gentle, giving nature.My little daughter had carried some treasured pennies into the store with us one day. As we were paying the cashier we noticed that she walked over to the door where another little girl was standing with her parents. Watching her out of the corner of his eye, my husband admonished, "Be careful and don't hurt the little girl."

I noticed that the little girl was smiling and clutching something tightly in her hand. Briefly, she opened her hand, revealing a shiny penny. Their eyes met in a bond of friendship. They smiled at each other and waved goodbye. Not even one word had been spoken audibly, yet they departed friends.

Children are simple. Their hearts have not yet been clouded by materialism and worldly things, making them more able to appreciate the simple joy life offers. Their expressions of gratitude are simple and direct. One evening, I fought back tears as my little three year old daughter prayed to her Father, "Thank thee for Jesus, because I love Him." That was all. Just a simple, heartfelt prayer of thanks. I was touched.

The simple faith of children is inspiring, and something each of us would be wise to learn from. While running errands one afternoon, my purse came up missing. "Where's my purse?" I asked my daughter.

"You leave it in the store," she said.

"No, I couldn't have!" I frantically searched the car and all the packages, but it was not there. I bowed my head and prayed for help. Hearing my plea, my daughter assured me, "Don't worry, Mama. Jesus will help you find it." I hurried back to the last store I had been in, which was a few miles away. I found the shopping cart where I had left it, and my purse still inside." At times when adults are frustrated because they choose to rely on their own wit and effort, faithful children are on their knees seeking help, and trusting that it will be given.

Children have a thirst to learn the truth. Incessantly, they question, "Why?" Peter wrote, "*Wherefore laying aside all malice, and all guile, and hypocrisies, and envies, and all evil speakings, As newborn babies, desire the sincere milk of the word, that ye may grow thereby.*" (1 Peter 2:1-2) The prophet Joseph Smith possessed this childlike attribute and went to his Father in prayer. Because of his questions and thirst for the "sincere milk of the word" the fullness of the gospel was restored to earth.

Once while traveling home with my son, he asked, "Why did Heavenly Father need a helper?" I asked him what he meant. "You know, like Jesus," he said, "Why did Heavenly Father need Jesus to help him?" For a half hour I enjoyed a splendid spiritual experience as I explained to my young son in simple terms, the mediation and the atonement of the Savior, and why it was necessary.

His ability to understand these profound truths was amazing. Deuteronomy 6:6-7 says, "*And these words, which I command thee this day, shall be in thine heart: And thou shalt teach them diligently unto thy children, and shalt talk of them when thou sittest in thine house, and when thou walkest by the way, and when thou liest down, and when thou risest up.*"

Often adults tend to underestimate the ability children have to understand gospel truth. We began sharing scripture stories with our son when he was not yet three years old. We were concerned about how much he would comprehend. The first night, we shared the story of Jesus healing the blind man, from the New Testament Scripture Stories. I carefully chose words he would understand. When I encountered the word "blind", I explained that the man couldn't see because his eyes didn't work. I knew he wouldn't understand the word fountain, so I substituted it with something familiar to him -- "swimming pool." The next night as we prepared to read with him, he insisted on telling us the story. Pointing to each picture, he retold it. "This man can't see. His eyes don't work. So Jesus made mud wiff dirt and put it on his eyes. He said go wash in the swimming pool. The man say, 'Thank you! Thank you, now I can see!" These spirits, so fresh from heaven, are able to grasp gospel concepts with astounding ease.

Children, because of their size, must always look up to those who would guide them. We should learn from the stature of children to humbly look up to Him who would lead us home.

In his stirring discourse to his people, King Benjamin taught, "*For the natural man is an enemy to God, and has been from the fall of Adam, and will be forever and ever, unless he yields to the enticings of the Holy Spirit, and putteth off the natural man and becometh a saint through the atonement of Christ the Lord, and becometh as a child, submissive, meek, humble, patient, full of love. willing to submit to all things which the Lord seeth fit to inflict upon him, even as a child doth submit to his father.*" (Mosiah 3:19)

I overheard my son one day, burst into tears and tell his friends, "Please don't tell. I promise not to do it again! Promise not to tell." I couldn't understand the rest of the conversation, so I questioned him later. He refused to tell me what he had done. I figured that this was a great opportunity to teach him about repentance. "I don't need to repent yet," he informed me, "I'm not eight yet." He knew enough to know that he wasn't yet accountable, but he didn't yet understand the value of this very important gospel principle. I mentally searched for a way to explain repentance to him in a way that he could understand.

I explained that when Adam and Eve had transgressed the laws of God, they had tried to hide it from Him. But Heavenly Father knows everything we have done, and not only is it wrong to try to hide our sins from Him, it is also useless. I could tell that he felt pain for what he had done, and I explained there was only one way to make the hurt go away. Only repentance could make those painful, guilty feelings disappear. He burst into tears and told me what he had done. (After racking my mind to know what great sin he had committed, I must admit that I was rather relieved to know he had climbed the neighbor's tree without permission.) When he submitted, and relieved himself of the burden, the pain went away.

"I feel peace," he told me later. And I could tell that he did.

When just a toddler, one of my son's favorite games was wrapping himself in a blanket. "Here's a present for you, Mama," he would call out. "Come and unwrap it." I would slowly unwrap the package and examine each part carefully; the toes, the legs, the belly, until at last I reached his face. "Oh, it's my boy!" I would shout. He would giggle and then wrap himself up again. "Its a present!" Oh, if he only knew, I thought, what a wonderful gift he really was! But then, maybe he did know.

What a blessing, that in His eternal plan of salvation, God would entrust to us the lives of His precious children; that man might be reminded of heaven through the wisdom of innocents.

TELL IT TO CHILDREN

Would you set a precious truth among the stars?
Then write it large upon the hearts of children.
They will remember.

Have you visions of a finer, happier world?
Tell it to children!
They will build it for you.

Have you a word of hope for poor, blind,
stumbling human kind?
Then give it not to stupid blundering men,
Give it to children.

In their clear, untroubled minds,
it will reflect itself a thousand fold,
Somewhere a Lincoln plays and learns
and watches with bewildered gaze,
This strange procession of mismannered souls.

Have you a ray of light to offer him?
Then give it and some day it will help
To make the torch which he will use
To light the world to freedom and to joy!

Author Unknown

Published in: *I Have a Heavenly Father,* Course 3 Sunday School Manual, 1971, Church of Jesus Christ of Latter-day Saints, page 127

TWO PRAYERS

Last night my little boy confessed to me
Some childish wrong;
And kneeling at my knee,
He prayed with tears--
"Dear God, make me a man
Like Daddy -- wise and strong;
I know you can."

Then while he slept
I knelt beside his bed
Confessed my sins,
And prayed with low-bowed head --
"O God, make me a child
Like my child here--
Pure, guileless,
Trusting Thee with faith sincere."

Andrew Gillies
1870 -1942

Published in *Masterpieces of Religious Verse*, ed. by James Dalton Morrison, copyright by Harper &Row, New York, 1948

ADDITIONAL REFERENCES

Proverbs 21:14	A gift in secret pacifieth anger
Matthew 6:24	Ye cannot serve God and mammon
Matthew 7:16	Ye shall know them by their fruits
Matthew 25:35-40	Serve God by serving one another (See also Mosiah 2:17)
Mark 12:41-44	The widow's mites
Luke 12:33-34	Lay up treasures in heaven (See also Helaman 5:8, 3 Nephi 13:20, D&C 6:27.)
Luke 14:33	He who forsaketh not all cannot be disciple
Luke 22:24-27	Whoever is chief among you is servant (See also D&C 50:26)
Galatians 5:13	By love serve one another
Ephesians 6:6-8	Serve not to please men but as service as to the Lord
James 1:27	Pure religion is serving one another
1 Peter 2:21	Christ suffered, leaving an example
1 John 3:18	Do not love in word only but in deed
Mosiah 4:15	Teach children to serve
Alma 5:41	Those who do good follow the shepherd
Moroni 7:48	Pray for charity to become like Him
D&C 6:13,33	Do good and be saved
D&C 42:29-31	If we love Him we will serve Him
D&C 58:27	Be anxiously engaged
D&C 64:33	Be not weary in well doing
Article of Faith 13	We believe in doing good

Old Testament Stories
- Abraham and the Sacrifice of Isaac
- Jonah

New Testament Stories
- The Rich Young Man
- Paul Learns About Jesus

Book of Mormon Stories
- King Benjamin
- Alma and His People Escape
- Alma's Mission to Ammonihah
- Peace in America

FOR WE HAVE SEEN HIS STAR

The intent of the Wise Men is stated simply, "When they were come into the house, they saw the young child with Mary his mother, and fell down, and worshipped him." (Matthew 2:11) These men were wise enough to understand just how big this little Child was.

Perhaps more than any other story in scripture, the tale of the Wise Men's visit to the Christ child has received more speculation than any. Many suppositions and legends have been accepted as truth. Men have created for them homelands, number and ancestral lineage. Diverse legends have designated race, names and physical descriptions. Even their skulls were allegedly found by Bishop Reinald in the twelfth century, and can be viewed in the cathedral at Cologne, each bedecked with a golden crown of jewels. The fact is, we know very little about these men. Their entire story is related in twelve short verses in the second book of Matthew. Legends about their rank, where they came from, how many there were, when they arrived and what their names were are mere speculation, for the Bible contains no information on these matters.

Who were these men and what do we really know about them? We know that they must have been men of importance, for they were able to obtain an audience with King Herod to make their inquiry, *"Where is he that is born King of the Jews? for we have seen his star in the east and are come to worship him."* (Matthew 2:2) The word "East" might be more accurately rendered as "at its rising", and "king" as "The Messiah" or "The Anointed One." So, their question was more likely, *"Where is the child that is born, the Messiah of the Jews? for we have seen his star at its rising and have come to worship him."* (See The

Life of Christ, Frederic W. Farrar, Salt Lake City: Bookcraft, 1994, p. 48 footnote # 1; See also JST Matthew 2:2)

The Greek translation of Matthew uses the word "Magi" instead of Wise Men. Elder Bruce R. McConkie explained that the term Magi was "applied to a priestly caste or order of ancient Media or Persia...Their religion centered around star gazing and astrology; they worshipped fire, had a religion filled with taboos and spells and were versed in magic. The very word 'magic' is one which was used originally to designate the ritual and learning practiced by Persian Magi." (*Mormon Doctrine*, Bruce R. McConkie, Salt Lake City: Bookcraft, 1966 p. 462) The name Magi was later applied to Oriental soothsayers or astrologers who were known to have frequently visited the Western countries.

Because of the Greek translation, "Magi"and the fact that they had seen a star, many assumed that the Wise Men were Magi from this ancient cult. However, there is no historical basis to support this assumption. It would be more plausible to believe instead, that they were devout and righteous men, who possessed and were familiar with ancient books of scripture, for they were aware of a star which would signal the Messiah's birth. Though the Bible contains no clear prophecy of the sign of a star, Numbers 24:17 makes allusion to it. "*.... there shall come a Star out of Jacob, and a Scepter shall rise out of Israel.*" However, it is not known from which prophecy they obtained their knowledge of the promised star.

Anciently, the Greeks and Romans believed that both the birth and death of great men were accompanied by the appearance and disappearance of heavenly bodies. Because of this belief, many false Christ's were accepted. (See *The Life of Christ,* Frederic W. Farrar, p. 52) Many have supposed that perhaps the Wise Men, too, held this belief. The Book of Mormon, however, clearly states that the appearance of a new star would be a sign in the western hemisphere of Christ's birth. (See Helaman 14:5) From what the Wise Men said to King Herod, it appears that they, also, held the conviction that a star would be the sign of the child's birth for they called it "his star", and it was for this reason they had come seeking Him.

It was common knowledge throughout Palestine that the Messiah would be born in Bethlehem. After hearing the things the Wise Men told him, Herod and all Jerusalem were troubled. Subsequently, he gathered together all of the chief priests and scribes and demanded of them where the Christ should be born. They told him that the prophets had written that the Messiah would be born in Bethlehem of Judea. As stated in Micah 5:2 "*But thou, Bethlehem Ephratah, though thou be little among the thousands of Judah, yet out of thee shall he come forth unto me that is to be ruler in Israel; whose goings forth have been from of old, from everlasting.*" (See also John 7:42, 1 Samuel 16:1)

Many erroneously assume that it was their pagan beliefs combined with ancient prophecy which led the Wise Men to the Christ child. The Latter-Day Saint belief, however, is that the Wise Men were not men from some apostate cult, but were knowledgeable, righteous, and spiritually sensitive men, who had been granted the privilege and divine mission to find the Christ child, offer Him gifts, and bear witness that the Son of God had been born in the flesh. They may have been representatives, or even prophets, from a branch of the Lord's people somewhere east of Palestine. They seem to have been led by the Spirit, and by ancient prophecy to the home of the Child, and then returned to their homeland to bear witness that the Messiah had indeed been born upon the earth. (See *L.D.S. Bible Dictionary*, Magi p. 727-728 and Wise Men from the East p. 789)

That they were righteous men is evidenced by the fact that they watched for a star, and knew of its significance, while others did not. They were sensitive enough to the Spirit to be warned of God in a dream about the evil intentions of the king. Rather than seek a reward their privileged information might command, they were obedient to divine instruction and returned home a different way.

The assumption that these men were kings probably comes from the valuable gifts which they offered along with a scripture from Isaiah 60:3 which says, "*And the Gentiles shall come to thy light, and kings to the brightness of thy rising.*" However, there is no scriptural proof that the Wise men were actually kings.

Where did the Wise Men come from? A prophecy from Psalms 72:10 states: "*The kings of Tarshish and of the isles shall bring presents: the kings of Sheba and Seba shall offer gifts.*" From this scripture, along with the fact that frankincense and myrrh are products of Arabia, many have deduced that the Wise Men were kings from that country. They may have come from Persia, Mesopotamia, Chaldea, Ethiopia, India or one of the many other Eastern countries, and opinions of Bible scholars differ greatly as to their origin.

How many Wise Men were there? Two traditions have existed about their number. Augustine and Chrysostom believed that there were twelve, but the more common belief is that there were three, probably stemming from the three gifts which they brought. Since the original word from which "Wise Men" was translated is plural, it can be assumed that there were at least two. Also, the Lord's law of witnesses would require that there be at least two. "*In the mouth of two or three witnesses shall every word be established.*" (2 Corinthians 13:1, See also Deuteronomy 17:6, 19:15, Matthew 18:15-16, John 8:12-29) However, there may have been a great number of "Wise Men" who traveled to Bethlehem to pay homage to the Infant King.

It was the Venerable Bede, an English Benedictine monk and scholar, (673?-735) who assigned names, ages, and descriptions to the Wise Men, while other traditions and legends provide their genealogies.

Melchior supposedly was an old man with white hair and long beard, and was a descendant of Shem. Caspar, a descendant of Ham, was a ruddy and beardless young man. Balthasar, a dark skinned man in the prime of his life is believed to be a descendant of Japeth. Ham, Japeth and Shem are three of the sons of Noah. Perhaps, to help each person relate more personally to these Wise Men, their representations conveniently depict three periods of life, and three areas of the globe. (See *The Life of Christ*, Frederic W. Farrar p.50)

When did the Wise Men arrive? Traditionally, January sixth, is celebrated as the date of the arrival of the Wise Men. The exact date of their arrival is uncertain, but it is more likely that they arrived several months after the birth of the Savior, which through modern revelation we know was April sixth.

Eight days after His birth, the new parents took Jesus to the temple to be circumcised according to Jewish law. Some time following the forty days required for Mary's purification under the law of Moses, the family traveled to the temple again. Mary went to the temple for two reasons. The law stipulated that every first born male should be called holy to the Lord, and that day, Jesus was presented in the temple to be redeemed. Mary also needed to be purified under the Mosaic law. This required a burnt offering, (as a symbol of devotion) and a sin offering. (for the remission of sin) The sin offering required the sacrifice of either a pair of turtle doves or two young pigeons.

That day, Simeon and Anna, two more witnesses, testified of the divinity of the Holy Child. Simeon had been promised that he would see the Christ before he died. The day of the Baby's presentation, Simeon was directed by the Spirit to go to the temple. Anna, on the other hand, served daily in the temple, heard Simeon's testimony, and gave thanks likewise to the Lord.

Luke makes no mention of the Wise Men's visit but tells us in 2:39, "*And after they had performed all things according to the law of the Lord, they returned into Galilee, to their own city Nazareth.*"

After traveling to Nazareth, the family then returned to Bethlehem, where Jesus was sought by the Wise Men. Why Joseph made the 180 mile trip to Nazareth and back, no one knows. Perhaps he had decided to make Bethlehem his permanent home and had returned to collect his belongings, or take care of unfinished business.

It was following their return from Nazareth to Bethlehem, that the Wise Men finally arrived. J. Reuben Clark in *Our Lord of the Gospels*, places the family's trip to Nazareth and back at two to three months following the Savior's birth. The scriptures tell us that the Wise Men arrived at the house rather than the stable, and that Jesus was a young child, not an infant. (See Matthew 2:11)

The legends, suppositions, and folklore about the Wise Men could undoubtedly fill volumes. Although the answers to where they came from, who they were, when they arrived and how many Wise Men there actually were are unknown; the "why" of their visit is clearly made known. This, after all, is the most important reason for their mention in scripture. First, they brought gifts. "Bring gifts" translated from original Greek means to render tribute.

The intent of the Wise Men is stated simply, "*when they were come into the house, they saw the young child with Mary his mother, and fell down, and worshipped him.*" (Matthew 2:11) Before treasures were opened, before the precious gifts were presented, they had fallen to their knees in humble and reverent worship. This is a most significant and moving fact about these men who had earned the title of "Wise" Men.

"*The offering of gifts to a superior in rank, either as to worldly status, or recognized spiritual endowment, was a custom of early days and still prevails in many Oriental lands. It is worthy of note that we have no record of these men from the east offering gifts to Herod in his palace; they did, however, impart of their treasure to the lowly Infant, in whom they recognized the King they had come to seek.*" (James E. Talmage, *Jesus the Christ*, 33d. ed., Salt Lake City: The Church of Jesus Christ of Latter-day Saints, 1973, p. 108)

Myrrh and frankincense are aromatic resins which come from plants indigenous to those eastern countries. They were used in medicines, perfumes, and incense, and were very costly. These three gifts, were a fitting tribute for a king. Perhaps, the grandeur of these gifts overshadows the more important reasons for the Wise Men's visit to the Christ Child.

Through the Wise Men, God had established yet another witness. Simple shepherds claimed to have seen angels announcing His birth. Two humble people in the temple had seen Him and testified of His divinity. Now, men of a noble class were also witness to His birth. Theirs was an important witness which the aristocracy may have had a harder time dismissing.

These men were wise enough to understand just how big this little Child was. With their eyes steadfastly fixed on a promised star, they had traveled a great distance, leaving homes, families and occupations to seek the Promised Child. Now, with their backs to the star which had guided their journey, they returned home; but not in darkness. Within their hearts, was "*the true Light.*" (John 1:9) "*the Light of the world*". (John 8:12)

Some months ago, I talked to a pair of missionaries from a different religion who had come proselyting at our home. They admonished me to worship God in the way that He desired to be worshipped. That caused me to reflect a great deal about the manner in which I worship. How is it that God wants to be worshipped? What gifts should we offer Him?

When Jesus was asked what the greatest of all the commandments was, he replied, "*Thou shalt love the Lord thy God with all thy heart, and with all thy soul, and with all thy mind. This is the first and great commandment. And the second is like unto it, Thou shalt love thy neighbor as thyself.*" (Matthew 22:37-39)

At the last supper, knowing the events which would soon transpire, Jesus told his disciples, "*A new commandment I give unto you, That ye love one another; as I have loved you.*" (John 13:34) A new commandment? Love was not a new commandment! John said that the message of love had been taught from the beginning. (See 1 John 3:11) The law of Moses commanded its followers to love their neighbor as themselves. (See Leviticus 19:18)

Jesus' mission was to fulfill the law of Moses and add to that a higher law. The law of "*an eye for an eye,*" was replaced with the command to "*love thine enemies.*" (See Matthew 5:38-44) The law of love previously had required that we love others as we love ourselves. Jesus was now giving a higher standard which required men to love one another as *He* has loved us!

President Harold B. Lee wisely said, "*Life is God's gift to man. What we do with our life is our gift to God.*" (*Favorite Quotations from the Collection of Thomas S. Monson,* Salt Lake City: Deseret Book, 1985, p. 250)

The apostle James wrote, "*Pure religion and undefiled is this, To visit the fatherless and widows in their affliction, and to keep himself unspotted from the world.* " (James 1:27) "One who practices pure religion soon discovers it is more rewarding to lift a man up than to hold him down." (Marvin J. Ashton, *Ensign,* November 1982, p. 65)

As we contemplate how we might best worship God and His Son, Jesus Christ, we must remember that the greatest gift anyone can offer to God is a pure life, filled with service and love for others. For, "*when ye are in the service of your fellow beings, ye are only in the service of your God.*" (Mosiah 2:17)

References:

Bruce R. McConkie, *The Mortal Messiah,* Salt Lake City: Deseret Book, 1980

Frederic W. Farrar, *The Life of Christ,* originally published London, England: Cassell & Company, 1874. Reprinted Salt Lake City: Bookcraft, 1994

James E. Talmage, *Jesus The Christ,* Salt Lake City: The Church of Jesus Christ of Latter-day Saints, 1973

Bruce R. McConkie, *Mormon Doctrine,* Salt Lake City: Bookcraft Inc., 1966

Bible Dictionary, Salt Lake City: The Church of Jesus Christ of Latter-day Saints, 1979

WISE MEN

It was wise men who foretold His coming.
'Twas the wise who awaited His birth.
And the wise from afar
Who followed the star,
To the Savior, at last come to earth.

It was wise men who followed His footsteps.
The wise gathered to learn of His will,
'Twas the wise who believed,
While the world was deceived.
It's the Wise Men who follow Him still.

'Twas the wise who declared, "He is risen!"
After suffering death on the hill.
With their lamps burning bright,
Through the darkness of night,
It is wise men who watch for Him still.

It is wise men who know of His glory.
It is Wise Men who praise Him and sing,
"One day each knee will bow,
To confess humbly, Thou,
Art Jesus the Savior and King!"

Sharon Velluto

WHAT SHALL I BRING?

The Wise Men brought three treasured gifts,
Of frankincense, and gold.
A tribute of their finest goods,
A wonder to behold.

Then, reverently, the Wise Men bowed
To reverence the small King.
I muse, were I a Wise Man then
Which gift I'd choose to bring.

But what of now?-- How can I bow
To give my rendering?
What gift befitting, thine to me?
There's no such offering!

Yet, what I have, I offer thee,
My gifts of laud and praise.
My gold, my frankincense and myrrh--
Devotion to thy ways.

Sharon Velluto.

ADDITIONAL REFERENCES

Psalms 82:6 .... We are children of God
Matthew 18:3,10,14 .... Become as children
Matthew 19:14 .... Value of children to God
Mark 9:37 .... By receiving a child we receive Christ
Luke 17:12-19 .... Jesus cleanses ten lepers, one returns
Romans 5:15-18, 6:23 .... Gift of the atonement
Romans 8:16-17 .... We are the children of God
1 Corinthians 7:7 .... Everyone has his gift of God
2 Corinthians 9:15 .... Thanks be to God for His gift
Philippians 4:6 .... With thanksgiving let requests be known
1 Timothy 4:14 .... Gifts of Spirit (See also 2 Timothy 1:6)
James 1:17 .... Every good gift is from above (See also Moroni 7:12-13, Psalms 85:12)
Alma 34:38 .... Live in thanksgiving daily
Alma 37:37 .... Always render thanks to God
Moroni 10:30 .... Lay hold upon every good gift
D&C 46, Moroni 10 .... Gifts of the Spirit
Article of Faith 7 .... List of spiritual gifts

Old Testament Stories
Jesus Makes The Earth
The Ten Commandments

New Testament Stories
Jesus is Resurrected
Simon and the Priesthood

Book of Mormon Stories
Jesus Christ Blesses the Children

Doctrine and Covenants Stories
Joseph and Oliver are Given the Priesthood

A REASON FOR REJOICING

"Be ready always to give an answer to every man that asketh you a reason of the hope that is in you..." (1 Peter 3:15)

Before leaving on my mission, a dear friend gave me some wise counsel. He told me that as I taught people the principles of the gospel, I should also teach how that principle could enrich and bless their lives. His simple suggestion has made a great impact on my life and has caused me to approach the gospel in a different way than I might have otherwise. It has made me reflect a great deal on the blessings which have come to me as a member of The Church of Jesus Christ of Latter-day Saints, and has helped me to appreciate more fully those blessings. Too often, many of us take our membership in the Church for granted, never fully realizing what a treasure we have within our grasp. Society desperately searches for answers which have been taught within the Church for many years. Millions of God's children are longing for direction the and answers which we already have; answers which exist in their purity within the gospel of Jesus Christ.

The Apostle Peter counseled, *"Be ready always to give an answer to every man that asketh you a reason of the hope that is in you..."* (1 Peter 3:15)

What are the blessings which have come to me as a member of Christ's Church? How have I grown? What have I learned? How has my life been made better because of my membership in the Church? What is the reason for my rejoicing? To answer these questions I need only to ponder what my life might have been without the gospel.

There are so many spiritual and eternal blessings which come from living the gospel that it is impossible to enumerate all of them. Most people recognize and are aware of the eternal blessings which are given to the obedient, yet, in the pursuit of eternal blessings, we often fail to recognize the immediate and practical blessings which come to us daily. These are the blessings which I would like to emphasize-- the more temporal blessings which have played such an important part of my life —blessings which have helped me to avoid many of the pitfalls and problems of the world, and have brought me peace.

"But learn that he who doeth the works of righteousness shall receive his reward, even peace in this world, and eternal life in the world to come." (D&C 59:23)

First: My life has been richly blessed by good friends who shared my same ideals, my same principles, my same values. These are friends who have supported me, lifted me, encouraged me and given me wise counsel throughout my life. As a youth, there were so many activities such as dances, plays, sports, parties and camps, within the Church, that I didn't feel I needed to search for fulfillment in other places. This helped me to avoid many of the problems which I might have encountered otherwise. It gives me some measure of comfort, now that I have children of my own, to know that they too can avoid much of the wickedness in the world around them through wholesome activities provided within the Church, and the support of good friends.

Second: The Church has given me many opportunities for growth and development. I had a missionary companion who told me that this was one of the things which had attracted her most about to the Church. In the church she belonged to, she felt that she was no longer progressing. She felt dissatisfied and had decided to study to become a nun. She felt this might provide her the opportunities for growth and service which she yearned for. When she learned that in the Church of Jesus Christ of Latter-Day Saints she would be given a chance to serve and grow, she was overjoyed and decided to join the Church. Often we take callings and opportunities to serve for granted.

This is a church of participation and because of this there are many possibilities for growth. When I think for even a moment of the things I have learned through Relief Society, the Young Women's program, the camp program, and various callings I have held within the Church, I am overwhelmed. There is great growth which comes through work, service and accepting responsibility.

As a young girl, I was extremely timid. The Church afforded me many opportunities to develop my talents and leadership abilities. Through callings in the Church I have developed faith in myself, as well as the ability to communicate with others.

Jesus commanded that we love and serve our fellow man. He said, *"For I have given you an example, that ye should do as I have done to you."* (John 13:15) His gospel requires that we feed the hungry, clothe the naked, and visit the sick. For some of us, developing altruism and compassion can be difficult. When so many people desperately need help, it is hard to decide which causes to support and how we can best serve others. A wise and loving Father provided for this in His gospel plan. Through the payment of fast offerings, serving in the welfare program, home and visiting teaching etc., we learn to reach out and help others.

Third: Because of the great importance the Church places on family, we receive much counsel on how to become better parents, spouses and neighbors. We are taught how to create a loving atmosphere in our homes, and unity within our families. The Church considers the family an eternal unit which continues to exist long after death. The bonds of eternal marriage inspire us to resolve problems within our marriage and family. Our families are one of life's most exquisite treasures and one of mortality's most important duties. The help and counsel we receive through lessons and from our Church leaders is invaluable.

Fourth: The Church is like a large family. When we encounter problems and difficulties we can find help and comfort from people who care about us. We can also turn to inspired leaders for help and inspiration.

Fifth: By following the counsel given in the Word of Wisdom, we receive many blessings of health as well as many spiritual blessings. With all the counsel and innovations about diet and nutrition available in the world today, I find it very comforting to have a plan given by One who knows our bodies better than anyone, for He was the creator of them.

Sixth: When we are obedient to the law of tithing the Lord gives us many financial blessings. The Lord has invited us to put Him to the test. *"Bring ye all the tithes into the storehouse, that there may be meat in mine house, and prove me now herewith, saith the Lord of hosts, if I will not open you the windows of heaven and pour you out a blessing, that there shall not be room enough to receive it. And I will rebuke the devourer for your sakes, and he shall not destroy the fruits of your ground; neither shall your vine cast her fruit before the time in the field, saith the Lord of hosts."* (Malachi 3:10)

The brother of Jared was blessed to see the finger of the Lord after he had exercised great faith. I know of no other commandment our Father has given where we may more clearly witness His hand, than through the payment of tithing. There have been numerous occasions that the Lord has stretched forth His hand to bless and protect our family, and I believe these were direct blessings which came to us as a result of paying tithing.

Seventh: The law of chastity provides us with a moral compass. Obedience to this law not only protects us from many of the diseases rampant in the world today, but it develops trust and happiness within the marriage relationship, while its counterpart, immorality, breeds distrust, and unhappiness. It is a great blessing to associate with people who hold these same convictions, and who share the same standards of morality.

Eighth: In the Church, if we are worthy, we can receive a special blessing, called a Patriarchal Blessing. Often, these blessings give personal advice, warn of things which should be avoided and give admonition of endeavors which should be pursued. These blessings give words of comfort and strength during times of trouble or trial. For me, this blessing has been of profound help, guidance, direction and comfort. A Patriarchal Blessing is one of the most generous and special of all the blessings which have been bestowed upon us by a kind and loving Heavenly Father who knows us intimately and loves us deeply.

Ninth: One of the greatest blessings which God has given to His children is that of the priesthood. Though the priesthood is a great spiritual blessing, it also blesses our lives temporally. Many times our family has felt the need to call upon our Father for His blessings through this wonderful gift of priesthood power. Our prayers were heard, and our lives were blessed.

Tenth: The blessing of scripture. At times, I think we tend to forget what a practical blessing the scriptures can be. It is comforting to know that while the theories in the schools of psychology and sociology may change quite drastically over a period of 15 to 20 years, the word of the Lord remains constant and unchangeable. The counsel and inspired writings within the pages of the holy scriptures can give us practical guidance for our daily lives, challenges and problems.

Elder Neal A Maxwell said, "*Many reject the scriptures, the moral memory of mankind, and then declare absolutely the absence of absolutes. Others reject the light of the gospel and then grump over the growling darkness. Still others cut themselves off from God and lament the loneliness of the universe.*" (*Ensign*, May 1983, p. 10) The word of God is a light in the darkness, a comfort during struggle, peace during the storm.

I have a great love for the Bible --- the stories, the doctrine, the counsel. But in this marvelous book, there are many passages which are difficult to understand. We have been blessed with a divine key for opening those passages up to our understanding. The revelation and knowledge given to us in the Book of Mormon, Doctrine and Covenants and The Pearl of Great Price can help us to understand many of these things which remain a mystery to others. Truly, as prophesied, these books go hand in hand not only to testify of truth, but to help us live happier and more fulfilling lives. (See Ezekiel 37:16-20)

Eleventh: The gospel has given direction to my life -- a path to follow. It has given me the answers to important questions. The gospel has taught me who I am. It has taught me my purpose for being here, and has given me the hope of what will follow this life. But, even more important to me is the fact that the gospel offers me the hope of whom I may become.

There are many people who desperately search for the answers to these questions; answers which can give strength, security and direction in this troubled world.

When we die, I imagine that we will not be concerned by how much money we earned, what type of clothes we wore or the number of commodities we possessed. We will not even be concerned about how happy or sad we were, but we will wonder what truly worthwhile things we have accomplished. The gospel gives us each the opportunity to accomplish many truly worthwhile and noble things.

Twelfth: The gift of the Holy Ghost. I don't think any of us fully realize how important the gift of the Holy Ghost is to our daily lives. The Spirit warns us of danger, prompts and directs us to make correct choices, teaches us the truth, and guides us to know what to say or do to help family members, neighbors and others. The Holy Ghost can bring us peace. For me, this is one of the most wonderful blessings which Heavenly Father has given me. In this world of turmoil, the blessing of peace, and guidance from on high are of infinite worth. "*But the Comforter, which is the Holy Ghost, whom the Father will send you in my name, he shall teach you all things, and bring all things to your remembrance, whatsoever I have said unto you. Peace I leave with you, my peace I give unto you; not as the world giveth, give I unto you. Let not your heart be troubled, neither let it be afraid.*" (John 14:27) This gift of peace doesn't mean that we will have a life free from trials. It does mean that regardless of the problems we may face, the assurance is given that we can find peace.

Thirteenth: The gift of commandments. Often, we tend to think of commandments as a burden instead of a blessing. I believe that Heavenly Father is watching and waiting for every opportunity available to bless His children. Every commandment which God has given to us was for the purpose of blessing and enriching our lives both temporally and eternally. Through obedience to His commandments, we learn the truth of His doctrine and it makes us free. (See John 3:21, 8:32)

Fourteenth: A prophet of God. It is a great blessing to be led by a living prophet. He knows our day and the troubles we face. Through inspiration, he and other inspired Church leaders can warn us of approaching danger and teach us how to live richer and more abundant lives.

Fifteenth: The cleansing power of the sacrament and the gift of repentance. It is a wonderful gift of God to be given the means whereby we can cleanse ourselves, have the burden of sin lifted, find peace of mind and feel whole once again. Forgiveness truly is a divine miracle.

Sixteenth: The gift of testimony. Though this is a personal and deeply spiritual gift, it is also a practical one. To live life with the assurance that your path is right, that God lives and answers prayer, that Jesus was His Son, that "*death is a comma, not an exclamation point*" gives security and peace of mind. (See Neal A Maxwell, *Ensign*, May 1983, p.10)

This is but a brief list of some of the more practical blessings we receive when we live in obedience to gospel principles. The list of blessings is endless. This is the reason for the hope which is in me, the reason for my rejoicing. The gospel is wonderful, it is practical, it is spiritual, it is true.

CONVERSATION WITH A THREE YEAR OLD

...little children do have words given unto them many times, which confound the wise and learned. (Alma 32:23)

"Who maked your body?" my little three year old daughter asked me.

"Heavenly Father did," I told her, giving her another spoonful of cereal.

She chewed for a minute and then asked, "What you sayed when He gived you your body."

"I said, 'Thank you, but couldn't you have made a thinner, more streamlined model?'" I joked. (Of course, I knew He had nothing to do with that!) I gave her another spoonful of cereal.

"Who maked your head?" she asked next.

"Heavenly Father did," I told her.

"What you sayed to Him when He gived you your head?" she asked.

"I said, 'Thank you, but couldn't you have given me one that remembered things a little better?'" She missed the second joke, as well as the first, and went on with her questioning.

"Who maked your feet?" she asked.

Another spoonful of cereal, "Heavenly Father did," I said, trying to think up some other sarcastic remark, when it occurred to me that I wasn't showing much gratitude for what I had.

"Who maked your eyes?" she asked.

"Heavenly Father did," I said.

"What you sayed to Him when He gived you your eyes?" she asked me.

"I said, 'Thank you for all the wonderful things I can see!'" I told her.

"Like what? " she asked, her mouth full of cereal.

"Like you!" I told her and she laughed.

"Who maked your ears?"

"Heavenly Father did," I told her.

"What you tell Him?"

"I said, 'Thank you for all the wonderful things I can hear!'" I told her.

"Like panos?" she asked.

"Yes," I said. "Like pianos and my little girl's questions!"

She laughed again. "Who maked your mouth?" she continued.

"Heavenly Father," I told her. "What can we do with our mouth?" I asked her giving her another spoonful of cereal.

"I can say,'I love you!'" she replied. "Who gived you your hands?"

"Heavenly Father did. What good things can we do with our hands?" I asked.

"I can color," she offered.

"What you sayed when Heavenly Father maked my legs?" she asked.

I told her, "I said, 'Thank you, for making my little girl's legs so she can dance and run..'"

"I have two legs!" she informed me.

"Yes, aren't you glad? It would be hard to dance with just one!"

"What did you tell Heavenly Father when He maked my body."

I instantly remembered how I felt when that tiny little bundle was first placed in my arms, the tears of gratitude which overflowed. I was silent a minute and swallowed back the lump in my throat. I told her simply, "I said, 'Thank you, Heavenly Father.'"

She asked, "What you say when He make my brudder's body?"

"I told Him,'Thank You.'" I told her again.

"What you say when He maked your arms?" she questioned.

"I said, 'Thank you, but I wish I had four arms."

She gave me a funny look and shook her head, "No!" she said.

"What Heavenly Father say when He make my fingers?" she asked.

I told her,"He said, 'Here are ten fingers. Do good things with them!"

"Like what?" she wanted to know.

"What can you do with your fingers?" I asked.

" I can say I Love you!" she told me.

"How can you do that?" I laughed, a little puzzled by her reasoning.

Then, pretending to sign with her hands, she placed both hands upon her chest and then pointed to me. "I Love You." she said matter-of -factly.

"And I love you!" I told her giving her a big hug. "I'm sure glad Heavenly Father gave me my arms so I could hug you!" She squeezed me even tighter. "Last bite." I said.

She chewed and swallowed it and ran off to play, and I was made a little better that day because of the conversation I had with a three year old.

HANDS

Loaded with bundles I open the door.
Only two hands! I wish I had four
Two hands to carry things,
One for the door.
And one for my toddler...
I'd then wish for four.
I'd want them to double.
I sure could use eight,
For cleaning, and cooking,
And laundry, but wait...
Rather than wishing
For what I have not...
I just should give thanks
For the two that I've got.

Sharon Velluto

HEAVEN'S GIFT

One of Heaven's greatest gifts
To man, is a small child;
A whisper from God's presence
An angel — undefiled.

Sent to bless and teach us
Of God's eternal plan,
To help us to more clearly see
The measure of a man.

With wide-eyed morning wonder
Rich lessons they impart.
The hug and kiss of innocence
Soon melts an icy heart

Reflecting things we tell them,
And miming things we do,
Teaching us about ourselves,
And bits of heaven too.

They teach us of forgiveness,
Of love, humility.
The Master used a little child
To show what we should be.

Eternal realms are mirrored
In these meek ones, without guile
Yes, One of Heaven's greatest gifts
To man, is a small child.

Sharon Velluto

ALL THAT I HAVE

Of all the treasures life holds in her hands,
There isn't one which I can call my own.
While heaven graciously bequeaths the grant,
I stand indebted to the Heavenly Throne.

Though works of art or writ may bear my name,
Though worldly wealth or fame lies in my hand,
Eternity reminds me that these things
Are temporary as the shifting sand.

All things I now possess are but a loan —
My breath my inspiration and my song.
Contrite, I feel compelled to humbly bow
And render thanks to Whom they all belong.

To think of family, teachers, leaders, friends
Who have labored, led and loved me on my way,
Impels me to give thanks for those whose lives
Inspire and lift and guide my life today.

To Him who gave me hands for work and toil,
Who blessed me with both heart and eyes to see,
I owe all that I have, all that I am.
And everything I ever hope to be.

Sharon Velluto

PERSPECTIVE

Do not bemoan the furnace;
the hot refiners fire;
Be grateful for the tempering
that helps you to aspire

Do not complain life's journey
is steep and all uphill
Appreciate the very fact
you can climb higher still

Do not praise just the sunshine,
but also blackest night;
For sometimes it's the darkest hour
which sheds the greatest light.

All metal must be heated
and tempered to be bent.
The rugged, upward climb builds strength
far more than the descent.

And there, atop the mountain
are vistas rich and new.
One sees more from God's vantage point.
Be grateful for the view!

So, thank God for the furnace
and for the upward climb.
Be glad God cares enough for you
to temper, and refine.

Sharon Velluto

GRATITUDE

More than simple courtesy,
It is a command
To cultivate a grateful heart,
Acknowledging God's hand.

More than for His glory,
Commandments given men
Are meant to lift and bless their lives
And draw them close to Him.

A thankful heart remembers
God's goodness and His grace.
And though they try, they realize
Their debt can't be repaid.

A grateful man is happy
For all that he's been given;
Enumerating all God's gifts
His soul approaches heaven.

A grateful man is faithful
Through Heaven's smile or rod
He finds serenity and peace.
He knows and trusts His God.

Gratitude reminds us
Of our place within His plan.
This great command was given
For the benefit of man.

Sharon Velluto

ADDITIONAL REFERENCES

Genesis 2:18, 24.......................... It is not good for man to be alone,
(See also Moses 3:18,24; Abraham 5:14-16, 18)
Malachi 4:6................................ Elijah will come to turn hearts of children to fathers
Mark 10:2-12............................ Jesus explains the law of marriage
1 Corinthians 11:11-12.............. Neither is man without woman, or woman without man
1 Corinthians 13:4..................... Charity suffereth long and is kind
Ephesians 3:14-19...................... We all belong to the family of God
1 Thessalonians 3:12.................. Abound in love one toward another
1 John 4:16-21........................... He who loveth God loveth his brother
Moroni 7:42-47.......................... Faith, hope, charity
Moroni 8:17............................... Charity is everlasting love
D&C 131:2................................. Everlasting covenant of marriage

Old Testament Stories
Before the Old Testament

New Testament Stories
Before the New Testament

Book of Mormon Stories
Lehi's Dream
Alma Counsels His Sons
King Benjamin

Doctrine and Covenants Stories
Before the Doctrine and Covenants

CHRISTMAS EVE

God has given us no greater blessing than that of belonging to a loving and loyal family-- and it will always be so, always and forever. Richard L. Evans

Oh sure, we knew the rules alright, my four sisters, three brothers and I. We even respected those rules. The rules of Christmas Eve!

1. We knew that no matter how badly we wanted to see what was under that Christmas tree on Christmas morning, we couldn't wake anyone up until 6:00 A.M.

2. We knew that we had to let the baby sleep so everyone's day would be happier.

3. We knew that there would never be a better time because we knew we always had each other.

You see, for as long as I can remember, all of us brothers and sisters slept in the same room on Christmas Eve. Well, okay, so we didn't sleep, but we sure had fun! We would tell stories, sing Christmas songs and keep each other alert to any and all noises that might possibly be Santa.

We took turns making trips to the bathroom, (all legitimate of course) and returned with tales of the shapes and shadows we saw in the dark under the tree as we passed. We huddled together weaving our imaginations into beautiful patterns of anticipation and excitement.

There was even one year we turned all the clocks in the house forward one hour trying to shorten the suspense. If Mom and Dad's clock had been synchronized with the rest of the clocks in the house, our plan may have worked!

Oh, what magic filled those nights! I can still see the sparkle in the eyes of my brothers and sisters, and that memory floods my heart with warmth.

We live in separate houses now, with families of our own. We see the same sparkle in the eyes of our loved ones. We have passed on our beloved traditions to a new generation.

Now, they know, along with us, that no matter how badly you want to see under the Christmas tree on Christmas morning, you can't wake anyone up until 6:00 A.M. They know you may have to let the baby sleep so everyone's day can be happier.

And they know that there will never be a better time because they know we will always have each other.

THE FIGHT FOR FREEDOM AND FAMILY

"The time will come when only those who believe deeply and actively in the family will be able to preserve their families in the midst of the gathering evil around us. (*Ensign*, November 1980, pp. 4-5)

In the Book of Mormon, we read about a Captain Moroni, one of the most brilliant military leaders of all time. He is described as a "*strong and a mighty man... of perfect understanding;" a man "firm in the faith of Christ.*" Mormon writes, "*Yea verily, verily I say unto you, if all men had been, and were, and ever would be like unto Moroni, behold the very powers of hell would have been shaken forever; yea the devil would never have power over the hearts of the children of men.*" (Alma 48:11-13, 17)

On the other hand, Amalickiah, the leader of the enemy forces, is described as a "*man of cunning device and a man of many flattering words, that he led away the hearts of many people to do wickedly*" (Alma 46:10) Amalickiah used treachery, deceit and murder to obtain position and power. It seemed there was nothing he would not do in order to get what he wanted.

Even though the Lamanite army greatly outnumbered them, Moroni's military genius led the Nephites to victory. He rent his coat and wrote upon it, "*In memory of our God, our religion, and freedom, and our peace, our wives, and our children.*" (Alma 46:12) He called it "The Title of Liberty," and inspired his people to enter into a covenant to protect their land and freedom. He hoisted the banner upon every tower as a reminder of the covenant they had made.

Captain Moroni instructed his people to fortify each city by erecting large walls, and forts for places of resort. He built up the land of Jershon, one of the central and most important cities, and took up his main defensive position there. He then sent messengers to the prophet Alma to inform him of their plans and to ask for his counsel. When Moroni's men returned they told him Alma had revealed that the Lamanites were not going to attack the stronghold of Jershon, but instead, planned to attack the smaller and weaker city of Manti on the outskirts of the Nephite lands. Immediately Moroni sent reinforcements to protect the city of Manti.

Moroni made improvements in the Nephite armor making them more than a match, man for man over their enemy. Moroni also sent men to watch the enemy, and inform him of any Lamanite movement.

Long before we came to this earth, there was another war in which all of us fought. There was a great leader who was a "*man of cunning device and a man of many flattering words,*" who tried to lead many of God's children to do wickedly. He sought to destroy the plan of God, and the liberty and agency which God had granted unto them.

President Ezra Taft Benson declared, "*The one great revolution in the world is the revolution for human liberty. This was the paramount issue in the great council in heaven before this earth life. It has been the issue throughout the ages. It is the issue today.*" (*Conference Report*, October 1962, pp. 14-15) Without liberty all progression, human and spiritual, stops.

Often because of the subtleness of the war, we fail to see that the tactics, and motivations are the same; one side desires to bring souls into the bondage of sin, while the other fights to defend and protect their families, their liberty, and their rights of worship. That war over the souls of men continues today.

Satan, by fraud, treachery and deceit has obtained power over many of the souls of men. "*There is no crime he would not commit, no debauchery he would not set up, no plague he would not send, no heart he would not break, no life he would not take, no soul he would not destroy.*" (J. Reuben Clark, Jr., *Conference Report*, October 1942)

In this battle, the enemy outnumbers us, and knows our strongholds and our weaknesses. But we have a great Captain at our head; one who is "*strong and mighty and of perfect understanding.*" President Joseph F. Smith wrote, "*God is the greatest man of war of all, and his Son is next unto him, and their warfare is for the salvation of the souls of men.*" (*Conference Report.* Oct. 1914, page 129. See also *Gospel Doctrine*, Salt Lake City: Deseret Book, page 57)

Moroni was inspired by this great Captain of war, and employed the same strategies to protect and save his people as does our Father in Heaven.

Knowing that men are strengthened by making and keeping covenants, Heavenly Father has asked all who are willing to follow His "standard" to make and keep sacred promises, and has planted a "title" as a reminder of the promises we have made. Temples and the sacrament are both visual reminders of these covenants.

He has called inspired leaders; fathers, bishops, stake presidents, apostles and prophets, to help us identify the enemy's plan of attack, and teach us how resist his cunning temptations.

He has built up forts, as a resort for safety. We have been counseled to "Stand in holy places!" (See D&C 87:8, 2 Chronicles 35:5) Here in these fortresses we are not only given refuge and protection, but are armed with strategies, knowledge, strength and motivation to combat the enemy forces.

Heavenly Father knows of the enemy's plans

and has repeatedly cautioned us, through our great leaders, to build up, and fortify our families. Back in 1915, the Lord's prophets began telling us to fortify our families by holding regular Family Home Evenings, but the counsel to fortify and teach our families the laws of God dates back to Adam. (See Moses 6:57-58) We cannot be complacent and leave the efforts of fortification to chance hoping someone else will do it for us. If not fortified, Satan will attack, and he will conquer Manti.

President Marion G. Romney cautioned, "*As we bear this great responsibility, we must not be so busy with feeding, clothing, housing and otherwise looking after the temporal needs of our children that we neglect the important things, the things calculated to fortify them against the evils of the world and prepare them for eternal life.*" (*Ensign*, January 1985, page 4)

We have been offered a mighty suit of armor, designed to fit over and protect the vital parts of our body. However, it is up to us to put it on and to fit it carefully to our children. "*Put on the whole armour of God, that ye may be able to stand against the wiles of the devil. For we wrestle not against flesh and blood, but against powers, against the rulers of the darkness of this world, against spiritual wickedness...Wherefore take unto you the whole armour of God, that ye may be able to withstand in the evil day, and having done all, to stand. Stand therefore, having your loins girt about with truth, and having on the breastplate of righteousness; And your feet shod with the preparation of the gospel of peace; Above all, taking the shield of faith, wherewith ye shall be able to quench all the fiery darts of the wicked. And take the helmet of salvation..*" (Ephesians 6:11-17)

The design for each piece of armor was not accidental. It was carefully considered. Identical pieces of armor are listed in nearly every book of scripture. (See Isaiah 59:17, Isaiah 61:10, 2 Nephi 1:23, D&C 27:15-18) Wearing the breastplate of righteousness over the heart can dramatically effect our decision to follow the Lord. Having our loins girt about with truth will protect us from immorality. Protecting our eyes, ears and mind with the helmet of salvation will help us have clearer perspective and focus on the kingdom of God. Having our feet shod with the preparation of the gospel of peace can move us to positive action. The movable shield of faith protects each vital spiritual organ from the fiery darts of the adversary.

This is not all. Heavenly Father has not left us defenseless, but has given us a very powerful weapon to fight the enemy — the sword of the Spirit. (See Ephesians 6:17) There exists no more powerful weapon with which we can fight the forces of evil than the witness of the Holy Ghost and the power of pure testimony. "*For the word of God is quick and powerful, and sharper than any two edged sword piercing even to the dividing asunder of soul and spirit, and of the joints and marrow, and is a discerner of the thoughts and intents of the heart... For by fire and by the sword will the Lord plead with all flesh; and the slain of the Lord shall be many.*" (Hebrews 4:12, Isaiah 66:16)

We, like Captain Moroni are fighting: "*In memory of our God, our religion, and freedom, and our peace, our wives,* (and husbands) *and our children.*" (Alma 46:12 Parentheses added) Our battle against the evil forces attacking our families and threatening our spiritual freedom today is no less real than was Moroni's battle. Never before has the devil been so well organized. Never before has he had access to such powerful munitions. God's commandments are being attacked on every front as the devil tries to break down the very moral standards which give us strength. Carefully and cunningly he "lulls" us into thinking evil is acceptable. The battle for the preservation of the family, must be fought with the highest spiritually technological weapons and protective armaments available. We must use the armor the Lord has provided and trust in the great spiritual weapons he has provided. Families must be fortified and resist the movement to down play the significance of family. The battle for the preservation of the family must be fought with all the energy of soul. An apathetic show of resistance will offer little more protection than a firecracker in a nuclear war.

We will not retreat though our numbers may be few
When compared with the opposite host in view;
But an unseen power will aid me and you
In the glorious cause of truth.

Fear not though the enemy deride;
Courage, for the Lord is on our side.
We will heed not what the wicked may say,
But the Lord alone we will obey.

Evan Stephens 1854-1930 Hymns # 243, verse 2

"*Yea verily, verily I say unto you, if all men had been and were, and ever would be like unto Moroni, behold, the very powers of hell would have been shaken forever; yea the devil would never have power over the hearts of the children of men.*" (Alma 48:17)

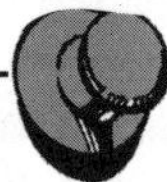

Sickness of Spirit in a family is carried to the office or classroom just as surely as the flu.

Neal A Maxwell

Deposition of a Disciple
Salt Lake City; Deseret Book, 1976 page 20

MARRIAGE, HOME AND FAMILY

God consecrated families
as part of His great plan.
Created to ennoble and
exalt the soul of man.

The God of Heav'n himself decreed:
"Man should not be alone."
A helpmeet given with the command
they twain should be as one.

The foundation of a family
surpasses all of time;
More ancient that the world itself.
Its mission is divine.

Our Heavenly Father smiles upon
the home where love prevails;
A place where heav'n and earth can meet —
where peace and virtue dwell.

Marriage, home and family
are God's appointed plan
To bless and teach His children
to be ever more like Him.

Eternal worlds hang balanced —
all society depends
On how His children understand
and follow His great plan.

Sharon Velluto

TALLY SHEET

When all the tally sheets are made
from since the world began,
What would you guess to have
The greatest influence on man?

A congress or a kitchen?
A law or lullaby?
Great threats and pow'rful treaties?
A mother's wise reply?

In truth there is no law on earth
no jail, no chastening rod,
Can ever equal in its pow'r
a child taught to love God.

When in the end the family
endures the spoils of earth,
No tally sheet can calculate
Just what a good home's worth!

Sharon Velluto

Inspired by the writings of Neal A. Maxwell
Ensign, May 1978, pp. 10-11

TWO AND A HALF

Hold him a little longer,
Rock him a little more,
Tell him another story
(You've only told him four).
Let him sleep on your shoulder,
Rejoice in his happy smile,
He is only two and a half
For such a little while!

Author Unknown

Cleaning and scrubbing can wait till tomorrow
For children grow up, we've learned to our sorrow
So cobwebs be quiet,
Dust go to sleep,
I'm rocking my baby, and babies don't keep.

Author Unknown

CIRCLES

A young mother and a new father,
Admiring their fine newborn son;
Whose cheeks bear the kisses of Heaven,
A circle anew has begun.

Embraced within circles of caring,
The warmth of a father's embrace,
A comforting hug from a mother
Who washes a sad, tear-stained face,

Circles of Ring-Around-Rosies
Joining with children in play,
Circles around dinner tables
Discussing events of the day,

Circles to learn of God's teachings,
Circles which train and prepare,
Circles of God's holy priesthood,
Circles of families in prayer,

Circles which lift and encourage,
Circles which strengthen and cheer,
Certainly circles in heaven,
Begin with the circles formed here.

Sharon Velluto

Wreath Cookies

Cream: 1/2 Cup butter or margarine and 1/2 Cup sugar
Mix In: 1/2 Cup shortening and 1 egg
Add: 3 Cups flour
1 tsp. vanilla
1& 1/2 tsp. almond extract (optional)
1 tsp salt

Divide the dough in half. Add a few drops of green food coloring to one half of the dough and work it in. Take a small ball of dough from each half of the dough and roll it into ropes. Twist the two colored ropes together and form them into a circle making a wreath. Bake at 375 degrees for 10 minutes..

These recipes go with Activity # 3 , page 31 .

Cookie Play dough

Cream: 1 Cup margarine and 1& 1/4 Cups sugar
Add: 4 1/4 Cups flour
1 tsp. baking soda
Mix In: 3 eggs
2 tsp. cream of tartar
2 tsp. vanilla extract

Use the same instructions as above, or color the whole batch of dough green and let the children "get creative." This is a stiff dough and even works when the "cookie sculptures" are rather thick. Bake at 375 degrees for 10 minutes.

Signora Albano's Cookies

Cream: 2 & 1/2 Cups sugar and 1& 1/4 Cup margarine
Add: 7 Cups flour
2 Tablespoons baking powder
Mix in: 5 eggs
2 Tablespoons vanilla
1/4 Cup orange juice (fresh squeezed)*
Orange peel

* Lemon juice or almond extract is also good.
These cookies can also be molded and shaped as desired.
Bake 375 degrees for 10 minutes.

ADDITIONAL REFERENCES

Psalms 27:1	The Lord is my light and salvation
Psalms 112:4	To the upright, there ariseth light
Isaiah 9:2	The people who walked in darkness have seen a great light
Isaiah 60:19	The Lord shall be an everlasting light
Matthew 25	Parable of the 10 virgins
John 1:4,5,9	Jesus is the light which lighteth every man
John 3:19-21	Men loved darkness more than light
John 11:9-10;12:46	Jesus is the light of the world
1 Corinthians 13:12	Now we see through a glass darkly
James 1:17	All good gifts come from the Father of lights
1 Peter 2:9	God hath called his people out of darkness
1 John 1:5	God is light, in him is no darkness at all
1 Nephi 17:13	Christ will be a light in the wilderness
3 Nephi 8-11	Nephites spend three days in total darkness
Ether 3	The brother of Jared needs light for their ships
Moroni 7:12-19	A guide for discerning between good and evil
D&C 6:21	The light shineth in darkness
D&C 84:44-46	The spirit giveth light to every man
D&C 88:48-50	Christ is the true light
D&C 88:67	If your eye be single, your body shall be filled with light
D&C 93:2,9,37	Light and truth forsake the evil one
See Mormon Doctrine	Light, Light of Christ, Light of the World.
See Bible Dictionary	Light of Christ p. 725

Ensign
May 1978, pp. 14-16, *Ye Shall Know the Truth*, Tanner
May 1981, pp. 28-30, *Light and Truth*, Burton
May 1977, pp. 43-45, *The Light of Christ*, Romney

New Testament Stories
The Ten Young Women

Book of Mormon Stories
Lehi's Dream
The Signs of Christ's Birth
The Signs of Christ's Crucifixion
Jesus Christ Appears to the Nephites
Jesus Christ Blesses the children
The Jaredites Travel To The Promised Land

Doctrine and Covenants Stories
Joseph Smith's First Vision

MY LITTLE LIGHT

I have a little light
which shines inside of me.
And though I feel it there,
it's something I can't see.

It shines when I am good,
and when I choose the right.
It feels secure and warm.
I love my little light.

But when my choice is wrong,
this little light grows dim.
I feel so dark inside.
My light can't shine within.

I want my light to shine.
And I know just the way.
Repent of what I've done
and choose a better way!

Sharon Velluto

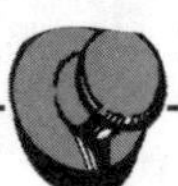

Let no pleasure tempt thee, no profit allure thee, no ambition corrupt thee, to do anything which thou knowest to be evil; so shalt thou always live jollily; for a good conscience is a continual Christmas.

Benjamin Franklin
1706-1790

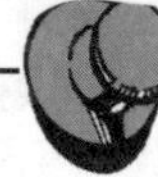

When life seems just a dreary grind,
And things seem fated to annoy,
Say something nice to someone else
And watch the world light up with joy.

Author Unknown

ADJUDICATION

To every man an All Wise God has given
A confidant, a comrade, a true friend,
A light divine, a voice within his soul,
A conscience to accuse and to defend.

Though others by his pretense be deceived,
Though his reputation carefully be bought,
The impostor stands condemned by two who know.
He cannot fool himself — nor mock his God.

The tribunal of the conscience ne'er permits
Exoneration of the guilty one.
Condemned by his own self, the sentence giv'n
To bear his soul's reproach for what was done.

This friend of conscience urges change and growth;
The rising above worldly praise or pelf.
Though other friendships wane — the man who's true
Enjoys a peaceful friendship with himself.

The gift of conscience graciously was giv'n
To enlighten and ennoble souls of men.
Ignored he stands to prosecute and judge.
When heeded he becomes man's dearest friend.

Sharon Velluto

TWO OVERTURES

Two symphonies which ever play
Inside each human breast;
Dissonant, discordant notes
Embroiling with unrest.

Two undulating overtures,
Though similar in sound;
One inspires a soul to change,
The other drags him down.

While one voice rings of worthlessness,
Of failure, forfeiture,
The other sings, "Begin anew,
Revise, resolve, endure!

"Two arias, so similar
A message would imbue.
Man's challenge to give ear and then
Discern between the two.

Sharon Velluto

Inspired by the writings of Neal A. Maxwell
Notwithstanding My Weakness, *Ensign*, November 1976, pages. 12-14

SIGHT

Bartimaeus sat alone on Jericho's lush highway side.
Holding up an earthen bowl to beg alms of those passing by.
Blank expression, vacant eyes, an invalid, deprived of sight;
Hearing Jesus passed his way, began to plead with fervent might.

"Jesus, Son of David, please have mercy upon me," he cried.
When many charged him hold his peace,he louder for attention vied,
Jesus stopped, stood resolute, said, "Call the man to come to me."
"Be of comfort, rise," they said, "Behold, the Master calleth thee."

With faltering steps and outstretched arms they led him to the Savior's feet.
Then Jesus asked him, "What wilt thou that I should now do unto thee?"
"Lord," the blind man said to Him, "Oh, Lord, that I might have my sight."
"Go thy way. In faith be whole," He said, restoring blessed light.

Then Bartimaeus looked upon the first thing that he ever saw:
The face of One he knew to be the Son of David — Son of God.
Bartimaeus then arose and followed Him who gave him sight.
In praises glorifying God, both eyes and heart receiving light.

Sharon Velluto

THE HOLD-UP

And herein do I exercise myself, to have always a conscience void of offense toward God, and toward men. (Acts 24:16)

A few years ago, tape recorder and notebook in hand, I began to take my grandmother's oral history. She told of high adventure as her family, Mormon colonists in Mexico, had been driven out by Pancho Villa, and when as a young married woman, the house had caught fire, and by herself, she had loaded almost everything they owned into a metal baby crib and pushed it out the door. She told of romance when she met her tall, dark and very handsome husband who had died more than thirty years ago, and of the love she still felt for him. I listened with intent as she told of childhood experiences, accidents, illnesses, schools etc.

She told of different jobs she had held: weeding beets, Penny's, Postmaster, and Simpson's Market down on the corner. I vaguely remembered her working at Simpson's when I was younger. She told of a night when she had been held up at gunpoint by two teenage boys. Mr. and Mrs. Simpson, the owners, always locked up the store themselves, but this particular night they had other obligations and had left my grandmother to do it. They had given her instructions about where to hide the money, and how to lock up. Just before closing time around 9:00 P.M., two boys came into the store. Both wore red, knit hunting caps on their heads and a dark blue bandanna over their face. One of them held a gun to Grandma's stomach and forced her into the back room, while the other unloaded the till. "There was only about $400.00," Grandma said, "but that was a lot of money back then. The store didn't make much, and they couldn't afford to lose it."

She looked at the young man who held the gun to her stomach." He had eyebrows, just about like Bruce," (her son) she said. "His face was covered up, all but his eyes. I could see his eyes. I looked at him and said, 'What would your mother say if she knew you were doing things like this?' And he said, 'Shut your mouth lady!'"

The robbers ordered her to stay on the floor of the back room, until they had gone. "I didn't stay there though," she said. "I walked out to where the cash register was. Posters covered almost all of the windows, and I stooped down and looked underneath them. Those guys pointed the gun at me again, so, of course, I ducked a little deeper, and they drove off."

I was incredulous. I laughed, "You didn't really say that?" I asked her. "Yes," she announced straightening her shoulders. "Yes, that's just what I said." I couldn't believe it. Of all the things I might say if I were being held at gun point, (for instance, "Please don't hurt me!") of all the things that would have run through my mind, "What would your mother say if she knew you were doing things like this?" wouldn't have been my first choice, in fact, I doubt it would have even crossed my mind.

However, as I learned more about my grandmother, by doing her history, that statement, "What would your mother say...," though hilarious to me at first, now seems a very natural one. Grandma had a deep respect for her parents, and worked to earn their respect in return.

When I had asked her what were some of her saddest memories while growing up, she told of a day her father had called her out onto the front porch to talk to her. Her father, my great-grandfather, was a brick mason. He had bid a large job, a school in Nevada with another man. The man had forgotten to figure in the price of the steel when he placed his bid. Because of this man's mistake, they had lost the job, and my great-grandfather had been forced into bankruptcy. He lost everything, his car, his business, everything except his house. Sadly, he told his daughter that he would not be able to buy the dress she wanted for her high school graduation. Grandma asked her father for permission to buy a dress on credit, and after graduation she would get a job to pay it off. "I think Dad felt worse about it than I did. He was sad," she said, "and I was sad to see him sad." He trusted his daughter and gave his permission. Grandma continued, "I went to Mrs. Christiansen and she charged a graduation dress to me. Many years later, while riding to Provo with her son, I told him how much his mother's kindness had meant to me."

Grandma valued greatly the trust and faith her father had placed in her and, like her father, her word was her bond. "I got a job at Penny's," she recalled, "and paid the dress off."

As I listened to my grandmother express the feelings of love and respect she felt for her parents, I realized it was not a strange thing at all for her, being held at gunpoint, to look into the eyes of that young man and ask, 'What would your mother say if she knew you were doing things like this?'

I guess Grandma didn't realize that not everyone was blessed to have the honest and upright parents which she did, and not everyone held them in as high esteem.

I believe, very mortal man which has been born upon this earth, brought with him innate feelings of love and respect for our Heavenly Parents. Each child was born with a light, a little voice inside which looks into our heart and asks, "What must your Father think when He sees you doing things like this?" Of course, not everyone listens to that voice. That is the problem with society. There are those who are able to ignore those promptings and say, 'Just shut your mouth, lady!' until they reach that point of spiritual deafness when they can no longer hear the voice.

That voice, the light of Christ, was given to every man so that all men could be held accountable before God for their own actions. Without that voice which prompts one to do right, and warns against evil, no man could be held accountable for his actions. This light, often called conscience, was given to bless, and exalt man, and lead him in the paths of righteousness. Though it may be easy at times to stifle the voice, it is nevertheless real and unmistakable. Whether man chooses to do evil or to do good, each must ultimately answer the voice within his soul, the voice which looks deep into his heart and asks,

"*What must your Father think when He sees you doing things like this?*"

OPEN YOUR EYES

We wait for light, but behold obscurity; for brightness, but we walk in darkness. We grope for the wall like the blind...and stumble at noonday as in the night. (Isaiah 59:9-10)

Every year, in the spring, my fifth grade class did physical fitness testing. The particular program we tested for had three award levels: gold, silver and bronze. One of my students had achieved the gold level in every event except the fifty yard dash. He was so close, yet wasn't able to cross that line within the allotted time. We went out at recess time so he could practice, and I timed him. I think, by the time we finished testing that year, perhaps, I wanted him to earn that award almost as badly as he wanted it. Each time he tried, I hoped, and, each time he just barely missed the time limit, I felt badly. The deadline for turning in the final results was approaching. I showed him ways to start which might cut a few seconds off his time. I ran him against some of the faster runners in the class, hoping that would quicken his pace. On the day the results were to be turned in, I took the entire class out one final time, to complete the testing for any of the students who were just a little shy of getting an award. Everyone in the class knew how badly this boy wanted the award. We had all seen his efforts. All of his classmates sat on the sideline cheering for him, encouraging him. Every time he came in just a little short, he begged for just one more shot. The bell to dismiss was about to ring, and I allowed him one final attempt. He selected someone to run against and they both lined up at the starting line.

"On your mark. Get set. Go!" I cried, hoping this would be the time. His start was great, and I could tell he was giving it all he had. Then he started to veer to the right, and didn't correct himself. He kept running. Next to our track were large cement planters about three feet tall, and about three feet in diameter. He got dangerously close, and I shouted for him to stop. He didn't hear me and kept running. I shouted again, but it was too late. He ran at full speed right into the planter. He hit it at about his hip socket and went sprawling into the pot along with the scrawny tree inside. I ran over to see if he was all right. He was sore, and a little bruised.

"What were you doing?" I asked.

"I closed my eyes," he said. "I thought I could run faster."

I couldn't believe that anyone would attempt to run a race with their eyes closed! Without physical light it is impossible to see the things around us or to know where we are going.

The scriptures record, "*In the beginning God created the heaven and the earth. And the earth was without form and void; and darkness was upon the face of the deep. And the Spirit of God moved upon the face of the waters. And God said, Let there be light: and there was light. And God saw the light, that it was good: and God divided the light from the darkness.*" (Genesis 1:1-4)

When God created the earth, He knew the importance of light for man's existence. Deprived of light man would cease to exist. Not only is light essential for physical life, it is also necessary for spiritual life. Each of God's spirit children was endowed with a special gift of light. This light is called the "Light of Christ," or the "Light of Truth."

"*In the beginning was the Word, and the Word was with God, and the Word was God. In him was life; and the life was the light of men. And the light shineth in darkness; and the darkness comprehendeth it not. ...That was the true Light, which lighteth every man that cometh into the world.*" (John 1:1,4,5,9) Though some may foolishly choose to close their eyes to the light, nevertheless, it is undeniably there.

Two vivid examples from my mission helped me to understand the power of this light and just how much it effects our lives for the good, when choose to accept and heed its guidance; and how detrimental to our growth it can be, when we choose to close our eyes to it.

My companion and I had been teaching a wonderful lady. Her face almost seemed to glow while we visited with her. She loved learning, and absorbed the truth. Some of my richest spiritual experiences occurred while teaching this lovely sister. I remember her nearly jumping out of her chair after one discussion and proclaiming, "Has anyone ever taught this to the Pope? Someone needs to tell the Pope!" But then something happened. On one visit, we returned and she told us that she had decided not to be baptized. We talked with her for a long time. She told us that she didn't want to hear any more about the Church.

The glow had gone from her face and her expression and countenance felt so very dark. It was with sadness that my companion and I left a solemn, final testimony. I had loved this sister and had worked with her for months. I continued to write to her, but she never returned my letters. I do not know whatever became of her. I only knew she had turned against the "Light of Truth" and by choice had denied herself and her family of the wonderful blessings of gospel light.

During the latter part of my mission I taught another young seventeen year old girl. She accepted the gospel message, and described the warmth she felt when she had read and prayed about the Book of Mormon. Yet it was with some uncertainty, that she entered the waters of baptism. A few days following her baptism, my companion and I went back to visit her. During this interval of time, she had met with missionaries from another church, who had grilled her. They had convinced her that she had made a terrible mistake, and had taught her all the things they perceived to be false doctrine, taught by our Church. This young girl hurled their accusations at us one after another and we tried to explain the truth to her, but she didn't buy it. Finally, I stopped her and I asked, "Paola, how did you feel when these missionaries taught you?"

"I felt cold and confused and dark," she told us.

"How did you feel when you listened to our message?" I asked.

"I felt warm and good," she explained. "Paola," I asked, "how do you think you can tell which message is the truth?"

Suddenly the light of understanding came into her eyes. I will never forget the impression it left with me, to see her face. "I understand," she said.

Paola continued to attend church and learn its principles line upon line. The last letter I received from her told of her mother's baptism. Her mother had been bitterly opposed to her daughter's baptism and now, she too is enjoying the blessings of the gospel.

The light of Christ is real. It enlightens every person willing to heed its prompting.

Recently, as a personal goal, I began an art project; a drawing in colored pencil of the Savior holding a small child in His arms. I graduated with a B.A. in art and design, but have not had the chance to do much the past few years, and had never tried anything serious in colored pencil. My husband, an accomplished artist counseled me every time he passed, "Remember your light source. That is what determines your shadows and makes things look real and three dimensional. Otherwise everything looks flat. You are relying too much on instinct. Remember your light source."

One night, I was working on Jesus' robe, and having some difficulty. "Remember your light source," he told me again. He grabbed a white dish towel and draped it over his arm, forming the folds of the robe, and stood next to the light. "See," he said, pointing out the highlights, cast shadows and reflected light of each fold." I carefully copied each shadow and patch of highlight onto my paper, each now very clear and distinct.

The light of Christ can help us understand and to discern more clearly the difference in shadow and highlight. When we close our eyes to spiritual light, we close our minds to knowledge and understanding. Ours is the choice to either close our eyes to the light, run in darkness and then suffer the consequences; or we can open our eyes and follow Him "*who hath called you out of darkness into his marvelous light.*" (1 Peter 2:9)

May we all 'Remember our light source,' and run this race with our eyes open, and fixed on the finish line.

ADDITIONAL REFERENCES

1 Samuel 16:7............. Man looks on the outward appearance, the Lord looks on the heart
Isaiah 13:12................. I will make a man more precious than fine gold
Jeremiah 1:4-19.......... Jeremiah is afraid when called to be prophet
Jonah 4....................... God explains to Jonah the worth of His children
Matthew 9:9-13........... Matthew, a tax collector is called as disciple
Luke 9:56..................... The Son of man is not come to destroy men's souls but to save
Luke 14:7-17............... The parable of the great supper
Luke 19:2-8................. Zacchaeus is invited to dine with Jesus
John 13:4-17............... Jesus gives an example of service
Acts 10-11(10:9-16)... What God has cleansed, that call not thou common
Romans 5:8.................. While we were yet sinners Christ died for us
Ephesians 6: 6-8......... Paul teaches about service
James 1:22-2:26......... Discourse on service
Revelation 2:19........... The Lord knows our acts of service
Alma 36....................... God understands Alma's worth. Alma explains his conversion
D&C 18:10.................... The worth of souls is great in sight of God
Moses 1:39................... God's work is to bring to men immortality, and eternal life
Abraham 3:22-26......... God explains to Abraham the infinite worth of the souls of man

Old Testament Stories
Young David
Job

New Testament Stories
Jesus Christ Is Born
The Man With The Evil Spirits
The Pharisee and the Publican
The Widow's Mites

Book of Mormon Stories
Alma the Younger Repents

TRUSTING IN HIS HAND

A Tribute to a Friend

A few years ago, a very dear friend of mine was diagnosed with cancer. After a long, bout of pneumonia which doctors couldn't seem to clear up, they decided to do some further testing and discovered a large inoperable tumor, the size of a softball, lodged next to her lung.

My friend's first reaction was disbelief and grief, which later was transformed to optimism and courage. She was a beautiful girl, with long thick dark hair, and always seemed to wear a smile. She was an accomplished pianist and was the accompanist for the ward choir. Only twenty seven years old when first diagnosed, and with two small children, she fought a courageous battle for almost three years. All were impressed with her cheerful attitude and perseverance.

It was difficult to watch as the cancer robbed her of nearly everything — everything but her attitude about life. The first thing to go was her hair. The chemotherapy caused it to fall out in great hands full and radiation left her complexion a little splotched. It burned her throat and left her with a persistent cough.

As the cancer progressed, it weakened her muscles and robbed her of the ability to play the piano. Finally, she became so weak that she could no longer care for her little two year old son when he woke up each night. Her two children and husband stayed with her in-laws while she was cared for by her own parents.

One day she told me, "Heavenly Father really protects and blesses you when something like this happens." She seemed to have the serenity and peace to accept God's will, perhaps more than any of us who watched her suffer. She telephoned often, just to talk, and always seemed to turn the conversation from her own troubles to talk about my life, and the challenges I was facing. She would not permit people to cry, and said one of the things that bothered her the most about this trial was the pain and suffering her illness had caused for others, even though she had not been at fault.

She said once, "I miss some of the silliest things. I went on a drive with my sister, and we stopped at a gas station to fill up the car. There was a mother who had her two little children in the back seat. She jumped out and began to pump her gas. How I wished I could do that — take my two children for a ride in the car and get out and pump my own gas. I wish I could go out and weed my garden — just dig in the dirt a bit." All of the things which I take for granted, which are even a drudgery at times, were the things she missed the most.

One day she took me into her bedroom. Here were the few of her treasured possessions which had not been put into storage.

On her wall was a picture of the Savior. "I love that one," she told me, "because He is smiling." Next to the picture, she had posted some of her favorite thoughts and quotations.

One was an adaptation of a quote by Charles Swindoll which said, "*The longer I live, the more I realize the impact of attitude on life. Attitude, to me, is more important than facts. It is more important than the past, than education, than money, than circumstances, than failures, than successes, than what other people think or say or do. It is more important than appearance, giftedness or skill. It will make or break a company... a church... a home. The remarkable thing is we have a choice every day regarding the attitude we will embrace from that day. We cannot change our past... we cannot change the fact that people will act in a certain way. We cannot change the inevitable. The only thing we can do is play on the string we have, and that is our attitude... I am convinced that life is 10 percent what happens to me and 90 percent how I react to it. And so it is with you... we are in charge of our Attitudes.*" (Adapted from *Strengthening Your Grip*,, Charles R. Swindoll,1982, Word, Inc., Dallas, Texas.) Mr. Swindoll further stated, "*I believe that the single most significant decision I can make on a day-to-day basis is my choice of attitude .... Attitude keeps me going or cripples my progress. It alone fuels my fire or assaults my hope. When my attitudes are right, there's no barrier too high, no valley too deep, no dream too extreme, no challenge too great for me.*" (Ibid. Used with permission.)

My friend had first hand experience with attitude. Though every thing which she held most dear was gradually taken from her by this dreaded disease, it could not rob her of her attitude, it could not take away who she was deep down inside.

Cancer gradually stole her breath, her ability to speak and communicate with others and finally took her life. But it did not take her memory, — the memory of her smile, her cheerfulness, her optimism, her courage and above all, her trust in the purposes of God; these will always remain.

HIS PLAN

Each life is filled with mysteries
So hard to understand,
Because, we do not always know
How God works out His plan.

In the furnace of affliction
When from its depths we cry;
Or when life takes what matters most
And leaves us asking, "Why?"

Then sweet comes the assurance
As God helps us to see
That in His love, He'll always do
What's best for you and me.

Sharon Velluto

THE GREAT POTATO DISCOURSE

Yea, I know that I am nothing; as to my strength I am weak; therefore I will not boast of myself, but I will boast of my God, for in his strength I can do all things... (Alma 26:12)

I was very amused one evening as my husband and a friend talked about a mutual friend from their home town. We all laughed as they talked about his famous counsel which many of the members there call,"The Great Potato Discourse."

Basically, the speech says: "There are so many blessings available through the gospel that it is incredible what it can make of you. If you don't avail yourself of these blessings you have the intelligence of a Potato!" It loses a lot in the translation. In their local dialect, "Si proprie na' patana!" made us all laugh, even though I have never met this friend of theirs.

The next day, while studying the words of King Benjamin, I was surprised to see that King Benjamin had given a similar "Potato Discourse," but, he took it much further. "*And now after ye have known and have been taught all these things, if ye should transgress and go contrary to that which has been spoken, that ye do withdraw yourselves from the Spirit of the Lord, that it may have no place in you to guide you in wisdom's paths that ye may be blessed, prospered, and preserved — I say unto you, that the man that doeth this ..*" is a potato! Well, no, King Benjamin didn't actually use *those* words, he said: "*I say unto you, that the man that doeth this, the same cometh out in open rebellion against God; therefore he listeth to obey the evil spirit and becometh an enemy to righteousness; therefore, the Lord has no place in him, for he dwelleth not in unholy temples.*" (Mosiah 2:36-37)

King Benjamin was much more severe than my

husband's friend. He told his people they were less than potatoes -- they were 'dirt.' *"And now I ask, can ye say aught of yourselves? I answer you, Nay. Ye cannot say that ye are even as much as the dust of the earth; but behold, it belongeth to him who created you.... I would that ye should remember and always retain in remembrance, the greatness of God, and your own nothingness, and his goodness and long-suffering towards you, unworthy creatures..."* (Mosiah 2:25, 4:11)

King Benjamin was emphatic in his teachings that without God, man is nothing -- less than nothing, in fact we are deeply in debt. "*I say unto you my brethren, that if you should render all the thanks and praise which your whole soul has power to possess, to that God who has created you...I say unto you that if ye should serve him who has created you from the beginning, and is preserving you from day to day, by lending you breath.. I say, if ye should serve him with all your whole souls yet ye would be unprofitable servants. And behold, all that he requires of you is to keep his commandments... therefore, if ye do keep his commandments he doth bless you and prosper you. And now in the first place, he hath created you, and granted unto you your lives, for which ye are indebted to him. And secondly, he doth require that ye should do as he hath commanded you; for which if ye do, he doth immediately bless you; and therefore he hath paid you, And ye are still indebted unto him, and are, and will be, forever and ever; therefore, of what have ye to boast?... ye are eternally indebted to your heavenly Father...* " (Mosiah 2:20-24, 34) King Benjamin taught that not only is man nothing -- he is even less than dirt. Not only is he in debt -- he is an enemy to God. "*For the natural man is an enemy to God, and has been from the fall of Adam, and will be forever and ever, unless he yields to the enticings of the Holy Spirit, and putteth off the natural man and becometh a saint through the atonement of Christ, the Lord, and becometh as a child, submissive, meek, humble, patient, full of love, willing to submit to all things which the Lord seeth fit to inflict upon him, even as a child doth submit to his father.*" (Mosiah 3:19)

When we fully realize our fallen nature and our nothingness, we are prompted to ask with the Psalmist, "*What is man, that thou art mindful of him?"* (Psalms 8:4) Without God, man is nothing, less than nothing. The hope which lies in the gospel of Jesus Christ is, even though man is 'nothing,' his Maker created him to be 'something!' We were not placed on this earth by chance, but by design. (See Esther 4:14) If we will allow Him, through the gift of His Son, God can help us to make something of our nothingness.

The most amazing part about the "Great Potato Discourse" was the story behind it. This young man had been quite worldly. He ran a business in the open market in Italy selling fish. He was illiterate, which was common for such an occupation, yet, among his co-workers he was uncommon in his expensive tastes in clothing and his popularity with women. Though he had surrounded himself with many worldly things, he still had a nagging feeling that something was missing. His efforts to compensate for what he felt he lacked inside were futile.

His sister was a member of the Church and lived in France. Initially, this young man had no interest in the Church. He frequently visited his sister and upon returning home from one of these visits, he met with the missionaries who taught him the gospel, and he determined to be baptized.

Gradually, his life began to change. A few years after his baptism, now, in his thirties, he decided to serve a mission. He packed his bags and left behind the things of the world and entered with full heart into the service of the Lord. He began to have a burning desire to understand the gospel more fully and to be a good missionary. He asked his companion, (this friend of my husband's) to teach him to read. Using the Book of Mormon as his text, he learned to read and write. After completing an honorable mission, he returned home, a mighty servant of God. Later on a trip to the temple he met a wonderful girl from Spain. They were later married and are now raising a righteous family, who also love the Lord.

This young man truly learned the meaning and import of the Savior's words, "*He that findeth his life shall lose it; and he that loseth his life for my sake shall find it.*" (Matthew 10:39) He had experienced for himself how the gospel can transform people, and make of them something which, alone, they could not make of themselves. It was this deep conviction which prompted the 'Great Potato Discourse.' " If you don't avail yourself of these blessings, *si proprie na' patana.*"

Through the gospel of Jesus Christ, His atoning sacrifice, and the merciful gift of repentance man can transform his life of nothingness to become the "something" God created Him to be.

A BAG OF TOOLS

Isn't it strange
That princes and kings,
And clowns that caper
In sawdust rings,
And common people like you and me
Are builders for eternity?

Each is given a bag of tools,
A shapeless mass,
A book of rules;
And each must make --
Ere life is flown --
A stumbling block
Or a stepping stone.

R.L. Sharpe

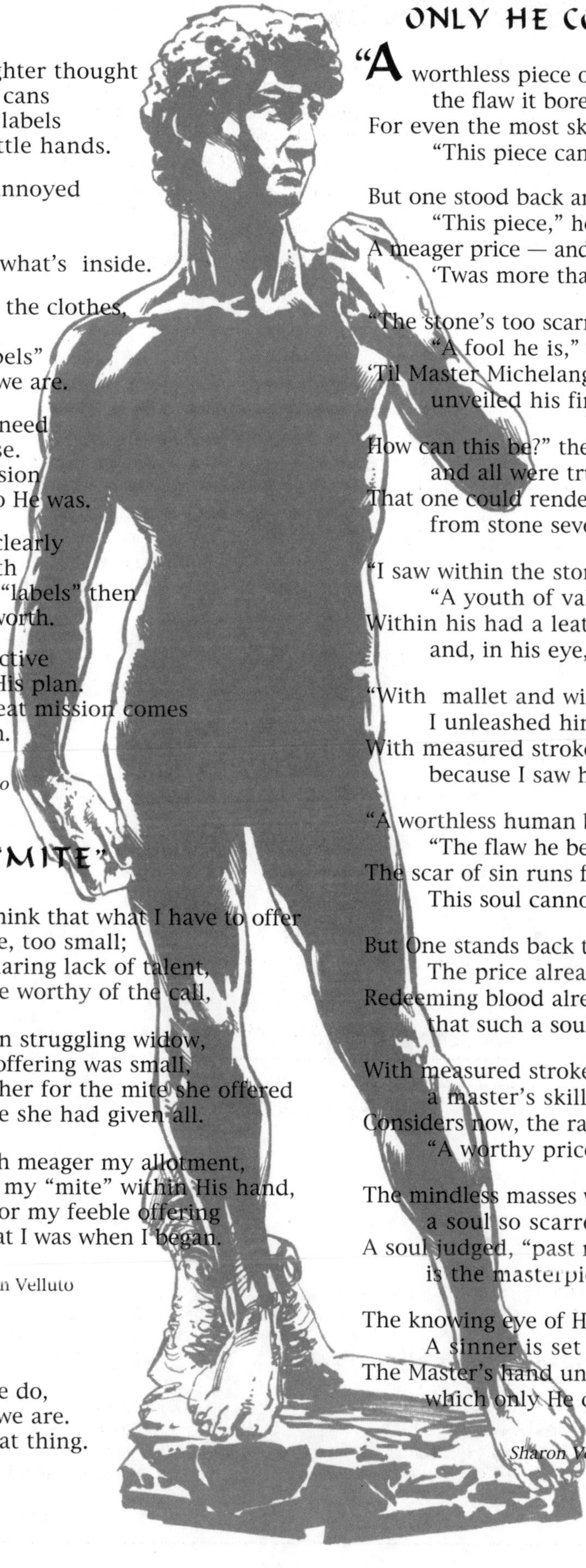

LABELS

My helpful little daughter thought
she'd take all of my cans
And remove each of the labels
with such careful little hands.

Although, at first a bit annoyed
I came to realize
A label can be helpful,
but, it can't change what's inside.

Within a house, beneath the clothes,
inside a fancy car,
Beneath all of these "labels"
we remain just who we are.

Our Savior never felt in need
of labels in His cause.
He succeeded in his mission
for He knew just who He was.

If we could sense more clearly
our noble, royal birth
We wouldn't need these "labels" then
to comprehend our worth.

It gives me faith, perspective
when I understand His plan.
And strength for this great mission comes
by knowing who I am.

Sharon Velluto

MY "MITE"

When I'm prone to think that what I have to offer
Insignificant, inadequate, too small;
When I tremble at my glaring lack of talent,
Thinking others far more worthy of the call,

I'm reminded of a certain struggling widow,
One who also knew her offering was small,
And the Master praised her for the mite she offered
Knowing with her tribute she had given all.

I'm assured that although meager my allotment,
When with faith, I place my "mite" within His hand,
That His compensation for my feeble offering
Makes me more than what I was when I began.

Sharon Velluto

Goodness consists not
in the outward things we do,
but in the inward thing we are.
--- To be good is the great thing.

Edwin H. Chapin
1814 - 1880

ONLY HE COULD SEE

"A worthless piece of stone," they judged.
the flaw it bore too grave
For even the most skillful hands,
"This piece cannot be saved."

But one stood back and eyed the stone.
"This piece," he asked, "How much?"
A meager price — and both agreed,
'Twas more than fair for such.'

"The stone's too scarred," they murmured.
"A fool he is," they smirked,
'Til Master Michelangelo
unveiled his finished work.

How can this be?" they wondered.
and all were truly awed,
That one could render such a work,
from stone severely flawed.

"I saw within the stone," he said,
"A youth of valor -- strong.
Within his had a leather sling,
and, in his eye, a song."

"With mallet and with chisel,
I unleashed him from his lair.
With measured stroke, I cut him loose,
because I saw him there."

"A worthless human being," they judge.
"The flaw he bears too grave.
The scar of sin runs far too deep.
This soul cannot be saved!"

But One stands back to eye the man.
The price already paid;
Redeeming blood already spilt,
that such a soul be saved.

With measured stroke and painful blow,
a master's skillful touch
Considers now, the ransom paid,
"A worthy price for such."

The mindless masses wonder how
a soul so scarred by sin --
A soul judged, "past redemption,"
is the masterpiece within ?

The knowing eye of Heaven smiles.
A sinner is set free.
The Master's hand unveiling one,
which only He could see.

Sharon Velluto

ADDITIONAL REFERENCES

Leviticus 26:3,6,12...... If ye walk in My statutes,.... I will give give peace in the land
Job 22:21...................... Acquaint thyself with God, be at peace
1 Kings 19:11-12........ Elijah hears the still small voice
Psalms 85:8................. The Lord will speak peace to his people
Isaiah 11:6................... The wolf shall dwell with the lamb
Isaiah 52:7 .... How beautiful are feet that publish peace (See also Mosiah 15:18)
Isaiah 54:13................. Thy children shall be taught of the Lord, great shall be the peace
Matthew 3:13-17.......... The baptism of Jesus
Matthew 5:9.................. Blessed are the peacemakers
Mark 4:35-41............... Jesus stills the storm
Romans 2....................... God shall render to man according to his deeds
Romans 5:11................. Repentance brings peace
Romans 8:6................... To be spiritually minded is life and peace.
Romans 14:19............... Let us follow things that make for peace
Romans 15:13............... Now the God of hope fill you with peace
1 Corinthians 14:33..... God is not author of confusion
Galatians 5:13-26........ Paul discusses the fruits of the Spirit
1 Nephi 20:22.............. There is no peace unto the wicked
Alma 38:8, 36:5-24...... Alma repents, and feels peace
Alma 58:11.................. The assurances of the Lord bring peace
4 Nephi 1:2, 15............ No contentions in the land because of the love of God
D&C 6 esp. vs. 23........ Oliver Cowdery's prayer answered with a feeling of peace
D&C 39:5-6.................. The Holy Ghost teaches peaceable things
D&C 85:6..................... The still small voice whispers through and pierces all things
D&C 88:125................. Charity is the bond of peace
D&C 138:18-24............ Joseph F.Smith's vision of the redemption of the dead

Old Testament Stories
Elijah Talks With Jesus

New Testament Stories
Jesus is Baptized

Book of Mormon Stories
Peace In America

Doctrine And Covenants Stories
Joseph Smith and Oliver Cowdery

Ensign, November 1984, p. 33-34 Howard W. Hunter tells the history the hymn *"Master the Tempest is Raging."*

IN SEARCH OF PEACE

With armaments and treaties,
spy satellites, police,
With programs and with prisons,
men try to purchase peace.

More cannons, ships and airplanes;
convinced that, "might makes right."
Rejecting the commands of God
ensures their dreadful plight,

To live a life devoid of peace,
in anguish, worry, fear;
Encaged by bars of hatred
just because they would not hear.

When right pervades the souls of men
with justice, mercy, light;
Perpetuating peace, good will
--- then will "right make might."

If all men learned and lived God's truth
their peace would never wane.
But, seeking from another source
they search for peace in vain.

Long ago, the Prince of Peace taught
righteousness brings rest,
And peace throughout the world begins
within each human breast.

Sharon Velluto

PRAYER FOR PEACE

Lord, make me an instrument of they peace;
Where there is hatred, let me sow love;
Where there is injury pardon;
Where there is doubt, faith;
Where there is despair, hope;
Where there is darkness, light;
Where there is sadness, joy.

O Divine Master, grant that I may not so much seek
To be consoled, as to console;
To be understood, as to understand;
To be loved, as to love;
For it is in giving that we receive,
It is in pardoning that we are pardoned,
And it is in dying that we are born to eternal life.

St.. Francis of Assisi
1182-1226

CONQUESTS

We've conquered deserts, explored the moon,
Surveyed the ocean floor.
Encouraged arts, humanities,
And flown from shore to shore.

We've eradicated smallpox,
Sent news across the sea,
Bridged barriers of language,
With our vast technology.

Culture, commerce, science,
Surging higher, deeper, more;
Advancing all mankind to levels
Only dreamed before.

Yet social ills endure, unchanged
Envy, anger, greed
Since earth began, to conquer self
Remains our greatest need.

To span the gulf of selfishness
Suspicion, hate or pride,
To break down walls of prejudice,
Put jealousy aside.

The Savior, master of Himself
Resisted worldly snares;
To demonstrate a better way:
To love, to serve, to share.

The elements were subject to
The Master's word divine.
The waves were stilled, disease gave way,
And water turned to wine.

The dead, the halt, the deaf, the blind
Were healed at His command.
The poor, down trod and hungry
All were nourished by His hand.

If fearlessly men lived like Him
All fear and strife would cease.
If only men could conquer self
The world would be at peace.

Sharon Velluto

Inspired by the writings of President Spencer W. Kimball
The Teachings of Spencer W. Kimball, page 416

THE PRINCE OF PEACE

In Bethlehem, in David's town,
the night was dark and still.
Some humble shepherds watched their flocks
upon a nameless hill.
They huddled round a crackling fire;
their faithful watch to keep.
A whistling wind, the tinkling bells,
the bleating of the sheep.

The soft glow of a bright, new star
which bathed the town with light,
This was a night, unlike the rest;
this was the night of nights!
Astonished shepherds gazed in awe,
and trembled, sore afraid.
As heavenly host in radiant light
the proclamation made.

Good news for the transgressor,
the broken and forlorn;
Glad tidings of great joy — this night,
the Prince of Peace is born.
This babe, the Great Physician, sent
to heal the shattered soul.
Affirming with His healing touch
that faith can make men whole.

Peace was on the Savior's lips,
and peace was in His gaze.
"Peace, be still!" with outstretched hand
He calmed the troubled waves.
"Peace I leave you," Jesus said,
while in that upper room.
"Peace unto you," he spake again,
as victor o'er the tomb.

And those of us when called upon
to bear life's chastening rod
Still hear His whisper, "Peace, be still,
and know that I am God."
Within His hand He holds the world!
His power will not cease!
Acquaint thyself with Him —
the Prince of Everlasting Peace.

Sharon Velluto

See: Isaiah 9:6, Luke 2:14, Matthew 9:12, Mark 5:34, John 16:33, Mark 4:39, John 20:19, D&C 101:16, Job 22:21

PSALMS XXIII: 1-4

The Lord is my shepherd; I shall not want.
He maketh me to lie down in green pastures;
he leadeth me beside the still waters.
He restoreth my soul;...
Yea, though I walk through the
valley of the shadow of death ,
I will fear no evil;
for thou art with me;
thy rod and thy staff
they comfort me.

THE PEACEMAKER CAKE

This activity tells a story while making a yummy Christmas treat.

(To be used with Activity Idea #5 , Page 37)

Peacemaker Cake
(Gingerbread)

Prepare the ingredients ahead of time.
Preheat oven to 350 degrees.

Ingredients:

1 cup sugar	1&1/2 Tb.. baking powder
1 cup butter	1& 1/2 Tb.. baking soda
2 tsp cinnamon	2 Cups Molasses
2 tsp ginger	2 eggs
1 tsp powdered cloves	5 cups flour
1 & 3/4 cups milk	1 tsp salt
1/4 cup vinegar	Whipped topping

The day started out well enough. Nick, the year old baby was calm for most of the morning. Mother put him down for his nap at the usual time and all was peaceful and cheerful.

Cream together the butter and sugar

Then Andrew and Angela, the twins began to argue. "Stay out of my things," Angela snapped. "I didn't touch your silly stuff," Andrew argued. Their spicy words made the day feel a little darker.

Mix in cinnamon, ginger and cloves

Mother asked them to quit arguing but they only remembered for a short while. They were both in very sour moods. No, the day didn't feel very good at all.

Pour the vinegar into the milk, and watch while it curdles, then pour it on top of the dark mixture but do not stir yet.

Their arguing woke the baby and when mother asked them to be kind to one another, they continued to argue in whispers so that she couldn't hear. But even though their words could not be heard, their anger toward each other was seen and felt by the rest of the family.

Add baking powder and baking soda and watch it bubble

Mother asked Andy and Angela to help her. She sent them up to clean their room. Instead of cleaning, they continued to bicker and argue. Mother was frustrated and upset. She walked the crying baby and listened to the twins yell at each other. The atmosphere in their home was sour, and dark, and gloomy.

Add the molasses and mix

Sarah returned home from playing with her friend. When she walked in the door, she could tell that something was wrong. She took the crying baby from her mother and offered to rock him so mother could fix dinner. Sarah had a heart of gold.

Crack eggs into mixture and stir

Sarah was a peacemaker and didn't like it when her home felt dark. Her cheerful helpful attitude always made things seem lighter.

Add flour and mix

When the baby was finally asleep, Sarah went into the twins' room. She helped them to clean up their mess. When they had finished Sarah sat down to talk to them. "Jesus said that we are the salt of the earth." she started. The twins asked Sarah what that meant. She explained, "Salt adds flavor and makes things taste better," Sarah explained. "If we try to live as Jesus taught us and to love one another, we are like the salt which makes things taste better."

Add salt

"If we stick together, and love and help one another," she went on, "even when things get hot, life can still be sweet."

Pour into a greased 9 X 13 pan and put into the oven. 350 degrees for about 35-40 minutes, or until a knife, after inserting, comes out clean. Top with whipped topping and serve.

THE PUZZLE

The wind and the waves shall obey thy will, Peace be still.
Whether the wrath of the storm tossed sea, or demons or men or whatever it be
No water can swallow the ship where lies The Master of ocean and earth and skies.
They all shall sweetly obey thy will; Peace be still. (Mary Ann Baker, *Hymns* #105)

"Ooooh!" I said, "I'm going to tickle you to pieces." My little three year old daughter and I had been rolling and playing on the bed, but she stopped and looked at me very seriously.

"If you cut my head off," she said, "you won't have a little girl any more." I laughed, not quite understanding what had prompted such a remark and I said, "No, I would never cut your head off! I love my little girl!" I gave her a hug.

Still troubled by what I had just said, she continued very seriously, "If you cut me into pieces, I will be a puzzle." I laughed, but, to my little daughter it wasn't funny. She didn't want to be a puzzle! I guess that is the last thing any of us want -- to be a puzzle. We want to be whole.

When ministering among the Nephites Jesus asked the question, "*What manner of men ought ye to be?*" and then he answered his own inquiry saying,"*Even as I am.*" (3 Nephi 27:27)

He told them, "*Therefore I would that ye should be perfect even as I, or your Father who is in heaven is perfect.*" (3 Nephi 12:48. See also Matthew 5:48) In the Hebrew language, the word perfect is often translated as "whole."

We read in the scriptures of many people with physical ailments who came to Jesus for help. After healing them, the Savior often responded, "*Thy faith hath made thee whole.*"

The gospels recount the story of a woman, who had been ill for twelve years. She had spent all she had on physicians who were unable to help her. Her condition grew worse. When she heard of Jesus, she said, "*If I may touch but his clothes, I shall be whole...*" She struggled through the crowd which thronged Jesus and reached out to touch the hem of His coat. Immediately, she felt the plague leave. Jesus sensed what had happened and turned around asking, "*Who touched my clothes?*" He looked around to see who had done it. The woman recognized that she had been healed and "*fearing and trembling,*" *fell at His feet and* "*told him all the truth.*" Jesus then said to her, "*Daughter, thy faith hath made thee whole; go in peace, and be whole of thy plague.*" (Mark 5:25-34. Underlining added)

"*While he yet spake, there cometh one from the ruler of the synagogues house, saying to him, Thy daughter is dead; trouble not the Master. But when Jesus heard it, he answered him, saying,* "*Fear not; believe only, and she shall be made whole.*" (Luke 8:48)

In Jerusalem there was a pool surrounded by five porches, where many of the afflicted gathered and lay to wait for the moving of the water. "*For an angel went down at a certain season into the pool, and troubled the water; whosoever then first after the troubling of the water stepped in was made whole of whatsoever disease he had.*" Among the blind, halt, and withered, lay a man who had suffered for thirty eight years with an infirmity. Jesus, knowing that he had suffered with this condition for a long time was moved with compassion and asked, "*Wilt thou be made whole?*" One can almost sense the pleading in his voice as he replies, "*Sir, I have no man, when the water is troubled, to put me into the pool: but while I am coming, another steppeth down before me.*" Perhaps the man expected Jesus to wait there with him and carry him to the pool. Jesus answered, "*Rise, take up thy bed, and walk. And immediately the man was made whole...*" (John 5:2-9)

Wherever Jesus went, the sick, the weary and the infirm sought Him. "*And when they were gone over, they came into the land of Gennesaret. And when the men of that place had knowledge of him, they sent out into all that country round about, and brought unto him all that were diseased; And besought him that they might only touch the hem of his garment; and as many as touched were made perfectly whole.*" (Matthew 14:34-36) "*And whithersoever he entered, into villages, or cities, or country, they laid the sick in the streets, and besought him that they might touch if it were but the border of his garment: and as many as touched him were made whole.*" (Mark 6:56)

Whoever had sufficient faith in the Savior, was made "whole." Not only did Jesus heal those with physical ailments, but he healed the spiritually infirm as well. In the Book of Mormon we read of a young man by the name of Enos who went to the Lord seeking help for an aching spirit. He was the son of a mighty prophet, and as he reflected on the words of his father, they began to weigh heavily upon his heart. He recorded, "*And my soul hungered... and I kneeled down before my Maker, and I cried unto him in mighty prayer and supplication for mine own soul.*" Enos prayed all day long and into the night. He records, "*And there came a voice unto me, saying; Enos, thy sins are forgiven thee, and thou shalt be blessed.... wherefore, my guilt was swept away. And I said: Lord, how is it done? And he said unto me; Because of thy faith in Christ, whom thou hast never before heard nor seen.... wherefore, go to, thy faith hath made thee whole.*" (Enos 1: 2-8)

In order to enter into the Kingdom of God, a man must be clean and pure. "*And no unclean thing can enter into his kingdom.*" (3 Nephi 27:19) We must be "perfect." We must be "whole." It is vain to hope or falsely assume that anyone will be permitted to enter into His kingdom simply because his goodness outshines his badness. God has made it clear that we must be "perfect." By ourselves, this is an impossible task. Only through faith in Jesus Christ can we be made "*whole.*"

Faith in Jesus Christ is the first principle of the gospel. It is absolutely essential. Elder A. Theodore Tuttle said, "*I am a product of a household of faith. I learned faith in my home...I need that faith now as much as I ever did.*

"*I think we all do. We're not going to survive this world, temporally or spiritually, without increased faith in the Lord — and I don't mean a positive attitude — I mean downright solid faith in the Lord Jesus Christ. That is the one thing that gives vitality and power to otherwise rather weak individuals.*" (*Ensign,* November 1986, p. 73)

Faith in Jesus Christ is more than an acknowledgement that He lives, more than a profession of belief. Faith in Jesus Christ is a moving power.

Each of us stand before the Lord, imperfect, halt, withered, maimed, or as debtors. So, why is faith in Jesus Christ so essential, and how can that faith make us " *whole?*"

First, faith in Jesus Christ offers us a standard of reference. It moves us to rise above ourselves. Faith in Christ inspires us to strive to more fully live by the precepts He taught, to do His will, '*in earth as it is in heaven.*' (See Matthew 6:10) It inspires us to deal with others honestly. It prompts us to be more charitable, more forgiving and less judgmental. Faith in Jesus Christ not only inspires us to be better but also gives us the power to reach beyond our own capabilities. Through Him our weaknesses can become strengths. (See Ether 12:27, Acts 3:16)

President David O. McKay said, "*Spirituality is the consciousness of victory over self, and of communion with the infinite. Spirituality impels one to conquer difficulties and acquire more and more strength. To feel one's own faculties unfolding and truth expanding the soul is one of life's sublimest experiences.*" (Llewelyn McKay, *Stepping Stones to an Abundant Life.* Salt Lake City: Deseret Book Co. 1971, p. 99)

When our Faith in Christ moves us to stop and compare ourselves to this standard of perfection, our faults begin to stare us in the face. This moves us to repentance. Alma called this "*faith unto repentance.*" (See Alma 34:17) Through the process of repentance we begin to root out the natural man and begin the process of spiritual "rebirth." Sincere repentance instills a deep personal desire to change, and to distance oneself from evil. Once one experiences the joy which comes from receiving a forgiveness of sins, he will naturally seek to retain a remission of sins; to keep himself free from spiritual debt and bondage. Faith in Christ moves us to be forgiving of others, especially when we understand how merciful the Lord has been in pardoning our own faults. Faith in the atoning sacrifice of Jesus Christ, faith unto repentance, sanctifies and makes us "whole."

Faith in Christ helps us to understand His goodness, knowledge, power, purpose, mercy and love. When we understand that He loves us and wants the best for us, we can place our complete trust in Him.

President Ezra Taft Benson said, "*Faith in Jesus Christ consists of complete reliance on Him. As God, He has infinite power, intelligence, and love. There is no human problem beyond his capacity to solve. Because He descended below all things (see D&C 122:8), He knows how to help us rise above our daily difficulties.*

"*Faith in Him means believing that even though we do not understand all things, He does. We therefore, must look to Him "in every thought; doubt not, fear not.*" (D&C 6:36) (*Ensign,* November 1983, p. 8)

This kind of faith helps us to carry on through the storm knowing that whatever comes, the Lord is in control. "The Lord of hosts hath sworn, saying, Surely as I have thought, so shall it come to pass; and as I have purposed, so shall it stand." (Isaiah 14:24)

President Howard W. Hunter said, "*I suppose we have all had occasion, individually or collectively, to cry out on some stormy sea, 'Master, carest thou not that we perish?'...Our faith should remind us that he can calm the troubled waters of our lives... On the sea of Galilee, the stirring of the disciples' faith was ultimately more important than the stilling of the sea...*" (President Howard W. Hunter, *Ensign*, November 1984, pp. 33-34)

President Spencer W. Kimball wrote, "*There are depths in the sea which the storms that lash the surface into fury never reach. They who reach down into the depths of life where, in the stillness, the voice of God is heard, have the stabilizing power which carries them poised and serene through the hurricane of difficulties.*" (*Ensign* January, 1974, p. 17)

I was deeply moved by the faith of one such sister. She was expecting twins and started into early labor. The doctors worked, but could not halt the labor. She was given a priesthood blessing and with firm faith, she awaited the outcome. Two tiny babies, a boy and a girl, were delivered. The boy barely over two pounds, and the girl just under two. In the weeks which followed, the doctors and nurses worked to save their lives. Nurses came to the hospital on their day off, and called on off hours to see how the babies were. It became necessary for the little girl to undergo open heart surgery. The bishop gave the tiny baby a blessing, and felt inspired to say that "all will be well." Days passed, desperate days, and finally this humble sister was called to the hospital. For the first time in three weeks she was allowed to hold her tiny daughter in her arms. She rocked her and kissed her tiny head, as she quietly passed from this life. The Spirit whispered peace and she knew that this was the way things were supposed to be. Afterwards, the bishop came to their house to talk. He was a little confused and confessed, "I don't understand. I felt prompted to say that everything would be okay." With deep conviction, this sister told her leader, "Bishop, it is okay. Everything is okay." Through the years that have followed, this sister has recognized that the loss of her little daughter has given added strength and determination to live her life so that she may be counted worthy to have her entire family together throughout eternity. "I think," she said, "if you look at things before they happen, you feel that you could never make it, but when you are called to pass through it, Heavenly Father gives the strength and peace to see you through."

"Why is it expedient that we center our confidence, our hope, and our trust in one solitary figure? Why is faith in Him so necessary to peace of mind in this life and hope in the world to come?

"Our answers to these questions determine whether we face the future with courage, hope and optimism or with apprehension, anxiety, and pessimism.... Only Jesus Christ is uniquely qualified to provide that hope, that confidence, and that strength to overcome the world and rise above human failings. To do that, we must place our faith in Him and live by His laws and teachings. " (President Ezra Taft Benson, *Ensign*, November 1983, p. 6)

In times of grief and sorrow, or when sin makes us ache, only a deep and abiding faith in Jesus Christ can make us "*whole.*"

"*Jesus Christ is called the Prince of Peace* (See Isaiah 9:6) *and his message is a message of peace to the individual and to the world. The gospel of Jesus Christ is the plan of life which will restore peace to the world, remove inner tensions and troubles, and bring happiness to the human soul. It is the greatest philosophy of life ever given to man.*" (Franklin D. Richards, *Ensign*, November 1983 p. 57)

There are many different terms and phrases used to describe this state of inner peace and wholeness: grounded, solid, in tune, in harmony, at peace, "at one."

In His great intercessory prayer, Jesus prayed, "*Holy Father, keep through thine own name those whom thou hast given me that they may be one as we are, Neither pray I for these alone, but for them also which shall believe on me through their word. That they all may be one; as thou Father art in me, and I in thee, that they also may be one in us; that the world may believe that thou hast sent me. And the glory which thou gavest me I have given them; that they may be one, even as we are one; I in them, and thou in me, that they may be made perfect in one...*" (John 17:11,20-23. See also: Acts 17:26, Romans 12:5, 1 Corinthians 6:17, Galatians 3:28, Ephesians 2:14-19, D&C 50:43 Moses 6:68, 7:18)

Happiness and peace are found only when we are in harmony with ourselves, our God and our fellowman. This feeling of peace and harmony -- of being "at-one" with ourselves and our God, can only come through the gift of the atonement which Christ made in our behalf.

There will come a day, a glorious resurrection day when all men will rise from the grave. Their spirit will be restored to their body. After long years of waiting, physically they will be made "*whole.*" Then each individual will stand before God to be judged. Those who have exercised faith in Jesus Christ, a faith which has moved them to abide by His teachings, a faith which impelled them to sanctify themselves, a faith which has caused them to trust Him, will have the glorious privilege of kneeling before Him, knowing that "*faith in Him hath made them whole.*" Paul wrote, "*For by grace are ye saved through faith; and that not of yourselves; it is the gift of God.*" (Ephesians 2:8)

There are many who believe that they are "past redemption." The scars are too deep, their "infirmity" too great to ever be healed. If one will probe the center of his aching heart, he will hear the voice of the Savior, pleading to the Father to forgive those who sought His life. If he quietly listens, he will hear the Savior's admonition, "*Fear not; believe only, and ye shall be made whole.*" (Luke 8:48)

Jesus Christ offers healing. There is no infirmity He cannot heal, no storm He cannot calm. He offers rest to the weary, and peace to the troubled soul.

In the words of the Apostle Paul, "*Finally, brethren, farewell. Be perfect, be of good comfort, be of one mind, live in peace; and the God of love and peace shall be with you.*" (2 Corinthians 6:17)

Additional References: Romans 14:23, 1 Corinthians 2:5, Ephesians 4:13, Mosiah 3:9-12, Ether 12:12

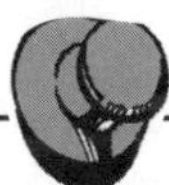

Peace is a triumph of correct principles."

Elder Marvin J. Ashton
Ensign, November 1985, p.71

ADDITIONAL REFERENCES

Job 14:14, 19:26-27................. Job teaches about the resurrection
Psalms 118:7........................... I shall not die, but live
Isaiah 25:8.............................. He shall swallow up death in victory
Isaiah 53:5.............................. With his stripes we are healed
Ezekiel 37:12........................... I will open the graves and cause you to come up
Hosea 13:14............................. I will ransom them from power of grave
Luke 22:44............................... Being in agony.. his sweat was as great drops of blood
Acts 24:15............................... There shall be a resurrection of the dead
1 Corinthians 6:14.................... God will raise us up
1 Corinthians 15:19-22........... Paul teaches about resurrection
2 Nephi 9:6-26......................... Nephi explains the atonement
Mosiah 3:7............................... He shall suffer great anguish, and bleed at every pore
Mosiah 16:7-11........................ Amulek teaches about salvation and resurrection
Alma 7:11-16........................... Alma teaches of Christ's atonement
Alma 11:42-44......................... The spirit and the body shall be reunited
Alma 42: 2-28.......................... Alma explains the fall, atonement, mercy and justice
D&C 18:10-13.......................... Christ suffered that men might come unto Him

New Testament Stories
Jesus Suffers in the Garden of Gethsemane
Jesus Is Crucified
Jesus Is Resurrected

Book of Mormon Stories
King Benjamin
Abinadi and King Noah
Jesus Appears to the Nephites

Doctrine and Covenants Stories
Jesus Will Come To Earth Again

Ensign, April 1977, *The Mediator,* Boyd K. Packer, page 54

Optional Materials, Chapter 24, *The Sacramental Covenant,* page 157

IT PLEASED HIM

Father behold the sufferings and death of him who did no sin, in whom thou wast well pleased; behold the blood of thy Son which was shed, the blood of him whom thou gavest that thyself might be glorified; (D&C 45:4)

While reading from the book of Isaiah, I ran across a very intriguing scripture. Speaking of the Messiah, Isaiah wrote, "*...He is despised and rejected of men; a man of sorrows, and acquainted with grief; and we hid as it were our faces from him; he was despised, and we esteemed him not. Surely he hath borne our griefs, and carried our sorrows; yet we did esteem him stricken, smitten of God and afflicted. But he was wounded for our transgressions, he was bruised for our iniquities; the chastisement of our peace was upon him; and with his stripes we are healed. All we, like sheep have gone astray; we have turned every one to his own way; and the Lord hath laid on him the iniquities of us all. He was oppressed, and he was afflicted, yet he opened not his mouth; he is brought as a lamb to the slaughter, and as a sheep before her shearers is dumb so he opened not his mouth. He was taken from prison and from judgement;... he was cut off from the land of the living;... And he made his grave with the wicked, and with the rich in his death; because he had done no evil, neither was any deceit in his mouth.*"

Then Isaiah makes a most peculiar statement. "*Yet it pleased the Lord to bruise him; he hath put him to grief.*" (See Isaiah 53:10) I wondered, how was it possible that such grief and agony could please a loving Father. Was this a mistranslation or a mistake by Isaiah? Yet only one verse later he writes, "*He shall see the travail of his soul, and shall be satisfied.*" In other scriptures, the Lord expresses his indignation at innocent blood being spilt. So how was it possible that the sufferings of his beloved and innocent Son could please him?

My mind raced back to a few years ago, when

our young son was very ill. His fever was so high that he just laid listlessly and stared at us through glazed and glassy eyes. Three times we took him to the clinic that night and the following day. The effects of the medications were only temporary. After several tests were done, a blood culture indicated there was bacteria in the bloodstream. The doctors determined that it was necessary to do a spinal tap, since that particular bacteria causes meningitis.

For hours he had been poked and prodded, and was already frightened. The doctors asked my husband to hold him still, bending his back into a bowed shape, so they could insert the long needle into his spine without injuring him. I was to hold his arms and legs still. I was right down by his little face, trying to reassure him. He looked at me as if I had betrayed him. I knew that he must have wondered why I was holding him down while these doctors hurt him.

For a parent, watching a child suffer can be one of the most horrible and painful of all of life's experiences. So, why would a Father who prized His Son, say that it "pleased" him to bruise him, that it "satisfied" him to see him suffer?

I remember over and over telling my little boy, "It will be all right. The doctors will make you better." That was my motivation, the only thing that enabled me to bear watching him suffer. I hoped that the doctors could make him well. I held him down and watched him suffer because I knew it would be for his benefit.

For our Heavenly Father, it "pleased" Him to bruise his Son, only because He knew how much this sacrifice could benefit all of His other children. For *"with his stripes we are healed..."* (Isaiah 53:5) *When thou shalt make his soul an offering for sin he shall see his seed, he shall prolong his days, and the pleasure of the Lord shall prosper in his hand...by his knowledge shall my righteous servant justify many; for he shall bear their iniquities. Therefore will I divide him a portion with the great... because he hath poured his soul unto death; and he was numbered with the transgressors; and he bore the sins of many, and made intercession for the transgressors."* (Isaiah 53:10-12)

Because Jesus Christ endured the suffering and anguish which he did, He made it possible for us to return to the presence of God, clean and pure. And so Isaiah wrote that it *"pleased the Lord to bruise him... He shall see the travail of his soul and be satisfied."*

For me, Isaiah's statement is a window into heaven. To think that God so loved the world, --- He so loved you and I, that He would not only watch His Son suffer, and voluntarily give Him as a sacrifice for us, but that it would "*please*" Him to do so, helps me begin to realize the great love our Heavenly Father feels for each of his children.

"For God so loved the world, that he gave his only begotten Son, that whosoever believeth in him should not perish, but have everlasting life. For God sent not his son into the world to condemn the world; but that the world through him might be saved." (John 3:16-17) *"But God commendeth his love toward us, in that, while we were yet sinners, Christ died for us. For if we were enemies, we were reconciled to God by the death of his Son."* (Romans 5:8,10) *"This is a faithful saying and worthy of all acceptation, that Christ Jesus came into the world to save sinners; of whom I am chief."* (1 Timothy 1:15)

I stand all amazed at the love Jesus offers me,
Confused at the grace that so fully he
proffers me.
I tremble to know that for me he was crucified,
That for me, a sinner, he suffered, he bled
and died.

I marvel that he would descend from his
throne divine
To rescue a soul so rebellious and proud as mine,
That he should extend his great love unto
such as I,
Sufficient to own, to redeem and to justify.

I think of his hands pierced and bleeding
to pay the debt!
Such mercy, such love, and devotion can I forget?
No, no, I will praise and adore at the mercy seat,
Until at the glorified throne I kneel at his feet.

Oh it is wonderful that he should care for me
Enough to die for me!
Oh it is wonderful, wonderful to me!

** I think of our Father who watched His Son's*
suffering
That it pleased Him to give to the world such an
offering.
The infinite ransom paid by his Son's sacrifice,
That we through His blood be redeemed and
be sanctified.

Oh it is wonderful that he would care for me
Enough to give for me
His own begotten Son who gave his life for me!

Cecil Frances Alexander, [1811-1895]
Hymns # 193

* Fourth verse added.

THE KIND FRIEND

...he offereth himself a sacrifice for sin, to answer the ends of the law, unto all those who have a broken heart and a contrite spirit; (2 Nephi 2:7)

There once was a young man who wanted a grand house. He had but little money. Still, he learned of a way he could get what he desired. The king was allowing each of his servants to take possession of a house, with the promise that they would take stewardship over the house and its grounds and help others who may be in need. Then at an appointed time, each steward would pay the allotted price for the house based on his faithfulness to the king's requests. Upon payment, each servant would become sole owner of the home and grounds. At this time each steward would be entitled to an inheritance from the king as he judged them worthy after observing what each had done with his responsibilities.

All people in the kingdom were excited, but none was happier than the poor young man who yearned for a grand house. With little thought to the commitment he was making, he hurried through the process which made him a steward over a new house.

When at first he saw the house that was to be his stewardship, he was disappointed, It was a nice house, but not what he had been imagining. It was similar to all those around it, yet, he felt it was not as nice in some ways. He felt frustrated when he looked around at his neighbors' houses getting even nicer as they worked to upgrade their homes and yards. Each neighbor worked individually on their own responsibilities, but also helped one another with different work around the area. He didn't join in to help others because he felt there was so much that needed to be done for himself.

It wasn't long before he realized many things were falling into disrepair. He could not keep up with all the things he felt needed to be done. Discouragement overwhelmed him as he recognized things weren't the way he wanted them to be. He spent less and less time caring for the house and grounds. What he had thought would make him the happiest didn't seem to make him happy at all.

The appointed time for payment to the king came nearer. As the man looked at the condition of the house, he felt sure that it was of little value. He felt he would owe less than the allotted price for it. To his surprise, however, he found that he would owe as much as any of his neighbors whose homes seemed far nicer than his. As the day approached, he knew he would be unable to pay his debt. He was ashamed that he had not prepared better.

As he went before the king to give an accounting of his stewardship, he begged for more time to prepare to pay his debt. He pleaded for mercy. The king gently asked, "What has changed, that you feel time will help? In the beginning, didn't you promise you would pay at this time? Did you not know this day would come? Have you kept your promise to care for the property and help others? How have you kept your stewardship over the home and gardens?"

In despair the man hung his head, for he knew the answers to all of the questions the king had asked. He replied sadly, "I have been a slothful servant, yet I still desire to serve thee."

The king was a just man. He reminded the inexperienced young man that in fairness to all, justice must be served. The king sorrowed in his heart, but he knew the choice had been made long before by this young man to disregard the agreement made with the king. With breaking heart, the loving king demanded payment with the words, "I wanted you to succeed. I gave you all the opportunities I could. I have loved you and I always will, but the payment must be made that my word remains true. I have tried to be just to all, and in doing so, if I went against my word now, I would be a liar."

At that moment, a kind friend stepped forward to the right side of the king. He addressed the king respectfully, "I will pay the debt for him."

In awe, the young man tried to remember where he had seen the kind face of this devoted friend before. Why would this friend do such a thing for him? With painful memory he recalled that he had refused help from this friend before. On occasion, he had refused to help this man also --- this same great man who now offered to pay the price for him to the king.

What gratitude swept over the young man as the king accepted the offer of this selfless friend and allowed him to pay the debt!

Side by side, the young man and his beloved friend worked repairing his house. He learned that although it was his responsibility to make his home the best it could be, he found that he could use his talents to help others, and in turn allow others to use their talents to help him. In thankfulness, the now wiser young man asked what he could do for his cherished friend in return.

The reply was simple and beautiful. "If you desire to repay me, care for others the way I care for you."

STONE

With guard and stone securely set
'twas foolish to assume
His influence and teachings
could be sealed up in a tomb!

What grave could hold him prisoner?
What stone could ever stay
God's Son who held life in His palm?
What door could bar His way?

And so that great and massive stone
was moved by God's decree.
Christ opened up death's prison doors,
and set the sinner free.

His influence will flood the earth,
and reach to every land;
A great stone which cannot be stopped
by man's unhallowed hand!

Sharon Velluto

EMPTY

Nameless graves and faceless names;
Ominous, in countless rows
Tombs and vaults and crosses stand.
Each crypt filled with mold'ring bones.

One sepulcher, though nondescript,
Stands unique among the rest.
It looms abandoned, desolate.
Empty — and of corse divest.

An angel who rolled back the stone
To the grieving mourners said,
"He is not here! The risen Lord
Can not be found among the dead!"

Still tombs and vaults and crosses stand;
Biding Resurrection Day,
When open tombs stand rows on rows.
Vacant crypts and empty graves.

Because that tomb stands empty now,
Assuring shrine of life reborn!
A promise man shall rise from death
One glorious Resurrection Morn!

Sharon Velluto

TWO KEYS

Victorious over Darkness,— Heav'n prevailed,
And in His hand, God held two precious keys.
Bitter and discountenanced, Hell vowed,
"Although this battle's o'er, I will not cede."

"The battle for the souls of men goes on!
One day I'll be possessor of the keys."
The Heavens wept when Satan was cast down;
The master of destruction and deceit.

Forbidden fruit — and Purgatory boasts,
"The purpose of creation unfulfilled!
"One key of hell, the other key of death,
He held, and two imposing doors were sealed.

With haughty laugh, deriding Heaven's plan;
And, insolent he vaunted his great prize.
The two great keys of death clutched in his hand,
With turgid fist he waved them at the skies.

Omniscient God, with wise farseeing eye,
Provision made in His judicious plan,
To confiscate -- secure again the keys;
To free the body and the soul of man.

Through innocent and expiating blood,
To free the felon from the chains of sin;
Through resurrection's miracle unlock
The grave -- and death's unyielding hold on men.

The blood was spilt and life's last breath went out.
Infernal grave could hold the dead no more.
The Savior seized the keys of death and hell,
And opened up those two imposing doors.

Triumphant over sin and o'er the grave;
The penitent from prison's walls expelled!
Exultant voices sing and praise the name
Of Him, who holds the keys to death and hell!

Sharon Velluto

HE IS NOT HERE!

Jesus is risen! He is not here!
Thus spake the angel -- testament clear.

Seek not the living -- with those who sleep.
Message of gladness! Woman don't weep.

Sepulcher empty -- Victory dear!
Jesus is risen! He is not here!

Sharon Velluto

ADDITIONAL REFERENCES

Exodus 16:1-35.............. The Israelites are fed with manna in the wilderness
1 Kings 17:6.................... Elijah is fed by ravens
1 Kings 19:1-12.............. Elijah is fed before hearing the still small voice
Psalms 105:39-42........... God feeds the Israelites while in the wilderness
Matthew 4:3-4.................. Temptation of Jesus and His response (See Deuteronomy 8:3)
Matthew 16:5-12.............. Jesus warns His disciples to beware of leaven of Pharisees
Matthew 26:26-29........... Institution of the sacrament (See also Luke 22:19, 3 Nephi 18:5-12)
Mark 6:32-44.................. Jesus feeds the multitude (See also Mark 8: 14-21, Matthew 15:29-39
Luke 14:15-24................. The parable of great supper
John 4:31-34................... I have meat ye know not of
John 6.............................. Discourse on bread of life
1 Corinthians 10:1-6....... All did eat the same spiritual meat
Revelation 2:7,17............. Those who overcome will eat of hidden manna
1 Nephi chapters 8,11..... Lehi's vision of the tree of life
2 Nephi 9:51.................... Feast on that which perisheth not
2 Nephi 31:20-32:6......... Feast on the words of Christ
Alma 5:33-34................... Eat of the bread of life freely

Old Testament Stories
The Israelites in the Wilderness

New Testament Stories
Jesus feeds 5000 people

Book of Mormon Stories
Jesus Christ Teaches about the Sacrament and Prayer

SO CLOSE AND YET....

And no man receiveth a fullness unless he keepeth his commandments. He that keepeth his commandments receiveth truth and light, until he is glorified in truth and knoweth all things. (D&C 93:27-28)

My little three year old had heard the message on our answering machine numerous times. He picked up his little toy phone and repeated, "If you'd like to make a call, please hang up and try again. If you need a sister, please hang up and dial the operator." (I was expecting at the time and it sounded like a pretty good proposition to me.) He had understood, but not quite. He was, "so close and yet so far away."

Generally, being close just isn't good enough, in fact, at times it can be dangerous, and even deadly. Consider a medical diagnosis which is almost correct, a piano which almost has all of the keys, the game deciding shot which almost went in, a compass reading which is almost right, an antibiotic which almost kills the bacteria, the parachute that almost opened.

In the spiritual sense, just being close doesn't suffice either. Several times when Jesus was questioned about doctrine, He responded, "*Ye do err not knowing the scriptures.*" (See Matthew 22:29, Mark 12:24,27) This must have been a great insult to the Pharisees and Scribes whose lives were dedicated to the study of the "law and the prophets." They did "know" the scriptures in the mental sense, but lacked the spiritual understanding for their proper application. They were so versed in the law that they had come to believe that their knowledge of it could save them. Jesus' stinging reply to them was, "*Search the scriptures; for in them ye think ye have eternal life: and they are they which testify of me. And ye will not come to me, that ye might have life.*" (John 5:39-40)

In the wilderness, Israel had been fed with manna, seven days a week for forty years. They often referred to manna as the 'bread of angels,' or 'bread from heaven.' The Jews mistakenly attributed this miracle to Moses. They had read the prophesies of a great Messiah who would come to redeem them, and in Jesus' day there were many who believed that when the Messiah came, He also, would feed them miraculously.

When Jesus fed the multitude with two fish and five loaves of bread, many believed that He was the promised Messiah. They had awaited the day when a mighty ruler would lead them, and feed them, and free them from bondage. Zealously, they tried to force Jesus to be their king. (See John

6:15) They had understood enough to follow Him and to desire His leadership, but did not understand fully what His mission was. They were "close, but yet so far away."

Jesus refused their earthly crown of honor. This confused and frustrated many of Jesus' disciples. The following day they sought for Him again. Jesus reproved them saying, "*Ye seek me, not because ye saw my miracles, but because ye did eat of the loaves, and were filled. Labour not for the meat which perisheth, but for that meat which endureth unto everlasting life, which the Son of man shall give unto you.*" (John 6:26-27)

The people asked Jesus what they needed to do, that they "might work the works of God." (John 6:28) Jesus told them simply that the thing which God required of them was that "ye believe on him whom he hath sent." (John 6:29)

The people wanted Jesus to prove that He was, indeed, whom He claimed to be. If He truly was the Son of God, then surely He was greater than Moses and should be able to do miracles mightier than those of Moses, whom they said, fed their fathers for forty years with manna. Jesus corrected them. It was not Moses, but God, who had sent the manna. Now, the Father was offering them the true bread from heaven. "*For the bread of God is he which cometh down from heaven, and giveth life unto the world...I am the bread of life: he that cometh unto me shall never hunger; and he that believeth on me shall never thirst.*" (John 6:33,35. See also John6:51, 53-56)

Many of His followers didn't understand this doctrine, saying "*This is an hard saying; who can hear it?*" Jesus responded, "*It is the spirit that quickeneth; the flesh profiteth nothing: the words which I speak unto you, they are spirit and they are life... No man can come unto me except it were given unto him of my Father.*" And, "*from that time many of his disciples went back, and walked no more with him.*" (John 6:60, 63, 65- 66) They had understood only with their eyes, rather than the heart, the significance of the miracle Jesus performed.

We live in a world of counterfeits which imitate so closely in their appearance the real thing that many are easily fooled. There are those who purchase counterfeit goods thinking that there really is such a small difference, that it doesn't really matter anyway. While this may be true of a piece of clothing or a bottle of perfume, it is not true in spiritual things. A counterfeit ticket will not guarantee a seat in the arena to see the ball game, any more than a counterfeit system can take us to heaven. Today we are being bombarded by many worldly philosophies which dangerously approximate the truth; philosophies which are "so close, and yet so far away." Satan, the master of deceit, masterfully intermingles truth with other philosophies to appeal to the senses of men.

There are many who accept Christ and His gospel, but with some reservation. They readily accept His message, but reject Him as the Son of God. One publicly declares that a belief in Christ's teachings of the brotherhood of man is the way to world peace, but privately does not believe that men are truly brothers. Another advocates and teaches the saving and eternal doctrines Jesus taught, but his heart cannot unconditionally accept Jesus as the Savior and Son of God, for, he says, "that would place Christ above himself and who knows but what another may come tomorrow who will teach things even greater." Others praise Jesus as a great teacher and spiritual leader, but deny His divinity. There are still others who have established their personal lists of the doctrines they are willing to accept and lists of other commandments they are not willing to embrace. They profess to believe, crying, 'Lord, Lord,' but fail to reflect in their daily lives His teachings. Most of us recognize that it is much easier to profess than to live His teachings. It is much easier to "be in the church" than to have the "church in us." However, the closer we come to living His doctrine, the more we come to understand who Jesus really was.

Society is filled with people willing to offer guidance, counsel and advice. Shelves are filled with self-help books. And, in our yearning for for the "quick fix" to our problems, these solutions can be very appealing, but often may be like the antibiotic which almost worked. The symptoms subside or may even go away for a while, but eventually come back, and often are more severe than before.

Solutions for the problems and conflicts in our lives which come directly from God, the fountain of truth, who knows us better than anyone, are not "quick fixes" but lasting solutions.

I have found that God's answers are generally quite simple. They may be a few words whispered to the mind, a thought or idea from a church meeting, a passage of scripture or conference talk which seems to jump from the page into the heart.

These answers are sometimes so simple that one may wonder, "Why didn't I think of that?" Or, perhaps, like Naaman, the leper, who was told to wash himself in the Jordan River, some may tend to underestimate or discount the solutions. The remedy the prophet Elisha gave to Naaman seemed so simplistic and foolish that, at first, Naaman chose to ignore it. (See 2 Kings 5:1-14) Some may even take credit for the idea as being their own.

Another challenging aspect of receiving solutions from the Lord is that, generally, these solutions need to be "taken with a good dose of humility," for pride impedes their application and diminishes their effectiveness, much like a medication which needs to be taken on an empty stomach to achieve its full effect.

The Lord's solutions usually require some work or effort on our part; somewhat like "physical therapy" which can at times be painful and difficult. Jesus taught that those who would "*do*" God's will would "*know*" of the doctrine. (See John 7:17) Often there must be a good deal of "living of doctrine" before the "understanding of doctrine" comes.

It is not only foolish, but also dangerous to not follow directions on a prescribed medication. It is equally hazardous spiritually to think that anyone is free to pick and choose to obey only the commandments which are the easiest or most convenient. Just as an antibiotic needs to be taken in its entirety , so the gospel must be lived in its fullness. If God had felt that we could live sufficiently well with only a partial knowledge of the truth, he never would have restored the fullness of the gospel to the earth.

The solutions which come from the Lord, pinpoint directly the problem and give an exact solution. It is interesting to note that David, Moses and the brother of Jared each had a very different problem. David's problem was Goliath. Moses needed to provide water for a thirsting people, and the brother of Jared needed light for his barges. For each of them, part of the prescribed solution involved a rock. It was the way each rock was used to resolve the problem which differed. David's rocks and sling wouldn't have done Moses much good to provide water for the Israelites. The rock which Moses used may have sunk the Jaredite barges. The Lord knows exactly our needs, and offers always the exact solution. If taken as prescribed, these God-given solutions not only effectively treat ailments, but often change lives for the better. Sometimes, they may not take away the problem, but instead, alleviate suffering and give needed strength. They may help us to increase faith and patience; enable us to see with clearer perspective; or help us to be more grateful, compassionate, or understanding.

Jesus taught, "*This is the bread which cometh down from heaven, that a man may eat thereof, and not die. I am the living bread which came down from heaven: if any man eat of this bread, he shall live for ever:*" (John 6:50-51)

Practically speaking, what did Jesus mean by this ? The eternal sense of this statement is that "*there is none other way nor name given under heaven whereby man can be saved in the kingdom of God.*" (2 Nephi 31:21) But, what does His message mean for our day to day lives; the here and the now?

To eat of the bread of life, is to believe in and accept Jesus Christ as the literal Son of God, the Savior of the world, without reservation; to strive with the "whole soul" to apply the gospel principles in our daily lives; and obey His commandments.

Jesus taught "*And this is life eternal, to know thee the only true God, and Jesus Christ, whom thou hast sent.*" (John 17:3) At first glance this seems pretty simple, but John counsels, "*And hereby we do know that we know him, if we keep his commandments.*" (1 John 2:3)

One of my favorite scripture stories is in Luke 24. It takes place shortly after Jesus' resurrection. on the road to Emmaus. Two of his disciples were traveling along the road, talking about Jesus' death, when He appeared to them. "*But their eyes were holden that they should know him not.*" (Luke 24:16) Jesus asked them why they were so sad. They were surprised and asked, "*Art thou only a stranger in Jerusalem, and hast not known the things which are come to pass?*" Then they related to him the awful things which had occurred, and said, "*But we trusted that it had been he which should have redeemed Israel.*" After talking with them for a while, Jesus said, "*O fools and slow of heart to believe all that the prophets have spoken.*" Then, "*beginning at Moses and the prophets, he expounded unto them in all the scriptures the things concerning himself.*" (See Luke 24:18-27)

These were men who once had "*known*" Jesus, had listened to his teachings and had followed him. But, now, they didn't recognize him. Here they were, so close to the one whom they had followed and loved, but yet so far away. Impressed by his teachings, they asked him to stay with them. When He sat down to eat with them, He took bread and blessed it. "*Their eyes were then opened and they knew him; and he vanished out of their sight. And they said one to another, did not our heart burn with in us, while he talked with us by the way, and when he opened to us the scriptures?*" (See Luke 24:13-32) That day, they came to *know* Jesus not only with their eyes and ears, but with their hearts.

Following His discourse on the bread of life, knowing that many had now rejected Him and His doctrine, Jesus asked the twelve, "*Will ye also go away?*" Peter answered for all of them, "*Lord, to whom shall we go? thou hast the words of eternal life. And we believe and are sure that thou art that Christ, the Son of the living God.* " (John 6: 67-69)

Jesus is the Promised Messiah, the Savior, and Son of God. He is the life, the truth and the way. (See John 14:6) No one can come unto the Father but through Him. There is no other path, no other person, no other doctrine, no other way.

LIVING BREAD

Nephi didn't say devour,
Or munch, or chew, or gnaw.
He measured his words carefully
A metaphor to draw.

He didn't say to nibble,
To snack, or graze, or piece,
To gulp, or gorge, or gobble.
The word he chose was "feast."

He recognized the words of Christ
Are bounteous and grand--
By feasting we internalize,
And come to understand,

How delicious are His teachings
Souls are gratified and fed
By living truths which perish not
His Word — Our Living Bread.

Sharon Velluto

DO I HUNGER AFTER RIGHTEOUSNESS?

Do I hunger after righteousness?
Do I feast upon the word?
Do I thirst for living water
Offered freely by the Lord?

Do I feel the yearning Mary felt
To seek the needful thing?
Do I relish Holy Scripture?
Do I long to know the King?

Am I awed and honored by
His invitation,"Come to me."
'To share His yoke... To take His name...'
Do those thoughts humble me?

Do I approach the table
To partake of broken bread
With humble spirit, contrite heart,
A longing to be fed?

Is my store of oil sufficient,
My lamp burning and well-trimmed?
And does the flame which flickers there
Reflect belief in Him?

Do I praise Him for His mercy,
For His sacrifice, His love?
Do I hunger after righteousness?
Not enough.--- no, not enough!

Sharon Velluto

Scripture Muffins

3/4 cup	2 Nephi 26:25......	(milk)
1/2 cup	1 Kings 17:12.......	(oil)
1	Isaiah 10:14........	(egg)
2 cups	1 Kings 4:22.........	(flour)
1/2 cup	Jeremiah 6:20......	(sugar)
1 1/2 tsp	Amos 4:5..............	(baking powder)
1/2 tsp	1 Corinthians 4:6....	(baking soda)
1 tsp	Mark 9:50............	(salt)
1 cup	Proverbs 7:2.........	(grated apple or applesauce)

Fill muffin cups 2/3 full. Bake at 400 degrees for 18-20 minutes.

These recipes are to be used with Activity Idea # 3, page 41

Scripture Cookies

3/4 cup	Judges 5:25..............	(butter)
1/2 tsp	D&C 101:39..............	(salt)
1/2 cup	Exodus 16:31............	(honey)
1 cup	D&C 89:17................	(oatmeal)
1/2 cup	Jeremiah 6:20............	(sugar)
1 cup	1 Samuel 30:12.........	(raisins)
1	Isaiah 10:14..............	(eggs)
1/2 cup	Numbers 17:8...........	(almonds)
2 & 1/2 Cup	1 Kings 4:22............	(flour)
1/2 tsp	1 Kings 10:10...........	(nutmeg_
1/2 tsp	1 Corinthians 4:6.......	(baking soda)
1 tsp	Amos 4:5..................	(baking powder)

Drop by teaspoon onto a greased cookie sheet and flatten slightly. Bake at 375 degrees for 10-12 minutes. But first read History of Joseph Smith 1:37 and D&C 133:11

ADDITIONAL REFERENCES

2 Kings 5:1-14..........	Naaman the leper is cleansed
Psalms 51..................	David pleads to be made clean
Isaiah 1:16-20..........	Israel commanded to become clean
Isaiah 12:3...............	With joy draw water from the well
Isaiah 55:1................	Come and drink; salvation is free (See also 2 Nephi 9:50)
John 3:1-7...............	Jesus explains baptism to Nicodemus
John 5:3-9................	A man waiting for the moving of the water is healed
John 4:5-42.............	Jesus teaches a Samaritan woman at the well
John 6:53-63...........	How a man can eat and drink of Christ's flesh and blood
1 Corinthians 1-6....	Drink of the spiritual drink
Titus 3:4-7..............	We are saved by the washing of regeneration
Revelation 7:17.........	The Lamb shall feed them and lead them to living waters
Revelation 22:17.......	Whosoever will, let him take the water of life freely
1 Nephi 11:25...........	The fountain of living water is a representation of the love of God
Mosiah 3;18.............	Men drink damnation unless they humble themselves
Moroni 7:10-24.........	Moroni explains bitter and good fountains
D&C 10:62-67..........	An invitation to partake of the waters of life
D&C 63:23...............	The obedient will be given the mysteries
D&C 133:29.............	In deserts found pools of living water

Old Testament Stories

The Israelites in the Wilderness
Forty Years In The Wilderness
The Prophet Elisha: Three Miracles (Third Miracle)

CAN YOU IMAGINE?

Blessed are they which do hunger and thirst after righteousness; for they shall be filled. (See Matthew 5:6)

Can you imagine an announcement read from the pulpit one Sunday morning of a change in policy; that members would be able to partake of the sacrament only one week during the year? What do you imagine might happen? Wards would probably announce the event for months in advance. Home teachers and visiting teachers would also carry the message. It is likely that this meeting would be better attended that even Mother's Day, Christmas or Easter. There would probably be a feeling of reverence not previously felt during the sacrament.

Can you imagine what might happen if a similar announcement were read, stating that the Church had sufficient funds and the sacred opportunity of paying tithing would be limited to only a small percentage of the membership? Anyone interested in having this opportunity should give written request of participation to their bishop within the week. Can you imagine how our perception of the law of tithing may change?

Can you imagine a testimony meeting where no one was allowed to stand and voice the feelings in their hearts, but instead, had to remain sitting to meditate for the full meeting? How many would feel in their hearts something pulling them to their feet, to express their personal testimony to others?

Such suppositions are preposterous and absurd, because each of them involves sacred blessings which come to members who are faithful and obedient in living the precepts of the gospel.

Yet, when God's children choose to ignore commandments or fail to recognize the hand of the Lord, these blessings are often withheld from them. The prophet Jeremiah understood the pain and longing which come from being unable to bear testimony. Because of the hardness of the hearts of his people, for a time he refrained from bearing testimony. His words are poignant. *"Oh Lord...I am in derision daily, every one mocketh me. For since I spake, I cried out, I cried violence and spoil; because the word of the Lord was made a reproach unto me, and a derision, daily. Then I said, I will not make mention of him, nor speak any more in his name. But his word was in mine heart as a burning fire shut up in my bones, and I was weary with forbearing, and I could not stay."* (Jeremiah 20:7-9)

President Joseph Fielding Smith wrote, "*We should fully and sincerely comprehend the fact that no requirement, request, or commandment made of man by the Father or Son is given except for the purpose of advancing man on the path of eternal perfection. Never at any time has the Lord given to man a commandment which was not intended to exalt him and bring him nearer to eternal companionship with the Father and the Son. Too many of us receive the commandments of the Lord in the spirit of indifference or with the attitude of mind toward them that they have been given for the sole purpose of depriving us of some comfort or pleasure without any real profit to be derived in the observance of them.*

"Every covenant, contract, bond, obligation, and commandment we have received by revelation and coming from the Almighty has the one purpose in view, the exaltation and perfection of the individual who will in full faith and obedience accept it. He that receiveth a commandment with doubtful heart, and keepeth it with slothfulness, the same is damned,' (D&C 58:29) the Lord has said. Unfortunately there are a great many who receive covenants in that way." (*Doctrines of Salvation*, Salt Lake City: Bookcraft, volume 1, pages. 155-56)

Spiritually speaking, when there is a banquet constantly spread before us, we have a tendency to piece a little here and there, but not to "feast." We have a tendency to be complacent, even take for granted the bounteous blessings of the gospel. It seems there is great difficulty in ease. Much strength is derived from the struggle to gain root. Often spiritual things become habit, which in some ways is good. But, when one stops being appreciative of these sacred opportunities and blessings, or becomes negligent in fulfilling his responsibilities, he will be held accountable for it.

Many prophets have admonished us to be careful of ease. Amos wrote, " *Woe unto them that are at ease in Zion...*" (Amos 6:1) And Alma similarly admonished, "*Do not let us be slothful because of the easiness of the way; for so it was with our fathers.*" (Alma 37:46)

Israel had been repeatedly admonished to repent and turn to the Lord. During their difficulties, they tended to be more obedient, but during times of ease, they became complacent and neglected the counsel of the prophets and the law of the Lord. Lehi, Isaiah, Jeremiah and many other prophets testified of the destruction of Jerusalem. But things were going well for the people. They were a prosperous and strong nation, and disbelieved the words of the prophets. However, just as the prophets had said, Jerusalem was overthrown, their sacred temple spoiled and Israel was scattered and taken into bondage.

For almost seventy years the Israelites served as slaves, first to the Assyrians and then to the Babylonians who conquered Syria, and established a world empire.

Jeremiah had prophesied, that after seventy years of Babylonian captivity the Jews would be gathered again to rebuild their homeland. To the Jews, Jeremiah's prophecy probably seemed as unlikely as the prophecies foretelling their destruction. Now, they were a small, weak and impoverished nation surrounded by large and powerful countries. How could they possibly expect that this prophecy would be fulfilled? But, with God, all things are possible. (See Matthew 19:26, Mark 10:27, Luke 18:27)

In Persia, about 550 BC, a great leader by the name of Cyrus, in just ten years had become master over the Median empire and began moving westward conquering one nation after another. When he came against Babylon, they opened their gates to his armies, and surrendered to them without even a battle.

For two centuries, Persia was the most powerful state in the world. But, Cyrus was a merciful king, unlike the rulers which Israel had previously known. He began a policy of treating those subject to him with consideration, instead of tyrannizing them, or holding them in subjection by force. People under his rule were loyal because they liked Cyrus and trusted him. Thus, his was a reign of peace. Cyrus was particularly sympathetic to the religions of conquered people.

Nearly one hundred and forty years before the destruction of the temple in Jerusalem, Isaiah had prophesied, "*That saith of Cyrus, He is my shepherd, and shall perform all my pleasure: even saying to Jerusalem, Thou shalt be built and to the temple, Thy foundation shall be laid. Thus saith the Lord to his anointed, to Cyrus, whose right hand I have holden, to subdue nations before him; and I will loose the loins of the kings to open before him the two leaved gates; and the gates shall not be shut.*" (Isaiah 44:28-45:1)

Can you imagine what Cyrus must have felt when he read this prophesy, which called him by name, and told him that he had been called of God to perform this great work?

Cyrus was so impressed with Isaiah's prophecy, that he determined to see it fulfilled. He made a declaration: "*Thus saith Cyrus king of Persia, The Lord God of heaven hath given me all the kingdoms of the earth; and he hath charged me to build him an house at Jerusalem, which is in Judah. Who is there among you of all his people? his God be with him, and let him go to Jerusalem,... and build the house of the Lord God of Israel, (he is the God,) which is in Jerusalem.*" (Ezra 1:2-3)

Wilford Woodruff wrote, "*To trace the life of Cyrus from his birth to his death, whether he knew it or not, it looked as though he lived by inspiration in all his movements.*" (*Journal of*

Discourses, London: Latter-day Saints Book Depot, 1854-86 vol. 22, p. 207 See also President Ezra Taft Benson, *Ensign* July 1972, pp.59-60)

The seemingly impossible had happened. The Jews were not only free to gather and rebuild their city and temple, but had the physical and monetary support of the most powerful king in the world. About forty to fifty thousand Jews went to Jerusalem, but the majority of them remained in Persia. When they arrived in Jerusalem, they found it inhabited by the Samaritans, who were a remnant of Israel who had intermarried with the Assyrians and adopted many of their pagan beliefs. Israel struggled constantly with the Samaritans who opposed the rebuilding of the city, and for nearly fifteen years ceased in their labors because of these difficulties. The Jews were discouraged that this temple was not as elegantly adorned as the first, and it lacked many essential things such as the Ark of the Covenant, and the glory of the Lord. Many who remembered the first temple, were 'disconsolate' and wept in discouragement. (See Ezra 3:12-13 and *The Life and Works of Flavius Josephus Antiquities of the Jews*, book.. 11, chapter.4, paragraph .2)

Many thought it more important to begin to rebuild their homes, and to earn money for their own livelihood than to spend their time, money and energy in rebuilding the Lord's house. Their land was struck with a great famine. The prophet Haggai declared, "*Now therefore thus saith the Lord of hosts; Consider your ways, Ye have sown much and bring in little; ye eat, but ye have not enough; ye drink but ye are not filled with drink; ye clothe you, but there is none warm; and he that earneth wages earneth wages to put it into a bag with holes. Thus saith the Lord of hosts; Consider your ways. Go up to the mountain, and build the house; and I will take pleasure in it, and I will be glorified saith the Lord.*" (Haggai 1:5-8)

God assured the people, that their obedience to His commandments was of more importance than the splendor of the building. (See Haggai 2:3-9)

The Israelites took heart and began again to work on the temple. It was completed exactly seventy years after the destruction of the first temple, just as Jeremiah had prophesied. Psalm 48 is a song, or poem, which celebrates the restoration of Jerusalem.

With the permission of the Persians, Israel established a theocratic government, run by priests. However, the Israelites had lived for so long among the Babylonians and Persians, that they had intermarried and adopted many of the pagan beliefs. Ezra, Nehemiah and the prophets were now faced with the challenge of renewing covenants, and cleansing the apostates from among the people. "*Ezra had prepared his heart to seek the law of the Lord, and to do it, and to teach in Israel statutes and judgments.*" (Ezra 7:10)

Many of the scriptures had been lost or destroyed during the Babylonian captivity, and Ezra began the painstaking task of gathering all of the scriptures he could find and determining which version was the most correct. The people gathered "*as one man,*" in the streets to hear the word read to them. Most had never had the opportunity to hear the law. Ezra stood on some type of pulpit, above the people, and opened the book. The entire congregation stood and praised the Lord. The law was read from "*morning to midday*" and "*the ears of the people were attentive.*" (See Nehemiah 8:1-9) Upon hearing the law, they were so overcome that they wept. Some wept for joy at receiving again the law of God which had been lost to them. Some wept in sorrow for those parts of the law which had been neglected by them, and others wept because they were unable to understand what was read. There were many different languages and dialects spoken by the people and many weren't able to understand the scriptures. Ezra was a scribe, and together with other scribes, translated the scriptures into different languages so all could hear and understand the word of God in their own tongue.

Ezra realized that simply having the scriptures was not enough, they needed to be understood.

Can you imagine being deprived of temple blessings for 70 years? Can you imagine hearing the scriptures for the first time in your life?

The Lord has admonished, "*Let the solemnities of eternity rest upon your minds.*" (D&C 43:34)

President Spencer W. Kimball said, "*From the beginning, people of the world have existed in alternating light and shadow, but most of the time in the grayness or darkness of the shadows, with relatively short periods of light.*

"*The Lord is eager to see their first awakening desires and their beginning efforts to penetrate the darkness. Having granted freedom of decision, He must permit man to grope his way until he reaches for the light. But when men begin to hunger, when arms begin to reach, when knees begin to bend and voices become articulate, then and not until then does the Father push back the horizons, draw back the veil and make it possible for men to emerge from dim, uncertain stumbling to sureness in the brilliance of the heavenly light.*" ("To His Servants the Prophets," *Instructor*, August 1960, page 256. See also *The Teachings of Spencer W. Kimball,* Salt Lake: Bookcraft, 1982, page 423)

The Savior taught, "*Blessed are they which do hunger and thirst after righteousness; for they shall be filled.*" (See Matthew 5:6)

Nephi was a great example of one who possessed this thirst. He wrote, "*Having great desires to know of the mysteries of God, wherefore I did cry unto the Lord; and behold he did visit me, and did soften my heart that I did believe all the words which had been spoken by my father; wherefore I did not rebel against him like unto my brothers.*" (1 Nephi 2:16)

With similar sentiment the Psalmist wrote, "*O how I love thy law! it is my meditation all the day. Thou through thy commandments hast made me wiser than mine enemies... I have refrained my feet from every evil way, that I might keep thy word, I have not departed from thy judgments: for thou hast taught me. How sweet are thy words unto my taste! yea, sweeter than honey to my mouth! Through thy precepts I get understanding; therefore I hate every false way. Thy word is a lamp unto my feet, and a light unto my path.*" (Psalms 119:97-98, 101-105)

Do we really appreciate the blessings we have been given? Can you imagine the tables being turned? Can you imagine that you were the one living without the gospel, while your neighbor enjoyed its blessings. What if you and your ancestor, who died without the gospel, were to change places, and it was you waiting for him to complete your work? Would all the things which consume our time and energy seem as important to us? Personally, I would hope my neighbor would be more diligent in sharing the gospel than I am, and that my descendent would be more anxiously engaged in securing eternal blessings for me than I have been for them.

Elder F. Burton Howard said, "*I know now that it is not so much the haste of one's journey but rather what he does along the way which determines whether he will arrive at his destination.... Our testimonies, our greatest blessings, our membership and activity in Christ's church — all of these we owe to the often unremembered and always unnumbered hundreds who gave their time and their patience and their love to us when we were trying to find our way in the desert. They brought living water to us, or to our parents, or to our parents' parents. Whether we know it or not, whether we like it or not, whether we are grateful or not, we are where we are because of others.* (*Ensign*, May 1981, p. 72)

How fortunate we are to have available to us the blessings of the fullness of the gospel. These blessings, though offered to us freely, have been afforded us through the great, personal sacrifice of others. We should learn to better appreciate them and to let that appreciation move us to share these blessings with others.

There are rich blessings which come to those who "drink of the waters." President Marion G. Romney speaking of the blessings which come from reading the scriptures said, "*There is another reason why we should read the Book of Mormon: By doing so we will fill and refresh our minds with a constant flow of that 'water"'which Jesus said would be in us 'a well of water springing up into everlasting life.' (John 4:14) We must obtain a continuing supply of this water if we are to resist evil and retain the blessing of being born again... Drink deeply from the divine fountain itself.*

"I feel certain that if, in our homes, parents will read from the Book of Mormon prayerfully and regularly, both by themselves and with their children, the spirit of that great book will come to permeate our homes and all who dwell therein. The spirit of reverence will increase; mutual respect and consideration for each other will grow, The spirit of contention will depart. Parents will counsel their children in greater love and wisdom. Children will be more responsive and submissive to the counsel of their parents. Righteousness will increase. Faith, hope, and charity — the pure love of Christ — will abound in our homes and lives, bringing in their wake peace, joy, and happiness." (*Ensign*, May 1980, pages. 66-67)

He leads me to green pastures
And to the water's brink,
Living waters, offered freely
If I but choose to drink.

COME TO THE WELL

Come to the well and drink from its depths.
Come dip thy bucket and try
A sweet living water-- a balm to the soul,
In a vast, never-ending supply.

Come to the fountain and fill up thy cup
With water which cleanses the soul--
Water to wash away tarnish of sin,
To heal, to redeem, to make whole.

Come to the well, any soul who is parched;
Those who wander the dry arid waste.
Come to the oasis, and there quench thy thirst
With pure water — delicious to taste.

Drink of His word, learn and follow His way;
Live His truths which will bring inner peace.
Come to the well of salvation and drink
Living waters which never will cease.

Sharon Velluto

ADDITIONAL REFERENCES

Psalms 24:7.................... And the King of glory shall come in
Psalms 34:20.................. Not one of His bones shall be broken
Psalms 95:3.................... Fot the Lord is a great King
Psalms 132 :11............... The Messiah will be of lineage of David
Isaiah 6:1-5.................... Mine eyes have seen the King
Isaiah 9:6........................ And the government shall be upon his shoulders
Isaiah 43:15.................... I am the Lord.. your Holy One... the creator..your King
Jeremiah 10:10............... The Lord is a true God, a living God and an everlasting King
Daniel 2:44..................... The God of heaven shall set up a kingdom
Zechariah 14:9................ The Lord shall be king over the earth
Malachi 1:14................... I am a great King saith the Lord
Matthew 25:34................ Then shall the King say... Come ye blessed of my Father
Matthew 27:11................ Pilate asks, Art thou the King of the Jews?
(See also Mark 15:2, Luke 23:3, John 18:33)
John 1:49........................ Nathanael receives a witness that Jesus is the King of Israel
Acts 17:1-9..................... People are angered when Paul teaches there is another
1 Timothy 1:17............... Unto the King eternal be honor and glory
1 Timothy 6:15............... Jesus Christ will reign as King of kings, and Lord of lords
Mosiah 3:5...................... Lord Omnipotent dwell in tabernacle of clay
Alma 5:50....................... Behold the glory of the King
D&C 29:11...................... I will dwell in righteousness 1000 years
(See also D&C 43:29,76:63)
D&C 45:53-59................ The Lord shall come in glory to be their king and lawgiver
D&C 76:22-23................ Joseph and Sidney Rigdon bear testimony of Jesus
D&C 128:22-23............... Let the heavens and earth praise the Eternal King

Article of Faith 10 Christ will reign on earth

Old Testament Stories
The Prophets Tell About Jesus

New Testament Stories
Before The New Testament

Book Of Mormon Stories
Jesus Christ Comes To America

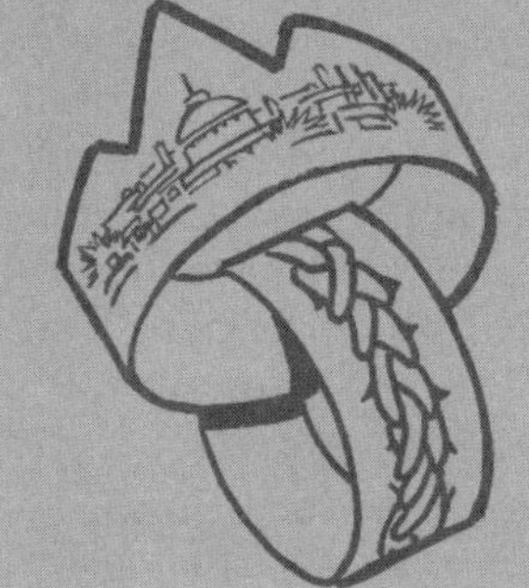

NATHANAEL AND THE PREACHER

Jesus saith unto him, I am the way, the truth, and the life; no man cometh unto the Father, but by me. (John 14:6)

"You're very late, Nathanael."

"I know," the boy answered.

"I was worried. I expected you back hours ago."

"I know. I'm sorry, Mother," he said. The boy's dark eyes seemed to be focused on something distant and uncertain. He set the burlap wrapped parcel on the rough wooden table. Sweat beaded on the boy's forehead. His face was gaunt and pale.

"You got the fish?"

The boy nodded.

"You shouldn't spend so much time by the sea. The wind and the chill are not good for you," the woman said, pushing a coarse graying strand of hair away from her face with the back of her hand. She continued kneading the mass of dough.

"I know," said the boy. "but there was a man there at the shore today. A man not like any other I have yet seen."

His mother stopped kneading and looked up, a tired expression on her face. She looked far older than she actually was. Life had been hard and had taken its toll. "What sort of man?" she asked suspiciously.

The boy hesitated and began, "There was a crowd, a huge crowd of people. He tried to talk above the crowd but there was too much confusion, and no one could hear. Everyone was reaching out to touch him, be close to him. So, he got in a boat. It was his friend's boat, I guess. He cast out, a short distance from the shore and taught the people. There were scores of them. They sat on the hot bank or stood along the shore in the scorching sun listening to him teach for well over an hour."

The woman continued kneading as she listened to her son. He was a sickly boy, and perhaps she was overly concerned with his health, overly protective. He was nearly seventeen now, but looked much younger. The boy had dark curly hair and was of very slight frame. His bony knees and elbows protruded from under his worn cloak.

The boy paused and looked at his mother. "Mother," he asked, "do you believe in the Messiah?"

The woman bristled, as if an old wound had been opened. She sighed, "I used to, Nathanael. But,..." she paused, " I'm not certain what I believe any more."

"But the prophets, Mother... The prophets have all testified of Him."

The woman was silent as she searched for words to explain. Finally, she began. "Nathanael, about thirty years ago, I guess, someone began a rumor, a rumor of shepherds seeing angels. Angels which told them the King had been born. The Messiah had come. For a while, there was a feeling among our people... a fire of hope which burned in everyone's heart. Imagine, the Messiah born, and living among us. Perhaps it was the star, that bright new star in the sky that caused some of the commotion. So many centuries had passed since the prophets began to testify of Him. And angels. No one had admitted to seeing angels for nearly four hundred years. Everyone was talking about it, discussing it, arguing about it.

At the well. At the market. Everywhere we went. Some believed. Some didn't." She shaped the dough into a ball and laid a clean white cloth on top of it. She wiped her hands on a towel and sat down beside her son at the table.

"Well," she went on, "that rumor worried Herod, the tetrarch." She paused and looked at him. "He was a wicked man, Nathanael, a more wicked man I have never seen. At least, I guess that's what caused him to do it."

"Do what, Mother?" Her eyes glistened with both rage and pain. Her voice was sharp. "He ordered all the baby boys two years and younger to be slain. Your brother was three, but he was small like you. The soldiers didn't believe me. They slaughtered them all. They..." Her voice broke and she stopped, unable to go on. She buried her head into her arms and wept.

Both were silent for a long while.

"Mother," the boy finally began, "today, after that man finished teaching, he told his friend to cast into the sea for a draught of fish. His friend argued with him. Said they had been out all night and hadn't taken anything. They had just finished cleaning those big nets. And he looked really tired. The teacher didn't say anything, just looked his friend in the eye. So his friend finally agreed, and said if that's what he wanted him to do, he would do it. So they cast out into the sea, not even a furlong, and the preacher called to them to let down their nets. Mama, when they did, there were so many fish that they couldn't lift them up. They tried to drag them to the shore, but the nets broke. So they called to their friends and filled another boat clear full of fish also. Both boats began to sink. His friends were stupefied. They all just looked at each other and then at the preacher. We were all surprised. Everyone was surprised. The preacher's friend fell to his knees and cried, 'Depart from me, for I am a sinful man.' Then the man said something about 'Follow me and I will make you great fishermen." They just left their nets, the fish and everything and followed him."

Again there was silence. "Nathanael," the woman began gently, "don't believe everything you see."

"But, Mother, I saw it with my own eyes."

"Nathanael, not all men are honest. They have ways. Ways to trick young, gullible minds like yours. Just don't believe everything you see. That's all."

She stood up, unwrapped the fish, and began to gut them. "The fish are fresh," she said, absentmindedly.

"Yes, Mama," he returned, with a knowing nod. His eyebrows were drawn together as he pondered the curious event. Seeing his mother's solemn expression, he decided to change the subject. "Mother," he asked, "did I have other brothers?"

She shook her head. "No," she said, "you had three sisters. One died at birth, and one died with a fever."

"And what about the other one?" he asked.

His mother had never talked of these things before. Her face was etched with pain and anger. She sighed deeply and began, "She went to get water at the well. She was only twelve. She stayed a long time, and didn't come back. Your father went to look for her. He found her broken body by the well. Your father carried her back home. She was delirious. Kept saying, 'Romans. Help me. Roman soldiers.' Your father was beside himself. He left that night, perhaps to seek revenge. I never found out what happened to him. He never returned."

The woman picked up the cleaned fish, and carried them outdoors. Nathanael followed her. She dropped the fish one by one onto the glowing red coals. They sizzled and popped.

"Yes," she said with a distant look in her eyes. "I used to believe in a Messiah. I even thought with the star and the rumor and all, that maybe he had come. But, Nathanael, we are still in bondage to these cursed Romans. Nothing has changed. Didn't the prophecy say the Messiah would be our deliverer -- that he would free us? The prophets said that Messiah would be a mighty ruler, a king who would establish peace. Just because someone guesses where the fish are swimming, well, that doesn't make him a king now, does it?

Nathanael, shook his head. "No, I guess it doesn't. But Mother, they say..." He stopped, sensing it was best not to continue this conversation.

They ate their meal in silence. The boy pondered the miracle he had witnessed, while his mother sat silent, fighting back bitter tears and angry thoughts which had festered through these many years, locked tightly and carefully inside.

They didn't speak much for the remainder of the evening. The boy rose early the next morning, and quietly left before his mother awoke. He returned late at night and said nothing. In the days and weeks that followed, Nathanael became increasingly illusive and quiet. His mother suspected, but never dared talk to him about the strange preacher, fearing she may distance her son even more. One night Nathanael didn't return home. His mother was sick with worry. She watched and waited all the next day, hoping and praying that her son, her only son would return home safely. Late that night he crept into the house and crawled into bed. The woman pulled the woolen blankets up to her face to muffle the sobs. Sobs of relief, and sorrow, and fear; fear that she was losing her only son to an unknown preacher.

Finally, she heard his relaxed and rhythmic breathing and she too fell into a deep sleep.

Early the next morning, his mother awoke just as Nathanael was leaving. "Nathanael," she said quietly through the darkness. The boy turned with a start.

"I didn't want to wake you." he said.

"Nathanael, I worry about you."

"I am well enough off, Mother." he assured her.

"Where is it that you have been these days?" she asked.

"The teacher, Mother. I have been following the rabbi."

"Nathanael, why don't you spend this day with me. We haven't talked much for so long. I need your company today."

Nathanael turned and came back into the house. He laid his cloak on the bed and sat at the table. "All right," he said. "If you wish."

His mother looked relieved, and smiled warmly at him. She rose and pulled a shawl about her shoulders and shivered." "It is cold this morning," she said. "Perhaps it is best you stay home today. They sky is cloudy, it looks like it will rain."

Nathanael sat quietly as his mother prepared something to eat. She put four small loaves of bread onto the table, some sweet curds and a small bit of fresh honey. "The bread is fresh," she said. "I baked it yesterday. I traded some for honey at the market. I hoped you would stay with me today." She looked at him and smiled warmly.

The woman sat, bowed her head and gave thanks for the food. Then, Nathanael began to eat hungrily. "Nathanael," she began, "tell me about this preacher."

"His name is Jesus. He comes from Nazareth."

"From Nazareth?" she asked, "Why then is he in Capernaum?"

"He travels all over, Mama, to teach. He teaches a different doctrine. Different from the Scribes, or the Pharisees, anyway. His manner is so gentle, yet he so is strong." He paused to think for a moment. "Mother, he seems to know more, so much more than anyone I've ever heard. I listen to his stories, and I understand, but I sense there are many things I do not understand, something much deeper. You know," the boy said, "Perhaps, it is not so much what he teaches, but how I feel when I listen to him. Mother, I feel that he is teaching the truth, something even higher than the law. He lives what he teaches. And, -- he has power. God's power."

The woman chewed and swallowed a piece of bread. "What do you mean?" she asked.

"Just yesterday, he was in someone's house teaching. I was without the door trying to hear. I couldn't get in. The crowd was too big. No one else could enter the house. I saw four men carrying a bed, with a sick man on it. They tried to push past the people but no one would move to let them through, so they climbed the stairs to the roof, and began to tear the thatch and tiling from the roof. The Master stopped teaching and looked up. The men lowered the man down through the hole. I heard the Master say in a loud voice, 'Son, thy sins be forgiven thee.' Then he told the man to take up his couch and walk. And he did. Mama, the man got off his couch, picked it up and he walked right past me. His friends came down from the roof shouting for joy. The Pharisees were angry. Said the preacher had blasphemed God. But, I think they are really angry that many of their own followers are leaving to follow this man."

"Nathanael," the woman looked at her son with pleading eyes. "Can't you see that this all could be set up. Prearranged."

"No, Mother," the boy argued. "I don't think so. That man was sick. I could see. And then he was well. And he left glorifying God."

"Nathanael," I have seen men act.."

"No, Mother. Some weeks ago, another man came to him, a leper. His skin crawled with festering sores, his flesh and hair were yellow. His nails had fallen off, and his nose and ears and teeth had all begun to rot away. Mother, he was the walking dead. He cried, 'Unclean,' as he approached. We all moved back. But the preacher,... he did not move. There was an incredible stench about this man as he drew near. He fell at the Rabbi's feet and cried, 'Lord, if thou wilt, thou canst make me clean.' And the Master stood there quietly for a moment, looking upon him with deep compassion, and then replied, 'I will. Be thou clean.' The man remained there, kneeling at the Master's feet, as if he were utterly drained of strength, and hope. Immediately, the loathsome sores quit weeping and began to shrink. As we watched, Mama. As we watched. The crowd gathered around him and we all watched. The man knelt there and held out his arms in front of him, turning them back and forth in the sun to look at them. He watched the sores shrink and disappear .In just a few moments they were gone. He was clean! You should have seen his eyes, Mother, as he watched his own flesh become clean again. He put his hands to his face, and felt his mouth, and his nose and his ears. They were healed. His teeth and gums, were completely restored. His nose and ears were whole again. The leprosy was gone. He began to cry, and to tremble and to praise God. It wasn't acting, Mama. It wasn't a trick."

Nathanael looked into his mother's eyes. "The Master is good and kind."

His mother sat silent, studying the intent expression on her son's face. They heard a noise in the distance, which grew louder and louder. They both hurried outside the house so they could see. Far down the dusty road, Nathanael and his mother could see a large crowd of people approaching. "It is the Master!" Nathanael exclaimed.

A bearded man in a simple robe approached their house. He seemed a most ordinary man. A more ordinary man the woman had never seen. The preacher hesitated for a brief moment and looked at Nathanael. The woman noticed immediately the man's eyes. There was something in his eyes. She turned to watch Nathanael's reaction. He turned to her and asked, "Mother, may I go? May I follow him?"

His mother nodded reluctantly, and watched as her son joined the crowd.

Nathanael didn't return for several days.

When he finally came home, he looked weary but peaceful; his countenance and demeanor so serene that his mother hesitated to talk with him.

"Nathanael," she began, "I'd like us to move to Nain, to be near my sister. It would do you good. It is twenty miles away from this lake. It would be warmer there, less humid."

"But, Mother,..." Nathanael protested.

"Please Nathanael," she pleaded.

He sat quietly and then sadly nodded his head in agreement.

"Tomorrow," she said. "We will leave tomorrow."

Neither the woman or Nathanael talked of the preacher again. The days and weeks passed. Nathanael seemed distant and withdrawn. He seemed more feeble and lethargic than the woman had ever seen him. She encouraged him to go out, to meet people, but he seemed uninterested.

One morning he lay listless in his bed. The woman called to him to get up. He only moaned and rolled to his side. She walked to his bed and laid a hand on his forehead, "Nathanael?" He was hot, so hot. She bathed a rag in water and laid it on his forehead. She soaked another rag and bathed his thin arms, again and again. His hollow eyes stared blankly at her. She held a cup to his lips to make him drink, but the water just trickled out of his mouth and rolled down the side of his face. She covered him with an extra blanket and ran out the door to her sister's house.

"Nathanael.., " she cried. "He is sick. Very sick. Please go find someone to help."

The woman hurried back to Nathanael's side. His breathing was shallow and irregular. "Oh, Nathanael," the woman choked, the tears running freely down her cheeks. "You are all that I have. You are the only earthly thing I possess which is important to me." She sobbed. "I thought to save you from being hurt by the preacher, and brought you here. But... Oh, Nathanael, what have I done?" She lifted his chin toward her face. "Look at me. Nathanael, please look at me."

The boy did not respond. He was struggling now for breath. His eyes opened wide. He gave a final sigh and shuddered. His body relaxed and went limp.

"Nathanael!" the woman screamed and threw herself on top of her son. "No, Nathanael, No."

When her sister and the physician entered the tiny room, they found the woman, hunched in a ball on the floor beside his bed, his bony hand pressed to her cheek. She sobbed uncontrollably, "My son. I have killed my only son! I tried to spare him hurt and I have killed him!"

The woman's sister prepared the body for burial, and the mourners gathered at the small house for the funeral procession. The woman walked blindly at the end of the procession, her face veiled. She leaned against her sister for support, as they trudged toward the burial plot which was to hold her son's frail body.

The procession stopped as they reached the gates of the city. "What is it?" the woman asked. Her sister replied, "There is a large crowd gathered without the gate. We will wait until they pass." The woman bowed her head, her body racked with great gulping sobs. As the crowd passed, the woman felt a hand on her arm and she looked up. It was the man, the preacher. She looked into his eyes and quickly looked away in shame and grief, choking back the bitter sobs.

"Weep not," he said, his voice calm and comforting.

He walked to the bier and looked upon her son, with a kindness and compassion she had never before beheld, and said in a firm voice, "Young man, I say unto thee, arise."

The boy coughed once, and began to breathe, a deep gulping breath followed by quick shallow breathing. The men carrying the bier placed it on the ground, and stepped back, watching in amazement. The boy sat up. A bewildered look crossed his face. He looked about and his eyes met those of the preacher. "Master," he exclaimed. "Master."

The woman sank to her knees, in uncontrollable sobs of relief, and disbelief. She looked up into the eyes of the preacher and tried to utter her thanks, but she was too overwhelmed, and the words would not come out. The preacher looked at her and smiled, a most gentle, knowing, compassionate smile. He lifted the boy to his feet and led him to where his mother knelt. The boy bent down and tenderly wrapped his arms around his mother's shaking frame. She bathed his face with kisses and tears. The woman looked up again and caught the Master's gaze. "Thank you," she managed to whisper. "Thank you." The preacher said nothing, just nodded and looked intently upon her.

A low hushed murmur issued from the crowd. Then, the preacher quietly beckoned for them to follow him, leaving the woman and her son kneeling on the dusty road, surrounded by their family.

No one spoke or moved for quite some time. The woman cradled her son in her arms, repeating his name again and again.

Finally, they arose. Nathanael and his mother walked home silently together, the boy's frail arm supporting his mother.

The following morning, the boy arose early. His mother still slept. He shook her shoulder and quietly said, "Mother, I wish to follow the Master."

His mother nodded. "Yes," she said. "Yes.

"He started for the door. "Nathanael," she called, "There is a satchel with some fresh bread, cheese and dried fish." She pointed to the table. "Take it with you." she urged.

"Thank you, mother," he said and bent to kiss her cheek.

Nathanael returned home occasionally and his mother eagerly awaited his visits. He shared with her marvelous stories of how the blind and deaf and halt and withered had been healed just by the touch of the Lord's gentle hand. He told of multitudes being fed miraculously, of demons being cast out and how the preacher had been expelled from his own city of Nazareth. He told her the stories and parables he had heard the Master teach, and she listened with great interest.

On one trip home Nathanael and his mother made plans to journey together to Jerusalem for the Passover. They would stay with one of his mother's distant cousins, and would eat the sacred meal with them. Nathanael and his mother both hoped they would meet the preacher there, even though the city would be crowded with thousands of visitors.

Nathanael and his mother joined a large caravan which was also traveling to Jerusalem for the feast. They would be safer making the 120 mile trip in the company of others. They arrived at dusk on the fourth day of the week.

The woman's cousin, Joanna, and her husband, Jonathan, greeted Nathanael and his mother warmly. Joanna was a thin woman with long black hair and fiery eyes. Her husband was tall and a bit fairer. It seemed to Nathanael that the man wore a permanent scowl. Joanna and her husband owned a moderate house on the outskirts of the city, much more well furnished than that of Nathanael and his mother. They sat to relax and exchange small talk, and to catch up on news of recent events.

Nathanael and his mother chose not to speak of the miracle of which they had been a part, but spoke instead of their journey to Jerusalem.

Then they listened intently as Joanna excitedly described some of the events of the week. On the first day of the week, a man had ridden into Jerusalem from the way of Bethany on the back of a donkey. Masses of people had gathered within the city gates and had bowed to him, shouting praises and lauding him as the 'Son of David.' They had thrown their coats upon the ground for the animal to walk upon, just as the prophet had foretold. This had really excited the Pharisees and Priests. They were all enraged. The following day the same man had returned. He had gone to the temple and overturned all of the tables, and many of the sacrificial animals were freed. "This man, " she mused, "has caused quite a stir among the people. It served them right, though," she said, "The thieves! But, I don't understand how he thinks he has the authority to do such a thing? It's ..."

Her husband cut her off. "It is an outrage! That is what it is. The man is a trouble maker. He has been here before stirring up the people, making blasphemous remarks. He violates the sabbath and our laws of cleanliness. He claims to be the Son of the Holy God, and then pollutes himself by eating with Publicans and sinners."

Nathanael and his mother listened with interest. "I wonder if it could be the preacher," the woman said.

"You know this man?" Joanna asked.

"If it is the same man," Nathanael's mother nodded, but, sensed that it was best to offer no more.

Jonathan glared coldly at the three of them. Joanna quickly changed the subject. "You must be exhausted. Let me show you to your beds."

As she led them to their room, Joanna whispered, "Jonathan despises this man. It is best not to talk of him." Nathanael and his mother both nodded.

Early on the morning of the fifth day, the first

morning of the feast, Nathanael went out to search for the Master but saw and heard nothing of him.

Nathanael's mother and Joanna worked to prepare the Passover meal which was to be eaten that evening. Later Nathanael went with Jonathan to the temple where they both presented themselves according to custom and made the required sacrifice for the family. The Passover dinner began after the sun had set and continued well into the evening.

Early the next morning Nathanael left to see if he could locate the preacher. Generally the preacher was easy to find because of the crowds which followed him.

Nathanael didn't return all day. Around noon the sky grew dark, and a thick, eerie blackness settled over the land, and remained for three long hours. His mother worried when Nathanael still did not return.

As evening fell, Nathanael burst through the door, "Mother, they have crucified him! They have killed the Master!" he said breathlessly. "Last night at midnight, the Sanhedrin held an illegal trial, so none of us would know. They beat and flogged him. They mocked him as 'King of the Jews,' and, placed a crown of thorns on his head. He did nothing. He wouldn't say anything to defend himself. He did nothing!" The boy's face was etched with concern and pain, his eyes filled with confusion. "He is dead, Mother. The Master is dead!"

Both of them sat silent trying to comprehend what had happened. Finally, Nathanael spoke, "I don't understand. What went wrong, Mother? All of us who followed him, believed in him, to whom do we turn now? Where do we go? We believed he was the Messias."

His mother reached out and placed a hand on her son's bronzed arm. "Son," she said, her voice firm with conviction, "Jesus of Nazareth, the preacher, I believe He is the Christ. I believe He is the King we have waited for, but, somehow, I don't think that His kingdom was of this world. Nathanael, the day he freed you from death and the grave, I knew the liberation which was prophesied was different from what I had understo od it to be. I looked into his eyes and I knew. I knew that I had misunderstood the prophesies."

"My son," she continued quietly, her voice soft but filled with surety, "this man has freed the blind from worlds of darkness. He has freed the deaf from their world of silence. He has freed the withered and ailing from their prisons of pain with just his touch. Those who once begged in the streets were freed to live their life with hope. Those possessed of demons and those bound by sin, have been freed. They all have been freed. Don't you see, Son? He has not released us from Roman bondage but he has set us free. He has truly set us free. That day, as I looked upon him, I felt somehow renewed inside, and I knew this was no ordinary man. There is so much we don't understand, so much which I do not understand. But this much I know. Jesus of Nazareth, He is the Christ, Nathanael. He must be the Christ."

Nathanael sat quietly and nodded, He knew that it was as his mother said.

"Son," the woman said quietly, "We must trust that somewhere there is an answer, and we must wait patiently to find it. This man had power to restore life. He restored your life. His mission could not have ended with his death. It is the Sabbath and we can do nothing now, but on the morrow we will find an answer."

Nathanael arose at dawn the following day. He had been awake all night. He wandered the streets aimlessly as he pondered what had happened. He wondered why would God send His Son, and allow Him to be murdered? Now, his direction, his anchor, had been stripped from him. Where was he to go now? What was he to do? He felt lost and bewildered. He sat on a rock near the well. The boy noticed that several people were already leaving Jerusalem. It seemed strange for them to be leaving even before the feast of unleavened bread was finished. Otherwise the streets were quiet.

Several women hurried past him. He recognized one of them as a follower. He had been a guest once in her house. They were excitedly discussing something and hurried by, not even noticing him. Nathanael jumped up. "Wait," he called.

The women turned and looked at him blankly. Then the light of recognition crept across her face. "Nathanael," the woman greeted him warmly. She was intensely happy. Her face was glowing. The boy searched for words to express the questions which weighed heavily on his mind.

"Nathanael," she burst out, "He is risen! The Lord is risen from the dead! We have seen him, Nathanael! Early this morning. The tomb was empty, and He was there! He has instructed his disciples to go to Galilee where He will meet them."

The woman embraced him warmly. The doubts, and uncertainty which a moment ago had consumed him, melted away. She put both hands on his shoulders and looked into his eyes. "He is risen!" she repeated. "We must go and tell the others," she said.

His mother had been right. The Master's mission had not ended with His death. This remarkable man who had power over life and death, was alive again. The Messiah, risen from death!" Nathanael ran to tell her.

Note: It may be helpful to explain to children that this story is a fictional account, adapted from the New Testament account in Luke:7:11-17. The characters names were selected because they are common to that period of time.

SO IT WAS DONE

'Twas written a virgin shall bring forth a son, (Isaiah 7:14)
His birthplace a city called Bethleh'm, (Micah 5:2)
And from David's line would the Promised One come, (Jeremiah 23:5,)
So it was written. So it was done. (Isaiah 11:1)

A new star appeared as the prophets foretold, (Numbers 24:17)
His name meant salvation to those of His fold, (Isaiah 7:14)
Honored as king with fine treasures and gold,
And all was fulfilled as the prophecy told.

Come to open blind eyes, to heal and to save, (Isaiah 42:7)
Sent to atone, that the ransom be paid, (Hosea 13:14)
To redeem us from sin, and to open the grave, (Ezekiel 37:12)
All in fulfillment of prophecy made.

He entered Jerusalem riding a foal, (Zechariah 9:9)
And multitudes bowed down and prayed as He rode, (Mark 11: 1-11)
Hosannas rang out for their King they did know. (Matthew 21:4-11)
All in accordance as prophets foretold.

As sheep before shearer, a silent defense, (Isaiah 53:7)
His back and His cheek to the smiters extends, (Isaiah 50:6)
Wounded and bruised in the house of His friends, (Zechariah 13:6)
They mocked and abused, pierced His feet and His hands. (Psalms 22:16)

Forsaken, and for thirty pieces betrayed, (Psalms 22:1)
The bargain agreed to, the silver was weighed, (Zechariah 11:12)
Cast in the temple, the potter was paid, (Zechariah 11:13)
Exacting in detail of prophecy made.

With the wicked His grave, with the rich made His tomb, (Isaiah 53:9)
Lots cast for His vesture, divided and strewn, (Psalms 22:18)
Forewarned and admonished God's seers importuned
Smitten, the Shepherd. Ensured was their doom. (Zechariah 13:7)

In vision seers witnessed the life of God's Son.
The law He fulfilled, and the victory won.
Prophetically teaching of things yet to come.
As it was written, — So it is done.

Sharon Velluto

MOSES, BUILDER, SAVIOR, KING

They wanted a monarch, a powerful king
To free from oppression, redemption to bring;
A strong, mighty warrior, a ruler supreme,
And God sent His Son, -- a meek Nazarene.

Subservient, beaten, enslaved and suppressed,
They prayed for a builder, to seek for redress
To build up the kingdom which once they had known.
God answered their prayers with the Carpenter's Son.

They watched for a Moses, deliverer strong--
To feed them with manna, avenge every wrong,
To lead them in battle, by miracle fed.
Then scorned and derided God's Heavenly Bread.

They wanted a ruler with staff firm and proud,
A pillar of fire, a heavenly cloud,
A guide for their pathway, a lamp for the night.
They turned from the Way, and the Truth, and the Light.

They crowned Him with thorns and derided His claim.
Enduring their mocking, the scourging, the shame;
He hung on the cross, just a meek Nazarene.
Their Moses, their Builder, their Savior, their King.

Sharon Velluto

CROWN

No regal crown,
No scepter proud,
No royal robe.
No praising crowd.

With reed in hand
And robe of shame
They jeered and scoffed
And mocked His claim.

Then spit on Him
With hateful scorn
And crowned Him King
With plated thorn.

Men's crowns are passed
From sire to son.
Immortal crowns
Are always won.

Christ won the crown
Through sacrifice
His blood won us
A crown of life.

Sharon Velluto

PARADOX

Descended He below all things
To know how he could lift us up.
And bought for us the sweetest gift
When He partook the bitter cup.

Submission made him conqueror,
Although a servant, reigned as King.
The giving of His mortal life
Unlocked the grave, removed death's sting.

It's strange tho think that such a Man
Had not a place to lay His head.
The greatest King to grace the earth
Once lay in lowly manger bed.

Descended He, a powerful God,
To dwell as lamb, with bear and fox,
The Greatest came and served as Least;
As God's supernal paradox.

Sharon Velluto

YET I KNOW

I have not seen the stable,
nor the town of Bethlehem,
Nor visited Gethsemane,
or seen Jerusalem.

I've never walked in Galilee
where often He repaired.
I needn't view the paths He walked
to know that He was there.

I didn't sit upon the Mount
with that vast multitude.
Yet, still I know within my heart
That what He taught was true.

I did not see His miracles
of which I've read so much.
I've never knelt beneath His hand,
yet, I have felt His touch.

I did not see the angel
nor the tomb they said was His.
I've never seen the risen Lord,
yet, still I know He lives.

I've felt of His redeeming power;
the peace and hope it brings.
I know that Jesus is the Christ--
our Savior, Lord and King.

Sharon Velluto

ADDITIONAL REFERENCES

Genesis 22:1-19.................. Abraham was a type pointing to Christ
Genesis chaps. 37,39, 41-45 Joseph sold to Egyptians, becomes ruler, sees family again (A type of Christ)
Amos 3:7.............................. God reveals all His secrets to prophets
Jonah 1-3............................. Story of Jonah (See also Matthew 12:39-41; Luke 11:29-30)
Matthew 5:17-19................. Jesus came to fulfill the law of the prophets
Jacob 4:5.............................. The law of Moses points to Christ
Mosiah 13:28-35................. Abinadi prophecies of Christ's fulfillment of the law
3 Nephi 1:13, 18, 20........... The prophecy of Samuel is fulfilled
Ether 3:4-16........................ The brother of Jared sees the finger of God
D&C 1:37-38........................ God speaks by the mouth of His servants
D&C 128:12-13................... Baptism is a likeness of resurrection
D&C 138:11-16................... Joseph F. Smith's vision of Spirit World (Note esp. vs. 13)
Moses 1:6,16....................... Moses converses with God and is tempted of Satan
Moses 5:5-8......................... Adam's sacrifice was a similitude of the sacrifice of Christ
Articles of Faith 5-9 Proper authority, Church organization, continuing revelation

Old Testament Stories
Abraham and the Sacrifice of Isaac
Joseph
The Prophet Moses
Jonah
The Prophets tell about Jesus

New Testament Stories
Prophets tell of Jesus

Book of Mormon Stories
How We Got the Book of Mormon
Lehi Warns the People
King Benjamin
Abinadi and King Noah
Samuel the Lamanite Tells about Jesus Christ
The Signs of Christ's Birth
The Signs of Christ's Crucifixion
The Jaredites Leave Babel
The Jaredites Travel to the Promised Land
The Destruction of the Jaredites

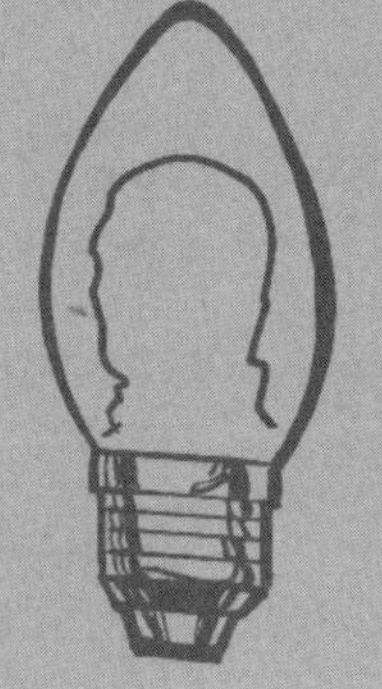

Doctrine and Covenants Stories
Joseph Smith's First Vision
Joseph and Oliver Are Given the Priesthood
The Prophet Is Killed

WE THANK THEE, OH GOD FOR MAP AND COMPASS!

I will raise them up a Prophet from among their brethren, like unto thee, and will put my words in his mouth; and he shall speak unto them all that I shall command him. (Deuteronomy 18:18)

I wouldn't call orientation one of my strong points. No, disorientation better describes me. Oh, if I'm given a map, I can find longitude and latitude or scale of miles -- but put me inside of a shopping mall and I am lost. If I can't see those wonderful Wasatch Mountains in the east of my home town, I completely loose my bearings.

During my mission, I was forever walking into someone's bedroom or closet, thinking it to be an exit. When I was transferred to a new city, I was usually lucky enough to have a companion who knew her way around. But, once, during the later part of my mission, my luck ran out. My Jr. companion had been in the city only a short time, and this city had a most "unique" layout. There were no mountains. There was no 100 South or 500 West, like those wonderful, Utah streets I was used to. Each street had a name, and each house had a number, and usually, they were not marked very clearly. I was lost. Completely lost.

After we wandered aimlessly for a few days, I announced to my companion that we needed to buy a map. The next morning, we located on the map where we were and where we needed to go. We determined what bus we needed to take and which street the bus stop was on. We were on our way. We got on the bus, content that we were finally going somewhere. My companion watched for the street we were to exit on, but nothing looked familiar to her. Before we realized it, we were at "*Capolinea*," the end of the line. We had taken the correct bus, and waited on the correct street. We had just waited on the wrong side of the street and had taken the bus in the wrong direction. We waited for the bus to make the return trip. We had wasted the entire morning going nowhere.

Over the next few days, we were doomed to repeat the same mistake several times, due to the Senior companion's excellent "orientation skills." The map did us absolutely no good, when we didn't know which direction we were supposed to be going.

I felt badly wasting so much of the Lord's valuable time going nowhere. And we had a standing joke about asking directions from one of the residents. Ninety-nine percent of the time they told you to go "Sempre diritto!" Always forward. Well, if you walk forward far enough you eventually fall into the ocean!

Finally, I figured out a solution to our dilemma. A compass! I purchased one and kept it in my pocket at all times. If ever I was unsure which direction I needed to go, I pulled my "Liahona" out of my pocket to figure it out.'

Not wanting to look too much like a misguided tourist, I tried to be as inconspicuous as possible. But, it wasn't long before the elders found out about my problem, and they teased me mercilessly. But, I didn't really mind, because I never again wasted valuable time, taking a bus "somewhere" and arriving "nowhere."

Maps are invaluable tools for travelers who are unfamiliar with an area. We keep a map in our car at all times.

Knowing that we would be "sojourners" in an unfamiliar land, God has blessed mankind with the best maps available -- the holy scriptures.

Many, however, still choose to wander aimlessly about, refusing help from this heavenly road map.

But, even the best road map is useless without knowing which direction to travel. So many in the world today are troubled and confused, with a giant maze of unfamiliar and ill-marked streets. They try to find meaning and direction for their lives, only to find that they have traveled in the wrong direction to "Capolinea," wasting valuable time. There are many who are willing and anxious to interpret the "road map" for us and send us on our misguided way.

The Lord recognized our desperate need for a "compass" and sent a prophet.

Anyone willing to disregard criticism from skeptics, and heed his counsel can receive divine guidance, as if it fell from the lips of the Lord himself. "*What I the Lord have spoken, I have spoken, and I excuse not myself; and though the heavens and the earth pass away, my word shall not pass away, but shall all be fulfilled, whether by mine own voice or by the voice of my servants, it is the same.*" (D&C 1:37-38)

Armed with both map and compass we can be sure of safe passage if we will but follow carefully the directions.

Oh, what a blessing it is to be guided by a prophet of God! What a blessing it is to receive direction for our lives from someone who can positively point the way.

We thank thee, Oh God, for map and compass,
To guide us through this muddled maze,
We give thanks for the map of holy scripture,
And the Compass who leads us in Thy ways.

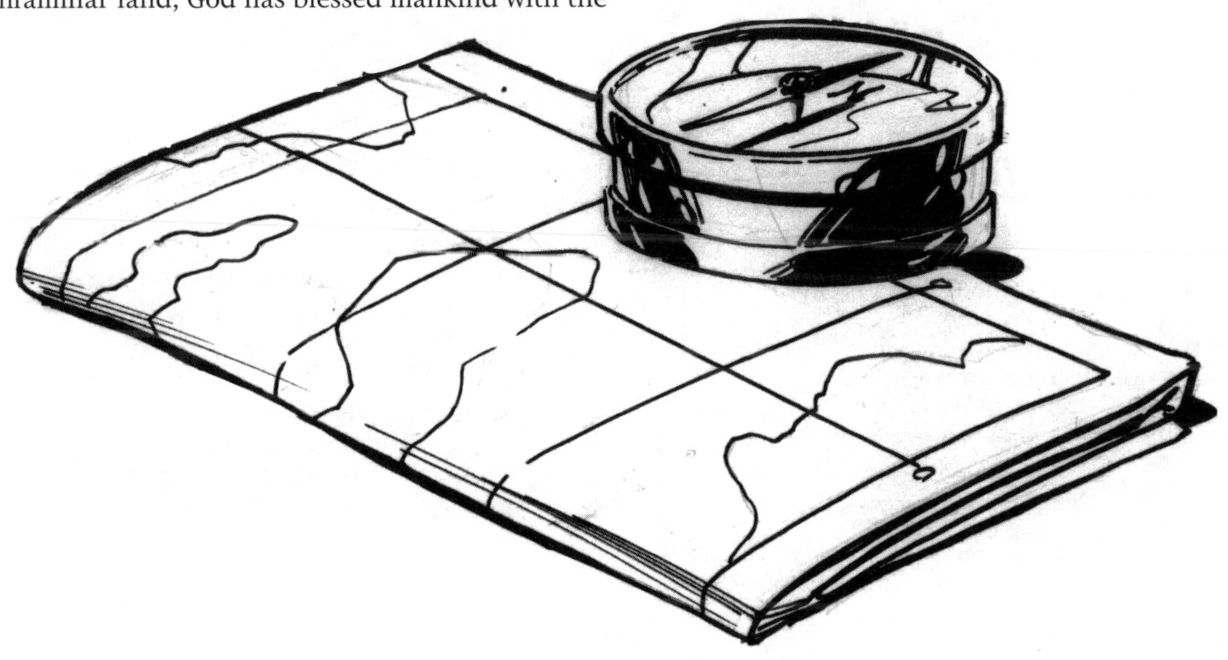

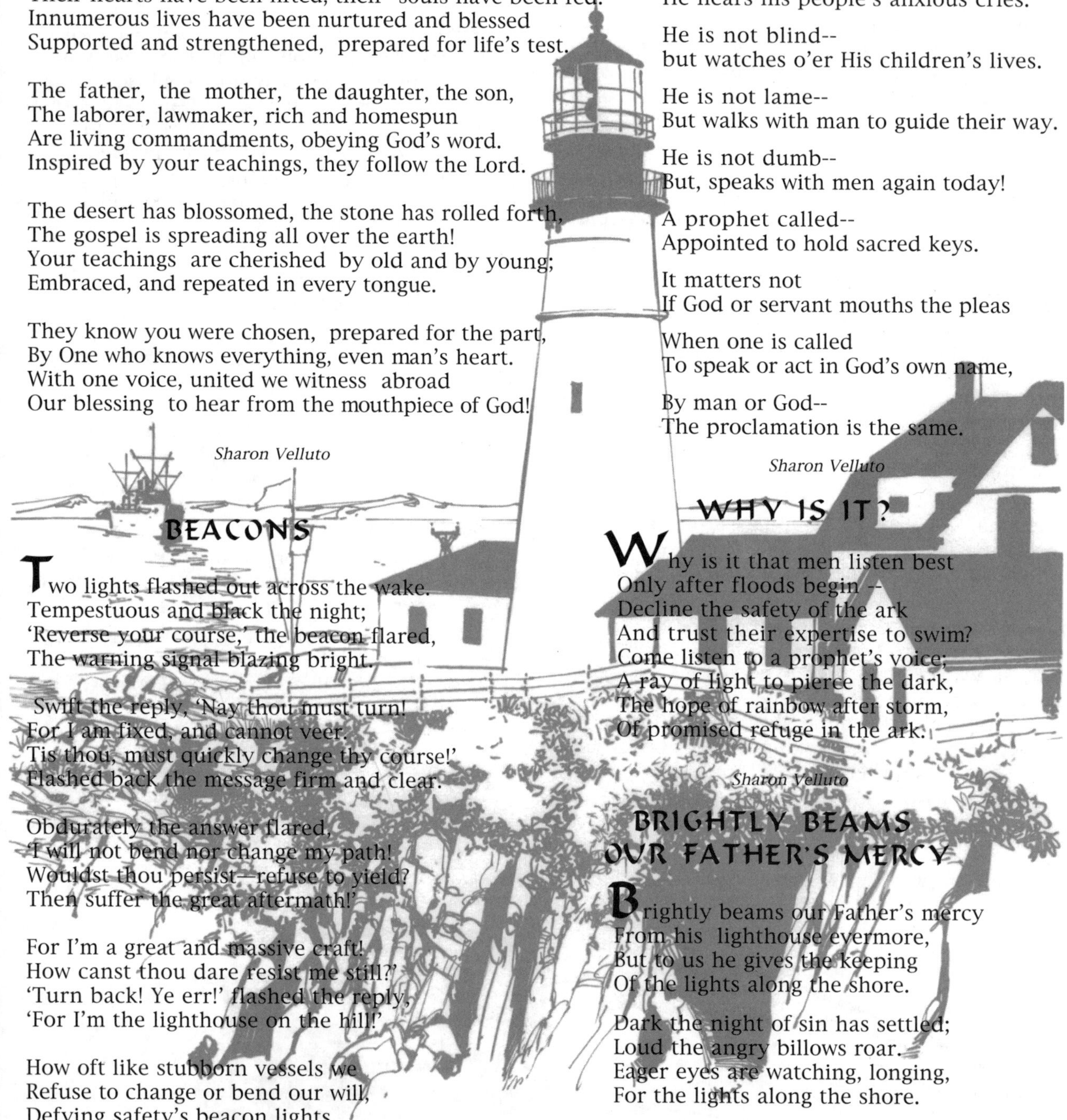

A PROPHET'S WORD

So many are living by what you have have said.
Their hearts have been lifted, their souls have been fed.
Innumerous lives have been nurtured and blessed
Supported and strengthened, prepared for life's test.

The father, the mother, the daughter, the son,
The laborer, lawmaker, rich and homespun
Are living commandments, obeying God's word.
Inspired by your teachings, they follow the Lord.

The desert has blossomed, the stone has rolled forth,
The gospel is spreading all over the earth!
Your teachings are cherished by old and by young;
Embraced, and repeated in every tongue.

They know you were chosen, prepared for the part,
By One who knows everything, even man's heart.
With one voice, united we witness abroad
Our blessing to hear from the mouthpiece of God!

Sharon Velluto

BEACONS

Two lights flashed out across the wake.
Tempestuous and black the night;
'Reverse your course,' the beacon flared,
The warning signal blazing bright.

Swift the reply, 'Nay thou must turn!
For I am fixed, and cannot veer.
Tis thou, must quickly change thy course!'
Flashed back the message firm and clear.

Obdurately the answer flared,
'I will not bend nor change my path!
Wouldst thou persist—refuse to yield?
Then suffer the great aftermath!'

For I'm a great and massive craft!
How canst thou dare resist me still?'
'Turn back! Ye err!' flashed the reply,
'For I'm the lighthouse on the hill!'

How oft like stubborn vessels we
Refuse to change or bend our will,
Defying safety's beacon lights
Sent from the lighthouse on the hill.

Or recklessly ignore the voice
Which God declared is as His own;
A prophet -- revelation's beam;
His lighthouse which can guide us home.

Sharon Velluto

*This poem was inspired by a story I once heard. I apologize that I no longer remember where I heard it, or who told it.

REALIZATION

God is not deaf--
He hears his people's anxious cries.

He is not blind--
but watches o'er His children's lives.

He is not lame--
But walks with man to guide their way.

He is not dumb--
But, speaks with men again today!

A prophet called--
Appointed to hold sacred keys.

It matters not
If God or servant mouths the pleas

When one is called
To speak or act in God's own name,

By man or God--
The proclamation is the same.

Sharon Velluto

WHY IS IT?

Why is it that men listen best
Only after floods begin --
Decline the safety of the ark
And trust their expertise to swim?
Come listen to a prophet's voice;
A ray of light to pierce the dark,
The hope of rainbow after storm,
Of promised refuge in the ark.

Sharon Velluto

BRIGHTLY BEAMS OUR FATHER'S MERCY

Brightly beams our Father's mercy
From his lighthouse evermore,
But to us he gives the keeping
Of the lights along the shore.

Dark the night of sin has settled;
Loud the angry billows roar.
Eager eyes are watching, longing,
For the lights along the shore.

Trim your feeble lamp, my brother;
Some poor sailor, tempest tossed
Trying now to make the harbor,
In the darkness may be lost.

Let the lower lights be burning;
Send a gleam across the wave.
Some poor fainting, struggling seaman
You may rescue, you may save.

Philip Paul Bliss
1838-1876 Hymns # 335

ADDITIONAL REFERENCES

Matthew 21:3	The parable of vineyard
Matthew 23:11	He that is greatest among you shall be your servant
Mark 12: 30-31	The two great commandments (See also Matthew 22:37-40)
Luke 2	The Christmas story
Luke 22:19-20	This is my body which is given for you
John 4:7-41 (esp. vs. 10)	Jesus teaches the Samaritan woman that He is the gift of God
John 11:25	I am the resurrection and the life
John 14:2	In my Father's house are many mansions
John 14:21,23, 27	If ye love me, keep my commandments and receive peace
John 15:9-14	Greater love hath no man
Romans 6:23	The gift of God is eternal life through Jesus Christ (See also D&C 6:13, 14:7)
Philippians 4:4	Rejoice in the Lord
1 John 4:7-11	God is love
1 Nephi chapters 8 &15	Lehi's vision of tree of life and its interpretation

Old Testament Stories
The Prophets Tell about Jesus

New Testament Stories
Jesus Christ is Born
Jesus is Crucified
Jesus is Resurrected

Book of Mormon Stories
Lehi's Dream
King Benjamin
Alma Teaches about Faith and the Word of God
Samuel the Lamanite Tells about Jesus Christ
The Signs of Christ's Birth
The Signs of Christ's Crucifixion
Jesus Christ Appears to the Nephites
Jesus Christ Blesses the Children
Jesus Christ Teaches and Prays with the Nephites
Jesus Christ Blesses His Disciples

EXCERPTS FROM THE SACRAMENTAL COVENANT

by Melvin J. Ballard

For I know that my redeemer liveth, and that he shall stand at the latter day upon the earth; And though after my skin worms destroy this body, yet in my flesh shall I see God; ...Whom I shall see for myself, and mine eyes shall behold, and not another... (Job 19:25-27)

It is written in the scriptures that God so loved the world that He gave His Only Begotten Son to die for the world, that whosoever believes on Him,... and keeps His commandments, shall be saved....

While we give nothing, perhaps, for this atonement and this sacrifice, nevertheless, it has cost someone something, and I love to contemplate what it cost our Father in heaven to give us the gift of His Beloved Son, that worthy Son of our Father, who so loved the world that He laid His life down to redeem the world, to save us and to feed us spiritually while we walk in this life, and prepare us to go and dwell with Him in the eternal worlds.

I think as I read the story of Abraham's sacrifices of his son Isaac that our Father is trying to tell us what it cost him to give His Son as a gift to the world. You remember the story of how Abraham's son came after long years of waiting and was looked upon by his worthy sire, Abraham, as more precious than all his other possessions; yet, in the midst of his rejoicing, Abraham was told to take this only son and offer him as a sacrifice to the Lord. He responded. Can you feel what was in the heart of Abraham on that occasion? You love your son just as Abraham did; perhaps not quite so much, because of the peculiar circumstances, but what do you think was in his heart when he started away from Mother Sarah, and they bade her goodbye? What do you think was in his heart when he saw Isaac bidding farewell to his mother to take that three days' journey to the appointed place, where the sacrifice was to be made? I imagine it was about all Father Abraham could do to keep from showing his great grief and sorrow at that parting, but he and his son trudged along three days toward the appointed place, Isaac carrying the fagots that were to consume the sacrifice. The two travelers rested, finally, at the mountainside, and the men who had accompanied them were told to remain, while Abraham and his son started up the hill.

The boy then said to his father: "Why, Father, we have the fagots; we have the fire to burn the sacrifice; but where is the sacrifice?"

It must have pierced the heart of Father Abraham to hear the trusting and confiding son say: "You have forgotten the sacrifice." Looking at the youth, his son of promise, the poor father could only say; "The Lord will provide."

They ascended the mountain, gathered the stones together, and placed the fagots upon them. Then Isaac was bound, hand and foot, kneeling upon the altar. I presume Abraham, like a true father, must have given his son his farewell kiss, his blessing, his love, and his soul must have been drawn out in that hour of agony toward his son who was to die by the hand of his own father. Every step proceeded until the cold steel was drawn, and the hand raised that was to strike the blow to let out the life's blood, when the angel of the Lord said: "It is enough."

Our Father in heaven went through all that and more for in His case the hand was not stayed. He loved his Son, Jesus Christ, better than Abraham ever loved Isaac, for our Father had with Him His Son, our Redeemer, in the eternal worlds, faithful and true for ages, standing in a place of trust and honor, and the Father loved him so dearly, and yet He allowed this well-beloved Son to descend from His place of glory and honor, where millions did Him homage, down to the earth, a condescension that is not within the power of man to conceive, He came to receive the insult, the abuse, and the crown of thorns. God heard the cry of His Son in that moment of great grief and agony, in the garden when, the pores of His body opened and drops of blood stood upon Him, and He cried out: "Father, if thou be willing, remove this cup from me."

I ask you, what father and mother could stand by and listen to the cry of their children in distress, in this world, and not render assistance? I have heard of mothers throwing themselves into raging streams when they could not swim a stroke to save their drowning children, rushing into burning buildings to rescue those whom they loved.

We cannot stand by and listen to those cries without its touching our hearts. The Lord has not given us the power to save our own. He has given us faith, and we submit to the inevitable, but He had the power to save, and He loved His Son, and He could have saved Him. He might have rescued Him from the insult of the crowds. He might have rescued Him when the crown of thorns was placed upon His head. He might have rescued Him when the Son, hanging between two thieves, was mocked with, "Save thyself, and come down from the cross. He saved others; himself he cannot save." He listened to all this. He saw that Son condemned; He saw Him drag the cross through the streets of Jerusalem and faint under its load. He saw the Son finally upon Calvary; He saw His body stretched out upon the wooden cross; He saw the cruel nails driven through hands and feet, and the blows that broke the skin, tore the flesh, and let out the life's blood of His Son. He looked upon that.

In the case of our Father, the knife was not stayed, but it fell, and the life's blood of His Beloved Son went out. His Father looked on with great grief and agony over His Beloved Son, until there seems to have come a moment when even our Savior cried out in despair: "My God, my God, why hast thou forsaken me?"

In that hour I think I can see our dear Father behind the veil looking upon these dying struggles until even he could not endure it any longer; and, like the mother who bids farewell to her dying child, and has to be taken out of the room so as not to look upon the last struggles, so He bowed His head, and hid in some part of His universe, His great heart almost breaking for the love that He had for His Son. Oh, in that moment when He might have saved His Son, I thank Him and praise Him that He did not fail us, for He had not only the love of His Son in mind, but He also had love for us. I rejoice that He did not interfere, and that His love for us made it possible for Him to endure to look upon the sufferings of His Son and give Him finally to us, our Savior and our Redeemer. Without Him, without His sacrifice, we would have remained, and we would never have come glorified into His presence. And so this is what it cost, in part, for our Father in heaven to give the gift of His Son unto men.

How do I appreciate the gift? If I only knew what it cost our Father to give His Son, if I only knew how essential it was that I should have that Son and that I should receive the spiritual life that comes from that Son, I am sure I would always be present at the sacrament table to do honor to the gift that has come unto us, for I realize that the Father has said that He, the Lord, our God, is a jealous God — jealous lest we should ignore and forget and slight His greatest gift unto us.

I know that no man or woman shall ever come to stand in the presence of our Father in heaven, or be associated with the Lord Jesus Christ, who does not grow spiritually. Without spiritual growth we shall not be prepared to enter into the divine presence. I need the sacrament. I need to renew my covenant every week. I need the blessing that comes with and through it. I know that what I am talking about is true. I bear witness to you that I know that the Lord lives. I know that He has made this sacrifice and this atonement. He has given me a foretaste of these things.

I recall an experience which I had two years ago, bearing witness to my soul of the reality of His death, of His crucifixion, and His resurrection, that I shall never forget. I bear it to you;...not with a spirit to glory over it, but with a grateful heart and with thanksgiving in my soul. I know that He lives, and I know that through Him men must find their salvation, and that we cannot ignore this blessed offering that He has given to us as the means of our spiritual growth to prepare us to come to Him and be justified.

Away on the Fort Peck Reservation where I was doing missionary work with some of our brethren, laboring among the Indians, seeking the Lord for light to decide certain matters pertaining to our work there, and receiving a witness from Him that we were doing things according to His will, I found myself one evening in the dreams of the night in that sacred building the temple. After a season of prayer and rejoicing I was informed that I should have the privilege of entering into one of those rooms to meet a glorious Personage, and, as I entered the door, I saw, seated on a raised platform, the most glorious Being my eyes have ever beheld or that I have conceived existed in all the eternal worlds. As I approached to be introduced, he arose and stepped towards me with extended arms, and he smiled as he softly spoke my name. If I shall live to be a million years old, I shall never forget that smile. He took me into his arms and kissed me, pressed me to his bosom and blessed me, until the marrow of my bones seemed to melt! When he had finished, I fell at his feet, and, as I bathed them with my tears and kisses, I saw the prints of the nails in the feet of the Redeemer of the world. The feeling that I had in the presence of Him who hath all things in His hands, to have His love, His affection, and His blessing was such that if I ever can receive that of which I had but a foretaste, I would give all that I am, all that I ever hope to be to feel what I then felt!

...I would be ashamed, I know, as I felt then, to stand in His presence and try to offer any apology or any excuse for not having kept His commandments and honored Him by bearing witness, before the Father and before men, that I believe in Him, and that I take upon me His blessed name, and that I live by and through Him spiritually.

...I see Jesus not now upon the cross, I do not see his brow pierced with thorns nor His hands torn with the nails, but I see Him smiling, with extended arms, saying to us all: "Come unto me!"

Excerpt from "The Sacramental Covenant," delivered at the M.I.A. Conference June 8, 1919 and reprinted in *Melvin J. Ballard Crusader for Righteousness*, Salt Lake City: Bookcraft, 1966 pp. 131-139. Used with permission.

CHRISTMAS GREETINGS

Frohliche Weihnachten Bruder, Freund!

One Christmas on the battle front,
Fields lightly dusted with the snow,
And "no-man's" land between the trench
Lay deathly quiet, hushed and low.

A silence, not of peacefulness;
But poison, malice, hatred, fear,
And memories of bloody war
Still echoed through the frosted air.

One serviceman the silence broke
By hoisting up in painted scrawl
A small hand-painted sign which read
"A Merry Christmas, One and All!"

A puzzled laugh, then a reply
"Frohliche Weihnachten, Bruder, Freund!"
Their sign was lifted in the air
A Christmas greeting, crudely penned.

Another sign, with a response,
They corresponded for a while,
Then climbed out from dismal trench
Exchanging handshakes, greetings, smile.

Forgetfulness erased the hate,
And, for the moment conflict ceased,
Changing enemies to friends,
Replacing war with blessed peace.

Inspired and lifted by the day
Which celebrates the sacred birth
Of Him who truly lived the song,
"Good will to men, and peace on earth."

Opposing forces --- yet alike
Each man with home and wife and son,
These men who worshipped the same God,
On Christmas Day, became as one.

Sharon Velluto

Poem adapted from the writings of President Spencer W. Kimball.
See *The Teachings of Spencer W. Kimball*, Salt Lake City; Bookcraft, 1982, p. 419

THE LANGUAGE OF CHRISTMAS

Natal, Noel, and Navidad;
The words all mean the same.
Frohliche, feliz, or merry;
Like sentiments proclaim.

For Christmas speaks one native tongue,
Of peace, and love, and joy.
Men's lives are elevated by
The life of one small Boy.

When hearts are moved to follow Him;
To give as He has given;
Forgiveness, kindness, charity,
We catch a glimpse of heaven.

Sharon Velluto

KEEPING CHRISTMAS

When all the ornaments are boxed
and tinsel put away,
Be careful not to package up
the spirit of this day.

The peace and joy of Christmas time —
the willingness to give,
Much more than fleeting reverie —
Ideals by which we live!

May warmest Christmas wishes,
and, the greetings we impart --
Remain a Christmas greeting card
inscribed upon our heart.

And may the Christmas story that
each one of us hold dear,
Be cherished, and embraced, and lived
each day throughout the year.

May the mem'ry of His message,
and the spirit of this day
Remain forever in our hearts
and ne'er be put away.

Sharon Velluto

PONDER THESE THINGS

"Fear not," the angel told Mary,
"for thou shalt bring forth a Son.
And thou shalt call His name Jesus."
Mary asked, "How shall this be done?"

"With God there is nothing impossible,"
the angelic herald assured.
"Be it unto me," Mary answered,
"according to thy holy word."

Her cousin Elizabeth hailed her,
"Among women, most blessed thou art!"
Mary marveled at her salutation,
and pondered those things in her heart.

Mary heard the announcement of shepherds;
an angel who gave as a sign,
"A small swaddled Babe in a manger.
Messiah, and Savior divine!"

From the East there came others who sought Him:
who followed the light of a star.
Mary saw how they bowed there in worship,
and pondered these things in her heart.

As a young boy, He taught in the temple,
and later turned water to wine.
Each wonder affirming her witness,
she pondered God's holy design.

Grief stricken she watched as He suffered,
and died upon Calvary's hill.
She rejoiced when she heard, "He is risen!"
and pondered God's promise fulfilled.

Herein lies the message of Christmas,
the mother of God humbly taught,
That we labor to follow his teachings,
and ponder these things in our heart.

Sharon Velluto
(See Luke 2:19, 51)

Cards & Activities

CLARIFICATION OF COPYRIGHT

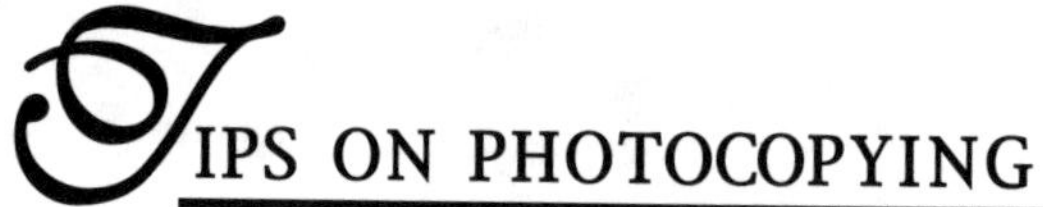

TIPS ON PHOTOCOPYING

When photocopying, make sure the machine you are using is set to the proper light/dark level. The materials printed on colored cardstock require a lighter setting in order to reproduce correctly. Red cardstock will not reproduce properly. Therefore, an extra copy of the poinsettia petals are printed on white cardstock for your convenience. (See page 269)

ORDERING ADDITIONAL COPIES

To order additional packets of ornaments send a check or money order in the amount of U.S. $5.95 per packet. For each packet add U.S. $2.00 for shipping and handling within the United States, and U.S $2.50 for Canada.) Utah residents add U.S. $0.38 sales tax per packet. (Prices subject to change without notice.)

Send your orders to:

SVI Inc.
P.O. Box 1663
WEST JORDAN, UT 84088
U.S.A.

Please note: Extra packets are not available for the materials labeled "Cards and Activities."

Find us on the World Wide Web at: www.velluto.com/ccc

A LIGHT TO REMEMBER HIM: To be used with activity #1, page 3

PUT UP A STAR: To be used with activity #3 page 3

STREET SIGNS: To be used with activity #5, page 3

TREASURES IN HEAVEN GAME: To be used with activity #2, page 7.

You participate in family scripture study Forward 2 Steps	You show reverence during the prayer Forward 2 Steps
You say personal prayers Forward 2 Steps	You give service to someone in need Forward 3 Steps
You help a friend to choose the right Forward 3 Steps	You help someone who is less fortunate Forward 3 Steps
You tell the truth even though you might get in trouble Forward 3 Steps	You pay your tithing cheerfully Forward 2 Steps
You help a younger brother or sister Forward 2 Steps	You treat others and their belongings with respect Forward 2 Steps

TREASURES IN HEAVEN GAME: To be used with activity #2, page 7.

You are kind to someone who needs a friend

Forward 3 Steps

You help someone who is new in your class

Forward 2 Steps

You defend someone whom others are making fun of

Forward 3 Steps

You invite someone to come to church with you

Forward 3 Steps

You help without being asked, or expecting to be paid

Forward 3 Steps

You are cheerful

Forward 2 Steps

You pray for others

Forward 3 Steps

You share

Forward 3 Steps

You say "no" when someone wants you to do wrong

Forward 3 Steps

You do a secret act of service for someone

Forward 3 Steps

TREASURES IN HEAVEN GAME: To be used with activity #2, page 7.

You brag that you are better than someone else

Back 1 Step

You cheat on a test

Back 1 Step

You come home later than you promised

Back 1 Step

You refuse to do an errand

Back 1 Step

You get angry when asked to help

Back 1 Step

You blame others for something you did

Back 1 Step

You take something without asking for permission

Back 1Step

You don't let others take their turn

Back 1 Step

You fight with your brothers and sisters

Back 1 Step

You gossip about someone

Back 1 Step

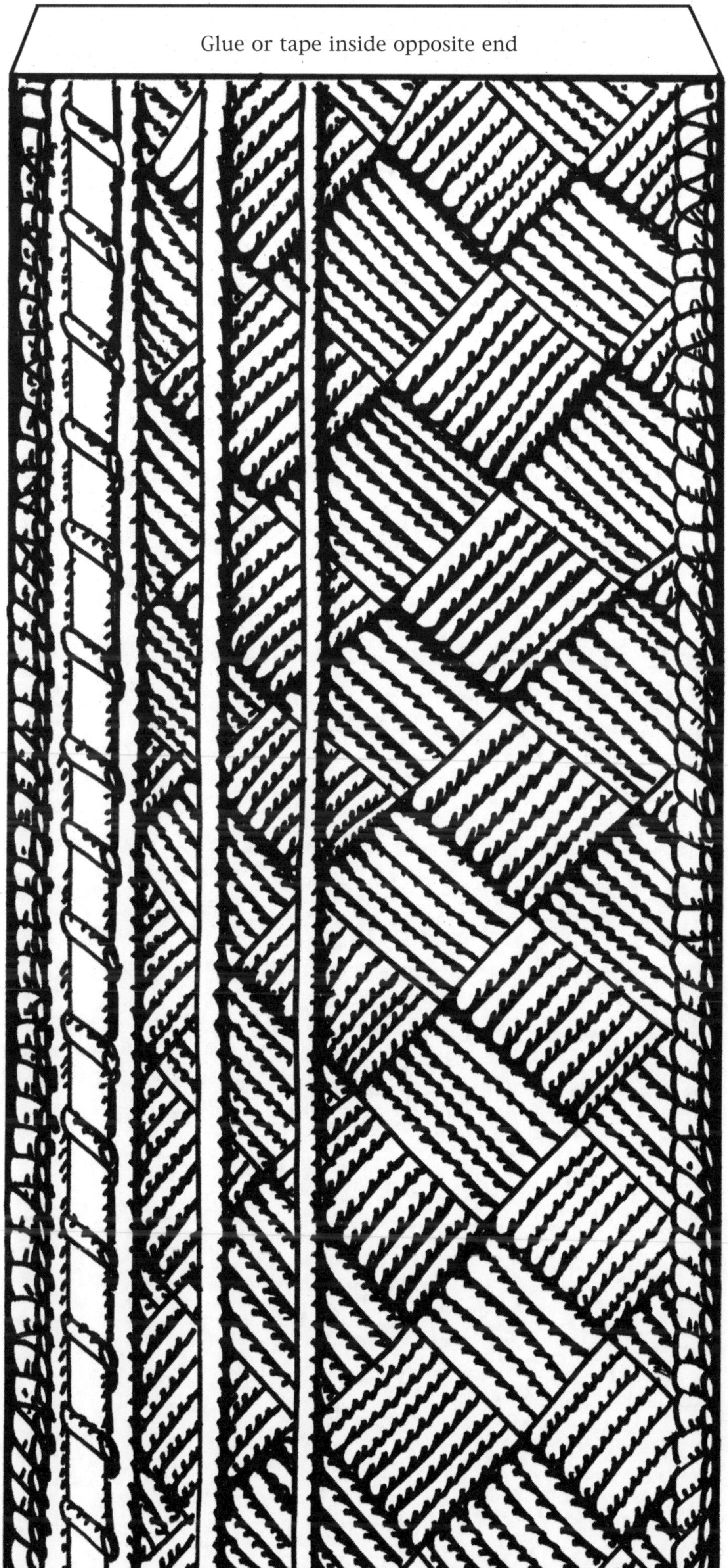

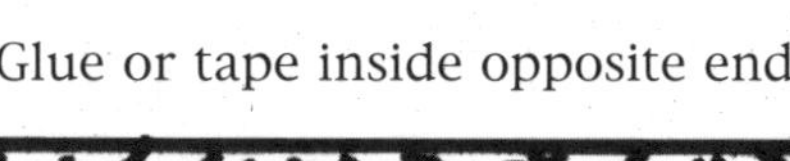

Use with activity #2 , page 9

BUSHEL: Cut out picture of bushel basket. Connect the two ends, gluing tab to back side as marked. Slide over a one pint jar. Put the jar on top of a lit candle. The flame will go out when all the oxygen in the bottle has been consumed. Adult supervision required.

WHO'S THAT ANGEL? GAME: To be used with activity #2, page 15.

After the death of Jesus, his disciples continued to preach the gospel. Two of these disciples were thrown into prison. I came at night and opened the prison doors.

(Acts 5:14-20)

Who were these two men?

I was sent from God to help a righteous young man and his younger brother. He had great faith and chose to obey God's commandments. His two older brothers were wicked and disobedient. Once when this young man was trying to teach them, they began to beat him and his younger brother with a rod. I came to stop the brothers from hurting these two young men. *(Nephi 3:27-31)*

Who were the two righteous men and who were the two wicked brothers?

I am an angel who was sent to a righteous young man to restore the Aaronic Priesthood to the earth.

(D&C 13:1, Joseph Smith History 1:69)

Who am I?

Bonus: Who were the three beings who later came to restore the Melchizedek Priesthood?

(D&C 27:12, 128:20)

God called two young men as prophets to go and preach to some wicked people. The people wouldn't listen and became very angry. They threw these two men into prison. But God protected them. They were encircled by fire and spoke with angels.

(Helaman 5:19-48)

Who were these two men?

John the Revelator, saw in vision an angel who would come to the earth bringing the everlasting gospel.

Who was that angel?

(Revelation 14: 6)

I am an angel who was sent to bring a joyous message to a woman who was not able to have children. I told her that she would have a son, and warned her that she was not to drink wine, or eat anything unclean. Also, I told her that she should never cut the boy's hair. The child would be a Nazarite chosen of God and would begin to deliver Israel from the Philistines. *(Judges 13)*

Who was the woman's son?

We were three special messengers of God whom he sent to restore sacred priesthood keys to the earth. We appeared at the dedication of the Kirtland Temple to restore these keys.

(D&C 110)

Who were we?

Bonus: What keys did we come to restore?

The Syrian army was very powerful and wicked. They had surrounded the city of Dothan where the prophet and his servant were staying. They wanted to capture them. We stood atop the mountains surrounding the city. The prophet saw us but his servant did not. The prophet told his servant not to worry for there were more on their side than with the Syrians. At first the servant doubted the prophet, until he too, saw us there. *(2 Kings 6:8-19)*

Who was the prophet?

WHO'S THAT ANGEL? GAME: To be used with activity #2, page 15.

When I came to give my message, those who saw me were extremely frightened. I didn't mean to frighten them. I had exciting news. In fact, everyone in heaven was excited. After I gave my message, I was joined by many other angels, and we all rejoiced together!

(*Luke 2:8-14*)

Who did I come to and what was my message?

I was an angel sent from God to an obedient father and son. They loved each other very much, but both of them loved God enough to yield their wills to His. God asked the father to do the most difficult thing which could ever be asked of him. When the father proved his obedience to God by complete, humble submission, I told him that it was enough. He and his son were blessed.

(*Genesis 22:2-18*)

Who were they?

I am an angel who helped a man in deep trouble. He had continued to pray to God three times a day, even after the King had made a law forbidding prayer. God sent me because the man was in great danger of being eaten alive.

(*Daniel 6:7-23*)

Who is the man I saved by the power of God?

My name means *Man of God.* I brought messages to several people. I helped a young man understand a dream. I told an old man of a miracle which was about to take place in his life. I came to a woman with news which would change the world. She was truly blessed among women. While I lived as a mortal man upon the earth, I was known as Noah.

(*Daniel 8:16, 9:21; Luke 1:11-19, 26-38; Bible Dictionary: Angels, page 608; HC 3:386*)

Who am I?

Because of the faith of a faithful father, I was sent to warn a group of young men who were trying to destroy the Church. They were so shocked, they fell to the ground. One couldn't speak or move. His friends carried him back to his father, who fasted and prayed that his son would regain his strength. His prayers were answered. The young man and his friends repented and began teaching others about Jesus Christ and repentance.

(*Mosiah 27:11-32*)

Who were these young men?

I am an angel who was sent to help a rebellious man to obey God's will. I stood in his way, preventing him from going astray. The man couldn't see me, but his donkey could, and wouldn't move. The man beat the donkey to make her move forward. The donkey then spoke to the man! She asked him what she had done to deserve this beating. The man's eyes were opened and he could see me. I gave him the message God had sent me to give.

(*Numbers 22:21-35*)

Who was the man?

I was a messenger sent from God to a young man only eighteen years old. I taught him on several occasions. When I lived on earth, I was given charge of some sacred records. I wrote on them and protected them. When my life was in danger, I hid them in a hill. Many years later, I told this young man where I had hidden these plates.

(*Joseph Smith History 1:30-59*)

My name is ____________.

I came to three men who really needed some help. The king had commanded all his people to worship a golden image he had made. These three young men knew it was wrong, and stayed true to their God and their beliefs. My name isn't given in the scriptures, but here's another clue to help you figure out who the three men were: "When you're hot you're hot, and when you're not you're not!"

(*Daniel 3*)

Who were the 3 young men?

To be used with activity #4, page 17. (See instructions on back)

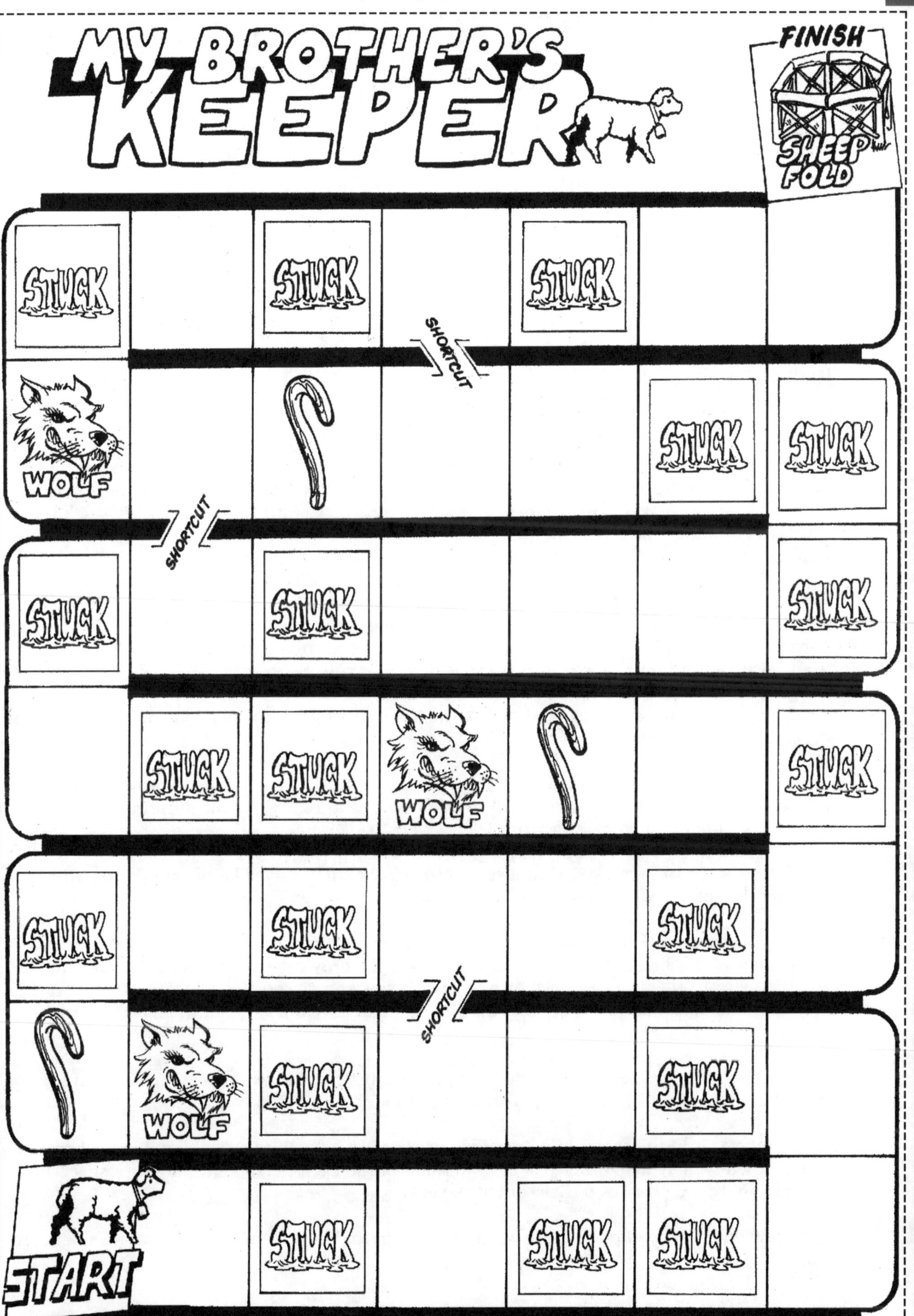

MY BROTHERS KEEPER

INSTRUCTIONS

MARKERS: Use different colored buttons, beads, small pieces of paper etc. for playing pieces. Cotton balls may be glued to the buttons to make them look like sheep.

Use three pennies in a cup to determine the spaces advanced. Pour the pennies out. All coins landing on heads are the number of spaces advanced.

OBJECTIVE: This is a game of family members against the board. The objective of the game is to get all pieces to the finish line safely. If all members become stuck, the family loses.

1. On the first roll, all players must move their own piece out of the starting block, whether it lands on "stuck" or not.

2. After their piece is out of the starting block and onto the playing board, each player has the option of moving his own piece or of helping someone else. For example if the player rolls one head and will move forward one space into a place marked "stuck", instead of moving his own piece, he can use his move to help someone else to advance. The player's move must help the other player. A player cannot move another player's piece into a space marked "stuck." If the roll does not allow a person to help anyone else, the player rolling must be the one who advances into the place marked "stuck". He can, however, move another player's piece from "stuck" to another "stuck" further ahead. If a player has the option of helping two different people, he should always help the person who is the furthest behind. The entire number rolled must be used to move only one piece. It cannot be split to move two pieces. For example: if a player rolls a three, he cannot move one player two spaces and another player one space. Each play must be used. A player may not skip a turn because of a poor roll.

3. If a player lands on a space marked "stuck" he looses his turn until someone helps him by using their turn to free him.

4. There are three shortcuts marked. To take a shortcut, the player must land exactly on that space. If he is one space behind the space marked "short-cut" and rolls a two, he must move forward two spaces instead of taking the shortcut.

5. There are three places marked with a shepherd's crook. If a player lands on this space, he may help another player who is stuck" to move forward one space.

6. Three spaces are marked "Wolf". If a player lands on this space, another player must move to the same spot, by an exact roll to free him. This is the only time in the game that moving backwards is permissible. Once the player reaches the square marked "wolf," to assist his "brother," player who landed on "wolf" but must then continue to play the game until he reaches the "fold" again.

7. To enter the space marked "sheep fold" the player must roll the exact number. If a player is one space behind and rolls a two, the player may not enter "the sheep fold."

8. Once a player is in the sheep fold, he does not continue to roll unless all family members are stuck. Then he may help other players two times only. Each person entering the "sheep fold" will have only two chances to help other players.

9. The game ends when all players are within the sheep fold at the end, or when all members are stuck.

MUSIC CARDS: To be used with activity #7, page 19

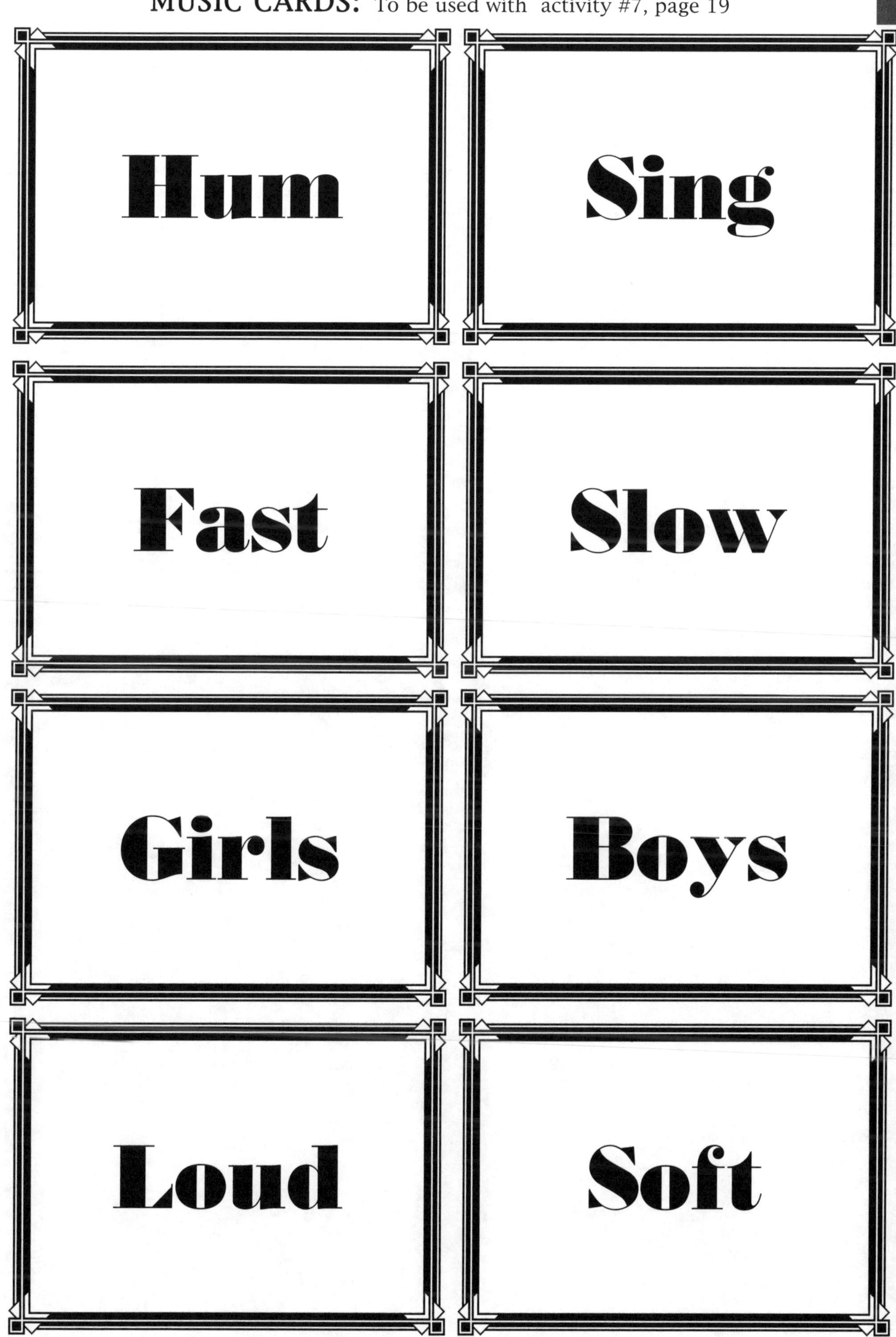

THE LAMB HUNT GAME: To be used with activity #2, page 23.

THE LAMB HUNT GAME: To be used with activity #2, page 23.

TREASURE HUNT CLUES: To be used with activity #1, page 25.

More to be desired are they than gold... sweeter also than honey and the honeycomb.

Psalms 19:10

And because my words shall hiss forth-- many of the Gentiles shall say; A Bible, A Bible We have got a Bible, and there cannot be any more Bible.

2 Nephi 29:3

Thou preparest a table before me in the presence of mine enemies; thou anointest my head with oil, my cup runneth over.

Psalms 23:5

Thy word is a lamp unto my feet, and a light unto my path.

Psalms 119:105

And he lighted upon a certain place and tarried there all night...and he took of the stones of that place and put them for pillows and lay down in that place to sleep.

Genesis 28:11

Therefore the kinsman said unto Boaz, Buy it for thee. So he drew off his shoe.

Ruth 4:8

In the sweat of thy face shalt thou eat thy bread till thou return to the ground; for dust thou art and unto dust shalt thou return.

Genesis 3:19

For the Pharisees, and all the Jews, except they wash their hands oft, eat not, holding the tradition of the elders.

Mark 7:3

And if any man will sue thee at the law, and take away thy coat let him have thy cloak also.

Matthew 5:40

But this is not all; ye must pour out your souls in your closets and your secret places, and in your wilderness.

Alma 34:26

Behold I stand at the door and knock; if any man hear my voice, and open the door, I will come in to him, and will sup with him and he with me.

Revelation 3:20

As cold waters to a thirsty soul, so is good news from a far country.

Proverbs 25:25

And he took butter and milk and the calf which he had dressed, and set it before them and he stood by them under the tree, and they did eat.

Genesis 18:8

And the key of the house of David, will I lay upon his shoulder; so he shall open and none shall shut; and he shall shut and none shall open.

Isaiah 22:22

Is there no balm in Gilead; is there no physician there? Why then is not the health of the daughter of my people recovered?

Jeremiah 8:22

As the fining pot for silver, and the furnace for gold; so is a man to his praise.

Proverbs 27:21

ACTION WORDS GUESSING GAME: To be used with activity #2, page 25.
(See answers on the back)

Sing, Born, Receive Hosanna! Hosanna! Oh. let us gladly sing,	**Gleaming, Dreaming, Rang, Heard** Angel's story rang with glory	**Went, Took, Place, Close** I think he took great care.
Heard, Singing, Echoing And the mountains in reply, echoing their joyous strain.	**Looked, Lay, Asleep** The stars in the heavens looked down where he lay	**Receive, Prepare, Sing** Let every heart prepare him room
Come, Behold, Adore Come and behold him, born the King of angels	**Sing, Reconciled, Join** Join the triumph of the skies	**Heard, Play, Repeat** And wild and sweet the words repeat, Of peace on earth Good will to men
Say, Lay, Keeping In fields where they lay keeping their sheep	**Sleep, Shineth, Met** Yet in thy dark streets shineth the everlasting light	**Come, Bending, Touch** From angels bending near the earth to touch their harps of gold
Sleep, Quake, Stream Shepherds quake at the sight, Glories stream from heaven afar	**Watched, Seated, Shone** The angel of the Lord came down and glory shone around	**Hush, Came, Dwell** A story I'll tell, How little Lord Jesus on earth came to dwell
Come, See, Bring Our finest gifts we bring	**Sleeping, Greet, Keeping** Whom angels greet with anthems sweet	**Wish, Bring, Go** Good tidings we bring to you and your kin
Lead, Guide, Walk Has given me an earthly home	**Think, Read, Called** How he called little children like lambs to the fold	**Wants, Shine, Please** To shine for him each day
Called, Chosen, Witness Chosen e'er to witness for his name	**Built, Came, Washed** The rains came down and the floods came up	**Trying, Following, Love** I'm trying to love as he did

Answer:
When Joseph Went to Bethlehem
Children's Song Book
Page 38

Answer:
Stars were Gleaming
Children's Song Book
Page 37

Answer:
Samuel Tells Of The Baby Jesus
Children's Song Book
Page 36

Answer:
Joy To The World
Hymns # 201

Answer:
Away In A Manger
Children's Song Book
Page 42

Answer:
Angels We Have Heard on High
Hymns # 203

Answer:
I Heard The Bells On Christmas Day
Hymns # 214

Answer:
Hark! The Herald Angels Sing
Hymns # 209

Answer:
Oh, Come all Ye Faithful
Hymns # 202

Answer:
It Came Upon A Midnight Clear
Hymns # 207

Answer:
O Little Town of Bethlehem
Hymns # 208

Answer:
The First Noel
Hymns # 213

Answer:
Oh, Hush Thee My Baby
Children's Song Book
Page 48

Answer:
While Shepherds Watched Their Flocks By Night
Hymns # 211

Answer:
Silent Night
Hymns # 204

Answer:
We Wish You A Merry Christmas
Traditional

Answer:
What Child Is This?
Traditional

Answer:
The Little Drummer Boy
Traditional

Answer:
Jesus Wants Me For A Sunbeam
Children's Song Book
Page 60

Answer:
I Think When I Read That Sweet Story
Children's Song Book
Page 56

Answer:
I Am A Child Of God
Children's Song Book
Page 2

Answer:
I'm Trying To Be Like Jesus
Children's Song Book
Page 78

Answer:
The Wise Man Built His House
Children's Song Book
Page 281

Answer:
Called To Serve
Children's Song Book
Page 174

FLAMES: To be used with activity #5, page 33.

PIES: To be used with activity #3, page 37.

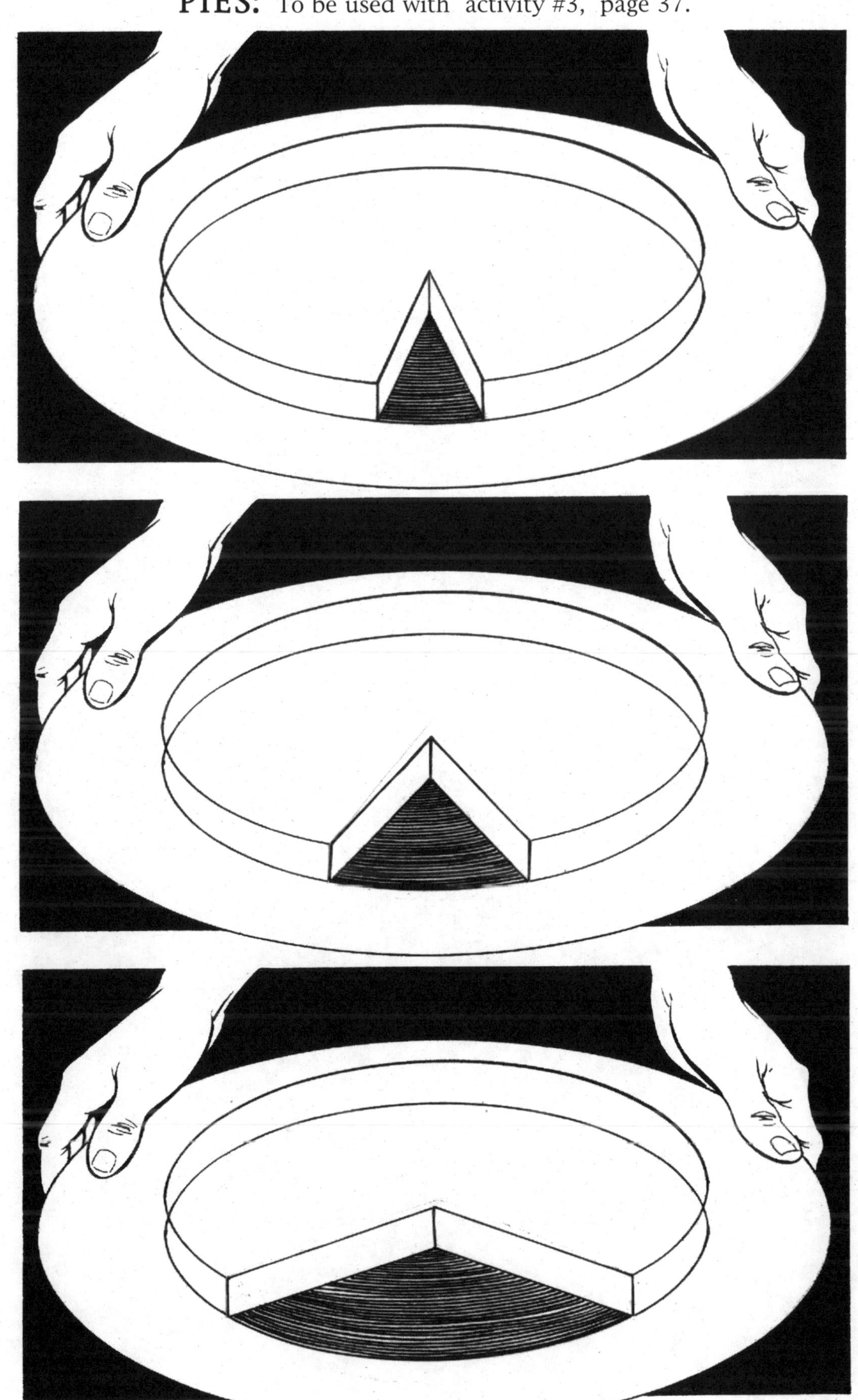

PROPHET TRIVIA: To be used with activity #4, page 47.

JOSEPH SMITH JR.

First President of the Church
(From Jan. 1832 to June 1844)

BIRTH: December 23, 1805, Sharon, Vermont
HEIGHT/WEIGHT: 6'0" 200-210 lbs.
PHYSICAL TRAITS: Brown hair, blue eyes, walked with a limp
ANCESTRY: English, Scottish
OCCUPATION: Farmer
MISSIONS: 4 (Missouri, Canada, Michigan, Eastern States)
AGE SUSTAINED APOSTLE: 23
YEARS AS GENERAL AUTHORITY: 15
AGE SUSTAINED AS PROPHET: 26
YEARS AS PROPHET: 12 and 1/2
DEATH: June 27, 1844, Carthage, Illinois
AGE AT DEATH: 38
BOOKS/SELECTIVE WORKS: History of the Church, Teachings of the Prophet Joseph Smith,, Lectures on Faith
FAMILY: Married Emma Hale, 11 Children, complete list of wives unavailable
OTHER INTERESTING FACTS:
Contracted typhus fever as a child

BRIGHAM YOUNG

Second President of the Church
(From Dec. 1847 to Aug. 1877)

BIRTH: June 1, 1801, Whittingham, Vermont
HEIGHT/WEIGHT: 5'10" 185-200 lbs.
PHYSICAL TRAITS: Reddish hair, wore beard in later years.
ANCESTRY: English
OCCUPATION: Glazier, Carpenter
MISSIONS: 3 (Canada, Eastern States, Britain)
AGE SUSTAINED APOSTLE: 34
YEARS AS GENERAL AUTHORITY: 42 and 1/2
AGE SUSTAINED AS PROPHET:46
YEARS AS PROPHET: 30
DEATH: August 29, 1877, Salt Lake City, Utah
AGE AT DEATH: 76
BOOKS/SELECTIVE WORKS: Discourses of Brigham Young
FAMILY: Married Miriam Works, Mary Ann Angell, Lucy Ann Decker, Harriet E.C. Cook, Augusta Adams, Clara Decker, Olive Grey Frost, Louisa Beaman, Clarissa Ross, Emily Partridge, Emeline Free, Margaret Marcia Allen, Susan Snively, Margaret Pierce, Ellen Rockwood, Marcia Lawrence, Martha Bowker, Zina D. Huntington,

(BRIGHAM YOUNG continued)

Naomah K.J. Carter, Mary Jane Bigelow, Lucy Bigelow, Eliza R. Snow, Eliza Burgess, Harriet Barney, Harriet Amelia Folsom, Mary Van Cott, Ann Eliza Webb. (27 wives) 57 children

OTHER INTERESTING FACTS:

Mother died when he was 14 years. old.
Served as Governor of Utah.
Sent first telegram over new overland telegraph
Started Juvenile Instructor for Sunday School
Organized Sunday School
Organized Young Women's and Young Men's Organizations
Organized Brigham Young Academy (B.Y.U.)
Ordained four sons as Apostles while serving as prophet.
Drove last spike in Utah Central Railroad
Nauvoo Temple dedicated (by Orson Hyde)
Presided over St. George Temple dedication

QUOTES:

If we follow a compass, the needle of which does not point correctly, a very slight deviation in the beginning will lead us, when we have traveled some distance, far to one side of the true point for which we are aiming.

Work as if everything depends on you; Pray as if everything depends on God.

Each will find that happiness in this world mainly depends on the work he does, and the way in which he does it.

This is the right place.

The most effectual way to establish the religion of Heaven is to live it, rather than to die for it. I think I am safe in saying that there are many of the Latter-day Saints who are more willing to die for their religion than to live it faithfully.

There is not an individual upon the earth but what has within himself ability to save or to destroy himself.

(JOSEPH SMITH JR. continued)

OTHER INTERESTING FACTS:

Contracted typhus fever as a child
Translated gold plates in about 90 days.
Elected as Lieutenant Governor.
Organized Relief Society.
Ran for President of the United States.
Translated scrolls found with mummies.
Dedicated Kirtland Temple.

QUOTES:

I teach them correct principles and they govern themselves.

And now after the many testimonies which have been given of him, this is the testimony last of all which we give of him: That he lives! For we saw him, even on the right hand of God; and we heard the voice bearing record that he is the Only Begotten of the Father-- That by him, and through him, and of him, the worlds are and were created, and the inhabitants thereof are begotten sons and daughters unto God.

The standard of truth has been erected; no unhallowed hand can stop this work from progressing. Persecutions may rage, mobs may combine, armies may assemble, calumny may defame; but the truth of God will go forth boldly, nobly and independent, till it has penetrated every continent, visited every clime, swept every country and sounded in every ear, till the purposes of God shall be accomplished, and the Great Jehovah shall say the work is done.

Happiness is the object and design of our existence and will be the end thereof, if we pursue the path that leads to it.

JOHN TAYLOR

Third President of the Church
(From Oct. 1880 to July 1887)

BIRTH: November 1, 1808, Milnethorpe, England
HEIGHT/WEIGHT: 5'11" 180 lbs.
PHYSICAL TRAITS: Gray eyes, beard
ANCESTRY: Scottish, Welsh, French
OCCUPATION: Framer, wood turner, Methodist preacher
MISSIONS: 4 (Britain, France & Germany, Deseret, Eastern States)
AGE SUSTAINED APOSTLE: 30
YEARS AS GENERAL AUTHORITY: 49
AGE SUSTAINED AS PROPHET: 71
YEARS AS PROPHET: 6 years 9 months
DEATH: July 25, 1887, Kaysville, Utah
AGE AT DEATH: 78
BOOKS/SELECTIVE WORKS: The Gospel Kingdom, The Mediation and the Atonement
FAMILY: Married Leonora Cannon, Elizabeth Kaighin, Jane Ballantyne, Mary Ann Oakley, Sophia Whitaker, Harriet Whitaker,Margaret Young. 35 children

WILFORD WOODRUFF

Fourth President of the Church
(From Apr. 1889 to Sep. 1898)

BIRTH: March 1, 1807, Farmington, Connecticut
HEIGHT/WEIGHT: 5'8" 170 lbs.
PHYSICAL CHARACTERISTICS: Blue eyes, beard
ANCESTRY: English
OCCUPATION: farmer
MISSIONS: 5 (Southern States, Fox Islands, Britain, Europe, Eastern States)
AGE SUSTAINED APOSTLE: 32
YEARS AS GENERAL AUTHORITY: 59
AGE SUSTAINED AS PROPHET:82
YEARS AS PROPHET: 9 and 1/2
DEATH: September 2, 1898, San Francisco, California
AGE AT DEATH: 91
BOOKS/SELECTIVE WORKS: Discourses of Wilford Woodruff
FAMILY: Married Phoebe Whittemore Carter, Mary Ann Jackson, Emma Smith, Sarah Brown, Sarah Delight Stocking. 33 children
OTHER INTERESTING FACTS:
Read of Mormonism in a newspaper article
Lived with Joseph Smith a while after his baptism

(WILFORD WOODRUFF continued)

Was called to preside over first completed temple in Utah.
Baptized for signers of Declaration of Independence.
Issued Manifesto to discontinue plural marriage
Organized Genealogical Society
Fast Day changed from first Thursday to first Sunday
Ordained one son as Apostle
Dedicated Salt Lake Temple
Wrote a very extensive diary which has served as an important source of Church history
Suffered from a series of accidents, illnesses and brushes with death
Made a pronouncement that affected temple work. Before this most people were being sealed to one of the prophets. He recommended that members be sealed to their parents instead.

QUOTES:

I have had visions. I have had revelations. I have seen angels, but the greatest of all is the still small voice.

I feel to say little else to the Latter-day Saints... than to call upon them to build these temples now under way, to hurry them to completion. The dead will seek after you as they have after us in St. George. They called upon us knowing that we held the keys and power to redeem them.

I have broken both legs, one of them in two places; both arms,both ankles, my breastbone, and three ribs; I have been scalded, frozen and drowned; I have been in two water wheels while turning under a full head; I have passed through a score of other hairbreadth escapes. The repeated deliverances from all these remarkable dangers I ascribe to the mercies of my Heavenly Father. In recalling them to mind I always feel impressed to render the gratitude of my heart, with thanksgiving and joy to the Lord. I pray that the remainder of my days may pass in His service, in the building up of His kingdom.

(JOHN TAYLOR continued)

OTHER INTERESTING FACTS:

He was in the Carthage jail when Joseph Smith was murdered and sang *A Poor Wayfaring Man* at the prophet's request.
He was shot but a pocket watch saved his life.
Under his direction the Book of Mormon was translated in French and German.
Organized Primary
Under his leadership the Pearl of Great Price was accepted as scripture.
Counseled some Saints to move to Mexico to avoid persecution for having plural wives.
Wrote several poems while in exile which were set to music and sung as hymns for many years.
Church properties became possession of U.S. government
Dedicated Logan Temple, Manti Temple
Ordained one son as Apostle
Died in exile

QUOTES:

I felt that the Lord had preserved me by a special act of mercy; that my time had not yet come, and that I still had a work to perform upon the earth.

The Kingdom of God or nothing.

If you do not magnify your calling, God will hold you responsible for those you might have saved had you done your duty

Endeavor to make your homes a little heaven, and try to cherish the good Spirit of God. Then let us as parents train up our children in the fear of God and teach them the laws of life. If you do, we will have peace in our bosoms, and peace in our families, and peace in our surroundings.

LORENZO SNOW

Fifth President of the Church
(From Sep. 1898 to Oct. 1901)

BIRTH: April 3, 1814, Mantua, Ohio
HEIGHT/WEIGHT: 5'6" 125-130 lbs.
PHYSICAL TRAITS: Gray eyes, beard
ANCESTRY: English
OCCUPATION: Educator
MISSIONS: 7 (Ohio, Southern States, Britain, Europe, Hawaii, Holy Land, Lamanites)
AGE SUSTAINED APOSTLE: 34
YEARS AS GENERAL AUTHORITY: 52
AGE SUSTAINED AS PROPHET: 84
YEARS AS PROPHET: 3
DEATH: October 10, 1901, Salt Lake City, Utah
AGE AT DEATH: 87
BOOKS/SELECTIVE WORKS: Biography and Family Records of Lorenzo Snow
FAMILY: Married Charlotte Squires, Mary Adaline Goddard, Sarah Ann Prichard, Eleanor Houtz, Harriet Amelia Squires, Caroline Horton, Mary Elizabeth Houtz, Phoebe Amelia Woodruff, Sarah Minnie Jensen. 40 children

JOSEPH F. SMITH

Sixth President of the Church
(From Oct. 1901 to Nov. 1918)

BIRTH: November 13, 1838, Far West, Missouri
HEIGHT/WEIGHT: 5'11" 185-195 lbs.
PHYSICAL TRAITS: Brown eyes,long full beard, wore glasses
ANCESTRY: English, Scottish
OCCUPATION: Farmer
MISSIONS: 5 (Hawaii, Britain, Hawaii, Europe, Hawaii)
AGE SUSTAINED APOSTLE: 27
YEARS AS GENERAL AUTHORITY: 52
AGE SUSTAINED AS PROPHET: 62
YEARS AS PROPHET: 17
DEATH: November 19, 1918, Salt Lake City, Utah
AGE AT DEATH: 80
BOOKS/SELECTIVE WORKS: Gospel Doctrine
FAMILY: Married Levira Annett Clark Smith, Julina Lambson, Sarah Ellen Richards, Edna Lambson, Alice Ann Kimball, Mary Taylor Schwartz. 48 children (3 adopted)
OTHER INTERESTING FACTS:
Son of Hyrum Smith who was murdered when Joseph F. was 6 years old

(JOSEPH F. SMITH Continued)

Drove team of oxen across the plains when 8-10 years old
Orphaned at 14 years old
First mission when 15 years old
Salt Lake High Council 21 years old
Second Counselor to three prophets: John Taylor, Wilford Woodruff, Lorenzo Snow'
Under his direction The *Children's Friend* established.
Directed Saints to observe Family Home Evening (1915)
Elected to United States Senate
Church cleared of debt for first time
Ordained sons Hyrum Mack Smith and Joseph Fielding Smith, (10th prophet) as apostles
Vision about redemption of dead (canonized 1976)
Seminary Program started (1912)
Dedicated temple sites in Cardston, Canada and Laie, Hawaii

QUOTES:

While I was thus engaged, my mind reverted to the writings of the apostle Peter... As I pondered over these things which are written, the eyes of my understanding were opened, and the Spirit of the Lord rested upon me and I saw the hosts of the dead, both small and great.

Not one child in a hundred would go astray if the home environment, example and training were in harmony with the truth of the Gospel of Christ, as revealed and taught to the Latter-day Saints.

There is too little religious devotion, love and fear of God in the home; too much worldliness, selfishness, indifference, and lack of reverence in the family.

Man is the child of God, formed in the divine image and endowed with divine attributes, and even as the infant son of an earthly father and mother is capable in due time of becoming a man, so the undeveloped offspring of celestial parentage is capable, by experience through ages and aeons, of evolving into a God.

(LORENZO SNOW Continued)

OTHER INTERESTING FACTS:

Served as a counselor to Brigham Young
Organized the Church in Italy
Jailed for 11 months for plural marriage
Started the *Improvement Era*
Called by revelation to St. George. Instructed Saints to be more diligent in paying tithing.

QUOTES:

These children are now at play, making mud worlds, the time will come when some of these boys, through their faithfulness to the gospel, will progress and develop in knowledge, intelligence and power, in future eternities, until they shall be able to go out into space where there is unorganized matter and call together the necessary elements, and through their knowledge of and control over the laws and powers of nature, to organize matter into worlds on which their posterity may dwell, and over which they shall rule as gods.

As man now is, God once was; As God now is, man may be.

The Lord has determined in His heart that He will try us until He knows what He can do with us.

The time has come for every Latter-day Saint, who calculates to be prepared for the future and to hold his feet strong upon a proper foundation, to do the will of the Lord and pay his tithing in full.

A Son of God, like God to be,
Would not be robbing Deity,
And he who has this hope within,
Will purify himself from sin.

Improvement Era, June 1919, page 661

HEBER J. GRANT

Seventh President of the Church
(From Nov.1918 to May 1945)

BIRTH: November 22, 1856, Salt Lake City, Utah
HEIGHT/WEIGHT: 6'0" 175-180 lbs.
PHYSICAL TRAITS: Gray eyes, short beard, wore glasses
ANCESTRY: English, Scottish, Dutch
OCCUPATION: Businessman
MISSIONS: 2 (Japan, Europe)
AGE SUSTAINED APOSTLE: 25
YEARS AS GENERAL AUTHORITY: 63
AGE SUSTAINED AS PROPHET: 62
YEARS AS PROPHET: 26 and 1/2
DEATH: May 14, 1945, Salt Lake City, Utah
AGE AT DEATH: 88
BOOKS/SELECTIVE WORKS: Gospel Standards
FAMILY: Married Lucy Stringham, Hulda Augusta Winters, Emily J. Harris Wells. 12 children
OTHER INTERESTING FACTS:
Father died nine days after his birth
Played baseball as a boy on several championship teams
Formed his own insurance company.
President of State Bank of Utah

GEORGE ALBERT SMITH

Eighth President of the Church
(From May 1945 to Apr. 1951)

BIRTH: April 4, 1870, Salt Lake City, Utah
HEIGHT/WEIGHT: 6'0" 160 lbs.
PHYSICAL TRAITS: Blue eyes, beard, wore glasses
ANCESTRY: English, Scottish
OCCUPATION: Businessman
AGE SUSTAINED APOSTLE: 33
YEARS AS GENERAL AUTHORITY: 48
MISSIONS: 3 (Southern Utah, Southern States, Europe)
AGE SUSTAINED AS PROPHET: 75
YEARS AS PROPHET: 6
DEATH: April 4, 1870, Salt Lake City, Utah
AGE AT DEATH: 81
BOOKS/SELECTIVE WORKS: Sharing the Gospel with Others, Teachings of George Albert Smith
FAMILY: Married Lucy Emily Woodruff. 3 children
OTHER INTERESTING FACTS:
Attends Brigham Young Academy at 12 years old
Investigated and approved scouting program, and served over 30 years on Salt Lake Boy Scout Council, and served on national executive council.

(GEORGE ALBERT SMITH continued)

With permission of President Grant began an Indian program.
Organized relief goods to be sent to Europe following WWII
Church membership reached one million
First Church president to appear on telecast of general conference

QUOTES:

When my life is over, I will be the product of my thoughts

I can think of nobody who has had a fuller life than I have had, and I don't say that boastfully, but gratefully; and I want to say to you that every happiness and every joy has been the result of keeping the commandments of God and observing his advice and counsel.

I desire to so order my life that I may be an uplift to all those with whom I come in contact.

I lost consciousness of my surroundings and thought I had passed to the Other Side...I saw a man coming towards me....and hurried my steps to reach him, because I recognized him as my grandfather...I remember how happy I was to see him coming. I had been given his name and had always been proud of it. When Grandfather came within a few feet of me, he stopped....He looked at me very earnestly and said. "I would like to know what you have done with my name."...I smiled and looked at my grandfather and said: " I have never done anything with your name of which you need be ashamed."

The [Era, March 1947,, *Sharing the Gospel With Others*, pp. 110--112)

(HEBER J. GRANT Continued)

Organized and presided over Japanese Mission
Dedicated Hawaii Temple, Alberta Temple, Arizona Temple
Main speaker when conference was first broadcast on radio
Institutes of religion in colleges started.
Established The Church Security Plan (Welfare Plan)
Suffered partial paralysis.

QUOTES:

There are two spirits striving with us always, one telling us to continue our labor for good, and one telling us that with the faults and failings of our nature we are unworthy.

There seems to be a power which the mother possesses in shaping the life of the child that is far superior, in my judgment, to the power of the father, and this is almost without exception...A mother's love seems to be the most perfect and the most sincere, the strongest of any love we know anything about.

The only safe ground is so far from danger as it is possible to get.

The aim of the Church is to help the people to help themselves. Work is to be re-enthroned as the ruling principle of the lives of our Church membership.

That which we persist in doing becomes easier to do, not that the nature of the thing has changed but our capacity to do has increased.

President Grant's motto
Actually written by
Ralph Waldo Emerson

We have no right to go near temptation, or in fact do or say a thing that we cannot honestly ask the blessing of the Lord upon...The Good Spirit will not go with us to the Devil's ground... We cannot handle dirty things and keep our hands clean.

DAVID O. MCKAY

Ninth President of the Church
(From Apr. 1951 to Jan. 1970)

BIRTH: September 8, 1873, Huntsville, Utah
HEIGHT/WEIGHT: 6'1" 195-200
PHYSICAL TRAITS: Hazel eyes, white flowing hair
ANCESTRY: Scottish, Welsh
OCCUPATION: Educator
MISSIONS: 3 (Britain, World, European Mission president)
AGE SUSTAINED APOSTLE: 32
YEARS AS GENERAL AUTHORITY: 64
AGE SUSTAINED AS PROPHET: 77
YEARS AS PROPHET: 18 years. 9 months
DEATH: January 18, 1970, Salt Lake City, Utah
AGE AT DEATH: 96
BOOKS/SELECTIVE WORKS: Gospel Ideals, Cherished Experiences, True to the Faith, Secrets of a Happy Life
FAMILY: Married Emma Ray Riggs. 7 children
OTHER INTERESTING FACTS:
President and valedictorian of class at University of Utah
Taught at Weber State Academy, and later served as principal

JOSEPH FIELDING SMITH

Tenth President of the Church
(From Jan. 1970 to July 1972)

BIRTH: July 19, 1876, Salt Lake City, Utah
HEIGHT/WEIGHT: 5'10" 165 lbs.
PHYSICAL TRAITS: Blue eyes, wore glasses
ANCESTRY: English, Scottish
OCCUPATION: Genealogist, historian
MISSIONS: 1 (Britain)
AGE SUSTAINED APOSTLE: 33
YEARS AS GENERAL AUTHORITY: 62
AGE SUSTAINED AS PROPHET: 93
YEARS AS PROPHET: 2 and 1/2
DEATH: July 2, 1972, Salt Lake City, Utah
AGE AT DEATH: 95
BOOKS/SELECTIVE WORKS: Doctrines of Salvation, Answers to Gospel Questions, The Progress of Man, The Way to Perfection
FAMILY: Married Louie E. Shurtliff, Ethel G. Reynolds, Jessie Ella Evans. 11 children
OTHER INTERESTING FACTS:
Grandson of Hyrum Smith (Joseph Smith's brother) and son of Joseph F Smith (6th prophet)

(JOSEPH FIELDING SMITH Continued)

Served as director and librarian for Genealogical Society, and as Church historian.
Dedicated Korea, Okinawa, Guam, and Philippines for the preaching of the gospel.
Family Home Evening officially designated for Monday night.
Ensign, New Era and *The Friend* began publication.
Dedicated Ogden and Provo temples.

QUOTES:

There is no cure for the ills of the world except the gospel of the Lord Jesus Christ. Our hope for peace, for temporal and spiritual prosperity, and for an eventual inheritance in the kingdom of God is found only in and through the restored gospel.

Motherhood lies at the foundation of happiness in the home, and of prosperity in the nation. God has laid upon men and women very sacred obligations with respect to motherhood, and they are obligations that cannot be disregarded without invoking divine displeasure.

If you ever make a mistake of judgment, let it be on the side of mercy.

The family is the most important organization in time or in eternity. Our purpose in life is to create for ourselves eternal family units... It is the will of the Lord to strengthen and preserve the family unit.

People die in bed, and so does ambition.

If this were the work of man, it would fail, but it is the work of the Lord and does not fail. And we have the assurance that if we keep the commandments and are valiant in the testimony of Jesus and are true to every trust, the Lord will guide and direct us and his Church in the paths of righteousness, for the accomplishment of his purposes.

(DAVID O. MCKAY Continued)

Dedicated China for the preaching of the gospel.
Dedicated Swiss Temple, Los Angeles Temple, New Zealand Temple, London Temple, Oakland Temple, Church College of Hawaii.
Established a uniform method for teaching the gospel
Family Home Evening inaugurated

QUOTES:

True happiness comes only by making others happy -- the practical application of the Savior's doctrine of losing one's life to gain it.

Pure hearts in a pure home are always in whispering distance of heaven...I know of no other place where happiness abides more securely than in the home. It is possible to make home a bit of heaven. Indeed I picture heaven as a continuation of the ideal home.

No other success can compensate for failure in the home.

No matter what they may be without, are your homes pure within?

Despite discouragement and disheartening conditions throughout the world, Christmas is the happiest season of the whole year. But let us ever keep in mind that people are most blessed whose daily conduct most nearly comports with the teachings and example of Jesus Christ our Lord and Savior, at whose birth was proclaimed:"Peace on earth, good will toward men."

True Christianity is love in action. There is no better way to manifest love for God than to show an unselfish love for one's fellowman.

Let us realize that the privilege to work is a gift, that the power to work is a blessing, that the love to work is success.

HAROLD B. LEE

Eleventh President of the Church
(From July 1972 to Dec. 1973)

BIRTH: March 28, 1899, Clifton, Idaho
HEIGHT/WEIGHT: 5'11" 175 lbs.
PHYSICAL TRAITS: Hazel eyes, wore glasses.
ANCESTRY: English, Irish, Scottish
OCCUPATION: Educator, Businessman
MISSIONS: 1 (Western States)
AGE SUSTAINED APOSTLE: 42
YEARS AS GENERAL AUTHORITY: 32
AGE SUSTAINED AS PROPHET: 73
YEARS AS PROPHET: 1 and 1/2
DEATH: December 26, 1973 Salt Lake City, Utah
AGE AT DEATH: 74
BOOKS/SELECTIVE WORKS: Stand Ye In Holy Places, Ye Are The Light of the World, Teachings of Harold B. Lee
FAMILY: Married Fern Lucinda Tanner, Freda Joan Jensen. 2 children
OTHER INTERESTING FACTS:
Began teaching in a one room school house.
Also worked as a principal and seminary teacher
Helped establish the Pioneer Stake welfare program with a warehouse for storage and distribution of food etc.

SPENCER W. KIMBALL

Twelfth President of the Church
(From Dec.1973 to Nov. 1985)

BIRTH: March 28, 1895, Salt Lake City, Utah
HEIGHT/WEIGHT: 5'6 1/2" 165 lbs.
PHYSICAL TRAITS: Brown eyes, wore glasses
ANCESTRY: English
OCCUPATION: Businessman
MISSIONS: 1 (Central States)
AGE SUSTAINED APOSTLE: 48
YEARS AS GENERAL AUTHORITY:42
AGE SUSTAINED AS PROPHET: 78
YEARS AS PROPHET: 12
DEATH: November 5, 1985, Salt Lake City, Utah
AGE AT DEATH: 90
BOOKS/SELECTIVE WORKS: Miracle of Forgiveness, Faith Precedes the Miracle, Teachings of Spencer W. Kimball
FAMILY: Married Camilla Eyring. 4 children
OTHER INTERESTING FACTS:
Chairman of the Church Indian Committee
Suffered and recovered from severe heart ailment, and later underwent open heart surgery. Operated on for cancer of throat 1 and 1/2 vocal cords removed.

(SPENCER W. KIMBALL Continued)

Under his leadership, 22 temples were dedicated:
Washington, Arizona, Sao Paulo, Tokyo, Seattle, Jordan River, Atlanta Georgia, Apia Samoa, Nuku'alofa Tonga. Santiago Chile, Papeete Tahiti, Mexico City, Boise, Sydney Australia , Manila Philippines, Dallas, Taipei Taiwan, Guatemala City, Frieberg, Stockholm Sweden, Chicago Illinois, Johannesburg South Africa
First quorum of seventy reconstituted
Dedicated Poland for Missionary work
First President to visit behind iron curtain
Two revelations added to Pearl of Great Price
Received revelation making Priesthood available to all worthy male members
L.D.S. edition of King James Bible and triple combination published. New hymnbook published
Consolidated meeting schedule instituted
Church museum and new Family History library dedicated

QUOTES:

When I ask for more missionaries, I am not asking for more testimony barren or unworthy missionaries... I am asking for missionaries who have been carefully indoctrinated and trained through the family and the organizations of the Church, and who come to the mission with a great desire...The question is frequently asked: Should every young man fill a mission? And the answer has been given by the Lord. It is "Yes." Every young man should fill a mission...

We can make our houses homes and our homes heavens.

DO IT!

Our responsibility is to lengthen our stride.

I remember that, without being pressured by anyone, I made up my mind while still a little boy that I would never break the Word of Wisdom.... Having made up my mind fully and unequivocally, I found it not too difficult to keep the promise to myself and my Heavenly Father...If every boy and girl would make up his or her mind,'I will not yield,' then no matter what the temptation is : 'I made up my mind. That's settled.'

(HAROLD B. LEE Continued)

Appointed to Salt Lake City commission.
Gave a series of radio sermons, later published as *Decisions for Successful Living*

QUOTES:

The trouble with the Latter-day Saints is we spend too much time confessing the other fellow's sins.

Don't try to live too many days at a time.

Life is God's gift to man. What we do with our life is our gift to God.

We get our answer from the source of power we list to obey. If we are keeping the commandments of the Devil, we will get the answer from the Devil. If we are keeping the commandments of god, we will get the commandments from our Heavenly Father for our direction and for our guidance.

There are no successful sinners. All must one day stand before God and be judged.

The most important work you will do for the Church will be within the walls of your own home.

We are not teaching lessons; we are preparing for a temptation which will surely come.

I don't believe scientists have discovered anything that God didn't already know.

I know that there are powers divine that reach out when all other help is not available.

EZRA TAFT BENSON

Thirteenth President of the Church
(From Nov. 1985 to May 1994)

BIRTH: August 4, 1899, Whitney, Idaho
HEIGHT/WEIGHT: 6'1" 200-210 lbs.
PHYSICAL TRAITS: Brown eyes, wore glasses
ANCESTRY: English, French
OCCUPATION: Farming, Secretary of Agriculture
MISSIONS: 2 (Great Britain, European Mission after WWII,) President European Mission
AGE SUSTAINED APOSTLE: 44
YEARS AS GENERAL AUTHORITY: 51
AGE SUSTAINED AS PROPHET: 86
YEARS AS PROPHET:8 and 1/2
DEATH: May 30, 1994, Salt Lake City, Utah
AGE AT DEATH: 94
BOOKS/SELECTIVE WORKS: Teachings of Ezra Taft Benson; A Witness and a Warning; God, Family, Country: This Nation Shall Endure
FAMILY: Married Flora Smith Amussen. 6 children
OTHER INTERESTING FACTS:
He didn't breathe at birth, and his grandmothers dipped him in warm and cold water until he finally cried.

HOWARD W. HUNTER

Fourteenth President of the Church
(From June 1994 to March 1995)

BIRTH: 14 Nov. 1907, Boise, Idaho
HEIGHT/WEIGHT: 6'0" 190 lbs.
***PHYSICAL TRAITS:** Brown eyes
ANCESTRY: Scottish, Scandinavian, American
OCCUPATION: Business, law
AGE SUSTAINED APOSTLE: 51
YEARS AS GENERAL AUTHORITY: 35 and 1/2
AGE SUSTAINED AS PROPHET: 86
YEARS AS PROPHET:9 months
DEATH: 3 Mar 1995, Salt Lake City, Utah
AGE AT DEATH: 87
BOOKS/SELECTIVE WORKS: That We Might Have Joy
FAMILY: Married Clara May Jeffs, Inis Stanton. 3 sons, (one died at 6 months old)
OTHER INTERESTING FACTS:
His father was not a member of the Church and would not give permission for Howard and his sister to be baptized until they were older.
At 12 years old, he was baptized in an indoor swimming pool.

(HOWARD W. HUNTER Continued)

Discovered he was color blind when he went to school.
Studied piano and violin as a child and won a marimba.
Also played drums, saxophone, clarinet, and trumpet.
Formed a group called *Hunter's Croonaders*. Played on cruise ship to Orient, later gave up music for family life.
Second person in Idaho to become an Eagle Scout
Guided implementation of computers for Family History Dept.
Overseer in negotiations to buy land for Jerusalem center and later dedicated it.
Presided over creation of the Church's 2,000th stake
Series of serious health problems: benign tumor removed, heart attack and bypass surgery, back surgery, bleeding ulcer, kidney failure but revived, gall bladder surgery, fell during a conference address breaking three ribs
Bomb threat made while speaking at B.Y.U. fireside.
Orlando Florida Temple dedicated.
*Information not available. Estimate made by comparing photos

QUOTES:

I invite all members of the Church to live with ever more attention to the life and example of the Lord Jesus Christ, especially the love and hope and compassion he displayed. I pray that we will treat each other with more kindness, more patience, more courtesy and forgiveness...(*Ensign* November 1994, page 8)

I invite the Latter-day Saints to look to the temple of the Lord as the great symbol of your membership...It is the deepest desire of my heart to have every member of the Church worthy to enter the temple. It would please the Lord if every adult member would be worthy of, and carry a current temple recommend.(*Ensign* November 1994, page 8)

Our first parents knew the pain and suffering of seeing some of their children reject the teachings of eternal life ...Our Father in Heaven has also lost many of his spirit children to the world; he knows the feelings of your heart ... Don't give up hope for a boy or a girl who has strayed. Many who have appeared to be completely lost have returned. We must be prayerful and, if possible, let our children know of our love and concern. (*Ensign*, November, 1983, page 64)

(EZRA TAFT BENSON Continued)

Played trombone, piano and sang vocal solos.
Nine temples dedicated during his administration and 10 more announced. Seoul Korea, Lima Peru, Buenos Aires Argentina, Denver Colorado, Frankfurt Germany, Portland Oregon, Las Vegas Nevada, Toronto Ontario, San Diego California
Presided over European Mission after WWII to distribute goods.
Served as U.S. Secretary of Agriculture to President Dwight D. Eisenhower
(For further information See: *Ensign*. January 1986, July 1994)

QUOTES:

The Lord works from the inside out. The world works from the outside in. The world would take people out of the slums. Christ takes the slums out of the people, and then they take themselves out of the slums. The world would mold men by changing their environment. Christ changes men, who then change their environment. The world would shape human behavior, but Christ can change human behavior.(*Ensign*, Nov.85, p.6)

You cannot do wrong and feel right.

Once you begin a serious study of the [Book of Mormon], you will find greater power to resist temptation. You will find the power to avoid deception. You will find the power to stay on the strait and narrow path..When you begin to hunger and thirst after those words, you will find life in greater and greater abundance. (*Ensign*, November 1986, page 7)

The antidote for pride is humility, meekness, submissiveness ...God will have a humble people. Either we can choose to be humble or we can be compelled to be humble...We can choose to humble ourselves by conquering enmity toward our brothers and sisters, esteeming them as ourselves, and lifting them as high or higher than we are...We can choose to humble ourselves by receiving counsel and chastisement...by forgiving those who have offended us...by rendering selfless service...by going on missions and preaching the word that can humble others,...by getting to the temple more frequently, by confessing and forsaking our sins and being born of God. We can choose to humble ourselves by loving God, submitting our will to His, and putting Him first in our lives. (*Ensign*, May 1989, pages 6-7)

GORDON B. HINCKLEY

Fifteenth President of the Church
(From Mar. 1995)

BIRTH: 23 June 1910, Salt Lake City, Utah
HEIGHT/WEIGHT: 5'10" 175 lbs.
***PHYSICAL TRAITS:** Blue-gray eyes, wears glasses
ANCESTRY: Welsh, English, Swiss, American
OCCUPATION: Media, writer, various Church committees
AGE SUSTAINED APOSTLE: 51
YEARS AS GENERAL AUTHORITY: Sustained Assistant to Twelve 6 Apr.1958
MISSIONS: 1 (Great Britain),
AGE SUSTAINED AS PROPHET: 84
BOOKS/SELECTIVE WORKS: Be Thou an Example, Faith the Essence of True Religion
FAMILY: Married Marjorie Pay, 5 children
OTHER INTERESTING FACTS:

Had whooping cough as a young child, suffered from asthma and allergies

Mother died of cancer when he was 20 years. old.

Before mission, he lost his entire savings when bank failed during great depression. Father and brother supported him on his mission. They also discovered some money which his mother had saved.

TRIVIA QUESTIONS

1. Do you share the same birth date with one of the prophets?
2. Are any of your family members the same height as one of the prophets?
3. Did one of the prophets serve in the same mission as your father, mother, brother or sister.
4. Which prophet was the oldest when called?
5. Which prophet lived the longest?
6. Which prophets had beards?
7. Which prophets wore glasses?
8. Which prophet was not born in the U.S.A.?
9. Which two prophets did not die in Utah?
10. Which prophets wrote books contained in the Doctrine and Covenants?
11. Who was the first prophet to be born in the Church?
12. Who was the first Prophet born in Salt Lake City?
13. Who was the first prophet to not practice plural marriage?
14. Which prophet first announced Family Home Evening?
15. Which prophet started the welfare plan?
16. Which Prophet organized the Young Women's and Young Men's organizations?
17. Which prophet organized the Primary organization?
18. Which was the first Church president to be heard on radio? On TV?
19. Which president worked to have the Scouting program approved in the Church?

Make up your own trivia questions

Note: While teaching a Sharing Time in Primary to familiarize the children with our Latter-day prophets, I was impressed that one young girl knew the names and something about each of the prophets. She knew more than any of her peers and even more than some of the teachers. Finally, we asked her how she knew all of this. "We play Sunday School," she said, "and I am the teacher."

The preceding information is offered to help all of us become more familiar with these great men. It is important to realize that many of the above facts, are merely trivia. We can never measure a prophet's greatness by height, statistics or length of term. A prophet who serves a great number of years is in no way greater than one who serves but a short time.

The Lord does not judge a man by these things, but knows the thoughts and intents of the heart. This is the measure of true greatness. Each prophet builds upon the foundation another has laid.

While we marvel at the great number of temples dedicated during the administration of President Kimball, we must also realize that had it not been for the revelation and subsequent teaching about he principle of tithing by President Lorenzo Snow, the Church could not have emerged from its debt, thus enabling the building of these temples. It was President Heber J. Grant, who dedicated the Hawaii temple, but the land had been dedicated by Joseph F. Smith 4 years earlier, and the fulfillment of that blessing to the Hawaiian Saints was partially due to the fact that President Smith had served a mission to Hawaii some 75 years earlier to prepare them for this great blessing.

It is under inspiration from the Lord that each prophet carries the Kingdom forward. When asked what the theme for his administration would be, President Hinckley said, "Carry on." It would be impossible for him to use this phrase had it not been for the great work of each of his predecessors, giving him and each of us something to "Carry on!" Each successive prophet will then build on the foundation left by President Hinckley, just as we will "Carry on" the work which others have commenced.

Sources: *Ensign*, December 1985, January 1986, February 1986, July 1994, May 1995, June 1995, April 1995

Emerson Roy West, *Profiles of the Presidents*, Revised Edition, Salt Lake City: Deseret Book, 1980

Gordon B. Hinckley Man of Integrity, 15th President of the Church, Salt Lake City:The Church of Jesus Christ of Latter-day Saints, 1995 (video)

Howard W. Hunter Prophet of God, Salt Lake City: The Church of Jesus Christ of Latter-day Saints 1994 (video)

(GORDON B. HINCKLEY Continued)

Organized the first use of media in the Church and is responsible for method of presentation used in temple ceremonies.
Wrote many of the pamphlets, tracts and books used by the Church.
Became a third counselor in the First Presidency to President Spencer W. Kimball
Has served as a counselor to three Church Presidents
Under the direction of Church Presidents for whom he served, and as Prophet, President Hinckley has either dedicated or rededicated all but 5 of the 47 temples.(Up to Dec. 1995)
Dedicated Bountiful Utah Temple, Mount Timpanogos Temple
* This is an estimate made by comparing photographs.

QUOTES:

CARRY ON!

This is a season to be strong. It is a time to move forward without hesitation, knowing well the meaning, the breadth, and the importance of our mission. It is a time to do what is right regardless of the consequences that might follow. It is a time to be found keeping the commandments.

Now my brethren and sisters, the time has come for us to stand a little taller, to lift our eyes and stretch our minds to a greater comprehension and understanding of the great millennial mission of this The Church of Jesus Christ of Latter-day Saints.

I recall getting to my knees before the Lord and asking for help in the midst of that very difficult situation. And there came into my mind those reassuring words, 'Be still and know that I am God.' I knew again that this was His work, and that He would not let it fail, and that all I had to do was work at it and do our very best, and that the work would move forward without let or hindrance of any kind.

We have work to do, you and I, so very much of it. Let us roll up our sleeves and get at it, with a new commitment, putting our trust in the Lord... We can do it, if we will be prayerful and faithful. We can do better than we have ever done before.

Cardstock Activity Pages & Ornaments

CLARIFICATION OF COPYRIGHT

This book is protected by United States copyright laws.

Permission is hereby granted *with purchase* to reproduce the materials found in the "Cards and Activities," and "Ornaments" sections, on a limited basis for personal use only.

Reproduction of the aforementioned materials to be used by large groups, is prohibited without prior written permission from the publisher.

Reproduction of any parts of this book for commercial use is expressly forbidden.

Copyright laws are for the protection of the authors, publisher, distributors and retailers. We appreciate the concern shown about the correct procedure for using this book.

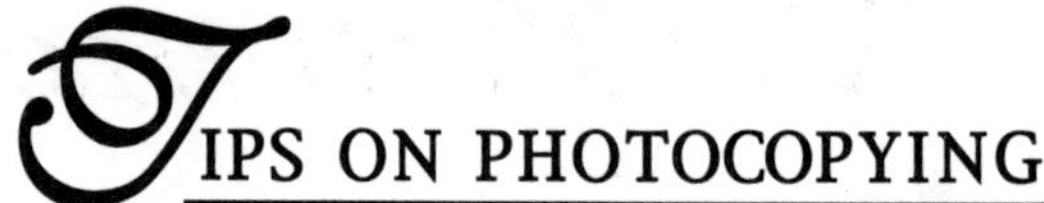

TIPS ON PHOTOCOPYING

When photocopying, make sure the machine you are using is set to the proper light/dark level. The materials printed on colored cardstock require a lighter setting in order to reproduce correctly. Red cardstock will not reproduce properly. Therefore, an extra copy of the poinsettia petals are printed on white cardstock for your convenience. (See page 269)

ORDERING ADDITIONAL COPIES

To order additional packets of ornaments send a check or money order in the amount of U.S. \$5.95 per packet. For each packet add U.S. \$2.00 for shipping and handling within the United States, and U.S \$2.50 for Canada.) Utah residents add U.S. \$0.38 sales tax per packet. (Prices subject to change without notice.)

Send your orders to:

SVI Inc.
P.O. Box 1663
WEST JORDAN, UT 84088
U.S.A.

Please note: Extra packets are not available for the materials labeled "Cards and Activities."

Find us on the World Wide Web at: www.velluto.com/ccc

SAMUEL THE LAMANITE
Flannel Board Figures

To be used with activity # 2, page 3,
and activity #1, page 49.

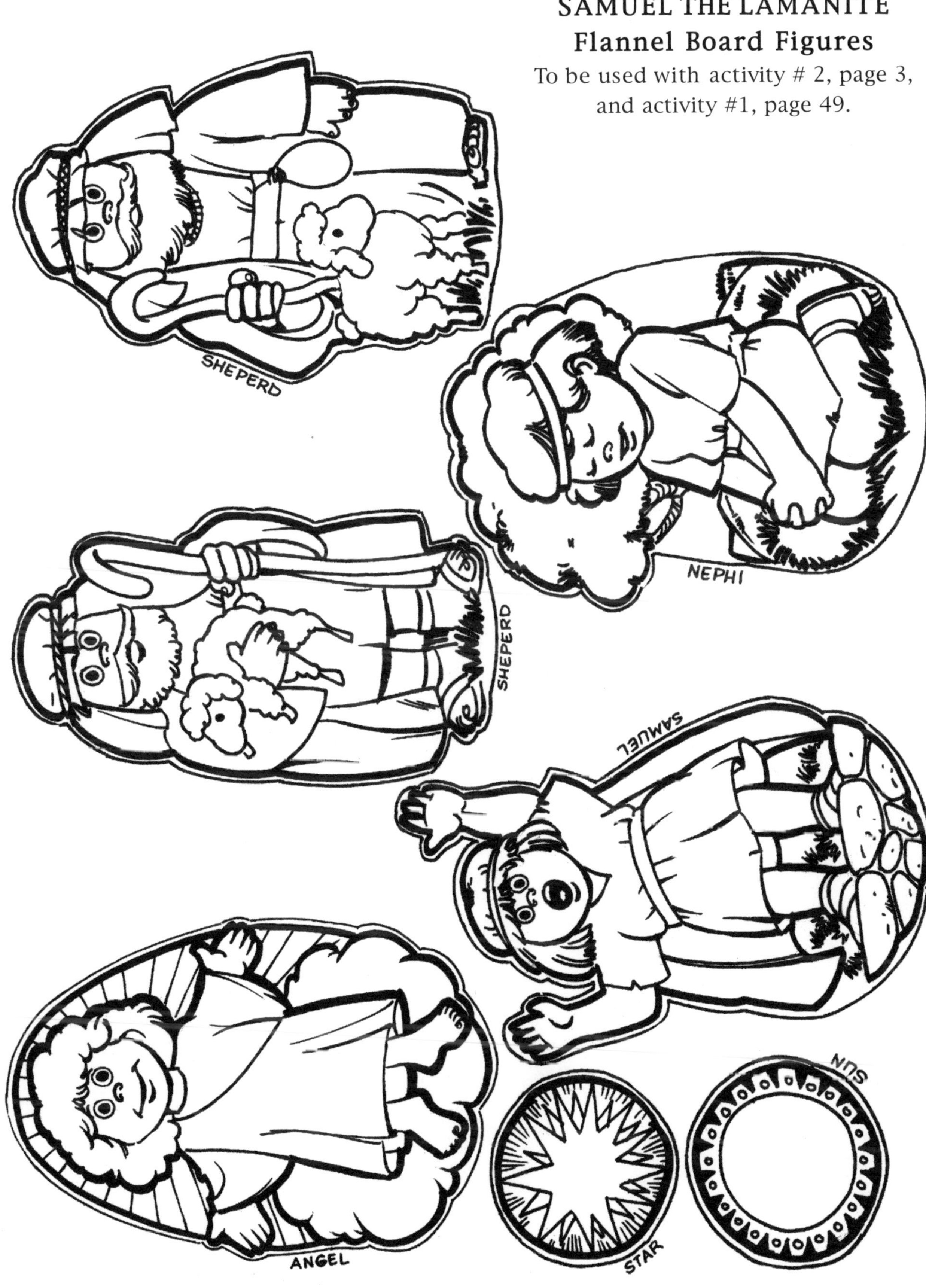

SAMUEL THE LAMANITE
Flannel Board Figures

To be used with activity # 2, page 3, and activity #1, page 49.

THE GOOD SAMARITAN
Flannel Board Figures

To be used with activity # 2, page 11.

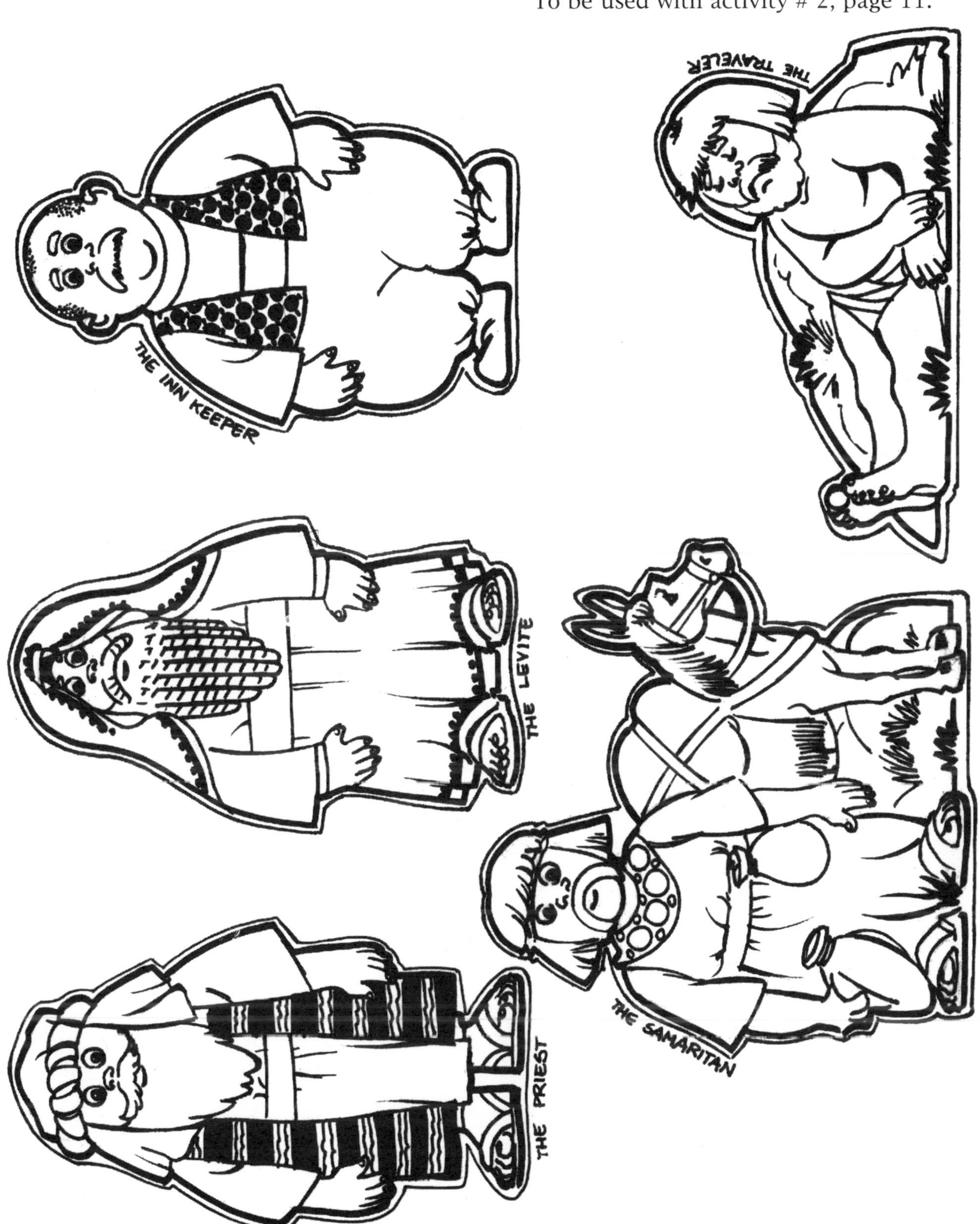

EMPTY BOX: To be used with activity # 6, page 11.

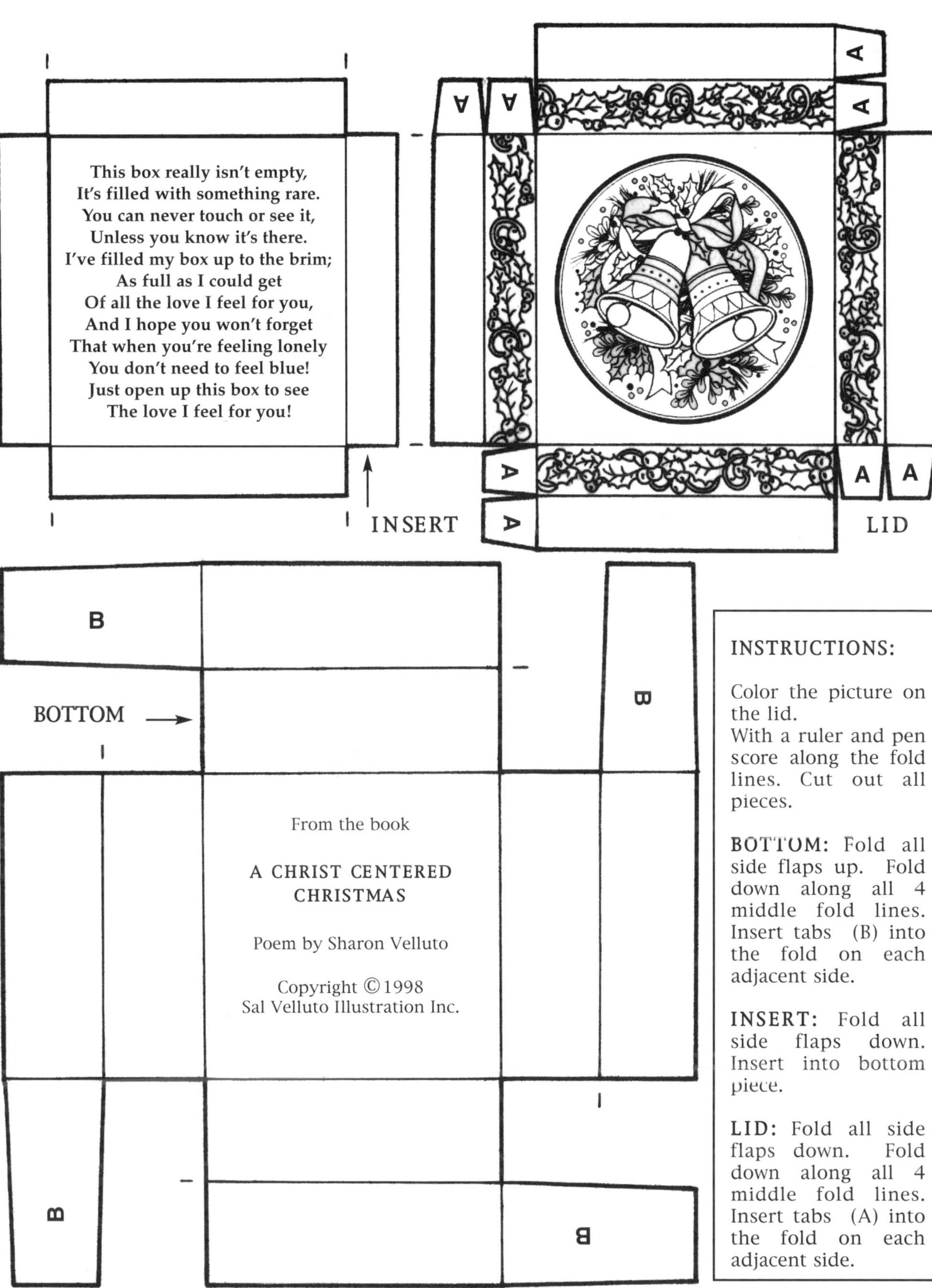

INSTRUCTIONS:

Color the picture on the lid.
With a ruler and pen score along the fold lines. Cut out all pieces.

BOTTOM: Fold all side flaps up. Fold down along all 4 middle fold lines. Insert tabs (B) into the fold on each adjacent side.

INSERT: Fold all side flaps down. Insert into bottom piece.

LID: Fold all side flaps down. Fold down along all 4 middle fold lines. Insert tabs (A) into the fold on each adjacent side.

SHOE: To be used with activity #2, page 27.

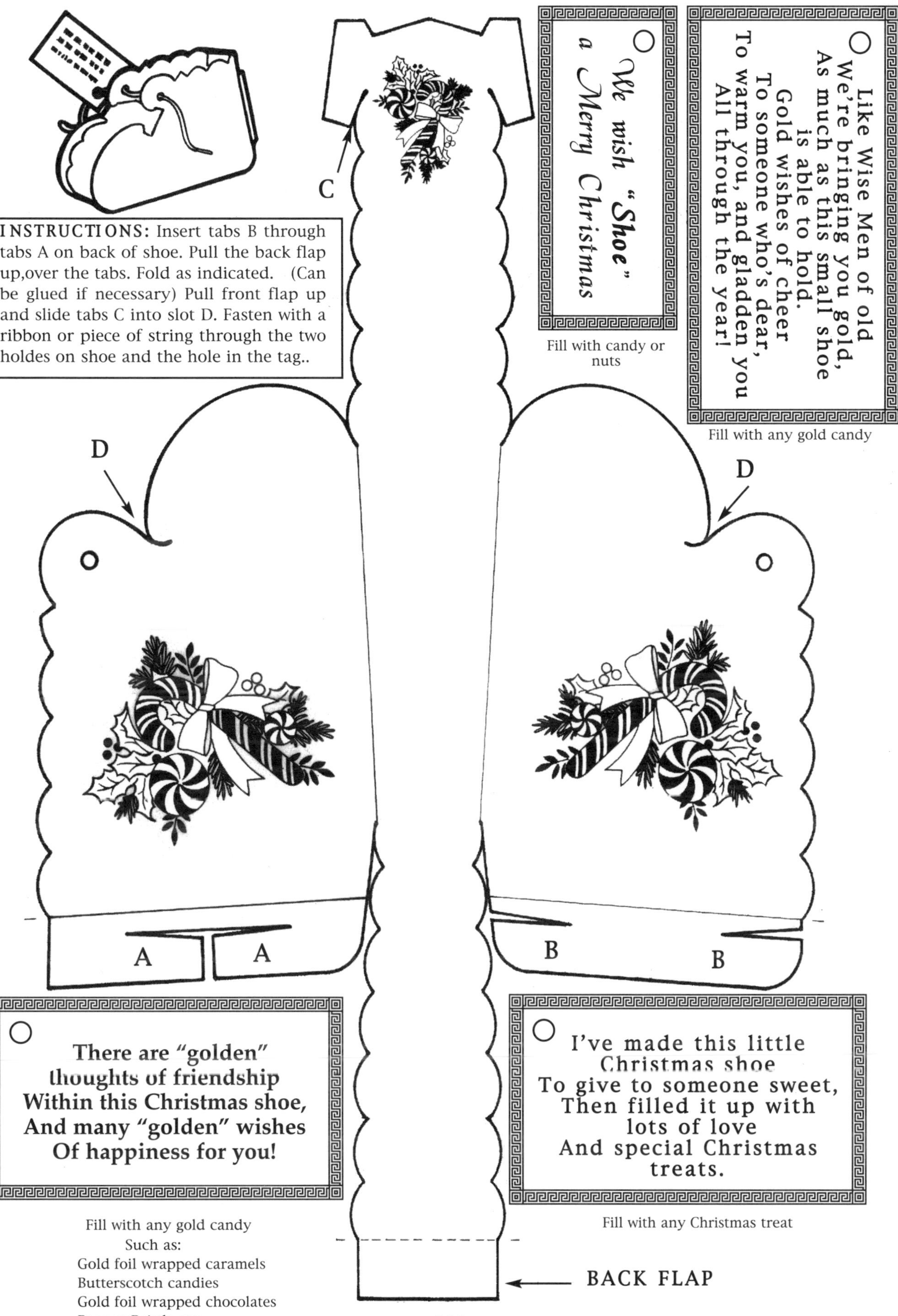

HOUSE UPON A ROCK: To be used with activity #3, page 43.

INSTRUCTIONS: Color the house. With a ruler and pen score along the fold lines. Cut out all pieces. Cut windows and door on three sides along the dotted lines. Position the window inserts behind the corresponding windows. Glue or tape into place. Fold the house to the inside along all fold lines, forming a box. Fold all tabs to the inside and glue. Open the windows to read the messages behind.

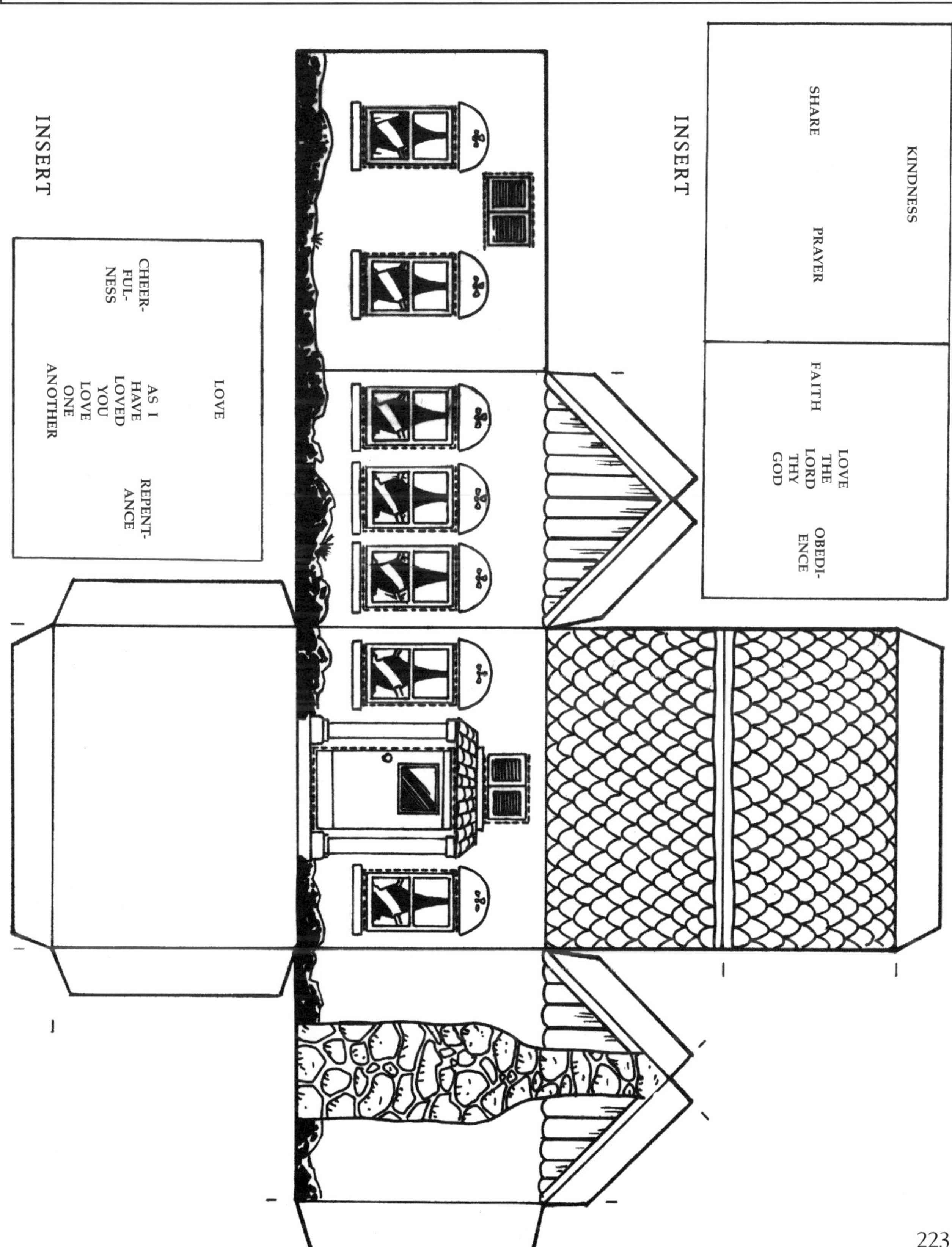

PICTURES OF THE PROPHETS:

To be used with activity #5, page 47.

SAMUEL STAR: With a ruler and pen score along the fold lines. Cut out pieces, and fold on fold lines, making two triangles. Glue. Invert one triangle and position it over the other so both Samuels are standing upright on each side of the star. Punch out hole on top of star, insert hook. *For embellishment, add a tassel and feathers to the bottom.*

Lesson 2

Lesson 9

ORNAMENTS ORNAMENTS ORNAMENTS ORNAMENTS ORNAMENTS ORNAMENTS

Christmas Carols

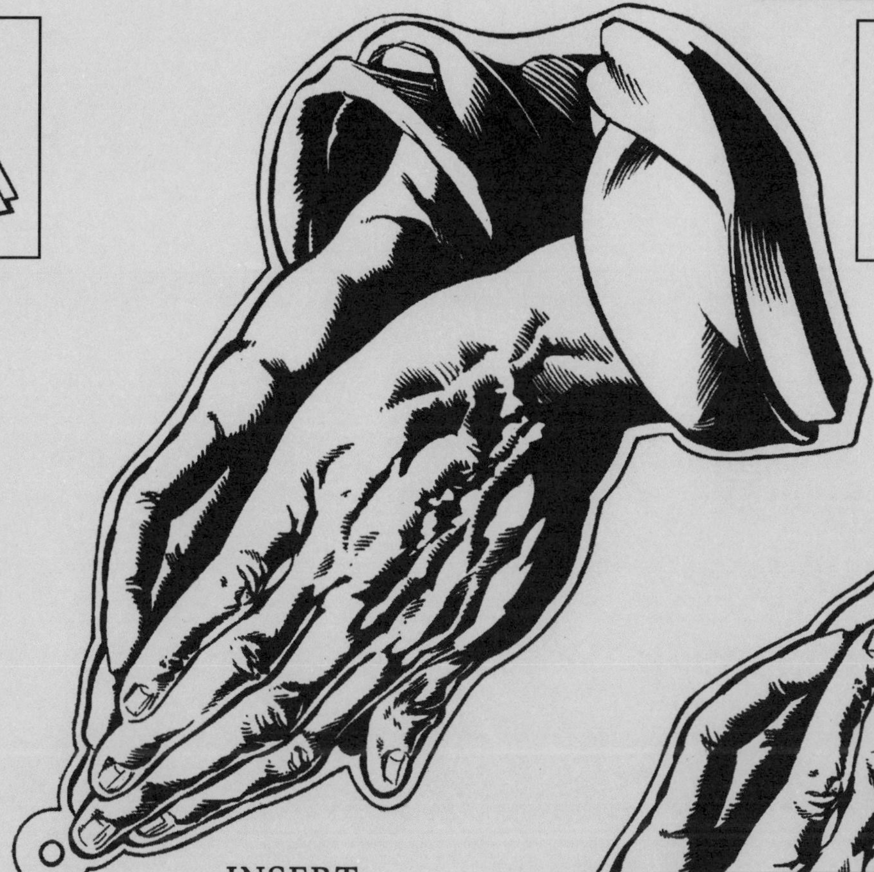

INSERT

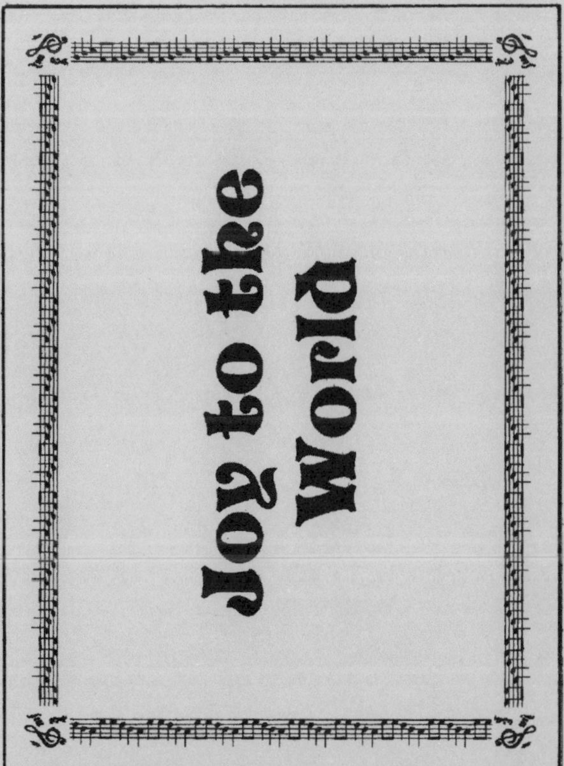

Joy to the World

HANDS: Color the pieces and cut out. Glue back to back. Punch hole and insert hook.

BOOK OF CAROLS: This ornament consists of 2 pieces, found on pages 231 and 245

With a ruler and pen score along the fold lines. Cut out pieces and fold. Fold the loop on the top of the cover and secure into place inside the cover. Staple or glue the inner music page and the cover, back to back, along the fold line. Punch hole and insert hook.

HOLLY/ HOLY: Color the pieces and cut out. Glue back to back. Punch hole and insert hook.

GOLD SNOWFLAKE: With a ruler and pen score along the fold lines. Punch holes before gluing! Cut out pieces and fold along fold lines. Glue one half of the first snowflake to one half of the second snowflake. Glue the third snowflake to the back of the two remaining halves. Insert hook.
To embellish, sprinkle with glitter, or paint with gold acrylic fabric paint.

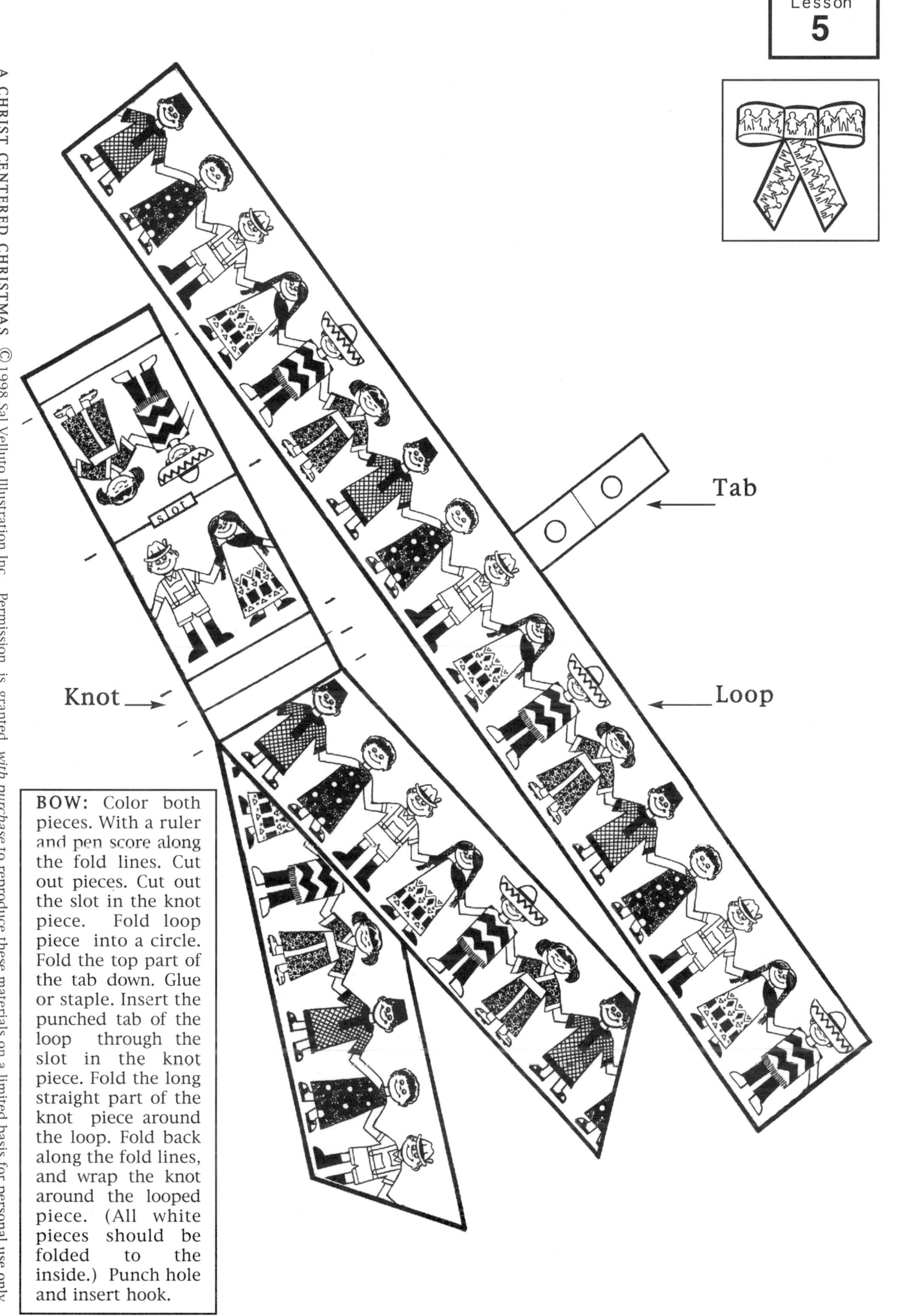

BOW: Color both pieces. With a ruler and pen score along the fold lines. Cut out pieces. Cut out the slot in the knot piece. Fold loop piece into a circle. Fold the top part of the tab down. Glue or staple. Insert the punched tab of the loop through the slot in the knot piece. Fold the long straight part of the knot piece around the loop. Fold back along the fold lines, and wrap the knot around the looped piece. (All white pieces should be folded to the inside.) Punch hole and insert hook.

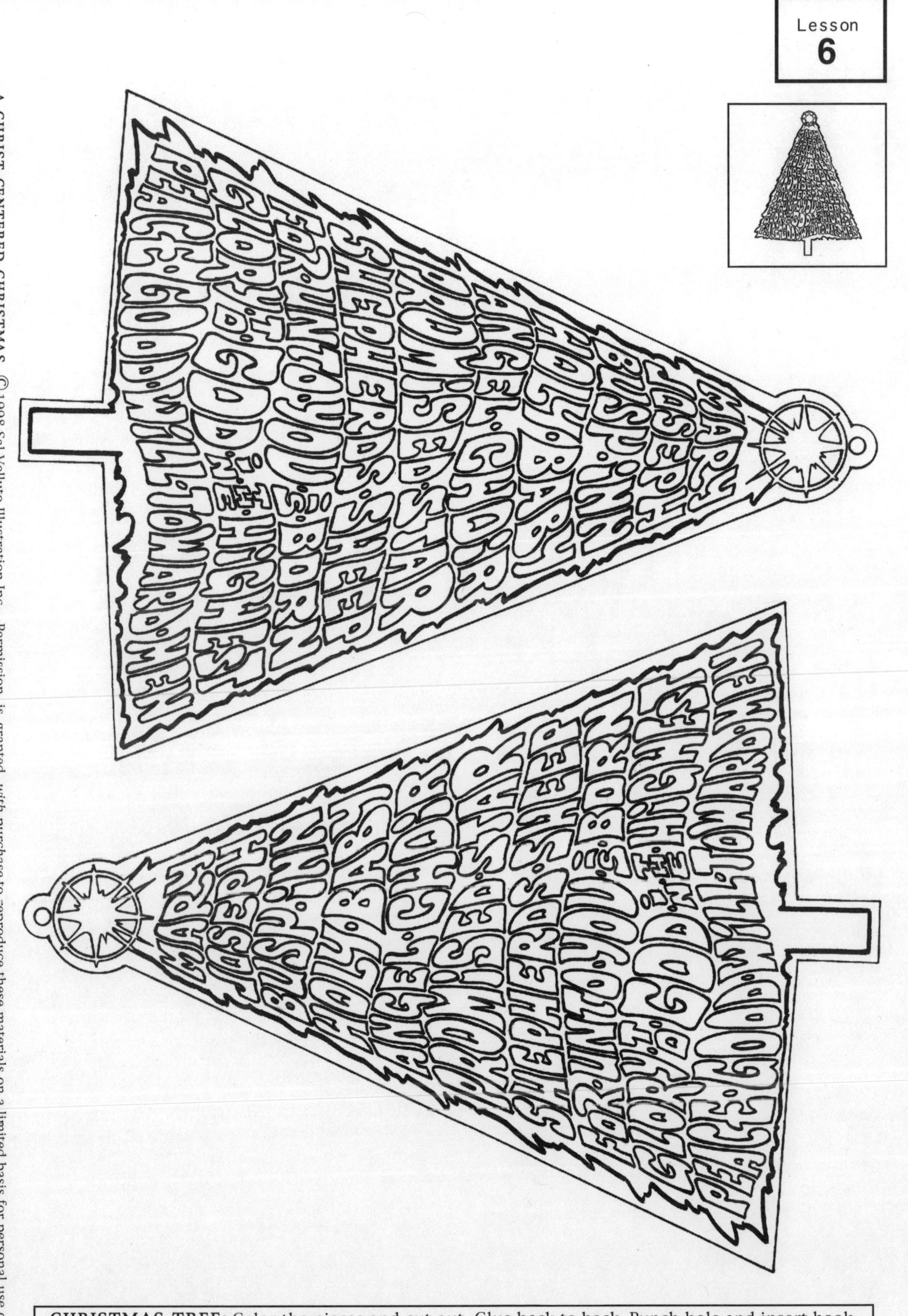

CHRISTMAS TREE: Color the pieces and cut out. Glue back to back. Punch hole and insert hook.

ANGEL: Color and cut out. Pull pieces of skirt into a cone shape and glue. Punch hole and insert hook. *To embellish, add curly hair.* (A hot glue gun works best) *Add small commercial jewels and lace to the dress.* (It is best to cover the angel with contact paper first.)

CROWN: Color the pieces and cut out. Roll the first crown to make a cylinder. Glue into place. Insert the second crown through the first. Form a second cylinder and glue into place. Punch hole and insert hook. *Another way to make this ornament : Fasten each crown onto the end of an eight inch piece of ribbon, so both crowns hang at the two ends. Tie a loop into the middle of the ribbon and insert hook.*

Lesson **8**

Lesson **20**

SHEPHERD/CANDY CANE: Color the pieces and cut out. Glue back to back. Punch hole and insert hook. *To embellish: Insert a candy cane (real or plastic) into shepherd's hand.*

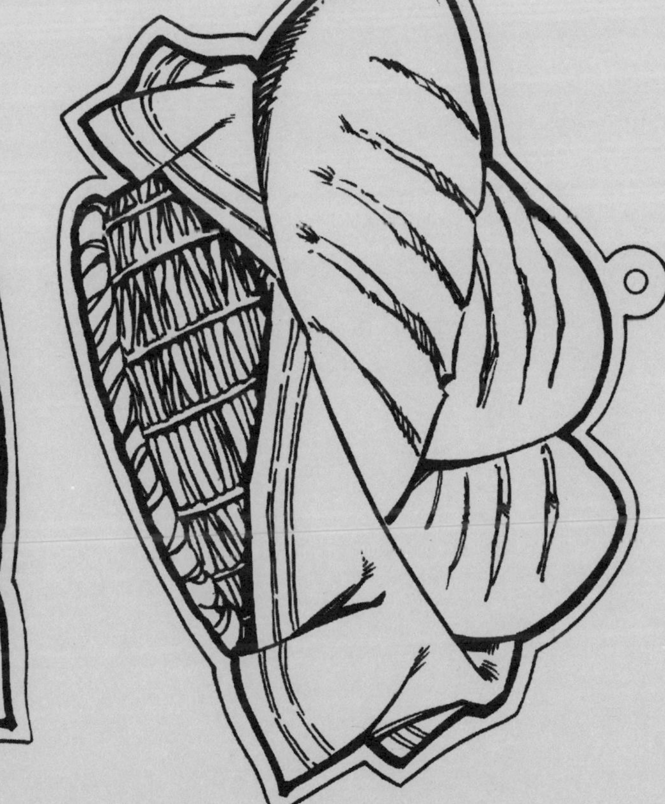

BREAD: Color the pieces and cut out. Glue back to back. Punch hole and insert hook.

Christmas Carols

BOOK OF CAROLS: This ornament consists of 2 pieces, found on pages 231 and 245

With a ruler and pen score along the fold lines. Cut out pieces and fold. Fold the loop on the top of the cover and secure into place inside the cover. Staple or glue the inner music page and the cover, back to back, along the fold line. Punch hole and insert hook.

POINSETTIA: This ornament consists of 4 pieces, found on pages 245, 261, and 267.

Cut out each piece and cut out the small circle in the red flower as marked. Tightly roll the yellow stamen, beginning at the end without tabs. Insert the stamen into the hole. Turn the tabs up and glue into place. Gently bend down the small pieces of the stamen so they turn somewhat outward. Glue the top flower (with stamen) onto the second flower, alternating petals. Glue the completed flower onto the green leaves. Punch hole and insert hook.

Lesson 10 Lesson 17

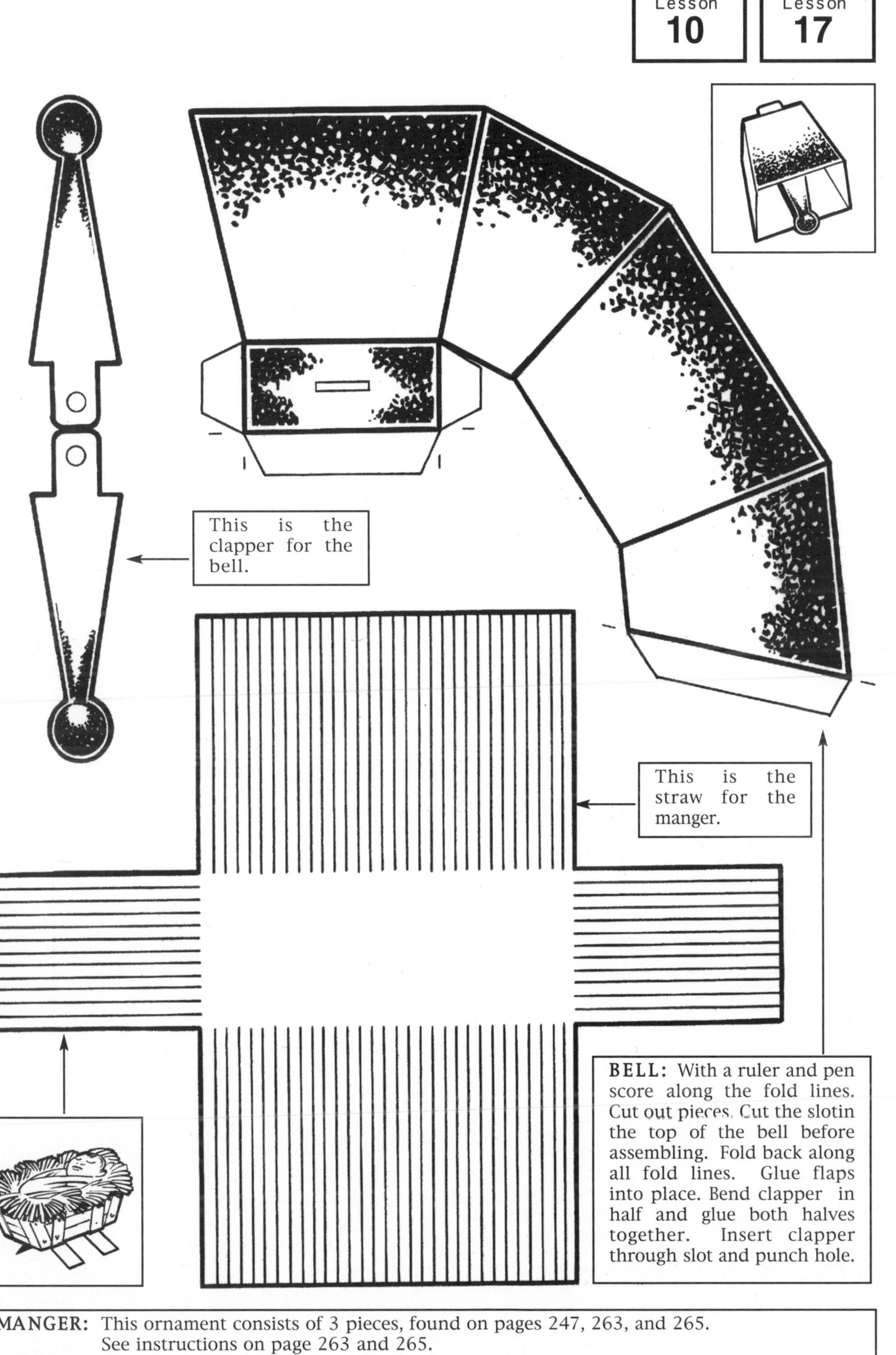

BELL: With a ruler and pen score along the fold lines. Cut out pieces. Cut the slotin the top of the bell before assembling. Fold back along all fold lines. Glue flaps into place. Bend clapper in half and glue both halves together. Insert clapper through slot and punch hole.

MANGER: This ornament consists of 3 pieces, found on pages 247, 263, and 265. See instructions on page 263 and 265.

EAR

EAR

TOP KNOT

TAIL

GLUE HEAD HERE

FRONT

BACK

Slit marks

SHEEP: Color and cut out pieces. Roll the bottom part of each leg inward and glue tabs into place. (Straws can be inserted into legs to add shape and strength) Fold the legs (at the slit mark, and bottom of fleece) up into the body, and glue into place. Insert tail piece into slot on back. Glue into place. Glue front and back pieces together. (A couple of cotton balls inside the body will keep the body a little more rounded) Overlap flaps on ears and glue or tape, making them curve forward. Glue them onto the back of the topknot. Overlap the flaps on the head making it curve backwards. Glue or tape in place. Glue the topknot and ears onto top of head over the slit. Glue head onto front of body as indicated. Punch hole and insert hook.

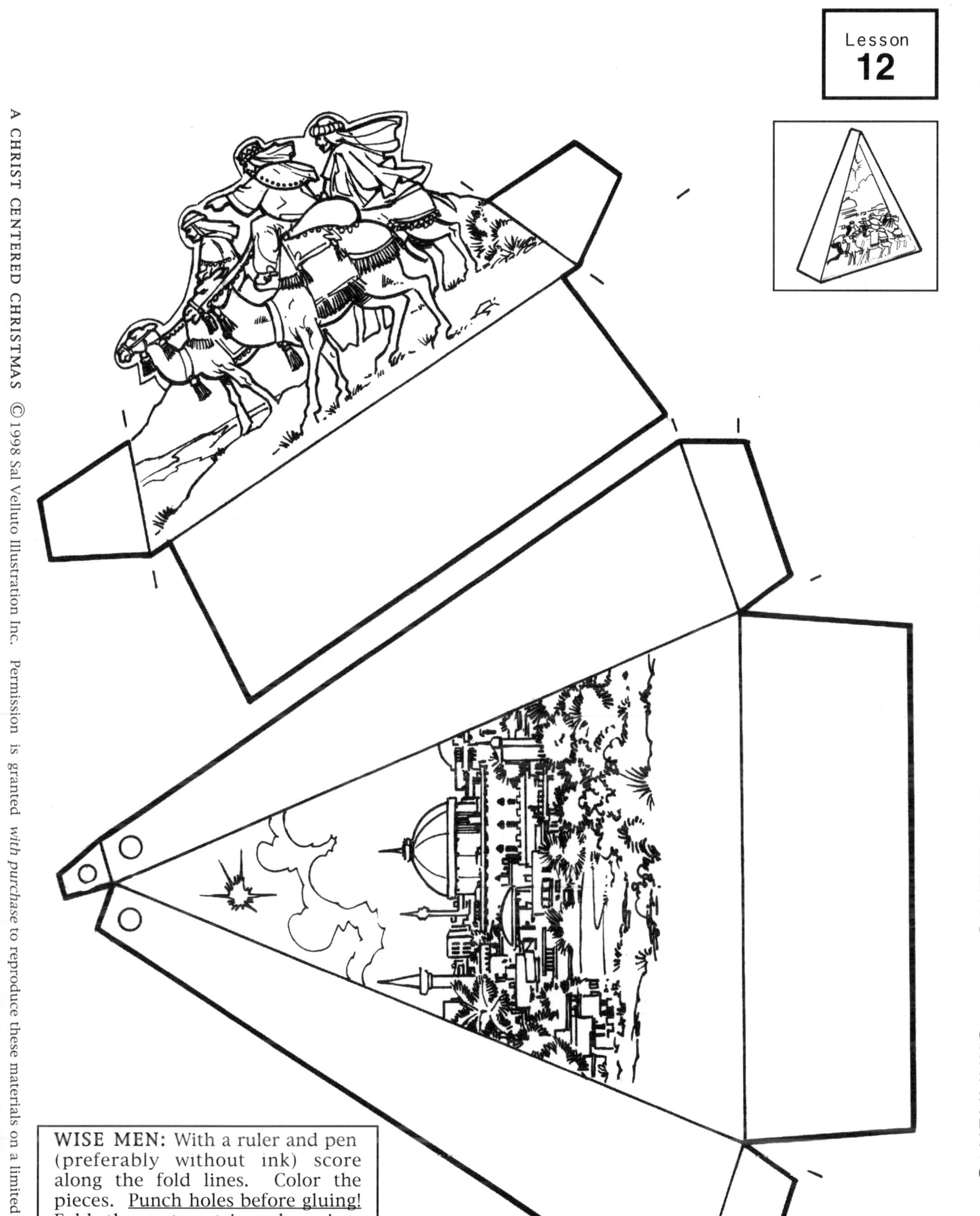

WISE MEN: With a ruler and pen (preferably without ink) score along the fold lines. Color the pieces. Punch holes before gluing! Fold the outer, triangular piece along fold lines, turning the flaps to the inside. (toward the picture) Glue the tab onto the inside rim of the triangle. Insert flaps on the piece with the Wise Men into the triangle. The Wise Men should sit on the outside edge. (Gently bow the bottom piece to insert completely) Insert hook.

To embellish add a metallic foil star, or a small jewel star. Run a thin ribbon around the outside of the triangle and tie a bow on the top.

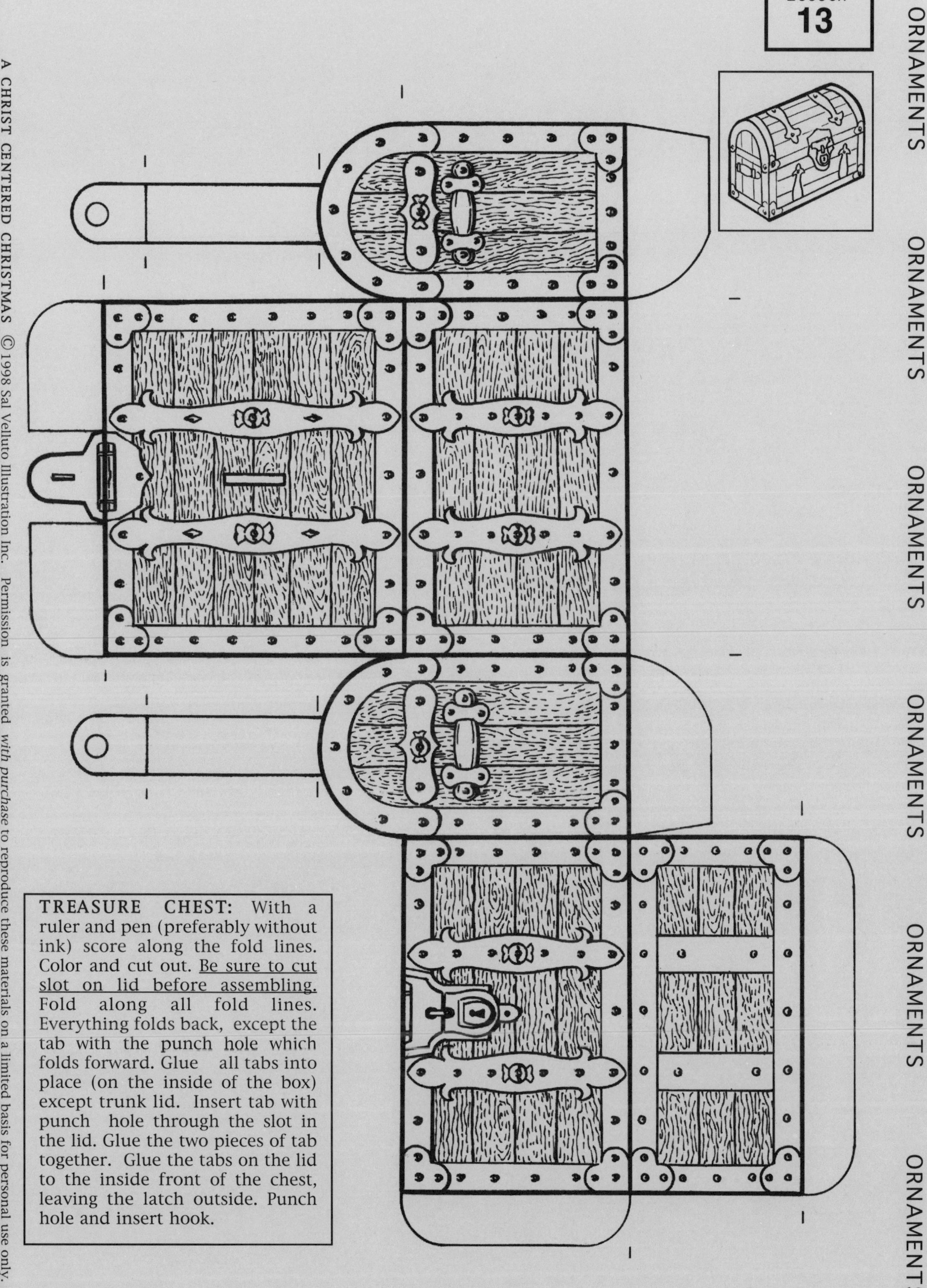

TREASURE CHEST: With a ruler and pen (preferably without ink) score along the fold lines. Color and cut out. <u>Be sure to cut slot on lid before assembling.</u> Fold along all fold lines. Everything folds back, except the tab with the punch hole which folds forward. Glue all tabs into place (on the inside of the box) except trunk lid. Insert tab with punch hole through the slot in the lid. Glue the two pieces of tab together. Glue the tabs on the lid to the inside front of the chest, leaving the latch outside. Punch hole and insert hook.

GIFT BOX: This ornament consists of 1 piece. (Three copies)

Color. Cut out ornament including oval hole. Select a picture of a blessing you have and position it beneath the hole. (This lesson emphasizes the blessing of children. A small photo of your child could be used. A child's drawing, or picture from a magazine could be used as well) Secure with tape or glue. Score fold lines. Fold and glue. Punch hole and insert hook.

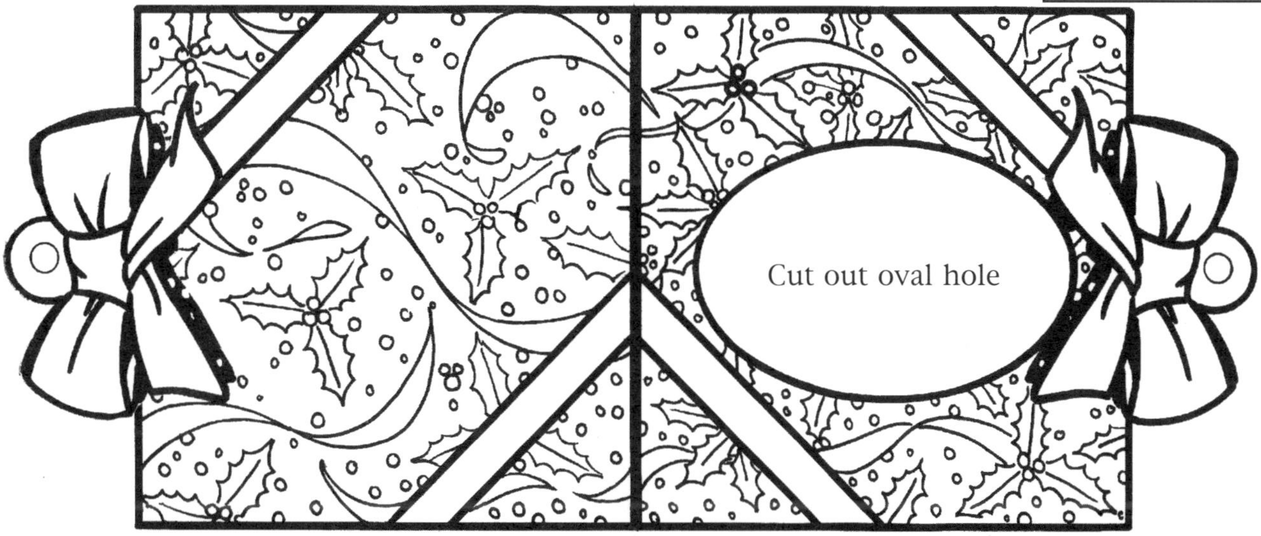

Cut out oval hole

Cut out oval hole

Cut out oval hole

WREATH:
Color the pieces and cut out. Glue back to back. Punch hole and insert hook.
Embellish by putting tiny drops of red acrylic paint for berries and painting the bow in gold or silver acrylic paint.

CANDLE: This ornament consists of 3 pieces, found on pages 259 and 261. See instructions on page 261.

CHRISTMAS LIGHTS: Score the fold line. Cut out piece. Glue back of one half to the other half. Punch hole and insert hook.

Tab

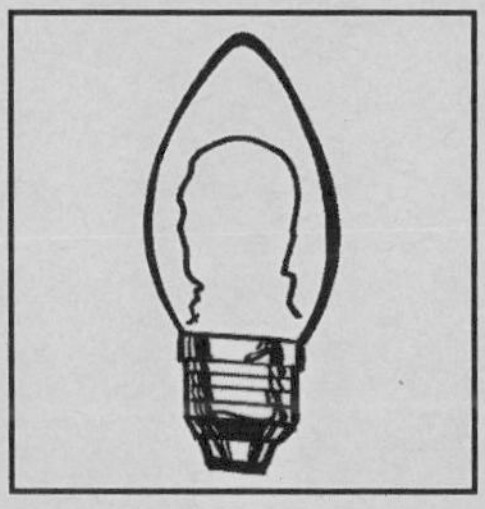

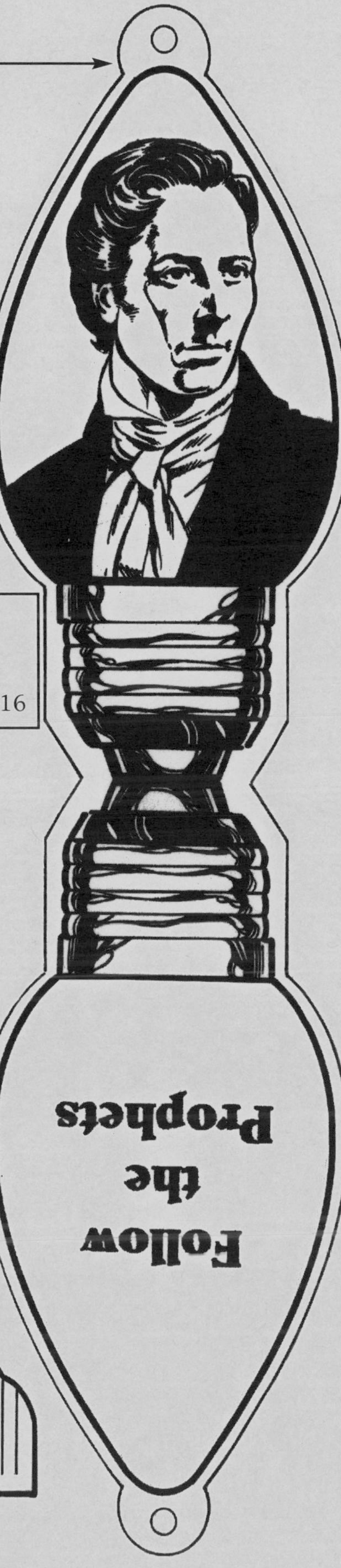

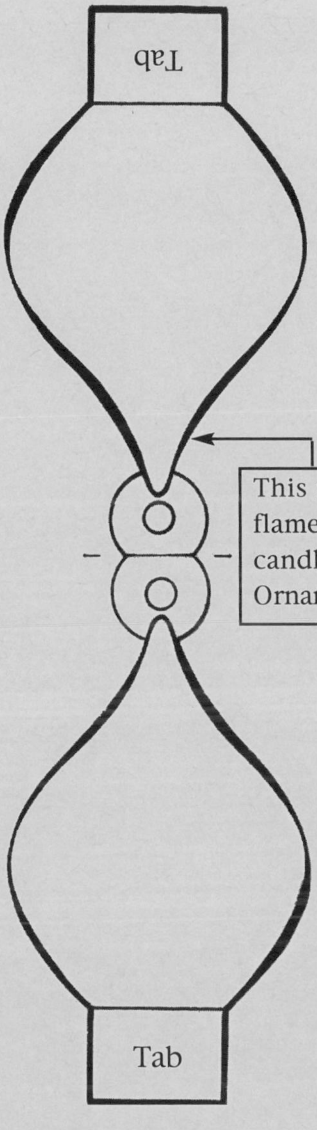

This is the flame to the candle. Ornament # 16

Tab

Follow the Prophets

POINSETTIA: This ornament consists of 4 pieces, found on pages 245, 261, 267. This piece is thc stamen. See complete instructions on page 267.

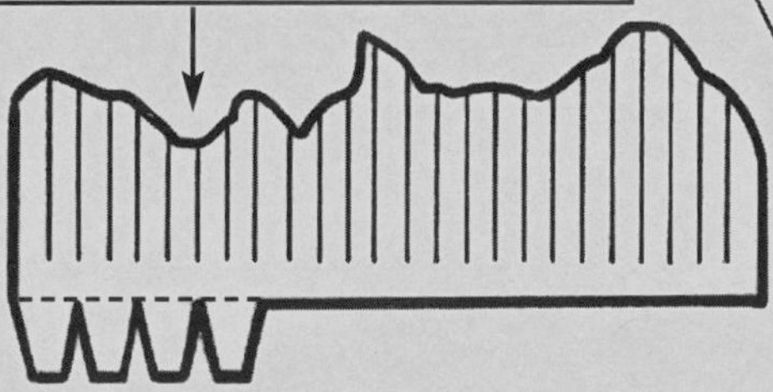

CANDLE: This ornament consists of 3 pieces, found on pages 259 and 261. With a ruler and pen score along the fold lines. Color and cut out the pieces. (You may want to color the back side of the leaves as well, since they will show.

CANDLE: Fold flame and glue the flame pieces back to back. (DO NOT glue the tabs) Insert the flame into the slot on the top flap of the candle and glue tabs in place. Fold sides of candle into a cube and secure the sides. (tab should be on the inside) Fold top two flaps in and secure. The flap with the flame is folded last.

CANDLE HOLDER: Glue tabs on each corner. (About half way) Turn the handle and insert into slot. Glue. Place the candle on the holder and glue in place. Gently bend the leaves so they fold down over the candle holder. Punch hole, and insert hook.

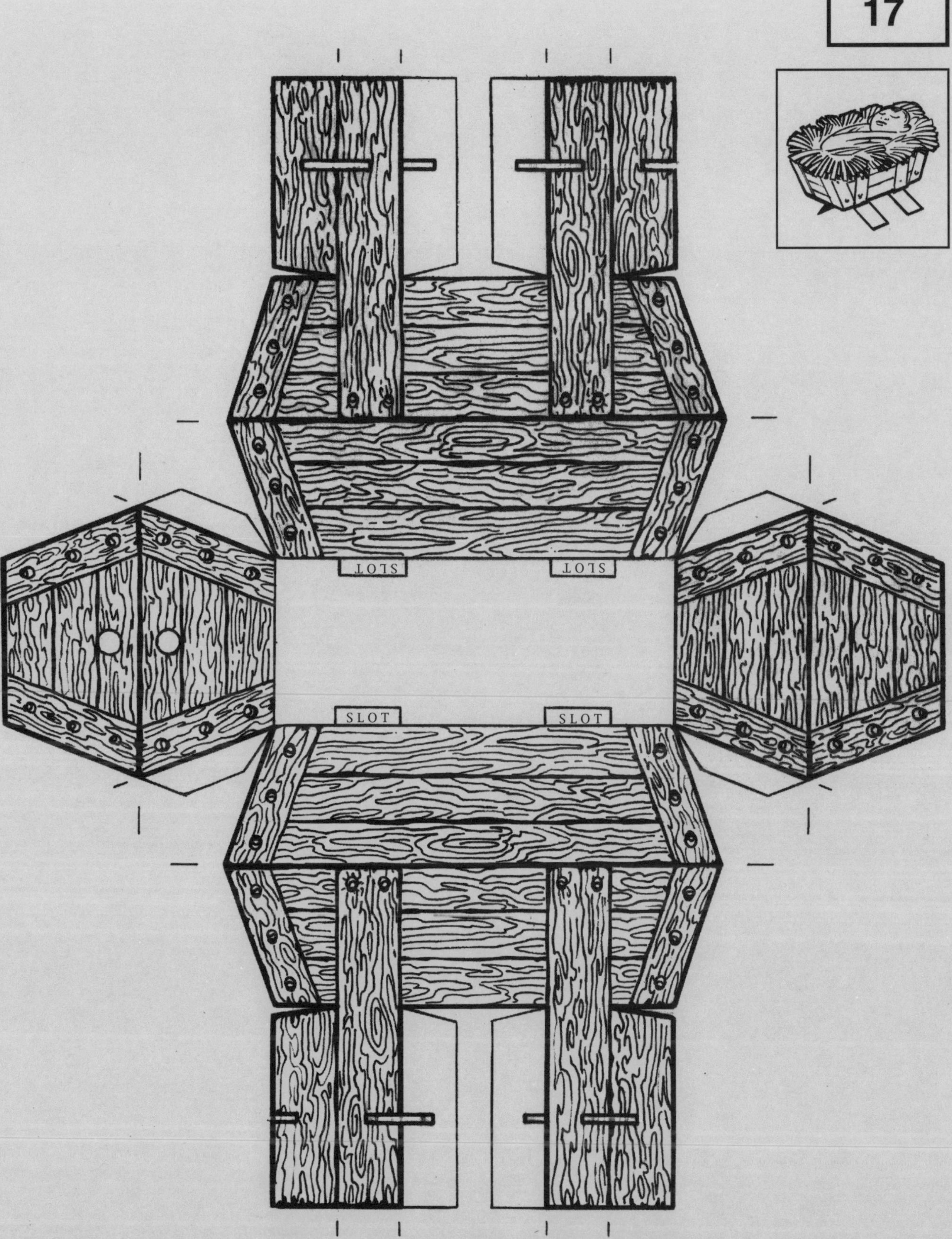

MANGER: This ornament consists of 3 pieces, found on pages 247, 263, 265. With a ruler and pen score along the fold lines. Color and cut out, including slots. <u>(slots are easier to cut after the piece is folded)</u>

<u>**LEGS:**</u> Fold white flap to the inside of each leg, fold the wood part over the top and glue. Fold the long sides of the manger and insert the legs through the slots. Fold the short sides along fold line. Insert tabs between upper and lower layers of long side. Glue. Glue short sides of manger securely. Cross legs by placing the slots of one leg inside the slots of the other leg. (Toothpicks can be inserted along the sides of the legs to add stability. Punch hole and insert hook.

(Continued on page 265)

(A)

(B)

(C)

This is the hanger piece for the dove ornament

RESTING POINT FOR WINGS

(Continued from page 263)

HAY: Cut out (all strands must be cut) and glue onto bottom of manger.

BABY: Color and cut out. Clip head as indicated. Overlap tab on one side of the head over the other and glue into place so that the head rounds outward. Fold tab and part A back. (A is actually the bottom) Glue tab (two or three cotton balls can be stuffed inside to make the baby hold its rounded shape. Fold bottom flap C up over the front of the baby and glue. Fold flap B over the top of C and glue. Glue baby on top of hay. Crinkle and shape the hay around the baby.

DOVE: With a ruler and pen score along the fold lines. Cut out. Fold in half along line. Push the beak of the bird through the loop in the wings. Bring the loop around and under the bottom of the belly, and then up over the tail. Rest the loop on the flat place between the wing and tail. Slide the wing into the slit. Fold and punch the hanger. Glue into place as indicated.

Lesson 19

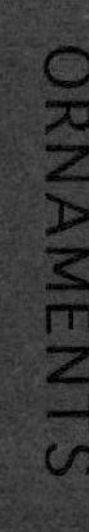

Only two sets of petals are required for this ornament. A third set is provided for your convenience.

POINSETTIA: This ornament consists of 4 pieces, found on pages 245, 261, and 267.
Cut out each piece and cut out the small circle in the red flower as marked.
Tightly roll the yellow stamen, beginning at the end without tabs. Insert the stamen into the hole. Turn the tabs up and glue into place. Gently bend down the small pieces of the stamen so they turn somewhat outward. Glue the top flower (with stamen) onto the second flower, alternating petals. Glue the completed flower onto the green leaves. Punch hole and insert hook.

Only two sets of petals are required for this ornament. A third set is provided for your convenience.

POINSETTIA:
Since the original page is printed on red cardstock, it will not reproduce when photocopied.

This is an additional page provided for the purpose of photocopying.

Copy onto red cardstock.

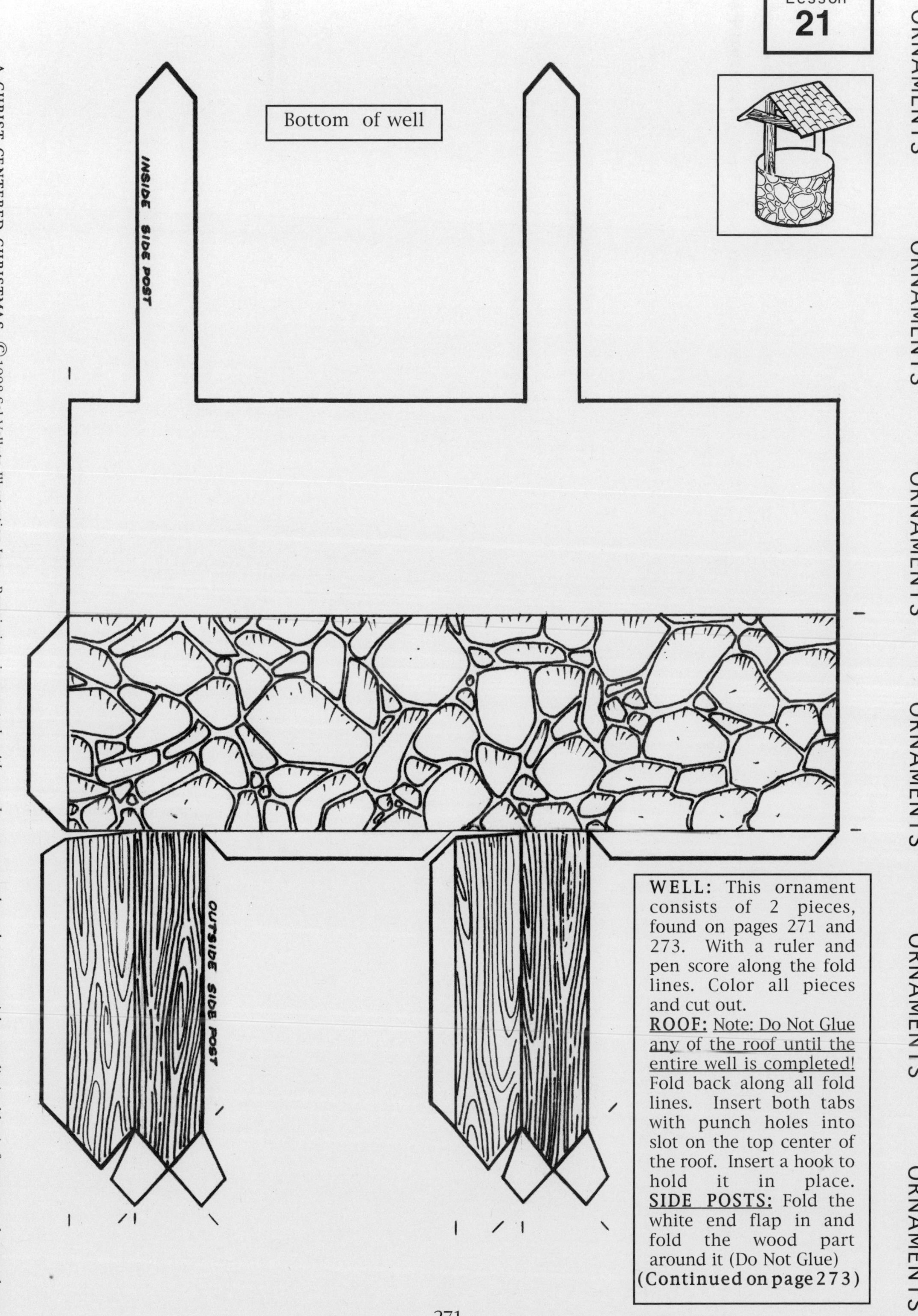

WELL: This ornament consists of 2 pieces, found on pages 271 and 273. With a ruler and pen score along the fold lines. Color all pieces and cut out.
ROOF: Note: Do Not Glue any of the roof until the entire well is completed! Fold back along all fold lines. Insert both tabs with punch holes into slot on the top center of the roof. Insert a hook to hold it in place.
SIDE POSTS: Fold the white end flap in and fold the wood part around it (Do Not Glue)
(Continued on page 273)

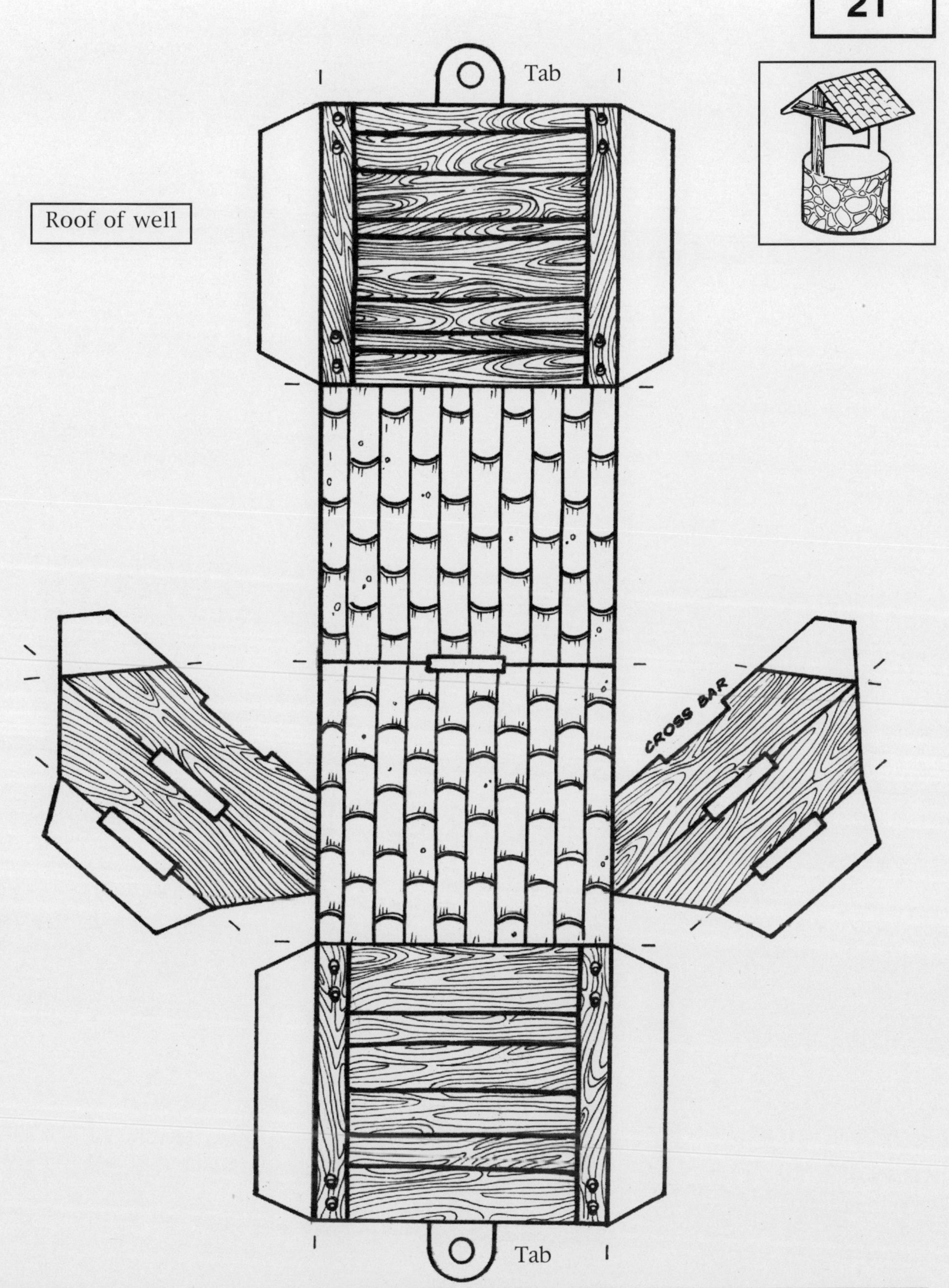

(Continued from page 271)

BOTTOM: Fold all tabs back (It is helpful to crease them with the edge of a scissor blade.) Fold in half along center line. Fold the side posts around the inner white post. Glue the tab on the inside. (Wooden popcicle sticks can be inserted for strength) Glue tabs on top of the well. Bend the well into a tube and glue the side tab inside th hollow opening. Fold the tabs on the side posts down and hold in place while inserting the side posts through both slots in the cross bar on the roof. Glue flaps on side posts between layers of roof. Glue all tabs on roof into place between the two layers of the roof. Glue tabs with punch hole. Punch and insert hook.

Lesson
24

NATIVITY: With a ruler and pen score along the fold lines. Color, cut out and punch holes! Glue back sides of C and D together. Glue the back sides of I and O together. (I= inside O= outside) Glue tabs into place on the back of the stable. Repeat the same procedure for the roof, making sure to glue the tabs at roof peak between the two layers.

Fold D to the bottom and glue the back over all flaps (which should already be glued in place) making sure the bottom tabs on the stable side are glued between layers A and B. Insert the tabs from section C into the slots on the side of the stable. Glue. Fold the tabs on Mary and Joseph piece back. Glue in place inside the stable. Insert hook.